Big-Data Analytics for Cloud, IoT and Cognitive Computing

Big-Data Analytics for Cloud, IoT and Cognitive Computing

Kai Hwang
University of Southern California, Los Angeles, USA

Min Chen
Huazhong University of Science and Technology, Hubei, China

Registered Office
John Wiley & Sons, Inc., 111 River Street, Hoboken, NJ 07030, USA
John Wiley & Sons Ltd, The Atrium, Southern Gate, Chichester, West Sussex, PO19 8SQ, UK

Editorial Office
The Atrium, Southern Gate, Chichester, West Sussex, PO19 8SQ, UK

For details of our global editorial offices, customer services, and more information about Wiley products visit us at www.wiley.com.

Wiley also publishes its books in a variety of electronic formats and by print-on-demand. Some content that appears in standard print versions of this book may not be available in other formats.

Library of Congress Cataloging-in-Publication Data

Names: Hwang, Kai, author. | Chen, Min, author.
Title: Big-Data Analytics for Cloud, IoT and Cognitive Computing/
   Kai Hwang, Min Chen.
Description: Chichester, UK ; Hoboken, NJ : John Wiley & Sons, 2017. |
   Includes bibliographical references and index.
Identifiers: LCCN 2016054027 (print) | LCCN 2017001217 (ebook) | ISBN
   9781119247029 (cloth : alk. paper) | ISBN 9781119247043 (Adobe PDF) | ISBN
   9781119247296 (ePub)
Subjects: LCSH: Cloud computing–Data processing. | Big data.
Classification: LCC QA76.585 .H829 2017 (print) | LCC QA76.585 (ebook) | DDC
   004.67/82–dc23
LC record available at https://lccn.loc.gov/2016054027

Cover Design: Wiley
Cover Images: (Top Inset Image) © violetkaipa/Shutterstock;(Bottom Inset Image) © 3alexd/Gettyimages;(Background Image) © adventtr/Gettyimages

Set in 10/12pt WarnockPro by Aptara Inc., New Delhi, India

Printed in the UK

Contents

About the Authors *xi*
Preface *xiii*
About the Companion Website *xvii*

Part 1 Big Data, Clouds and Internet of Things *1*

1   **Big Data Science and Machine Intelligence** *3*
1.1   Enabling Technologies for Big Data Computing *3*
1.1.1   Data Science and Related Disciplines *4*
1.1.2   Emerging Technologies in the Next Decade *7*
1.1.3   Interactive SMACT Technologies *13*
1.2   Social-Media, Mobile Networks and Cloud Computing *16*
1.2.1   Social Networks and Web Service Sites *17*
1.2.2   Mobile Cellular Core Networks *19*
1.2.3   Mobile Devices and Internet Edge Networks *20*
1.2.4   Mobile Cloud Computing Infrastructure *23*
1.3   Big Data Acquisition and Analytics Evolution *24*
1.3.1   Big Data Value Chain Extracted from Massive Data *24*
1.3.2   Data Quality Control, Representation and Database Models *26*
1.3.3   Big Data Acquisition and Preprocessing *27*
1.3.4   Evolving Data Analytics over the Clouds *30*
1.4   Machine Intelligence and Big Data Applications *32*
1.4.1   Data Mining and Machine Learning *32*
1.4.2   Big Data Applications – An Overview *34*
1.4.3   Cognitive Computing – An Introduction *38*
1.5   Conclusions *42*
          Homework Problems *42*
          References *43*

2   **Smart Clouds, Virtualization and Mashup Services** *45*
2.1   Cloud Computing Models and Services *45*
2.1.1   Cloud Taxonomy based on Services Provided *46*
2.1.2   Layered Development Cloud Service Platforms *50*
2.1.3   Cloud Models for Big Data Storage and Processing *52*

2.1.4   Cloud Resources for Supporting Big Data Analytics   *55*
2.2   Creation of Virtual Machines and Docker Containers   *57*
2.2.1   Virtualization of Machine Resources   *58*
2.2.2   Hypervisors and Virtual Machines   *60*
2.2.3   Docker Engine and Application Containers   *62*
2.2.4   Deployment Opportunity of VMs/Containers   *64*
2.3   Cloud Architectures and Resources Management   *65*
2.3.1   Cloud Platform Architectures   *65*
2.3.2   VM Management and Disaster Recovery   *68*
2.3.3   OpenStack for Constructing Private Clouds   *70*
2.3.4   Container Scheduling and Orchestration   *74*
2.3.5   VMWare Packages for Building Hybrid Clouds   *75*
2.4   Case Studies of IaaS, PaaS and SaaS Clouds   *77*
2.4.1   AWS Architecture over Distributed Datacenters   *78*
2.4.2   AWS Cloud Service Offerings   *79*
2.4.3   Platform PaaS Clouds – Google AppEngine   *83*
2.4.4   Application SaaS Clouds – The Salesforce Clouds   *86*
2.5   Mobile Clouds and Inter-Cloud Mashup Services   *88*
2.5.1   Mobile Clouds and Cloudlet Gateways   *88*
2.5.2   Multi-Cloud Mashup Services   *91*
2.5.3   Skyline Discovery of Mashup Services   *95*
2.5.4   Dynamic Composition of Mashup Services   *96*
2.6   Conclusions   *98*
         Homework Problems   *98*
         References   *103*

3   **IoT Sensing, Mobile and Cognitive Systems**   *105*
3.1   Sensing Technologies for Internet of Things   *105*
3.1.1   Enabling Technologies and Evolution of IoT   *106*
3.1.2   Introducing RFID and Sensor Technologies   *108*
3.1.3   IoT Architectural and Wireless Support   *110*
3.2   IoT Interactions with GPS, Clouds and Smart Machines   *111*
3.2.1   Local versus Global Positioning Technologies   *111*
3.2.2   Standalone versus Cloud-Centric IoT Applications   *114*
3.2.3   IoT Interaction Frameworks with Environments   *116*
3.3   Radio Frequency Identification (RFID)   *119*
3.3.1   RFID Technology and Tagging Devices   *119*
3.3.2   RFID System Architecture   *120*
3.3.3   IoT Support of Supply Chain Management   *122*
3.4   Sensors, Wireless Sensor Networks and GPS Systems   *124*
3.4.1   Sensor Hardware and Operating Systems   *124*
3.4.2   Sensing through Smart Phones   *130*
3.4.3   Wireless Sensor Networks and Body Area Networks   *131*
3.4.4   Global Positioning Systems   *134*
3.5   Cognitive Computing Technologies and Prototype Systems   *139*
3.5.1   Cognitive Science and Neuroinformatics   *139*
3.5.2   Brain-Inspired Computing Chips and Systems   *140*

3.5.3   Google's Brain Team Projects   *142*
3.5.4   IoT Contexts for Cognitive Services   *145*
3.5.5   Augmented and Virtual Reality Applications   *146*
3.6   Conclusions   *149*
         Homework Problems   *150*
         References   *152*

Part 2   Machine Learning and Deep Learning Algorithms   *155*

4   Supervised Machine Learning Algorithms   *157*
4.1   Taxonomy of Machine Learning Algorithms   *157*
4.1.1   Machine Learning Based on Learning Styles   *158*
4.1.2   Machine Learning Based on Similarity Testing   *159*
4.1.3   Supervised Machine Learning Algorithms   *162*
4.1.4   Unsupervised Machine Learning Algorithms   *163*
4.2   Regression Methods for Machine Learning   *164*
4.2.1   Basic Concepts of Regression Analysis   *164*
4.2.2   Linear Regression for Prediction and Forecast   *166*
4.2.3   Logistic Regression for Classification   *169*
4.3   Supervised Classification Methods   *171*
4.3.1   Decision Trees for Machine Learning   *171*
4.3.2   Rule-based Classification   *175*
4.3.3   The Nearest Neighbor Classifier   *181*
4.3.4   Support Vector Machines   *183*
4.4   Bayesian Network and Ensemble Methods   *187*
4.4.1   Bayesian Classifiers   *188*
4.4.2   Bayesian Belief Networks   *191*
4.4.3   Random Forests and Ensemble Methods   *195*
4.5   Conclusions   *200*
         Homework Problems   *200*
         References   *203*

5   Unsupervised Machine Learning Algorithms   *205*
5.1   Introduction and Association Analysis   *205*
5.1.1   Introduction to Unsupervised Machine Learning   *205*
5.1.2   Association Analysis and A priori Principle   *206*
5.1.3   Association Rule Generation   *210*
5.2   Clustering Methods without Labels   *213*
5.2.1   Cluster Analysis for Prediction and Forecasting   *213*
5.2.2   K-means Clustering for Classification   *214*
5.2.3   Agglomerative Hierarchical Clustering   *217*
5.2.4   Density-based Clustering   *221*
5.3   Dimensionality Reduction and Other Algorithms   *225*
5.3.1   Dimensionality Reduction Methods   *225*
5.3.2   Principal Component Analysis (PCA)   *226*
5.3.3   Semi-Supervised Machine Learning Methods   *231*

5.4   How to Choose Machine Learning Algorithms?   *233*
5.4.1   Performance Metrics and Model Fitting   *233*
5.4.2   Methods to Reduce Model Over-Fitting   *237*
5.4.3   Methods to Avoid Model Under-Fitting   *240*
5.4.4   Effects of Using Different Loss Functions   *242*
5.5   Conclusions   *243*
        Homework Problems   *243*
        References   *247*

6   Deep Learning with Artificial Neural Networks   *249*
6.1   Introduction   *249*
6.1.1   Deep Learning Mimics Human Senses   *249*
6.1.2   Biological Neurons versus Artificial Neurons   *251*
6.1.3   Deep Learning versus Shallow Learning   *254*
6.2   Artificial Neural Networks (ANN)   *256*
6.2.1   Single Layer Artificial Neural Networks   *256*
6.2.2   Multilayer Artificial Neural Network   *257*
6.2.3   Forward Propagation and Back Propagation in ANN   *258*
6.3   Stacked AutoEncoder and Deep Belief Network   *264*
6.3.1   AutoEncoder   *264*
6.3.2   Stacked AutoEncoder   *267*
6.3.3   Restricted Boltzmann Machine   *269*
6.3.4   Deep Belief Networks   *275*
6.4   Convolutional Neural Networks (CNN) and Extensions   *277*
6.4.1   Convolution in CNN   *277*
6.4.2   Pooling in CNN   *280*
6.4.3   Deep Convolutional Neural Networks   *282*
6.4.4   Other Deep Learning Networks   *283*
6.5   Conclusions   *287*
        Homework Problems   *288*
        References   *291*

Part 3   Big Data Analytics for Health-Care and Cognitive Learning   *293*

7   Machine Learning for Big Data in Healthcare Applications   *295*
7.1   Healthcare Problems and Machine Learning Tools   *295*
7.1.1   Healthcare and Chronic Disease Detection Problem   *295*
7.1.2   Software Libraries for Machine Learning Applications   *298*
7.2   IoT-based Healthcare Systems and Applications   *299*
7.2.1   IoT Sensing for Body Signals   *300*
7.2.2   Healthcare Monitoring System   *301*
7.2.3   Physical Exercise Promotion and Smart Clothing   *304*
7.2.4   Healthcare Robotics and Mobile Health Cloud   *305*
7.3   Big Data Analytics for Healthcare Applications   *310*
7.3.1   Healthcare Big Data Preprocessing   *310*
7.3.2   Predictive Analytics for Disease Detection   *312*

7.3.3   Performance Analysis of Five Disease Detection Methods   *316*
7.3.4   Mobile Big Data for Disease Control   *320*
7.4   Emotion-Control Healthcare Applications   *322*
7.4.1   Mental Healthcare System   *323*
7.4.2   Emotion-Control Computing and Services   *323*
7.4.3   Emotion Interaction through IoT and Clouds   *327*
7.4.4   Emotion-Control via Robotics Technologies   *329*
7.4.5   A 5G Cloud-Centric Healthcare System   *332*
7.5   Conclusions   *335*
         Homework Problems   *336*
         References   *339*

8   Deep Reinforcement Learning and Social Media Analytics   *343*
8.1   Deep Learning Systems and Social Media Industry   *343*
8.1.1   Deep Learning Systems and Software Support   *343*
8.1.2   Reinforcement Learning Principles   *346*
8.1.3   Social-Media Industry and Global Impact   *347*
8.2   Text and Image Recognition using ANN and CNN   *348*
8.2.1   Numeral Recognition using TensorFlow for ANN   *349*
8.2.2   Numeral Recognition using Convolutional Neural Networks   *352*
8.2.3   Convolutional Neural Networks for Face Recognition   *356*
8.2.4   Medical Text Analytics by Convolutional Neural Networks   *357*
8.3   DeepMind with Deep Reinforcement Learning   *362*
8.3.1   Google DeepMind AI Programs   *362*
8.3.2   Deep Reinforcement Learning Algorithm   *364*
8.3.3   Google AlphaGo Game Competition   *367*
8.3.4   Flappybird Game using Reinforcement Learning   *371*
8.4   Data Analytics for Social-Media Applications   *375*
8.4.1   Big Data Requirements in Social-Media Applications   *375*
8.4.2   Social Networks and Graph Analytics   *377*
8.4.3   Predictive Analytics Software Tools   *383*
8.4.4   Community Detection in Social Networks   *386*
8.5   Conclusions   *390*
         Homework Problems   *391*
         References   *393*

         Index   *395*

About the Authors

Kai Hwang is Professor of Electrical Engineering and Computer Science at the University of Southern California (USC). He has also served as a visiting Chair Professor at Tsinghua University, Hong Kong University, University of Minnesota and Taiwan University. With a PhD from the University of California, Berkeley, he specializes in computer architecture, parallel processing, wireless Internet, cloud computing, distributed systems and network security. He has published eight books, including *Computer Architecture and Parallel Processing* (McGraw-Hill 1983) and *Advanced Computer Architecture* (McGraw-Hill 2010). The American Library Association has named his book: *Distributed and Cloud Computing* (with Fox and Dongarra) as a 2012 outstanding title published by Morgan Kaufmann. His new book, *Cloud Computing for Machine Learning and Cognitive Applications* (MIT Press 2017) is a good companion to this book. Dr Hwang has published 260 scientific papers. Google Scholars has cited his published work 16,476 times with an h-index of 54 as of early 2017. An IEEE Life Fellow, he has served as the founding Editor-in-Chief of the *Journal of Parallel and Distributed Computing* (JPDC) for 28 years.

Dr Hwang has served on the editorial boards of IEEE *Transactions on Cloud Computing* (TCC), *Parallel and Distributed Systems* (TPDS), *Service Computing* (TSC) and the *Journal of Big Data Intelligence*. He has received the *Lifetime Achievement Award* from *IEEE CloudCom* 2012 and the *Founder's Award* from IEEE *IPDPS* 2011. He received the 2004 *Outstanding Achievement Award* from *China Computer Federation* (CCF). Over the years, he has produced 21 PhD students at USC and Purdue University, four of them elevated to IEEE Fellows and one an IBM Fellow. He has chaired numerous international conferences and delivered over 50 keynote speech and distinguished lectures in IEEE/ACM/CCF conferences or at major universities worldwide. He has served as a consultant or visiting scientist for IBM, Intel, Fujitsu Reach Lab, MIT Lincoln Lab, JPL at Caltech, French ENRIA, ITRI in Taiwan, GMD in Germany, and the Chinese Academy of Sciences.

Min Chen is a Professor of Computer Science and Technology at Huazhong University of Science and Technology (HUST), where he serves as the Director of the Embedded and Pervasive Computing (EPIC) Laboratory. He has chaired the IEEE Computer Society Special Technical Communities on Big Data. He was on the faculty of the School of Computer Science and Engineering at Seoul National University from 2009 to 2012. Prior to that, he has worked as a postdoctoral fellow in the Department of Electrical and Computer Engineering, University of British Columbia for 3 years.

Dr Chen received Best Paper Award from IEEE ICC 2012. He is a Guest Editor for *IEEE Network, IEEE Wireless Communications Magazine*, etc. He has published 260 papers including 150+ SCI-indexed papers. He has 20 ESI highly cited or hot papers. He has published the book: *OPNET IoT Simulation* (2015) and Software Defined 5G Networks (2016) with HUST Press, and another book on *Big Data Related Technologies* (2014) in the Springer Series in Computer Science. As of early 2017, Google Scholars cited his published work over 8,350 times with an h-index of 45. His top paper was cited more than 900 times. He has been an IEEE Senior Member since 2009. His research focuses on the Internet of Things, Mobile Cloud, Body Area Networks, Emotion-aware Computing, Healthcare Big Data, Cyber Physical Systems, and Robotics.

Preface

Motivations and Objectives

In the past decade, the computer and information industry has experienced rapid changes in both platform scale and scope of applications. Computers, smart phones, clouds and social networks demand not only high performance but also a high degree of machine intelligence. In fact, we are entering an era of big data analysis and cognitive computing. This trendy movement is observed by the pervasive use of mobile phones, storage and computing clouds, revival of artificial intelligence in practice, extended supercomputer applications, and widespread deployment of *Internet of Things* (IoT) platforms. To face these new computing and communication paradigm, we must upgrade the cloud and IoT ecosystems with new capabilities such as machine learning, IoT sensing, data analytics, and cognitive power that can mimic or augment human intelligence.

In the big data era, successful cloud systems, web services and data centers must be designed to store, process, learn and analyze big data to discover new knowledge or make critical decisions. The purpose is to build up a big data industry to provide cognitive services to offset human shortcomings in handling labor-intensive tasks with high efficiency. These goals are achieved through hardware virtualization, machine learning, deep learning, IoT sensing, data analytics, and cognitive computing. For example, new cloud services appear as *Learning as a Services* (LaaS), *Analytics as a Service* (AaaS), or *Security as a Service* (SaaS), along with the growing practices of machine learning and data analytics.

Today, IT companies, big enterprises, universities and governments are mostly converting their data centers into cloud facilities to support mobile and networked applications. Supercomputers having a similar cluster architecture as clouds are also under transformation to deal with the large data sets or streams. Smart clouds become greatly on demand to support social, media, mobile, business and government operations. Supercomputers and cloud platforms have different ecosystems and programming environments. The gap between them must close up towards big data computing in the future. This book attempts to achieve this goal.

A Quick Glance of the Book

The book consists of eight Chapters, presented in a logic flow of three technical parts. The three parts should be read or taught in a sequence, entirely or selectively.

- **Part I** has three chapters on data science, the roles of clouds, and IoT devices or frameworks for big data computing. These chapters cover enabling technologies to explore smart cloud computing with big data analytics and cognitive machine learning capabilities. We cover cloud architecture, IoT and cognitive systems, and software support. Mobile clouds and IoT interaction frameworks are illustrated with concrete system design and application examples.
- **Part II** has three chapters devoted to the principles and algorithms for machine learning, data analytics, and deep learning in big data applications. We present both supervised and unsupervised machine learning methods and deep learning with artificial neural networks. The brain-inspired computer architectures, such as IBM SyNapse's TrueNorth processors, Google tensor processing unit used in Brain programs, and China's Cambricon chips are also covered here. These chapters lay the necessary foundations for design methodologies and algorithm implementations.
- **Part III** presents two chapters on big data analytics for machine learning for healthcare and deep learning for cognitive and social-media applications. Readers should master themselves with the systems, algorithms and software tools such as Google's DeepMind projects in promoting big data AI applications on clouds or even on mobile devices or any computer systems. We integrate SMACT technologies (*Social, Mobile, Analytics, Clouds and IoT*) towards building an intelligent and cognitive computing environments for the future.

Part I: Big Data, Clouds and Internet of Things
    Chapter 1: Big Data Science and Machine Intelligence
    Chapter 2: Smart Clouds, Virtualization and Mashup Services
    Chapter 3: IoT Sensing, Mobile and Cognitive Systems
Part II: Machine Learning and Deep Learning Algorithms
    Chapter 4: Supervised Machine Learning Algorithms
    Chapter 5: Unsupervised Machine Learning Algorithms
    Chapter 6: Deep Learning with Artificial Neural Networks
Part III: Big Data Analytics for Health-Care and Cognitive Learning
    Chapter 7: Machine Learning for Big Data in Healthcare Applications
    Chapter 8: Deep Reinforcement Learning and Social Media Analytics

Our Unique Approach

To promote effective big data computing on smart clouds or supercomputers, we take a technological fusion approach by integrating big data theories with cloud design principles and supercomputing standards. The IoT sensing enables large data collection. Machine learning and data analytics help decision-making. Augmenting clouds and supercomputers with *artificial intelligence* (AI) features is our fundamental goal. These AI and machine learning tasks are supported by Hadoop, Spark and TensorFlow programming libraries in real-life applications.

The book material is based on the authors' research and teaching experiences over the years. It will benefit those who leverage their computer, analytical and application skills to push for career development, business transformation and scientific discovery in the big data world. This book blends big data theories with emerging technologies on smart clouds and exploring distributed datacenters with new applications. Today, we see cyber physical systems appearing in smart cities, autonomous car driving on the roads, emotion-detection robotics, virtual reality, augmented reality and cognitive services in everyday life.

Building Cloud/IoT Platforms with AI Capabilities

The data analysts, cognitive scientists and computer professionals must work together to solve practical problems. This collaborative learning must involve clouds, mobile devices, datacenters and IoT resources. The ultimate goal is to discover new knowledge, or make important decisions, intelligently. For many years, we have wanted to build brain-like computers that can mimic or augment human functions in sensing, memory, recognition and comprehension. Today, Google, IBM, Microsoft, the Chinese Academy of Science, and Facebook are all exploring AI in cloud and IoT applications.

Some new neuromorphic chips and software platforms are now built by leading research centers to enable cognitive computing. We will examine these advances in hardware, software and ecosystems. The book emphasizes not only machine learning in pattern recognition, speech/image understanding, language translation and comprehension, with low cost and power requirements, but also the emerging new approaches in building future computers.

One example is to build a small rescue robotic system that can automatically distinguish between voices in a meeting and create accurate transcripts for each speaker. Smart computers or cloud systems should be able to recognize faces, detect emotions, and even may be able to issue tsunami alerts or predict earthquakes and severe weather conditions, more accurately and timely. We will cover these and related topics in the three logical parts of the book: *systems, algorithms* and *applications*. To close up the application gaps between clouds and big data user groups, over 100 illustrative examples are given to emphasize the strong collaboration among professionals working in different areas.

Intended Audience and Readers Guide

To serve the best interest of our readers, we write this book to meet the growing demand of the updated curriculum in Computer Science and Electrical Engineering education. By teaching various subsets of nine chapters, instructors can use the book at both senior and graduate levels. Four university courses may adopt this book in the subject areas of *Big Data Analytics (BD), Cloud Computing (CC), Machine Learning (ML)* and *Cognitive Systems (CS)*. Readers could also use the book as a major reference. The suggested course offerings are growing rapidly at major universities throughout the world. Logically, the reading of the book should follow the order of the three parts.

The book will also benefit computer professionals who wish to transform their skills to meet new IT challenges. For examples, interested readers may include Intel engineers working on *Cloud of Things*. Google brain and DeepMind teams develop machine learning services including autonomic vehicle driving. Facebook explores new AI features, social and entertainment services based on AV/VR (*augmented and virtual realities*) technology. IBM clients expect to push cognitive computing services in the business and social-media world. Buyers and sellers on Amazon and Alibaba clouds may want to expand their on-line transaction experiences with many other forms of e-commerce and social services.

Instructor Guide

Instructors can teach only selected chapters that match their own expertise and serve the best interest of students at appropriate levels. To teach in each individual subject area (BD, CC, ML and CS), each course covers 6 to 7 chapters as suggested below:

Big Data Science (BD):{1, 2, 4, 5, 6, 7, 8}; **Cloud Computing** (CC): {1, 2, 4, 5, 6, 7, 8}; **Machine Learning** (ML):{1, 4, 5, 6, 7, 8}; **Cognitive Systems** (CS):{1, 2, 3, 4, 6, 7, 8}.

Instructors can also choose to offer a course to cover the union of two subject areas such as in the following 3 combinations.

{**BD, CC**}, {**CC, CS**}, or {**BD, ML**}, each covering 7 to 8 chapters. All eight chapters must be taught in any course covering three or more of the above subject areas. For example, a course for {**BD, CC, ML**} or {**CC, ML, CS**}, must teach all 8 chapters. In total, there are nine possible ways to use the book to teach various courses at senior or graduate levels.

Solutions Manual and PowerPoint slides will be made available to instructors who wish to use the material for classroom use. The website materials will be available in late 2017.

About the Companion Website

Big-Data Analytics for Cloud, IoT and Cognitive Computing is accompanied by a website:

www.wiley.com/go/hwangIOT

The website includes:

- PowerPoint slides
- Solutions Manual

Part 1

Big Data, Clouds and Internet of Things

1

Big Data Science and Machine Intelligence

CHAPTER OUTLINE

1.1 Enabling Technologies for Big Data Computing, 3
    1.1.1 Data Science and Related Disciplines, 4
    1.1.2 Emerging Technologies in the Next Decade, 7
    1.1.3 Interactive SMACT Technologies, 13
1.2 Social-Media, Mobile Networks and Cloud Computing, 16
    1.2.1 Social Networks and Web Service Sites, 17
    1.2.2 Mobile Cellular Core Networks, 19
    1.2.3 Mobile Devices and Internet Edge Networks, 20
    1.2.4 Mobile Cloud Computing Infrastructure, 23
1.3 Big Data Acquisition and Analytics Evolution, 24
    1.3.1 Big Data Value Chain Extracted from Massive Data, 24
    1.3.2 Data Quality Control, Representation and Database Models, 26
    1.3.3 Big Data Acquisition and Preprocessing, 27
    1.3.4 Evolving Data Analytics over the Clouds, 30
1.4 Machine Intelligence and Big Data Applications, 32
    1.4.1 Data Mining and Machine Learning, 32
    1.4.2 Big Data Applications – An Overview, 34
    1.4.3 Cognitive Computing – An Introduction, 38
1.5 Conclusions, 42

1.1 Enabling Technologies for Big Data Computing

Over the past three decades, the state of high technology has gone through major changes in computing and communication platforms. In particular, we benefit greatly from the upgraded performance of the Internet and World Wide Web (WWW). We examine here the evolutional changes in platform architecture, deployed infrastructures, network connectivity and application variations. Instead of using desktop or personal computers to solve computational problems, the clouds appear as cost-efficient platforms to perform large-scale database search, storage and computing over the Internet.

This chapter introduces the basic concepts of data science and its enabling technologies. The ultimate goal is to blend together the sensor networks, RFID (radio frequency identification) tagging, GPS services, social networks, smart phones, tablets, clouds and Mashups, WiFi, Bluetooth, wireless Internet+, and 4G/5G core networks with the

Big-Data Analytics for Cloud, IoT and Cognitive Computing, First Edition. Kai Hwang and Min Chen.
© 2017 John Wiley & Sons Ltd. Published 2017 by John Wiley & Sons Ltd.
Companion Website: http://www.wiley.com/go/hwangIOT

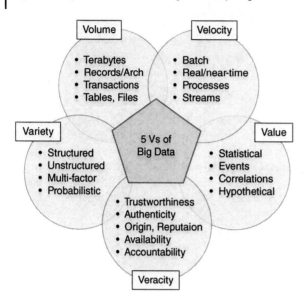

Figure 1.1 Big data characteristics: Five V's and corresponding challenges.

emerging Internet of Things (IoT) to build a productive big data industry in the years to come. In particular, we will examine the idea of technology fusion among the SMACT technologies.

1.1.1 Data Science and Related Disciplines

The concept of data science has a long history, but only recently became very popular due to the increasing use of clouds and IoT for building a smart world. As illustrated in Figure 1.1, today's big data possesses three important characteristics: data in large volume, demanding high velocity to process them, and many varieties of data types. These are often known as the five V's of big data, because some people add two more V's of big data: one is the veracity, which refers to the difficulty to trace data or predict data. The other is the data value, which can vary drastically if the data are handled differently.

By today's standards, one Terabyte or greater is considered a big data. IDC has predicted that 40 ZB of data will be processed by 2030, meaning each person may have 5.2 TB of data to be processed. The high volume demands large storage capacity and analytical capabilities to handle such massive volumes of data. The high variety implies that data comes in many different formats, which can be very difficult and expensive to manage accurately. The high velocity refers to the inability to process big data in real time to extract meaningful information or knowledge from it. The veracity implies that it is rather difficult to verify data. The value of big data varies with its application domains. All the five V's make it difficult to capture, manage and process big data using the existing hardware/software infrastructure. These 5 V's justify the call for smarter clouds and IoT support.

Forbes, Wikipedia and NIST have provided some historical reviews of this field. To illustrate its evolution to a big data era, we divide the timeline into four stages, as shown in Figure 1.2. In the 1970s, some considered data science equivalent to data logy, as noted by Peter Naur: "The science of dealing with data, once they have been established, while the relation of the data to what they represent is delegated to other fields and sciences."

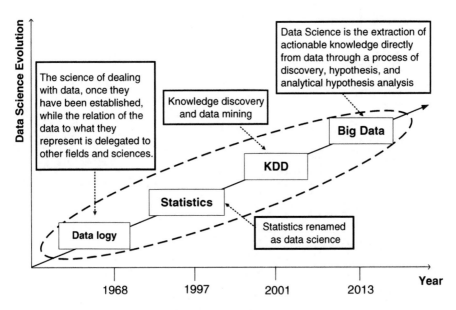

Figure 1.2 The evolution of data science up to the big data era.

At one time, data science was regarded as part of statistics in a wide range of applications. Since the 2000s, the scope of data science has become enlarged. It became a continuation of the field of data mining and predictive analytics, also known as the field of knowledge discovery and data mining (KDD).

In this context, programming is viewed as part of data science. Over the past two decades, data has increased on an escalating scale in various fields. The data science evolution enables the extraction of knowledge from massive volumes of data that are structured or unstructured. Unstructured data include emails, videos, photos, social media, and other user-generated contents. The management of big data requires scalability across large amounts of storage, computing and communication resources.

Formally, we define data science as the process of extraction of actionable knowledge directly from data through data discovery, hypothesis and analytical hypothesis. A data scientist is a practitioner who has sufficient knowledge of the overlapping regimes of expertise in business needs, domain knowledge, analytical skills and programming expertise to manage the end-to-end scientific process through each stage in the big data life cycle.

Today's data science requires aggregation and sorting through a great amount of information and writing algorithms to extract insights from such a large scale of data elements. Data science has a wide range of applications, especially in clinical trials, biological science, agriculture, medical care and social networks, etc [1]. We divide the value chain of big data into four phases: namely data generation, acquisition, storage and analysis. If we take data as a raw material, data generation and data acquisition are an exploitation process. Data storage and data analysis form a production process that adds values to the raw material.

In Figure 1.3, data science is considered as the intersection of three interdisciplinary areas: computer science or programming skills, mathematics and statistics, and

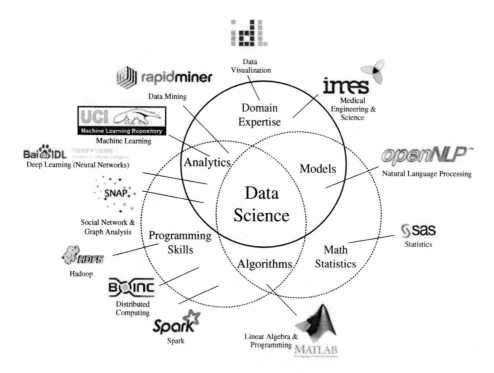

Figure 1.3 Functional components of data science supported by some software libraries on the cloud in 2016.

application domain expertise. Most data scientists started as domain experts who are mastered in mathematical modeling, data mining techniques and data analytics. Through the combination of domain knowledge and mathematical skills, specific models are developed while algorithms are designed. Data science runs across the entire data life cycle. It incorporates principles, techniques and methods from many disciplines and domains, including data mining and analytics, especially when machine learning and pattern recognition are applied.

Statistics, operations research, visualization and domain knowledge are also indispensable. Data science teams solve very complex data problems. As shown in Figure 1.3, when ever two areas overlap, they generate three important specialized fields of interest. The modeling field is formed by intersecting domain expertise with mathematical statistics. The knowledge to be discovered is often described by abstract mathematical language. Another field is data analytics, which has resulted from the intersection of domain expertise and programming skills. Domain experts apply special programming tools to discover knowledge by solving practical problem in their domain. Finally, the field of algorithms is the intersection of programming skills and mathematical statistics. Summarized below are some open challenges in big data research, development and applications:

- Structured versus unstructured data with effective indexing;
- Identification, de-identification and re-identification;

Figure 1.4 Hype cycle for emerging high technologies to reach maturity and industrial productivity within the next decade. (Source: Gartner Research, July 2016, reprinted with permission.) [19]

- Ontologies and semantics of big data;
- Data introspection and reduction techniques;
- Design, construction, operation and description;
- Data integration and software interoperability;
- Immutability and immortality;
- Data measurement methods;
- Data range, denominators, trending and estimation.

1.1.2 Emerging Technologies in the Next Decade

Garnter Research is an authoritative source of new technologies. They identify the hottest emerging new technologies in hype cycles every year. In Figure 1.4 we examine Gartner's Hype Cycle for new emerging technologies across many fields in 2016. The time taken for an emerging technology to become mature may take 2 to 10 years to reach its plateau of productivity. By 2016, the most expected technologies are identified at the peak of the hype cycle. The top 12 include cognitive expert advisors, machine learning, software defined security, connected home, autonomous vehicles, blockchain, nanotube electronics, smart robots, micro datacenters, gesture control devices, IoT platforms, and drones (commercial UAVs).

As identified by the dark solid circles, most technologies take 5 to 10 years to mature. The light solid circles, such as machine learning, software defined anything (SDx) and natural language answering, are those that may become mature in 2 to 5 years' time. Readers should check hype cycles released in previous years to find more hot technologies. The triangles identify those that may take more than 10 years of further development. They are 4-D printing, general-purpose machine intelligence, neuromorphic hardware, quantum computing and autonomous vehicles, etc. Self-driving cars were a hot topic in 2016, but may need more time to be accepted, either technically or legally. The enterprise taxonomy and ontology management are entering the disillusion stage, but still they may take a long shot at becoming a reality.

Other hot technologies, like augmented reality and virtual reality, resulted in disillusionment, but they are heading towards industrial productivity now. At the early innovation trigger stage, we observe that Wifi 11.ac and context brokering are rising on the horizon, together with Data broker PaaS (dbrPaaS), personal analytics, smart workplace, conversational user interfaces, smart data discovery, affective computing, virtual personal assistant, digital security and people-literate technology. Many other technologies on the rising edge of the expectation curve include 3-D bio-printing, connected homes, biochips, software-defined security, etc. This hype cycle does include more mature technologies such as hybrid cloud computing, cryptocurrency exchange and enterprise 3-D printing identified in previous years.

Some of the more mature technologies such as cloud computing, social networks, near-field communication (NFC), 3-D scanners, consumer telematics and speech recognition, that have appeared in hype cycles released from 2010 to 2015, do not appear in Figure 1.4. The depth of disillusionment may not be bad, because as interest wanes after extensive experiments, useful lessons are learned to deliver products more successfully. Those long-shot technologies marked by triangles in the hype cycle cannot be ignored either. Most industrial developers are near-sighted or very conservative in the sense that they only adopt mature technologies that can generate a profitable product quickly. Traditionally, the long-shot or high-risk technologies such as quantum computing, smart dust, bio-acoustic sensing, volumetric displays, brain–human interface and neurocomputers are only heavily pursued in academia.

It has been well accepted that technology will continue to become more human-centric, to the point where it will introduce transparency between people, businesses and things. This relationship will surface more as the evolution of technology becomes more adaptive, contextual and fluid within the workplace, at home, and interacting with the business world. As hinted above, we see the emergence of 4-D printing, brain-like computing, human augmentation, volumetric displays, affective computing, connected homes, nanotube electronics, augmented reality, virtual reality and gesture control devices. Some of these will be covered in subsequent chapters.

There are predictable trends in technology that drive computing applications. Designers and programmers want to predict the technological capabilities of future systems. Jim Gray's "Rules of Thumb in Data Engineering" paper is an excellent example of how technology affects applications and vice versa. Moore's Law indicates that the processor speed doubles every 18 months. This was indeed true for the past 30 years. However, it is hard to say that Moore's Law will hold for much longer in the future. Gilder's Law indicates that the network bandwidth doubled yearly in the past. The tremendous price/performance ratio of commodity hardware was driven by the smart phone, tablets and notebook markets. This has also enriched commodity technologies in large-scale computing.

It is interesting to see the high expectation of IoT in recent years. The cloud computing in mashup or other applications demands computing economics, web-scale data collection, system reliability and scalable performance. For example, distributed transaction processing is often practised in the banking and finance industries. Transactions represent 90% of the existing market for reliable banking systems. Users must deal with multiple database servers in distributed transactions. How to maintain the consistency of replicated transaction records is crucial in real-time banking services. Other complications include shortage of software support, network saturation and security threats in these business applications.

A number of more mature technologies that may take 2 to 5 years to reach the plateau are highlighted by light gray dots in Figure 1.4. These include biochip, advanced analytics, speech-to-speech translation, machine learning, hybrid cloud computing, cryptocurrency exchange, autonomous field vehicles, gesture control and enterprise 3-D printing. Some of the mature technologies that are pursued heavily by industry now are not shown in the 2016 hype cycle as emerging technologies. These may include cloud computing, social networks, near-field communication (NFC), 3-D scanners, consumer telematics and speech recognition that appeared in the hype cycles in last several years.

It is interesting to see the high expectation of IoT in recent years. The cloud computing in mashup or hybrid clouds has already been adopted in the mainstream. As time goes by, most technologies will advance to better stages of expectation. As mentioned above, the depth of disillusionment may not be too bad, as interest wanes after extensive experiments, and useful lessons are learned to deliver products successfully. It should noted that those long-shot technologies marked by triangles in the hype cycle may take more than 10 years to become an industrial reality. These include the rising areas of quantum computing, smart dust, bio-acoustic sensing, volumetric displays, human augmentation, brain–human interface and neuro-business popular in the academia and research communities.

The general computing trend is to leverage more and more on shared web resources over the Internet. As illustrated in Figure 1.5, we see the evolution from two tracks of system development: HPC versus HTC systems. On the HPC side, supercomputers

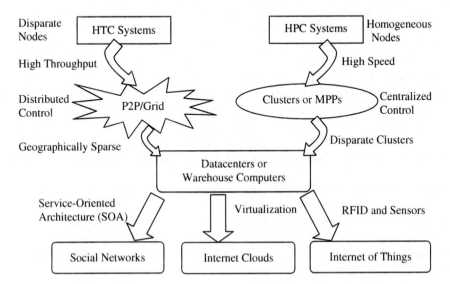

Figure 1.5 Evolutional trend towards parallel, distributed and cloud computing using clusters, MPPs, P2P networks, computing grids, Internet clouds, web services and the Internet of things. (HPC: high-performance computing; HTC: high-throughput computing; P2P: peer-to-peer; MPP: massively parallel processors; RFID: Radio Frequency Identification [2].)

(massively parallel processors, MPP) are gradually replaced by clusters of cooperative computers out of a desire to share computing resources. The cluster is often a collection of homogeneous compute nodes that are physically connected in close range to each other.

On the HTC side, Peer-to-Peer (P2P) networks are formed for distributed file sharing and content delivery applications. Both P2P, cloud computing and web service platforms place more emphasis on HTC rather than HPC applications. For many years, HPC systems emphasized raw speed performance. Therefore, we are facing a strategic change from the HPC to the HTC paradigm. This HTC paradigm pays more attention to high-flux multi-computing, where Internet searches and web services are requested by millions or more users simultaneously. The performance goal is thus shifted to measure the high throughput or the number of tasks completed per unit of time.

In the big data era, we are facing a data deluge problem. Data comes from IoT sensors, lab experiments, simulations, society archives and the web in all scales and formats. Preservation, movement and access of massive datasets require generic tools supporting high performance scalable file systems, databases, algorithms, workflow and visualization. With science becoming data centric, a new paradigm of scientific discovery is based on data intensive computing. We need to foster tools for data capture, data creation and data analysis. The cloud and IoT technologies are driven by the surge of interest in the deluge of data.

The Internet and WWW are used by billions of people every day. As a result, large datacenters or clouds must be designed to provide not only big storage but also distributed computing power to satisfy the requests of a large number of users simultaneously. The emergence of public or hybrid clouds demands the upgrade of many datacenters using larger server clusters, distributed file systems and high-bandwidth networks. With massive smart phones and tablets requesting services, the cloud engines, distributed storage and mobile networks must interact with the Internet to deliver mashup services in web-scale mobile computing over the social and media networks closely.

Both P2P, cloud computing and web service platforms emphasize high-throughput over a large number of user tasks, rather than high performance as often targeted in using supercomputers. This high-throughput paradigm pays more attention to the high flux of user tasks concurrently or simultaneously. The main application of the high-flux cloud system lies in Internet searches and web services. The performance goal is thus shifted to measure the high throughput or the number of tasks completed per unit of time. This not only demands improvement in the high speed of batch processing, but also addresses the acute problem of cost, energy saving, security and reliability in the clouds.

The advances in virtualization make it possible to use Internet clouds in massive user services. In fact, the differences among clusters, P2P systems and clouds may become blurred. Some view the clouds as computing clusters with modest changes in virtualization. Others anticipate the effective processing of huge datasets generated by web services, social networks and IoT. In this sense, many users consider cloud platforms a form of utility computing or service computing.

1.1.2.1. Convergence of Technologies

Cloud computing is enabled by the convergence of the four technologies illustrated in Figure 1.6. Hardware virtualization and multicore chips make it possible to have

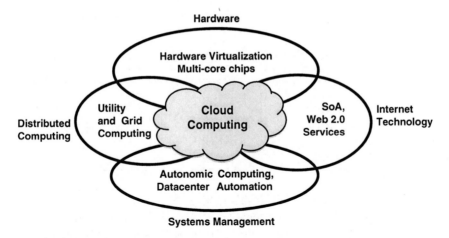

Figure 1.6 Technological convergence enabling cloud computing over the Internet. (Courtesy of Buyya, Broberg and Goscinski, reprinted with permission [3])

dynamic configurations in clouds. Utility and grid computing technologies lay the necessary foundation of computing clouds. Recent advances in service oriented architecture (SOA), Web 2.0 and mashups of platforms are pushing the cloud to another forward step. Autonomic computing and automated datacenter operations have enabled cloud computing.

Cloud computing explores the muti-core and parallel computing technologies. To realize the vision on data-intensive systems, we need to converge from four areas: namely hardware, Internet technology, distributed computing and system management, as illustrated in Figure 1.6. Today's Internet technology places the emphasis on SOA and Web 2.0 services. Utility and grid computing lay the distributed computing foundation needed for cloud computing. Finally, we cannot ignore the widespread use of datacenters with virtualization techniques applied to automate the resources provisioning process in clouds.

1.1.2.2. Utility Computing

Computing paradigms are attributed to different characteristics. First, they are all ubiquitous to our daily lives. Reliability and scalability are two major design objectives. Second, they are aimed at autonomic operations that can be self-organized to support dynamic discovery. Finally, these paradigms can be mixed with QoS (quality of service) and SLA (service-level agreement), etc. These paradigms and their attributes realize the computer utility vision.

Utility computing is based on a business model, by which customers receive computing resources from cloud or IoT service providers. This demands some technological challenges, including almost all aspects of computer science and engineering. For example, users may demand new network-efficient processors, scalable memory and storage schemes, distributed OS, middleware for machine virtualization, new programming models, effective resource management and application program development. These hardware and software advances are necessary to facilitate mobile cloud computing in various IoT application domains.

Table 1.1 Differences of three cloud service models from the on-premise computing in resources control under user, vendor and shared responsibilities.

Resources Types	On-Premise Computing	IaaS Model	PaaS Model	SaaS Model
App Software	User	User	Shared	*Vendor*
Virtual Machines	User	Shared	Shared	*Vendor*
Servers	User	*Vendor*	*Vendor*	*Vendor*
Storage	User	*Vendor*	*Vendor*	*Vendor*
Networking	Shared	*Vendor*	*Vendor*	*Vendor*

1.1.2.3. Cloud Computing versus On-Premise Computing

Additional computing applications are primarily executed on local hosts on premises. They appear as desktops, deskside, notebooks or tablets, etc. On-premise computing differs from cloud computing mainly in resources control and infrastructure management. In Table 1.1, we compare three cloud service models with the on-premise computing paradigm. We consider hardware and software resources in five types: storage, servers, virtual machines, networking and application software, as listed in the left-hand column of Table 1.1. In the case of on-premise computing at local hosts, all resources must be acquired by the users except networking, which is shared between users and the provider. This implies a heavy burden and operating expenses on the part of the users.

In the case of using an IaaS cloud like AWS EC2, the user only needs to worry about application software deployment. The virtual machines are jointly deployed by user and provider. The vendors are responsible for providing the remaining hardware and networks. In using the PaaS clouds, like Google AppEngine, both application codes and virtual machines are jointly deployed by user and vendor and the remaining resources are provided by the vendors. Finally, when the SaaS model is using the Saleforce cloud, everything is provided by the vendor, even including the app software. In conclusion, we see that cloud computing reduces users' infrastructure management burdens from two resources to none, as we move from IaaS to PaaS and SaaS services. This clearly shows the advantages for users in separating the application from resources investment and management.

1.1.2.4. Towards a Big Data Industry

As shown in Table 1.2, we had a database industry in the 1960 to 1990s. At that time most data blocks were measured as MB, GB and TB. Datacenters became widely in use

Table 1.2 Evolution of the big data industry in three development stages.

Stage	Databases	Data Centers	Big Data Industry
Time Frame	1960–1990	1980–2010	2010 and Beyond
Data Sizes	MB – GB -TB	TB – PB - EB	EB – ZB - YB
Market Size and Growth Rate	Database market, Data/Knowledge Engineering	$22.6 B market by IDC 2012, (21.5% growth)	$34 B in IT spending (2013), 4.4 M new big data jobs (2015), Gartner predicts it to exceed 100 B by 2020

from 1980 to 2010, with datasets easily ranging from TB to PB or even EB. After 2010, we saw the gradual formation of a new industry called big data. To process big data in the future, we expect EB to ZB or YB. The market size of the big data industry reached 34 billion in 2013. Exceeding 100 billion in big data applications is within reach by 2020.

1.1.3   Interactive SMACT Technologies

Almost all applications demand computing economics, web-scale data collection, system reliability and scalable performance, such as in the banking and finance industries described above. In recent years, five cutting-edge information technologies: namely Social, Mobile, Analytics, Cloud and IoT, have become more demanding, known as the SMACT technologies. Table 1.3 summarizes the underlying theories, hardware, software and networking advances, and representative service providers of these five technologies. We will study these advances in subsequent chapters.

1.1.3.1.   The Internet of Things

The traditional Internet connects machines to machines or web pages to web pages. The IoT refers to the networked interconnection of everyday objects, tools, devices or computers [4]. The things (objects) of our daily life can be large or small. The idea is to tag every object using radio-frequency identification (RFID) or related sensor or electronic technologies like GPS (global positioning system). With the introduction of IPv6 protocol, there are 2^{128} IP addresses available to distinguish all objects on the Earth, including all mobile, embedded devices, computers and even some biological objects. It is estimated that an average person is surrounded by 1000 to 5000 objects on a daily basis.

The IoT needs to be designed to track 100 trillion static or moving objects simultaneously. For this reason, the IoT demands unique addressability of all objects on the Earth. The objects are coded or labeled and IP-identifiable. They are instrumented and interconnected by various types of wired or wireless networks. In some cases they can interact with each other intelligently over the network. The term Internet of Things (IoT) is a physical concept. The size of the IoT can be large or small, covering local regions or a wide range of physical spaces. An IoT is not a just virtual network or logical network or peer-to-peer (P2P) network in cyber space. In other words, the IoTs are built in the physical world, even though they are logically addressable in cyberspace.

Communication among objects can be done in a variety of ways: For example, H2H refers to human-to-human, H2T for human-to-things, T2T for things-to-things, etc. The importance is to connect any things at any time and any place at low cost. By anything connections, we refer to between PCs, H2H (not using PCs but using mobile devices), H2T (using generic equipment) and T2T. By any-place connections, we refer to all the PCs, indoors, outdoors and on the move. By any-time, we imply connections at any time period: day time, night time, outdoor and indoors, and on the move, etc. The dynamic connections will grow exponentially into a new universal network of networks, called IoT. The IoT is strongly tied to specific application domains. Different application domains are embraced by different community circles or groups in our society. We simply call them the IoT domains or IoT networks accordingly.

Table 1.3 SMACT technologies characterized by basic theories, typical hardware, software tooling, networking and service providers needed.

SMACT Technology	Theoretical Foundations	Hardware Advances	Software Tools and Libraries	Networking Enablers	Representative Service Providers
Mobile Systems	Telecommunication, Radio Access Theory, Mobile Computing	Smart Devices, Wireless, Mobility Infrastructures	Android, iOS, Uber, WeChat, NFC, iCloud, Google Player	4G LTE, WiFi, Bluetooth, Radio Access Networks	AT&T Wireless, T-Mobile, Verizon, Apple, Samsung, Huawei
Social Networks	Social Science, Graph Theory, Statistics, Social Computing	Datacenters, Search Engines and WWW Infrastructure	Browsers, APIs, Web 2.0. YouTube, Whatsapp, WeChat, Massager	Broadband Internet, Software- Defined Networks	Facebook, Twitter, QQ, Linkedin, Baidu, Amazon, Taobao
Big Data Analytics	Data Mining, Machine Learning, Artificial Intelligence	Datacenters, Clouds, Search Engines, Big Data Lakes, Data Storage	Spark, Hama, DatTorrent, MLlib, Impala, GraphX, KFS, Hive, Hbase,	Co-Location Clouds, Mashups, P2P Networks, etc.	AMPLab, Apache, Cloudera, FICO, Databricks, eBay, Oracle
Cloud Computing	Virtualization Parallel and Distributed Computing	Server clusters, Clouds, Virtual Machines, Interconnection networks.	OpenStack, GFS, HDFS, MapReduce, Hadoop, Spark, Storm, Cassandra	Virtual Networks, OpenFlow Networks, Software-defined Networks	AWS, GAE, IBM, Salesforce, GoGrid Apache, Azure Rachspace, DropBox
Internet of Things (IoT)	Sensing Theory, Cyber Physics, Navigation, Pervasive Computing	Sensors, RFID, GPS, Robotics, Satellites, Zigbee, Gyroscope	TyneOS, WAP, WTCP, IPv6, Mobile IP, Android, iOS, WPKI, UPnP, JVM	Wireless LAN, PAN, MANET, WLAN Mesh, VANet, Bluetooth	IoT Council, IBM, Healthcare, SmartGrid, Social Media, Smart Earth, Google, Samsung

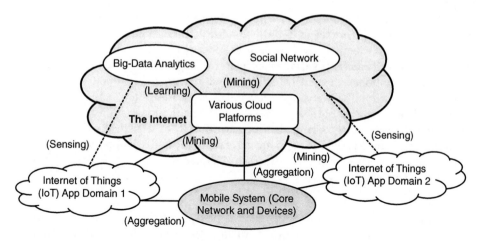

Figure 1.7 Interactions among social networks, mobile systems, big data analytics and cloud platforms over various Internet of Things (IoT) domains.

1.1.3.2. Interactions among SMACT Subsystems

Figure 1.7 illustrates the interactions among the five SMACT technologies. Multiple cloud platforms work closely with many mobile networks to provide the service core interactively. The IoT networks connect any objects including sensors, computers, humans and any IP-identifiable objects on the Earth, The IoT networks appear in different forms in different application domains. The social networks, such as Facebook and Twitter, and big data analytics systems are built within the Internet. All social, analytics and IoT networks are connected to the clouds via the Internet and mobile networks, including some edge networks like WiFi, Ethernet or even some GPS and Bluetooth data.

We need to reveal the interactions among these data-producing, transmission or processing subsystems in the mobile Internet system. In Figure 1.7, we label the edges between subsystems by the actions taking place between them. We briefly introduce below these interactive actions for five purposes: i) data signal sensing is tied to the interactions among IoT and social networks with the cloud platforms; ii) data mining involves the use of cloud power for effective use of captured data; iii) aggregation of data takes place between the mobile system; iv) IoT domains; and vi)the processing clouds. Machine learning forms the basis for big data analytics.

1.1.3.3. Interactions among Technologies

Large amounts of sensor data or digital signals are generated by mobile systems, social networks and various IoT domains. Sensing of RFID, sensor network and GPS generated data is needed to capture the data timely and selectively, if unstructured data were to be disrupted by noises or air loss. IoT sensing demands high quality of data, and filtering is often used to enhance the data quality. Chapter 3 is dedicated to various sensing operation in the IoT system:

- **Data Mining:** Data mining involves the discovery, collection, aggregation, transformation, matching and processing of large datasets. Data mining is a fundamental operation incurred with the big data information system. The ultimate purpose is knowledge discovery from the data. Both numerical, textual, pattern, image and video data can be mined. Chapter 2 will cover the essence of big data mining in particular.

- **Data Aggregation and Integration:** This refers to data preprocessing to improve data quality. Important operations include data cleaning, removing redundancy, checking relevance, data reduction, transformation and discretization, etc.
- **Machine Learning and Big Data Analytics:** This is the foundation to use cloud's computing power to analyze large datasets scientifically or statistically. Special computer programs are written to automatically learn to recognize complex patterns and make intelligent decisions based on the data. Chapters 4, 5 and 8 will cover machine learning and big data analytics.

1.1.3.4. Technology Fusion to Meet the Future Demand

The IoT extends the Internet of computers to any object. The joint use of clouds, IoT, mobile devices and social networks is crucial to capture big data from all sources. This integrated system is envisioned by IBM researchers as a "smart earth" [22], which enables fast, efficient and intelligent interactions among humans, machines and any objects surrounding us. A smart earth must have intelligent cities, clean water, efficient power, convenient transportation, safe food supplies, responsible banks, fast telecommunications, green IT, better schools, health care and abundant resources to share. This sounds like a dream, which is yet to become a reality in the years to come.

In general, mature technology is supposed to be adopted quickly. The combined use of two or more technologies may demand additional efforts to integrate them for the common purpose. Thus integration may demand some transformational changes. In order to enable innovative new applications, core technology transformation presents a challenge. Disruptive technology is even more difficult to be integrated due to higher risk. They may demand more research and experimentation or prototyping efforts. This takes us on to consider technology fusion by blending different technologies together to complement each other.

All five SMACT technologies are deployed within the mobile Internet (also known as wireless Internet). The IoT networks may appear in many different forms at different application domains. For example, we may build in IoT domains for national defense, healthcare, green energy, social media and smart cities, etc. Social networks and big data analysis subsystems are built in the Internet with fast database search and mobile access facilities. High storage and processing power are provided by domain-specific cloud services on dedicated platforms. We still have a long way to go before we see widespread use of domain-specific cloud platforms for big data or IoT applications in the mobile Internet environment.

1.2 Social-Media, Mobile Networks and Cloud Computing

This section gives an overview of social networks, mobile devices and radio-access networks of all sorts for short-range and wide-range communications and data movement. Social and mobile cloud computing will be assessed. More detailed treatment of these topics can be found in Chapters 4, 7, 8 and 9.

Table 1.4 Summary of popular social networks and web services provided.

Social Network, Year and Website	Registered Active Users	Major Services Provided
Facebook, *2004* *http://www.facebook.com*	*1.65 billion users, 2016*	*Content sharing, profiling, advertising, events, social comparison, communication, play social games, etc.*
Tencent QQ *in China, 1999* *http://www.qq.com*	*853 million users, 2016*	*An instant messaging service, on-line games, music, ebQQ, shopping, microblogging, movies, WeChat, QQ Player, etc.*
Linkedin, *2002,* *http://www.linkedin.com*	*364 million users, 2015*	*Professional services, on-line recruiting, job listings, group services, skills, publishing, influences, advertising, etc.*
Twitter, *2006* *http://www.twitter.com*	*320 million users, 2016*	*Microblogging, news, alerts, short messages, rankings, demographics, revenue sources, photo-sharing, etc.*

1.2.1 Social Networks and Web Service Sites

Most social networks provide human services such as friendship connections, personal profiling, professional services, entertainment, etc. In general, the user must register to become a member to access the website. Users can create a user profile, add other users as "friends", exchange messages, post status updates and photos, share videos and receive notifications when others update their profiles. In addition, users may join common-interest user groups, organized by workplace, school or college, or other characteristics, and categorize their friends into lists such as "People From Work" or "Close Friends", etc. In Table 1.4, we compare several popular social networks and introduce their services briefly.

Facebook is by far the largest social networking service provider, with over 1.65 billion users. The Tencent QQ network is the second largest social network based in China. The QQ network has over 800 million users. It is really the Facebook in China, with extended services such as email accounts, entertainment and even some web business operations. Linkedin is a business-oriented social network providing professional services. It is highly used by large business enterprises in recruiting and search for talent. Twitter offers the largest short text message and blogging services today. Other sites are on-line shopping networks or tied to special interest groups.

Example 1.1 Facebook Platform Architecture and Social Services Provided
With 1.65 billion active users worldwide in 2016, Facebook keeps huge personal profiles, tags and relationships as social graphs. Most users are in the US, Brazil, India, Indonesia, etc. The social graphs are shared by various social groups on the site. This website has attracted over 3 millions active advertisers with $12.5 billion revenue reported in 2014. The Facebook platform is built with a collection of huge datacenters with a very large storage capacity, intelligent file systems and searching capabilities. The web must resolve the traffic jams and collisions among all its users. In Figure 1.8(a), the infrastructure of the Facebook platform is shown.

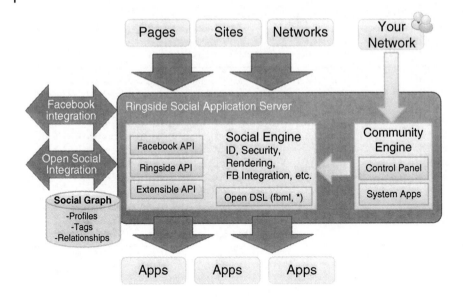

(a) Facebook infrastructure

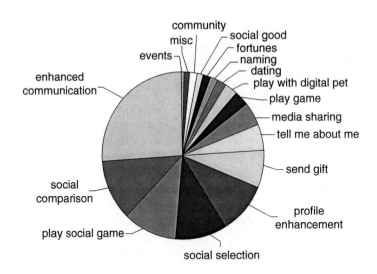

(b) Facebook application distribution

Figure 1.8 The Facebook platform offering over 2.4 millions of user applications [6].

The platform is formed with a huge cluster of servers. The requests are shown as pages, sites and networks entering the Facebook server from the top. The social engine is the core of the application server. This social engine handles IS, security, rendering and Facebook integration operations. Large numbers of APIs are made available to benefit users to use more than 2.4 millions of applications. Facebook has acquired

Table 1.5 Service functionality of the Facebook platform.

Function	Short Description
Profile Pages	Profile picture, bio information, friends list, user's activity log, public messages
Graph Traversal	Access through users' friends list on profile pages, with access control
Communication	Send and receive messages among friends, instant messaging, and micro blogging
Shared Items	Photo album with built-in access control, embedded outside videos on profile page
Access Control	Access control levels: Only me, Only friends, Friends of friends, and Everyone
Special APIs	Games, calendars, mobile clients, etc.

Insragram, WhatsApp, Qculus VR and PrivateCore applications. The social engine executes all user applications. Open DSL is used to support application executions. The service functionalities of Facebook include six essential items, as summarized in Table 1.5.

Facebook provides blogging, chat, gifts, marketplace, voice/video calls, etc. Figure 1.8(b) shows the distribution of Facebook services. There is a community engine that provides networking services to users. Most Facebook applications are helping users to achieve their social goals, such as improved communication, learning about self, finding similar others, engaging in social play and exchanges. Therefore, Facebook appeals more in the private and personal domains. ∎

1.2.2 Mobile Cellular Core Networks

A cellular network or mobile network is a wireless network distributed over land areas called cells, each served by at least one fixed-location transceiver, known as a cell site or base station. In a cellular network, each cell uses a different set of frequencies from neighboring cells, to avoid interference and provide guaranteed bandwidth within each cell. Mobile communications systems have revolutionized the way people communicate, joining together communications and mobility. Figure 1.9 shows the progress of mobile core networks for wide-range communications, having gone through five generations of development, while short-range wireless communication has also upgraded in data rate, QoS and applications during the same period.

Evolution of wireless access technologies has just entered the fourth generation (4G). Looking at the past, wireless access technologies have followed different evolutionary paths aimed at performance and efficiency in a high mobile environment. The first generation (1G) has fulfilled the basic mobile voice communication needs, while the second generation (2G) has introduced the capacity and coverage. The third generation (3G) is a quest for data at higher speeds to open the gates for truly "mobile broadband" experience. The fourth generation (4G) provides access to a wide range of telecommunication services, including advanced mobile services, supported by mobile and fixed networks, which are fully packet switched with high mobility and data rates.

As the mobile communications industry traveled a long way from 2G to 4G, now 5G aims to change the world by connecting anything to anything. Different from its

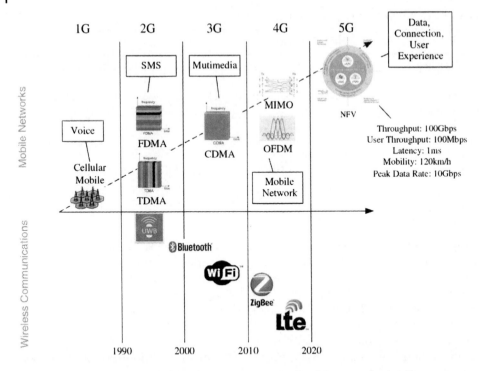

Figure 1.9 Mobile core networks for wide-range communications have gone through five generations, while short-range wireless networks upgraded in data rate, QoS and applications.

previous versions, the research of 5G is not only focusing on new spectrum bands, wireless transmissions, cellular networking, etc., for an increase in capacity. It will be an intelligent technology to interconnect the wireless world without barriers. To meet the requirements of the 5G to enable higher capacity, higher rate, more connectivity, higher reliability, lower latency, larger versatility and application-domain specific topologies, new concepts and design approaches are needed. Current standardization work for 4G may influence the introduction of promising radio features and network solutions for 5G systems.

New network architectures, extending beyond heterogeneous networks and exploiting new frequency spectrum (e.g. mmWave), are emerging from research laboratories around the world. In addition to the network side, advanced terminals and receivers are being developed to optimize network performances. Splitting the control and data planes (currently studied in 3GPP) is an interesting paradigm for 5G, together with massive multi-input multi-output (MIMO), advanced antenna systems, software-defined networking (SDN), Network Functions Virtualization (NFV), Internet of Things (IoT) and cloud computing.

1.2.3 Mobile Devices and Internet Edge Networks

Mobile devices appear as smart phones, tablet computers, wearable gear and industrial tools. Global users of mobile devices exceeded 3 billions in 2015. The 1G devices, used in the 1980s, were mostly analog phones for voice communication only. The 2G mobile networks began in the early 1990s. Digital phones appeared accordingly for both voice and data communications. As shown in Figure 1.9, 2G cellular networks appear as GSM, TDMA, FDMA and CDMA, based on different division schemes to allow multiple callers to access the system simultaneously. The basic 2G network supports 9.6 Kbps data with circuit switching. The speed was improved to 115 Kbps with packet radio services. Up to 2015, 2G networks were still in use in many developing countries.

Since 2000, 2G mobile devices have been gradually replaced by 3G products. The 3G networks and phones are designed to have 2 Mbps speed to meet the demand of multimedia communications through the cellular system. The 4G LTE (Long Term Evolution) networks appeared in the 2000s. They were targeted to achieve a download speed of 100 Mbps, upload speed of 50 Mbps and a static speed of 1 Gbps. The 3G system is enabled by better radio technology with MIMO smart antennas and OFDM technology. The 3G systems have received widespread deployment now, but could be replaced gradually by 4G networks. We expect the mixed use of 3G and 4G networks for at least another decade. The 5G networks may appear beyond 2020 with a target speed of at least 100 Gbps.

1.2.3.1. Mobile Core Networks

The cellular radios access networks (RAN) are structured hierarchically. Mobile core networks form the backbone of today's telecommunication systems. The core networks have gone through four generations of deployment in the past three decades. The 1G mobile network was used for analog voice communication based on the circuit switching technology. The 2G mobile network started in the early 1990s to support the use of digital telephones in both voice and data telecommunications exploring packet switching circuits. Famous 2G systems are the GSM (Global System for Mobile Communications) developed in Europe and the CDMA (Code Division Multiple Access) system developed in the US. Both GSM and CDMA systems are deployed in various countries.

The 3G mobile network was developed for multimedia voice/data communications with global roaming services. The 4G system started in the early 2000s based on the LTE and MIMO radio technologies. The 5G mobile networks are still under heavy development, which may appear in 2020. The technology, peak data rate and driven applications of the five generations of cellular mobile networks are summarized in Table 1.6. Speedwise, the mobile systems improved from 1 Kbps to 10 Kbps, 2 Mbps and

Table 1.6 Milestone mobile core networks for cellular telecommunication.

Generation	1 G	2 G	3 G	4 G	5 G
Radio and Networks Technology	Analog phones, AMPS, TDMA	Digital phones GSM, CDMA	CDMA2000, WCDMA, and D-SCDMA	LTE, OFDM, MIMO, software-steered radio	LTE, Cloud-based RAN
Peak Mobile Data Rate	8 Kbps	9.6–344 Kbps	2 Mbps	100 Mbps	10 Gbps–1 Tbps)
Driving Applications	Voice Communication	Voice/Data Communication	Multimedia Communication	Wide band Communication	Ultra-speed Communication

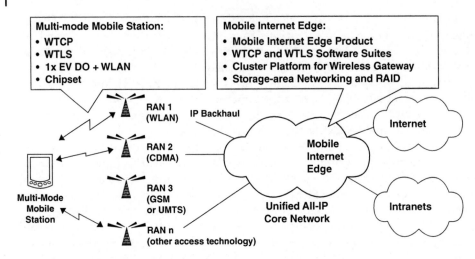

Figure 1.10 The interactions of various radio-access networks (RANs) with the unified all-IP based mobile core network, Intranets and the Internet.

100 Mbps in four generations. It is projected that the upcoming 5G system may achieve a 1000 increase in data rate to 100 Gbps or higher. The 5G system may be built with remote radio head (RRH) and virtual base stations installed in CRAN (Cloud-based Radio Access Networks).

1.2.3.2. Mobile Internet Edge Networks

Most of today's wireless and mobile networks are based on radio signal transmission and reception at various operating ranges. We call them radio access networks (RANs). Figure 1.10 illustrated how various RANs are used to access the mobile core networks, which are connected to the Internet backbone and many Intranets through mobile Internet edge networks. Such an Internet access infrastructure is also known as the wireless Internet or mobile Internet by the pervasive computing community. In what follows, we introduce several classes of RANs known as WiFi, Bluetooth, WiMax and Zigbee networks. Generally speaking, we consider several short-range wireless networks, such as wireless local-area network (WLAN), wireless home-area network (WHAN), personal-area network (PAN) and body-area network (BAN), etc. These wireless networks play a key role in mobile computing and IoT applications.

1.2.3.3. Bluetooth Devices and Networks

Bluetooth is a short-range radio technology named after a Danish King dating back to the 9th century. A Bluetooth device operates in 2.45 GHz industrial scientific medical band, as specified by IEEE 802.15.1 Standard. It transmits omni-directional (360°) signals with no limit on line of sight, meaning data or voice can penetrate solid non-metal object. It supports up to 8 devices (1 master and 7 slaves) in a PAN called *Piconet.* Bluetooth devices have low cost and low power requirements. The device offers a data rate of 1 Mbps in *ad hoc* networking with 10 cm to 10 meters in range. It supports voice or data communication between phones, computers and other wearable devices. Essentially, Bluetooth wireless connections are replacing most wired cables between computers and their peripherals such as mouse, keyboard and printers, etc.

1.2.3.4. WiFi Networks

WiFi access point or WiFi networks are specified in the IEEE 802.11 Standard. So far, they have appeared as a Series of 11 a, b, g, n, ac and ay networks. The access point broadcasts its signal in a radius of less than 300 ft. The closer it is to the access point, the faster will be the data rate experienced. The maximum speed is only possible within 50–175 ft. The peak data rates of WiFi networks have improved from less than 11 Mbps in 11b to 54 Mbps in 11g and 300 Mbps in 11n networks. The 11n and 11ac network applies OFDG modulation technology with the use of multiple input and multiple output (MIMO) radio and antenna to achieve its high speed. WiFi enables the fastest WLAN in a mesh of access points or wireless routers. They offer almost free access to the Internet within 300 ft at many locations today.

1.2.4 Mobile Cloud Computing Infrastructure

Mobile devices are rapidly becoming the major service participants nowadays. There is a shift of user preferences from traditional cell phones and laptops to smart phones and tablets. Advances in the portability and capability of mobile devices, together with widespread 3G/4G LTE networks and Wi-Fi accesses, have brought rich mobile application experiences to the end users. Mobile cloud computing is a model for elastic augmentation of mobile device capabilities via ubiquitous wireless access to cloud storage and computing resources. This is further enhanced by context-aware dynamic adaption to the changes in the operating environment. Figure 1.11 shows a typical mobile environment for offloading large jobs to remote clouds from mobile device holders.

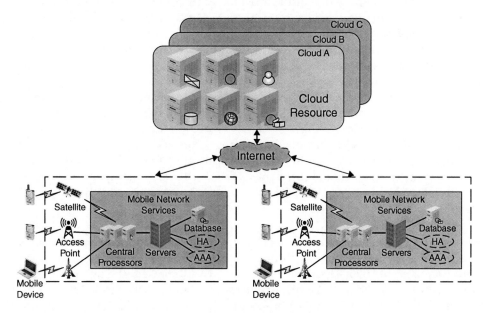

Figure 1.11 The architecture of a mobile cloud computing environment.

With the support of mobile cloud computing (MCC), a mobile user basically has a new cloud option to execute its application. The user attempts to offload the computation through WiFi, cellular network or satellite to the distant clouds. The terminal devices at the user end have limited resources, i.e. hardware, energy, bandwidth, etc. The cellphone itself is infeasible to finish some compute-intensive tasks. Instead, the data related to the computation task is offloaded to the remote cloud. Special cloudlets were introduced to serve as wireless gateways between mobile users and the Internet. These cloudlets can be used to offload computations or web services to remote clouds safely. Details of cloudlets for mobile clouds will be described in Chapter 2.

1.3 Big Data Acquisition and Analytics Evolution

Big data analytics is the process of examining large amounts of data of a variety of types (big data) to uncover hidden patterns, unknown correlations and other useful information. Such information can provide competitive advantages over rival organizations and result in higher business intelligence or scientific discovery, such as more effective marketing, increased revenue, etc. The primary goal of big data analytics is to help companies make better business decisions by enabling data scientists and other users to analyze huge volumes of transaction data that may be left untapped by conventional business intelligence (BI) programs.

1.3.1 Big Data Value Chain Extracted from Massive Data

Data science, data mining, data analytics and knowledge discovery are closely related terms. In many cases, they are used interchangeably. These big data components form a big data value chain built up of statistics, machine learning, biology and kernel methods. Statistics cover both linear and logistic regression. Decision trees are typical machine learning tools. Biology refers to artificial neural networks, genetic algorithms and swarm intelligence. Finally, the kernel method includes the use of support vector machines. These underlying theories and models will be studied in Chapters 4, 5 and 6. Their applications will be covered in Chapters 7, 8 and 9.

Compared with traditional datasets, big data generally includes masses of unstructured data that need more real-time analysis. In addition, big data also brings about new opportunities for discovering new values, helps us to gain an in-depth understanding of the hidden values, and incurs new challenges, for example on how to effectively organize and manage such data. At present, big data has attracted considerable interest from industry, academia and government agencies. Recently, the rapid growth of big data mainly comes from people's daily life, especially related to the Internet, Web and cloud services.

Example 1.2   Expected Growth of Big Data from 2010 to 2020 and Economic Gains
The size of a big dataset varies with time. Table 1.7 shows some representative data sizes from 2010 to 2020. These numbers simply give the reader the impression of a steady increase with time. By the 2015 standard, a dataset of 1 TB is labeled as big data. The massive volumes bring in values in economic gains as revealed in the bottom rows. Just location sensitive applications can deliver $800 billion revenue in 10 years. Big data

Table 1.7 The Growth of big data from 2010 to 2020 and expected economic value in two typical big data applications.

Big Data Sources, Observed Growth in Data Size and Year	Data Size
Global data generated in 2 days in 2011	1.82 ZB
Pictures uploaded to Facebook in 2014	759 million pieces
Storage capacity of American manufacturing industry in 2010	966 PB
Number of RFID tags scanned in 2011 to 2020	12 million to 209 billion
Data captured during a computer geek's 2.450 million hours	200 TB
Personal location data services could reach the level of $800 billion dollars in 10 years	
Savings from healthcare analysis and treatment could exceed $300 billion dollars in the US	

applied for healthcare may save $300 billions in medical expenses in the US. The big data industry is gradually shaping up over time. ∎

At present, data has become an important production factor that could be comparable to material assets and human capital. As multimedia, social media and IoT are fast evolving, business enterprises will collect more information, leading to an exponential growth of data volume. Big data will have a huge and increasing potential in creating values for businesses and consumers. The most critical aspect of big data analytics is big data value. We divide the value chain of big data into four phases: data generation, data acquisition, data storage and data analysis. If we take data as a raw material, data generation and data acquisition are exploitation processes, as data storage must use clouds or datacenters. Data analysis is a production process that utilizes the raw material to create new value.

The rapid growth of cloud computing and IoT also triggers the sharp growth of data. Cloud computing provides safeguarding, access sites and channels for data assets. In the paradigm of IoT, sensors worldwide are collecting and transmitting data to be stored and processed in the cloud. Such data in both quantity and mutual relations will far surpass the capacities of the IT architectures and infrastructure of existing enterprises, and its real-time requirement will greatly stress the available computing capacity. The following example highlights some representative big data values driven by the massive data volume involved.

1.3.1.1. Big Data Generation

The major data types include Internet data, sensory data, etc. This is the first step of big data. Given Internet data as an example, huge amounts of data in terms of searching entries, Internet forum posts, chatting records and microblog messages, are generated. Those data are closely related to people's daily lives, and have similar features of high value and low density. Such Internet data may be valueless individually but, through the exploitation of accumulated big data, useful information such as habits and hobbies of users can be identified, and it is even possible to forecast users' behaviors and emotional moods.

Moreover, generated through longitudinal and/or distributed data sources, datasets are more large-scale, highly diverse and complex. Such data sources include sensors, videos, clickstreams, and/or all other available data sources. At present, main sources of big data are the operation and trading information in business enterprises, logistics and sensing information in the IoT, human interaction information and position information in the Internet world, and data generated in scientific research, etc.

1.3.2 Data Quality Control, Representation and Database Models

In Table 1.8, we summarize interesting properties and attributes that affect the data quality. We introduce the methods, architectures and tools for big data analysis. Our studies by no means cover all progress made in this field. We identify the key concepts and some representative tools or database models used in this context. Big data sources come from business transactions, textual and multimedia contents, qualitative knowledge data, scientific discovery, social media and sensing data from IoT. The quality of the data is often poor due to the massive volume, data variety due to unpredictable data types, and data veracity for lack of traceability.

The quality control of big data involves a circular cycle of four stages: i) we must identify the important data quality attributes; ii) to access the data relies on the ability to measure or assess the data quality level; iii) then we must be able to analyze the data quality and their major causes; and finally iv) we need to improve the data quality by suggesting concrete actions to take. Unfortunately, none of these tasks are easy to implement. In Table 1.8, we identify the important attributes towards data quality control. Among these data quality control dimensions, the intrinsic attributes and representational and access control mechanisms are equally important.

Data can be represented in many different ways. Four major representation models are suggested for big data: i) the <key, value> pairs is often used to distribute data in MapReduce operations (to be presented in Chapter 5). The Dynamo Volldemort is a good example to use key-value pairs; ii) table lookup or relational database such as

Table 1.8 Attributes for data quality control, representation and database operations.

Category	Attributes	Basic Definitions and Questions To Ask
Intrinsic and Contextual	Accuracy and Trust	Data correctness and credibility: true, fake or accurate?
	Integrity and Reputation	Biased or impartial data? Reputation of data source?
	Relevance and Value	Data relevance to task at hand and value added or not?
	Volume and Completeness	Data volume tested and any value present?
Representation	Easy to Comprehend	Data clarity and easy to understand without ambiguity?
	Interpretability and Visualization	Data well represented in numbers, textual, graphs, image, video, profiles or metadata, etc.?
Accessibility and Security	Access Control	Data availability, access control protocols, easy to retrieve?
	Security Precautions	Restricted access or integrity control from alteration or deletion?

Google's BigTable and Cassandra software; iii) graphic tools like GraphX used in Spark for social graph analysis, and iv) special database systems such as MongoDB, SimpkleDB and CouchDB commonly used by the big data community.

1.3.3 Big Data Acquisition and Preprocessing

Loading is the most complex procedure among the three, which includes operations such as transformation, copy, clearing, standardization, screening and data organization. A virtual database can be built to query and aggregate data from different data sources, but such a database does not contain data. On the contrary, it includes information or metadata related to actual data and its positions. Such two "storage-reading" approaches do not satisfy the high performance requirements of data flows or search programs and applications. Compared with queries, data in such two approaches is more dynamic and must be processed during data transmission.

Generally, data integration methods are accompanied with flow processing engines and search engines:

1) **Data Selection:** Select a target dataset or subset of data samples on which the discovery is to be performed.
2) **Data Transformation:** Simplify the datasets by removing unwanted variables. Then analyze useful features that can be used to represent the data, depending on the goal or task.
3) **Data Mining:** Searching for patterns of interest in a particular representational form or a set of such representations as classification rules or trees, regression, clustering, and so forth.
4) **Evaluation and knowledge representation:** Evaluate knowledge pattern, and utilize visualization techniques to present the knowledge vividly.

1.3.3.1. Big Data Acquisition

This includes data collection, data transmission and data pre-processing. As the second phase, data acquisition also includes data collection, data transmission and data pre-processing. During big data acquisition, once we collect the raw data, we utilize an efficient transmission mechanism to send it to a proper storage management system to support different analytical applications. The collected datasets may sometimes include much redundant or useless data, which unnecessarily increases storage space and affects the subsequent data analysis. Table 1.9 summarizes major data acquisition methods and preprocessing operations.

For example, high redundancy is very common among datasets collected by sensors for environmental monitoring. Data compression technology can be applied to reduce the redundancy. Therefore, data pre-processing operations are indispensable to ensure

Table 1.9 Some big data acquisition sources and major preprocessing operations.

Collection Sources	Logs, sensors, crawlers, packet capture and mobile devices, etc.
Preprocessing Steps	Integration, Cleaning and Redundancy elimination
Data Generators	Social Media, Enterprises, Internet of Things, Internet, Bio-Medical, Government, scientific discovery, environments, etc.

efficient data storage and exploitation. Data collection is to utilize special data collection techniques to acquire raw data from a specific data generation environment. Many common data collection and generation sources and data generators are introduced below.

1.3.3.2. Log Files

CAs are one widely used data collection method, and log files are record files automatically generated by the data source system, so as to record activities in designated file formats for subsequent analysis. Log files are typically used in nearly all digital devices. For example, web servers record in log files the number of clicks, click rates, visits, and other property records of web users. To capture activities of users at the websites, web servers mainly include the following three log file formats: public log file format (NCSA), expanded log format (W3C) and IIS log format (Microsoft).

All three types of log files are in the ASCII text format. Databases other than text files may sometimes be used to store log information to improve the query efficiency of the massive log store. There are also some other log files based on data collection, including stock indicators in financial applications and determination of operating states in network monitoring and traffic management.

1.3.3.3. Sensors

Sensors are common in daily life to measure physical quantities and transform physical quantities into readable digital signals for subsequent processing (and storage). Sensory data may be classified as sound wave, voice, vibration, automobile, chemical, current, weather, pressure, temperature, etc. Sensed information is transferred to a data collection point through wired or wireless networks, for applications that may be easily deployed and managed, for example video surveillance system.

1.3.3.4. Methods for Acquiring Network Data

At present, network data acquisition is accomplished using a combination of web crawler, word segmentation system, task system and index system, etc. Web crawler is a program used by search engines for downloading and storing web pages [28]. Generally speaking, web crawler starts from the uniform resource locator (URL) of an initial web page to access other linked web pages, during which it stores and sequences all the retrieved URLs. Web crawler acquires a URL in the order of precedence through a URL queue and then downloads web pages, and identifies all URLs in the downloaded web pages, and extracts new URLs to be put in the queue.

This process is repeated until the web crawler is stopped. Data acquisition through a web crawler is widely applied in applications based on web pages, such as search engines or web caching. Traditional web page extraction technologies feature multiple efficient solutions and considerable research has been done in this field. As more advanced web page applications are emerging, some extraction strategies are used to cope with rich Internet applications. The current network data acquisition technologies mainly include traditional Libpcap-based packet capture technology, zero-copy packet capture technology, as well as some specialized network monitoring software such as Wireshark, SmartSniff and WinNetCap.

1.3.3.5. Big Data Storage

Big data storage refers to the storage and management of large-scale datasets while achieving reliability and availability of data accessing. The explosive growth of data has more strict requirements on data storage and management. We consider the storage of big data as the third component of big data science. The storage infrastructure needs to provide information storage service with reliable storage space, and it must provide a powerful access interface for query and analysis of a large amount of data.

Considerable research on big data promotes the development of storage mechanisms for big data. Existing storage mechanisms of big data may be classified into three bottom-up levels: file systems, databases and programming models. File systems are the foundation of the applications at upper levels. Google's GFS is an expandable distributed file system to support large-scale, distributed, data-intensive applications. GFS uses cheap commodity servers to achieve fault tolerance and provides customers with high-performance services. GFS supports large-scale file applications with more frequent reading than writing. However, GFS also has some limitations, such as a single point of failure and poor performances for small files. Such limitations have been overcome by Colossus, the successor of GFS.

In addition, other companies and researchers also have their solutions to meet the different demands for storage of big data. For example, HDFS and Kosmosfs are derivatives of open source codes of GFS. Microsoft developed Cosmos to support its search and advertisement business. Facebook utilizes Haystack to store the large amount of small-sized photos. Taobao also developed TFS and FastDFS. In conclusion, distributed file systems have become relatively mature after years of development and business operation. Therefore, we will focus on the other two levels in the rest of this section.

1.3.3.6. Data Cleaning

Data cleaning cleanses and preprocesses data by deciding strategies to handle missing fields and alter the data as per the requirements. Data cleaning is a process to identify inaccurate, incomplete or unreasonable data, and then to modify or delete such data to improve data quality. Generally, data cleaning includes five complementary procedures: defining and determining error types, searching and identifying errors, correcting errors, documenting error examples and error types, and modifying data entry procedures to reduce future errors.

During cleaning, data formats, completeness, rationality and restriction should be inspected. Data cleaning is of vital importance to keep data consistency, which is widely applied in many fields, such as banking, insurance, retail industry, telecommunications and traffic control. In e-commerce, most data is electronically collected, which may have serious data quality problems. Classic data quality problems mainly come from software defects, customized errors or system mis-configuration. Some consider data cleaning in e-commerce by using crawlers and regularly re-copying customer and account information.

The problem of cleaning RFID data is examined next. RFID is widely used in many applications, for example inventory management and target tracking. However, the original RFID features low quality, which includes a lot of abnormal data limited by the physical design and affected by environmental noise. The probabilistic model was developed to cope with data loss in mobile environments. We could build a system to automatically correct errors of input data by defining global integrity constraints.

1.3.3.7. Data Integration

Data integration is the cornerstone of modern commercial informatics, which involves the combination of data from different sources and provides users with a uniform view of data. This is a mature research field for traditional database. Historically, two methods have been widely recognized: data warehouse and data federation. Data warehousing includes a process named ETL (Extract, Transform and Load). Extraction involves connecting source systems, selecting, collecting, analyzing and processing necessary data. Transformation is the execution of a series of rules to transform the extracted data into standard formats. Loading means importing extracted and transformed data into the target storage infrastructure.

1.3.4 Evolving Data Analytics over the Clouds

Big data analytics is the process of examining large amounts of data of a variety of types (big data) to uncover hidden patterns, unknown correlations and other useful information. Such information can provide competitive advantages over rival organizations and result in higher business intelligence or scientific discovery, such as more effective marketing, increased revenue, etc. Big data sources must be protected in web server logs and Internet clickstream data, social media activity reports, mobile-phone call records and information captured by sensors or IoT devices. Big data analytics can be done with the software tools commonly used as part of advanced analytics disciplines such as predictive analytics and data mining.

In Figure 1.12, we specify the goals and requirements of today's cloud analytics evolved from the basic analysis used in handling small data in the past. In the past, we handled "small data" objects in terms of MB to GB, as shown on the left-hand side of Figure 1.12. On the *x*-axis, we evolve from small data to "big data", which ranges from TB to PB based

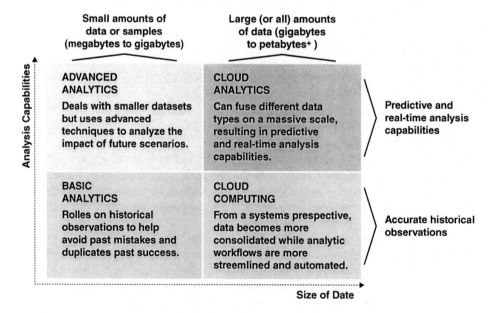

Figure 1.12 The evolution from basic analysis of small data (MB to GB) in the past to sophisticated cloud analytics over today's big datasets (TB~PB).

on the 2015 standard. On the *y*-axis, we show the analytics capability in two ascending levels: accurate historical observations versus predictive and real-time analysis capabilities. The performance space is divided into four subspaces:

1) The **basic analysis** of small data relies on historical observations to help avoid past mistakes and duplicate past successes.
2) The **advanced analytics** system on small data is improved from the basic capability to use advanced techniques to analyze the impact of future scenarios.
3) As we move to **cloud computing**, most existing clouds provide a better coordinated analytics workflow in a streamlined and automated fashion, but still lack predictive or real-time capabilities.
4) For an ideal **cloud analytics** system, we expect to handle scalable big data in streaming mode with real-time predictive capabilities.

Traditional data analysis means the use of proper statistical methods to analyze massive first-hand data and second-hand data, to concentrate, extract and refine useful data hidden in a batch of chaotic data, and to identify the inherent law of the subject matter, so as to develop functions of data to the greatest extent and maximize the value of the data. Data analysis plays a huge guidance role in development plans for a country, as well as understanding customer demands and predicting market trends by business enterprises. Big data analysis can be deemed as the analysis of a special kind of data. Therefore, many traditional data analysis methods may still be utilized for big data analysis. Several representative traditional data analysis methods are examined in the following, many of which are from statistics and computer science.

In general, we build a cloud for big data computing with a layered structure, as illustrated in Figure 1.13. At the bottom layer, we have the cloud infrastructure management

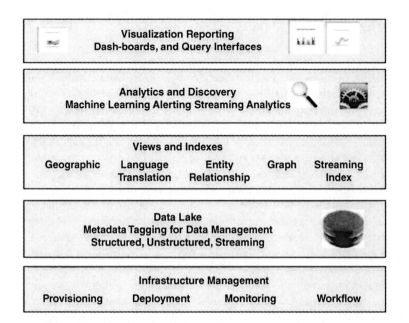

Figure 1.13 Layered development of cloud platform for big data processing and analytics applications.

control, which handles resources provisioning, deployment of agreed resources, monitoring the overall system performance and arranging the workflow in the cloud. All big data elements collected from all sources form the data lake. Data could be structured or unstructured or come-and-go in streaming mode. This lake stores not only raw data but also the metadata for data management.

At the middle layer, we need to provide views and indexes to visualize and access data smoothly. This may include geographic data, language translation mechanisms, entity relationship, graphs analysis and streaming index, etc. At the next higher level, we have the cloud processing engine which includes data mining, discovery and analytics mechanisms to perform machine learning, alerting, and data stream processing operations. At the top level, we have to report or display the analytics results. This includes visualization support for reporting with dashboards and query interfaces. The display may take the form of histograms, bar graphs, charts, video, etc.

1.4 Machine Intelligence and Big Data Applications

In this section, we try to link machine intelligence to big data applications. Machine intelligence is attributed to smart clouds applied IoT sensing, and data analytics capabilities. First, we reveal the relationship between data mining and machine learning. Then we give an overview of important big data applications. Finally, we present the key concept of cognitive computing and their applications.

1.4.1 Data Mining and Machine Learning

We classify data mining into three categories: association analysis, classification and cluster analysis. Machine learning techniques are divided into three categories: supervised learning, unsupervised learning and other learning methods including reinforcement learning, active learning, transfer learning and deep learning, etc.

1.4.1.1. Data Mining versus Machine Learning

Data mining and machine learning are closely related to each other. Data mining is the computational process of discovering patterns in large datasets involving methods at the intersection of artificial intelligence, machine learning, statistics and database systems. The overall goal of the data-mining process is to extract information from a dataset and transform it into an understandable structure for further use. Aside from the raw analysis step, it involves database and data management aspects, data pre-processing, model and inference considerations, interestingness metrics, complexity considerations, post-processing of discovered structures, visualization and online updating.

Machine learning explores the construction and study of algorithms that can learn from and make predictions on data. Such algorithms operate by building a model from example inputs in order to make data-driven predictions or decisions, rather than following strictly static program instructions. These two terms are commonly confused, as they often employ the same methods and overlap significantly. Machine learning is closer to applications and end user. It focuses on prediction, based on known properties learned from the training data. As shown in Figure 1.14, we divide machine learning techniques into three categories: i) supervised learning such as regression model,

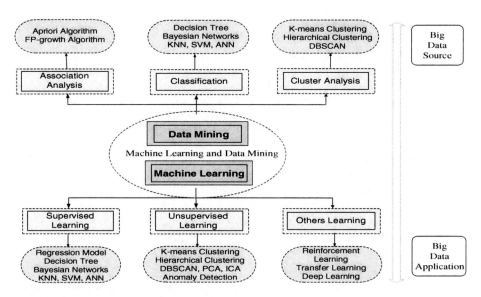

Figure 1.14 The relationship of data mining and machine learning.

decision tree, etc.; ii) unsupervised learning, which includes clustering, anomaly detection, etc.; and iii) other learning, such as reinforcement learning, transfer learning, active learning and deep learning, etc.

Data mining is closer to the data source. It focuses on the discovery of unknown properties of the data, which is also considered as the analysis step of knowledge discovery in databases. As shown in Figure 1.14, the typical data mining techniques are classified into three categories: i) association analysis includes Apriori algorithm and FP-growing algorithm; ii) classification algorithm includes decision tree, support vector machine (SVM), k-nearest-neighbor, Naïve Bayesian, Bayesian belief network and artificial-neural-network (ANN), etc.; and iii) clustering algorithm includes K-means and density-based spatial clustering of applications with noise.

The analysis of big data is confronted with many challenges but the current research is still in the beginning phase. Considerable research efforts are needed to improve the efficiency of data display, data storage and data analysis. The research community demands a more rigorous definition of big data. We demand structural models of big data, formal description of big data, and a theoretical system of data sciences, etc. An evaluation system of data quality and an evaluation standard of data computing efficiency should be developed.

Many solutions of big data applications claim they can improve data processing and analysis capacities in all aspects, but there exists no unified evaluation standard and benchmark to balance the computing efficiency of big data with rigorous mathematical methods. The performance can only be evaluated by an implemented and deployed system, which could not horizontally compare advantages and disadvantages of various solutions. Before and after the use of big data, the efficiencies are also hard to compare. In addition, since data quality is an important basis of data preprocessing, simplification and screening, it is another urgent problem to effectively evaluate data quality.

The emergence of big data triggers the development of algorithm design, which has transformed from a computing-intensive approach into a data-intensive approach. Data transfer has been a main bottleneck of big data computing. Therefore, many new computing models tailored for big data have emerged and more such models are on the horizon. Machine intelligence is critical to solve challenging issues existing in big data applications. Machine intelligence is obtained through machine learning.

- **Supervised Machine Learning**: includes the following categories:
  a) **Regression Model:** Decision Tree, SVM;
  b) **Bayesian Classifier:** Hidden Markov Model;
  c) **Deep Learning:** to be explained in Chapter 8.
- **Unsupervised Machine Learning**: includes:
  a) **Dimension Reduction:** Principal component analysis (PCA);
  b) **Clustering:** finding a partition of the observed data in the absence of explicit labels indicating a desired partition. Chapter 7 will be devoted to these unsupervised models.
- **Other Machine Learning techniques**:
  a) **Reinforcement Learning: Markov decision processes (MDPs)** provide a mathematical framework for modeling decision making in situations where the outcomes are partly random and partly under the control of a decision maker.
  b) **Transfer Learning:** Through transfer learning, the time-consuming and labor-intensive processing costs can be reduced extensively. After a certain time of labeling and validation through transfer learning, the training sets are established. Among various key big data technologies, machine intelligence is the key component. The machine learning techniques for big data computing will be studied in detail in Chapters 3, 4 and 5.

1.4.2 Big Data Applications – An Overview

A large number of big data applications have been reported in the literature. We will treat big data and cloud applications in Part III of this book. Here in Table 1.10, we simply give a global overview of various big data applications. The US National Institute of Standards and Technology (NIST) has identified 52 application cases of big data application. These tasks are grouped into 9 categories. As a matter of fact, many data driven applications have emerged in the past two decades. For example, business intelligence has become a prevailing technology in business applications. Network search engines are based on a massive data-mining process. We briefly introduce these applications as follows:

1.4.2.1. Commercial Applications

The earliest business data was generally structured data, which was collected by companies from old systems and then stored in RDBMSs. Analytical technologies used in such systems prevailed in the 1990s and were intuitive and simple, for example reports, instrument panels, special queries, search-based business intelligence, online transaction processing, interactive visualization, score cards, predictive modeling and data mining. Since the beginning of the 21st century, networks and websites have provided a unique opportunity for organizations to have online display and directly interact with customers.

Table 1.10   Application categories of big data: from TBs to PBs (NIST 2013).

Category	Brief Description	Example Applications
Government	National Archives and Records, Federal/State Administration, Census Bureau, etc.	CIA, FBI, Police Forces, etc.
Business and Commercial	Finance in Cloud, Cloud Backup, Mendeley (Citations), Web Search, Digital Materials, etc.	Netflix, Cargoing shipping, On-line shopping, P2P
Defense and Military	Sensors, Image surveillance, Situation Assessment, Crisis Control, Battle management, etc.	Pentagon, Home Security Agency
Health Care and Life Science	Medical records, Graph and Probabilistic analysis, Pathology, Bioimaging, Genomics, Epidemiology, etc.	Body-Area Sensors, Genomics, Emotion control
Deep Learning, Social media	Self-driving car, geolocate images/cameras, Crowd Sourcing, Network Science, NIST benchmark datasets	Machine learning, Pattern Recognition, Perception, etc.
Scientific Discovery	Sky Surveys, Astronomy and Physics, polar science, Radar Scattering in Atmosphere, Metadata, Collaboration, etc.	Large Hadron Collider at CERN and Belle Accelerator in Japan
Earth Environment	Earthquake, Ocean, Earth Observation, Ice sheet Radar scattering, Climate simulation datasets, Atmospheric turbulence identification, Biogeochemistry.	AmeriFlux and FLUXNET gas sensors, IoT for smart earth
Energy Research	New Energy Resources, Wind power, Solar systems, green computing, etc.	SmartGrid Project

Abundant products and customer information, including click stream data logs and user behavior, etc., can be acquired from the websites. Product layout optimization, customer trade analysis, product suggestions and market structure analysis can be conducted by text analysis and website mining technologies. The quantity of mobile phones and tablet PC first surpassed that of laptops and PCs in 2011. Mobile phones and Internet of Things based on sensors are opening a new generation of innovation applications, and searching for larger capacity of supporting location sensing, people oriented and context operation.

1.4.2.2.   Network Applications

The early Internet mainly provided email and webpage services. Text analysis, data mining and webpage analysis technologies have been applied to the mining of email content and building search engines. Nowadays, most applications are web-based, regardless of their application field and design goals. Network data accounts for a major percentage of the global data volume. Web has become the common platform for interconnected pages, full of various kinds of data, such as text, images, videos, pictures and interactive content, etc. Advanced technologies are in great demand in semi-structured or unstructured data.

For example, the image analysis technology may extract useful information from pictures, for example face recognition. Multimedia analysis technologies are applied to automated video surveillance systems for business, law enforcement and military applications. Online social media applications, such as Internet forums, online communities, blogs, social networking services and social multimedia websites, etc., provide users with great opportunities to create, upload and share content. Different user groups may search for daily news and publish their opinions with timely feedback.

1.4.2.3. Big Data in Scientific Applications

Scientific research in many fields is acquiring massive data with high-throughput sensors and instruments, such as astrophysics, oceanology, genomics and environmental research. The US National Science Foundation (NSF) has recently announced the BIGDATA Research Initiative to promote research efforts to extract knowledge and insights from large and complex collections of digital data. Some scientific research disciplines have developed massive data platforms and obtained useful outcomes.

For example, in biology, iPlant applies network infrastructure, physical computing resources, coordination environment, virtual machine resources, and inter-operative analysis software and data service to assist research, educators and students, in enriching all plant sciences. iPlant datasets have high varieties in form, including specification or reference data, experimental data, analog or model data, observation data and other derived data. Big data has been applied in the analysis of structured data, text data, website data, multimedia data, network data and mobile data.

1.4.2.4. Application of Big data in Enterprises

At present, big data mainly comes from and is mainly used in business enterprises, while BI and OLAP can be regarded as the predecessors of big data application. The application of big data in business enterprises can enhance their production efficiency and competitiveness in many aspects. In particular, in marketing, with correlation analysis of big data, business enterprises can accurately predict the behavior of consumers.

On sales planning, after comparison of massive data, business enterprises can optimize their commodity prices. On operation, such enterprises can improve their operation efficiency and operation satisfaction, optimize the input of the labor force, accurately forecast personnel allocation requirements, avoid excess production capacity and reduce labor costs. On supply chain, using big data, business enterprises may conduct inventory optimization, logistic optimization and supplier coordination, etc., to mitigate the gap between supply and demand, control budgets and improve services.

Example 1.3   Banking Use of Big Data in Financing and e-Commerce Applications
In the finance community, the application of big data has grown rapidly in recent years. For example, China Merchants Bank utilizes data analysis to recognize that such activities as "Multi-times score accumulation" and "score exchange in shops," are effective for attracting quality customers. By building a customer loss early warning model, the bank can sell high-yield financial products to the top 20% customers in loss ratio so as to retain them. As a result, the loss ratios of customers with Gold Cards and Sunflower Cards have been reduced by 15% and 7%, respectively.

By analyzing customers' transaction records, potential small and micro-corporate customers can be effectively identified. Utilizing remote banking, cloud referral platforms can help implement cross-selling, and considerable performance gains have been observed in recent years. Obviously, the most classic application is in e-commerce. Tens of thousands of transactions are conducted in Taobao and the corresponding transaction time, commodity prices and purchase quantities are recorded every day.

More importantly, such information matches age, gender, address and even hobbies and interests of buyers and sellers. Data Cube of Taobao is a big data application on the Taobao platform, through which merchants can be aware of the macroscopic industrial status of the Taobao platform, market conditions of their brands and consumers' behaviors, etc., and accordingly make production and inventory decisions. Meanwhile, more consumers can purchase their favorite commodities at more preferable prices.

The credit loan of Alibaba automatically analyzes and judges whether to provide loans to business enterprises through the acquired enterprise transaction data by virtue of big data technologies, while manual intervention does not occur in the entire process. It is disclosed that, so far, Alibaba has lent more than RMB 30 billion Yuan, with the rate of bad loans at only about 0.3\%, which is a great deal lower than those of other commercial banks. ∎

1.4.2.5. Healthcare and Medical Applications

The healthcare industry is growing rapidly and medical data is a continuously and rapidly growing complex data, containing abundant and various information values. Big data has unlimited potential for effectively storing, processing, querying and analyzing medical data. The application of medical big data will profoundly influence human health. The IoT is revolutionizing the healthcare industry. Sensors collect patient data, then microcontrollers process, analyze and communicate the data over wireless Internet. Microprocessors enable rich graphical user interfaces. Healthcare clouds and gateways help analyze the data with statistical accuracy. A few simple examples are given below. More on health care IoT and big data applications will be studied in Chapters 4, 5, 8 and 9.

Example 1.4   Big data Applications in Healthcare Industry
Aetna Life Insurance Company selected 102 patients from a pool of 1000 patients to complete an experiment to help predict the recovery of patients with metabolic syndrome. In an independent experiment, it scanned 600,000 laboratory test results and 180,000 claims through a series of detection test results of metabolic syndrome of patients in three consecutive years. In addition, it summarized the final result into an extreme personalized treatment plan to assess the dangerous factors and main treatment plans of patients.

In this way, doctors may reduce morbidity by 50% in the next 10 years, by prescribing statins and helping patients to lose weight by as much as 5 lb, or suggesting patients should reduce the total triglyceride in their bodies if the sugar content in their bodies is over 20%. The Mount Sinai Medical Center in the US utilizes technologies of Ayasdi, a big data company, to analyze all genetic sequences of *Escherichia Coli*, including over 1 million DNA variants, to know why bacterial strains resist antibiotics. Ayasdi's technology uses Topological data analysis, a brand new mathematic research method, to understand data characteristics.

HealthVault of Microsoft offers an excellent application of medical big data launched in 2007. The goal is to manage individual health information in individual and family medical equipment. Presently, health information can be entered and uploaded with mobile smart devices and imported into individual medical records by a third-party agency. In addition, it can be integrated with a third-party application with the software development kit (SDK) and open interface. ∎

1.4.2.6. Collective Intelligence

With the rapid development of wireless communication and sensor technologies, mobile phones and tablet computers have integrated more and more sensors, with increasingly stronger computing and sensing capacities. As a result, crowd sensing is taking to the center stage of mobile computing. In crowd sensing, a large number of general users utilize mobile devices as basic sensing units to conduct coordination with mobile networks for distribution of sensed tasks and collection and utilization of sensed data. The goal is to complete large-scale and complex social sensing tasks. In crowd sensing, participants who complete complex sensing tasks do not need to have professional skills.

Crowd sensing modes represented by Crowdsourcing have been successfully applied to geotagged photograph, positioning and navigation, urban road traffic sensing, market forecasting, opinion mining and other labor-intensive applications. Crowdsourcing, a new approach to problem solving, takes a large number of general users as the foundation and distributes tasks in a free and voluntary way. Crowdsourcing can be useful for labor-intensive applications, such as picture marking, language translation and speech recognition.

The main idea of Crowdsourcing is to distribute tasks to general users and to complete tasks that users could not individually complete or do not anticipate to complete. With no need for intentionally deploying sensing modules and employing professionals, Crowdsourcing can broaden the sensing scope of a sensing system to reach the city scale and even larger scales. Crowdsourcing was applied by many companies before the emergence of big data. For example, P&G, BMW and Audi improved their R&D and design capacities by virtue of Crowdsourcing.

In the big data era, Spatial Crowdsourcing is a hot topic. The operation framework of Spatial Crowdsourcing is shown as follows. A user may request the service and resources related to a specified location. Then the mobile users who are willing to participate in the task will move to the specified location to acquire related data (i.e. video, audio or pictures). Finally, the acquired data will be sent to the service requester. With the rapid growth of mobile devices and the increasingly complex functions provided by such devices, it is forecast that Spatial Crowdsourcing will be more prevalent than traditional Crowdsourcing, for example Amazon Turk and Crowdflower.

1.4.3 Cognitive Computing – An Introduction

The term cognitive computing is derived from cognitive science and artificial intelligence. For years, we have wanted to build a "computer" that can compute as well as learn by training, to achieve some human-like senses or intelligence. It has been called a "brain-inspired computer" or a "neural computer". Such a computer will be built with special hardware and/or software, which can mimic basic human brain functions such as handling fuzzy information and perform affective, dynamic and instant responses. It can handle some ambiguity and uncertainty beyond traditional computers.

To this end, we want a cognitive machine that can model the human brain with the cognitive power to learn, memorize, reason and respond to external stimulus, autonomously and tirelessly. This field has been also called "neuroinformatics". Cognitive computing hardware and applications could be more affective and influential by design choices to make a new class of problems computable. Such a system offers a synthesis, not just of information sources but of influences, contexts and insights. IBM describes the systems that learn at scale, reason with purpose and interact with humans.

Cognitive computing hardware and applications could be more affective and influential by design choices to make a new class of problems computable. Such a system offers a synthesis not just of information sources but of influences, contexts and insights. In other words, cognitive computing systems make some well-defined "context" computable. IBM describes the systems that learn at scale, reason with purpose and interact with humans naturally.

1.4.3.1. System Features of Cognitive Computing

In a way, a cognitive system redefines the relationship between humans and their pervasive digital environment. They may play the role of assistant or coach for the user, and they may act virtually autonomously in many situations. The computing results of a cognitive system could be suggestive, prescriptive or instructive in nature. Listed below are some characteristics of cognitive computing systems:

- **Adaptive in learning:** They may learn as information changes, and as goals and requirements evolve. They may resolve ambiguity and tolerate unpredictability. They may be engineered to feed on dynamic data in real time, or near real time.
- **Interactive with users:** Users can define their needs as a trainer of the cognitive system. They may also interact with other processors, devices and cloud services, as well as with people.
- **Iterative and stateful**: They may redefine a problem by asking questions or finding additional source input if a problem statement is ambiguous or incomplete. They may "remember" previous interactions iteratively.
- **Contextual in information discovery**: They may understand, identify and extract contextual elements such as meaning, syntax, time, location, appropriate domain, regulations, user's profile, process, task and goal. They may draw on multiple sources of information, including both structured and unstructured digital information, as well as sensory inputs such as visual, gestural, auditory or sensor provided.

1.4.3.2. Differences with Current Computers

Cognitive systems differ from current computing applications in that they move beyond tabulating and calculating based on preconfigured rules and programs. Although they are capable of basic computing, they can also infer and even reason based on broad objectives. Cognitive computing systems can be extended to integrate or leverage existing information systems and add domain or task-specific interfaces and tools. Cognitive systems leverage today's IT resources and coexist with legacy systems into the future. The ultimate goal is to bring computing even closer to human thinking and become a fundamental partnership in human endeavors.

Table 1.11 Related fields to neuroinformatics and cognitive computing.

Subject Areas	Brief Description of The Field	Technology Support
Artificial Intelligence	Study of cognitive phenomena to implement the human intelligence in computers	Pattern recognition, robotics, computer vision, speech processing, etc.
Learning and Memory	Study of human learning and memory mechanisms and build them in future computers	Machine learning, database systems, memory enhancement, etc.
Languages and Linguistics	Study of how linguistic and language are learned and acquired, and how to understand novel sentences	Language and speech processing, machine translation, etc.
Perception and Action	Study of the ability to take in information via the senses such as vision and hearing, etc. Haptic, olfactory and gustatory stimuli fall into this domain	Image recognition and understanding, behavioral science, brain imaging, psychology and anthropology
Neuro-informatics	Neuroinformatics stands at the intersection of neuroscience and information science	Neurocomputers, artificial neural nets, deep learning, aging, disease control, etc.
Knowledge Engineering	The study of big data analysis, knowledge discovery, transformation and creativity process	Datamining, data analytics, knowledge discovery and system construction

Cognitive science is interdisciplinary in nature. It covers the areas of psychology artificial intelligence, neuroscience and linguistics, etc. It spans many levels of analysis from low-level machine learning and decision mechanisms to high-level neural circuitry to build brain-modeled computers. Related fields to neuroinformatics and cognitive computing are summarized in Table 1.11. In Chapter 3 and subsequent chapters, we will further explore these cutting-edge technologies.

1.4.3.3. Applications of Cognitive Machine Learning

Cognitive computing platforms have emerged and become commercially available, and evidence of real-world applications is starting to surface. Organizations have adopted and used these cognitive computing platforms for the purpose of developing applications to address specific use cases, with each application utilizing some combination of available functionality. Examples of such real-world cases include: i) speech understanding; ii) sentiment analysis; iii) face recognition; iv) election insights; v) autonomous driving; and vi) deep learning applications. Many more examples are available in cognitive computing services. These demystify the possibilities into real-world applications. Figure 1.15 lists all important cognitive machine learning applications.

Among these big data applications:

a) object recognition;
b) video interpretation;
c) image retrieval;

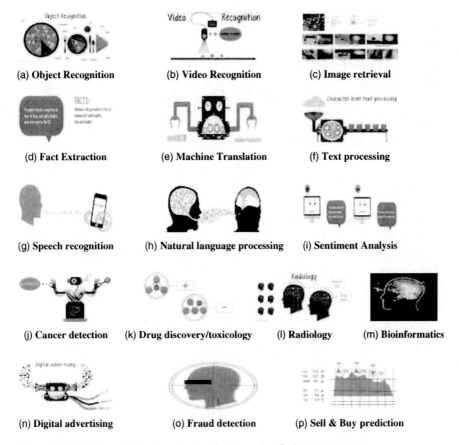

Figure 1.15 Machine and deep learning applications classified in 16 categories.

are related to machine vision applications. Text and document tasks include:

a) fact extraction;
b) machine translation; and
c) text comprehension.

On the audio and emotion detection side, we have:

a) speech recognition;
b) natural language processing, and
c) sentiment analysis tasks.

In medical or healthcare applications, we have:

a) cancer detection;
b) drug discovery;
c) toxicology and radiology; and
d) bioinformatics.

Additional information on cognitive machine learning applications can be found on the youtube website: www.youtube.com/playlist?list =PLjJh1vlSEYgvGod9wWiydum Yl8hOXixNu

In business and financial applications, we have (n) digital advertising, (o) fraud detection and (p) sell and buy prediction in market analysis. Many of these cognitive tasks are awaiting automation. Some of the identified applications involve plenty of raw data in text of trillions of words in various languages, visual data in billions of images and videos, audio in 400 days of speech, user queries and marketing messages, plus knowledge and social media graphs in billions of labeled tuples.

1.5 Conclusions

This chapter introduces the basic definitions and key concepts of big data science and cognitive computing. The purpose is to prepare our readers for studying the in-depth treatment in subsequent chapters. Smart clouds are supported by IoT sensing and big data analytics. More coverage of smart clouds is given in Chapters 3, 4 and 9. We emphasize the interactions or fusion of the SMACT technologies for big data processing. Social-media networking and mobile access of the cloud services are introduced in Section 1.2. These topics will be further studied in Chapters 2, 3, 8 and 9. We introduce basics of data mining, machine learning, data analytics and cognitive computing in Sections 1.3 and 1.4. These big data topics are further studied in subsequent chapters.

Homework Problems

1.1 Briefly characterize the differences in the following computing paradigms and technologies: Clouds, datacenters, virtualization, supercomputers, Internet technologies, web services, utility computing and service computing:
  a) Cloud computing versus supercomputing applications?
  b) What are the similarity and differences between clouds and datacenters?
  c) The conventional Internet versus the Internet of things?
  d) What is utility computing versus service computing?
  e) Why is virtualization crucial to the use of today's clouds?

1.2 Hype cycle is updated every year. You have learned from Figure 1.4 about the progress up to July 2016. Check with the Wikipedia with the latest Gartner Report on Hype Cycle and discuss the new changes compared with the 2016 report.

1.3 This homework requires you to do some research. Write an updated assessment report of the SMACT technologies. Discuss the strength and weakness and pros/cons of each technology. You need to dig out a few relevant technical reports or white papers from relevant industries, especially from major industrial players such as Facebook, AT&T, Google, Amazon and IBM, etc. Reading some published papers at leading *ACM/IEEE Magazines or Conferences* would be useful to make insightful assessment with concrete evidence.

1.4 Compare conventional on-premise desktop computing with the three cloud service models: IaaS, PaaS and SaaS. The resources and user application software are divided in five categories: user applications, virtual machines, servers, storage and networking. Each resource category could be controlled by user, vendor, or shared between user and vendor. Indicate appropriate control labels as User, Vendor and Shared in these four computing models. Justify your labels with reasoning.

1.5 After studying the basic concept of mobile clouds in Section 1.2.4, try to answer the following questions with an updated survey of the major providers of mobile cloud services. Checking Wikipedia under mobile clouds or mobile cloud computing may be helpful in finding the answers. Additional information can be also found in *IEEE MobileCloud Conferences* or the Special issue on Mobile Cloud Computing in *IEEE Transactions on Cloud Computing or Service Computing*.

1.6 Briefly explain the problems (challenges) associated with four "V's" of big data characteristics. (1) Volume, (2) Velocity, (3) Variety, and (4). Veracity. Discuss the resources demand and associated processing requirement and limitations.

1.7 In data science, what are the intersection field of the application domain expertise and the field of mathematics or statistics background? Also explain the intersection field of programming skills and the required mathematics or statistics background.

1.8 Consider the following two cloud/IoT service applications, and find out more examples from the literature about smart cities in Example 1.5 and healthcare cloud services in Example 1.4. You need to report your findings on how machine learning and big data analytics can help out in their success stories.

1.9 Explain why big data can be more cost-effectively handled by clouds than by using supercomputers. Why big data scientists require domain expertise. Also explain the differences in supervised versus unsupervised machine learning techniques.

1.10 In Figure 1.3, we have identified a number of software tools provided by various companies or research centers. Consider the following three software packages: The MatLab library for computing algorithms, the UCI machine learning repository for data analytics, and the OpenNLP for natural language processing. Find out from their websites or the literature about their functionalities and usage requirements for big data computing.

References

1 B. Baesens, *Analytics in a Big Data World: The Essential Guide to Data Science and its Applications*. Wiley, 2015.
2 L. Barroso and U. Holzle, The datacenter as a computer: An introduction to the design of warehouse-scale machines. In: *Synthesis Lectures on Computer architecture*. M. Hill (ed.), Morgan Claypool, 2009.

3 R. Buyya, J. Broberg and A. Goscinski (eds), *Cloud Computing: Principles and Paradigms*. Wiley Press, US, February 2011.

4 H. Chaouchi, *The Internet of Things*. Wiley, 2010.

5 M. Chen, *Big Data Related Technologies*. Springer Computer Science Series, 2014.

6 S. Farnham, *The Facebook Association Ecosystem*. O'Reilly Radar Report, 2008.

7 J. Gobbi, R. Buyya, S. Marusic and M. Palaniswarni, Internet of Things (IoT): A vision, architectural elements, and future directions. *Future Generation Computer Systems*, 29, 1645–1660, 2013.

8 J. Han, M. Kamber and J. Pei, *Data Mining: Concepts and Techniques*, Third Edition. Morgan Kaufmann, 2012.

9 U. Hansmann, et al., *Pervasive Computing: The Mobile World*, Second Edition. Springer, 2003.

10 T. Hey, S. Tansley and K. Tolle (eds), *The Fourth Paradigm: Data-Intensive Scientific Discovery*. Microsoft Research, 2009.

11 M. Hilber and P. Lopez, The world's technological capacity to store, communicate and compute information. *Science*, 332(6025), 2011.

12 K. Hwang, G. Fox and J. Dongarra, *Distributed and Cloud Computing*. Morgan Kaufamann, 2011,

13 K. Hwang and D. Li, Trusted cloud computing with secure resources and data coloring. *IEEE Internet Computing*. October 2010.

14 R, Liu, *Introduction to Internet of Things*. Science Press, Beijing, 2011.

15 H. Karau, et al., *Learning Spark: Lightning Fast Data Analysis*. O'Reily, 2015.

16 M. Rosenblum and T. Garfinkel, Virtual machine monitors: current technology and future trends. *IEEE Computer*, May 2005, 39–47.

17 S. Ryza, et al., *Advanced Analytics with Spark*. O'Reily, 2015.

18 J. Smith and R. Nair, *Virtual Machines: Versatile Platforms for Systems and Processes*. Morgan Kaufmann, 2005.

19 Hype Cycle, http://www.gartner.com/newsroom/id/2819918

20 Mark Weiser, The computer for the 21st century. *Scientific American*, 1991.

21 Y. Li, and W. Wang, Can mobile cloudlets support mobile applications? *IEEE INFOCOM*, April 2014, 1060–1068.

22 J. Kelley, III, Computing, Cognition and The Future of Knowing, IBM Corp, October 2015. http://www.research.ibm.com/software/IBM Research/multipmedia/Computing_Cognition_WhitePaper.pdf

2

Smart Clouds, Virtualization and Mashup Services

CHAPTER OUTLINE
2.1 Cloud Computing Models and Services, 45
2.1.1 Cloud Taxonomy based on Services Provided, 46
2.1.2 Layered Development Cloud Service Platforms, 50
2.1.3 Cloud Models for Big Data Storage and Processing, 52
2.1.4 Cloud Resources for Supporting Big Data Analytics, 55
2.2 Creation of Virtual Machines and Docker Containers, 57
2.2.1 Virtualization of Machine Resources, 58
2.2.2 Hypervisors and Virtual Machines, 60
2.2.3 Docker Engine and Application Containers, 62
2.2.4 Deployment Opportunity of VMs/Containers, 64
2.3 Cloud Architectures and Resources Management, 65
2.3.1 Cloud Platform Architectures, 65
2.3.2 VM Management and Disaster Recovery, 68
2.3.3 OpenStack for Constructing Private Clouds, 70
2.3.4 Container Scheduling and Orchestration, 74
2.3.5 VMWare Packages for Building Hybrid Clouds, 75
2.4 Case Studies of IaaS, PaaS and SaaS Clouds, 77
2.4.1 AWS Architecture over Distributed Datacenters, 78
2.4.2 AWS Cloud Service Offerings, 79
2.4.3 Platform PaaS Clouds – Google AppEngine, 83
2.4.4 Application SaaS Clouds – The Salesforce Clouds, 86
2.5 Mobile Clouds and Inter-Cloud Mashup Services, 88
2.5.1 Mobile Clouds and Cloudlet Gateways, 88
2.5.2 Multi-Cloud Mashup Services, 91
2.5.3 Skyline Discovery of Mashup Services, 95
2.5.4 Dynamic Composition of Mashup Services, 96
2.6 Conclusions, 98

2.1 Cloud Computing Models and Services

The concept of cloud computing has evolved from cluster, grid and utility computing. Cluster and grid computing leverage the use of many computers in parallel. Cloud computing leverages elastic resources to satisfy a large number of users. The key driving

Big-Data Analytics for Cloud, IoT and Cognitive Computing, First Edition. Kai Hwang and Min Chen.
© 2017 John Wiley & Sons Ltd. Published 2017 by John Wiley & Sons Ltd.
Companion Website: http://www.wiley.com/go/hwangIOT

forces behind cloud computing are the ubiquity of broadband and wireless networking, falling storage costs, and progressive improvements in Internet computing software.

Cloud users are able to demand more resources at peak workload, reduce their costs, experiment with new services and remove unneeded capacity. The cloud service providers can increase the system utilization via multiplexing, virtualization and dynamic resource provisioning. Cloud frees up users to focus on user applications and create business values by outsourcing the job execution to the cloud providers.

2.1.1 Cloud Taxonomy based on Services Provided

Clouds are enabled by the progress in the hardware, software and networking technologies summarized in Table 2.1. These technologies play instrumental roles in making cloud computing a reality. Most of these technologies have matured to meet the increasing demand. In the hardware area, the rapid progress in multi-core CPUs, memory chips and disk arrays has made it possible to build faster datacenters with huge storage space. Resource virtualization enables rapid cloud deployment with HTC and disaster recovery capabilities.

The progress in providing Software as a Service (SaaS), Wed 2.0 standards and Internet performance have all contributed to the emergence of cloud services. Today's clouds are designed to serve a large number of tenants over massive volumes of data. The availability of large-scale, distributed storage systems lays the foundation for today's datacenters.

Cloud computing has resulted from progress made in license management and automatic billing techniques. Private clouds are easier to secure and more trustworthy within an organization. Once the private clouds become mature and better secured, they can be open or converted to public clouds. Therefore, the boundary between public and private clouds could be blurred in the future. Most very likely, most future clouds will be hybrid in nature.

Table 2.1 Cloud technologies in hardware, software and networking.

Technology	Requirements and Benefits
Fast Platform Deployment	Fast, efficient and flexible deployment of cloud resources to provide dynamic computing environment to users
Virtual Clusters on Demand	Virtualized cluster of VMs provisioned to satisfy user demand as workload changes
Multi-Tenant Techniques	SaaS distributes software to a large number of users for their simultaneous use and resource sharing if so desired
Massive Data Processing	Internet search and web services often require massive data processing, especially to support personalized services
Web-Scale Communication	Support e-commerce, remote education, telemedicine, social networking, digital government and digital entertainment, etc.
Distributed Storage	Large-scale storage of personal records and public archive information demand distributed storage over the clouds
Licensing and Billing Services	License management and billing services greatly benefit all types of cloud services in utility computing

2.1.1.1. Cloud Development Trends

Many executable application codes are much smaller than the web-scale datasets they process, and cloud computing avoids large data movement during execution. This will result in less traffic on the Internet and better network utilization. The core of a cloud is the server cluster (or VM cluster). The cluster nodes are used as compute nodes. A few control nodes are used to manage and monitor of the cloud activities. The scheduling of user jobs on a cloud is required to assign the work to virtual clusters created for users. The gateway nodes provide the access points of the service from the outside world. These gateway nodes can be also used for security control of the entire cloud platform.

In physical clusters, users expect static demand of resources. Clouds are designed to face fluctuating workloads and thus demand variable amounts of resource dynamically. Datacenters and supercomputers do have some similarities and distinctions. In the case of datacenters, the scaling is a fundamental requirement. The datacenter server clusters are built with low-cost servers. For example, Microsoft has a datacenter in the Chicago area with 100,000 8-core servers housed in 50 containers. In a supercomputer, a separate storage disk array is used, while a datacenter uses local disks attached to server nodes.

The cloud offers significant benefit to IT companies by freeing them from the low level task of setting up the hardware (servers) and managing the system software tools. Cloud computing applies a virtual platform with elastic resources put together by on-demand provisioning of hardware, software and datasets, dynamically. The main idea is to move desktop computing to a service-oriented platform using server clusters and huge databases at datacenters. Cloud computing leverages its low cost and simplicity to both providers and users.

2.1.1.2. Generic Cloud Architecture

A security-aware cloud architecture is shown in Figure 2.1. The Internet cloud is envisioned as a massive cluster of servers. These servers are provisioned on demand to

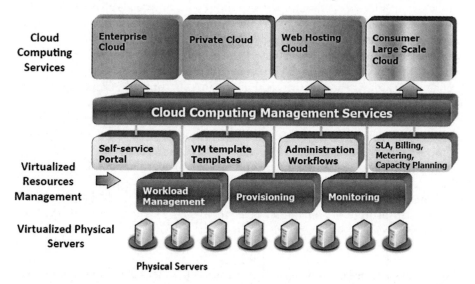

Figure 2.1 A generic architecture of a cloud computing system, where physical servers are virtualized as VM instances under the control of a resources management system.

perform collective web services or distributed applications using datacenter resources. The cloud platform is formed dynamically by provisioning or de-provisioning of servers, software and database resources. Servers in the cloud can be physical machines or virtual machines. User interfaces are applied to request services. The provisioning tool carves out the cloud system to deliver the requested service.

Essentially, the bottom layer of physical servers is the hardware and hosting machine infrastructure. The top layer includes the cloud applications for user services. In the middle layer the applications are often called middleware for virtualization and resources management purposes. In addition to building the server cluster, the cloud platform demands distributed storage and accompanying services. The cloud computing resources are built in datacenters, which are typically owned and operated by a third-party provider.

Consumers do not need to know the underlying technologies. In a cloud, software becomes a service. The cloud demands a high degree of trust of massive data retrieved from large datacenters. We need to build a framework to process large-scale data stored in the storage system. This demands a distributed file system over the database system. Other cloud resources that are added into a cloud platform include the storage area networks, database systems, firewalls and security devices. Web service providers offer special APIs that enable developers to exploit Internet clouds. Monitoring and metering units are used to track the usage and performance of resources provisioned.

2.1.1.3. Virtual Machines

Multiple VMs can be started and stopped on-demand on a single physical machine to meet accepted service requests, hence providing maximum flexibility to configure various partitions of resources on the same physical machine to different specific requirements of service requests. In addition, multiple VMs can concurrently run applications based on different operating system environments on a single physical machine, since every VM is isolated from each another on the same physical machine. In-depth treatment of VMs and containers are given in Sections 2.2 and 2.3 subsequently.

The software infrastructure of a cloud platform must handle all resource management and do most of the maintenance, automatically. Software must detect the status of each node, server joining and leaving. and do the tasks accordingly. Cloud computing providers, like Google and Microsoft, have built a large number of datacenters worldwide. Each datacenter may have thousands of servers. The location of the datacenter is chosen to reduce power and cooling costs. Thus, the datacenters are often built close to hydroelectricity power stations. The cloud physical platform builder is more concerned about the performance/price ratio and reliability issues than the shear speed of performance.

Some common characteristics are listed below, based on what are defined by the US NIST (National Institute of Standard and Technology) for cloud operations. We will cover these requirements in subsequent chapters:

- Massive scale in terms of number of servers use, often in tens of hundreds or up to a million;
- Homogeneity in component servers use, often low-cost ×-86 servers;

- Virtualization of servers is heavily used to provide multi-tenant user services;
- Lost-cost commodity software such as using Linux-based hosts;
- Resilient computing is required with fault-tolerance fast disaster recovery;
- Geographical distribution of multiple datacenters to reduce access latency;
- The cloud operation is often service oriented to provide infrastructure, platforms and applications;
- Advanced security and data protection are necessary, enforced in service-level agreements.

To support the above, today's cloud systems must be featured with: i) resources pooling; ii) measurable services; iii) rapid elasticity in system reconfiguration; and iv) broadband network access. All of the above features are needed to support IaaS, PaaS and SaaS services models for all public, provide, hybrid and community clouds. Overall, the user demands on-demand self-service in any cloud construction. Four families of cloud platforms are characterized below:

- **Public Clouds**: A public cloud is built over the Internet, which can be accessed by any user who has paid for the service. Public clouds are owned by service providers. They are accessed by subscription. Well-known public clouds include the Google App Engine (GAE), Amazon Web Service (AWS), Microsoft Azure, IBM Blue Cloud, Salesforce Sales Clouds, etc. These providers offer a publicly accessible remote interface for creating and managing VM instances within the system.
- **Community Clouds:**This is a growing subclass of public clouds. These clouds appear as a collaborative infrastructure shared by multiple organizations with some common social or business interest, scientific discovery, high availability, etc. Community clouds are often built over multiple datacenters. In recent years, community clouds have grown rapidly in education, business enterprises and government sectors to meet the growth of big data applications.
- **Private Clouds:** The private cloud is built within the domain of an intranet owned by a single organization. Therefore, they are client owned and managed. Private clouds give local users a flexible and agile private infrastructure to run service workloads within their administrative domains. A private cloud is supposed to deliver more efficient and convenient cloud services. Private clouds may wish to retain greater customization and organizational control.
- **Hybrid Clouds:** A hybrid cloud is built with all cloud families. Private clouds support a hybrid cloud model by supplementing local infrastructure with computing capacity from an external public cloud. For example, the research compute cloud (RC2) is a private cloud owned by IBM. The RC2 interconnects the computing resources at 8 IBM Research Centers scattered across the US, Europe and Asia. A hybrid cloud provides access to clients, partner networks and third parties.

In summary, public clouds promote standardization, preserve capital investigation and offer application flexibility. The private clouds attempt to achieve customization and offer higher efficiency, resiliency, security and privacy. The hybrid clouds operate in the middle with some compromises in resource sharing. In general, the private clouds are easier to manage, while public clouds are easier to access. The trend of cloud development is that more and more clouds will be hybrid.

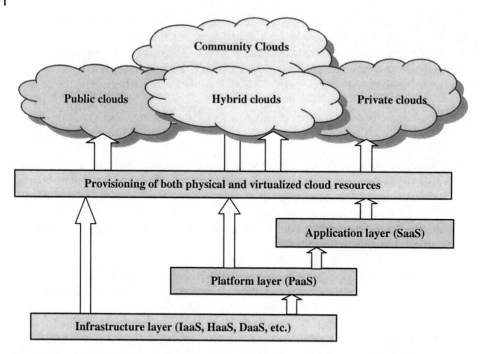

Figure 2.2 Layered architectural development of the cloud platform for IaaS, PaaS and SaaS applications over the Internet.

2.1.2 Layered Development Cloud Service Platforms

Cloud computing benefits the service industry and advances the business computing with a new paradigm. It has been forecasted that global revenue in cloud computing may reach $150 billion by 2013 from the $19 billion reported in 2009. The basic advantages of cloud computing lie in providing ubiquitous services, resource efficiency and application flexibility. Users are able to access and deploy applications from anywhere in the world at very competitive costs.

The architecture of a cloud is developed at three layers: infrastructure, platform and application, as demonstrated in Figure 2.2. These three development layers are implemented with virtualization and standardization of hardware and software resources provisioned within the cloud. The services to public, private and hybrid clouds are conveyed to users through the networking support over the Internet and intranets involved. It is clear that the infrastructure layer is deployed first to support IaaS type of services. This infrastructure layer serves as the foundation to build the platform layer of the cloud for supporting PaaS services. In turn, the platform layer is a foundation to implement the application layer for SaaS applications.

The infrastructure layer is built with virtualized compute, storage and network resources. The abstraction of these hardware resources is meant to provide the flexibility demanded by users. Internally, the virtualization realizes the automated provisioning of resources and optimizes the infrastructure management process. It should be noted that not all cloud services are restricted to a single layer. Many applications may apply resources at mixed layers. After all, the three layers are built from bottom up with a dependence relationship.

The platform layer is for general purposes and repeated usage of the collection of software resources. This layer provides the users with an environment to develop their applications, to text the operation flows and to monitor the execution results and performance. The platform should be able to assure the users of scalability, dependability and security protection. In a way, the virtualized cloud platform serves as a "system middleware" between the infrastructure and application layers of the cloud.

The application layer is formed with a collection of all needed software modules for SaaS applications. Service applications in this layer include daily office management work, such as information retrieval, document processing, and calendar and authentication services, etc. The application layer is also heavily used by business enterprises in business marketing and sales, consumer relationship management (CRM), financial transactions, supply chain management, etc.

From the provider's perspective, the services at various layers demand different amounts of function support and resource management by the providers. In general, the SaaS demands the most work from the provider, the PaaS in the middle, and IaaS the least. For example, Amazon EC2 provides not only virtualized CPU resources to users but also the management of these provisioned resources. Services at the application layer demand more work from the providers. The best example is the Salesforce CRM service in which the provider supplies not only the hardware at the bottom layer and the software at the top layer, but also provides the platform and software tools for user application development and monitory:

- **Infrastructure as a Service (IaaS):** This model puts together infrastructures demanded by users, namely servers, storage, networks and datacenter fabric. The user can deploy and run on multiple VMs running guest OS on specific applications. The user does not manage or control the underlying cloud infrastructure, but can specify when to request and release the needed VMs and data. The best IaaS examples are the AWS, GoGrid, Rackspace, Eucalyptus, flexscale, RightScale, etc.
- **Platform as a Service (PaaS):** This model provides the user to deploy user-built applications onto a virtualized cloud platform. PaaS include middleware, database, development tools and some runtime supports like Web 2.0 and Java, etc. The platform includes both hardware and software integrated with specific programming interfaces. The provider supplies the API and software tools (e.g. Java, Python, Web2.0, .Net). The user is freed from managing the cloud infrastructure. PaaS provides a programming environment to build and manage cloud applications. The best example of PaaS platforms are Google AppEngine, Windows Azure, Force.com, etc.
- **Software as a Service (SaaS):** This refers to browser-initiated application software delivered to thousands of paid cloud customers. The SaaS model applies to business processes, industry applications, CRM (consumer relationship management), ERP (business enterprise resources planning), HR (human resources) and collaborative applications. On the customer side, there is no upfront investment in servers or software licensing. On the provider side, costs are rather low, compared with conventional hosting of user applications. The best SaaS examples are Cloudera, Hadoop, salesforce.com, .NETService, Google Docs, Microsoft Dynamic CRM Service, SharePoint service, etc.

An Internet cloud is envisioned as a public cluster of servers provisioned on demand to perform collective web services or distributed applications using the datacenter resources. The cloud design objectives are specified below. Then we present the basic principles behind cloud architecture design.

2.1.2.1. Cloud Platform Design Goals

Scalability, virtualization, efficiency and reliability are the four major design goals of a cloud computing platform. Clouds support Web 2.0 applications. The cloud management receives the user request and finds the correct resources, and then calls the provisioning services which invoke resources in the cloud. The cloud management software needs to support both physical and virtual machines. Security in shared resources and shared access of datacenters also poses another design challenge.

The platform needs to establish a very large-scale HPC infrastructure. The hardware and software systems are combined together to make it easy and efficient to operate. The system scalability can benefit from cluster architecture. If one service takes a lot of processing power or storage capacity or network traffic, it is simple to add more servers and bandwidth. The system reliability can benefit from this architecture. Data can be put into multiple locations. For example, the user email can be put in three disks which expand to different geographical separate datacenters. In such situations, even if one of the datacenters crashes, the user data is still accessible. The scale of cloud architecture can be easily expanded by adding more servers and enlarging the network connectivity accordingly.

2.1.3 Cloud Models for Big Data Storage and Processing

The largest use of clouds is in the business service areas. Table 2.2 classifies various types of commercial clouds into five business categories, namely application, platform, compute/storage, co-location and network clouds. The representative cloud service providers are listed. We have already introduced the top three service layers as SaaS, PaaS and IaaS, respectively. The platform cloud provides the PaaS, which sits on top of the IaaS infrastructure. On the top category, the cloud offers software application services (SaaS). The implication is that we cannot launch SaaS applications without a

Table 2.2 Five business cloud services and representative providers.

Cloud Categories	Cloud Service Providers
Application Clouds	OpenTable, KeneXa, Netsuite, RightNow, Webex, Balckbaud, Consur Cloud, Telco, Omiture, Vocus, Microsoft OWA (office 365), Google Gmail, Yahoo! Hotmail
Platform Clouds	force,com, Google AppEngine, Facebook, IBM BlueCloud, postini, SQL Service, Twitter, postini, MicroSoft Azure, SGI Cyclone, Amazon EMR
Compute and Storage Clouds	Amazon AWS, Rackspace, OpSource, GoGrid, MeePo, Flexiscale, HP Cloud, Banknorth, VMware, XenEnterprise, iCloud
Co-Location Clouds	Savvis, Internap, Digital Realty, Trust, 365 Main
Network Clouds	AboveNet, AT&T, Qwest, NTTCommunications

cloud platform. The cloud platform cannot be built if the computing and storage infrastructures are not there. However, the developer can rent the lower level clouds to build the higher level platforms or application portals.

Two concrete example clouds are given below to highlight the commercial use of public clouds. More case studies of major clouds in different categories will be treated in Section 2.4.

Example 2.1 Apple iCloud for Storage, Backup and Many Personal Services

In 2011, Apple Inc. launched the iCloud as a cloud storage and cloud computing service. One of Apple's iCloud datacenters is located in Maiden, North Carolina. By 2015, the iCloud service had over 500 million users. iCloud provides its users with the means to store documents, photos and music on remote servers at Apple datacenters for download to iOS, Macintosh or Windows devices. The cloud shares and sends data to other users, and manages their Apple devices if lost or stolen.

The iCloud service also provides the means to wirelessly back up iOS devices directly to iCloud, instead of being reliant on manual backups to a host Mac or Windows computer using the iTunes services. The system also allows users to use AirDrop wireless service to share photos, music and games instantly by linking with their mobile accounts. It also acts as a data syncing center for email, contacts, calendars, bookmarks, notes, reminders (to-do lists), iWork documents, photos and other data. The backup iOS devices directly to iCloud, acting as a data syncing center and managing Apple devices if lost or stolen, are major improvements from the past using iTunes indirectly.

Big data types stored in iCloud include contacts, calendars, bookmarks, mail messages, notes, shared photo albums, iCloud photo library, my photo stream, iMessages, text (SMS) and MMS messages, etc. Documents saved in iCloud use iOS and Mac applications on the iCloud.com website. These data types and settings stored on your mobile devices (iPhones, iPads, etc.) are backed up by iCloud daily, even including purchase history for music, movies, TV shows, apps and books. The iCloud also offers an interesting feature to find friends. Users of *Find My Friends* share their location with the people they choose. Location is determined using GPS in the iOS device when Location Services are turned on.

Notification appears when a user requests another user to see where they are. Your location is sent from your device when someone requests to see your location. The feature can be turned on and off at any time. To locate a misplaced or stolen iPhone, you can play sound at maximum volume, and make flashing on screen even if it is muted. This feature is useful if the device has been mislaid. You can also flag the device in lost mode: The user can lock it with a passcode. People finding the phone can call the owner directly on the lost device. The system can also erase all sensitive iPhone records on a stolen phone. ∎

Example 2.2 Co-Location Cloud Services by Savvis

A co-location service deals with the management of datacenters, where the equipment, space and bandwidth are available for rental to retail customers. Co-location facilities provide space, power, cooling and physical security for the server, storage and networking equipment of multiple clouds that interact with each other via telecommunications and network service providers. Savvis is such a company, founded in 1996. They provide web hosting and co-location services, including the cloud housing and power supply, infrastructure management, networking and security services to both physical and network resources of many datacenters.

Apple was their first large customer. By leveraging the Apple Computer customer reference and testimonials, Savvis closed additional large contracts with other cloud providers. The company sells managed hosting and co-location services with more than 50 datacenters throughout North America, Europe and Asia, automated management and provisioning systems, and information technology consulting. By 2015, Savvis had approximately 2500 business and government customers. Savvis is positioned alongside 19 other web-hosting providers, including AT&T, Rackspace, Verizon Business, Terremark and Sungard in providing co-location cloud services.

In the past, the company had some ups and downs. In 2006, Savvis' content delivery network (CDN) services were booming. They grew rapidly with network assets, customer contracts and intellectual property used in Savvis' CDN business. Several lessons they have learned are in spam support allegations and security breaches on IaaS cloud management. One incidence was a charge of soliciting the business from spammers for profits. As a result of the negative media attention, Savvis resumed business using Spamhaus (a worldwide organization of spam fighters) to prevent customer spam attacks. ∎

Ian Foster defined cloud computing as follows:

> A large-scale distributed computing paradigm that is driven by economics of scale, in which a pool of abstracted virtualized, dynamically-scalable, managed computing power, storage, platforms and services are delivered on demand to external customers over the Internet [3].

Cloud computing offers an on-demand computing paradigm. Three basic cloud service models are given below. Figure 2.3 shows the cloud landscape with major cloud providers. All three cloud service models are applied.

Internet clouds offer four deployment modes: private, public, community and hybrid. These modes demand different levels of security implications. The different SLAs imply the security to be the shared responsibility of all the cloud providers, the cloud resource

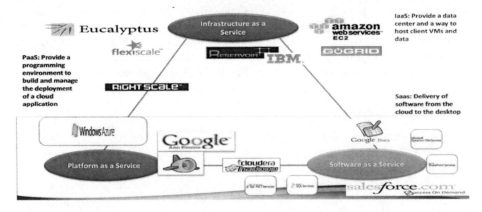

Figure 2.3 Three cloud service models deployed by major providers. (Reprinted with permission from Dennis Gannon, Keynote address in *IEEE Cloudcom2010*)

consumers and the third-party cloud enabled software providers. Advantages of cloud computing have been advocated by many IT experts, industry leaders and computer science researchers.

Cloud computing applies a virtualized platform with elastic resources on-demand by provisioning hardware, software and datasets, dynamically. The idea is to move desktop computing to a service-oriented platform using server clusters and huge databases at datacenters. Cloud computing leverages its low cost and simplicity that benefits both users and the providers. Machine virtualization has enabled such cost-effectiveness. Cloud computing intends to satisfy many user applications simultaneously. The cloud ecosystem must be designed to be secure, trustworthy and dependable. Otherwise, it may deter the users from accepting the outsourced services.

2.1.3.1 Big Data Storage Requirements

In 2015, the total data stored in all forms on Earth was estimated to be 300+ EB, with an annual growth rate of 28%. However, the total data transmitted among all possible sources is about 1900+ EB per year (http://www.martinhilbert.net/WorldInfo Capacity.html). In the past, most information items are expressed in analog format. Digital storage devices became popular from 2002 and replaced most analog devices quickly.

Table 2.3 shows that by 2007 only 6% (19 EB) were in analog and 94% (280 EB) were digital devices. Analog items are primarily stored on audio/video tapes (94%). Digital information spread across many different kinds of storage devices. PC/server hard drives have contributed the most (44.5%), including those used in large datacenters. The next are DVD and Blue Ray devices (22.8%). Clearly, the secondary storage devices still predominate in the storage spectrum.

2.1.4 Cloud Resources for Supporting Big Data Analytics

The cloud ecosystem is changing toward big data applications. Cloud computing, IoT sensing, database and visualization technologies are indispensable for analyzing big data. These technologies play a fundamental role in cognitive services, business

Table 2.3 Global information storage capacity in terms of total bytes in 2007.

Technology	Storage Devices	>Distribution
Analog, 19 EB, 6% of the total	Paper, film, audio tape and vinyl	6%
	Analog video tapes	94%
Digital, 280 EB, 94% of the total capacity	Portable media and flash drives	2%
	Portable hard disks	2.4%
	CDs and mini disks	6.8%
	Digital tapes	11.8%
	DVD and blue ray	22.8%
	PC/server hard disks	44.5%
	Others (memory cards, floppy disks, mobile phone, PDSs, cameras, video games, etc.)	> 1%

intelligence, machine learning, face recognition, natural language processing, etc. Multidimensional data arrays known as tensors, which can be handled by the TensorFlow library, are studied in Chapters 9 and 10. Additional technologies crucial to big data management include data mining, distributed file systems, mobile networks and cloud-based infrastructure.

In the US, the topological data analysis program supported by DARPA (Defense Advanced Research Project Agency) seeks the fundamental structure of massive datasets. To use big data analytics, most users prefer direct-attached storage such as solid state drive (SSD) and distributed disks in cloud clusters. The traditional storage area network (SAN) and network-attached storage (NAS) are too slow to meet big data analysis demands. Cloud designers must be concerned about system performance, commodity infrastructure, low cost and real-time responses to enquiries.

The cloud access latency problem is also of major concern in the use of clouds. Another concern is the scalability problem as the dataset grows dramatically. Shared storage has the advantage of being faster, but lacks scalability. Big data analytics practitioners prefer distributed storage in large clusters for its scalability and low-cost considerations. Big data for manufacturing demands an infrastructure for transparency. Predictive manufacturing offers an attractive approach toward near-zero downtime, availability and productivity.

2.1.4.1. Big Data Cloud Platform Architecture

Listed below are critical issues that must be addressed to design smart clouds for big data applications:

- **Preprocessing of unstructured data:** Traditional relational databases cannot support unstructured data, thus we demand NoSQL processing of incomplete data from noisy and dirty sources. These data are often short of veracity or not traceable. Many blogs or social exchanges cannot be easily verified, requiring data filtering and integrity control.
- **Social graphs, API, and visualization tools** are needed to handle unstructured social media data effectively. This demands cost-effective clouds and distributed file systems to aggregate, store, process and analyze big data. Bottom-up techniques are needed to uncover unknown structures and patterns.
- **Data analytics software tools** are needed in a big data cloud. In subsequent chapters, we will address some open-source or commercial tools for big data analysis. These tools must be integrated to maximize their collaborative effect. Business intelligence must be upgraded to inductive statistics or support predictive analytics in critical decision making.
- **Machine learning and cloud analytics algorithms** are greatly in demand for supervised or unsupervised machine or deep learning. These will be studied in Chapters 4, 5, and 6. Data scientists must have sufficient domain knowledge, statistical data mining, social science and programming skills. Thus it demands experts from crossover domains to work cooperatively.
- **Data governance and security** demand data privacy, integrity control, SLA compliance, accountability, and trust management, etc. Security control must be deployed on a global scale. Data privacy must be preserved down to fine-grain access control level.

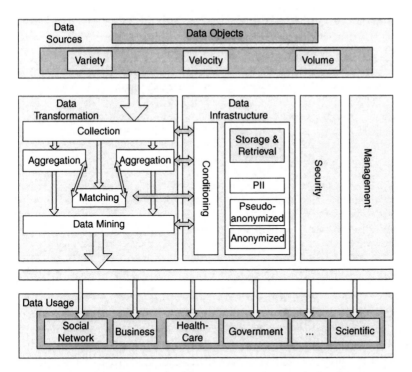

Figure 2.4 Conceptual architecture of a modern cloud system for big data computing applications.

2.1.4.2. Workflow in A Big Data Processing Engine

In Figure 2.4, we show the conceptual workflow in a typical data analytics cloud. The big data comes as data blocks or data streams from various sources from the top. The cloud platform resources are divided into four infrastructure parts: mainly used to store, retrieve, transform and process the data flowing through the large cluster of servers forming the cloud core. The resource management and security units control the security and are divided into two halves. On the right, data flow control mechanisms manage the data movement through the cloud engine on the left. This engine performs various data transformation functions, including collection, aggregation, matching and mining operations, before feeding the extracted or sorted data to various applications in the bottom box.

We consider some key requirements that should be performed by a smart cloud in typical big data computing applications. These cloud services are exercised at five layers: data sources, processing, access control, incident management and privacy protection shown as the row headings. Obviously, these mechanisms, policies and analytics capabilities must be built into a modern cloud analytics system. In particular, data privacy and cloud security become critically important among all five processing layers.

2.2 Creation of Virtual Machines and Docker Containers

Traditional datacenters are built with large-scale clusters of servers. Those big clusters are used not only for storing a large database but also for building fast search engines.

Table 2.4 Resources virtualization and representative software products.

Virtualization	Brief Description	Representative Products
Servers	Multiple VMs installed in servers to enhance the utilization rate of shred servers	XenServer, PowerVM, Hyper/V, VMware EXS Server, etc.
Desktop	Upgrade applications flexibility on PCs and workstations	VMware workstation, VMwarew ACE, XenDesktop, Virtual PC, etc.
Networks	Virtual private networks (VPN), virtual local area networks, virtual clusters in clouds	Intranet virtualization, OpenStack, Eucalyptus, etc.
Storage	Network storage and NAS virtualization for shared cluster or cloud applications	DropBox, Apple iCloud, AWS S3, MS One Drive, IBM Datastore, etc.
Application	Software process level virtualization, i.e. containers	Dock containers, XenApp, MS CRM, various Salesforce SaaS clouds, etc.

Ever since the introduction of virtualization, more and more datacenter clusters are being converted into clouds. Google, Amazon and Microsoft are all building their cloud platforms by this way. In this section, we cover the resource virtualization techniques. Both hypervisors and Docker engines are introduced. Virtualization can be done at the software process level, the host system level or at various extended levels.

Table 2.4 summarizes five resource virtualization levels. Some representative products are also listed. Among these, server virtualization is indispensable in converting a datacenter into an operating cloud to serve a large number of users at the same time. The main purpose of server virtualization is to upgrade the cluster elasticity and enhance the utilization of shared servers. Desktop virtualization attempts to provide application flexibility by individual users. Virtual storage and virtual networking make clouds even more powerful for co-location operations. Application virtualization refers to software process-level virtualization.

2.2.1 Virtualization of Machine Resources

The concept of computer virtualization started in the 1960s. It is a technique to abstract the machine resources logically at different architectural levels. Virtual memory is a typical example to expand the physical memory beyond its physical capacity by allowing page swapping between physical disks and virtual address space. In this section, we introduce the key concepts of hardware virtualization and other types of virtualization. It is fair to observe that no elastic clouds can be built to satisfy the multi-tenancy operations without resource virtualization.

2.2.1.1. Hardware Virtualization

This refers to the use of special software to create a virtual machine (VM) on a host hardware machine. This VM acts like a real computer with a guest OS. The host machine is the actual machine where the VM is executed, with the VM and host machine maybe running with different OSs. The software that creates VM on the host hardware are called hypervisors or virtual machine monitors (VMMs). Three hardware virtualization approaches are specified below:

- **Full virtualization:** This refers to a complete simulation or translation of the host hardware to some sort of virtual CPU, virtual memory or virtual disks for use by the VM using its own unmodified OS.
- **Partial virtualization:** This refers to the fact that some selected resource are virtualized and some are not. Therefore, some guest programs must be modified to run in such an environment.
- **Para-virtualization:** In this case, the hardware environment of the VM is not virtualized. The guest applications are executed in an isolated domains or sometimes caller software containers. The guest OS is no longer used. Instead, a VMM is installed at the user space to guide the execution of user programs.

2.2.1.2. Virtualization at Various Abstraction Levels

Five levels of abstraction are specified in Table 2.5 to implement VMs. At the ISA (instruction set architecture) level, VMs are created by emulating one given ISA by another. This approach gives the lowest performance due to the slow emulation process. However, it gives very high application flexibility. Some academic research on VMs use this approach like the Dynamo, etc.

The highest VM performance comes from virtualization at the bare-metal or OS levels. The famous hypervisor XEN creates virtual CPU, virtual memory and virtual disks right on top of the bare-metal physical devices. However, the hardware-level virtualization results in the most complexity. The best example of OS-level virtualization is the Docker containers. Virtualization at the run-time library and user application levels lead to an average performance. Creating VMs at user app level leads to a high degree of app

Table 2.5 Relative merits of virtualization at five abstraction levels.

Level of Virtualization	Functional Description	Example Packages	Merits, App Flexibility/ Isolation, Implementation Complexity
Instruction Set Architecture	Emulation of a guest ISA by host	Dynamo, Bird, Bochs, Crusoe	Low performance, high app flexibility, median complexity and isolation
Hardware-level Virtualization	Virtualization on top of bare metal hardware	XEN, VMWare, Virtual PC	High performance and complexity, median app flexibility and good app isolation
Operating System Level	Isolated containers of user app with isolated resources	Docker Engine, Jail, FVM,	Highest performance, low App flexibility and best isolation and average complexity
Run-Time Library Level	Creating VM via run-time library through API hooks	Wine, cCUDA, WABI, LxRun	Average performance, low app flexibility and isolation and low complexity
User Application Level	Deploy HLL VMs at user app level	JVM, .NET CLR, Panot	Low performance and app flexibility, very high complexity and app isolation

Table 2.6 Hypervisors or virtual machine monitors for generating virtual machines.

Hypervisor	Host CPU	Host OS	Guest OS	Architecture, Applications and User Community
XEN	x-86, x-86–64, IA-64	NetBSD, Linux	Linux, Windows, BSD, Linux, Solaris	Native Hypervisor (Example 1.6) developed at Cambridge University
KVM	x-86, x-86–64, IA-64, S390, PowerPC	Linux	Linux, Windows, FreeBSD, Solaris	Hosted Hypervisor based on para-virtualization at the user space
Hyper V	x-86 based	Server 2003	Windows servers	Windows based native hypervisor, marketed by Microsoft
VMWare Player, Workstation, VirtualBox	x-86, x-8-6-64	Any host OS	Windows, Linux, Darwin Solaris, OS/2, Free BSD	Hosted hypervisor with a para-virtualization architecture shown in Figure 1.20(c)

isolation at the expense of very complex implementation efforts by the users. We must use hypervisors to create VMs at the hardware level and the use of Docker containers at the Linux kernel level. Implementing VMs at the ISA, user or run-time library levels are mostly done by academia, but rarely practised in industry for their low performance.

Most virtualization use the software or firmware approach to generating the VMs. However, we can also use a hardware assisted approach to help virtualization. Intel has produced VT-x for this purpose, to improve the efficiency of its processors in the VM environment. This requires modification of the CPU to provide hardware support for virtualization. Other types of virtualization also appear in desktop virtualization, memory and storage virtualization, and various levels of virtualization are introduced in Table 2.6. Even one considers data and network virtualization. For example, the virtual private network (VPN) allows a virtual network to be created over the Internet. Virtualization enables the concept of cloud computing. The major difference between traditional grid computing and today's clouds lies in the use of virtualized resources.

2.2.2 Hypervisors and Virtual Machines

Traditional computers are called physical machines. Each physical host runs with its own OS. In contrast, a virtual machine (VM) is a software-defined abstract machine created by the virtualization process. In a physical computer running an OS, X executes application programs only specially tailored to the X platform. In other programs written for a different OS, Y may not be executable on the X platform. In using a VM, the guest OS could differ from the host OS. For example, the X-platform is an Apple OS and the Y-platform could be a Window-based computer. VMs offer a solution to bypass the software portability barrier.

2.2.2.1. Virtual Machine Architecture

The conventional computer has a simple architecture, as illustrated in Figure 2.5(a), where the OS manages all hardware resources at the privileged system space and all

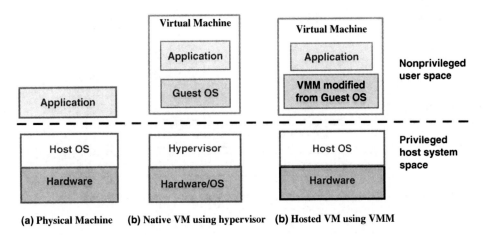

(a) Physical Machine   **(b) Native VM using hypervisor**   **(b) Hosted VM using VMM**

Figure 2.5 Two VM architectures compared with conventional physical machines.

applications run at the user space under the control of the OS. On a native VM, the VM consists of the user application control by a guest OS. This VM is created by the hypervisor installed at the privileged system space. This hypervisor sits right on top of the bare metal, as shown Figure 2.5(b). Multiple VMs can be ported to one physical computer. The VM approach expands the software portability beyond the platform boundaries. Bare-metal hypervisors run directly on the host hardware to manage the guest OS.

Another VM architecture is shown in Figure 2.5(c), known as hosted VM created by a VMM or a hosted hypervisor implemented on top of the host OS. The VMM is a middleware between the host OS and the user application. It replaces the guest OS used in a native VM. Thus the VMM abstracts the guest OS from the host OS. VMware Workstations, VM player and VirtualBox are examples of hosted VMs known as para-virtualization. In this case, the host OS is left unchanged and the VMM monitors the execution of the user application directly. Unless otherwise specified, we will consider only the native VMs produced by the bare-metal hypervisors.

Four hypervisors or VMMs are summarized in Table 2.6. The XEN is the most popular one used in almost all x-86 based PCs, servers or workstations. Hypervisor-created VMs are often heavily weighted, because they consists of the user application code (which could be only KB) plus a guest OS, which may demand GB of memory. The guest OS supervises the execution of the user applications on the VM. The KVM is a Linux Kernel-based VM. The Microsoft Hyper-V is used for Windows server virtualization. In other words, KVM is mostly used in Linux hosts, while Hyper V must be used in Windows hosts. This hypervisor involves OS integration at the lowest level. Malware and rootkits could post some threats to hypervisor security. Researchers from Microsoft and academia have developed some anti-rootkit Hooksafe software to protect the hypervisor from malware and rootkit attacks.

The VMware offers the three hosted hypervisors listed in Table 2.6. These hypervisors are better known as VMMs that perform the para-virtualization illustrated in Figure 2.5(c). VMware pioneered the virtualization software development. They started with a workstation version that can run with Windows and Linux hosts, which is really for full virtualization. Later, VMware launched the server ESX package for virtualization use in

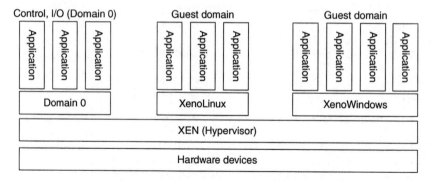

Figure 2.6 The XEN Architecture: Domain 0 for resources control and I/O and several guest domains (VMs) are created for housing user applications.

x.86 servers. This version requires no use of host OS to virtualize the resources. Now the cloud OS, vSphere, is entirely supported by VMware's own virtualization packages.

Generally speaking, some VMware VMM packages (players or VirtualBox) are not responsible for allocation resources for all user programs. They are used to allocate only restricted resources to selected applications. The VMM controls resources explicitly allocated to these selected special applications. In other words, the VMM is tied to selected processor resources. Not all processors satisfy VMM requirements. Specific limitations include the inability to trap some privileged instructions. This is the spirit of hardware-assisted virtualization.

Example 2.3   The XEN Hypervisor Architecture and Resources Control
The XEN is an open-source, micro-kernel hypervisor developed at Cambridge University. The XEN hypervisor implements all mechanisms, leaving the policy to be handled by a Domain 0, as shown in Figure 2.6. The XEN does not include any device drivers natively. The core components of an XEN system are the hypervisor, kernel and applications. The guest OS, which has the control ability, is called Domain0 and the others are called DomainU. Domain0 is a privileged guest OS of XEN. It is first loaded when XEN boots without any file system drivers.

The Domain0 is designed to access hardware directly and manage devices. Therefore, one function of Domain0 is to allocate and map hardware resources to the guest domains (DomainUs). For example, the XEN is based on Linux and its security level is higher. Its management VM is named domain 0, which has the privilege to manage other VMs implemented on the same host. If the domain 0 is compromised, the hacker can control the entire system. Special security policy is applied to secure domain 0. The domain 0, behaving like a hypervisor, allows users to create, copy, save, read, modify, share, migrate and rollback VMs as easily as manipulating a file. ∎

2.2.3   Docker Engine and Application Containers

Docker provides an OS-level virtualization on host machines running Linux, Mac OS and Windows. In this section, we introduce the Docker engine and Docker containers. Then we compare the implementation differences and discuss the relative strengths and

Figure 2.7 The Docker engine accessing the Linux kernel features for isolated virtualization of different application containers.

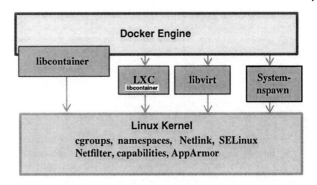

weaknesses between the bare-metal hypervisor-created VMs and Docker containers. Most datacenters are built with low-cost ×-86 servers on a large scale, so it is easy to see the growing interest of cloud builders and providers to switch to Docker containers for scalable user applications. However, the VMs are still useful in different types of applications. They may co-exist for an extended period of time.

2.2.3.1. Docker Engine

This is a virtualization software that runs between the host OS and the user application codes and their binaries and libraries. The Docker implements a high-level API to provide lightweight containers that run software processes in isolation. The Docker virtualization concept is illustrated in Figure 2.7. The Docker engine uses resources isolation features of the Linux kernel. The cgroups and kernel namespaces allow independent containers to run within separate Linux instances. These isolated containers avoid the overhead of creating VMs.

2.2.3.2. Docker Containers

Docker is an open-source project that automates the development of user applications as software containers. The Docker engine provides an additional layer of abstraction and automation of OS-level virtualization in Linux-based host platforms. Docker engine is written in Go language, running on the Linux platforms. Docker differs from the traditional VMs in that it consists of the application, plus its required binaries and library. Each application container takes about 10s of MB memory.

On the contrary, a hypervisor-generated VM may demand 10s of GB for hosting the guest OS in addition to the application codes. Docker containers are isolated, but may share OS and binaries and library, as shown in Figure 2.8(c). The obvious advantage is the light-weight containers versus the heavy-duty VMs, and each must have its own guest OS and bi/libraries. The contrast is demonstrated by the height disparity between the VMs and the containers in Figure 2.8 (a b). It may cost less to build and use containers than creating and using VMs. For this reason, Docker containers replace traditional VMs in major clouds. There is no guest OS needed to run the user applications. The containers apply the kernel's functionalities. The resource isolation including CPU, memory and block I/O, network, etc. is done through using separate namespaces for different applications.

Docker applies the kernel's virtualization features directly using the libcontainer library. This interface became available since Docker 0.9. The Doctor engine can also

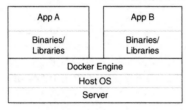

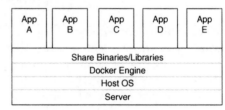

(a) Three hypervisor-created virtual machines (VMs) on the same hardware host, each VM is heavily loaded with its own guest OS and specific binaries and libraries.

(b) Each container is loaded with its own binaries/libraries which are not shared.

(c) The Docker engine creates many light-weight app containers, which are isolated, bur share OS

Figure 2.8 Hypervisor versus Docker engine for creating virtual machines and application containers, respectively.

access Linux kernel indirectly, through the use of interfaces: LXC (Linux Containers), the libvirt or system-spawn. Docker is an open-source project. The source code is entrusted to the GitHub website. The system is in appliance with the Apache 2.0 agreement. Docker engine generates light-weight virtualized containers on the Linux platform. The system is essentially a container generation and management engine. The Docker source code is small to fit most computers. It is implemented with Go language. For the clients, Docker assumes a client/server architecture.

2.2.4 Deployment Opportunity of VMs/Containers

In Table 2.7, we have summarized the properties of several hypervisors (XEN, KVM, Hyper V and VMware). These hypervisor-created VMs are compared with Docker

Table 2.7 Comparison between hypervisor-created VMs and Docker containers.

VM Type	Strength and Weakness	Suitable Applications
Hypervisor-created Virtual Machines	Higher app flexibility in launching different OS apps, but demand more memory and overheads to create and launch the VMs	More suitable for use in multiple apps without orchestration. VMs appeal to run on a wide variety of operating systems
Docker Containers	Light-weight application containers with low overheads to create and run with better protection under an isolated execution environment	More suitable for scalable use of the same app in multiple copies under orchestration. Works better with a particular OS version. It may save the operation costs of clouds

containers. It may cost less to build and to use containers than creating and using the VMs. For this reason, Docker containers may replace traditional VMs in some clouds. For example, AWS EC2 has already offered the ECS (Elastic Container Service) service. This allows users containers to implement their applications with significantly lowered memory demand and complexity. Using containers, resources are isolated, service restricted and processes provisioned to have a complete private view of the OS inside their own process ID space, file systems and network interfaces. For building highly distributed systems, the use of application containers can simplify the creation, security and management issues significantly, compared with the use of hypervisor-created VMs.

For example, a container can be booted and ready for application in 500 ms, while a hypervisor may boot in 20 seconds according to the OS used. In general, we can conclude that the lightweight containers are suitable for scalable use with multiple copies for cloud orchestration. This implies that containers are in favor of clustering and multiples. For example, containers act in favor of running multiple copies of a single application, say MySQL. The hypervisors are often more suitable for heavy duty applications that have limited cloud orchestration demand. If you want flexibility of running multiple applications, you use VMs.

Daemon interacts with three drivers in the Docker engine. Drivers control the creation of the container execution environment. The graphdriver is a container image manager, which communicates with the layered roots files associated with the containers created in the lower box. The networkdriver completes the container deployment. The execudriver is responsible for driving the container execution by working with the namespaces and cgroups in the libcontainer, which is written in Go language and used as a base to control all the containers created.

Finally, the containers are created at the lower box. The Docker uses Daemon as a manager and libcontainer as an executioner in generating the containers. The containers are similar in function as the VM under an isolated execution environment. In this process, the Docker container is created with low overheads, demands minimum memory, and is well protected with kernel isolation.

2.3 Cloud Architectures and Resources Management

In this section, we first study service-oriented architecture (SoA) for building public, private and hybrid clouds. Then we study the management issues in using the VMs and containers to build virtual clusters for use in cloud services. To this end, we present the three most popular cloud architectures, namely the AWS cloud, OpenStack and VMWare systems.

2.3.1 Cloud Platform Architectures

Most of today's clouds follow the SoA organization. In general, cloud architecture can be described by two layers of resources. The bottom layer is the static infrastructure, system boundary and user interface with the outside world. The upper layer is formed by dynamic resources such as VMs or containers under the management of cloud OS or control centers. In Table 2.8, we compare the three SoAs for building three types of clouds. The AWS cloud represents the most popular public cloud. The OpenStack is

Table 2.8 Comparison of three cloud platform architectures.

Cloud System Features	Amazon Web Service (AWS): Public Cloud	OpenStack Systems: Private Cloud	VMWare Systems: Hybrid Cloud
Service Model(s)	IaaS, PaaS	IaaS	IaaS, PaaS
Developer/Provider and Design	Amazon (Sec. 2.3.1 and 2.4.1–2.4.2	Rackspace/NASA and Apache (2.3.4)	VMWare (Sec. 2.3.5) Proprietary
Architecture Packages and Scale	Datacenters distributed as Availability Zones in various global Regions (Figure 2.11)	Small cloud at owner sites, licensed thru Apache (Figure 2.14)	Private clouds interacting with public clouds (Figure 2.17)
Cloud OS/ Software Support	Supporting both Linux and Windows machine instances with auto scaling and billing	Open source, extending from Eucalyptus and OpenNebula	vSphere and vCenter, supporting x-86 servers with NSX and vSAN
User Spectrum	General Public: Business Business Enterprises and Individual Users	Research Centers or Small Business	Business Enterprises and Large Organizations

used for private cloud construction in small business and protected communities. The commercial VMWare software packages are for building hybrid clouds used by large business enterprises and organizations.

The SoA architecture differs from the traditional computer architecture in many ways. The components in a traditional computer system are tightly coupled. This has restricted application flexibility and makes it difficult to maintain the system. The concept of SoA started with IBM, HP and Microsoft in early 2000. The principle of SoA is hinged on loose coupling among the service blocks of a system. Service interfaces are designed to link various service modules. This will free up the binding effects of the system, enabling higher scalability and modular grow and maintenance. That is exactly what a cloud system should have. Amazon CEO Bezzop has pushed the SoA idea into the development of the AWS cloud, which has proven successful among all public clouds.

The AWS cloud is built with a global infrastructure of many datacenters located in different regions of the world. For example, the AWS core, EC2 (elastic compute cloud), has nine regional sites worldwide. Within each region, they group the datacenters into availability zones (AZ). Each AZ is built with at least three datacenters, 50 KM distance from each other. The multi-datacenter approach greatly enhances the performance, reliability and fault tolerance of the AWS cloud. Amazon global infrastructure distributes resources, as shown in Figure 2.9. There are a large number of edge datacenters that can

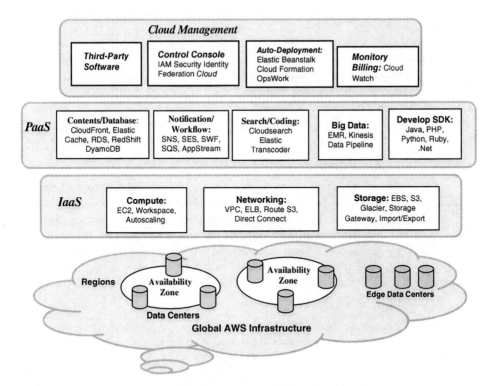

Figure 2.9 The AWS public cloud consisting of the top management layer, PaaS and IaaS platforms, and the global infrastructure built over datacenters in availability zones located at various regions globally.

be added into AWS cloud operations. AWS cloud has started to provide IaaS services in computer and storage functions.

Now the services have also been extended to the PaaS level. The PaaS services are meant to support big data, database and data analytics operations. A large number of service modules are built into both IaaS and PaaS platforms of AWS. The details of these services will be presented in Section 2.4.2 in several categories. Special service interfaces are designed to provide communications among the service modules. The combined IaaS+PasS services are also supported by Microsoft Azure and Google clouds. At the top of Figure 2.9, the cloud management coordinates the entire cloud operation in terms of monitory, security, billing and the use of third-party software. We will further study the components of AWS cloud in Section 2.4.

2.3.2 VM Management and Disaster Recovery

Cloud infrastructure management involves several issues. First, we consider the VM management from independent service jobs. Then we consider how to execute third-party cloud applications:

- **Independent Service Management:** Independent services request facilities to execute many unrelated tasks. Commonly, the APIs provided are web services that the developer can use conveniently. In AWS EC2, the SQS (Simple Queue Service) is constructed to provide a reliable communication service between different providers. Even endpoint does not run while another entity has posted a message in the SQS. By using independent service providers, the cloud applications can run different services at the same time.
- **Running Third-party Applications:** Cloud platform is often used to execute third-party applications. As current web applications are often provided by using Web 2.0 form, the programming interfaces are different from those used in runtime libraries. The APIs act as services. Web service application engines are used by the programmers for building third-party applications. The web browsers are the user interface for end users.
- **Hardware Virtualization:** In a cloud system, hypervisors are often used to virtualize the hardware resources to create VMs. System-level virtualization demands a special kind of software which simulates the execution of hardware and runs even unmodified operating systems. Virtualized servers, storage and networks are put together to yield a cloud computing platform. The cloud development and deployment environments should be consistent to eliminate runtime problems. The VMs installed at a cloud computing platform are mainly used for hosting third-party applications. Virtual machines provide the flexible runtime services to free the users from worrying about the system environment.

By using VMs, high application flexibility is often a primary advantage over traditional computer systems. As the VM resources are shared by many users, we need a method to maximize user's privilege and keep the provisioned VMs in an isolated execution environment. Traditional sharing of cluster resources is often set up statically before run time, but such sharing is not flexible. Users cannot customize the system for interactive applications and OS is often the barrier on software portability. Virtualization allows the

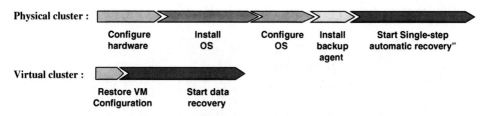

Figure 2.10 Recovery overhead on a physical cluster compared with that for a virtual cluster.

user to have full privilege while keeping them fully separated. In this sense, the Docker containers are better isolated than using hypervisor created VMs. Virtualization can benefit a cloud system by achieving high availability, disaster recovery, dynamic load leveling, flexible resources provisioning and scalable computing environments.

2.3.2.1. VM Cloning for Disaster Recovery

Virtual machine (VM) technology requires advanced disaster recovery schemes. One scheme is to recover a physical machine (PM) by another PM. A second scheme is to recover a VM by another VM. As shown in the top time line of Figure 2.10, the traditional disaster recovery from PM to PM is slow, complex and expensive. The total recovery time is attributed to the hardware configuration, installing and configuring of the OS, installing the backup agents, and the long time required to restart the PM. To recover a VM platform, the installing and configuration times for OS and backup agents are eliminated. Therefore, we end up with a much shorter disaster recovery time, about 40% of that to recover the PMs.

The cloning of VMs offers an effective solution. The idea is to make a clone VM on a remote server for every running VM on a local server. Among all cloned VMs, only one needs to be active. The remote VM should be in a suspended mode. A cloud control center should be able to activate this cloned VM in case of failure of the original VM, taking a snapshot of the VM to enable live migration with minimum time. The migrated VM runs on a shared Internet connection. Only updated data and modified states are sent to the suspended VM to update its state. Security of the VMs should be enforced during the live migration of VMs.

2.3.2.2. Live VM Migration Steps

In a cluster built with mixed nodes of host and guest systems, the normal way of operation is to run everything on the physical machine. When a VM fails, its role could be replaced by another VM on a different node, as long as they both run with the same guest OS. In other words, a physical node can fail over to a VM on another host. This is different from physical-to-physical failover in a traditional physical cluster. The advantage is to enhance failover flexibility. The potential drawback is that a VM must stop playing its role on a failing host node. However, this problem can be dealt with by live VM migration. Figure 2.11 shows the process of life migration of a VM from a host A to host B. The migration is done by copying the VM state file from the storage area to the host machine.

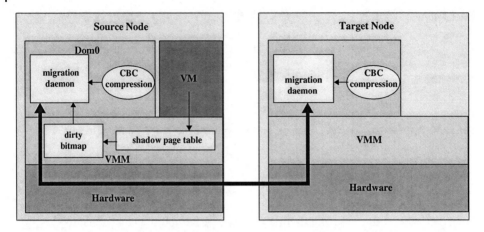

Figure 2.11 Live migration of VM from the Dom0 domain to that of an XEN-enabled target host.

Example 2.4   Live Migration of VMs between Two Xen-Enabled Hosts

Xen supports live migration. It is a useful feature and natural extension to virtualization platforms that allows for the transfer of a VM from one physical machine to another, with little downtime of the services hosted by the VM. Live migration transfers the working state and memory of a VM across a network when it is running. Xen also supports VM migration by using a mechanism: Remote Direct Memory Access (RDMA).

It speeds up the VM migration by avoiding TCP/IP stack processing overhead. RDMA implements a different transfer protocol where origin and destination VM buffers must be registered before any transfer operations reduce it to a "one sided" interface. Data communication over RDMA does not need to involve CPU, caches or context switches. This allows migration with minimum impact on guest operating systems and hosted applications. Figure 2.11 shows the design of compression algorithm for VM migration

Migration daemons are responsible for performing migration. Shadow page tables in the VMM layer trace modifications to memory page in migrated virtual machines during the pre-copy phase. Corresponding flags are set in a dirty bitmap. At the start of each pre-copying round, the bitmap is sent to the migration daemon. Then, the bitmap is cleared and the shadow page tables are destroyed and recreated in the next round. The system resides in the management VM of Xen. Memory pages denoted by bitmap are extracted and compressed before being sent to the destination. The compressed data are then de-compressed on the target.   ∎

2.3.3   OpenStack for Constructing Private Clouds

To convert server clusters or datacenters into private clouds, Eucalyptus is certainly the pioneer from the University of Santa Barbara. This is an open-source software for building clouds on large-scale clusters of servers. The stable version was released in 2010 and available to the general public. The OpenStack is extended from Eucalyptus with much more software support. Let us examine the functionality of Eucalyptus first. Then we present the progress with OpenStack.

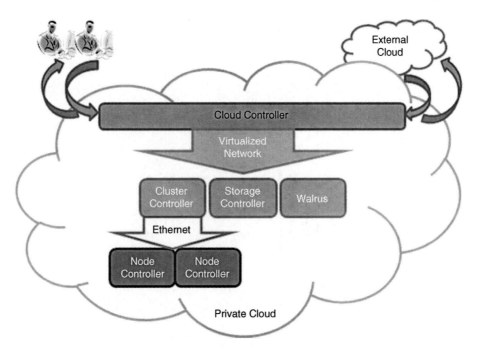

Figure 2.12 The Eucalyptus for building private cloud by establishing a virtual network over the VMs linked through Ethernet and the Internet.

Example 2.5   Eucalyptus for Virtual Networking of Private Cloud

This is an open-source software system (Figure 2.12) for supporting IaaS clouds. The system mainly supports virtual networking and management of virtual machines. Virtual storage is not supported. It has been used widely in building private clouds that can interact with end users through Ethernet or the Internet. The system also supports interactions with other private cloud or public clouds over the Internet. The system is short of security and features for general-purpose grid or cloud applications.

The designer claims that "Eucalyptus" stands for "Elastic Utility Computing Architecture for Linking Your Programs to Useful System". In terms of functionality, the Eucalyptus serves like AWS APIs, therefore it can interact with EC2. It provides a storage API to emulate the Amazon S3 API for storing user data and VM images. The Eucalyptus is installed on Linux-based platforms. It is compatible with EC2 and S3 in SOAP, REST and Query services. The CLI and Web portal services can be applied with Eucalyptus. ∎

Table 2.9 lists a number of open-source software packages for building mostly IaaS cloud platforms. The eCloud Foundry and ApplScale also support PaaS clouds. Most packages can create VMs over the Linux hosts. Almost all packages are compatible with EC2 and S3 services offered by AWS. They all use Xen and KVM. The VMware hypervisors are used in Eucalyptus, Cloud Foundry, ApplScale and vSphere/4. Among these, we choose to review the OpenStack to assess the capability of cloud construction software.

Open Stack was introduced by Rackspace and NASA in July 2010. The ultimate goal is to create a massively scalable and secure cloud software library for building clouds. By far, currently, 200+ companies have joined the OpenStack Project. The project offers

Table 2.9 Open source cluster management software systems.

Software	Cloud Type, License	Language used	Linux/ Windows	EC2/S3 Compatibility	XEN/KVM/ VMWare
Eucalyptus	IaaS, Rackspce	Java, C	Yes/Yes	Yes/Yes	Yes/Yes/Yes
Nimbus	IaaS, Apache	Java, Python	Unknown	Yes/No	Yes/Yes/Unknown
Cloud Foundry	PaaS, Apache	Ruby, C	Yes/No	Yes/No	Yes/Yes/Yes
OpenStack	IaaS, Apache	Python	Yes/Unknown	Yes/Yes	Yes/Yes/Unknown
OpenNebua	IaaS, Apache	C, C++, Ruby, Java, lex, yacc, Shellscript	Yes/Unknown	Yes/Unknown	Yes/Yes/Unknown
ApplScale	Paas, BSD	Python, Ruby, Go	Unknown	Yes/Yes	Yes/Yes/Yes

free open-source software under Apache license. OpenStack cloud software is written in Python. The system is updated every six months.

2.3.3.1. OpenStack Compute (Nova)

This is the OpenStack Compute module. Nova is a controller to set up the internal fabric of any IaaS cloud by creating and managing large clusters of virtual servers. The system applies with KVM, VMware, Xen, Hyper-v, Linux container LXC and bare-metal HPC configurations. The architecture for Nova is based on the concepts of shared-nothing and messaging-based information exchange. Hence most communications in Nova are facilitated by message queues. To prevent blocking, such as some components waiting for a response from others, deferred objects are introduced to enable callback when a response is received. The AMQP offers such an advanced messaging queuing proto-col. The cloud controller applies http and AMQP protocols to interact with other Nova nodes or the AWS S3.

Nova was implemented in Python while utilizing a number of externally supported libraries and components. This includes Boto, an Amazon API provided in Python, and Tornado, a fast HTTP server used to implement the S3 capabilities in OpenStack. The API Server receives http requests from Boto, converts the commands to and from the API format, while forwarding requests to the cloud controller. The cloud controller maintains the global state of the system, assuring authorization while interacting with the User Manager via the LDAP. The Nova system interacts with the S3 service and man-ages participating nodes and storage workers. In addition, Nova integrates networking components to manage private networks, public IP addressing, VPN connectivity and firewall rules.

2.3.3.2. OpenStack Storage (Swift)

This is a scalable redundant storage system over multiple disks spread over large dat-acenter servers. The Swift solution is to build around a number of interacting compo-nents, including a proxy server, a ring, an object server, a container server, an account server, replication, updaters and auditors. The proxy server enables look ups to the loca-tion of the accounts, containers or objects in Swift storage rings and route the request. Thus any object is streamed to or from an object server through the proxy server.

A ring represents a mapping between the names of entities stored on disk and their physical location. Separate rings are created for different accounts, containers and objects. Objects are stored as binary files with metadata stored in the file's extended attributes. This requires the underlying filesystem choice for object server support, which is often not the case for standard Linux installations. To list objects, a container server is utilized. Listing of containers is handled by the account server. Redundancy (thus fault tolerance) is achieved thru data replications over distributed disks.

2.3.3.3. Other OpenStack Functional Modules

Block Storage (Cinder) provides persistent block-level storage devices for use with OpenStack compute instances managed by the Dashboard. Networking (Neutron) offers a system for managing networks and IP addresses in a cloud deployment, and gives users self-service ability over network configuration. Dashboard (Horizon) provides admin-istrators and users a graphical interface to access, provision and automate cloud-based resources. Identity Service (Keystone) provides a central directory of users mapped to

OpenStack services. It acts as a common authentication system across the cloud OS and can integrate with existing backend directories like LDAP.

2.3.4 Container Scheduling and Orchestration

Docker users would like to scale a large number of containers across many hosts. Clustered hosts present some management challenges. This demands the use of Docker schedulers and orchestration tools. First, we identify the challenges and then examine the OpenStack Magnum, one of the container tools that can help managing Docker containers to yield scalable performance. Orchestration is a broad concept that involves container scheduling, cluster management, and even the provisioning of additional hosts.

2.3.4.1. Container Scheduling

Docker containers need to be loaded into the hosts to meet the service demand. Scheduling is the ability for a Docker administrator to load a service file into a host that establishes how to run a specific container. Cluster management is needed to control a group of hosts, which includes the adding or removal of hosts from a cluster. The cluster manager must first obtain the loading information about the current state of the hosts and their loaded containers. The container scheduler must have access to each host in the cluster. Host selection is a big problem for the container scheduler and the host information. This selection process should be as automatic as possible. The container functionality and the host workload need to be matched with load balancing in a cluster.

2.3.4.2. Container Orchestration Tools

Cluster management software like OpenStack is meant to support container scheduling. Advanced scheduling demands container grouping and optimization. The administrator must manage the group containers as a single application. Grouping containers may demand the synchronization of the start and stop time. Another issue is host provisioning, which refers to the timely and smooth joining of a new host to an existing cluster. Six popular tools for container scheduling and cluster management are summarized in Table 2.10. The Swarm and compose are developed by Docker teams. The Kubernetes is developed by Google to label, group and set container groups.

Table 2.10 Host provisioning and container scheduling tools.

Tool Name	Brief Description of Tool Functionality
fleet	Scheduling and cluster management component of the CoreOS
marathon	Scheduling and service management component of a Mesosphere installation
Swarm	Docker's robust scheduler to spin up containers on provisioned hosts
mesos	Apache mesos abstracts and manage the resources of all hosts in a cluster
Kubernetes	Google's scheduler over the containers running on your cloud infrastructure
compose	Docker's tool that allows group management of containers, declaratively

2.3.4.3. OpenStack Orchestration (**Magnum**)

This is an OpenStack API service developed by the OpenStack container team. The purpose is to make container orchestration engines such as Docker and Kubernetes available as first-class resources on the OpenStack. The Magnum applies the Docker Heat to orchestrate an OS image which contains Docker and Kubernetes. Magnum runs the image either in VMs or bare metal in a cluster configuration. More details can be found in https://github.com/stackforge/magnum/release/tag/2015.1.0b2 OpenStack containers are reviewed in http://eavesdrop.openstack.org/irclogs/%23openstack-containers/

Magnum is designed for OpenSrack cloud operators to use. The purpose is to offer a self-service solution to provide containers to cloud users as managed hosted services. Magnum supposes to create application containers to run with existing Nova instances, Cinder Volumes and Trove Databases. The major innovations are the ability to scale an application to a specific number of instances, to cause the application to re-spawn an instance in the event of a failure, automatically, and to pack application together more effectively than using heavy-duty VMs. More details of Magnum operations can be found in https://wiki.openstack.org/wiki/Magnum

Multiple Nova instances are used. Docker Heat, Kubernetes/Swarm, OpenStack Heat and Micro OS (Fedora Atomic, Core OS) are used as components. The Docker Heat does not provide a resource scheduler, but is specific to Docker that uses Glance to store container images. Layered images are supported by Heat. The major components in Magnum controller node are the Magnum API and Conductor and OpenStack Heat, which controls the Cloud Unit, Kunernetes/Swarm and Docker in Nova instances to function in a coordinated manner.

2.3.5 VMWare Packages for Building Hybrid Clouds

VMWare is the first company supported virtualization of ×-86 servers, with VMWare products mainly used to support more than an 80% market share of enterprise clouds or hybrid clouds. Their cloud OS products appear as vSphere kernels and vCenter interfaces. Figure 2.13 shows the VMWare vRealize management platform for supporting hybrid construction.

The virtual environments supported include the vSphere for computing purposes, NSX for SDN (server domain name) and vSAN for distributed storage applications. These virtual environments are managed in four subsystems: business, automation, operations and extensibility of the hybrid cloud. Large numbers of service modules are built into these subsystems. The main purpose is to build vSphere- or vCenter-based private clouds that can work external public clouds jointly as most hybrid clouds will do.

In what follows, we present the functions of vSphere/4 as a proprietary OS released by VMware. This OS is used to create VMs and aggregate them into virtual clusters as elastic resources. The vSphere/4 uses the hypervisors ESX and ESXi from VMware. Furthermore, vSphere/6 supports virtual storage in addition to virtual networking and protecting data. The proprietary vSphere is compared with the open-source Eucalyptus in Table 2.11. The Eucalyptus supports XEN and KVM virtualization and mainly the virtual networking of VMs or containers.

Example 2.6   VMware vSphere 6: A Commercial Cloud OS for Hybrid Clouds
The vSphere 4 is a hardware and software ecosystem developed by VMware, released in April 2009. The vSphere extends from the earlier virtualization software products

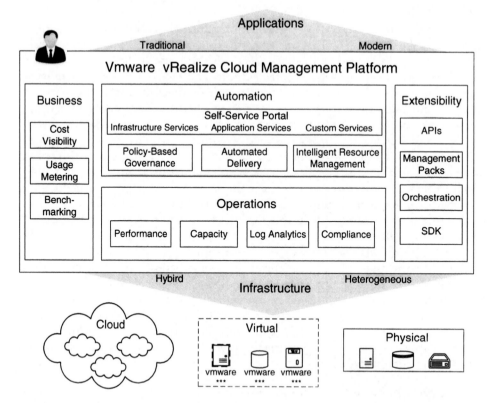

Figure 2.13 VMware cloud platform built with vSphere, NSX and vSAN, working as a hybrid cloud with AWS.

Table 2.11 Eucalyptus and vSphere/6 for cloud resource management.

OS Platform	Resources being Virtualized, Web link	Client APIs	Hypervisor	Cloud Interface	Special Features
Eucalyptus, Linux, BSD	Virtual networking, (Example 2.7) http://www.eucalyptus.com/	EC2 WS, CLI	XEN, KVM	EC2	Virtual clustering with hierarchical control
vSphere/6, Linux, Windows, Proprietary	Virtualizing OS for datacenters (Example 2.8), http://www.vmware.com/products/vsphere/products/vsphere/	CLI, GUI, Portal, WS	VMware ESX, ESXi	VMware vCloud partners	Data protection, vStorage, VMFS, DRM, High availability

by VMWare, namely the workstation virtualization, ESX for server virtualization, and virtual infrastructure for server clusters. The system interacts with user applications via an interface layer, called vCenter managed by VMware. The main use of vSphere is to offer virtualization support and resource management of datacenter resources in building enterprise clouds. VMware claims that the system is the very first cloud OS that supports availability, security and scalability in general-purpose cloud services.

The vSphere 4 is built with two functional software suites: the infrastructure services right on top of the hardware and the application services toward user applications. The infrastructure services are shown at the bottom. This suite has three component packages, mainly for virtualization purposes. The vCompute is supported by ESX, ESX1 and DRS virtualization libraries from VMWare. The vStorage is supported by VMS and thin provisioning libraries. The vNetwork offers distributed switching and networking functions. These packages interact with the hardware servers, disks and networks in the datacenter. These infrastructure functions also communicate with other external clouds.

The application services are also divided into three groups: namely availability, security and scalability. The availability support includes the VMotion, Storage VMotion, HA (high availability), Fault Tolerance and Data Recovery from VMWare. The security package supports vShield Zones and VMSafe. The scalability package has been built with DRS and Hot Add. Interested readers are referred to the vSphere 4 website for more details of these component software functions. To fully understand the use of VSphere 4, users must also learn how to use the vCenter interfaces in order to link with existing applications or to develop new applications. ∎

2.4   Case Studies of IaaS, PaaS and SaaS Clouds

Cloud computing delivers infrastructure, platform and software (application) as services, which are made available as subscription-based services in a pay-as-you-go model to consumers. The IaaS, PaaS and SaaS models form three pillars on top of Cloud Computing solutions which are delivered to end users. All the three models allow the user to access the services over the Internet, relying entirely on the infrastructures of the cloud service providers.

The IaaS clouds allow users to use virtualized IT resource for computing, storage and networking. In short, the service is performed by rented cloud infrastructure. The user can deploy and run his own applications over his chosen OS environment. The user does not manage or control the underlying cloud infrastructure but has control over the OS, storage, deployed applications and possibly select networking components. This IaaS model encompasses the storage as a service, compute instances as a service, and communication as a service. Some representative IaaS providers are listed in Table 2.12. More details of Amazon EC2 and S3 services are given in Examples 2.7 and 2.8.

These models are offered based on various service-level agreements (SLAs) between the providers and users. In a broad sense, the SLA for cloud computing is addressed in terms of the service availability performance and data protection and security aspects. The SaaS is applied at the application end using special interfaces by users or clients. At the PaaS layer, the cloud platform must perform billing services and handling of job queuing, launching and monitor services. At the bottom layer of IaaS services,

Table 2.12 IaaS clouds and their infrastructures and service offerings (August 2015).

Cloud Name	Virtual Machine Instance Configurations	API and Access Tools
Amazon EC2	Each instance has 1-20 EC2 processors, 1.7–15 GB memory and 160 TB storage	CLI or Web Service (WS) portal
GoGrid	Each instance has 1–6 CPUs, 0.5–8 GB memory and 30–480 GB storage	REST, Java, PHP, Python, Ruby
Rackspace Cloud	Each instance has a 4-core CPU, 0.25–16 GB memory and 10–620 GB storage	REST, Python, PHP, Java, C#, .NET
Flexiscale in UK	Each instance has 1–4 CPUs, 0.5–16 GB memory, and 20–270 GB storage	Web console

databases, compute instances, file system and storage must be provisioned to yield to user demands.

2.4.1 AWS Architecture over Distributed Datacenters

The AWS cloud architecture is shown in Figure 2.9. The AWS provides extreme flexibility (virtual machines) for the users to execute their own applications. Elastic load balancing automatically distributes incoming application traffic across multiple Amazon EC2 instances and allows users to avoid non-operating nodes and to equalize the load on functioning images. Both Auto Scaling and Elastic Load Balancing are enabled by CloudWatch, which monitors running instances. CloudWatch is a web service that provides monitoring for AWS cloud resources, starting with Amazon EC2. It provides customers with visibility into resource utilization, operational performance and overall demand patterns – including metrics such as CPU utilization, disk reads and writes, and network traffic.

Amazon offers a Relational Database Service RDS with a messaging interface. The Elastic MapReduce capability is equivalent to Hadoop running on the basic EC2 offering. AWS Import/Export allows us to ship large volumes of data to and from EC2 by shipping physical disks; it is well known that this is often the highest bandwidth connection between geographically distant systems. The CloudFront implements a content distribution network. Amazon DevPay is a simple-to-use online billing and account management service.

The Flexible Payments Service (FPS) provides developers of commercial systems in AWS with a convenient way to charge Amazon's customers that use such services built on AWS. Customers can pay using the same login credentials, shipping address and payment information they already have on file with Amazon. The Fulfillment Web Service allows merchants to access Amazon cloud through a simple web services. Many AWS services are studied in the next section.

Example 2.7   AWS Elastic Compute Cloud (EC2) for IaaS

The structure of the Elastic Compute Cloud (EC2) is shown in Figure 2.14. The EC2 supports many cloud services, with a cluster of machine instances. Both Linux and Windows instances are available. The Amazon Machine Images (AMI) offers the templates to create machine instances of various types. Public AMIs can be freely used by any user. The private AMIs are created for the owner's private use only. The paid AMIs

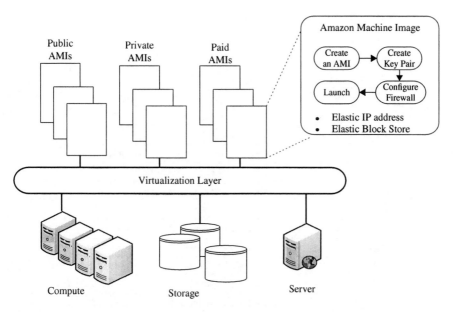

Figure 2.14 The EC2 execution environment where Amazon Machine Image (AMI) can be created from public, private or paid pools with security protection.

can be shared among users with some payment between the users and owners. The AMI launch cycle is shown in the blowout box, where security is enforced with instance-access firewalls.

Automatic scaling and load balancing among the instances are supported in EC2. The machine instances provisioned in an EC2 cluster are selected upon user demand. The cluster configuration should match with the workload anticipated. We will study scale-out and scale-up strategies for EC2 configuration control in Chapter 6. Auto Scaling allows you to scale your EC2 size up or down automatically, according to some threshold conditions. The number of EC2 instances in a cluster is driven by workload demand. Auto Scaling is particularly well suited for applications that experience frequent variability in workload. The scaling technique is automatically triggered by Amazon Cloud-Watch and available at no additional charge to the users beyond the use of the Cloud-Watch. ∎

2.4.2 AWS Cloud Service Offerings

Three tables are given below to summarize the offerings by AWS in three major service areas. Table 2.13 specifies the compute, storage and database band networking (IaaS) services. Table 2.14 specifies the application, mobile and analytics services offered by the AWS cloud. These are related PaaS offerings. In terms of services provided, the AWS is no longer just a pure IaaS cloud. We briefly introduce the AWS services below. By far, the EC2 and S3 are the most popular IaaS services provided by AWS. Many other IaaS clouds, private or public, are also trying to make their cloud systems compatible with EC2 and S3. The RDS service supports relational SQL services. The Dynamic DB

Table 2.13 Compute, storage, database and networking services in AWS cloud.

Category	Offering	Service Modules or Short Description
Compute	EC2	Virtual servers in the AWS cloud
	Lambda	Run code in response to events
	EC2 Container Service	Run and manage Docker containers
Storage and Content Delivery	S3	Scalable storage in the AWS cloud
	Elastic File System	Fully management file system for EC2
	Storage Gateway	Integrate on-premises IT facilities with cloud storage
	Glacier	Archive storage in the AWS cloud
	CloudFront	Global content delivery network
Database	RDS	MySQL, Postgres, Oracle, SQL server
	DynamicDB	Predictable and scalable NoSQL data store
	ElastiCache	In-memory Cache
	Redshift	Managed petabyte-scale warehouse service
Networking	VPC	Virtual private cloud as isolated cloud resources
	Direct Connect	Dedicated Network Connection to AWS
	Route S3	Scalable DNS and domain name registration

Table 2.14 Application, mobile and analytics services in the AWS cloud.

Category	Offering	Service Modules or Short Description
Application Services	SQS	Message queue services
	SWF	Workflow service for coordinating app components
	AppStream	Low latency application streaming
	Elastic Transcoder	Easy-to-use scalable media transcoding
	SES	Email sending and receiving service
	CloudSearch	Managed search service
	API Gateway	Build, deploy and manage APIs
Mobile Services	Cognito	User identity and app data synchronization
	Device Farm	Test Android, Fire OS and iOS apps on devices in the cloud
	Mobile Analytics	Collect, view and export app analytics
	SNS	Simple push notification service
Analytics Services	EMR	Managed elastic Hadoop (MapReduce) framework
	Kinesis	Real-time processing of streaming data
	Data Pipeline	Orchestration for data-driven workflows
	Machine Learning	Build machine learning prediction solutions

supports NoSQL operations over unstructured big data. The networking services support virtual clustering of the network resources.

Example 2.8   AWS S3 Architecture with Block-Oriented Data Operations

Amazon S3 provides a simple storage service that can be used to store and retrieve any amount of data, at any time, from anywhere on the web. S3 provides the object oriented storage service for users. Users can access their objects through SOAP protocol with any browser. The S3 execution environment is shown in Figure 2.15. The fundamental operation unit of S3 is an object, which is attributed to value, meta and access control. Each object is stored in a bucket and retrieved via a unique and developer-assigned key. The bucket is the container of the object.

Authentication mechanisms are provided to ensure that data is kept secure from unauthorized access. Objects can be made private or public, and rights can be granted to specific users. The default download protocol is http. There is no data transfer charge between Amazon EC2 and S3 within the same Region. The steps to use S3 are: i) create a bucket at region where your bucket and object(s) reside to optimize latency, minimize costs or address regulatory requirements; ii) upload Objects to your bucket, where your data is backed by the Amazon SLA; and iii) the access controls are optional to grant others access to your data from anywhere in the world. ■

Table 2.14 lists 15 application-oriented service offerings by AWS. Many of these are of the SaaS type, except users can request their own customized server clusters to run

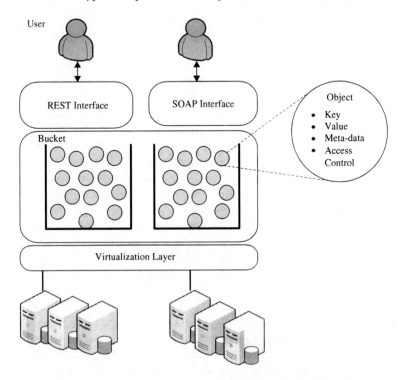

Figure 2.15 The Amazon S3 storage service for holding unlimited data objects.

these applications. The application services cover message queuing, real-time streaming, email sending, searching, synchronization, mobile and analytics workflow orchestration operations. Most of these are newly added features to the AWS cloud. The mobile services help user synchronizes their mobile data with the rented S3 storage. Mobile analytics are provided to analyze these data for decision making or responses. The SNS service handles the push notification servers between mobile phones and the S3 service.

The AWS platform supports many smaller clients and large companies to build their leased clouds to run their business to make a profit out of a huge number of Internet users. One good example is DropBox, which applied the S3 for a long time to provide their backup data storage operations before they built their own datacenter storage. The analytics services are newly added. They apply EMR using Hadoop or Spark. Real-time streaming and support of the orchestration of containers are also provided.

2.4.2.1. Amazon Machine Learning

Amazon Machine Learning (ML) offers a service that allows data scientists to use machine learning technology. Amazon ML provides visualization tools and wizards that guide the user through the process of creating prediction models. This frees up the developers from learning complex ML algorithms and software tools. The Amazon ML makes it easy to obtain predictions using simple APIs. The user does not have to implement custom prediction generation code, or manage any infrastructure.

The Amazon ML is based on highly scalable technology which has been used by Amazon for years. The service applies powerful algorithms to create ML models by finding patterns in users' training datasets. Then users apply these prediction models to a large dataset under testing for generating prediction results. The AWS claims that these services can generate billions of predictions daily. These predictions are served in real time and at high throughput. With Amazon ML, big data analytics is performed without upfront hardware or software investment. The user simply pays as he goes. Users can start small and scale up as their application workflow increases.

Listed below are some predictive analytics services provided by AWS: Fraud detection, customer churn prediction, content personalization, propensity modeling for marketing campaigns, document classification, and automated solution recommendation for customer support. Interested readers may want to access their website for details: https://aws.amazon.com/machinbe-learng/ The following example presents one of such applications of the Amazon ML services in commercial housing applications.

A large number of individual, small business or transient users are using EC2 instances based on their needs, dynamically. In fact, AWS provides research oriented universities with promotion grants for students to learn from practice on AWS cloud. Other public clouds, such as Azure and Google computer engines, are providing the same service for beginners. According to the authors, with teaching of cloud computing at the University of Southern California, hands-on experience plays a vital role for students to learn cloud computing operations, software environment and programming skills. A number of homework problems are included in this book, which are designed to serve that purpose.

2.4.3 Platform PaaS Clouds – Google AppEngine

To develop, deploy and manage the execution of applications using the provisioned resources demands a cloud platform with all required software environments. Such a cloud platform includes the operating system and run-time library support. This has triggered the creation of the PaaS model to enable the user to develop and deploy his user applications. Cloud platform services offered by five providers are given in Table 2.15. These PaaS service providers include Google AppEngine, Microsoft Azure, Force.com, Amazon Elastic MapReduce, and Aneka in Australia.

The platform cloud is an integrated computer system consisting of both hardware and software infrastructures. The user application can be developed on this virtualized cloud platform using some of the programming languages and software tools supported by the provider (e.g. Java, Python, .Net). The user does not manage the underlying cloud infrastructure. The cloud provider supports user application development and the testing on a well-defined service platform. This PaaS model enables the means to have a collaborated software development platform for users from different parts of the world. This model also encourages the third party to provide software management, integration and service monitoring solutions.

2.4.3.1. The Google App Engine

Google is one of the larger cloud application providers, although the fundamental service program is private and the outside people could not use the Google infrastructure to build their own service. The building blocks of Google cloud computing applications include the Google File System for storing large amounts of data, MapReduce programming framework for application developers, Chubby for distributed application lock services and BigTable as a storage service for accessing the structural or semi-structural data. With these building blocks, Google has built many cloud applications.

Famous GAE applications include the Google Search Engine, Google Docs, Google Earth, gmail, etc. These applications can support a large amount of users simultaneously. The user can interact with Google applications with the web interface provided by each

Table 2.15 Public clouds offering platform-as-a-service (PaaS) services (August 2015).

Cloud Name	Languages and Developer Tools	Programming Models supported by provider	Target Applications and Storage Option
Google AppEngine	Python, Java and Eclipse-based IDE	MapReduce, Web programming on demand	Web applications and BigTable Storage
Salesforce.com Force.com	Apex, Eclipse-based IDE, Web-based Wizard	Workflow, Excel-like, Web programming on demand	CRM and add-on App development for Business
Microsoft Azure	NET, Azure tools for MS Visual Studio	Dryad, Twister, .NET Framework	Enterprise and Web Applications
Amazon Elastic MapReduce	Hive, Pig, Cascading, Java, Ruby, Perl, Python, PHP, R, and C++	MapReduce, Hadoop, Spark,	Data Processing, eMail, and e-Commerce, S3 and WorkDocs

application. Third-party application providers can use the App Engine to build the cloud applications for providing services. The applications are all run in the Google datacenters. Inside each datacenter, there might be thousands of server nodes to form different clusters (see the previous section). Each cluster can run multiple purpose servers. Typical configuration of a cluster can run the Google file system, MapReduce jobs, as well as BigTable servers for structure data. Extra services such as Chubby for distributed locks can also run in the clusters.

Google App Engine runs the user program on Google's infrastructure. As a platform running third-party program, the application developer no longer needs to worry about the maintenance of servers. The Google App Engine can be comprehended as the combination of several software components. The front end is an application framework which is similar as other web application frameworks such as ASP, J2EE or JSP. Currently, Google App Engine supports the Python and Java programming environments. The applications can run similarly as in the web application containers. The frontend can be used as the dynamic web serving infrastructure, which can provide the full support to common technologies.

Google has the world's largest search engine facilities. They have extensive experience in massive data processing that has led to new insights into datacenter design and novel programming models that scale to incredible sizes. The user can interact with Google applications via the web interface provided by each application. Third party but as discussed earlier with MapReduce, this infrastructure is applicable to many other areas. Google has hundreds of datacenters and has installed over 460,000 servers worldwide. For example, 200 Google datacenters are used at any one time for a number of cloud applications. Data items are stored in text, images and video and are replicated to tolerate faults or failures. Here we discuss Google's App Engine (GAE), which offers a PaaS platform supporting various cloud and web applications.

Example 2.9   Google AppEngine for PaaS Services with load Balancing
Google has pioneered the cloud development by leveraging the large number of datacenters they operate. For example, Google pioneered cloud services in gmail, Google Docs, Google Earth, etc. These applications can support a large amount of users simultaneously with high availability. Notable technology achievements include the Google File System (GFS), MapReduce, Bigtable, Chubby, etc. The GAE is becoming a common platform for many small cloud service providers. This platform specializes in supporting scalable (elastic) web applications. GAE enables users to run their applications on a large number of datacenters associated with Google's search engine operations. Figure 2.16 shows the major building blocks of the Google cloud platform, which has been used to deliver the cloud services highlighted above.

The GFS is used for storing large amounts of data. MapReduce is for use in application program development. Chubby is used for distributed application lock services. BigTable enables application providers to use the App Engine for building cloud applications. The applications all run in datacenters under tight management by Google engineers. Inside each datacenter, there are thousands of servers forming different clusters. Google App Engine supports many web applications. One is the storage service to store the application specific data in the Google's infrastructure.

The data can be persistently stored in the backend storage server while still providing the facility for queries, sorting and even transactions similar to the traditional

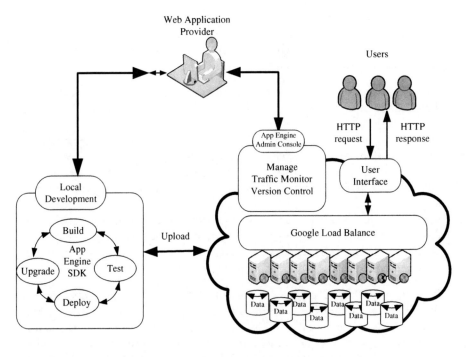

Figure 2.16 Google AppEngine platform for PaaS operations with load balancing.

database systems. The Google App Engine provides the Google's specific services such as the gmail account service. In fact, such a service is the login service, i.e. applications can use the gmail account directly. This can eliminate the tedious work of building the customized user management components in web applications. Thus, web applications built on top of the Google App Engine can use the APIs authenticating users and sending email using Google Accounts. ∎

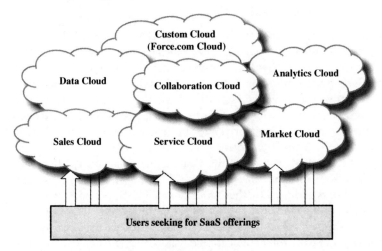

Figure 2.17 Seven Salesforce cloud service offerings: all for SaaS applications except the custom cloud offering PaaS applications.

2.4.3.2. Functionality of Google App Engine

The GAE platform is built with five major components. The GAE is not an infrastructure platform but rather an application development platform for users. We introduce below the component functionalities, separately:

a) The **datastore** offers an object-oriented, distributed, structured data storage service based on the Bigtable techniques. The datastore secures data management operations.
b) The **application runtime environment** offers a platform for scalable web programming and execution. It supports two development languages: Python and Java.
c) The **software development kit** (SDK) is used for local application development. The SDK allows users to execute test runs of local applications and upload application codes.
d) The **administration console** is used for easy management of the user application development cycle, instead of being used for physical resource management.
e) The **GAE Web service infrastructure** provides special interfaces to guarantee flexible use and management of storage and network resources by the GAE.

Google offers essentially free GAE services to all gmail account owners. You can register for a GAE account or use your gmail account name to sign up for the service. The service is free within a quota. If you exceed the quota, the page instructs you how to pay for the service. Then, you download their SDK and read the Python or the Java Guide to get started. GAE accepts Python, Ruby and Java programming languages. The platform does not provide any IaaS services. This model allows the user to deploy user-built applications on top of the cloud infrastructure, which are built using the programming languages and software tools supported by Google (e.g. Java, Python). Azure does this similarly for the .Net and Azure platform. The user does not manage the underlying cloud infrastructure. The cloud provider supports all application development, testing and operations.

2.4.4 Application SaaS Clouds – The Salesforce Clouds

This SaaS refers to browser-initiated application software over thousands of cloud customers. Services and tools offered by PaaS are utilized in the construction of applications and management of their deployment on resources offered by IaaS providers. SaaS model provides the software applications as a service. As a result, on the customer side, there is no upfront investment in servers or software licensing. On the provider side, costs are kept low, compared with conventional hosting of user applications. The customer data is stored in the cloud that is either vendor proprietary or publically hosted. Table 2.16 summarizes four SaaS cloud platforms.

The best examples of SaaS services include the Google gmail and docs, Microsoft SharePoint, and the CRM software from Salesforce.com. They are all very successful in promoting their own business and used by thousands of small businesses in their day-to-day operations. Providers like Google and Microsoft offer integrated IaaS and PaaS services, whereas others such as Amazon and GoGrid offer pure IaaS services. Third-party providers, such as Manjrasoft, offer application development and deployment services on top of commercial clouds. Another well-known SaaS cloud is the Outlook Web Access (OWA), or known as the Office 365, offered by Microsoft for cloud-hosted email services.

Table 2.16 Four SaaS cloud platforms and their service offerings (August 2015).

Model	Amazon AWS	Google AppEngine	Microsoft Azure	Salesforce
Platform Support	AWS EC2, S3, EMR, SNS, etc.	GAE, GFS, BigTable, MapReduce, etc.	Azure, .NET service, Dynamic CRM,	Salesforce.com, Force.com, Online CRM, Gifttag
SaaS Offerings	Elastic Beanstalk, Code-Deploy, OpsWorks, Code-Commit, Code Pipeline, Mobile Analytics	Gmail, Docs, YouTube, WhatApp	Live, SQL, Office"365 (OWA), Hotmail	Sales, Service, Market, Data, Collaboration, Analytics,
Security Features	CloudWatch, Trusted Advisor, Identity/Access Control	Chubby locks for security enforcement	Replicated Data, Rule-based access control	Adm./Record security, Use Metadata API
APIs and Languages	API Gateway, LatinPig	Web-based Adm. Console, Python	Azure portal, .net Framework	Apex, Visualforce, AppExchange, SOSL, SOQL

To discover new drugs through DNA sequence analysis, Eli Lily Company has used Amazon's EC2 and S3 platform with provisioned server and storage clusters. The goal is to conduct high-performance biological sequence analysis without using an expensive supercomputer. The benefit of this IaaS application is a reduced drug deployment time with much lower cost. Another good example is *New York Times* applying Amazon, EC2 and S3 services to retrieve useful pictorial information quickly from millions of archival articles and newspapers. The *New York Times* has significantly reduced their time and costs in getting the job done. Many startup cloud companies provide some SaaS services with rented platforms like AWS.

The following is a review of SaaS and PaaS services offered by Salesforce.com. This company was established in 1999 to provide on-line solutions to SaaS, mainly in CRM applications. Initially, they used third-party cloud platforms to run their software services. Gradually, the company launched its own Force.com as a PaaS platform that can execute many SaaS applications or help users to develop add-on applications under PaaS support.

Example 2.10   SaaS Cloud Services Offered by Salesforce Company
Recently, Salesforce has subdivided its CRM service into seven specific cloud service categories: namely Sales Cloud, Service Cloud, Data Cloud, Market Cloud and Collaboration Cloud, Analytics Cloud and Custom Cloud, as illustrated in Figure 2.17. Among these, all provide SaaS applications, except the PaaS Custom Cloud, also known as the Force.com.

We briefly introduce their functionalities as follows:

- **Sales Cloud:** for CRM SaaS applications for managing customer profile, tracking opportunities, optimizing campaigns, etc.;
- **Service Cloud:** a cloud-based customer service SaaS. Allowing companies to create, track and route service cases, including social media networking services;
- **Market Cloud:** providing social marketing SaaS applications. Allows companies to identify sales leads from social media, discover advocates, etc.;
- **Data Cloud:** for acquiring and managing CRM records;
- **Collaboration Cloud:** for use by business collaborators;
- **Analytics Cloud:** for sales performance analysis based on machine learning;
- **Custom Cloud:** a PaaS platform for creating add-on applications on top of the standard CRM applications.

■

2.5   Mobile Clouds and Inter-Cloud Mashup Services

This section is devoted to understanding the state-of-the-art in mobile clouds and their application. The material presented is highly relevant to mobile devices, wireless Internet and IoT sensing technologies and platforms.

2.5.1   Mobile Clouds and Cloudlet Gateways

As shown in Figure 2.18, the user carrying a mobile device moves across heterogeneous mobile computing environments, such as cellular networks, mobile *ad hoc* networks, body area networks, vehicular networks, etc. However, the resource-constrained nature

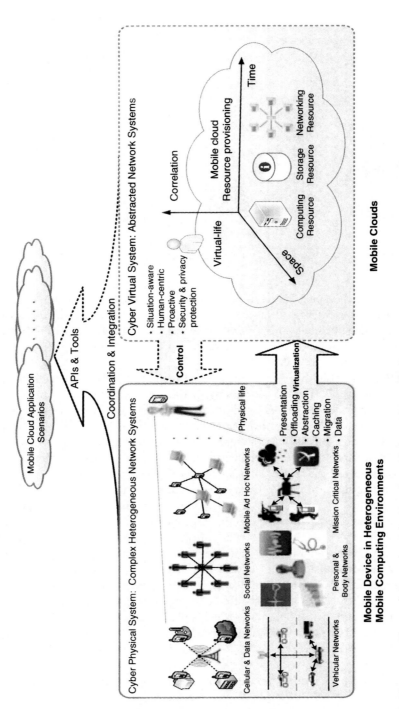

Figure 2.18 The capabilities of mobile device are enhanced by mobile clouds in a heterogeneous mobile computing environment.

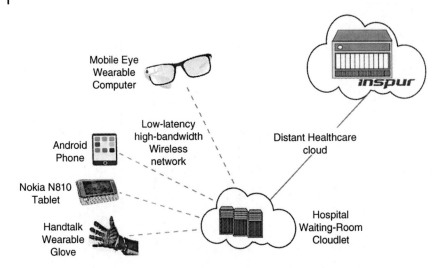

Figure 2.19 Virtual-machine based cloudlets for mobile cloud computing applications.

of the mobile device, especially the limited battery life, has been a stumbling block for the user to enjoy the further improvements of mobile applications and services. Special cloudlets [21] were introduced to serve as wireless gateways between mobile users and the Internet. These cloudlets can be used to offload computations or web services to remote clouds safely.

The combination of mobile communication and mobile clouds is paving the way to many more useful applications in our daily life. In other word, heavy-duty computations initiated by "small" mobile devices could be carried out by "large" clouds. For example, the user moves in the physical world. Meanwhile, the abundant data is collected through IoT sensing in various mobile environments. These sensing signals must be directed to the cloud for data storage. Virtualized data objects are created in the cloud for the user. By taking advantage of the abundant resources in the cloud platforms, data mining and machine learning algorithms are often developed to analyze the mobile user's situation and to take timely action proactively. In the bottom of Figure 2.19, a cyber physical system (CPS) is deployed to perform integrated execution of many mobile applications.

Recently, researchers at Carnegie-Mellon University, Microsoft, AT&T and Lancaster University have proposed a low-cost infrastructure to enable cloud computing using mobile devices. The idea is called Cloudlet, which offers a resource-rich portal for upgrading mobile devices with cognitive abilities to access distant clouds, as demonstrated in Figure 2.19. This portal should be designed as trustworthy and to use virtual machines to explore location-aware cloud applications. The idea can be applied for opportunity discovery, fast information processing, and intelligent decision making on the road, etc. Cloudlet makes it possible for mobile devices to access the Internet cloud easily in cost-effective mobile computing services.

The idea of using cloudlets for mobile cloud computing is illustrated in Figure 2.20. Both mobile devices and centralized clouds or datacenters have shortcomings in supporting mobile computing. The mobile handsets face a resource property problem with limited CPU power, storage capacity and network bandwidth on smart phones or tablet computers. Mobile devices cannot be used to handle large datasets. On the other hand, the distant cloud on the Internet faces the WAN latency problem.

How to solve these two-sided problems is the challenge of the cloudlets to be deployed at public sites such as coffee shops, bookstores and hospital waiting rooms for easy access, just like the convenience provided by access points for WiFi services to connect to the Internet. Widely deployed cloudlets enable distributed cloud computing and extended resource handling at convenience stores, classrooms or users on the move. The idea is to use the cloudlet as a flexible gateway or portal to access the distant cloud. The cloudlet can be implemented on PCs, workstations or low-cost servers. The major innovation lies in using VM-based flexibility to handle requests from different mobile devices.

2.5.1.1. Fast VM Synthesis in Cloudlets

A prototype of cloudlet by the name Kimberley was built at CMU. This prototype synthesizes a VM overlay in the cloudlet host. They have reported the fast VM synthesis time to be less than 100 seconds. In other words, they create VM overlay in transient cloudlets, which is customized to bind cloud resources in the distance to satisfy the user need. A small VM overlay is delivered by mobile devices to cloudlets that already possess a base VM. The VM overlay plus the base VM creates a special execution environment for the mobile device to launch its cloud applications through the cloudlet portal. Trust and security issues are also major factors in cloudlet deployment.

Data protection includes file/log access control, data coloring and copyright compliance. Disaster recovery is also needed to be secure from being lost through hardware/software failures. Cloud security can be enforced with establishing the root of trust, securing VM provisioning process, software watermarking, and the use of firewalls and IDSs at host and network levels. Recently, trust overlay networks and reputation systems have been suggested to protect datacenters in trusted cloud computing.

The architecture of a cloudlet mesh is shown in Figure 2.20. All cloudlets are WiFi-enabled. Each cloudlet server has an embedded WiFi access point. Each cloudlet connects many mobile devices within the WiFi range. The cloudlets are interconnected by wireless links to form a mesh. All cloudlets operate essentially as gateways at the edge network of the Internet. Multiple cloudlets can widen the wireless coverage range to serve many more mobile devices. Collaborative defense is suggested to use many cloudlets collectively to build a shield to deter intruders and attackers. Finally, caching and load balancing are practiced to upgrade the QoS and throughput during multi-task offloading to the remote clouds.

Mobile devices are subject to virus or network worm attacks. Encryption may not be the best solution for mobile devices, due to its limited computing power and energy consumption constraints. Some special software tools are available to resist virus or worm attacks on mobile devices. This may involve authentication, URL checking and spam filtering. With large storage and backup services, mobile users will offload these duties to the clouds.

2.5.2 Multi-Cloud Mashup Services

A cloud mashup is composed of multiple services with shared datasets and integrated functionalities. For example, the EC2 provided by Amazon Web Service (AWS), the

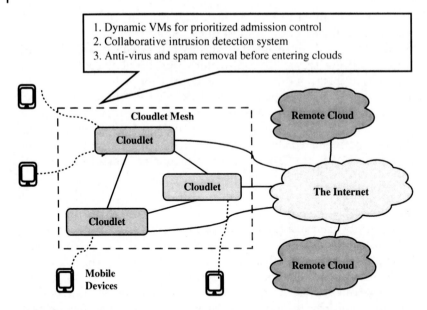

Figure 2.20 Cloudlet mesh architecture for securing mobile cloud computing.

authentication and authorization services provided by Facebook, and the MapReduce service provided by Google, can all be mashed up to deliver real-time, personalized driving route recommendation service. To discover qualified services and compose them with guaranteed Quality of Service (QoS), we propose an integrated skyline query processing method for building up cloud mashup applications. We use a similarity test to achieve optimal localized skyline.

This mashup method scales well with the growing number of cloud sites involved in the mashup applications. Faster skyline selection, reduced composition time, dataset sharing and resources integration assure the QoS over multiple clouds. We experimented with the Quality of Web Service (QWS) benchmark over 10,000 Web services along six QoS dimensions. By utilizing block-elimination, data-space partitioning and service similarity pruning, the skyline process is shortened by one-third, when compared with two state-of-the-art methods.

Cloud mashups have grown rapidly with the introduction of Web 2.0, service-oriented architectures, and big data management. Large cloud datasets are subject to mashup within inter-cloud services. Mashup applications face an increasing demand for personalized web/cloud services. Many public or commercial cloud providers compete to satisfy requests of mashup services. The main difficulty comes from the fact that there could be a combinatorial number of possibilities. Consequently, the optimal selection of component services is an NP-hard problem and only some sub-optimal composite services can be generated.

To this end, skyline operators and the MapReduce paradigm have been suggested to support the inter-cloud mashup selection and composition. Previous research integrates the aforementioned two powerful tools to accelerate the service composition process and to achieve high QoS. The goal is to upgrade cloud mashup services and promote the use of big data analytics. The skyline method is especially attractive to discover qualified

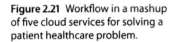

Figure 2.21 Workflow in a mashup of five cloud services for solving a patient healthcare problem.

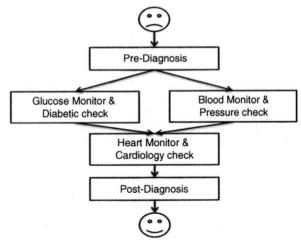

Web services in a multi-attribute decision-making process. The quality of composing Web services in a cloud mashup can be greatly enhanced by faster MapReduce skyline query processing.

A cloud mashup is built on top of multiple providers of web, cloud and big data services. The term refers to a composite cloud application that applies and aggregates datasets or functionalities from more than one source or provider. The motivation is to provide more application agility and scalability by expanding cloud computing with other Internet applications or web services. The design objective is to offer an integrated service by combining several cloud services with related web services offered by social networks and mobile platforms. For example, a cloud mashup can be integrated to form a workflow using Amazon AWS, DropBox, Twitter and Facebook services, jointly. Cloud mashups are built by choosing specific API and data types governed by some desired service functionalities.

Example 2.11   Mashup of Multiple Cloud Services in Healthcare Applications
Suppose each of the tasks is handled by an infirmary service deployed on a separate cloud. The five cloud services form a mashup providing integrated services as a workflow linked by the directed edges in the DAG (directed acyclic graph) in Figure 2.21. A composite service request is sent to the cloud mashup for making such an online healthcare plan. The output of the workflow is the complete process up to the satisfaction of the patient.

Each task could be one service provided by one or more web/cloud-based platform. Every candidate service is selected from a large service space supported by various cloud functions. For example, some infirmary services are deployed on a cloud with a fast response time and satisfactory diagnosis result but at a high cost. Patients with similar symptom need to choose a combination of those five infirmary services considering the total waiting time and cost involved in the five tasks.

In real-life applications, the difficulty lies in the pool of available cloud services being very large. Even worse, a medical check might involve far more tasks compared to the five tasks. If multiple patients choose the same service of the same cloud provider, the

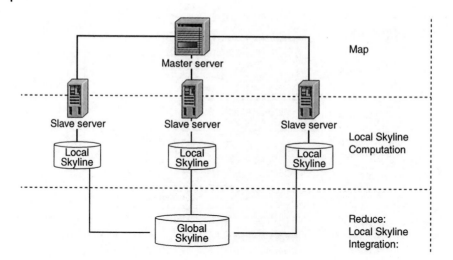

Figure 2.22 MapReduce model for selecting skyline services to optimize the QoS.

waiting list would be long. Correspondingly, the waiting time and cost become unpredictable. Therefore, an efficient method should be developed to help a user to choose a composed workflow of cloud services as a guaranteed QoS. ∎

Figure 2.22 illustrates the idea of optimized skyline query processing in three parts: skyline selection, similarity test and service composition. We select skyline services based on block elimination partitioning of the data space. The skyline may produce a large number of candidate services. To discover the best choice in each skyline subspace, a skyline relaxation method can be used to consider only the representatives in each subspace. The purpose is to accelerate the subsequent QoS-assured services composition.

These three component service classes form a composite cloud service. To reduce the composition time, similarity testing among compatible skyline selections can be used in various skyline sectors. The purpose is to remove redundancy using skyline representatives. Finally, we compose the mashup service as an integrated package for users. The QoS and QoE specify the desired performance requirements in the mashup services.

2.5.2.1. Quality of Mashup Service (QoMS)

QoS directly evaluates different performance metric attributes of composite mashup services. Take the "online healthcare planner" as an example. We can consider the waiting time, service time, cost, reputation, reliability and availability for each task. The response time is a major factor of QoS, since it accounts for the communication traffic when a user accesses the services and has a large impact on the service quality. The duration of composite service calculated by CPA is neither the optimal nor the actual duration, but it is a best-so-far evaluation method during the composition procedure. The first three attributes of a composite service, waiting time, service time and cost, depend not only on those of its elementary tasks but the operations in between; while the last three, i.e. the reputation, reliability and availability, are derived from its elementary attributes.

2.5.2.2. Quality of Experience (QoE)

How customers are satisfied with the solutions provided by the composite service is a critical evaluation of QoE. For example, the whole medical plan made by the planner is the solution of the composite service, and quality of the medical plan depends on the solutions of each task t_i, that is, the medical treatment applications, the cloud service providers, etc. It lacks, to the best of our knowledge, incorporation of the solution quality into the service composition procedure. People may argue that "reputation" can be used to incorporate how users are satisfied, but it is in terms of the service rather than looking down into its solution.

We define the criteria of QoE as the percentile satisfaction level to solutions of a service's solution. As labeled into the node, each solution is given a score denoting the customer specified solution quality. The methods of scoring the solution quality fall into two categories: statistics-based or profile-based. The statistics-based methods score a solution from customer voting or reviewing comments. The profile-based methods dynamically estimate a customer's satisfaction level, using for example pair comparison, and keep a user specific profile. Using statistics-based and profile-based methods, labeling the service scores can be offered either offline or online. The scores can be provided in advance or dynamically generated during the composition process.

2.5.3 Skyline Discovery of Mashup Services

Given a set Q of data points in d-dimensional QoS space, each dimension represents a performance attribute with values properly ordered. Suppose the lower-valued points are better than the higher-valued ones. A data point P_j is dominated by P_i, if P_i is better than or equal to P_j in all dimensions. Furthermore, P_i must be better than P_j in at least one dimension. All data points that are not dominated by any other point from a subset are called the skyline. For instance, let us pick two dual dimension points (10, 20) and (20, 10). Because the points do not dominate one another, the two points are parts of the skyline.

In the d-dimensional space, a skyline is really a surface that is closest to the origin of the coordinated space. Intuitively, all points on the skyline are more desirable than all off-skyline data points. A skyline query selects the best or most interesting points in all dimensions. There are several works applying MapReduce to upgrade the computing efficiency with scalable performance in large-scale skyline query processing. Our approach is based on a novel block-elimination method. Furthermore, we propose a variant of the MapReduce method by adding a process between Map and Reduce. The idea is illustrated in Figure 2.22 in three steps:

1) **The Map Process:** Service data points are partitioned by the master server (e.g. UDDI) into multiple data blocks based on the QoS demand. The data blocks are dispatched to slave servers for parallel processing.
2) **Local Skyline Computation:** In this process, each slave server generates the local skylines from service data points on its own subdivided data blocks.

3) **The Reduce Process:** In this process, local skylines generated by all the slave servers are merged and integrated into a global skyline, which applies to all services being evaluated.

The quality of the selected skyline services depends on the efficiency of the local skyline computation and the performance of the integration process. Thus, the efficiency and QoS of the MapReduce skyline process depends mainly on how to explore the distributed parallelism to accelerate the Map stage. The efficiency of the mapping depends on data space partitioning. The service data points are partitioned into divided regions. The goal is to achieve load balancing, to fit into the local memory, and to avoid repeated computations when old services are dropped and new services are added dynamically. Before the process of Reduce, we introduce a middle process (local skyline computation) at Step 2.

The reason is that computing skyline services is expensive if the number of candidate services is extremely large. By introducing the middle process, only local skyline services are delivered to the Reduce process at step 3. This will decrease largely the number of services to be processed at the Reduce stage. MapReduce is effective to speed up the skyline query processing process. We need to compare pairwise services in parallel. With MapReduce, the new service is first mapped into a group and added into the local skyline computation. Then all local skylines are integrated into the global skyline at the Reduce stage. We have adopted the skyline method to solve the QoS problem in two earlier works. We evaluate three MapReduce versions of the BNL (Block Name Label) skyline algorithm based on three different data space partitioning schemes.

Consider two service data points s_1, s_2, in the QoMS space Q. The service s_1 dominates service s_2, if s_1 is better than or equal to s_2 in all attribute dimensions of Q. Furthermore, s_1 must be better than s_2 in at least one attribute dimension. The subset S of services form the skyline in space Q, if all service points on the skyline are better than or equal to other services along all attribute dimensions. In other words, all skyline services are not dominated by any other service in the space Q. We evaluate three MapReduce skyline methods, denoted as MR-grid, MR-angular and MR-block, where MR stands for MapReduce in all figure labels and text body. Three MapReduce skyline algorithms are specified based on the three data partitioning schemes shown in Figure 2.23(a,b,c). The x-axis and y-axis are two attribute dimensions that favor lower values.

The MR-grid algorithm contains two stages: i) Partitioning Job, in which we divide the data space into some disjoint subspaces and compute the local skyline of each subspace; and ii) Merging Job, in which we merge all local skylines to compute the global skyline. Empirically, the number of partitions is set as (2 times of nodes) in the MR-grid algorithm. In the MR-grid, the QoS parameter values in all of the dimensions are used to do the partitioning. For example, we separate the dual-dimensional data space into 16 blocks according to the response time of each service in Figure 2.23(a). This method is easy to implement, while many redundant computations exist in this method. This method needs to balance the workload in the Reduce process.

2.5.4 Dynamic Composition of Mashup Services

The MR-grid is introduced in Algorithm 2.1 below. The whole service space is firstly partitioned into N disjoint sections. Points within one partition are sent to one Map Task, and each Map Task can process one or more partitions. Map Task outputs the

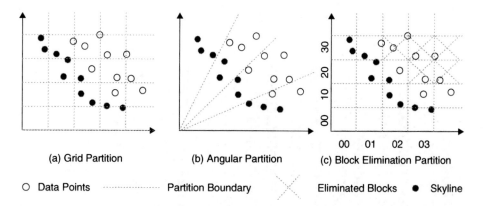

(a) Grid Partition (b) Angular Partition (c) Block Elimination Partition

○ Data Points ·············· Partition Boundary ✕ Eliminated Blocks ● Skyline

Figure 2.23 Three data partitioning methods for MapReduce skyline query processing. (Reprinted with permission from F. Zhang, K. Hwang, et al. 2016 [23]).

partition number as a key, and a list of local skylines of that particular partition as a value. At the reduce phase, all the local skylines are processed through a Reduce Task, and Global skyline is therefore generated. The angular partitioning method was originally proposed by DK design. We emphasize the composition of skyline selected services, which aims at achieving optimized QoMS with respect to a given set of resources and cost constraints.

The block-elimination algorithm is improved from the Grid Partition algorithm in section *C*. Consider a diagonal list of squares, where the services inside the left-down grid cell dominate the services inside its right-up grid cell. Take Figure 2.23(c) as an example. Cell (1, 2) has two points, therefore all the rest of the points along the diagonal line, for example Cell (2, 3) and Cell (3, 4), can be eliminated without further processing. The algorithm checks all the cells with at least one coordinate value equaling to zero. The block-based elimination method reduces a few blocks in step 1, and the other two methods (Angle and Grid) do not reduce any block. The Point Reduction Rate (PPR) is measured by the aggregated local skyline points that are rolled over to step 2, over the total number of points. The Block Reduction Rate (BRR) is defined as the blocks containing local skyline points that are rolled over to step 2, over the total number of blocks. In Figure 2.29, we chose three groups of data based on randomly distributed data density.

We define Skyline Ratio (CR) as the number of pairs of all of the blocks that need to be pairwise compared over the total number of pairs that have to be calculated at step 2. All three performance metrics prefer low values to produce a narrowed down set of points for further analysis. For example, 100 P/Per Cube represents the high density of each space, meaning each small partition has approximately 100 points inside. Figure 2.24 plots the results for randomly distributed data in 4-D spaces. To evaluate the efficiency of various MapReduce skyline selection methods, we use the basic metric of processing time, which consists of both reduce time and map time. In summary, with a very large service cardinality of 10,000 data points over 10 attributes, our MR-block method outperforms the MR-grid and MR-angular methods by a factor of around 3 and 1.5, respectively.

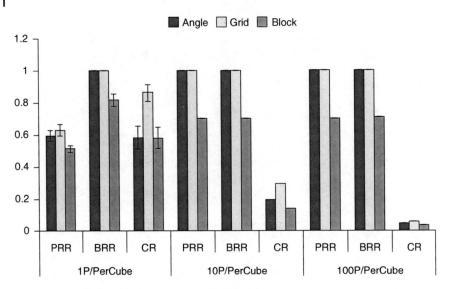

Figure 2.24 Relative performance of three MapReduce methods for cloud mashup performance (Reprinted with permission from F. Zhang, K. Hwang, et al., 2016. [23])

2.6 Conclusions

Cloud architecture was studied in this chapter. We considered clouds that can be applied to big data storage and processing in analytics applications. Then we devoted Sections 2.2 and 2.3 to virtualization techniques. Virtualization concepts are introduced with hypervisors and Docker containers, which lay the foundation for cloud construction and elastic management. Case studies of AWS, GAE and Salesforce clouds were given in Section 2.4. Then we introduced recent advances in cloud mashup services and software tools for applications.

Cloud mashup services are projected to grow rapidly in the coming decade due to the growing population of public clouds. We present skyline discovery and composition of cloud mashup services. In general, high performance promotes cloud productivity. The QoS in clouds is based on user preferences. For various cloud benchmarks and cloud performance modeling, readers are referred to Hwang's new book on *Cloud and Cognitive Computing: Principles, architecture, Programming,* to appear in 2017.

Homework Problems

2.1 Pick three IaaS cloud systems from the following: Amazon AWS, GoGrid, OpSource Cloud, Rackspace, HP Cloud, Banknorth and Fleiscale. Conduct in-depth studies beyond what you have read in this book. You need to dig out useful technical information by visiting the providers' websites or by searching through Google, Wikipedia and any open literature. The purpose is to report their latest progress in cloud technology, service offerings, software applications recently developed, business models applied, and success/failure lessons learned.

Make sure that your study report is technically rich in content and avoid sales pitches.

2.2 From the following PaaS clouds: Google Compute Engine, Force.com, postini, MS azure, NetSuite, IBM RC2, IBM Blue Cloud, SGIN Cyclone, and Amazon Elastic MapReduce, etc., pick three to engage in much deeper studies beyond what you have read in this book. You need to dig out useful technical information by visiting the providers' websites or by searching through Google, Wikipedia and any literature. The purpose is to report their latest progress in cloud technology, services offerings, software application developed, business model applied and success/failure lessons learned. Make sure that your study report is technically rich in content and avoid sales pitches.

2.3 Pick three SaaS cloud systems from the following: Consur, RightNow, Salesforce, Kenexa, Webex, Balckbaud, Netsuite, Omniture, Kenexa, Vocus, Google and Microsoft Azure. Conduct in-depth studies beyond what you have read in this book. You need to dig out useful technical information by visiting the providers' websites or by searching through Google, Wikipedia and any open literature. The purpose is to report their latest progress in cloud technology, service offerings, software applications recently developed, business models applied and success/failure lessons learned. Make sure that your study report is technically rich in content and avoid sales pitches.

2.4 Pick two Co-Location Cloud Services from the following: Savvis, Internap, NTTCommunications, Digital Realty, Trust and 365 main. Conduct in-depth studies beyond what you have read in this book. You need to dig out useful technical information by visiting the providers' websites or by searching through Google, Wikipedia and any open literature. The purpose is to report their latest progress in cloud technology, service offerings, software applications recently developed, business models applied and success/failure lessons learned. Make sure that your study report is technically rich in content and avoid sales pitches.

2.5 Check the AWS cloud website. Plan a real computing application using the Elastic computer cloud (EC2), the Simple Storage Service (S3), or the Simple queue service (SQS), separately. You must specify the resources requested and work out the costs charged by Amazon. Carry out the EC2, S3 and SQS experiments on the AWS platform and report and analyze the performance results measured. This homework could be extended into a term project done by a team of students.

2.6 In Examples 2.7 and 2.8, you have learned how the EC2 and S3 services are offered by AWS. Visit the website: https://www.aws.com for an update on the latest services and products from AWS. Dig out the functionality and application of additional services provided by AWS. Your report should be as technical as possible. Do not speculate, as everything you report must be substantiated with convincing evidence.

Optimized skyline query processing:

a) What is the Simple Notification Service (SNS) service on the AWS cloud? Explain how it works and the user interfaces for SNS on using the mobile phones to transmit and store photo streams on the S3.

b) What is Elastic MapReduce (EMR) on the AWS? How it is implemented? What language is applied to use EMR and how does it work with the Hadoop system?

2.7 A new AWS service is offered for virtualization using Docker Engine to create application software containers. The service is known as Amazon EC2 Container Service (ECS). Explain how it is done on the AWS cloud. Report the ECS applicability and discuss the experience in using containers and VM instances on EC2 instances.

2.8 VM and container cluster management of orchestration are hot topics among cloud providers and cloud clients. Pick one or more VM/container scheduling and orchestration tools from the following list: CorOS fleet, Mesosphere Marathon, Docker Swarm, Apache mesos, Google Kubernetes and Docker compose. The tools you pick should be mutually supportive in VM/container cluster management and orchestration. Conduct an in-depth study by visiting the company websites to discover their experiences in using these software tools. Write a short technical report based on your research findings.

2.9 The vSphere/4 covered in Example 2.6 is a solid cloud OS commercially available from VMware. Search the literature for reports of the porting and application experiences and measured performance by its clients or user groups. Write a short technical report to summarize your research findings.

2.10 Visit the iCloud website https://www.icloud.com or Wikipedia to find out the functionality and application services provided by Apple iCloud. In particular, answer the following questions on iCloud:

a) Briefly, specify the main services provided by iCloud. How many users are reported up to now?

b) What are the data types or information items that are handled by iCloud?

c) Explain the procedure to find an old friend using the *Find My Friend* service on the iCloud.

d) Explain the iCloud features *Find My iPhone* to locate your lost or stolen i-phone.

2.11 Compare strength, weakness and suitable applications of VMs created by hypervisors over bare metal with the application containers created by Docker engine on a Linux host. You should compare them along the lines of resources demands, creation overhead, execution modes, implementation complexity, execution environment, application isolation, OS flexibility and host platforms.

2.12 Pick two Network-as-a-Service (NaaS) clouds from the following: Owest, AT&T and Abovenet. Conduct in-depth studies beyond what you have read in the textbook. You need to dig out useful technical information by visiting the providers' websites or by searching through Google, Wikipedia and any other literature. The purpose is to report their latest progress in cloud technology, service offerings, software applications recently developed, business models applied and success/failure lessons learned. Make sure that your study report is technically rich in content and avoid sales pitches.

2.13 Consider the System Availability (A) of a server cluster in terms of three parameters: namely the mean time to failure (MTTF), the mean time to repair (MTTR) and a regular maintenance time (RMT). The MTTF reflects the average up time between two adjacent natural failures. The MTTR is the down time due to natural failure. The RMT refers to scheduled down time for hardware/software maintenance or update.

a) Given a cloud system with a demanded availability $A = 98\%$. If the MTTF is known to be 2 years (or $365 \times 24 \times 2 = 17{,}520$ hours) and the MTTR is known as 24 hours. What is the value of RMT in hours per month you can schedule for this cloud system?

b) Consider a cloud cluster of *3* servers. The cluster is considered available (or acceptable with a satisfactory performance level), if at least *k* servers are operating normally where $k \leq 3$. Assume that each server has an availability rate of *p* (or a failure rate of *1 − p*). Derive a formula to calculate the total cluster availability *A* (i.e. the probability that the cluster is available satisfactorily). Note that *A* is a function of *k* and *p*.

c) Given that each server has an availability $p = 0.98$. What is the largest minimum number of servers that must be available to achieve a total cluster availability *A*, which is higher than 96%? You have to check the effect of all possible values of *k* in part (b) in order to answer this question correctly.

2.14 We have studied the AWS and Salesforce cloud services. Visit their websites to dig out the detailed functionality and service features in the following service offerings by AWS, Google, Saleforce, Savvis and Apple icloud:

a) AWS Glacier, CloudFront, RDS, VPC, Direct Coonect, SQS, Elastic Transcoder, Cloud Search, API Gateway, Mobile Analytics, Data Pipeline, Kinesis, Machine Learning, Trusted Advisor, CloudWatch, WorkMail, Elastic Beanstalk, CodeCommit and Code Pipline;

b) Salesforce cloud services: Sales, Data, Market, Service, Collaborator, and Anlytics, and the custom cloud.

2.15 Learn about AWS container service and run the Amazon ECS sample container code. You need to take some screenshots to prove that you have done this correctly. You need to report what you have learned from this testing run.

Step 1: Learn about Amazon EC2 Container Service, watch the video here:
https://aws.amazon.com/ecs/
Look at the developer guide:
http://docs.aws.amazon.com/AmazonECS/latest/developerguide/Welcome.html

Step 2: Before using the service, set up the execution environment with Amazon ECS:

http://docs.aws.amazon.com/AmazonECS/latest/developerguide/get-set-up-for-amazon-ecs.html

Step 3: Get started with Amazon EC2 Container Service by creating a task definition, scheduling tasks, configuring a cluster in the ECS console via the link:

http://docs.aws.amazon.com/AmazonECS/latest/developerguide/ECS_GetSt arted.html

Step 4: Shut down the container and its host EC 2 instance:

http://docs.aws.amazon.com/AmazonECS/latest/developerguide/ECS_ CleaningUp.html

2.16 The Magnum in Example 6.11 is a good software project to realize container orchestration and host clustering on OpenStack Nova machine instances. Check with the OpenStack website to follow up with the latest release of the Magnum source codes. Write a short technical report to summarize your research findings.

2.17 The Eucalyptus presented in Example 2.5 is continuously upgraded to support the efficient management of IaaS cloud resources. Check with the Eucalyptus website to follow up with their latest development and porting experiences released by their registered user groups. Write a short technical report to summarize your research findings.

2.18 This problem asks you to practice mobile photo uploads to Amazon S3. Explore some SDK tools on the AWS for using either iOS phone or any Android phone to store photos on the Amazon S3 cloud and to notify AWS users using the SNS service. Report on the storage/notification service features, your testing results and app experiences. Check the website for Android SDK tools. Source: http://aws.amazon.com/sdkforandroid/ You can find iOS and Android SDK tools by checking /sdk-for-ios/ and /sdk-for-android/ similarly: Follow the following three steps to carry out your experiments:

Step 1: Download the Amazon AWS SDK for Android (or iOS) from the source URL.

Step 2: Check the sample code given in aws-android-sdk-1.6/samples/ S3_Uploader, which creates a simple application that lets the user upload images from phone to an S3 bucket in the user account.

Step 3: These images can be viewed by anyone with access to the URL shared by the user.

You need to perform the following operations and report the results in snapshots or using any performance metric you choose to display when using an Android phone. Similarly, for those students using Apple iOS phones:

1) Try to upload a selected data (image) to the AWS S3 bucket, using the Access key and Security Key credentials provided for the user. This will enable you as an AWS client.

2) Check if the S3 bucket exists with the same name and create the bucket and put the image in S3 bucket.

3) Show in Browser button and display the image in the browser.

4) Make sure the image is treated as an image file in the web browser.

    5) Create a URL, for the image in the bucket, so that it can be shared and viewed by other people.

    6) Comment on extended applications beyond this experiment.

2.19 Explain the differences in the following two machine recovery schemes. Comment on their implementation requirements, advantages and shortcomings and application potentials:

    a) Recovery of a physical machine failure by another physical machine;

    b) Recovery of a virtual machine failure by another virtual machine;

    c) Suggest a method to recover a VM from a failing physical machine.

2.20 The vSphere/6 covered in Example 2.6 is a solid cloud OS commercially available from VMware. Dig out from the literature reports on the porting and application experiences and measured performance by its clients or user groups. Write a short technical report to summarize your research findings.

References

1 B. Baesens, *Analytics in a Big Data World: The essential guide to data science and its applications*, Wiley, 2015.

2 L. Barroso and U. Holzle, The datacenter as a computer: An introduction to the design of warehouse-scale machines. In *Synthesis Lectures on Computer Architecture*, edited by M. Hill (ed.). Morgan Claypool, 2009.

3 R. Buyya, J. Broberg and A. Goscinski (eds), *Cloud Computing: Principles and Paradigms*. Wiley Press, USA, February 2011.

4 H. Chaouchi, *The Internet of Things*. Wiley, 2010.

5 M. Chen, *Big Data Related Technologies*. Springer Computer Science Series, 2014.

6 S. Farnham, *The Facebook Association Ecosystem*. O'Reilly Radar Report, 2008.

7 J. Han, M. Kamber and J. Pei, *Data Mining: Concepts and Techniques*, Third Edition. Morgan Kaufmann, 2012.

8 U. Hansmann, et al., *Pervasive Computing: The Mobile World*, Second Edition. Springer, 2003.

9 T. Hey, S. Tansley and K. Tolle (eds), *The Fourth Paradigm: Data-Intensive Scientific Discovery*. Microsoft Research, 2009.

10 M. Hilber and P. Lopez, The world's technological capacity to store. Communicate and compute information. *Science*, 332(6025), 2011.

11 K. Hwang, G. Fox and J. Dongarra, *Cloud Computing for Big Data Applications: A Hadoop, Spark and TensorFlow Approach*. Morgan Kaufmann Publisher, 2017.

12 K. Hwang and D. Li, Trusted cloud computing with secure resources and data coloring. *IEEE Internet Computing*, October 2010.

13 H. Karau, et al., *Learning Spark: Lightning Fast Data Analysis*. O'Reily, 2015.

14 M. Rosenblum and T. Garfinkel, Virtual machine monitors: Current technology and future trends. *IEEE Computer*, May 2005, 39–47.

15 S. Ryza, et al., *Advanced Analytics with Spark*, O'Reily, 2015.

16 J. Cao, K. Hwang, D. Li and A. Zomaya, Optimal multiserver configuration for profit maximization in cloud computing. *IEEE Trans. Parallel and Distributed Systems*, July 2013.

17 K. Hwang, S. Yue and X. Bai, Scale-out and scale-up techniques for cloud performance and productivity. *IEEE CloudCom, Workshop on Emerging Issues in Clouds.* Singapore, December 18, 2014.

18 K. Hwang and D. Li, Trusted cloud computing with secure resources and data coloring. *IEEE Internet Computing*, September 14, 2010.

19 K. Hwang, X. Bai, Y. Shi, M.Y. Li, W.G. Chen and Y.W. Wu, Cloud performance modeling with benchmark evaluation of elastic scaling strategies, *IEEE Transactions on Parallel and Distributed Systems*, January, 2016.

20 M. Satyanarayanan, P. Bahl, R. Caceres and N. Davies, The case for VM-based cloudlets in mobile computing. *IEEE Pervasive Computing*, 8(4), 14–23, 2009.

21 Y. Shi, S. Abhilash, and K. Hwang. Cloudlet mesh for securing mobile clouds from intrusions and network attacks. *The Third IEEE International Conference on Mobile Cloud Computing (MobileCloud)*, April, 2015, 109–118.

22 N. Yigitbasi, A. Iosup, D. Epema and S. Ostermann, C-Meter: A framework for performance analysis of computing clouds, *IEEE/ACM Proceedings of the 9th International Symposium on Cluster Computing and the Grid*, (CCGrid), 2009.

23 F. Zhang, K. Hwang, S. Khan, and Q. Malluhi, Skyline discovery and composition of multi-cloud mashup services, *IEEE Transactions on Service Computing*, September 2016.

3

IoT Sensing, Mobile and Cognitive Systems

CHAPTER OUTLINE

3.1   Sensing Technologies for Internet of Things, 105
 3.1.1   Enabling Technologies and Evolution of IoT, 106
 3.1.2   Introducing RFID and Sensor Technologies, 108
 3.1.3   IoT Architectural and Wireless Support, 110
3.2   IoT Interactions with GPS, Clouds and Smart Machines, 111
 3.2.1   Local versus Global Positioning Technologies, 111
 3.2.2   Standalone versus Cloud-Centric IoT Applications, 114
 3.2.3   IoT Interaction Frameworks with Environments, 116
3.3   Radio Frequency Identification (RFID), 119
 3.3.1   RFID Technology and Tagging Devices, 119
 3.3.2   RFID System Architecture, 120
 3.3.3   IoT Support of Supply Chain Management, 122
3.4   Sensors, Wireless Sensor Networks and GPS Systems, 124
 3.4.1   Sensor Hardware and Operating Systems, 124
 3.4.2   Sensing through Smart Phones, 130
 3.4.3   Wireless Sensor Networks and Body Area Networks, 131
 3.4.4   Global Positioning Systems, 134
3.5   Cognitive Computing Technologies and Prototype Systems, 139
 3.5.1   Cognitive Science and Neuroinformatics, 139
 3.5.2   Brain-Inspired Computing Chips and Systems, 140
 3.5.3   Google's Brain Team Projects, 142
 3.5.4   IoT Contexts for Cognitive Services, 145
 3.5.5   Augmented and Virtual Reality Applications, 146
3.6   Conclusions, 149

3.1   Sensing Technologies for Internet of Things

Integrating the digital world and physical world is the ultimate goal of IoT. This could be regarded as the third evolution of information industry. First, the network scale becomes very large in order to interconnect the enormous number of things in the physical world. Second, network mobility increases rapidly due to the pervasive use of mobile and vehicular devices. Third, the fusion of heterogeneous networks becomes deeper with various types of devices connected to the Internet. Furthermore, mobile Internet, cloud

Big-Data Analytics for Cloud, IoT and Cognitive Computing, First Edition. Kai Hwang and Min Chen.
© 2017 John Wiley & Sons Ltd. Published 2017 by John Wiley & Sons Ltd.
Companion Website: http://www.wiley.com/go/hwangIOT

computing, big data, software defined networking and 5G all have an impact on IoT development.

3.1.1 Enabling Technologies and Evolution of IoT

In Figure 3.1, we have identified many technologies that enable IoT infrastructure development for various applications. The supportive technologies are divided into two categories: i) the enabling technologies build up the foundations of IoT. Among the enabling technologies, tracking (RFID), sensor networks and GPS are critical; ii) the synergistic technologies play the supporting roles. For example, biometrics could be widely applied to personalize the interaction between humans and machine and objects. Artificial intelligence, computer vision, robotics and telepresence can make our life better automated in the future.

In 2005, the concept of IoT came into the limelight. The IoT should be designed to connect the world's objects in a sensory manner. The approach is to tag things through RFID, feel things through sensors and wireless networks, and think things by building embedded systems that interact with human activities. The IoT is now becoming a major thrust, not only in the research community but also in big industry like IBM and Google. The IoT is really enabled by many related technologies. To name just a few, pervasive computing, social-media clouds, wireless sensor networks, cloud computing, big data, machine to machine communications and wearable computing, etc.

In 2008, the US National Intelligence Council published a report on "Disruptive Civil Technologies", which also identified the IoT as a critical technology in US interests to 2025. Quantitatively speaking, the IoT should be designed to encode 50 to 100 trillion objects. Moreover, the IoT should be designed to follow the movement of those objects. With more than a 6 billion human population, means every person is surrounded by

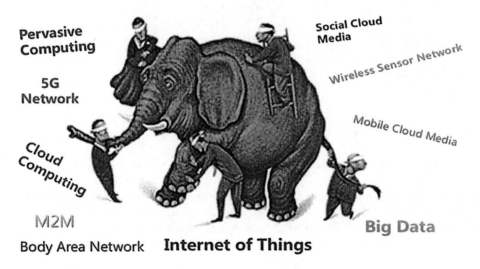

Figure 3.1 IoT enabling and synergistic technologies.

1000 to 5000 objects on a daily basis. Imagine how IoT can improve our interactions or convenience with everything (object) surrounding us.

3.1.1.1 Enabling and Synergistic Technologies

Over a period of 25 years, IoT development could become mature and more sophisticated. For example, supply chains could be more perfected in the first 10 years (2000–2010). Vertical market applications may be the next wave of advances. Ubiquitous positioning is expected to become a reality as we move toward 2020. Beyond that, a physical world web may appear to reach the ultimate goal of IoT. That goal is to achieve tremendous improvement in human abilities, societal outcomes, nation's productivity and the quality of life in general.

With an ever-increasing number of mobile devices and the resulting explosive mobile traffic, 5G networks call for various technology advances to transmit the traffic more effectively while changing the world by interconnecting a tremendous amount of mobile devices. However, mobile devices have limited communication and computation capabilities in terms of computation power, memory, storage and energy. In addition to the broadband bandwidth support from 5G, cloud computing needs to be utilized to enable mobile devices to obtain virtually unlimited dynamic resources for computation, storage and service provision that will overcome the constraints in the smart mobile devices. Thus, the combination of 5G and cloud computing technology are paving the way for other attractive applications.

With the support of mobile cloud computing (MCC), a mobile user basically has one more option to execute the computation of its application, i.e. offloading the computation to the cloud. Thus, one principal problem is under what conditions should a mobile user offload its computations to the cloud. The scenario of computation offloading at remote clouds requires a user to be covered by WiFi. Since the terminal device at the user end has limited resources, i.e. hardware, energy, bandwidth, etc., the cellphone itself cannot perform some compute-intensive tasks. Instead, the data related to the computation task can be offloaded to the remote cloud via WiFi or other high bandwidth channels.

Many IoT challenges are widely open, yet to be solved. Specific challenges include privacy, participatory sensing, data analytics, GIS (geographic information system) based visualization and cloud computing. Other areas are related to IoT architecture standardization, energy efficiency, security, protocols and Quality of Service. Standardization of frequency bands and protocols plays a pivotal role in accomplishing these goals. A roadmap of key developments for IoT research in the context of pervasive applications is shown in Figure 3.2. This diagram shows the growth of five key IoT application domains from 2010 to 2025.

In the early 2000s, IoT was primarily applied to expedite supply chain management. Vertical market and ubiquitous positioning applications have dominated IoT applications since 2010. Eventually, we will see the widespread use of IoT in a physical-world web, where teleoperations and telepresence will enable the monitoring and control of any remote objects. Ultimately, the IoT will enable the creation of a physical-world web that is connected to everything on Earth. This will make our daily lives convenient and well informed with the rest of the world. This will make smarter decisions, save human life, avoid disasters and reduce human burdens to a great extent. On the other hand, the

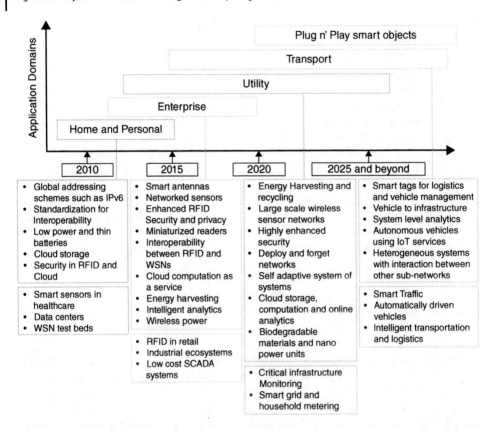

Figure 3.2 Projected IoT upgrade in five IoT application domains from 2010 to 2015. (Courtesy of Gubbi et al. 2013. [10]) Reproduced with permission of Elsevier.

rise of IoT brings some negative impacts. For example, we may lose privacy. Criminals or enemy powers could use IoT to stage even more destruction. Legal systems need to be established to prevent or avoid these negative IoT impacts.

3.1.2 Introducing RFID and Sensor Technologies

This section briefly introduces Radio Frequency Identification (RFID) and sensors. More details are given in Section 3.3 and 3.4. With the rapid advances in electronics, electromechanics and nanotechnologies, ubiquitous devices grow rapidly in quantity and smaller in physical size. These objects are referred to as "things", such as computers, sensors, people, actuators, refrigerators, TVs, vehicles, mobile phones, clothes, food, medicines, books, passports, luggage, etc. They are expected to become active participants in business, information and social processes. These participants can react autonomously in the physical world. They influence or trigger actions and create services with or without direct human intervention. There are lots of sensor devices for sensing and data collection. Each senor node could combine the functions of sensing, communications and local processing.

3.1.2.1 RFID Technology

The first step of enabling smart services is to collect contextual information about the environment, "things" and objects of interest. For example, sensors can be used to continuously monitor a human's physiological activities and actions such as health status and motion patterns. RFID technology can be utilized for collecting crucial personal information and storing it on a low-cost chip that is attached to an individual at all times. RFID is a radio-frequency (RF) electronic technology that allows automatic identification or location of objects, people and animals in a wide variety of deployment settings. In the past decade, RFID systems have been incorporated into a wide range of industrial and commercial systems, including manufacturing and logistics, retail, item tracking and tracing, inventory monitoring, asset management, anti-theft, electronic payment, anti-tampering, transport ticketing, supply-chain management, etc.

A typical RFID application consists of an RFID tag, an RFID reader and a backend system. With a simple RF chip and an antenna, an RFID tag can store information that identifies the object to which it is attached. There are three types of RFID tags, i.e. passive tags, active tags and semi-active tags. A passive tag obtains energy through RF signals from the reader, while an active tag is powered by an embedded battery, which enables larger memory or more functionality. Though a semi-active tag communicates with RFID readers like a passive tag, additional modules can be supported through an internal battery. When it comes within the proximity of an RFID reader, the information stored in the tag is transferred to the reader, and onto a backend system, which can be a computer employed for processing this information and controlling the operation of other sub-system(s).

3.1.2.2 Sensors and Sensor Networks

In the last decade, we have witnessed a growing interest in deploying the sheer number of micro-sensors that collaborate in a distributed manner on data gathering and processing. Sensor nodes are expected to be inexpensive and can be deployed in various environments. A wireless sensor network (WSN) consists of spatially distributed autonomous sensors to monitor physical or environmental conditions, such as temperature, sound, pressure, etc. and to cooperatively pass their data through the network to a main location. The sensor nodes form a multi-hop *ad hoc* wireless network. The biggest difference between WSN and cellular network is that WSN does not need a base station and each sensor node works as both transmitter and receiver. Due to limited resources at sensor nodes, routing in WSN is a challenging task, while minimizing energy consumption during data dissemination.

3.1.2.3 Wireless Sensor Network

A WSN is a group of specialized transducers with a communications infrastructure intended to monitor and record conditions at diverse locations. Commonly monitored parameters are temperature, humidity, pressure, wind direction and speed, illumination intensity, vibration intensity, sound intensity, power-line voltage, chemical concentrations, pollutant levels and vital body functions. A sensor network consists of multiple detection stations called sensor nodes, each of which is small, lightweight and portable. Every sensor node is equipped with a transducer, microcomputer, transceiver and power source. The transducer generates electrical signals based on sensed data.

The sensor processor handles input signals and stores or transmits the output. The transceiver can be hard-wired or wireless. The power for each sensor node is derived from the electric utility or from a battery. A sensor node may vary in size from that of a shoebox down to the size of a dust grain. The cost of sensor nodes also varies widely, ranging from hundreds of dollars to a few pennies, depending on the size of the sensor network and the complexity required of individual sensor nodes. Size and cost constraints on sensor nodes are often decided by energy, memory, computational speed and bandwidth of the sensors used.

The widely-used sensor technologies are the Zigbee devices specified in the IEEE 802.15.4 Standard [1]. The radio frequency applied in Zigbee results in low data rate, long battery life and secure networking. They are used mainly in monitory and remote control IoT or mobile applications. Many supermarkets, department stores and hospitals are installed with Zigbee networks. The data rate ranges from 20–250 Kbps. They can operate up to 100 meters. However, Zigbee devices can be networked together to cover a much large area. The Zigbee network is highly scalable. Zigbee networks are used in wireless home-area networks (WHAN). This technology is simpler to use and less expensive than Bluetooth or WiFi.

3.1.3 IoT Architectural and Wireless Support

Basic IoT architecture is introduced below in three layers, namely the sensing, networking and application layers. The IoT system is likely to have an event-driven architecture. In Figure 3.3, the IoT development is shown with a three-layer architecture. The top layer is formed by the driven applications. IoT applications for healthcare will be presented in Chapter 8. The bottom layer consists of various types of sensing and automatic

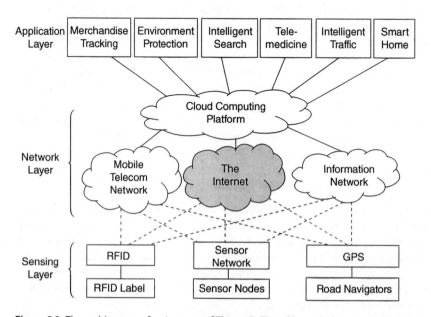

Figure 3.3 The architecture of an Internet of Things (IoT) and its underlying technologies.

information generation devices: namely sensors, ZigBee devices, RFID tags and road-mapping GPS navigators, etc. The sensing devices are locally or wide-area connected in the form of sensor networks, RFID networks and GPS systems, etc. Signals or information collected at these sensing devices are linked to the applications through the cloud computing platforms at the middle layer.

The signal-processing clouds are built over the mobile networks, the Internet backbone and various information networks at the middle layer. In the IoT, the meaning of a sensing event does not follow a deterministic or syntactic model. In fact, the service-oriented architecture (SoA) model is adoptable here. Large number of sensors and filters are used to collect the raw data. Various compute and storage clouds and grids are used to process the data and transform them into information and knowledge formats. The sensory data is used to put together a decision-making system for intelligence applications. The middle layer is also considered as a semantic web or grid. Some actors (services, components, avatars) are self-referenced.

3.2 IoT Interactions with GPS, Clouds and Smart Machines

This covers the networking requirements, including the wireless, wireline and mobile core networks. We will examine the local and global positioning systems and cloud-based radio access networks possible for 5G mobile systems. Finally, we will study four frameworks for IoT interactions with the rest of the world.

3.2.1 Local versus Global Positioning Technologies

The requirement to integrate the cyber world and physical world is higher than ever. Localization becomes the bridge to interconnect these two worlds. Given WSN as an example, together with location information, the sensory data becomes meaningful. There is a real WSN project named ZebraNet, for the use of biologists who want to track and study animals. However, without locations, animals cannot be tracked, thus not enabling further studies. As another example of ubiquitous computing, the location is critical to differentiate various scenarios for providing personalized services for users.

According to the capabilities of diverse hardware, we classify the measuring techniques into six categories (from fine- to coarse-grained): location, distance, angle, area, hop count and neighborhood. Among them, the most powerful physical measurement is directly obtaining the position without any further computation. GPS is such an infrastructure. We discuss the other five measurements in this chapter, with emphasis on the basic principles of the measuring techniques. Basically, distance-related information can be obtained by radio signal strength or radio propagation time, angle information by antenna arrays, and area, hop count and neighborhood information by the fact that radios only exist for nodes in the vicinity.

3.2.1.1 Local Positioning Technology

One method to determine the location of a device is through manual configuration, which is often infeasible for large-scale deployments or mobile systems. As a popular system, GPS is not suitable for indoor or underground environments and suffers from high hardware costs. Local positioning systems rely on high-density base stations being deployed, an expensive burden for most resource-constrained wireless *ad hoc* networks.

Limitations of the existing positioning systems motivate a novel scheme of network localization, in which some special nodes (a.k.a. anchors or beacons) know their global locations and the rest determine their locations by measuring the geographic information of their local neighboring nodes. Such a localization scheme for wireless multihop networks is alternatively described as "cooperative," "ad hoc," "in-network localization" or "self-localization."

Thus, network nodes cooperatively determine their locations by information sharing. The terms of "known" and "unknown" nodes refer to the nodes being aware and being unaware of their locations, respectively. Suppose a specific positioning process is one in which an unknown node determines its location based on the information provided by a number of known nodes. The unknown node is also known as a target node or a to-be-located node, while the known nodes as reference nodes.

Localization solutions consist of two basic stages: i) measuring geographic information from the ground truth of network deployment; and ii) computing node locations according to the measured data. Geographic information includes a variety of geometric relationships from coarse-grained neighbor-awareness to fine-grained internode rangings (e.g. distance or angle). Based on physical measurements, localization algorithms solve the problem: how to spread the location information from beacon nodes over a network-wide range.

Generally, the design of localization algorithms largely depends on a wide range of factors, including resource availability, accuracy requirements and deployment restrictions, and no particular algorithm is an absolute favorite across the spectrum. Due to hardware limitations, ranging is not always available for wireless devices. In such situations, range-free approaches are cost-effective alternatives, in which nodes merely know their neighbors.

Without direct distance ranging, the physical distance of a pair of nodes is estimated by the hop count or the proximity. The basic idea of hop count-based localization is to use hop-by-hop message delivery to calculate hop counts from nodes to anchors. The hop-count information is further converted to the distance estimates. Eventually, each node adopts trilateration or other methods to determine its location according to the estimated distances. Another possibility is to explore the relative proximity of nodes. When distance ranging is not available, the fact that one node is closer to some other node can aid the localization process.

3.2.1.2 Satellite Technology for Global Positioning

Global positioning is done with multiple satellites deployed in outer space. The deployment of satellites is shown in Figure 3.4. Each satellite continually transmits messages that include the transmission time and satellite position. A GPS receiver calculates its position by precisely timing the signals sent by satellites. The receiver uses the messages it receives to determine the transit time and computes the distance to each satellite using light speed. Each of these distances and the satellites' locations define a signal sphere. The receiver is located at the intersection signal spheres from multiple satellites. More details of GPS and other positioning technologies are given in Section 3.4.4.

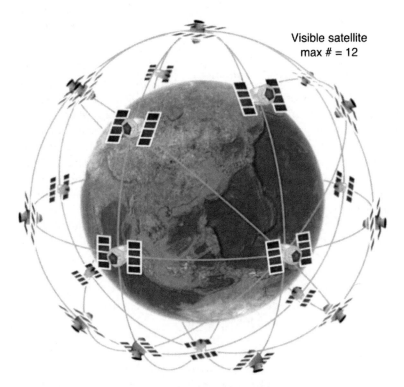

Visible satellite
max # = 12

Figure 3.4 The 24-satellite GPS architecture: the satellites circle the Earth twice per day in multiple layers of fixed orbits without interference to each other.

Example 3.1   GPS System Developed in the USA

The US GPS is built with three segments. The space segments are the satellites circulating in outer space. The user segments include any moving or stationary objects such as airplanes, ships and moving vehicles on the Earth's surface. The control segment includes some ground antennas and master and monitor stations on the Earth's surface that are scattered globally. The uplink and downlink data types are different. The computed signal travel time is used for displaying the receiver location. A number of applications for GPS do make use of this cheap and highly accurate timing, including time transfer, traffic signal timing and synchronization with cell phone base stations.

The US Air Force develops, maintains and operates the space and control segments of the GPS system. There are 24 satellites deployed around the Earth (Figure 3.4) in fixed orbits. The satellites orbit at an altitude of approximately 20,200 km. GPS satellites broadcast signals from space, by which each GPS receiver calculates its three-dimensional location (latitude, longitude and altitude) plus the current time. The space segment is composed of 24 satellites in medium Earth orbit and also includes the boosters required to launch them into orbit.

GPS satellites circle the Earth twice a day in precise orbits and transmit signals to the Earth. GPS devices on the ground receive these signals and use triangulation to calculate the user's exact location. In general cases, four satellites are required to locate a single point on the Earth's surface. The system was initially developed for military use in 1975.

Now the system, under strict regulation, is open for civilian and commercial use, mainly in vehicle tracking and navigation applications. ∎

3.2.2 Standalone versus Cloud-Centric IoT Applications

Typically, standalone IoT focuses on stable environments in which new applications would likely improve the quality of our lives: at home, while travelling, when sick, at work, when jogging and at the gym, just to cite a few. These environments are now equipped with objects with only primitive intelligence, mostly without any communication capabilities. Giving these objects the ability to communicate with each other and to elaborate the information perceived from their surroundings implies having different environments where a very wide range of applications can be deployed. These can be grouped into the following domains.

Transportation and logistics domain, healthcare domain, smart environment (home, office, plant) domain, personal and social domain; among the possible applications, we may distinguish between those either directly applicable or closer to our current living habits and those that are futuristic, which we can only imagine at the moment, since the technologies and/or our societies are not ready for their deployment. In the following subsections we provide a review of the short-medium term applications for each of these categories and a range of futuristic applications.

Example 3.2   A Smart Power Grid supported by the Internet of Things
A smart grid includes an intelligent monitoring system that keeps track of all electricity flowing in the system. Smart meters and sensors, a digital upgrade of current utility meters, track energy usage in real time so that both the customer and the utility company know how much is being used at any given time. Energy is paid for using "time of day" pricing, meaning electricity will cost more at peak times of use.

For example, when power is least expensive, the user can allow the smart grid to turn on selected home appliances such as washing machines or factory processes that can run at arbitrary hours. At peak times it could turn off selected appliances to reduce demand. More involved users will be able to use the smart meter to view energy usage remotely and make real-time decisions about energy consumption. A fridge or air conditioning system could be turned down remotely while residents are away.

With the development of WSNs, as well as low-power embedded systems and cloud computing, cloud-assisted IoT systems are gradually maturing to support smart and computation-intensive IoT applications involving a large amount of data. The home IoT applications can be upgraded by the emerging cloud computing environment. The scalable and elastic cloud-assisted framework shifts computation and storage into the network to reduce operational and maintenance costs. ∎

3.2.2.1 Cloud-Centric IoT System Applications

The information delivered from different domains (e.g. smart grid and healthcare) is difficult to understand and handle for the computer in the cloud service. With the support of a semantic model, an ontology-based approach can be used to implement information interaction and sharing in cloud-assisted home IoT. As shown in Figure 3.5, separate cloud systems can interoperate, with an additional root cloud providing different services for healthcare, energy management, convenience and entertainment, etc.

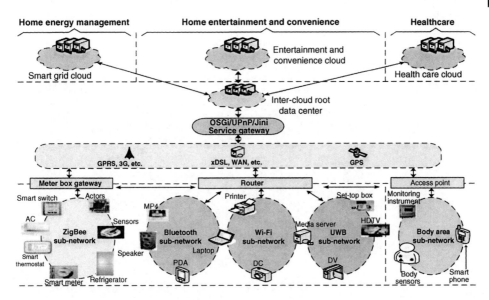

Figure 3.5 Cloud-centric IoT system for smart home environment.

The service gateway implements various technologies, protocols, standards and services to diversify communications capabilities and integrate devices. Currently, most service gateways implement well-defined software modes and systems, such as Jini, UPnP and OSGi. In addition, the communication of heterogeneous objects in IoT is a major problem, because different objects provide different information in different formats for different purposes. The semantic web technologies and models may also be used to help solve this problem. The semantic web technologies can be applied to facilitate communication in home IoT applications.

In recent years, cloud computing has provided novel perspectives in cloud-assisted technologies for distinct purposes. A cloud-assisted communication system may include multiple cloud systems operating with different policies to share resources, so that end-to-end QoS to users can be maintained, even in the event of large fluctuations in computing load that cannot be handled by a single cloud system. It is known that the previous architectures for IoT have not taken into account this cloud-assisted capability. In our view, it is an important factor for IoT to achieve functionality completeness. Therefore, compared to the previous survey literatures, we propose a cloud-assisted layer for the advancement of IoT architecture. The following example demonstrates the joint effort between Intel and China Mobile towards the development of 5G mobile core networks.

Example 3.3   Cloud-Based Radio Access Network (C-RAN) for 5G Mobile Systems
A large number of base stations are used in current 3G or 4G mobile core networks. They are facing a series of problems: namely bulky in physical size, slow in data rate, air losses during handover between cells, and demand appreciable power to keep them running smoothly without interruption. The C-RAN is joint project between Intel and China Mobile toward an efficient solution to these problems. The idea is illustrated in Figure 3.6. Details of this C-RAN architecture can be found in the white paper by Chen and Ran, 2011. [4]

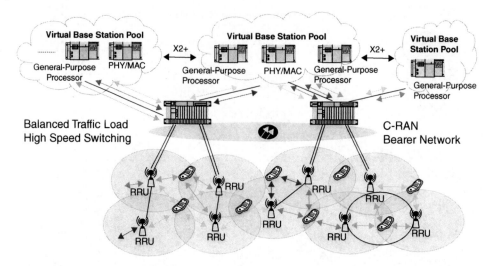

Figure 3.6 Conceptual architecture of a cloud-based radio access network (C-RAN). (Courtesy of China Mobile Research Institute, 2009.)

The bulky antenna towers used in a conventional based station are replaced by a large number of small remote radio heads (RRH), which operate with little power (even solar energy can do the job) and get easily distributed with high density in populated user areas. The control and processing in physical-based stations are replaced by using virtual base station (VBS) pools housed in a hierarchy of cloud-based switching centers. Balanced traffic load between the RRHs and the VBS pools is enabled by using high-speed optical transport networks and switches with fiber cables and microwave links.

The advantages of using C-RAN are summarized in four aspects: i) centralized processing resource pool can support 10–1000 cells with high efficiency; ii) cooperative radios are used in multi-cell joint scheduling and processing, which solve the air loss and handover problems; iii) C-RAN offers real-time services by targeting to open IT platform, resources consolidation and flexible multi-standard operation and migration; and iv) a green and clean mobile telecommunication is realized with much less power assumption, lower operating expenses and fast system rolling out. Many other companies are also building similar C-RAN systems, including CISCO and Korean Telecommunication. ∎

3.2.3 IoT Interaction Frameworks with Environments

As with any new kinds of "networks", IoT connects not only networked terminals such as mobile phones, computers and smart devices, but also daily life objects that until now have been to us just "un-networked things" or "inert objects". We first describe layer-based architecture for IoT, as shown in Figure 3.7.

- **Object sensing and information gathering**: The first step of enabling smart services is to collect contextual information about the environment, "things" and objects

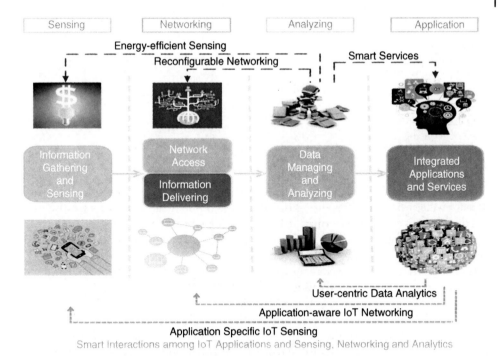

Figure 3.7 Interactions among IoT sensing, mobile monitoring and cloud analytics.

of interest. For example, sensors can be used to continuously monitor a human's physiological activities and actions such as health status and motion patterns. RFID techniques can be utilized for collecting crucial personal information and storing them on a low-cost chip that is attached to an individual at all times.

- **Information delivering**: Various wireless technologies can be used for delivering the information, such as wireless sensor networks (WSNs), body area networks (BANs), WiFi, Bluetooth, Zigbee, GPRS, GSM, cellular and 3G, etc. Such diverse communication techniques can accommodate more applications into the system.
- **Information processing for smart services**: Ubiquitous machines must process information in both "autonomic" and "smart" ways in order to provide pervasive and autonomic services. For example, the meaningless information could be filtered out according to the users' interests in social networks.

IoT sensing can interact with many other cyber systems, as illustrated in Figure 3.7. For example, the user can require personalized analytics performance based on specific data. The profile of sensing data and networking strategy can be adjusted based on application-specific requirements. Based on the intelligence obtained by data analytics, energy-efficient sensing can be achieved through the interaction between the sensing layer and analyzing layer; the data analytics also can benefit smart services. As for the network layer, the management functions (e.g. network function virtualization together with software defined networks) realized in the analyzing layer also has the potential to help operators satisfy tight service level agreements, accurately monitor and manipulate network traffic, and minimize operating expenses.

Table 3.1 Requirements of four IoT computing and communication frameworks.

Framework	WSN	M2M	BAN	CPS
Sensing Requirement	XXXX	XX	XXX	XXX
Networking Demand	XX	XXXX	XX	XXXX
Analyzing Complexity	XX	XX	XXX	XXXX
Application Industrialization	XXXX	XXX	XX	X
Security Demand	X	XX	XXX	XXXX

Through interfacing with WSNs, a wide range of information can be collected by sensors for M2M systems. Thus, in addition to M2M communications, machines also can act through the collected information by integrating with WSNs. With the capabilities of decision-making and autonomous control, M2M systems can be upgraded to CPS. Thus, CPS is an evolution of M2M by the introduction of more intelligent and interactive operations, under the architecture of IoT. Focusing on the different types of applications, IoT has different incarnations such as WSN, M2M, BAN and CPS.

In Table 3.1, we mark from one X to four X's (i.e. XXXX) to indicate the demand of different IoT frameworks on the relevant features listed in the row headings. More stars refer to higher demand of that particular feature under the column framework. CPS applications have the potential to benefit from massive wireless networks and smart devices, which would allow CPS applications to provide intelligent services based on knowledge from the surrounding physical world. We observe that WSNs are the very basic scenario of IoT. It is regarded as the supplement of M2M as the foundation of CPS. The CPS is evolved from M2M in intelligent information processing.

In what follows, we specify four wireless frameworks for the deployment of IoT applications. These appear as WSN, M2M, BAN and CPS, as briefed below:

- **Wireless Sensor Network (WSN):** It consists of spatially distributed autonomous sensors to monitor physical or environmental conditions, and to cooperatively pass their data through the network to a main location. WSNs, emphasizing the information perception through all kinds of sensor nodes, are the very basic scenario of IoT.
- **Machine to Machine (M2M) Communication:** Typically, M2M refers to data communications without or with limited human intervention, among various terminal devices such as computers, embedded processors, smart sensors/actuators and mobile devices, etc. The rationale behind M2M communications is based on three observations: i) a networked machine is more valuable than an isolated one; ii) when multiple machines are interconnected, more autonomous applications can be achieved; and iii) smart and ubiquitous services can be enabled by machine-type devices intelligently communicating with other devices at any time and anywhere.
- **Body-Area Network (BAN):** A new type of network architecture inherited from sensor networks by the use of novel advances in lightweight, small-size, ultra-low-power and intelligent monitoring wearable sensors, which continuously monitor a human's physiological activities and actions, such as health status and motion patterns.
- **Cyber Physical System (CPS):** It is a system of collaborating computational elements controlling physical entities.

3.3 Radio Frequency Identification (RFID)

RFID technology is a sort of non-contact information transfer mode realized by the radio frequency signals through space coupling (alternating magnetic field or electromagnetic field), and it achieves the purpose of automatic identification through the transferred information. In the late 1990s, an MIT group came up with the term of IoT. The progress of RFID has fueled up the IoT development. The US Auto-ID Center was the first to propose the concept of auto-ID tracking, which became one of the earliest forms of IoT deployment. In 2008, the US National Intelligence Council published a report on "Disruptive Civil Technologies", which identified the IoT as a crucial technology on national interest.

3.3.1 RFID Technology and Tagging Devices

RFID devices have varying sizes, power requirements, operating frequencies, amounts of rewriteable and nonvolatile storage, and software intelligence. They operate from a few centimeters to hundreds of meters. However, an internal power source is needed to enable large RFID devices to operate over large distances. Conversely, smaller RIFD devices do not need any power supply. RFID works through a combination of three functional components, i.e. RFID tag, RFID reader and reader antenna. Let us start with an example RFID.

3.3.1.1 RFID Tags

It consists of a tiny silicon chip and a small antenna. The tag's components are enclosed within plastic, silicon or sometimes glass. Data stored in the microchip waits to be read. Typically, the tag's antenna receives electromagnetic energy from an RFID reader. Using power harvested from the reader's electromagnetic field, the tag returns radio signals back to the reader. The reader picks up the tag's radio signals and interprets the frequencies into meaningful data.

There are three types of RFID tags, i.e. active, semi-active and passive. An active RFID tag contains a battery and can transmit signals autonomously. A passive RFID tag has no battery and requires an external source to provoke signal transmission. A semi-active RFID tag is actually a battery-assisted passive RFID tag. However, the battery is only activated when an RFID reader sends an energizing signal. Based on the radio frequency used, the passive RFID tags operate from low frequency (LF) to high frequency (HF), and to ultra high frequency (UHF) domains.

3.3.1.2 RFID Reader and Antenna

This is the device station that talks with the tags. A reader may support one or more antennae. Compared to the barcode, RFID has an important advantage, i.e. a reader device can detect objects without line of sight. Some RFID readers can identify multiple objects concurrently. An antenna is used to radiate the energy and then capture the return signal sent back from the tag. It can be integrated with a handheld reader device or connected to the reader by cable. The RFID reader antenna detects RFID tags similar to radar illuminating a target. However, RFID operates at shorter ranges.

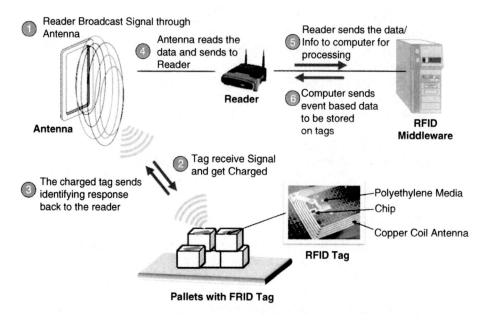

Figure 3.8 RFID readers retrieve product data on e-labels (RFID tags) placed on package boxes.

Example 3.4 RFID Technology for Merchandize Tagging or e-Labeling

Electronic labels or RFID tags appear on merchandize or shipping boxes. The e-label is made from polyethylene media housing small IC chips and printed circuitry driven by a copper coil antenna. The tag itself has no power supply attached to it. The tag is energized by signal waves broadcast from the reader antenna. Figure 3.8 shows a sequence of six events. Events 1 to 3 show the energization and handshaking between the reader and the tag. Events 4 to 6 show how the antenna reads the data on the label to the backend computer for processing.

The computer sends updated event-based data to be stored on tags for future use. The RFID in the middle is executed by the backend computer to complete the reading and updating process. Of course, the idea can be modified to serve other remote identification purposes. For example, RFID labels are also used in department stores, supermarkets, inventory searches, the shipping industry, etc. ∎

3.3.2 RFID System Architecture

RFID technology and products entered business applications in the 1980s. Now, the categories of RFID products increase considerably, various tags have been greatly developed with the cost constantly decreasing, and the industries with large-scale applications have started to expand. Derived from radar technology, RFID has an operating principle similar to that of radar. First, the reader sends out an electronic signal through the antenna, the tag emits the identification information stored internally after receiving the signal, then the reader receives and identifies the information sent back by the identification tag via the antenna, and finally the reader sends the identification result to the host.

A typical RFID system consists of an RFID tag, an RFID reader and a backend system. With a simple RF chip and an antenna, an RFID tag can store information that identifies the object to which it is attached. There are three types of RFID tags, i.e. passive tags, active tags and semi-active tags. A passive tag obtains energy through RF signals from the reader, while an active tag is powered by an embedded battery, which enables larger memory or more functionality. Though a semi-active tag communicates with RFID readers like a passive tag, additional modules can be supported through an internal battery. When it comes within the proximity of an RFID reader, the information stored in the tag is transferred to the reader, and onto a backend system, which can be a computer employed for processing this information and controlling the operation of other sub-system(s).

Example 3.5   Automobile Speeding Watch in a Typical Rule-Search RFID System
When a vehicle carrying a RFID tag is speeding on a highway, it passes a check point equipped with an RFID reader, and the identification data of the vehicle is transmitted to the RFID reader and backend system. The vehicle's ID is checked against the database at the backend. The system checks the database to issue the citation. In Figure 3.9(a), the vehicle is being monitored by a camera to check its speed. If the speed limit is exceeded, based on the traffic monitory rule, some actions are triggered, such as issuing a citation ticket to the vehicle driver. Alternatively, the vehicle may be chased by a police car to avoid endangering other drivers sharing the road.

In Figure 3.9(b), the rule-searching process is executed by such a speeding-check RFID system. The basic format of a rule consists of a simple conditional statement and a series of action codes: if {condition (environmental parameters), then {<action1 (parameter1)>, <action2 (parameter2)>, where environmental parameters (e.g. temperature or humidity sensed by some sensors) are used to determine whether the condition of a rule is satisfied. An action represents the operation that the system has against the running vehicle. Given the example in Figure 3.9(a), the rule-searching result could be: if {Speed > 120 km/hr} then {notify the police()}   ■

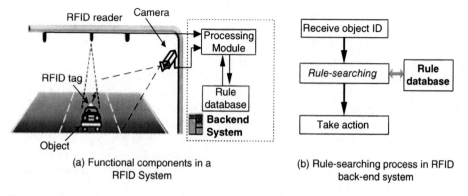

(a) Functional components in a
RFID System

(b) Rule-searching process in RFID
back-end system

Figure 3.9 A typical example of an RFID system applied to automobile speeding check.

3.3.3 IoT Support of Supply Chain Management

RFID technology plays an important role in business and the marketplace. Many industrial, government and community services can benefit from these applications. These include activities or initiatives to promote the development of better and more efficient societies, cities and governments. The typical RFID IoT applications includes retailing and logistics services and supply chain management.

3.3.3.1 Retailing and Logistics Services

Emergence of RFID applications depends strongly on adoption by retailers, logistics organizations and package-delivery companies. In particular, retailers may tag individual objects in order to solve a number of problems all at the same time: accurate inventories, loss control and ability to support unattended walk-through point of sale terminals (which promise to speed checkout, while reducing both shoplifting and labor costs). Cold-chain auditing and assurance could require tagging food and medicine with temperature-sensitive materials and/or electronics. Assuring or monitoring whether perishable materials are intact and/or need attention may entail communications among things such as refrigeration systems, automated data logging systems and human technicians.

For example, at the grocery store, you buy a carton of milk. The milk container will have an RFID tag that stores the milk's expiration date and price. When you lift the milk from the shelf, the shelf may display the milk's specific expiration date, or the information could be wirelessly sent to your personal digital assistant or cell phone. As you exit the store, you pass through doors with an embedded tag reader. This reader tabulates the cost of all the items in your shopping cart and sends the grocery bill to your bank. Product manufacturers know what you have bought and the store's computers know exactly how many of each product needs to be reordered.

Once you get home, you put your milk in the refrigerator, which is equipped with a tag reader. This smart refrigerator is capable of tracking all of the groceries stored in it. It can track the foods you use, how often you restock your refrigerator and can let you know when that milk and other foods spoil. Products are also tracked when they are thrown into a trash can or recycle bin. Based on the products you buy, your grocery store gets to know your unique preferences. Instead of receiving generic newsletters with weekly grocery specials, you might receive one created just for you.

3.3.3.2 Supply Chain Management

Supply Chain Management can be aided by an RFID system. The idea is to manage a whole network of related businesses or partners involved in product manufacturing, delivery and services as required by the end customers. At any given time, market forces could demand changes from suppliers, logistics providers, locations and customers, and from any number of specialized participants in a supply chain. This variability has significant effects on the supply chain infrastructure, ranging from the foundation layers of establishing the electronic communication between the trading partners to the more complex configuration of the processes, and the arrangement of work flows that are essential to the fast production process.

A supply line combines the processes, methodologies, tools and delivery options to guide collaborative partners to work in a sequence to conduct business with high

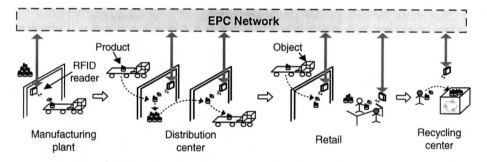

Figure 3.10 Supply chain management in a multi-partner business pipeline.

efficiency and delivery speed. The cooperative companies must work in step quickly as the complexity and speed of the supply chain increases due to the effects of global competition, rapid price fluctuations, surging of oil prices, short product life cycles, expanded specialization and talent scarcity. A supply chain is an efficient network of facilities that procures materials, transforms these materials to finished products and finally distributes the finished products to customers. The following example could explain how supply chain can be aided by the IoT, which is particularly tailored to promote business efficiency and fast growth.

Example 3.6   Supply Chain Management Aided by the Internet of Things

Supply chain management is a process used by companies to ensure that their supply chain is efficient and cost-effective. In Figure 3.10, the supply chain for the production and sales of consumer products is illustrated. The supply chain involves material or component suppliers, distribution centers, communication links, cloud datacenters, large number of retail stores, corporate headquarters (like Wal-Mart) and bank payments, etc. These are business partners that are linked by satellite, Internet, wired and wireless networks, truck, train or shipping companies, electronic banking, cloud providers, etc.

Sensors, RFID tags and GPS devices could be placed everywhere along the supply chain. The whole idea is to promote on-line business, e-commerce or mobile transactions. Supply chain management is comprised of five major stages of operations:

1) **Planning and Coordination:** A plan or strategy must be developed to address how a good or service can satisfy the needs of customers.
2) **Material and Equipment Supplies:** This phase involves building a strong relation with the raw material suppliers and also planning methods for shipping, delivery and payment.
3) **Manufacturing and Testing:** The product is tested, manufactured and scheduled for delivery.
4) **Delivery of Products:** Customer orders are taken and delivery of the goods is planned.
5) **After Sale Service and Returns:** At this stage customers may return defective products and the company also addresses customers' demands. Supply chain software is used by many companies for efficient supply chain management.   ∎

3.4 Sensors, Wireless Sensor Networks and GPS Systems

With the development of circuit design, signal processing and Micro-Electro Mechanical Systems (MEMS), various kinds of sensors are produced, from simple optical sensors and temperature sensors to complicated sensors such as carbon dioxide sensors, etc. To use which kind of sensors is usually determined by the specific application requirements. In general, processors interact with sensors through either analog signals or digital signals. Analog signal-based sensors output physically measured analog quantity such as voltage. The analog quantities must be digitalized before being used. Therefore, these sensors need external analog-digital converters as well as additional calibration technique. In digital signal-based sensors, the interaction between processors and sensors is simplified, since digital quantities are provided by sensors directly.

3.4.1 Sensor Hardware and Operating Systems

Sensors bridge the physical world and electronic systems. Sensors yield data in the form of analog or digitized signals that are fed to the sensor's node for immediate processing. However, depending on the circumstances, some form of specialized pre-processing or filtering can also take place beforehand, either as part of an algorithm implemented in the sensor node, or as part of an intermediate hardware component, although the former case has become prevalent.

We consider two categories of sensors: one for environmental surveillance and the other for body sensing. Environmental surveillance sensors are used to collect environmental information. Body sensors are deployed to gather vital body data. As shown in Table 3.2, typical environmental surveillance sensors include sensors for visible light, temperature, humidity, pressure, magnetism, acceleration, gyroscopic, sound, smoke, passive RF-optics, structured light, soil moisture, carbon dioxide (CO_2) gas, etc.

3.4.1.1 Inertial Motion Sensors

In this category, accelerometers and gyroscopes are by far the most common devices employed to estimate and monitor body posture, and miscellaneous human motion

Table 3.2 Characteristics of environmental surveillance sensors.

Manufacturer	Sensor	Voltage (V)	Power	Sampling Time
Taos	Visible light	2.7–5.5	1.9 mA	330 us
Dallas Semiconductor	Temperature	2.5–5.5	1 mA	400 ms
Sensirion	Humidity	2.4–5.5	550 uA	300 ms
Intersema	Pressure	2.2–3.6	1 mA	35 ms
Honeywell	Magnetism	Any	4 mA	30 us
Analog Devices	Acceleration	2.5–3.3	2 mA	10 ms
Panasonic	Sound	2–10	0.5 mA	1 ms
Motorola	Smoke	6–12	5 uA	–
Melixis	RF-Optics	Any	0 mA	1 ms
Li-Cor	Structured light	Any	0 mA	1 ms
Ech2o	Soil moisture	2–5	2 mA	10 ms

patterns. This capability is indispensable for many types of applications, especially in the realm of healthcare, sports and console gaming. To this end, accelerometers measure gravitational pull and inclination, whereas gyroscopes measure angular displacement. In general, their combined use yields orientation information and diverse user motion patterns.

3.4.1.2   Bioelectrical Sensors

These particular types of sensors are employed to measure electrical variations over the user/patient's skin that can be directly or indirectly correlated to the current activity or condition of a body organ. Electrocardiographic sensors are typical examples of these, which usually take the form of circular pads that are strategically placed around the human torso and extremities to monitor heart activity (ECG). Similar types of sensors placed over the skin are employed to measure the electrical activity of skeletal muscles (EMG) in order to help in the diagnosis of nerve and muscle disorders.

A body sensor node mainly consists of two parts: the physiological signal sensor(s) and the radio platform, to which multiple body sensors can be connected. The general functionality of body sensors is to collect analog signals that correspond to human's physiological activities or body actions. Such an analog signal can be acquired by the corresponding radio-equipped board in a wired fashion, where the analog signal is digitized. Finally, the digital signal is forwarded by the radio transceiver. The types of commercially available body sensors are listed as follows:

- **Electrochemical sensors:** These types of sensors generate an electrical output driven by a small chemical reaction between the sensor's chemical agent and bodily substance. A good example is the blood glucose sensor, which measures the amount of glucose circulating in the blood. Another example is the monitoring of carbon dioxide (CO_2) concentration levels in human respiration.
- **Optical sensors:** Devices that emit and receive light in both the visible and the infrared light bands are commonly employed in the non-invasive measurement of oxygen saturation in blood circulating in the human body. To this end, a pulse oximeter measures the degree of light absorption as light passes through the user/patient's blood vessels and arteries.
- **Temperature sensors:** This popular sensor type is placed over the skin in various places around the human body, and is routinely employed during physiological assessment of patients.

In a smart IoT environment, we may monitor and explore the physical world to the extreme. For example, humans can neither tolerate a temperature of over 1000 °C nor distinguish subtle changes of temperature. Therefore, the IoT for environmental protection has presented higher requirements on wide-range temperature measurement using heat-resistant sensors. Our daily life has been affected by extensive use of sensors, such as temperature and humidity sensors in an air conditioner, a temperature controller in a water heater, a sound controller for the lamp in a corridor, and a remote control for a TV set, etc.

Furthermore, sensors have been widely applied in fields such as environmental protection, medical health, industry and agriculture and military and national defense. A sensor is an apparatus or device that can sense the specified measure and convert it to a usable output signal according to a certain rule, and is generally constituted by sensing element, transduction element and basic circuit. The sensing element refers to the part in a sensor that can directly sense physical quantity; the transduction element converts the output of sensing element to circuit parameters (i.e. voltage and inductance); and finally the basic circuit converts the circuit parameters to electrical output.

3.4.1.3 Sensor Architecture Design

Figure 3.11(a) shows a typical sensor node with sensor, radio and memory modules. The sensor module consists of a sensor, a filter and an analog-to-digital converter (ADC). The sensor converts some form of energy to analog electric signals, which are bandpass-filtered and digitized by the ADC for further processing. We will discuss the radio systems for BANs and WPANs used for transmissions of sensed data in the next section. A sensor is easily confused with several concepts, such as sensor node, wireless sensor node and wireless sensor network. The sensor acts here as a signal converter.

The sensor node is usually called a sensor plus microprocessor, the function of which is to further convert the analog signal to the digital signal. The wireless sensor node further integrates the wireless communication chip, etc. on the basis of the traditional

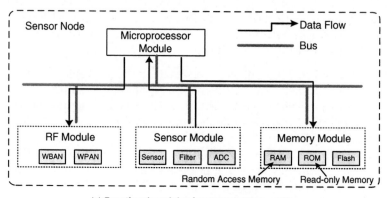

(a) **Functional modules in a smart sensor node.**

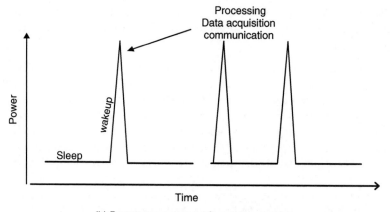

(b) **Power management in sensor nodes**

Figure 3.11 Power management in typical sensor operations.

sensor node: micro-operation systems such as TinyOS and Contiki are installed with some embedded programs to analyze and process the information received and transmit it via the network. If multiple wireless sensor nodes are placed to make them interconnect and form one *ad hoc* network, such a network is called a sensor network or a wireless sensor network.

3.4.1.4 Power Consumption

Wireless sensor nodes are generally deployed in the open air, so they cannot gain their power supply through wires. Therefore, their hardware design must consider energy saving as an important design objective. For example, under normal operating modes, the power of a typical sensor processor is between 3 and 15 mW. The periodic power management of a typical sensor is illustrated in Figure 3.11(b). The sleep, wake-up and processing spikes take the form of a periodic cycle, repeating within a fixed time interval. Most of time, the sensor is in sleep mode, with the device waking up periodically. The spike of power enables data collection and communication operations. Infrequently, triggering events are detected and they activate the sensor devices. The long life time of sensor operation may span over months to years, depending on whether the device is powered by solar energy or by other sustained energy sources.

3.4.1.5 Price and Size

Generally, a larger-scale network deployment requires a larger amount of sensor nodes to complete a complicated task. There is a tradeoff between node price and number of sensor nodes with a fixed budget. Therefore, their hardware design must consider cost-effectiveness as its critical design objective. Typically, wireless sensor nodes should be easy to transport and deploy, so their hardware design must regard micro-miniaturization as an important design objective. However, the limitation of node size also restricts the functions of the sensor nodes.

3.4.1.6 Flexibility and Expansibility

Sensor nodes are applied to different kinds of applications, so their hardware and software design must be flexible and expansible. In addition, flexibility and expansibility are important safeguards to realize the large-scale deployment of the sensor network. The hardware design of nodes should meet certain standard interfaces; for example, the interface of nodes and sensor plates make it beneficial to install sensors with different functions on nodes.

Moreover, the software design must be tailorable and able to install software modules with different functions according to the demands of different applications. Meanwhile, the design of software must also consider the extendibility of the system in time domains. For example, the sensor network should be able to add new nodes continuously, with this process not influencing the existing performance of the network. Another example is that node software should be able to update programs automatically through the network rather than redeploy each time after the deployed nodes are taken back and burned.

Table 3.3 compares the features of representative sensor platforms in terms of OS support, wireless standard and data rate, etc. We focus on operating system support, wireless standard used, maximum data rate, outdoor range and power level. These features of the system reveal the main characteristics of a sensor from the general application

Table 3.3 Comparison of typical sensor nodes in daily life applications.

Name	OS Support	Wireless Standard	Date Rate	Outdoor Range (m)
BAN node	TinyOS	IEEE 802.15.4	250 kbps	50
BTNode	TinyOS	Bluetooth	24 Mbps	100
eyesIFX	TinyOS	TDA5250	64 kbps	–
iMote	TinyOS	Bluetooth	720 kbps	30
iMote2	TinyOS or .NET	IEEE 802.15.4	250 kbps	30
IRIS	TinyOS	IEEE 802.15.4	250 kbps	300
Micaz	TinyOS	IEEE 802.15.4	250 kbps	75 to 100
Mica2	TinyOS	IEEE 802.15.4	38.4 kbps	>100
Mulle	TCP/IP or TinyOS	Any	250 kbps	>10
TelOS	TinyOS	Bluetooth or IEEE 802.15.4	250 kbps	75 to 100
ZigBit	ZDK	IEEE 802.15.4	250 kbps	3700

designer's perspective. We can see that all sensors achieve low power consumption, but possess low data rates ranging from 38.4 to 720 kbps, which is insufficient for large-scale body sensor networks or applications involving multimedia data traffic such as video streaming. The package running on the IEEE 802.15.4 ZigBee sensor has been widely adopted. Bluetooth turns out to be less energy inefficient. Interference from other radio devices sharing the 2.4 GHz ISM band may pose another problem when using them for building body-area networks.

3.4.1.7 Robustness

Robustness is an important safeguard to realize the long-time deployment of sensor networks. For common computers, if the system crashes, people can reboot it to recover the system; however, this is not useful for sensor nodes. Therefore, the design of the node program must be robust to guarantee that the nodes can work efficiently for a long time. For example, if the cost of the hardware design permits, we can adopt multi-form sensors, so that even if one kind of sensor breaks down, the other one can be used for the whole system. When designing software, we usually need to modularize the functions and have a total test of each function module before system deployment.

The next section is devoted to the selection of hardware components, communication interfaces, power supplies and operating systems for sensor module design and applications.

3.4.1.8 Energy-Supplying Devices

Generally, sensor nodes are battery-powered, which makes the nodes more easily deployed. In theory, a battery with 2000 mAh capacity can continue to output a 10 mA current for 200 hours. However, because of various factors such as voltage changes and environmental changes, the capacity of the battery cannot be utilized totally. Besides being battery-powered, nodes can also use renewable energy sources such as solar energy and wind energy. For example, under direct sunlight, a one-square-inch solar panel can provide 10 mW of electric energy; while under indoor lighting, the same panel can provide 10–100 uW electric energy.

The electric energy collected in the daytime can be used by the nodes at night. The key technology to utilize renewable energy is how to store it, with two kinds of technology presently in use. One is to use rechargeable batteries, their main advantages being that there is relatively less self-discharge and higher utilization rate of electric energy, and main disadvantages being that the charging efficiency is relatively lower and the charging times are limited. Another relatively new technology is to use ultra-capacitors, with their main advantages being that the charging efficiency is high and the charging times can reach 1 million. Also, they are not easily influenced by factors such as temperature and vibration.

Example 3.7 Networked Sensor Applications for Environmental Protection:
Many important environmental protection schemes can be supported by wireless sensor networks. Natural environment protection scenarios may include: i) seismic structure response to damage assessment after earthquakes; ii) contamination transport for pollution control; iii) ocean pollution control by monitoring marine microorganisms; and iv) ecosystem bio-complexity analysis through sensor monitory. These environmental protection scenarios require the use of a large number of micro-sensors, on-board processing and wireless interfaces feasible at very small scale, which can monitor phenomena up-close. These schemes enable spatially and temporally dense environmental monitoring. Large-scale distributed embedded sensing can now reveal some phenomenon, which has not been easily observed previously. ∎

3.4.1.9 Microprocessors

The microprocessor is the core responsible for computing in wireless sensing nodes. The present microprocessor chips also integrate internal storage, flash memory, module converters, digital Io, etc. This kind of deeply integrated characteristic makes them particularly suitable for use in the wireless sensing network. We are now going to analyze several processor key characteristics, which influence the whole operating performance of the nodes.

3.4.1.10 Communication Chips

Communication chips are important components of wireless sensing nodes. There are two main characteristics of the energy consumption of communication chips: one is that they consume the largest proportion of the energy in one wireless sensing node. For example, in the frequently-used TelosB Node, at present the current of CPU is only 50 0uA under normal circumstances, while the current reaches nearly 20 mA when the communication chips are sending and receiving data.

When communication chips with low power consumption are sending and receiving data, their energy consumption shows little difference. This means that as long as communication chips are open, they are consuming almost the same amount of energy whether they are sending and receiving data or not. Generally, the transmission distance of the communication chip is an important index for us to choose the sensing node. Their transmission distance is governed by the transmitted power of the chip.

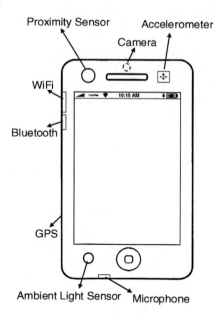

Proximity Sensor   Accelerometer

Camera

WiFi

Bluetooth

GPS

Ambient Light Sensor   Microphone

Figure 3.12 Sensor devices built inside a typical smart phone in 2016.

3.4.1.11   Operating System in Sensor Nodes

As the core of the sensor node software system, the node operation system provides the upper applications with hardware drives, resource management, task scheduling, programmatic interfaces, etc. The main characteristic that makes the node operation system different from the traditional one is that its hardware platform resource is really limited. Typical sensor node operation system includes TinyOS and MOS, etc. The sensor OS is extremely miniaturized and the TinyOS is the most widely-used in wireless sensing networks.

3.4.2   Sensing through Smart Phones

Regarding IoT sensing, a big change is happening around us, such as mobile phones now having directly integrated various sensors for sensing the physical world. As shown in Figure 3.12, more and more smart phones are equipped with devices such as GPS receiver, camera, sound recorder, thermometer, altimeter and barometer, etc. Due to the intrinsic capability of connection to the Internet in mobile environments, the smart phone enables sensor devices to be migrated to a global user group. Thus, the smart phone not only builds a bridge between sensor devices and the Internet, but also connects humans with social and cyber worlds, and so becomes an important element for IoT.

Nowadays, assessment of the user's health status is a promising research topic in the area of health IoT. There are various factors that can be used to make the assessment, such as mood, social interactions, sleeping habits, activity levels, perceived life satisfaction levels, etc. However, prior studies required face-to-face interactions between study coordinator and subject, thereby limiting the geographic reach and the scale of these studies.

Table 3.4 Sensors and usage installed at a typical smart phone.

Sensor/Data Name	Type	Sampling Period
Memory, CPU load, CPU utilization, Battery, Network traffic, Connectivity status	System	1 s
Geo-location	Sensor	10 s
Accelerometer, Magnetometer, Gyroscope	Sensor	100 ms
Proximity, Pressure, Light, Humidity, Temperature	Sensor	1 s
Phone Activity, SMS, MMS	User Activity	1 s
Screen state, Bluetooth, WiFi	User Activity	3 min

Table 3.4 shows several examples of data that can be captured by a smart phone. The sensors built into modern smart phones enable various information collections, such as physical activity, location, mobility patterns, social interactions (e.g. using proximity sensors) and heart rate. In addition, phone usage patterns and trends can also provide highly valuable context information. Such data include browsing histories, communication habits (calls, texting), social networking activities and app usage.

Example 3.8   Smart Phone or Smart Watch Features for Healthcare Applications
Various sensory data, such as accelerometer, GPS, SMS, camera, sound recorder, thermometer, altimeter and barometer, etc., can provide additional contextual information that are essential for a better understanding of trends and outliers in survey responses (e.g. mood-related survey responses can be different when submitted from home, the workplace, when on vacation, etc.). Also, smart phones make it easier to collect data over extended periods of time.

With digitalization of medical information and rapid distribution of smart devices, currently healthcare services are actively planned and developed based on smart devices. By 2015, 500 million smart phone users were expected to apply mobile health application, especially for exercise, diet and chronic disease management. Unlike most other chronic diseases, diabetes can be managed by the patient. Therefore, smart mobile device can be a universal tool for self-diabetes management because of its high penetration and functions.

A mobile healthcare application for Android OS was developed to provide self-diabetes management. The application consists of Diabetes management, Weight management, Cardio-cerebrovascular risk evaluation, Stress and depression evaluation and Exercise management. With the support of a smart phone or smart watch, various healthcare related data can be collected, such as Heart rate, Breathing Rate, Skin temperature, Duration time of sleep, Activity level (e.g. Static, Walking, Running), Facial expression video, etc.   ∎

3.4.3   Wireless Sensor Networks and Body Area Networks

As shown in Table 3.5, WSNs have been classified into 3 generations over the past 30 years. The sensors used in the first generation were mainly vehicle-placed or air-dropped single sensors. They were bulky, like a shoe box, and weighed several

Table 3.5 Three generations of wireless sensor networks.

WSN Features	First Gen. (1990s)	Sec. Gen. (2000s)	Third Gen. (2010s)
Manufacturers	Custom constructors, e.g. for TRSS	Crossbow Technology, Inc. Sensoria Corp, Ember Corp.	Dust, Inc. and others
Physical Size	Large shoe box and up	Pack of cards to shoe box	Dust particle
Weight	Kilograms	Grams	Negligible
Node architecture	Separate sensing, processing and communication	Integrated sensing, processing and communication	Integrated sensing, processing and communication
Topology	Point-to-Point, star	Client server, peer-to-peer	Peer to peer
Power supply lifetime	Large batteries; hours, days and longer	AA batteries; days to weeks	Solar; months to years
Deployment	Vehicle-placed or air-drop single sensors	Hand-placed	Embedded, sprinkled, left behind

kilograms. Networks assumed only-star or point-to-point topologies and were powered by large batteries that could last for hours or days. In the second generation, the sensors become smaller, like a pack of play cards, and weighed several grams, and the AA batteries lasted for days and weeks. They appeared in client-server or P2P configurations. The current generation are the size of dust particles, of negligible weight, and appear in P2P networks for embedded and remote applications.

Wireless *ad hoc* sensor networks apply a large number of (mostly stationary) sensors. Aside from the deployment of sensors at the ocean's surface or the use of mobile, unmanned, robotic sensors in military operations, most nodes in a smart sensor network are stationary. Networks of 10,000 or even 100,000 nodes are envisioned in the future and scalability becomes a demand. Low energy use is expected in the modern sensors. Since in many applications the sensor nodes will be placed in a remote area, service of a node may not be possible. In this case, the lifetime of a node is determined by the battery life, thereby requiring reduced energy expenditure or the use of solar energy to power the devices.

Advances in wireless communication technologies, such as wearable and implantable biosensors, along with recent developments in the embedded computing area, are enabling the design, development and implementation of body area networks. This class of networks is paving the way for the deployment of innovative healthcare monitoring applications. The differences between BAN and WSNs are listed as follows:

3.4.3.1 Deployment and Density

The number of sensor/actuator nodes deployed by the user depends on different factors. Typically, BAN nodes are placed strategically on the human body, or are hidden under clothing. In addition, BANs do not employ redundant nodes to cope with diverse types of failures. An otherwise common design provision is the conventional WSNs. Consequently, BANs are not node-dense. WSNs, however, are often deployed in places that may not be easily accessed by the operators, which requires that more nodes be placed to compensate for any node failures.

3.4.3.2 Data Rate

Most WSNs are employed for event-based monitoring, where events can happen at irregular intervals. By comparison, BANs are employed for registering a human's physiological activities and actions, which may occur in a more periodic manner, and may result in the applications' data streams exhibiting relatively stable rates.

3.4.3.3 Latency

This requirement is dictated by the applications, and may be traded for improved reliability and energy consumption. However, while energy conservation is definitely beneficial, replacement of batteries in BAN nodes is much easier done than in WSNs, whose nodes can be physically unreachable after deployment. Therefore, it may be necessary to maximize the battery life-time in a WSN at the expense of higher latency.

3.4.3.4 Mobility

BAN users may move around. Therefore, BAN nodes share the same mobility pattern, unlike WSN nodes that are usually considered stationary. BANs are commonly regarded as an enabling technology for a variety of applications, including health and fitness monitoring, emergency response and device control. Recent breakthroughs in solid-state electronics allow the creation of low-power, low-profile devices that can be modularly interconnected in order to create so-called sensor nodes comprised of one or more sensor devices, an MCU, and a radio transceiver that eliminates the need for wires to communicate with the node in order to transfer the collected data. BANs are merely at the beginning stage. Figure 3.13 illustrates a general architecture of a BAN-based health monitoring system.

In their most basic form, sensor devices operate by preloading MCUs with binary programs that access low-level hardware interfaces, which in turn obtain data from the actual sensor devices. Programs contain the necessary instructions for sensor devices

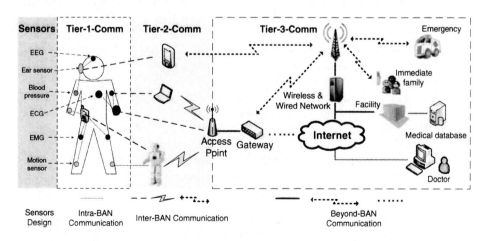

Figure 3.13 A three-tier architecture based on a BAN communications system.

to collect one or more readings in a particular time period. Raw sensor data can be subsequently processed in order to convert it to meaningful information that can be interpreted after it has been transmitted by the radio chip to an external device or system for further analysis. As their name implies, sensor nodes are meant to be either worn around or implanted in the human body.

Moreover, two or more sensor devices in their immediate vicinity can establish wireless links in order to coordinate their joint operation, thus creating a networked system. Therefore, the existing literature often refers to BANs as wireless BAN (WBAN) or Wireless Body Area Sensor Network (WBASN). The rest of this section introduces some of the most relevant advances in BAN technology, followed by a description of important technical challenges that researchers must tackle in order to make BANs efficient, reliable and economical.

This system monitors ECG: (electroencephalography) EEG, (electromyography) EMG, motion sensors and blood pressure sensors send data to nearby personal server (PS) devices. Then, through a Bluetooth/WLAN connection, these data are streamed remotely to a medical doctor's site for real-time diagnosis, to a medical database for record keeping, or to the corresponding equipment that issues an emergency alert. In this article, we separate the BAN communications architecture into three components.

Tier-1-Comm design (i.e. intra-BAN communications), Tier-2-Comm design (i.e. inter-BAN communications) and Tier-3-Comm design (i.e. beyond-BAN communications), are as shown in Figure 3.13. These components cover multiple aspects that range from low-level to high-level design issues, and facilitate the creation of a component-based, efficient BAN system for a wide range of applications. By customizing each design component, for example cost, coverage, efficiency, bandwidth, QoS, etc., specific requirements can be achieved according to specific application contexts and market demands.

3.4.4 Global Positioning Systems

Location-based service (LBS) is a key enabling technology for IoT applications. Most of the "things" in the IoT domain are interconnected via various wireless communication networks. When sensory data collected by IoT sensing technologies are sent to clouds, the associated location data is important. Without location information, the basic knowledge of the circumstance and users cannot be obtained, which results in the failure of the IoT applications. Thus, localization is a critical process.

One popular method to determine the location of a device is through Global Positioning Systems (GPS). An active GPS (aGPS) receiver can receive satellite signals and transmit position information to an aGPS control center. The aGPS is becoming the standard for companies who wish to monitor fleet vehicles as well as other heavy equipment. Real-time GPS tracking is practical for acquiring immediate and detailed information about large numbers of vehicles or objects that are being tracked. This could be the car rental business that provides cars for many customers. Real-time vehicle tracking processes are divided into the following four steps:

1) GPS receiver in each car accesses receiving signals from a network of satellites.
2) The collected satellite information is sent to the GPS center via mobile networks.
3) The control center enters calculated location information over global maps.

4) The control center sends commands to each unit to trigger alarms, stop engines, change direction or some personal messages, etc. Autonomous localization of GPS receivers is essential, since location makes the sensory data geographically meaningful.

Many applications and services of wireless networks directly or indirectly rely on location information. For IoT applications, localization is important since abundant data sensed through IoT are meaningless without locations for location-based services. Though GPS is a straightforward solution, it has two limitations for practical uses. First, the GPS signal is highly dynamic and unstable in indoor or dynamic environments, resulting in poor location accuracy. Second, it is costly to equip each sensor node with a GPS receiver for such a large-scale IoT system. A combined scheme that uses GPS and network localization simultaneously is recommended.

Each satellite is visible only by GPS receivers on certain parts of the Earth's surface. At different times, each receiver can see only a subset (about 6) of the satellites. Four satellites are sufficient to locate the receive position accurately. At different times, different satellite subsets will become visible to the receiver. The control segment is composed of a master control station and a host of dedicated and shared ground antennas and monitor stations. The user segment is composed of hundreds of thousands of US and allied military users of the secure GPS precise positioning services.

The ground GPS receiver calculates the 3-D location from four or more satellites with the help of a few ground reference stations and a master station, as shown in Figure 3.14. Essentially, the GPS receiver compares the time a signal was transmitted by a satellite with the time it was received. The time difference tells the GPS receiver how far away the

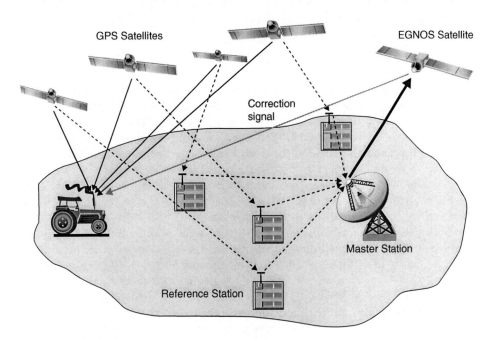

Figure 3.14 The ground GPS receiver calculates the 3-D location from four or more satellites with the help from a few ground reference stations and a master station.

satellite is. With distance measured from several satellites, the receiver can determine the user's position and display it on the unit's electronic map. Tens of millions of civil, commercial and scientific users are only allowed to use a degraded functionality of the so-called standard positioning services that cannot be used in hostile attack purposes.

3.4.4.1 Passive versus Active GPSs

The GPS tracking device makes it possible to track people, vehicles and other assets, anywhere on Earth. There are two types of GPS tracking systems, passive versus active. In passive tracking, the GPS is just a receiver, not a transmitter. Passive GPS tracking devices lack a transmission capability to send the GPS data from the vehicle. Therefore, the passive GPSs are also known as data loggers used primarily as recording devices. Active GPS tracking units incorporate a method to transmit the user information from a vehicle. Although satellite uplink of data is available, cellular data communication is the most common and cost effective. Automatic incremental updating provides a continuous source of tracking throughout a recording period. This provides current as well as historical logging positions.

Passive GPS tracking devices store GPS location data in their internal memory, which can then be downloaded to a computer for viewing at a later time, while active GPS tracking systems send the data at regular intervals to be viewed in real time. When real-time data is not required, passive GPS tracking devices tend to be favored more by individual consumers for their compact convenience and affordability. Concerned parents can install a GPS tracking unit just about anywhere in their teens' vehicles to monitor their driving habits and know where they have been going, and even law enforcement officials now rely on passive GPS tracking to trail criminal suspects and enhance civilian safety via electronic surveillance of parolees. Passive GPS tracking units also serve as a theft prevention and retrieval aid in consumer as well as commercial vehicles.

3.4.4.2 Operating Principles of GPS

Knowing the distance from receiver to a fixed-position satellite implies that the receiver is on the surface of a sphere centered at the satellite. With four satellites, the receiver location is detected at the intersection of four sphere surfaces. The intersection of two satellite spheres is generally a circle. This circle could be reduced to a single point, if the two spheres merely touch on their surfaces. Having found the two intersecting sphere surfaces, now we consider how the intersecting circle intersects with a third satellite sphere. A circle and a sphere surface intersect at zero, one or two points. With the receiver on the surface of the Earth, the receiver needs to choose the point which is closest to the receiver from the two intersecting points.

Obviously, the above triangulation method may result in some error in narrowing down to exactly one point with minimum inaccuracy. To locate the point accurately, the receiver has to use a fourth satellite to home in more precisely. The fourth satellite sphere will come very close to the final two intersecting points of the three satellite spheres. The final receiver location is thus decided by noting the closest point calculated from the two final points to the sphere surface of the fourth satellite. In the case of no error, the precise position is located. Otherwise some offset, say 10 meters from the exact location, can result from the error introduced. To further reduce errors, more satellite could be involved, but this would be rather costly.

Each satellite continually transmits messages that include: i) the time the message was transmitted; ii) precise orbital information (the ephemeris); and iii) the general system health and rough orbits of all GPS satellites (the almanac). A GPS receiver calculates its position by precisely timing the signals sent by GPS satellites high above the Earth's surface. A GPS receiver must be locked on to the signal of at least three satellites to calculate a 2-D position (latitude and longitude) and track movement. With four or more satellites in view, the receiver can determine the user's 3-D position (latitude, longitude and altitude).

Once the user's position has been determined, the GPS unit can calculate other information, such as speed, bearing, track, trip distance, distance to destination, sunrise and sunset time, and more. The receiver utilizes the messages it receives to determine the transit time of each message and computes the distances to each satellite. These distances along with the satellites locations are used to compute the position of the receiver. This position is displayed perhaps with a moving map display or latitude, longitude and elevation information. Many GPS units show derived information such as direction and speed calculated from positional changes.

3.4.4.3 Triangulation Location Calculation

This location calculation method is illustrated in Figure 3.15. The receiver uses messages received from four satellites to determine the satellite positions and time sent. The x, y and z components of position and the time sent are designated as $[x_i, y_i, z_i, t_i]$, where the index $i = 1, 2, 3$ or 4 denotes the satellite. Knowing when the message was received t_{ri}, the receiver computes the message's transit time as $t_{ri} - t_i$. Assuming the message traveled at the speed of light c, the distance traveled is calculated by $d_i = (t_{ri} - t_i) \times c$.

Having discussed how sphere surfaces intersect, we now formulate the equations for the case when errors are present. Let b denote the clock error or bias, the amount by which the receiver's clock is off. The receiver has four unknowns, the three components

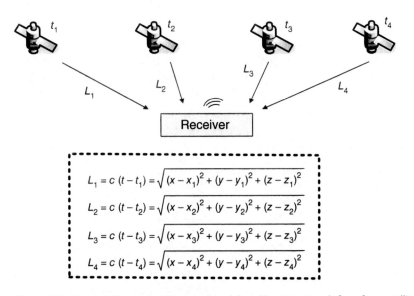

Figure 3.15 Triangulation method to calculate delayed location signals from four satellites.

of GPS receiver position and the clock bias $[x, y, z, b]$. The equation of the sphere surfaces is calculated by the following expression for i = 1, 2, 3, and 4:

$$(x - x_i)^2 + (y - y_i)^2 + (z - z_i)^2 = ([tr_i + b - t_i]c)^2 \tag{3.1}$$

A multidimensional root finding method such as the Newton–Raphson method can be used. This approach is to linearize around an approximate solution, say $[x^{(k)}, y^{(k)}, z^{(k)}, b^{(k)}]$ at iteration k, then solve four linear equations derived from the quadratic equations above to obtain the corresponding values at time instance of $k + 1$. The Newton–Raphson method converges faster than other position methods. When more than four satellites are available, the calculation can choose from four of the results shown in Figure 3.15. The error of position calculation is very sensitive to the clock error. Therefore, in the satellite-based navigation system, clock synchronization is critically important to minimize the location error.

Three satellites are sufficient to locate the receiver position, since the space has three dimensions and a position near the Earth's surface is always assumed. However, even a very small clock error multiplied by the light speed of satellite signals may result in a large positional error. Therefore, most receivers use four or more satellites to solve the receiver's location and time. The computed time is often hidden by most GPS applications, which use only the location information. A few specialized GPS applications do use the time for time transfer, traffic signal timing and synchronization of cell phone base stations.

Although four satellites are required for normal operation, if the 1-D variable is already known, a receiver can determine its position using only three satellites. For example, a ship or plane may have known elevation. Some GPS receivers may use additional clues or assumptions (i.e. reusing the last known altitude, dead reckoning, inertial navigation or including information from the vehicle computer) to give a less accurate (degraded) position when fewer than four satellites are available.

3.4.4.4 Worldwide Deployment Status

Table 3.6 summarizes four global positioning systems used today. In addition to the GPS deployed by the US, which is now open for global civilian applications by many countries, the Russians have deployed a GLONASS (Global Navigation Satellite System) for Russian military use exclusively. In the European Union, there is the Galileo positioning

Table 3.6 Four Global Positioning Systems in US, EU, Russia and China.

Features	GPS	GLONASS	Beidou	Galileo
Political entity	United States	Russia	China	European Union
Coding	CDMA	FDMA/CDMA	CDMA	CDMA
Orbital height	20,180 km (12,540 mi)	19,130 km (11,890 mi)	21,150 km (13,140 mi)	23,220 km (14,430 mi)
Period	11.97 hours (11 h 58m)	11.26 hours (11 h 16m)	12.63 hours (12 h 38m)	14.08 hours (14 h 5m)
Number of satellites	At least 24	31 (24 operational)	5 GEO, 30 MEO satellites	22 operational satellites supported

system. By 2015, China had launched 20 satellites toward a complete system, with 31 satellites planned for the 2020s.

3.5 Cognitive Computing Technologies and Prototype Systems

This section is devoted to the study of cognitive computing technologies and prototype systems. We check through the development processes of three experimental cognitive systems at the IBM Almaden Research Center, Google Brain Team Projects and the Chinese Academy of Sciences. Finally, we show how IoT contexts benefit cognitive services, and present the IoT context in cognition and recent cognitive devices such as AR glasses and VR headsets.

3.5.1 Cognitive Science and Neuroinformatics

Cognitive science is interdisciplinary in nature. It covers the areas of psychology, artificial intelligence, neuroscience and linguistics, etc. It spans many levels of analysis from low-level machine learning and decision mechanisms to high-level neural circuitry to build brain-modeled computers. In 2008, a fundamental concept of cognitive science was given by Paul Thagrad: "Thinking can best be understood in terms of representational structures in the mind and computational procedures that operate on those structures." In general, three approaches are adopted in cognitive computing applications:

1) Apply software library on clouds or supercomputers for machine learning and neuroinformatics studies.
2) Use representation and algorithms to relate the inputs and outputs of artificial neural computers.
3) Use neural chips to implement brain-like computers for machine learning and intelligence.

Neuroinformatics attempts to combine informatics research and brain modeling to benefit both fields of science. The traditional computer-based informatics facilitate brain data processing and handling. Through hardware and software technologies, we can arrange databases, modeling and communication in brain research. Or conversely, enhanced discoveries in neuroscience may invoke the development of new models of brain-like computers.

In Table 1.12, we have identified related fields to cognitive computing and neuroinformatics technologies. A major concern of AI research is to find out how human learning, memory, language, perception, action and knowledge discovery are handled. We hope to apply machine intelligence to help human decision making or make our daily lives activities safer, effective, efficient and comfortable, etc.

Example 3.9   Cognitive Science and Neuroinformatics at Academia and IBM Labs
McCulloch and Pitts developed the very first artificial neural network (ANN) model of computation inspired by the structure of biological neural networks. The first instance of cognitive science experiments were performed at the MIT Social Psychology Department using computer memory as models for human cognition. Much of the research

efforts on cognitive science were supported by the National Institute of Health in the USA.

IBM founded the Blue Brain Project in May 2005. The project was carried out on an 8000-processor Blue Gene/L supercomputer built by IBM. At that time, this was one of the fastest supercomputers in the world. The mission of the Blue Brain Project is to understand mammalian brain function and dysfunction through detailed simulations. The IBM projects cover the following aspects:

- **Databases**: 3-D reconstructed model neurons, synapses, synaptic pathways, micro-circuit statistics, computer model neurons and virtual neurons.
- **Visualization**: microcircuit builder and simulation results visualizator, 2-D, 3-D and immersive visualization systems are being developed.
- **Simulation environment**: a simulation environment for large-scale simulations of morphologically complex neurons on IBMI's Blue Gene supercomputer.
- **Simulations and experiments**: iterations between large-scale simulations of neocortical microcircuits and experiments.

∎

Traced back further, the IBM Watson Center had a Deep Blue project that led to the chess playing competition that defeated World Chess Champion Garry Kasparov in 1997. That was the world's first cognitive system built to work with traditional computer hardware. Recently, IBM announced that they will push cognitive services as a major thrust of effort in the next decade. The goal is to develop a cognitive industry to serve human societies and to promote global economy. We will cover the IBM synaptic chip development in building a brain-like computer in Section 3.5.2. Then, we will examine Google's Brain Team efforts in Section 3.5.3. Clouds and IoT technologies play a vital role in these industrial transformations.

3.5.2 Brain-Inspired Computing Chips and Systems

In this section, we study some new processor chips, non-von Neumann architecture and ecosystem development at IBM, Nividia, Intel and the China's Institute of Computing Technology for cognitive computing. Even though these projects are still at the research stage, they represent the emerging technologies which combine computing with cognition to augment human capacity and understanding of all kinds of environments surrounding us.

3.5.2.1 IBM SyNapse Program

IBM has a SyNapse research program, devoted to the development of new hardware and software for cognitive computing. This project has been supported by DARPA (Defense Advanced Research Projects Agency) in the US. In 2014, IBM unveiled a neurosynaptic computer chip design in *Science Magazine*, known as the TruthNorth processor. This processor can mimic the human brain's computing abilities and power efficiency. The chip design can enable wide-ranging applications, such as assisting vision-impaired people to navigate safely through their environment.

This chip could cram supercomputer-like powers into a microprocessor the size of a postage stamp. Rather than solving problems through brute-force mathematical calculations, the chip is designed to understand its environment, handle ambiguity and take action in real time and in context. It was estimated that an average human brain has 100 billion neurons and 100 to 150 trillion synapses. Modeled on the human brain, the TrueNorth chip incorporates 5.4 billion transistors, the most IBM has ever put on a chip [23]. The chip features 1 million programmable neurons and 256 million programmable synapses.

It was speculated that this synaptic chip could be applied to power small-and-rescue robots, automatically distinguish between voices in a meeting and create accurate transcripts for each speaker. It may even have the potential to issue tsunami alerts, monitor oil spills or enforce shipping lane rules. What is amazing is that the chip consumes only 70 milliwatts of power to perform the above functions, about the same level consumed by a hearing aid. The chip is still in the prototype stage.

It was announced at a conference that IBM may spend $3 billion to push for the future of such computer chips and explore its cognitive service potentials. It does not require the heavy computational loads for complex operations as in biological cognitive systems. For example, if a robot running with today's microprocessors is walking toward a pillar, it would depend on image processing and huge computing resources and power to avoid a collision. By comparison, a robot using a synaptic chip would steer clear of the danger by sensing the pillar, much as a person would do with little power consumption.

Experts believe an innovation like SyNapse's TrueNorth could help overcome the performance limits of the von Neumann architecture, the mathematics-based system at the core of almost every computer built since 1948. "It is a remarkable achievement in terms of scalability and low power consumption," said Horst Simon, the director of the US Department of Energy's Berkeley Lab and an expert on computer science. IBM expects the chip to help transform science, technology, business, government and society by enabling vision, audition and multi-sensory applications. This could be the first step in designing future computers based on the human brain model. Similarly, Nividia's graphics has leaned also in this direction to power supercomputer brains.

3.5.2.2 China's Cambricon Project

This project started as a joint research program between Dr Tianshi Chen at the Institute of Computing Technology, Chinese Academy of Sciences and Prof Oliver Tenam at French INRIA. The joint research team has developed a series of hardware accelerators, known as *Cambricon*, for neural network and deep-learning applications. The chip was built as a synaptic processor to power artificial neural computing in machine learning operations. The Cambricon stays away from the classic von Neumann architecture in order to match the special kind of operations performed in artificial neural network computations.

Machine-learning tasks are becoming pervasive in a broad range of systems, from embedded systems to datacenters. For example, deep-learning algorithms, using convolutional and deep neural networks (CNNs and DNNs to be treated in Chapter 6), take a long learning cycle to be usefully trained on a conventional computer. The Cambricon accelerator was designed to focus on large-scale CNN and DNN solutions. The joint ICT-INRIA team proved that it is possible to build accelerators with high throughput, capable of performing 452 GOP/s (key neural network operations in synaptic weight multiplications).

The chip was fabricated on a small footprint of 3.02 mm^2 and 485 mW silicon technology. The team has also worked out a new instruction set architecture (ISA) for efficient use of such a brain-like processor. This new ISA is specially tailored for neural network or cognitive computing. Compared with a 128-bit 2 GHz SIMD GPU accelerator, the accelerator chip achieved a speed 117 faster with 21 times reduction in power consumption. With an extended 64-chip machine-learning architecture, the team has shown a speed of 450 times over an array of GPU chips with a power reduction of 150 times.

Through multi-national efforts, human-oriented cognitive computing comes closer to a reality. It is interesting to watch the development of special purpose neuron-based synaptic processors in multi-core or many-core multiprocessor chips and the use of a massive number of such chips to build future cognitive supercomputers. We will study machine learning and deep learning algorithms in Chapters 4 to 6. Although these ML/DL algorithms are applied to today's clouds or server clusters, as covered in Chapters 7 to 9, they could be targeted to guide the design of future cognitive computing systems.

3.5.3 Google's Brain Team Projects

In research and industry, speech recognition is always in great demand. It would be nice to have an intelligent recording machine that could listen to human speech and produce documented textual reports. Similarly, the United Nations need to have automatic language translation systems, not only translation between text documents, but also between speeches and documented reports in different languages.

Example 3.10 Google's Brain Project on Developing New ML/DL Products
Google Brain project started in 2011 as a joint effort between Jeff Dean, Greg Corrado and Andrew Ng. Ng is interested in using deep learning techniques to crack the AI problems. They have built a large-scale deep learning software system, called DistBelief on top of Google's cloud computing infrastructure. In 2012, the *New York Times* reported that a cluster of 16,000 computers were used to mimic some aspects of human brain activity and had successfully trained itself to recognize a cat based on 10 million digital images taken from YouTube videos.

In 2013, Geoffrey Hinton joined Google, a leading researcher in the deep learning field. Subsequently, Google merged DeepMind Technologies and released TensorFlow. Notable Google products developed out of the Brain Team include the Android speech recognition system, Google photo search and video recommendations in YouTube. Figure 3.16 lists some of the service products developed at Google. The team has also worked on developing mobile and embedded machine intelligence applications, and started with Android and then iOS services. In addition, the brain team has worked with Google X and the Quantum Artificial Intelligence Lab at NASA in joint space programs.

In May 2016, Google announced a custom ASIC (application Specific integrated circuit) chip they have built specifically for machine learning tailored for TensorFlow programming. They installed the TPUs inside their data centers for more than a year, and achieved ten times in speed gains in machine learning operations. The TPU is a small circuit board inserted inside a hard drive attached to Google servers. The TPU is a pre-trained chip to support TensorFlow computing with a high volume of low-precision (e.g. 8 bit) arithmetic. The TPU is indeed programmable as TensorFlow program changes.

Multiple TPUs were used in the AlphaGo match to be discussed in Section 9.4. The TensorFlow offers a software platform for the deep learning applications to be covered in

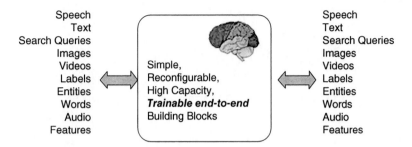

Figure 3.16 The promise of deep learning at Google's Brain Project (Reprinted with permission from a public slide presentation by Jeff Dean, 2016).

Section 7.5. The TPU accelerates TensorFlow computations. Android support of TensorFlow is available for mobile execution. iOS support will come soon. Intel has also optimized their high-end server processor for neural computing. We will assess Google DeepMind projects in Chapter 9. ∎

It is fair to say that deep neural networks play a crucial role in understanding speech, images, language and vision applications. Both pre-trained models or APIs must have low overheads and be easy to use in ML system development. In what follows, we check some of the deep learning systems developed by the Google Brain Team for various big data applications, as shown in Figure 3.17. Among these, we see DL applications in Android apps, drug discovery, gmail, image understanding, maps, natural language understanding, photos, robotics research, speech and YouTube among many others. Among the 50 internal product development teams at Google, the interest of using deep

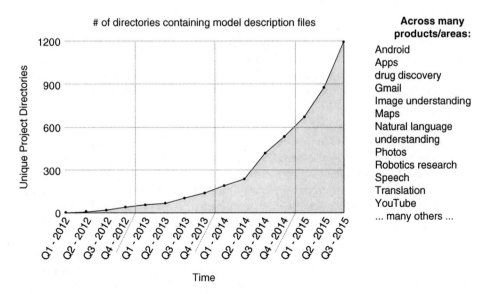

Figure 3.17 Growing use of deep learning at Google teams (Reprinted with permission from public presentation by Jeff Dean, 2016).

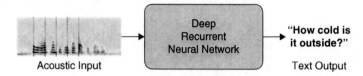

Figure 3.18 The concept of a Google speech recognition system built with deep recurrent neural networks.

learning has been measured by the number of unique project directories containing model description files.

In general, three approaches are adopted in cognitive computing apps:

1) Apply software library on clouds or supercomputers for machine learning and neuroinformatics studies.
2) Use representation and algorithms to relate the inputs and outputs of artificial neural computers.
3) Design hardware neural chips to implement brain-like computers for machine learning and intelligence.

In Figure 3.18, we demonstrate the idea of building a Google speech recognition system with deep recurrent neural networks (DRNN).

Here, acoustic speech signals are fed into the system as input. Through repeated learning from the DRNN system, text output as a question such as: "How cold is it outside?" is generated automatically. Apple's Siri system also has built such conversational capabilities. Deep convolutional neural networks have proven very useful for this purpose as well. In addition, object recognition and detection are of equal importance. This is part of the traditional field of pattern recognition and image processing domain. Deeper convolution and scalable object detection offer viable approaches to solve the problem on modern clouds.

Machine translation can be done by sequence-to-sequence learning processes with neural networks. Neural machine translation has been worked out at Google. Language modeling was also conducted with a 1 billion word benchmark. Another exciting area is automatic parsing grammar as a foreign language. The whole purpose of ANNs is to learn a complicated function from data. ANN has been a hot research field for at least 30 years.

Example 3.11   The Use of Google's ImageNet for Image Understanding
The ANN models, especially the deep convolutional neural networks (DCNN), have been reincarnated. They offer a collection of simple, trainable mathematical functions, that are compatible with many variants of machine learning. Figure 3.19 shows the ideas behind using a DCNN to recognize a "cat" or an "ocean" from thousand of classes over millions of photo images. Image captioning has been in high demand in Google search requests.

Searching a personal photo without tags is equivalent to the task of identifying 1 image out of 1000 different classes. The work was carried out at Google using the ImageNet. Another project using GoogleNet also emphasizes a deeper convolution approach in

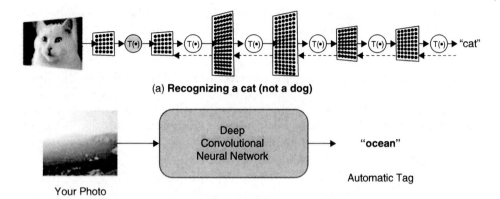

(a) **Recognizing a cat (not a dog)**

Deep
Convolutional
Neural Network

"ocean"

Automatic Tag

Your Photo

(b) **Distinguishing an ocean view from many other views**

Figure 3.19 Using a deep convolution neural network to understand particular images out of millions of photos belong to different or similar classes.

the inception area. Neural networks have made rapid progress in image recognition. The ImageNet project challenges many classification tasks. The Inception team using GoogLeNet achieved only 6.66% error in 2014. ∎

Another interesting area is to combine vision with translation or to combine vision with robotics intelligence. In other words, we want robots to go through a deep learning process by large-scale interactions. This is critical to the autonomous vehicle driving projects, which is actively pursued at Google, Baidu and other research centers. For example, we want the robots to learn hand-eye coordination through a deep learning system on board a car. Some progress has already been demonstrated in several on-going projects in the US and China.

3.5.4 IoT Contexts for Cognitive Services

In practice, the deployment of cognitive services relies on different contexts, such as location information which was used by services offered over the Internet in order to provide location-aware customization to users. Once the mobile devices (phones and tablets) became a popular and integral part of everyday life, context information (gravity, rotation vector, orientation, geomagnetic field, proximity, light, pressure, humidity and temperature, etc.) collected from sensors built into the devices (e.g. accelerometer, gyroscope, GPS, and pulse oximetry, etc.) were used to provide context-aware functionality. For example, built-in sensors are used to determine user activities, environmental monitoring, health and well-being, location and so on.

Today's context information is collected through social networking services (e.g. Facebook, Myspace, Twitter and WeChat, etc.) using mobile devices. Some context-aware applications are developed for activity predictions, recommendations and personal assistance. For example, a mobile application may offer location information retrieved from mobile phones to recommend nearby restaurants what a potential customer might like. Another example is Internet-connected refrigeration. The user can check the foods in the refrigerator remotely and decide what to purchase on the way home.

When the user leaves their workplace, the application autonomously does the shopping and guides the user to a particular shopping market so he can collect the goods it has already ordered. In order to perform such tasks, the application must fuse location data, user preferences, activity prediction, user schedules, information retrieved through the refrigerator (i.e. shopping list) and many more. In the light of the above examples, it is evident that the complexity of collecting, processing and fusing information has increased over time. The amount of information collected to aid decision making has also increased significantly.

In the IoT era, there will be a large number of sensors attached to everyday objects. These objects will produce large volumes of sensory data that have to be collected, analyzed, fused and interpreted. Sensory data produced by a single sensor will not provide the necessary information that can be used to fully understand the situation. Therefore, data collected through multiple sensors need to be fused. In order to accomplish sensor data fusion, contexts need to be tagged together with the sensory data to be processed and understood later. Therefore, context annotation plays a significant role in context-aware computing research.

3.5.4.1 IoT Contexts

Context-aware technology provides a methodology to evaluate the performance of an IoT solution. The evaluation is mainly based on three context-aware features in high-level: i) context-aware selection and presentation; ii) context-aware execution; and iii) context-aware-tagging. However, we have also enriched the evaluation framework by identifying sub-features under the above-mentioned three features. In Table 3.7 we give examples to evaluate IoT solutions in the smart city application domain.

The primary context data captured by IoT solutions are listed below: W denotes Web-based; M denotes Mobile-based; D denotes Desktop-based; and O denotes Object-based. We identify Touch (T), Gesture (G) and Voice (V) as three common mechanisms. M means that interactions are carried out through a PC or a smart phone. RT represents that an IoT solution processes data in real time, while A means that the IoT solution processes archival data. Other notations in Table 3.7 we have S for IoT sensing, E for energy, UD for user device, R for radio technology and N for notification. We introduce the name of the IoT project in the left-most column. The web page links are the most reliable references to a given IoT solution. Such links allow readers to probe further and explore the IoT technology more meaningfully.

3.5.5 Augmented and Virtual Reality Applications

Virtual reality (VR) is a computer technology that replicates an environment, real or imagined, and simulates a user's physical presence and environment to allow user interaction. Virtual realities artificially create sensory experience, which can include sight, touch, hearing and smell. The immersive environment needs to be similar to

Table 3.7 Representative IoT contexts in smart city applications.

IoT Project, Builder and (Website)	Primary Context	Secondary Context	Presentation Channel	User Interaction	Real Time Archival	Notification Mechanism	Learning Ability	Notification Execution
Waste Management Evevo (enevo.com)	Waste fill-level	Efficient routes to pick up waste	W	M	RT, A	N,R	ML,UD	E
Indoor Localization, Estimote (estimote.com)	Bluetooth signal strength, Beacon ID	Location, Distance	M	M	RT	N,R	UD	T,S,E
Parking Slot Management, ParkSight (streetline.com)	Sound level, Road surface temperature	Route for free parking slot	M,W	M	RT, A	N,R	ML,UD	T,S,E
Street Lighting, Tvilight (tvilight.com)	Light, presence, weather, events	Energy usage, patterns, lamp, etc	W	M	RT, A	N,A	ML,UD	T,S,E
Movement Analysis, Scene Tap (scenetap.com)	GPS, Video	Crowd profiling by location	M,W,D	M	RT	N,A	ML	T,S
Foot Traffic Monitoring (scanalyticsinc.com)	Floor level	Heat maps tracking movements	W	T,M	RT, A	N	ML,UD	S,E
Crowed Analysis, Livehoods (livehoods.org)	Foursquare check-ins cloud service	Social dynamics, large cities	W	M	RT, A	-	ML	E

Abbreviations: *M*: mobile, *W*: web services, *D*: desktop-base, *O*: object-oriented, *T*: touch technology, *S*: *IoT sensing*, *G*: gesture, *V*: voice, *RT*: real-time, *N*: notification, *A*: archival, *ML*: machine learning, *DU*: user device

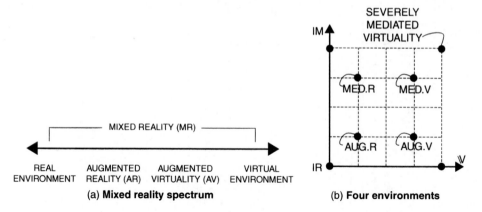

Figure 3.20 Spectrum from real environment to AR, AV and VR.

the real world in order to create a lifelike experience – for example, in simulations for pilot or combat training, it can differ significantly from reality, such as in VR games (Figure 3.20).

Augmented reality (AR) is a live view of a physical, real-world environment whose elements are augmented (or supplemented) by computer-generated sensory input such as sound, video, graphics or GPS data. It is related to a more general concept called mediated reality. As a result, the technology functions by enhancing our current perception of reality. By contrast, virtual reality replaces the real world with a simulated one. Augmentation is conventionally in real time and in a semantic context with environmental elements. A mixed reality sits anywhere between the extrema of the virtuality continuum, extending from the complete reality through to a complete virtual environment with augmented reality and augmented virtuality mixed together.

In Figure 3.20, four example points are shown: augmented reality, augmented virtuality, mediated reality and mediated virtuality on the virtuality and mediality axes. This includes, for example, diminished reality (e.g. computerized welding helmets that filter out and diminish certain parts of a scene), accelerometer, gyrometer, proximity sensor, and light sensors are built-in VR headsets, including the HTC Vive, Paystation VR and Samsung Gear VR, etc.

3.5.5.1 Video Games

The use of graphics, sound and input technology in video games can be incorporated into Virtual Reality. Several VR head mounted displays (HMD) have been released for gaming, including the Virtual Boy developed by Nintendo and iGlasses developed by Virtual I-O. Several companies are working on a new generation of VR headsets: Oculus Rift is a head-mounted display for gaming purposes, which was acquired by Facebook in 2014. One of its rivals was named by Sony as PlayStation VR (codenamed Morpheus). Valve Corporation announced their partnership with HTC Vive to make a VR headset capable of tracking the exact position of its user. Other AR/VR products can be found in Table 3.8.

Table 3.8 Recent AR/VR products developed by high tech companies.

Company	Product	Introduction
Microsoft	HoloLens	A pair of mixed reality head-mounted smart glasses by Microsoft. HoloLens gained popularity for being the first computer running the Windows Holographic platform.
Google	Google Cardboard	This is a VR platform by Google for use with a head mount for a smart phone. Named for its fold-out cardboard viewer, it is a low-cost system to encourage VR applications.
Facebook	Oculus Rift	Oculus Rift is a virtual reality headset developed and manufactured by Oculus VR, released March 28, 2016.
Samsung	Gear VR	The Samsung Gear VR is a mobile virtual reality headset developed by Samsung Electronics, in collaboration with Oculus, and manufactured by Samsung.
Sony	PlayStation VR	Known by the codename Project Morpheus during development, is a VR gaming head-mounted display developed by Sony Interactive Entertainment and manufactured by Sony.
HTC	HTC VIVE	This is a virtual reality headset developed by HTC and Valve Corporation in 2016. This is designed to utilize "room scale" technology to turn a room into 3-D space via sensors
Huawei	Huawei VR	Huawei honor VR was released on May 10, 2016 to match the honor V8 smart phone.
Alibaba	Buy + Plan	Buy+ program uses VR technology to generate interactive 3-D shopping environment with computer graphics systems and auxiliary sensors.

3.5.5.2 Education and Training

Strides are being made in the realm of education, although much still needs to be done. The possibilities of VR and education are endless and bring many advantages to pupils of all ages. A few are creating content that may be used for educational purposes, with most advances being made in the entertainment industry, but many understand and realize the future and the importance of education and VR. US Navy personnel use a VR parachute training simulator. The use of VR in a training perspective is to allow professionals to conduct training in a virtual environment where they can improve upon their skills.

3.6 Conclusions

The IoT has emerged rapidly to affect our daily life activities. The ultimate goal is to build a worldwide physical web that links everything together. IoT leads to smart classrooms, hospitals, marketplaces, department stores, streets, highways, cities and the Earth. In other words, we want to apply machine intelligence everywhere to aid or promote human safety, comfort, convenience and productivity. Cognitive science and services are also appearing. Both augmented reality (AR) and virtual reality (VR) may appear as commercial devices to expand human experiences in gaming, relaxation and creativity.

This chapter covers the progress of key technologies that make it possible to use smart devices, sensors, tags, phones, tablets, GPS, etc. everywhere and at any time. That is the dream of a paradise on Earth. We have shown how to apply IoT sensing capability in cloud computing with big data. Neural-based CPU chips are appearing at IBM research labs and at the Institute of Computing Technology in the China Academy of Sciences. The use of neuron-modeled computers for future machine learning and deep learning is no longer a dream. It is quite plausible to have innovative applications that involve IoT sensing and machine cognition in the near future.

Homework Problems

3.1 Answer the following two questions on IoT development in recent years:
  a) The early IoT technologies include 4 T's, namely Telemetry, Telemetering, Telenet and Telematics. Perform a literature survey of recent progress in IoT and report your findings.
  b) How are the following devices or techniques: sensors, smart phones, RFID labels/readers, bar code, 2-D QR code, or smart watch are used for data collection and sensing in IoT applications?

3.2 Answer the following two updated assessments of GPS technologies and four systems built in the US, Russia, the EU and China. Wikepedia may be a good source of quick information:
  a) What are the differences in civilian and military applications of various GPS systems?
  b) Report several interesting civilian applications of GPS services.
  c) What are the potential military applications of GPS capabilities?

3.3 Design a healthcare system which consists of body sensors and wearable devices to collect human physiological signals. This system should possess the following functions: real-time monitoring, disease prediction and early detection of chronic diseases. Also, you may need a monitoring and management system that can optimize the distribution of medical resources and facilitate the data sharing for such resources.

3.4 In recent years, video analytics became a hot topic, especially for security checks through video tracking, which is useful to protect personal and property safety. Traditional security technology emphasizes real-time response and the effectiveness of verification. So video presentation with high-resolution, no loss and low delay has been the main development direction of security industry over the past few years. Nowadays, we can see cameras for city surveillance everywhere.

With increasing use of high-definition cameras, how to effectively transmit the big amount of video data has become a key issue. In addition, tracking criminals to obtain their location information is time-consuming and labor-intensive. Describe how to use artificial intelligence and machine learning technology to analyze massive video samples, automatically track the target and find the moving path.

3.5 Parkinson's disease (PD) is a chronic disease caused by movement disorder of the central nervous system. Typically, gait is an important indicator to identify and evaluate PD. In order to evaluate gait changes in the elderly with PD continuously without human intervention, pressure of foot step can be measured when PD patients walk, and the mode of center of pressure (CoP) can be obtained. Try to figure out the differences of CoP between normal people and PD patients. Which statement is correct?

a) The pressure sensors are deployed under the PD patient's foot.

b) The pressure sensors are installed on the ground.

c) In order to obtain CoP, the pressure of front, middle or back parts of foot should be collected.

d) Measure the pressure data when PD patient is standing or walking.

3.6 The incidence of leukemia among young people has increased, which needs stem cell transplantation as the compulsory treatment. After the transplant, patients have to stay at home for 12 to 24 months. In order to skip arduous and unpleasant feelings of the patients during rehabilitation, a video system is designed to assist communication between patients and medical teams via smart phone, tablet or personal computer. Meanwhile, the personal data of the patients can be easily accessed through a web-based system. Especially, if a gaming element is added in such remote data retrieving system, the patients' mood can be improved during the daily report. With more practical and frequent healthcare data, the medical team can monitor the patient's health status more accurately and timely and provide more effective treatment.

1) About the video system, which statements are correct?

a. We need a highly flexible framework of data, in order to meet the requirements about custom health parameters.

b. External data sources transfer through the e-health data service bus to the database.

c. Data can only be hard to define, not soft definition.

d. Game is given priority with smart phones and tablets use, but can also be conducted on a web browser.

2) Video game system workflow includes three steps: data definition, create a configuration file, and plan a game task. When distributing small games to patients, the task can specify a group of patients with physical therapy practice according to their health status evaluated by a medical team. Write your thoughts on the above three steps.

3.7 Design an intelligent vehicle management system based on IoT, especially RFID technology. The system should enable automatic payment, such that a vehicle can go through an intersection without stopping. When the vehicle exits, the parking fee is deducted automatically.

3.8 This problem is related to using IoT to promote the green agriculture.

1) Based on a research study from the literature, elaborate on each of the following requirements:

    a. Real-time collection of a farm's environmental parameters like temperature, humidity, illumination, soil temperature, soil moisture and oxygen levels in a greenhouses or water beds, etc.

    b. Real-time intelligent decision on crop growth, and automatic opening or closing the environmental control equipment. The deployment of the system provides a scientific basis and effective means for agricultural monitoring, automatic control and intelligent management.

    c. The system will store and analysis the real-time monitoring data on the server to automatically open or close the specified device, such as remote control watering, switching shutter, adding oxygen or CO_2, etc.

2) About the solutions of building an intelligent agricultural system, discuss how to implement each solution with up-to-date wireless, sensor and GPS technologies:

    a. Wireless sensor network technology is applied in an intelligent agricultural system to achieve data collection and control.

    b. A smart agricultural greenhouse equipped with wireless sensors to monitor the environmental parameters like air/soil temperature, humidity, moisture, light and CO_2 concentration.

3.9 Answer the following two updated assessment of GPS technologies and four systems built in the USA, Russia, the EU and China. Wikepedia may be a good source of quick information:

    a) What are the differences between civilian and military applications of various GPS systems?

    b) Report several interesting civilian applications of GPS services.

    c) What are the potential military applications of GPS capabilities?

3.10 We have studied three IoT applications in Examples 3.1 to 3.8. Make some investigation and search for another meaningful IoT application. Submit an investigated report in similar depth as in the examples. Dig out as much technical information as you can from the literature or other sources. Report on the interesting IoT features, hardware and software advances, interaction models applied, and available performance results both quantitatively and qualitatively. Do not produce a hand-waving report. Everything you report must be substantiated with evidence and analysis.

References

1 P. Abouzar, K. Shafiee, D. Michelson and V.C.M. Leung, Action-based scheduling technique for 802.15.4/ZigBee wireless body area networks. *IEEE PIMRC*, Toronto, ON, September 2011.

2 Bluetooth Low Energy Specification, Bluetooth Special Interest Group, http://www.bluetooth.com

3 H. Cao, H. Li, L. Stocco and V.C.M. Leung, Wireless three-pad ECG system: Challenges, design and evaluations. *Journal of Communications and Networks*, 13(2), 113–124, 2011.

4 K. Chen and D. Ran, *C-RAN: The Road towards Green RAN*. White Paper, China Mobile Research Institute, Beijing, October 2011.

5 M. Chen, S. Gonzalez, A. Vasilakos, H. Cao and V. Leung, Body area networks: A survey. *ACM/Springer Mobile Networks and Applications* (MONET), 16(2), 171–193, 2010.

6 T. Chen and Z Du, et al., DianNao: A small-footprint high-throughput accelerator for ubiquitous *machine-learning. Proceedings of 19th International Conference on Architectural Support for Programming Languages and Operating Systems* (ASPLOS'14), 2014.

7 J. Dean, Large-scale Deep Learning for Intelligent Computer Systems, Slide Presentation, 2016

8 D, Gardner and G.M. Shepherd, A gateway to the future of neuroinformatics. *Neuroinformatics*, 2(3), 271–274, 2004.

9 E. Farella, A. Pieracci, L. Benini, L. Rochi and A. Acquaviva, Interfacing human and computer with wireless body area sensor networks: The WiMoCA solution. *Multimedia Tools and Applications*, 38(3), 337–363, 2008.

10 J. Gubbi, R. Buyya, S. Marusic and M. Palaniswami, Internet of things: A vision, architectural elements and future direction. *Future Generation of Computer Systems*, 29, 1645–1660, 2013.

11 S. González-Valenzuela, M. Chen and V.C.M. Leung, Mobility support for health monitoring at home using wearable sensors. *IEEE Trans. Information Technology in BioMedicine*, 15(4), 539–549, 2011.

12 I. Jantunen et al., Smart sensor architecture for mobile-terminal-centric ambient intelligence. *Sensors and Actuators A: Physical*, 142(1), 352–360, 2004.

13 E.A. Lee, Cyber physical systems: design challenges. *IEEE International Symposium on Object Oriented Real Time Distributed Computing*, 363–369, May 2008.

14 G. Lo, A. Suresh, S. Gonzalez-Valenzuela, L. Stocco and V.C.M. Leung, A wireless sensor system for motion analysis of Parkinson's disease patients. *Proceedings of the IEEE PerCom*, Seattle, WA, March 2011.

15 H. Li and J. Tan, Heartbeat driven medium access control for body sensor networks. *Proceedings of the ACM SIGMOBILE*, San Juan, Puerto Rico, 2007.

16 S. Liu, T. Chen, et al., Cambricon: An instruction set architecture for neural networks. *Proceedings of the 43rd ACM/IEEE International Symposium on Computer Architecture* (ISCA'16), 2016.

17 G.A. Miller, The cognitive revolution: a historical perspective. *Trends in Cognitive Sciences* 7: 141–144, 2004.

18 A. Milenkovic, C. Otto and E. Jovanov, Wireless sensor networks for personal health monitoring: Issues and an implementation. *Computer Communications*, 29(13–14), 2521–2533, 2006.

19 P. Merolla, et al., A million spiking neuron integrated circuit with a scalable network and interface. *Science*, 345(6197), 2014.

20 S. Pentland, Healthwear: Medical technology becomes wearable. *IEEE Computer*, 37(5), 42–49, 2004.

21 C. Perera, A. Zaslavsky, P. Christen and D. Georgakopoulos, Context aware computing for the Internet of Things: A survey, *IEEE Community Surveys Tutorials*, 16(1), 414–454, 2013.

22 TinyOS Website, available at http://tinyos.net/, 2011.

23 D. Terdiman, IBM's TrueNorth processor mimics the human brain, http://www.cnet.com/news/ibms-truenorth-processor-mimics-the-human-brain/, 2014.

24 N. Torabi and V.C.M. Leung, Robust license-free body area network access for reliable public m-health services. *Proceedings of the IEEE HealthCom*, Columbia, MO, June 2011.

25 A. Zaslavsky, C. Perera and D. Georgakopoulos, Sensing as a service and big data. *Proceedings of the International Conference Advanced Cloud Computing (ACC)*, Bangalore, India, 21–29, July 2012.

26 ZigBee Specification, ZigBee Alliance, 2005, http://www.zigbee.org

Part 2

Machine Learning and Deep Learning Algorithms

4

Supervised Machine Learning Algorithms

CHAPTER OUTLINE

4.1 Taxonomy of Machine Learning Algorithms, 157
    4.1.1 Machine Learning Based on Learning Styles, 158
    4.1.2 Machine Learning Based on Similarity Testing, 159
    4.1.3 Supervised Machine Learning Algorithms, 162
    4.1.4 Unsupervised Machine Learning Algorithms, 163
4.2 Regression Methods for Machine Learning, 164
    4.2.1 Basic Concepts of Regression Analysis, 164
    4.2.2 Linear Regression for Prediction and Forecast, 166
    4.2.3 Logistic Regression for Classification, 169
4.3 Supervised Classification Methods, 171
    4.3.1 Decision Trees for Machine Learning, 171
    4.3.2 Rule-based Classification, 175
    4.3.3 The Nearest Neighbor Classifier, 181
    4.3.4 Support Vector Machines, 183
4.4 Bayesian Network and Ensemble Methods, 187
    4.4.1 Bayesian Classifiers, 188
    4.4.2 Bayesian Belief Networks, 191
    4.4.3 Random Forests and Ensemble Methods, 195
4.5 Conclusions, 200

4.1 Taxonomy of Machine Learning Algorithms

Machine learning (ML) is an actionable discipline extended from the study of pattern recognition and computational learning theory in artificial intelligence (AI). This field is highly relevant to statistical decision making and data mining in building AI or expert systems. The key idea is to use computers to learn from data. For tedious or unstructured data, machines can often make better and more unbiased decisions than the human learner. Toward this end, we need to write a computer program based on a model algorithm. Learning from given data objects, we can reveal the categorical class or experience affiliation of future data to be tested. This concept essentially defines ML as an operational term rather than a cognitive term.

To implement the ML task, we need to explore or construct computer algorithms to learn from data and make predictions on data based on their specific features, similarity or correlations. ML algorithms are operated by building a decision-making model from

Big-Data Analytics for Cloud, IoT and Cognitive Computing, First Edition. Kai Hwang and Min Chen.
© 2017 John Wiley & Sons Ltd. Published 2017 by John Wiley & Sons Ltd.
Companion Website: http://www.wiley.com/go/hwangIOT

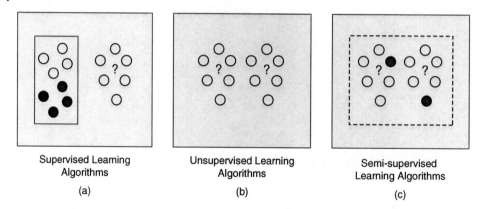

Figure 4.1 Machine learning algorithms grouped by different learning styles.

sample data inputs. The outputs of the ML model are the data-driven predictions or decisions. In Section 4.1.1, we classify ML algorithms by their learning styles. The style can be a supervised approach using some training data, or an unsupervised approach exploring hidden structures in data without training data. In Section 4.1.2, we group ML algorithms by their similarity in forms and functionality. Both supervised and unsupervised ML methods are plausible in real-life applications.

4.1.1 Machine Learning Based on Learning Styles

ML algorithms can be built with different styles in order to model a problem. The style is dictated by the interaction with the data environment expressed as the input to the model. The data interaction style decides the learning model that a ML algorithm can produce. The user must understand the roles of the input data and the model's construction process. The goal is to select the ML model that can solve the problem with the best prediction result. In this sense, ML sometimes overlaps with the goal of data mining. In Figure 4.1, we show three classes of ML algorithms based on different learning styles: supervised, unsupervised and semi-supervised. The style is hinged on how training data is used in the learning process:

- **Supervised learning:** The input data is called training data with a known label or result, which is depicted by the two types of circles in Figure 4.1(a) within the training data box. A model is constructed through training by using the training dataset. The model is improved by receiving feedback predictions. The learning process continues until the model achieves a desired level of accuracy on the training data. Future incoming data (without known labels) are tested on the constructed model. We will introduce various supervised ML algorithms in Section 4.1.3. Four major supervised algorithms are in subsequent sections.
- **Unsupervised learning:** All input data are not labeled with a known result, as shown in Figure 4.1(b). A model is generated by exploring the structures presented in the input data. This may be achieved by extracting general rules, going through a mathematical process to reduce redundancy, or organizing data by similarity testing. Example problems to be studied in Chapter 5 are clustering, dimensionality reduction and association rule.

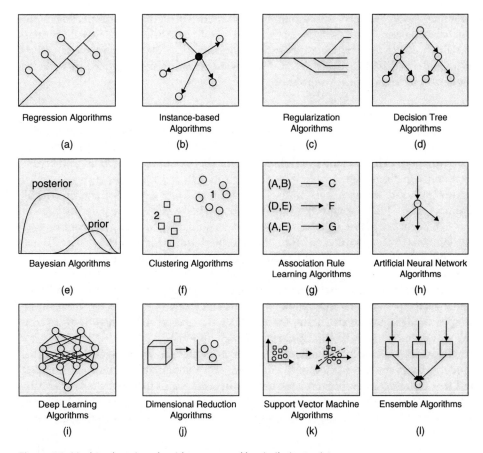

Figure 4.2 Machine learning algorithms grouped by similarity testing.

- **Semi-supervised learning:** In this case, the input data is a mixture of labeled and unlabeled examples, as shown in Figure 4.1(c). The model must learn the structures to organize the data to make predictions possible. Such problems and other ML algorithms will be described in Chapter 5 under different assumptions on how to model the unlabeled data.

4.1.2 Machine Learning Based on Similarity Testing

ML algorithms are distinguishable by applying different similarity testing functions in the learning process. For example, tree-based methods apply decision trees. The neural network is inspired by artificial neurons in a connectionist brain model. We could handle ML process subjectively by finding the best fit to solve the decision problem based on the characteristics in the processed datasets. Twelve categories of ML algorithms are briefly introduced below. The underlying key concepts are illustrated in Figure 4.2.

Some ML algorithms apply training data, including regression, decision trees, Bayesian networks and support vector machines. Other unsupervised algorithms apply no training dataset. Instead, they attempt to find hidden structures or properties in the entire input dataset. These include the clustering methods, association analysis, dimension reduction and artificial neural networks, etc. Some ML algorithms are covered in subsequent chapters, selectively. A lot of extensions from these ML algorithms will be summarized in Sections 4.1.3 and 4.1.4:

- **Regression:** this offers a supervised approach using statistical learning, as illustrated in Figure 4.2(a). Regression models the relationship between input data characteristics. The regression process is iteratively refined using an error criterion to make better predictions. This method minimizes the error between predicted value and actual experience in input data.
- **Instance-based learning:** this models a decision problem with instances or critical training data, as highlighted by the solid dots in Figure 4.2(b). The data instance is built up with a database of reliable examples. A similarity test is conducted to find the best match to make a prediction. This method is also known as memory-based learning, because representative data instances and similarity measures are stored in the database.
- **Regularization algorithms:** this method extends from the regression method that regulates the model to reduce complexity. This regularization process acts in favor of simpler models that are also better for generalization. Figure 4.2(c) shows how to sort the best prediction model among various design options.
- **Decision tree method:** this offers the decision model shown in Figure 4.2(d). The model is based on observation of the data's target values along various feature nodes in a tree-structured decision process. Various decision paths fork in the tree structure until a prediction decision is made at the leave node, hierarchically. Decision trees are trained on given data for better accuracy in solving classification and regression problems.
- **Bayesian methods:** these are based on statistical decision theory. It is often applied in pattern recognition, feature extraction and regression applications. A Bayesian network is shown in Figure 4.2(e), which offers a directed acyclic graph (DAG) model represented by a set of statistically independent random variables. Both prior and posterior probabilities are applied in making predictions. Again the model can be improved with the provision of a better training dataset.
- **Clustering Analysis:** this is a method based on grouping similar data objects as clusters. Two clusters are shown in Figure 4.2(f). Like regression, this method is unsupervised and modeled by using centroid-based clustering and/or hierarchal clustering. All clustering methods are based on similarity testing.
- **Association rule learning:** this is unsupervised with training data. Instead, the method generates inference rules that best explain observed relationships between variables in the data. These rules, as shown in Figure 4.2(g), are used to discover useful associations in large multidimensional datasets. These association patterns are often exploited by business enterprises or large organizations.
- **Artificial Neural Networks (ANN):** these are cognitive models inspired by the structure and function of biological neurons, as shown in Figure 4.2(h). The ANN tries to model the complex relationships between inputs and outputs. They form a class of pattern matching algorithms that are used for solving deep learning, regression and classification problems.

- **Deep Learning methods:** this extends from artificial neural networks by building much deeper and complex neural networks, as shown in Figure 4.2(i). Deep learning networks are built of multiple layers of interconnected artificial neurons. They are often used to mimic human brain processes in response to light, sound and visual signals. Deep learning will be studied in Chapter 5. This method is often applied to semi-supervised learning problems, where large datasets contain very little labeled data.

- **Dimensionality reduction:** this exploits the inherent structure in the data in an unsupervised manner. The purpose is to summarize or describe data using less information. This is done by visualizing multi-dimensional data with principal components or dimensions. Figure 4.2(j) shows the reduction from a 3-D e space to a 2-D data space. The simplified data can then be applied in a supervised learning method.

- **Support Vector Machines (SVM):** these are often used in supervised learning methods for regression and classification applications. Figure 4.2(k) shows how a hyperplane (a surface in a 3-D space) is generated to separate the training sample data space into different subspaces or categories. An SVM training algorithm builds a model to predict whether a new sample falls into one category or the other.

- **Ensemble methods:** these are models composed of multiple weaker models that are independently trained. The prediction results of these models are combined in Figure 4.2(l), which makes the collective prediction more accurate. Much effort is put into what types of weak learners to combine and the ways in which to combine them effectively. The ensemble model consists of mixed learners applying supervised, unsupervised or semi-supervised algorithms.

Table 4.1 summarizes six categories of machine learning algorithms by their functionality. Polynomial regression is a kind of regression method whose fitting function is a polynomial. The basic idea of stepwise regression is to bring variables in the model

Table 4.1 Classification of machine learning algorithms by functionality.

Functional Categories	Brief Description, Boldfaced Algorithms *are covered in this book*	Relevant Sections
Regression	Linear, Polynomial, Logistic, Stepwise, Exponential, MARS (Multivariate Adaptive Regression Splines)	4.2.1, 4.2.2
Instance-Based	KNN (k-nearest Neighbor), Neighboring, LVQ (Learning Vector Quantization), SOM (Self-Organizing Map), LWL (Locally Weighted Learning)	4.3.3, 4.3.4
Bayesian Networks	Naïve Bayesian, Gaussian, Multinomial, AODE (Averaged One-Dependence Estimators), BBN (Bayesian Belief Network), BN (Bayesian Network)	4.4.1, 4.3
Clustering	Clustering analysis, k-Means, Hierarchical Clustering, DBSCAN (Database Scan), Web-Cluster, COBWEB	5.2
Dimension Reduction	PCA (principal Component Analysis), MDS (Multi-Dimensional Scaling), SVD (Singular Value Decomposition), PCR (Principal Component Regression), and PLSR (Partial Least Squares Regression)	5.3
Ensemble	Neural Network, Bagging, Adaboost, Random Forests	4.4.3, 6.2.1

step by step, then we have to conduct an F-test before introducing each explanatory variable to confirm whether to introduce this variable to the model or not. Learning Vector Quantization (LVQ) is a neural network method based on the model. The idea of the Self-Organizing Map (SOM) is that a neural network will be portioned into different corresponding areas when accepting external inputs, where each area has different reflection to inputs and this procedure is completed automatically.

Gaussian Bayesian is a kind of Bayesian classification whose attributes are continual and follow the Gaussian distribution. Multinomial Bayesian is a special Naïve Bayesian, which uses polynomial distribution to compute the probability. Averaged one-dependence estimators (AODE) is a probabilistic classification learning technique. It was developed to address the attribute-independence problem of the popular naive Bayesian classifier. The grid-based clustering method first divides object space into finite units to construct a grid structure, then completes the clustering by this grid structure. This method is widely used because its incremental implementation is easy and it can process high-dimensional data.

COBWEB is a frequently-used and simple incremental clustering method based on the model. Singular Value Decomposition (SVD) is a method using singular value decomposition to reduce the dimension of sample space. Bagging uses the given method of choosing combinations (also called the weak classifier) to obtain an optimize solution (or class label) to improve the accuracy of classification. Adaboost is an iterative algorithm whose core idea is to train different weak classifiers for the same training set, and then combine these weak classifiers to constitute a stronger final classifier.

4.1.3 Supervised Machine Learning Algorithms

In a supervised ML system, the computer learns from a training dataset of {input, output} pairs. The input comes from sample data given in certain formats such as the credit reports of borrowers. The output may be discrete, such as "yes" or "no" to a loan application. The output could be also continuous, such as the probability distribution that the loan can be paid off in time. The ultimate goal is to work out a reliable ML model that can map or produce the correct outputs from new inputs that were unseen before. The ML system acts like a finely tuned predictor function $g(x)$. The "learning" system is built with a sophisticated algorithm to optimize this function. Given an input data x in a credit report of a borrower, the system will accurately make a loan decision for the bank.

In this section, we present four families of important supervised ML algorithms, as listed in Table 4.2, where the boldface ones will be studied in subsequent sections. The remaining algorithms are just listed for readers to explore further. In classification, inputs are divided into two or more classes, and the learner must produce a model that assigns unseen inputs to one or more of these classes. This is typically tackled in a supervised way. Spam filtering is a good example of classification, where the inputs are email (or other) messages and the classes are "spam" and "not spam". In regression, also a supervised problem, the outputs are continuous rather than discrete.

Decision trees are used as a predictive model, which maps observations about an item to conclusions about the item's target value. Support vector machines (SVMs) are built with a set of supervised learning methods, also often used in classification and regression. The Bayesian network is a statistical decision model that represents a set of random

Table 4.2 Supervised machine learning algorithms.

ML Algorithm Classes	Algorithm Names, boldfaced ones *are those covered in this book*	Relevant Sections
Regression	Linear, Polynomial, Logistic, Stepwise, OLSR (Ordinary Least Squares Regression), LOESS (Locally Estimated Scatterplot Smoothing), MARS (Multivariate Adaptive Regression Splines)	4.2.2, 4.2.3
Classification	KNN (k-nearest Neighbor), Trees, Naïve Bayesian, SVM (Support Vector Machine), LVQ (Learning Vector Quantization), SOM (Self-Organizing Map), LWL (Locally Weighted Learning)	4.3.3, 4.4.3
Decision Trees	Decision trees, Random Forests, CART (Classification and Regression Tree), ID3 (Iterative Dichotomiser 3), CHAID (Chi-squared Automatic Interaction Detection), ID3 (Iterative Dichotomiser 3), CHAID (Chi-squared Automatic Interaction Detection)	4.3.1, 4.4.3
Bayesian Networks	Naïve Bayesian, Gaussian, Multinomial, AODE (Averaged One-Dependence Estimators), BBN (Bayesian Belief Network), BN (Bayesian Network)	4.3.3, 4.3

variables and their conditional independencies via a directed acyclic graph (DAG). For example, a Bayesian network could represent the probabilistic relationships between diseases and symptoms. Given symptoms, the network can be used to compute the probabilities of the presence of various diseases. Many efficient algorithms that perform medical diagnosis exist in the healthcare industry.

4.1.4 Unsupervised Machine Learning Algorithms

Unsupervised learning is typically used in finding special relationships within the dataset. There are no training examples used in this process. Instead, the system is given a set of data to find the patterns and correlations therein. Table 4.3 lists some reported ML algorithms that operate without supervision. For example, association rules are generated from input data to identify close-knit groups of friends in a social network database.

Table 4.3 Some unsupervised machine learning algorithms.

Algorithm Class	Unsupervised ML Algorithm Names, boldface algorithms *are covered in this book.*	Relevant Sections
Association Analysis	A priori, Association Rules, Eclat, FP-Growth	5.1
Clustering	Clustering analysis, k-means, Hierarchical Clustering, Expectation Maximization (EM), Density-based Clustering	5.2
Dimensionality Reduction	PCA (principal Component Analysis), Discriminant Analysis, MDS (Multi-Dimensional Scaling)	5.3
Artificial Neural Networks (ANNs)	Perceptron, Back propagation, RBFN (Radial Basis Function Network)	6.2.1

In clustering, a set of inputs is to be divided into groups. Unlike supervised classification, the groups are not known in advance, making this an unsupervised task. Density estimation finds the distribution of inputs in some space. Dimensionality reduction simplifies the inputs by mapping them into a lower-dimensional space. ANNs appear in perceptron and back propagation prediction systems.

4.2 Regression Methods for Machine Learning

Regression analysis methods are introduced below for machine learning. First, we present the basic concepts and underlying assumptions. Then we study linear and logistic regression methods that have been applied in machine learning frequently. Both mathematical models and numerical examples are given to clarify the ideas and learning process involved.

4.2.1 Basic Concepts of Regression Analysis

Regression analysis methods apply mathematical statistics to establish dependent variables and independent variables in a machine learning process. It is essentially to perform a sequence of parametric or non-parametric estimations. In other words, the method finds the causal relationship between the input and output variables. Usually, the estimation function can be determined by experience using *a priori* knowledge or visual observation of the data. We need to calculate the undetermined coefficients of the function by using some error criteria. Furthermore, the regression method can be applied to classify data by predicting the category tag of the data.

The independent variables are the inputs of the regression process, also known as the predictors. The dependent variable is the output of the process. The aim of regression analysis is to understand how the typical value of the dependent variable changes when any independent variable varies, while the other independent variables are left unchanged. Thus, regression analysis estimates the average value of the dependent variable when the independent variables are fixed. The estimated value is a function of the independent variables known as the regression function, which can be described by a probability distribution.

Regression analysis is widely used in machine learning for prediction and forecasting. It is essentially to reveal the causal relationships between the independent and dependent variables. We have to be very careful to make such predictions, because causality may lead to illusions or false relationships that may in turn mislead the users. Most regression methods are parametric in nature and have a finite dimension in the analysis space. In this book, we will not deal with nonparametric regression analysis, which may be infinite-dimensional. Like many other machine learning methods, the accuracy or performance depends on the quality of the dataset used. This is related to the data generation process and the underlying assumptions made. In a way, regression offers estimation of continuous response variables, as opposed to the discrete response variables used in classification that demand higher accuracy.

In the formulation of a regression process, the unknown parameters are often denoted as β, which may appear as a scalar or a vector. The independent variables are denoted as X and the dependent variable as Y. When multiple dimensions are involved, these parameters are vector in form. A regression model establishes the approximated relation between X, β and Y as follows:

$$Y \approx f(X, \beta) \tag{4.1}$$

The function $f(X, \beta)$ is usually approximated by the expected value $E(Y|X)$. The regression function f is based on the knowledge of the relationship between Y and X. If no such knowledge is available, an approximated handy form is chosen for f.

Consider the vector of unknown parameters β to have k components. We have three models to relate the inputs to the output, depending on the relative magnitude between the number N of observed data points of the form (X, Y) and the dimension k of the sample space:

- When $N < k$, most classical regression analysis methods can be applied. Since the defining equation is underdetermined, there are not enough data to recover the unknown parameters β.
- When $N = k$ and the function f is linear, the equations $Y = f(X, \beta)$ can be solved exactly without approximation, because there are N equations to solve N components in β. The solution is unique as long as the X components are linearly independent. If f is nonlinear, many solutions may exist or no solution at all.
- In general, we have the situation that $N > k$ data points. This implies that there is enough information in the data to estimate a unique value for β in an overdetermined situation.

Example 4.1   Regression with a Necessary Set of Independent Measurements
This example helps the reader to understand the necessary number of independent data needed to perform the regression analysis of continuous data measurements. Consider a regression model which has four unknown parameters, $\beta_0, \beta_1, \beta_3$ and β_4. Suppose an experimenter performs 10 measurements all at exactly the same value of independent variable vector $X = (X_1, X_2, X_3, X_4)$. The regression analysis fails to give a unique set of estimated values for the four unknown parameters. In other words, the experimenter did not get enough information to perform the regression prediction.

Under these circumstances, the best we can do is to estimate the average value and the standard deviation of the dependent variable Y. Similarly, measuring at two different values of X would give enough data for a regression with two unknowns, but not for three or more unknowns. If the experimenter had performed measurements at four different values of the independent variable vector X, then regression analysis would provide a unique set of estimates for the four unknown parameters in β.   ■

In the case of $N > k$, the measurement errors ε_i are normally distributed. There exists an excess of information contained in $(N - k)$ measurements, known as the degrees of freedom of the regression. Listed below are three basic assumptions for regression analysis:

1) The sample is representative of the data space involved. The error is a random variable with a mean of zero conditional on the explanatory variables.
2) The independent variables are measured with no error. The predictors are linearly independent.

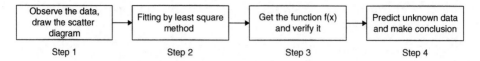

Observe the data, draw the scatter diagram	Fitting by least square method	Get the function f(x) and verify it	Predict unknown data and make conclusion
Step 1	Step 2	Step 3	Step 4

Figure 4.3 Major steps in linear regression.

3) The errors are uncorrelated and the variance of the error is constant across observations. If not, the weighted least squares methods may be used.

4.2.2 Linear Regression for Prediction and Forecast

Regression analysis is a statistical method that determines the quantitative relation where two or more variables are dependent on each other, including linear regression and nonlinear regression. If only one independent variable and one dependent variable are included in regression analysis, and if the approximate representation for the relation between the two can be conducted with a straight line, this kind of regression analysis is called unitary linear regression analysis. If two or more independent variables are included in regression analysis, and if there is linear relation between dependent variable and independent variables, then this is called multivariate linear regression analysis. The model of a linear regression is defined by $y = f(X)$, where $X = (x_1, x_2, \cdots, x_n)$ is a multi-dimensional vector and y is scalar variable. The linear regression is specified in Figure 4.3 in four steps.

4.2.2.1. Unitary Linear Regression Analysis

Consider a set of data elements in a 2-D sample space, $(x_1, y_1), (x_2, y_2), \cdots, (x_n, y_n)$. All points are mapped into a scatter diagram. If they can be covered, approximately, by a straight line, then we obtain the following linear regression expression:

$$y = ax + b + \varepsilon \tag{4.2}$$

where x stands for explanatory variable, y stands for explained variable, a and b are corresponding coefficients, and ε is the random error, which follows independent normal distribution with the same distribution with mean $E(\varepsilon)$ and variance $Var(\varepsilon)$. Then we need to work out the expectation by using a linear regression expression:

$$y = ax + b \tag{4.3}$$

Figure 4.4 shows residual error of unitary regression model. The main task for regression analysis is to conduct estimations for coefficient a and b through observations on

Figure 4.4 Unitary linear regression analysis.

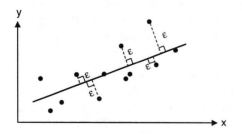

n groups of samples. The common method is the least square method, and its objective function is given by:

$$\min \; Q(\hat{a}, \hat{b}) = \sum_{i=1}^{n} \varepsilon_i^2 = \sum_{i=1}^{n} [y_i - E(y_i)]^2 = \sum_{i=1}^{n} (y_i - \hat{a}x_i - \hat{b})^2 \tag{4.4}$$

To minimize the sum of squares, we need to calculate the partial derivative of Q for $\hat{a}, \hat{b}$, and make them zero, as shown below:

$$\begin{cases} \dfrac{\partial Q}{\partial \hat{b}} = \sum_{i=1}^{n} (y_i - \hat{a}x_i - \hat{b}) = 0 \\[2mm] \dfrac{\partial Q}{\partial \hat{a}} = \sum_{i=1}^{n} (y_i - \hat{a}x_i - \hat{b})x_i = 0 \end{cases} \xrightarrow{\text{solve}} \begin{cases} \hat{a} = \dfrac{\displaystyle\sum_{i=1}^{n} (x_i - \bar{x})(y_i - \bar{y})}{\displaystyle\sum_{i=1}^{n} (x_i - \bar{x})^2} \\[4mm] \hat{b} = \bar{y} - \hat{a}\bar{x} \end{cases} \tag{4.5}$$

where $\bar{x}, \bar{y}$ are mean values for independent variable and dependent variable, respectively. Thus the specific expression for unitary linear regression analysis may be worked out. After working out the specific expression for the model, we want to know the fitting degree of that expression to the dataset, whether the expression can express the relation between the two variables, and whether it can be used in actual predictions. The closer R^2 (the coefficient of determination) is to 1, the better the fitting degree is, and the further R^2 is away from 1, the worse fitting degree is:

$$R^2 = 1 - \frac{\displaystyle\sum_{i=1}^{n} (y_i - \hat{y}_i)^2}{\displaystyle\sum_{i=1}^{n} (y_i - \bar{y}_i)^2}, \; 0 \geq R^2 \geq 1 \tag{4.6}$$

It should be noted that linear regression can be used not only for prediction but also for classification, but classification is only used in allusions to binary classification problems. When we calculate the regression equation $y = \hat{a}x + \hat{b}$, we may work out the estimated value of the dependent variable for each sample in the training dataset; the formula is $\hat{y} = \hat{a}x + \hat{b}$, thus it assumes two possible values:

$$class = \begin{cases} 1 & y_i > \hat{y}_i \\ 0 & y_i < \hat{y}_i \end{cases} \quad i = 1, 2, \cdots, n \tag{4.6}$$

The initial data (x_0, y_0) is used for classification. First, we determine $\hat{y}_0$ by using the dependent variable x_0, then we compare $y_0, \hat{y}_0$ to determine to which class it belongs. For multivariate linear regression, as studied below, this method is also applied to classify a dataset.

4.2.2.2. Multivariate Linear Regression Analysis

During solving actual problems, we will often encounter many variables. For instance, the scores of a student may be influenced by factors such as his or her earnestness in class, preparation before class and review after class; the health of a man is not only influenced by his environment, it is also related to his or her dietary habits at ordinary times. All these indicate that the model of unitary linear regression is not adapted to many conditions, so we make improvements to it and put forth a model of multivariate linear regression analysis, the structure of which is given below:

$$\begin{cases} y = \beta_0 + \beta_1 x_1 + \cdots + \beta_m x_m + \varepsilon \\ \varepsilon - N(0, \sigma^2) \end{cases} \tag{4.7}$$

Therefore, $\beta_0, \beta_1, \cdots, \beta_m, \sigma^2$ are unknown parameters, and ε complies with normal distribution where the mean value is 0 and the variance is equal to σ^2. By working out the expectation for the structure above, and we get the multivariate linear regression equation (substituted y for $E(y)$) as:

$$y = \beta_0 + \beta_1 x_1 + \cdots + \beta_m x_m \tag{4.8}$$

Its matrix form is given as $y = X\beta$, where $X = [1, x_1, \cdots, x_m]$, $\beta = [\beta_0, \beta_1, \cdots, \beta_m]^T$. Similarly, we need to estimate parameter β. Figure out $\hat{\beta}$ with the least square method. Its objective is given as

$$\min \ Q = \sum_{i=1}^{n} \varepsilon_i^2 = \sum_{i=1}^{n} (y_i - \beta_0 - \beta_1 x_{i1} - \cdots - \beta_m x_{im})^2 \tag{4.9}$$

To make the sum of squares, we need to make the partial derivative for β. This process gives

$$\begin{cases} \dfrac{\partial Q}{\partial \beta_0} = -2 \sum_{i=1}^{n} (y_i - \beta_0 - \beta_1 x_{i1} - \cdots - \beta_m x_{im}) = 0 \\[2mm] \dfrac{\partial Q}{\partial \beta_j} = -2 \sum_{i=1}^{n} (y_i - \beta_0 - \beta_1 x_{i1} - \cdots - \beta_m x_{im}) x_{ij} = 0 \\[2mm] j = 1, 2, \cdots, m \end{cases} \xrightarrow{\text{solve}} \hat{\beta} = (X^T X)^{-1} X^T Y \tag{4.10}$$

Therefore the final regression equation obtained is $y = X\hat{\beta} = \hat{\beta}_0 + \hat{\beta}_1 x_1 + \cdots + \hat{\beta}_m x_m$.

In fact, multivariate regression is an expansion and extension of unitary regression; they are identical in nature, but their range of applications is different. Unitary regression is an allusion to problems with one independent variable and one dependent variable, while multivariate regression is applicable to problems with multiple independent variables and one dependent variable.

Example 4.2   Healthcare Data Analysis with Linear Regression

With the improvement of the economy, more people are concerned about their health condition. As an example, obesity is reflected by the weight index. A fat person is more likely to have high blood pressure or diabetes. Using a linear regression model, we predict the relationship between obesity and high blood pressure.

Table 4.4 shows the dataset for body weight index and blood pressure of some people who received a health examination at a hospital in Wuhan, China. We conduct a preliminary judgment on what is the datum of blood pressure of a person with a body weight index of 24.

This is a prediction model with two variables, so the unitary linear regression may be considered. First, determine distribution of the data points, and draw a scatter diagram for body weight index–blood pressure with MATLAB, as shown in Figure 4.5.

Table 4.4 Data sheet for body weight index and blood pressure.

Id	Body Weight Index	Blood Pressure (mmHg)	Id	Body Weight Index	Blood Pressure (mmHg)
1	20.9	123	8	21.4	126
2	21.5	123	9	21.4	124
3	19.6	123	10	25.3	129
4	26	130	11	22.4	124
5	16.8	119	12	26.1	133
6	25.9	131	13	23	129
7	21.6	127	14	16	118

All data points are almost on or below the straight line, and they are linearly distributed. Therefore, the data space is modeled by a unitary linear regression process. By the least square method, we get a = 1.32 and b = 96.58. Therefore we have $y = 1.32x + 96.58$. A significance test is needed to verify whether the model will fit well with the current data. Then a prediction is made through calculation, so the mean residual and coefficient of determination of the model are: average error is 1.17 and $R^2 = 0.90$.

The mean residual is much less than the mean value 125.6 of blood pressure, and the coefficient of determination is close to 1. Therefore, it can be concluded that this regression equation is significant, and can fit well into the dataset, and that predictions may be conducted for unknown data on this basis. Results of the regression model are shown, as in Figure 4.5. The value of blood pressure of a person may be determined with the model obtained and given body weight index. Substitute 24 for x, and we can get the value of blood pressure of that person as $y = 1.32 \times 24 + 96.58 = 128$. ∎

4.2.3 Logistic Regression for Classification

Logistic regression is a linear regression analysis model in a broad sense, and may be used for prediction and classification. It is commonly used in fields such as data mining, automatic diagnosis for diseases and economical prediction. However, what calls for attention is that the Logistic Model may only be used to solve problems of dichotomy. As

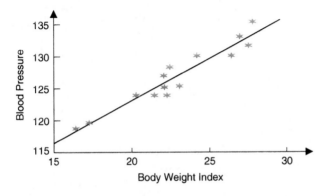

Figure 4.5 The relation between body weight and blood pressure.

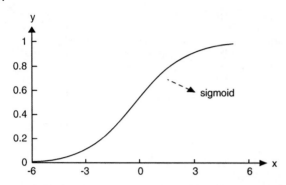

Figure 4.6 The curve of the sigmoid function applied in the regression method.

for logistic regression classification (LR classifier for short), the principle is to conduct classification to sample data with the logistic function; the expression for the logistic function (generally known as the sigmoid function) is expressed by

$$f(x) = \frac{1}{1 + e^{-z}} \tag{4.11}$$

As for that function, the domain of definition is $(-\infty, +\infty)$, and the value range is $(0, 1)$; therefore, we may regard the sigmoid function as the probability density function for sample data. Its function image is as Figure 4.6.

The image is sensitive, if $z = 0$, and not sensitive if $z \gg 0$ or $z \ll 0$; therefore, sample data may be concentrated at both ends of the sigmoid function by the use of intermediate feature z of the sample, thus they can be divided into two classes. This is the basic idea for logistic regression. Consider vector x with m independent variables $x = (x_1, x_2, x_3, \cdots, x_m)$. Each dimension of x stands for one attribute (feature) of sample data (training data). In logistic regression, multiple features of the sample data are combined into one feature by using the linear function:

$$z = \beta_0 + \beta_1 x_1 + \beta_2 x_2 + \cdots \beta_m x_m \tag{4.12}$$

By figuring out the probability of that feature in designated data, and utilizing the sigmoid function to act on that feature, we obtain the expression for the logistic regression defined below. The result is plotted in Figure 4.7.

$$\begin{cases} P(Y = 1|x) = \pi(x) = \dfrac{1}{1 + e^{-z}} \\ z = \beta_0 + \beta_1 x_1 + \beta_2 x_2 + \cdots \beta_m x_m \end{cases} \rightarrow \begin{cases} x \in 1, & \textit{if } P(Y = 1|x) > 0.5 \\ x \in 0, & \textit{if } P(Y = 0|x) < 0.5 \end{cases} \tag{4.13}$$

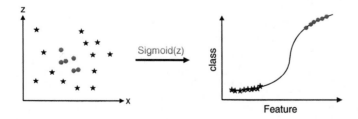

Figure 4.7 Principle of using logistic regression for classification purposes.

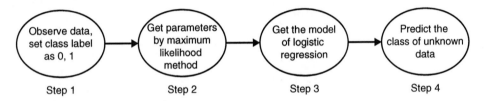

| Step 1 | Step 2 | Step 3 | Step 4 |

Figure 4.8 Four steps for the logistic regression process.

During combining of multiple features into one feature, we make use of the linear function, but we do not know the coefficient of the linear function (i.e. feature weight of sample data), so weight needs to be determined. Generally, maximum likelihood estimation is adopted to transform it into an optimization problem, and the coefficient is determined through the optimization method. In conclusion, general steps for logistic regression are as in Figure 4.8.

4.3 Supervised Classification Methods

The classification algorithm is often used in supervised machine learning. The input data is the training data. Every training data is given a specific label. For example, the label of "spam" or "legitimate mail" may be given to label each sample mail in the training set of a spam filtering system. Supervised learning needs to build a prediction model with an acceptable level of accuracy. The model keeps improving its accuracy by comparing predicted result with the labeled results from the training set. The model constantly adjusts its prediction mechanism until the predicted result reaches a specific level of accuracy.

Typically, the generation of a classifier model goes through three steps, as shown in Figure 4.9, for a two-class problem. Step 1 divides the sample dataset into two subsets (positive versus negative). The classified model is built by training at step 2. Finally, the model accuracy is determined by using a likelihood probability. In this section, we will study four families of supervised classification methods: namely the decision tree, rule-based classifier, nearest neighbor classifier and support-vector machines.

4.3.1 Decision Trees for Machine Learning

A decision tree offers a predictive model in both data mining and machine learning. We will concentrate on the machine learning using decision trees. The goal is to create a

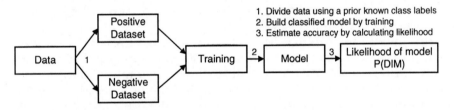

Figure 4.9 Three steps in building a classification model through sample data training.

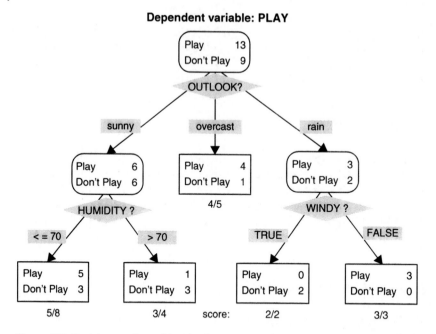

Figure 4.10 Decision tree for making the decision to play tennis or not with probability given at the leaf node.

model that predicts the value of an output target variable at the leaf nodes of the tree, based on several input variables or attributes at the root and interior nodes of that tree. Decision trees for classification are known as classification trees.

In a classification tree, leaves represent class labels and branches represent conjunctions of attributes that lead to the class labels. The target variable (output) can take two values (such as yes or no) or multiple discrete values (such as outcomes 1, 2, 3 or 4 of an event). The arcs from a node are labeled with each of the possible values of the attribute. Each leaf of the tree is labeled with a class or a probability distribution over the classes. Decision trees, where the target variable assumes continuous values (like real numbers), are called regression trees.

The decision tree follows a multi-level tree structure to make decisions at the leaf nodes of a tree. The concept is illustrated by the example in Figure 4.10. In this tree, we need to decide whether to go out playing tennis under various weather conditions. The weather conditions are indicated by three attributes: outlook, humidity and wind. The outlook is checked at the root, which has three possible outgoing arcs marked as sunny, overcast or rain. The humidity is fanning out to two arcs labeled as more than 70 or not. The wind values are simply true or false.

To traverse this tree, we start from the root to a leaf along a path of one or two levels. Inside each tree node, the target counts are given to determine the probability if a leaf node is reached. For example, if the outlook value is overcast, we reach a leaf node with a probability of 4/5 to play tennis. On the other hand, if the outlook is sunny and the humidity is above 70, we reach the leaf node at the extreme left with a probability of 5/8 to play tennis. Similarly, we can also reach other leaf nodes with different probabilities.

Figure 4.11 Decision tree for approving loan applications to bank customers.

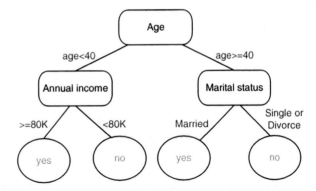

In the case of simple prediction decision, the target value could be just class labels (such as yes or no) without probability indicated, as seen in Example 4.3.

Example 4.3   Bank Loan Approval using Decision Tree with Training Data

Consider using the decision tree to make a decision on whether a bank will approve a loan application from its customer. The dataset is classified with three attributes: age, annual income and marital status. The internal node at each level tests on one attribute. Each leaf node represents one class decision: "yes" means approval and "no" for the opposite. Figure 4.11 shows the decision tree already built by the bank.

During constructing the decision tree, applicant age is considered first at the root node. Age partitions training samples into two categories: those less than 40 versus otherwise. The annual income attribute is then tested at the second level. Finally, marital status is used to make the decision on approving the loan or not.

Now, use the decision tree to test the acceptability of an applicant who is younger than 40 and with an annual income lower than $80,000. By traversing through the tree, we obtain the decision to deny the loan application. Obviously, the bank acts in favor of young applicants with higher income and for the older applicants who are not single or divorced. ∎

There are methods, ID3, C4.5 and CART, for choosing a top-down approach to constructing the decision tree from the training sample set. In general, the training sample set is recursively partitioned into smaller subsets. We only introduce the ID3 (Iterative Dichotomiser 3) algorithm below. The C4.5 is the improved successor of ID3 and the CART method combines classification and regression in the tree construction.

4.3.1.1.   ID3 Algorithm Tagging

The core idea of the ID3 algorithm takes the information gain of the attribute as the measure, and splits the attribute with the largest information gain after splitting, to make the output partition on each branch belong to the same class as far as possible. The measure standard of information gain is entropy, which depicts the purity of any example set. Given a training set S of positive and negative examples, the entropy function of S is defined as

$$Entropy(S) = -p_+ \log_2^{p_+} - p_- \log_2^{p_-}$$
(4.14)

Table 4.5 Training Dataset used in Example 4.4.

RID	Annual income($)	Age	Marital status	Class: load
1	70 K	18	Single	No
2	230 K	35	Divorce	Yes
3	120 K	28	Married	Yes
4	200 K	30	Married	Yes

where p_+ represents positive examples and p_- represents negative examples. If the target attribute possesses m different values, then the entropy of S relative to classifications of m classes is defined by

$$Entropy(S) = \sum_{i=1}^{m} -p_i \log_2^{p_i} \tag{4.15}$$

The measure standard of the effectiveness of training data is defined as the entropy, which is the standard for measuring training example set purity, and the above measure standard is called the "information gain". The information gain of an attribute shows the decrease of expected entropy caused by segmented examples. We define the gain $Gain(S, A)$ of an attribute A in set S as

$$Gain(S, A) = Entropy(S) - \sum_{v \in V(A)} \frac{|S_v|}{|S|} Entropy(S_v) \tag{4.16}$$

where $V(A)$ is the range of A, S is the sample set and S_v is the sample set with A value equal to v.

Example 4.4   Decision Tree Prediction using the ID3 Algorithm

Given a training set D with 500 samples, where the data format is shown in Table 4.5, and class label attribute "load" has two different values (i.e. {*yes*, *no*}), therefore there are two different categories (i.e. $m = 2$). Suppose category *C1* corresponds to "*yes*", and category *C2* corresponds to "*no*". There are 300 tuples in category "*yes*", and 200 tuples in category "*no*". And (root) node N is created for tuples in D. The information gain of each attribute must be calculated in order to find the split criterion of those tuples.

The entropy value is used to classify the tuples in D as

$$Entropy(D) = -\frac{2}{5} \log_2^{\frac{2}{5}} - \frac{3}{5} \log_2^{\frac{3}{5}} = 0.971 \tag{4.17}$$

Then we calculate the expected information demand of each attribute. For the income attribute of equal or greater than 80 K, there are 250 "*yes*" tuples and 100 "*no*" tuples. For the income attribute of less than 80 K, there are 50 "*yes*" tuples and 100 "*no*" tuples. When information gain is used, if the tuples are partitioned by annual income, the expected entropy for classifying the tuples in D is

$$Entropy_{income}(D) = \frac{7}{10} \times \left(-\frac{5}{7} \log_2^{\frac{5}{7}} - \frac{2}{7} \log_2^{\frac{2}{7}} \right) + \frac{3}{10} \times \left(-\frac{1}{3} \log_2^{\frac{1}{3}} - \frac{2}{3} \log_2^{\frac{2}{3}} \right) = 0.8797 \tag{4.18}$$

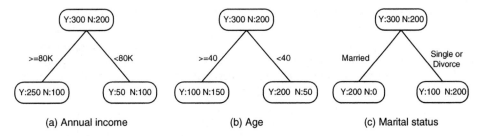

Figure 4.12 (a) Annual income (b) Age (c) Marital status

Figure 4.12 Decision tree partitions for three attributes in Example 4.4.

Therefore, the information gain of such a partition is expressed by

$$Gain(D, income) = Entropy(D) - Entropy_{income}(D) = 0.9710 - 0.8797 = 0.0913$$

$$(4.19)$$

The graphical representation is shown in Figure 4.12(a), the situation of age and marital statuses are as shown in Figures 4.12(b) and (c); similarly, information of age and marital status can be calculated. The attribute with the largest information gain is selected to construct the tree. From the above calculation, the information gain is the largest when using age attribute, therefore this attribute is selected to be the classification criterion. ∎

4.3.2 Rule-based Classification

Classification techniques have been applied in many fields, such as automatic text classification technique in information retrieval and search engines, and intrusion detection in the field of security. Researchers in the field of machine learning, expert systems, statistics and neural networks have put forward a number of specific classification forecasting methods. This section will focus on rule-based classification techniques.

The rule-based classifier is a technique to use a set of "if then…" rules to classify records, usually representing model rules in disjunctive normal form as given by $R = (r_1 \vee r_2 \cdots \vee r_k)$, where R means rule set, while r_i is the classification rule or disjunction. Consider the use of three prediction rules:

1) r_1: (Body temperature = Cold blood) → Non-mammalian
2) r_2: (Body temperature = Constant temperature) ∧ (Viviparity = Yes) → Mammalian
3) r_3: (Body temperature = Constant) ∧ (Viviparity = No) → Non-mammalian

Each classification rule is represented by r_i : $(Condition_i) \rightarrow y_i$. The left side of the rule is called the premise or rule antecedent, and the right side of the rule is called the conclusion or rule consequent. If a record meets a rule, we say that it was activated or triggered; or the record is covered by the rule. In general, the rule antecedent is represented by $Condition_i = (A_1 \ op \ v_1) \wedge (A_2 \ op \ v_2) \wedge \cdots (A_k \ op \ v_k)$, where each $(A_i \ op \ v_i)$ is called a conjunct and consists of attribute-value pairs and a logical operator (op), and generally $op \in \{=, \neq, <, >, \leq, \geq\}$.

For each class, there may be more than one rule that can apply. So, which rule is superior? In order to determine the quality of classification rules, we define the coverage precision function. For dataset D and classification rule: $r : A \rightarrow y$, rule coverage is defined as the proportion of records triggering rule r in D. Rule precision or confidence factor is defined as the proportion of records whose class label is equal to y in the records of triggering r. The mathematical formula is given as

$$
\begin{aligned}
Coverage(r) &= \frac{|A|}{|D|} \\
Accuracy(r) &= \frac{|A \cap y|}{|A|}
\end{aligned}
\tag{4.20}
$$

where $|A|$ is the number of records that meet the rule antecedent, $|A \cap y|$ is the number of records that meet both the rule antecedent and the rule consequent and $|D|$ is the total number of records.

Sometimes, we are not sure whether some of the rules in a given rule set are ineffective. Because some records can be triggered by more than one rule, this will lead to duplication of rules, while others may not be covered by any rule. Therefore, we consider two important properties to improve the applicability of the rules:

1) **Mutual exclusion rule:** If there are no rules triggered by the same record in the rule set R, it is said that rules in the rule set R are mutually exclusive. This property ensures that daily records are covered by one rule at most in R. The above rule set is a mutually exclusive one.
2) **Exhaustive rule:** if for any combination of property values, there is a rule in R to cover it, it is said that the rule set R is with exhaustive coverage. This property ensures that daily records are covered by one rule at least in R.

A rule set with both mutually exclusive and exhaustive properties ensures a record can be covered by one and only one rule. However, many rule sets cannot meet these two properties. If a rule set cannot meet the exhaustive property, a default rule r_d : $() \rightarrow y_d$ must be added to cover those uncovered records. If the antecedent of the default rule is empty, triggering will occur in case of the failure of all the rules and y_d is the default class. Often values of most of the classes of records are not covered by rules. If a rule set does not meet the mutually exclusive property, a record may be covered by more than one rule, and the classification of these rules may conflict; so how to determine the classification result of the record? The following two solutions are given:

1) **Ordered rules:** this kind of rule set is ordered from large to small in accordance with the rule priority, which is defined generally with precision, coverage and so on. When classifying, rules are scanned in sequence until a rule covering the record is found, and this rule will be the classification result of this record. General rule-based classifiers adopt this method.
2) **Unordered rules:** in this case, all rules are equal to each other. The rules are scanned successively, and after a record occurs, each will be chosen, and the one getting the most votes will be the final classification result of the record.

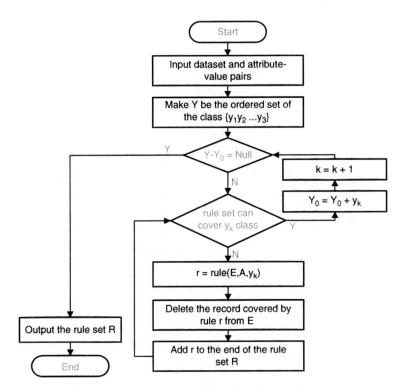

Figure 4.13 Sequential coverage and data flow for rule extraction.

4.3.2.1. Rule Extraction with Direct Rule

The sequential coverage algorithm is often used to directly extract rules from data, and the growth of rules is usually in a greedy manner based on some kind of evaluation measure. The algorithm extracts a class of rules at a time from the record containing more than one training data. A flow chart to illustrate the data flow is given in Figure 4.13. Here, E represents the training dataset, A is the attribute-value pairs $\{(A_j, v_j)\}$, and R is the rule set. First we input collection A of training dataset E and attribute-value pairs, then make Y the ordered set of the class $\{y_1, y_2, \cdots, y_k\}$, and $R = \{\}$ is the initial rule set. For each class y in Y, while the rule set can cover y class of training data, using function *Rule()* generates a rule r, deleting the record covered by rule r from E and adding r to the end of the rule set, namely $R = R \vee r$. Otherwise, end the circulation. Finally, add the default rule $() \rightarrow y_d$ to the end of the rule set.

The rule function is to extract a classification rule, which covers a larger number of positive examples with concentrated training, and covers none or only a few counter examples. In order to avoid exponential explosion, the function increases rules in a greedy manner. It first creates a rule r, and then constantly makes improvements to the rule until satisfying certain conditions; and then prunes the rule in order to improve its generalization error. Figure 4.14 shows a case of rule generation strategy from general to specific and from specific to general sample properties.

In general, set up an initial rule $r : \{\} \rightarrow y$, in which the rule antecedent is an empty set, and the consequent rule contains the target class. This rule covers all training set

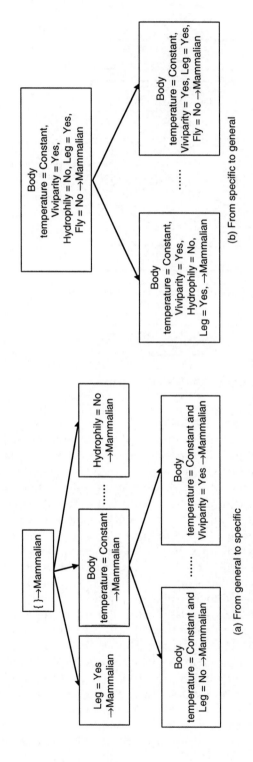

Figure 4.14 Rules generation strategies between general and specific properties.

records, so the quality is very poor. We can add new conjuncts to improve the quality of rules, which shall be continued until satisfying end conditions, such as conjuncts added cannot improve the quality of rules. We want to increase the rules in the strategy from general to specific, which can be conversed. That is, we can randomly select a positive example as the initial seed for rules increasing, and then delete a conjunct of rules to cover more positive examples to generalize rules until satisfying end conditions, such as rules appearing a counter example.

4.3.2.2. Rule Extraction from Decision Tree

Rule extraction from decision tree modeling is a common indirect method for rule extraction. In principle, each path of the decision tree from its root node to its leaf node may express a classification rule. Conditions for each path constitute the rule antecedent, while the class label of the leaf node constitutes the consequent rule. From the decision tree modeling in Figure 4.15, the following rule set is generated:

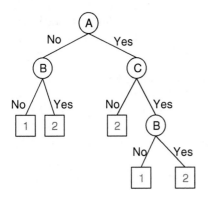
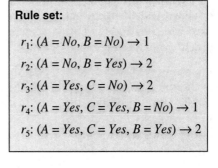

Rule set:

r_1: $(A = No, B = No) \rightarrow 1$

r_2: $(A = No, B = Yes) \rightarrow 2$

r_3: $(A = Yes, C = No) \rightarrow 2$

r_4: $(A = Yes, C = Yes, B = No) \rightarrow 1$

r_5: $(A = Yes, C = Yes, B = Yes) \rightarrow 2$

Figure 4.15 Rule set generated from using decision tree.

Taking r_2, r_3, r_5 and the following two rules into account:

$$r_6 : (B = Yes) \rightarrow 2$$
$$r_7 : (A = Yes) \wedge (C = No) \rightarrow 2$$

we find that r_2, r_3, r_5 may be replaced by r_6, r_7. In this way, it will be simpler to describe the decision tree modeling by the rules consisting of r_1, r_4, r_6, r_7. This is the content described by the C4.5 rule algorithm: first, use the decision tree to generate the rule set, then simplify the rule set and finally sort the rules.

Example 4.5 Diabetes Prediction using Rule-Based Classification

Table 4.6 shows a dataset of blood glucose (high, low), weight (overweight, normal), lipid content and diabetes (*yes, no*) from the physical examination of some people in Wuhan, based on which the corresponding rule sets may be constituted, and it will be convenient to classify people into two categories, i.e. the diabetic and the normal.

Table 4.6 Physical examination dataset for diabetes.

ID	Blood glucose	Weight	Blood lipid content (mmol/L)	Diabetic (Yes or No)
1	Low	Overweight	2.54	No
2	High	Normal	1.31	No
3	High	Overweight	1.13	No
4	Low	Normal	2.07	No
5	High	Overweight	2.34	Yes
6	High	Normal	0.55	No
7	Low	Overweight	2.48	No
8	High	Overweight	3.12	Yes
9	High	Normal	1.14	No
10	High	Overweight	8.29	Yes

First we need to determine the rule set and to classify people into two categories, i.e. the solvent and the insolvent, for which the consequent rule will be the diabetic (expressed with *Yes*) and the normal (expressed with *No*). Use the sequential coverage algorithm to generate rules.

1) Determine the classes {*Yes, No*}; and the normal people class to be (*No* class);
2) Use the strategy from general to specific to generate the rule { } → *No*;
3) Add the property of blood glucose (*A*), and generate the following rule: $r_1 : \{A = L\} \rightarrow No$;
4) Delete records with id of 1, 4 and 7, and add the above rules to the rule set *R*, then $R = \{r_1\}$;
5) Continue to add the property of weight (*B*), and generate $r_2 : \{A = H, B = Normal\} \rightarrow No$;
6) Delete records with id of 2, 6 and 9, and add rules to the rule set *R*, then $R = \{r_1, r_2\}$;
7) Consider blood lipid (*C*) and we get the rule: $r_3 : \{A = H, B = Overweight, C < 1.8\} \rightarrow No$;
8) Delete records with id of 3, and add rules to the rule set *R*, then $R = \{r_1, r_2, r_3\}$;
9) Inspect the diabetic class (*Yes* class);
10) Analyze it, and generate the following rule: $r_4 : \{A = H, B = Overweight, C > 1.8\} \rightarrow Yes$;
11) Delete records with id of 5, 8 and 10, and add rules to the rule set *R*, then $R = \{r_1, r_2, r_3, r_4\}$;
12) Now all training datasets have been deleted, so stop the circulation;
13) Finally, output the rule set R as follows:
14) From the above description, we get the following rule set:

$$r_1 : \{A = L\} \rightarrow No$$
$$r_2 : \{A = H, B = Normal\} \rightarrow No$$
$$r_3 : \{A = H, B = Overweight, C < 1.8\} \rightarrow No$$
$$r_4 : \{A = H, B = Overweight, C > 1.8\} \rightarrow Yes$$

■

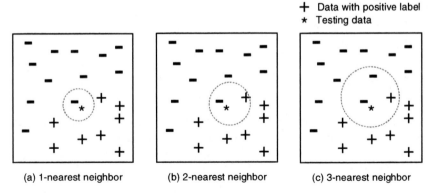

(a) 1-nearest neighbor   (b) 2-nearest neighbor   (c) 3-nearest neighbor

Figure 4.16 Instance of three kinds of nearest neighbors.

4.3.3 The Nearest Neighbor Classifier

The learning begins with the knowledge that the decision trees and rule-based classification have a training dataset with a mapping model built from input property to class
label. We call this the active learning method. However, we call the learning, when the
training dataset modeling is postponed until the test dataset can be used, the passive
learning method. The Rote classifier, a kind of passive learning method, will not classify the test data until it matches a certain training dataset instance completely. But the
method has an apparent disadvantage that most of the test data instances cannot be
classified, because no training dataset matches them. So an improved model called the
nearest neighbor classifier appears and we will give the details below.

The nearest neighbor classifier is used to find all the training dataset instances which
have the most similar properties as the test sample. The collection of these training
dataset instances is called the nearest neighbor of the test sample and the class labels are
determined according to these instances. So, the nearest neighbor classifier considers
each sample as the a n-dimensional point (total number of properties) dimension, and
determines the nearest neighbor between two given points. Generally, we use Euclidean
distance: $d(x, y) = \sum_{k=1}^{n} |x_k - y_k|$. An instance of three kinds of nearest neighbors are as
given in Figure 4.16.

It is very important to choose a proper distance threshold k. If k is too small, the nearest neighbor classifier tends to be affected by overfitting due to the noise from the training data; if k is too large, the nearest neighbor classifier may misclassify the test samples
because it contains data which are far from the nearest neighbor. We can determine the
class label of the test samples according to the class label in the nearest neighbor once
the nearest neighbor of the test samples is determined.

In the case where the class labels of the test samples are inconsistent with the coun-
terpart in the nearest neighbor, the class label in the nearest neighbor should be taken
as the class label of the test samples. In the case that some of the nearest neighbor samples are very important (e.g. the nearest neighbor with the smallest distance), the class
label choice can be carried out by the method of conferring weight coefficient. The two
methods of choosing the class label of test samples are called majority voting and

weighted distance voting respectively, of which the mathematical formulas are given by

$$
\begin{cases}
y = \underset{v}{\mathrm{argmax}} \sum_{(x_i, y_i) \in D_z} I(v = y_i) \\
y = \underset{v}{\mathrm{argmax}} \sum_{(x_i, y_i) \in D_z} w_i \times I(v = y_i)
\end{cases}
\tag{4.21}
$$

V means class label, D_Z means the nearest neighbor of the test sample, V_i is a class label of the nearest neighbor and $I(\cdot)$ is an indicator function defined as

$$
I(y_i) = \begin{cases} 1 & y_i = v \\ 0 & y_i \neq v \end{cases}
\tag{4.22}
$$

A flow chart is given in Figure 4.17. The variable k represents distance threshold, D is training dataset and z is test instance. First, we input k, D, z, then calculate the distance between the test instance and the training dataset sample. The samples whose $d\,(z, D)$ are lower than k are collected into set Dz. Then, making statistical use of the class label in Dz, we finally decide the class label of test instance by the majority voting method.

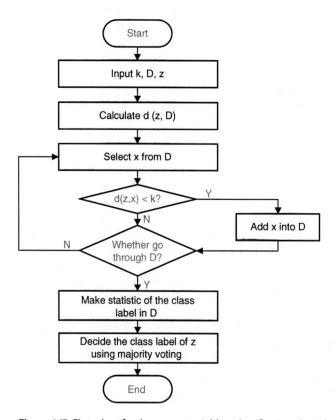

Figure 4.17 Flow chart for the nearest neighbor classification algorithm.

Table 4.7 Physical examination dataset for diabetes.

Id	Triglyceride (mmol/L)	Total cholesterol (mmol/L)	Hyperlipemia or not
1	1.33	4.19	No
2	1.31	4.32	No
3	1.95	5.02	Yes
4	1.86	5.17	Yes
5	1.30	537	Yes
6	1.30	4.36	No
7	2.04	4.42	Yes
8	1.45	4.68	No
9	1.35	4.41	Yes

Example 4.6   Hyperlipemia Prediction using Nearest Neighbor Algorithm

The hyperlipemia disease is attributed to two medical indexes: namely triglyceride and total cholesterol. Generally, people who have similar indexes may have similar health problems. We use nearest classifier to make a judgment as whether a patient has acquired hyperlipemia or not. Table 4.7 shows the dataset of triglyceride content, total cholesterol content and whether to have hyperlipemia (Yes, No) from nine potential patients. We consider those people to have hyperlipemia, if they have triglyceride content above 1.33 and a total cholesterol count above 4.32.

According to the problem, we can classify it by the nearest neighbor classifier with the test sample (1.33, 4.32). We set the threshold as 0.2 for this case and then the training dataset samples in the case of $id = 1$ is computed as $\sqrt{(1.33 - 1.33)^2 + (4.32 - 4.19)^2} = 0.13 < 0.2$.

The training dataset samples should be added into D_z. The training dataset sample in the case of $id = 2$ is $\sqrt{(1.33 - 1.31)^2 + (4.32 - 4.32)^2} = 0.02 < 0.2$. Thus, the training dataset samples should be added into D_z. The training dataset sample for $id = 3$ is computed as $\sqrt{(1.33 - 1.95)^2 + (4.32 - 5.02)^2} = 0.94 > 0.2$. Then, the training dataset samples should be discarded. With the remainder dealt with in the same manner, we obtain a collection of the nearest neighbors D_z as $D_z = \{x \mid id = 1, 2, 6, 9\}$.

There are Yes and No in the statistics of the nearest neighbor collection. Finally, we collect statistics of the above class label by a majority voting method, classifying those as No in the case of $id = 1$, 2 and 6 and those as Yes in the case of $id = 9$. The voting result is: $Yes = 1$, $No = 3$, which means the physically examined people are not suffering from hyperlipemia when the triglyceride content is 1.33 and the total cholesterol 4.32.   ∎

4.3.4   Support Vector Machines

The support vector offers another approach to classifying a multi-dimensional dataset. Samples on the margin are called the support vectors. We can use a straight line to separate the points in 2-D space, and use a plane to separate points in 3-D space. Similarly, we use the hyperplane to separate the points in high-dimensional space. We regard the

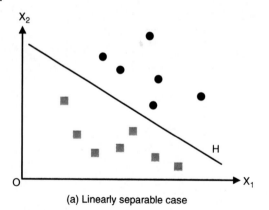

Figure 4.18 The concept of using SVM to classify between two classes of sample data.

(a) Linearly separable case

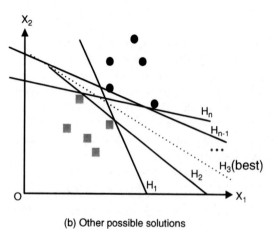

(b) Other possible solutions

points in the same area as one class, so that we can use SVM to solve the issues of classification. Whereas the original problem may be stated in a finite-dimensional space, it often happens that the sets to discriminate are not linearly separable in that space. For this reason, it is proposed that the original finite-dimensional space be mapped into a much higher-dimensional space, presumably making the separation easier in that space. Thus we can use the hyperplane to cluster these points in high-dimensional space.

4.3.4.1. Linear Decision Boundary

Consider a 2-D plane with two kinds of data, represented by red dots and blue dots, as Figure 4.18(a). These data are linearly separable, therefore one straight line is drawn between them. However, infinite straight lines can be drawn, as shown in Figure 4.18(b). How to find out the "best" line, i.e. the one with the minimum classification error? For example, consider the two-class problems in an n-dimensional space.

The two classes are separated by an $(n - 1)$-dimensional hyperplane, Consider a data point D is (X_1, y_1) $(X_{|D|}, y_{|D|})$, wherein, X_i is the training sample of n-dimension, with class label y_i. Each y_i can assume a value either of $+1$ for one class and/or -1 for the other classes. In this case, the $(n - 1)$-dimensional hyperplane is represented by

$$w^T x + b = 0 \tag{4.23}$$

Table 4.8 Dataset for using SVM in Example 4.8.

x_1	x_2	y
1	0.5	−1
0.5	1	−1
1	2	+1
3	1	+1
0.25	2	−1

where w and b are the parameters, and correspond to a straight line in the 2-D plane. It is certainly also hoped that the hyperplane can separate the two kinds of data, i.e. all the y_i corresponded by the data points on one side of the hyperplane are −1, and 1 on the other side. Make $f(x) = w^T x + b$, use $f(x) > 0$ point pairs for data points with y = 1, and $f(x) < 0$ point pairs for data points with y = −1.

Example 4.7   Classification using Support Vector Machine with Training Samples
The given 2-D data are as shown in the Table 4.8. Then one straight line $2x_1 + x_2 - 3 = 0$ can be found to separate the data in the table. The separating line is plotted in Figure 4.19. ∎

4.3.4.2.   Definition of Maximal Margin Hyperplane

Consider those squares and circles nearest to the decision boundary, as shown in Figure 4.20; adjust parameters w and b, and two parallel hyperplanes H_1 and H_2 can be represented by

$$H_1 : w^T x + b = 1 \qquad H_2 : w^T x + b = -1 \qquad (4.24)$$

The margin of the decision boundary is given by the distance between those two hyperplanes. To calculate the margin, make x_1 the data point on H_1, and x_2 the data

Figure 4.19 Sample space and a hyperplane solution for Example 4.7.

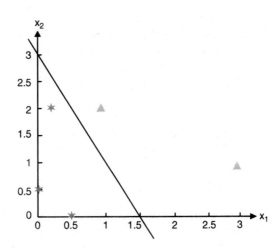

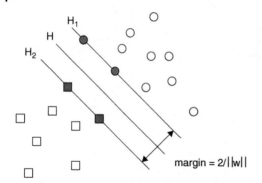

Figure 4.20 Linearly separating hyperplane with maximized margin from each class.

point on H_2, and insert x_1 and x_2 into the above formula, then margin d can be obtained by subtracting the formulas: $w^T(x_1 - x_2) = 2$, therefore: we have $d = \frac{2}{||w||}$

4.3.4.3. Formal SVM Model

The training phase of SVM includes estimation of parameters w and b from the training data, and the selected parameters must meet the following two conditions by

$$\begin{cases} w^T x_i + b \geq 1 & y_i = 1 \\ w^T x_i + b \leq -1 & y_i = -1 \end{cases} \tag{4.25}$$

Those two inequalities can be written as the following more compact forms as

$$y_i(w^T x_i + b) \geq 1 \quad i = 1, 2, \cdots, N \tag{4.26}$$

Maximization of the margin is equivalent to minimization of the following objective function:

$$f(w) = \frac{||w||^2}{2} \tag{4.27}$$

Therefore, SVM is obtained by finding the minimum objective function:

$$\min \frac{||w||^2}{2}, \quad subject\ to : y_i\left(w^T x_i + b\right) \geq 1 \quad i = 1, 2, ..., N \tag{4.28}$$

This is a convex optimization problem because the objective function is quadratic and the constraint condition is linear, and it can be solved through the standard Lagrange multiplier. We may need to adjust the model when the samples are not linearly insepa-rable. This situation is shown in Figure 4.21.

4.3.4.4. Non-linear Hyperplanes

As shown in the Figure 4.21, there exists an outlier (or noise), which make the sample space linearly inseparable. Some slack variable is introduced to avoid this case:

$$\begin{cases} w^T x_i + b \geq 1 - \xi_i & y_i = 1 \\ w^T x_i + b \leq -1 + \xi_i & y_i = -1 \end{cases} \tag{4.29}$$

With no restriction on misclassified samples on the boundary, the learning algorithm may find such a boundary with a wider margin by allowing many misclassified training

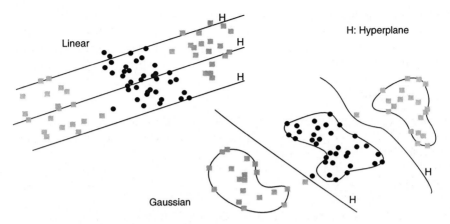

Figure 4.21 Nonlinear support vector machine.

samples. The objective function could be modified as flows to avoid boundaries with huge slack variable values:

$$f(w) = \frac{||w||^2}{2} + C\left(\sum_{i=1}^{N} \xi_i\right)^k \tag{4.30}$$

where C and k are parameters designated by the user, meaning the punishment to the misclassified training instances. That is to say, the more the outliers, the larger the objective function values. C means the weight of the outlier, therefore the final model is given as

$$\min\left\{\frac{||w||^2}{2} + C\left(\sum_{i=1}^{N} \xi_i\right)^k\right\} \tag{4.31}$$

Subject to : $y_i\left(w^T x_i + b\right) \geq 1 - \xi_i$ $i = 1, 2, \ldots, N, \xi_i \geq 0$

If we cannot find a hyperplane to separate the data, i.e. the above linear SVM cannot find a feasible solution, we need to extend the linear method: linear SVM is generally extended to nonlinear SVM through the following two steps: i) convert the input data to a space of higher dimension through nonlinear mapping; and ii) search the separating hyperplane in the new space. For example, when the low-dimensional linear data are inseparable, it can be mapped to a higher dimension to be separable after using the Gaussian function.

4.4   Bayesian Network and Ensemble Methods

Thomas Bayes invented the Bayesian methods for classification based on statistical decision theory. We introduce Naive Bayes and Bayesian Network in this section. These classifiers improve the accuracy of the classification when used in medical, financial and many other fields. We will introduce the basics of Bayesian classifier and Bayesian Belief networks in Sections 4.4.1 and 4.4.2. In some cases, a single machine learning algorithm cannot achieve the desired accuracy. The accuracy can be enhanced by combining multiple classifiers. That is known as an ensemble method in Section 4.4.3. In order to make reliable decisions, we can combine several simple weak machine learning methods with an accuracy greater than 50%.

4.4.1 Bayesian Classifiers

Consider a pair of random variables, X and Y. Their joint probability $P(X = x, Y = y)$ is expressed by $P(X, Y) = P(Y|X) \times P(X) = P(X|Y) \times P(Y)$, thus we have the inverse conditional probability:

$$P(Y|X) = \frac{P(X|Y)P(Y)}{P(X)} \tag{4.32}$$

This is the well-known Bayesian Theorem. During classification, the random variable is the class to be decided, and X is the attribute set. We need to compute the class probability $P(Y|X_0)$, given the attribute vector X_0 for a testing data item. The maximum value of Y corresponds to the class for testing data X_0. Consider an attribute vector $X = \{X_1, X_2, ..., X_k\}$, and l possible values (or classes) for random variable $Y = \{Y_1, Y_2, ..., Y_l\}$. We call $P(Y|X)$ the posterior probability and $P(Y)$ the prior probability of Y. We assume that all attributes are statistically independent. Thus we can compute the conditional probability as

$$P(X|Y = y) = \prod_{j=1}^{k} P(X_j|Y = y) \tag{4.33}$$

The naive Bayesian classifier calculates the posterior probability for each class Y by

$$P(Y|X) = \frac{P(Y)P(X|Y)}{P(X)} = \frac{P(Y)\prod_{j=1}^{k} P(X_j|Y)}{P(X)} \tag{4.34}$$

The Bayesian classification method predicts X to the class with the highest posterior probability. The posterior probability $P(Y_i|X)$, $i = 1, 2, ..., l$ for each combination of X and Y, then decides Y_r by finding $\max_{i=1,2,...,l} P(Y_i|X)$, and classify X to class Y_r. As $P(X)$ is the same for all classes, it is sufficient to find the maximum of the numerator $P(Y)\prod_{j=1}^{k} P(X_j|Y)$ in Equation 4.34. Thus, we just compute the following:

$$\max_{Y} P(Y)\prod_{j=1}^{k} P(X_j|Y) \tag{4.35}$$

The Naive Bayesian classification follows the six steps in Figure 4.22.

Example 4.8   Bayesian Classifier and Analysis of Detection Results

Given the following training dataset of animals, each data item can be labeled as mammal or non-mammal, but not both. Each data item is characterized by four independent attributes $A = <A1, A2, A3, A4> = <$*Give Birth, Can Fly, Live in Water, Have Legs*$>$. We need to build a Bayesian classifier model from the training set. The model will be applied

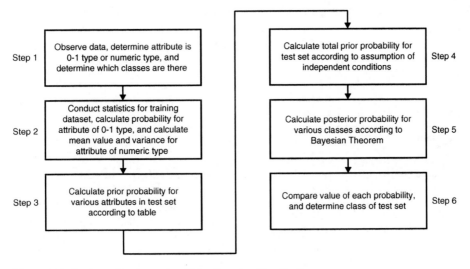

Figure 4.22 Computational steps in a Naive Bayesian Classification process.

to classify any unlabeled animal as either *mammals* (M) or *non-mammals* (N). Note that the attribute A3: "live in water" means the animal primarily lives in water, not just occasionally swims in the water. The value "sometimes in water" is considered a "no" entry in Table 4.9.

Table 4.9 Sample data in the training dataset for Example 4.8.

Name	Give Birth	Can Fly	Live in Water	Have Legs	Class
human	yes	no	no	yes	mammals
python	no	no	no	no	non-mammals
salmon	no	no	yes	no	non-mammals
whale	yes	no	yes	no	mammals
frog	no	no	sometimes	yes	non-mammals
komodo	no	no	no	yes	non-mammals
bat	yes	yes	no	yes	mammals
pigeon	no	yes	no	yes	non-mammals
cat	yes	no	no	yes	mammals
leopard shark	yes	no	yes	no	non-mammals
turtle	no	no	sometimes	yes	non-mammals
penguin	no	no	sometimes	yes	non-mammals
porcupine	yes	no	no	yes	mammals
eel	no	no	yes	no	non-mammals
salamander	no	no	sometimes	yes	non-mammals
gila monster	no	no	no	yes	non-mammals
platypus	no	no	no	yes	mammals
owl	no	yes	no	yes	non-mammals
dolphin	yes	no	yes	no	mammals
eagle	no	yes	no	yes	non-mammals

Using the samples in Table 4.10, we compute the prior probabilities: $P(M) = 7/20$ and $P(N) = 13/20$.

Consider an unlabeled testing data item characterized by an attribute vector: $A^* = <$ A1, A2, A3, A4$> = <$yes, no, yes, no$>$. First, we calculate the testing probability values as follows:

Table 4.10 Pre-test attribute probability for sample dataset in Table 4.9.

Features		Give Birth		Can Fly		Live in Water		Have Legs	
Probability		Yes	No	Yes	No	Yes	No	Yes	No
Counts	M	6	1	6	1	2	5	2	5
	N	1	12	10	3	10	3	4	9
Probability	M	6/7	1/7	6/7	1/7	2/7	5/7	2/7	5/7
	N	1/13	12/13	10/13	3/13	10/13	3/10	4/13	9/13

Since $P(M|A^*) > P(N|A^*)$, this creature with attribute vector A^* is detected as a mammal. In other words, such a creature that gives birth, cannot fly, lives in water, and has no legs is classified as a mammal. Now, let us analyze the accuracy of using the Bayesian classifier by testing four creatures using the above method. We list the following results as listed Table 4.11.

We obtain the posterior probabilities P(M|A1, A2, A3, A4) and P(N|A1, A2. A3, A4) for each of the four tested animals. Choose the class with highest probability as the predicted class. Comparing the predicted results with the actual creature classes in Table 4.11, we discover four possible prediction statuses in the right-hand column.

The TP (true positive) refers to a true case correctly predicted, TN (True Negative) for a true case incorrectly predicted, FP (False Positive) means a false case correctly predicted and FN (False negative) for the false case that is incorrectly predicted. By basing the comparison results in Table 4.11, we have the following performance results: TP = $2/4 = 0.5$, TN = $\frac{1}{4} = 0.25$, FP = 0, and FN = $\frac{1}{4} = 0.25$. Then we use two performance metrics to assess the accuracy of the Baysian classifier:

$$\text{Prediction accuracy} = (\text{TP} + \text{TN}) / (\text{TP} + \text{TN} + \text{FP} + \text{FN}) = 0.75$$
$$\text{Prediction error} = (\text{FP} + \text{FN}) / (\text{TP} + \text{TN} + \text{FP} + \text{FN}) = 0.25 \qquad \blacksquare$$

Table 4.11 Predicted results of four animals compared with their actual classes.

Animal Name	Give Birth	Can Fly	Live in Water	Have Legs	Predicted Class	Actual Class	Prediction Status
Dog	yes	no	no	yes	M	M	TP
Monostream	no	no	no	yes	N	M	FN
Alligator	no	no	yes	yes	N	N	TN
Horse	yes	no	no	yes	M	M	TP

Figure 4.23 Two Bayesian belief networks with two different numbers of variables.

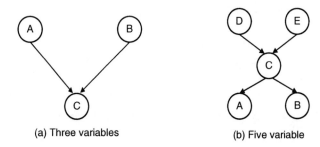

(a) Three variables   (b) Five variable

The accuracy or error comes from the weak assumption that all attributes are independent. In general, the larger the training set to cover all possible attribute vectors is, the higher is the prediction accuracy. Furthermore, if any of the individual conditional probability $P(A_i \mid C) = N_{ic} / N_c = 0$ due to the case that $N_{ic} = 0$ from the training dataset (Table 4.11), the entire posterior probability in Equation (4.34) becomes zero. This can be avoided by assuming an offset value $P(A_i \mid C) = (N_{ic}+1)/(N_c + c) = 1/(N_c + c)$, where c is the number of classes being considered. The performance metrics will be further studied in Chapter 8, when application of the Baysian classifier is used for chronic disease prediction.

4.4.2 Bayesian Belief Networks

Naive Bayesian networks assume that all attributes are statistically independent. This assumption is too strict in some cases. In order to relax this assumption, the Bayesian belief network is introduced with class conditional probability. The Bayesian belief network is a graphical representation of the relationship among attributes. There are two main components: i) a directed acyclic graph, representing the dependencies between the variables; and ii) a probability table, connecting each node and its parent node directly.

Consider three random variables, *A*, *B* and *C*, where *A* and *B* are independent of each other and both have a direct impact on the third random variable. So their relationship is represented by two DAGs in Figure 4.23(a). Consider five variables, *A*, *B*, *C*, *D* and *E*. The variables *A* and *B*, *D* and *E* are independent of each other, *D* and *E* have a direct impact on *C*, and variable *C* affects *A* and *B*. Thus, we obtain the DAG graph in Figure 4.23(b).

Consider the situation where variables are independent, namely the Naïve Bayesian Network, which is a special kind of Bayesian belief network. We use *Y* to denote the target class, $\{X_1, X_2, \cdots, X_d\}$ are its set of attributes, and the Bayesian belief network is shown in Figure 4.24.

Figure 4.24 Conditional independence assumption of Naive Bayesian classifier.

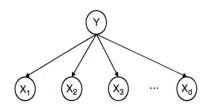

In order to indicate the relationship between the variables more vividly, we set rules as follows: if there is an arc from X to Y, then X is Y's parent and Y is the child of X; if an arc exists in the network from Y to Z, then X is the ancestor of Z, and Z is the offspring of X. For example, in Figure 4.23 (b), D is C's parent and the ancestor of A and B, while C is the children of D, and A and B is the offspring of D. In addition to the independence required by network topology, each node is associated with a probability table:

1) If node X has no parent node, this table contains only a priori probability $P(X)$.
2) If node X only has one parent node Y, this table contains conditional probability $P(X|Y)$.
3) If node X has multiple parent nodes $\{Y_1, Y_2, ..., Y_m\}$, this table contains conditional probability $P(X|Y_1, Y_2, ..., Y_m)$.

To sum up, Bayesian belief network modeling consists of two steps. First, create a network structure and then estimate the probability in the arcs. The network topology is obtained through encoding supported by subjective domain knowledge. The probability values are obtained by conditional probability. Algorithm 4.1 specifies a systematic procedure in using the Bayesian belief network.

Algorithm 4.1   Use of Bayesian Belief Network for Predictive Analytics

---

Input: d The number of variables, T General order of variables.
Output: Bayesian belief network topology
Procedure:
1) Consider $T = (X_1, X_2, \cdots, X_d)$ as one general order of variables
2) for I = 1 to d
3) Make as $X_{T(i)}$ i^{th} highest variable in T
4) Make $C(X_{T(i)})$ as the set of variables before $X_{T(i)}$
5) Eliminate all the variables in $C(X_{T(i)})$ with no impact on X_i with future knowledge
6) Draw an arc between remaining variables of $C(X_{T(i)})$ and $X_{T(i)}$
7) end
8) Output the drawn topological graph, namely Bayesian belief network topology.

Example 4.9   Use of Bayesian Belief Network in Diabetes Prediction
In general, diabetes is attributed to many factors such as obesity, family history, blood glucose, blood sugar and blood lipid, etc. These are also antecedents like obesity and family history. Other symptoms may be induced by blood glucose and blood sugar, also known as consequences. The Bayesian belief network can model the antecedents and consequences at the same time, while the Naive Bayesian network can only model the antecedents. Part of the physical examination data of patients is given in Table 4.12, where 1 indicates having the symptom and 0 otherwise.

According to experience and common sense, obesity and family history are both related to diabetes. The blood glucose and blood lipid are also related to diabetes. The attributes are ordered as $T = \{Obesity, family history, blood sugar, blood lipid, diabetes\}$ Based on the above analysis, we obtain the Bayesian belief network in Figure 4.25.

Table 4.12 Examination data for suspected diabetic patients.

Patient ID.	Obesity	Family history	Blood sugar	Blood lipid	Diabetes
1	1	0	1	1	1
2	0	1	1	0	0
3	1	1	0	1	0
4	0	0	0	0	1
5	0	0	0	0	0
6	1	0	1	0	1
7	1	1	1	1	1
8	0	1	0	1	0
9	0	0	1	0	0
10	1	1	1	1	1
10	0	1	0	0	0
12	1	0	0	1	0
13	1	0	1	0	0
14	0	0	0	0	0
15	0	1	1	1	1
16	0	0	0	0	0
17	0	0	0	0	0

According to the above topology map, we can simplify the conditional probability, for example $P(A|B) = P(A)$ because obesity (A) and family history (B) are independent of each other, and in combination with the given table, we can get the probability of diabetes. For example, $P(C|A,B)$, the calculation results of this probability table are presented in Table 4.13.

We can find out whether diabetes has effects on blood glucose and lipids, for example, the calculation results of probability table for $P(D,E|C)$ are presented as Table 4.14. Using the Bayesian conditional probability, we calculate whether there is the possibility of diabetes in some other cases. For example, suppose we detected some persons with high blood glucose and high blood fat, then what is the probability of the risk of diabetes? Namely $P(C = yes|D = yes, E = yes)$. It is clear that the known results make us release

Figure 4.25 Bayesian belief network for diabetics in Example 4.9.

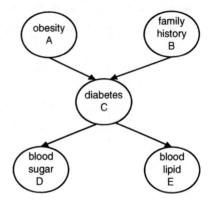

Table 4.13 Conditional probabilities for diabetic patients.

Obesity (A)	Family history (B)	Diabetics	No Diabetes
YES	YES	2/3	1/3
	NO	1/2	1/2
NO	YES	1/4	3/4
	NO	1/6	5/6

probability, which is in accordance with the Bayesian conditional probability theorem, then:

$$
\begin{cases}
P(C = yes|D = yes, E = yes) = \dfrac{P(D = yes, E = yes|C = yes)}{P(D = yes, E = yes)} \cdot P(C) = \dfrac{2/3}{4/17} \times \dfrac{6}{17} = 1 \\[3mm]
P(C = yes|D = yes, E = no) = \dfrac{P(D = yes, E = yes|C = no)}{P(D = yes, E = yes)} \cdot P(C) = \dfrac{0}{4/17} \times \dfrac{6}{17} = 0
\end{cases}
$$

$$(4.36)$$

The Bayesian belief network shows that the patient suffers from diabetes. Table 4.14 shows that an obese patient with a family history of diabetes, has the probability of diabetes of 2/3. Furthermore, with high blood glucose, the probability that the patient has diabetes is computed by

$$
\begin{aligned}
P(C &= yes|A = yes, B = yes, D = yes) \\
&= \frac{P(D = yes \mid C = yes, A = yes, B = yes)}{P(D = yes \mid A = yes, B = yes)} \times P(C = yes|A = yes, B = yes) \\
&= \frac{P(D = yes \mid C = yes)P(C = yes|A = yes, B = yes)}{\sum_i P(D = yes \mid C = yes)P(C = i|A = yes, B = yes)} \qquad i = yes, no \\
&= \frac{5/6 \times 2/3}{5/6 \times 2/3 + 1/6 \times 1/3} = \frac{10}{11}
\end{aligned}
$$

$$(4.37)$$

We conclude that such a patient has a high probability 10/11 of being diabetic. ∎

Table 4.14 Probability of blood glucose and lipids for diabetics patients.

Diabetics (C)	Blood glucose (D)	Blood lipids (E)	Probability (P)
YES	High	High	4/6
	High	Normal	1/6
	Normal	High	0/6
	Normal	Normal	1/6
NO	High	High	0/11
	High	Normal	3/11
	Normal	High	3/11
	Normal	Normal	5/11

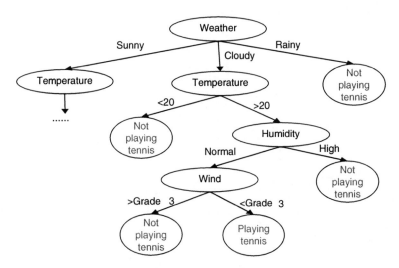

Figure 4.26 Decision tree for the tennis tournament.

4.4.3 Random Forests and Ensemble Methods

General classification techniques such as Bayesian networks, decision trees and support vector machines, use single classifiers obtained from training data to predict unknown class labels. Through the aggregation of multiple classifiers, classification accuracy is improved, and we call this technique an ensemble model or a combination of classifiers. Random forest as one of the combination classification methods is a kind of special combination method designated for decision tree classification.

Through the combination of multiple decision trees, the predictions are made, in which each tree is generated by a value of an independent set on the basis of random vector. For example, if we want to decide whether a certain day is suitable for playing tennis according to weather, temperature, humidity and wind conditions, you have the decision tree shown in Figure 4.26. Now, using multiple decision trees to increase the accuracy, we can divide the four attributes into multiple groups of attributes, such as {weather, humidity, wind}, {temperature, humidity, wind}, {weather, temperature} and so on, as shown in Figure 4.27.

In this way, one decision tree can be divided into three decision trees, when decision making every single decision tree will correspond to a result: playing tennis, or not playing tennis. In this way, we get three decision-making results, then find out which result has the most votes, and the final result is the one with the most votes. For example, under the case {sunny, greater than 20 degrees, high air humidity, no wind} shall we play tennis? With the decision tree in Figure 4.26, we know the results of the first, the third decision tree method is not playing tennis and the result of the second decision tree is playing tennis. As playing tennis gets 1 vote and not playing tennis gets 2 votes, so the final result is not playing tennis.

The method under which a random vector is obtained from random attributes is similar as described above, then the random vector is used to construct the decision tree, and once the decision tree is constructed, majority voting results are used to combine predictions, which is known as Forest-RI, among which RI refers to t-random input

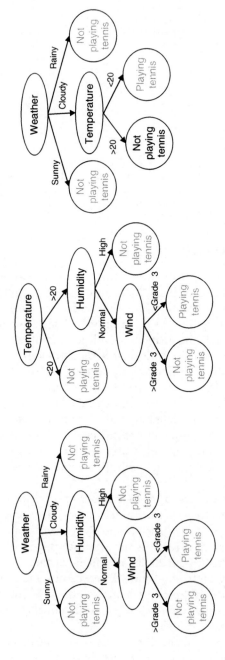

Figure 4.27 Random forest decision for playing tennis under various weather conditions.

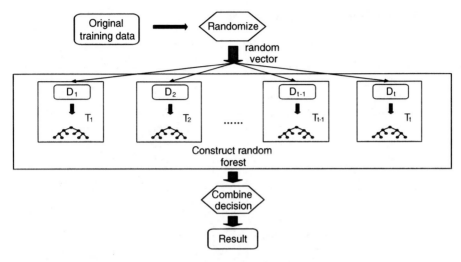

Figure 4.28 The process of using random forest for ensemble decision making.

selection. The strength of the random forest decision obtained by this method is dependent upon the dimension of the random vector, namely the number of characteristic numbers obtained by each tree, F, usually $F = log_2 d + 1$, where d is the total number of attributes.

If the number of the original attributes, d, is too small, it is difficult to select a random independent set of attributes to construct the decision tree. A method to increase the space of attributes is to create the linear combination of features, using L input attributes of the linear combination to create a new attribute, and then using created new attributes to form a random vector, and finally to construct the multiple pieces of decision tree. This random forest decision-making method is called as Forest-RC. The general process of random forest decisions is as in Algorithm 4.2. The process of random forest establishment is shown in Figure 4.28.

Algorithm 4.2   Use of Random Forests for Decision Making in Classification

---

Input: R: forecast sample, L: attribute matrix
Output: The decision results
Procedure:
1) Calculate the vector dimension F
2) Create F-dimension random attribute vector to constitute the collection, C
3) The decision tree is constructed according to the elements C, and a random forest is established
4) Make decision in every decision tree
5) Calculate and output the final results with the most votes
6) End

Example 4.10   Diabetics Prediction using the Random Forests Model
Part of the physical examination data of a real-life hospital from central China is represented in Table 4.15, and collection of data includes body weight, blood sugar, lipid

Table 4.15 Part of physical examination data from a Wuhan Hospital.

No.	Weight (A) (kg)	Blood sugar (B) (mmol/L)	Blood lipids (C) (mmol/L)	Diabetes (D)
1	68.4	17.5	7.7	1
2	64.3	4.7	1.33	0
3	65.4	8.6	2.48	0
4	62.0	14.3	4.67	1
5	81.5	8.5	0.82	1
6	58.3	5.0	1.99	0
7	55.2	4.6	0.86	0
8	84.3	5.8	2.34	1
9	85.6	5.9	2.54	0
10	54.7	5.7	2.63	1

content and whether the patient is suffering from diabetes (1: patients, 0: normal). The physical index data for a person is {weight: 60, blood sugar: 6.8, blood lipids: 1.5}, whether it can be found that the person is suffering from diabetes.

In order to improve the prediction accuracy, we can consider making predictions with the random forest method. We need to determine the dimension of the random vector $F = log_2 d + 1 = 2$. Considering the attributes in the example are few, and in order to make the correlation between random vectors lower, we can determine the following three random vectors: {weight, blood sugar}, {weight, blood lipid} and {blood sugar, blood lipid}. Then the sequence of several properties is determined as below. It is determined by the information entropy. The property whose information entropy increases the most is at the top of the decision tree, and the like (there are detailed introductions about this in the section on decision trees).

$$Entropy(D) = -\frac{1}{2}\log_2\frac{1}{2} - \frac{1}{2}\log_2\frac{1}{2} = 1$$

$$Entropy(A) = \frac{1}{2} \times \left(-\frac{3}{5}\log_2\frac{3}{5} - \frac{2}{5}\log_2\frac{2}{5}\right) + \frac{1}{2} \times \left(-\frac{3}{5}\log_2\frac{3}{5} - \frac{2}{5}\log_2\frac{2}{5}\right) = 0.9710$$

$$Entropy(B) = \frac{4}{10} \times \left(-\frac{3}{4}\log_2\frac{3}{4} - \frac{1}{4}\log_2\frac{1}{4}\right) + \frac{6}{10} \times \left(-\frac{2}{6}\log_2\frac{2}{6} - \frac{4}{6}\log_2\frac{4}{6}\right) = 0.8755$$

$$Entropy(C) = \frac{7}{10} \times \left(-\frac{4}{7}\log_2\frac{4}{7} - \frac{3}{7}\log_2\frac{3}{7}\right) + \frac{3}{10} \times \left(-\frac{1}{3}\log_2\frac{1}{3} - \frac{2}{3}\log_2\frac{2}{3}\right) = 0.9651$$

The entropy increases of blood sugar, blood lipids and weight are respectively:

$$\Delta Entropy(A) = Entropy(D) - Entropy(A) = 0.0290$$
$$\Delta Entropy(B) = Entropy(D) - Entropy(B) = 0.1245$$
$$\Delta Entropy(C) = Entropy(D) - Entropy(C) = 0.0349$$

Therefore, the content of blood sugar and blood lipids is more important, and it should be placed closer to the root of the decision tree. The order is blood sugar, blood lipid and weight. We can build the following random forest, as shown in Figure 4.29.

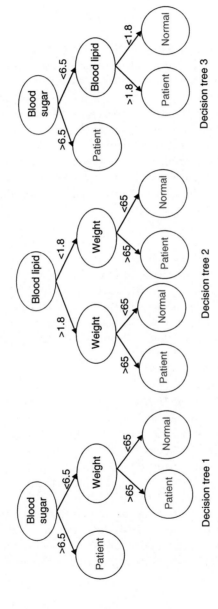

Figure 4.29 Diabetes random forest representation.

The examination index is {weight: 60, blood sugar 6.8, blood lipid: 1.5}, and according to the decision tree 1 for the patient, the result is YES, the decision tree 2 is NO, and the decision tree 3 is YES. The final situation is 2 votes for *yes* and 1 vote for *no*, so the preliminary result indicates that the person is suffering from diabetes. ∎

4.5 Conclusions

Machine learning becomes in high demand with the rise of data science and the big data industry. The taxonomy of ML algorithms is introduced to distinguish among supervised, unsupervised and semi-supervised families. The supervised ML algorithms studied in this chapter are more often used than the unsupervised ones to be studied in Chapter 5. Machine learning methods studied in these two chapters are applied for big data analytics. Deep learning is treated in Chapter 6 when artificial neural networks are introduced. Regression and classification algorithms are supervised by training data. Similarly, training is practised in using decision trees, support vector machines and Bayesian networks. In Chapter 5, we will learn how to choose ML learning algorithms, including unsupervised ones. Readers are encouraged to learn further by solving the homework problems.

Homework Problems

4.1 There are a group of women, with no direct information about their measured weights. Figure out a method to predict their weight order without asking them in person. What are the attributes or features to be used in your prediction process? For example, the attributes can be the height, age, race, wealth or other related factors. Justify the feasibility of your learning model for predicting their weights with some degree of accuracy.

4.2 Consider the density of Nitric Oxide (NO), an air pollutant, in an urban environment where vehicles discharge NO during their movement. The pollution in the air is proven harmful to human health. The NO density is attributed to vehicle traffic, temperature, air humidity and wind velocity. Table 4.16 shows environmental data collected in various observed areas. Use the linear regression method to estimate the NO density with a data vector of {1436, 28.0, 68, 2.00}.

4.3 The user information of a smart phone is given in Table 4.17. For each day, the collected average data include total call duration (minutes), mobile traffic volume (MB), number of incoming calls, and whether the user is at home or outside (1: home, 0: outside). Given a testing data of (A: 90, B: 60, C: 8), determine whether this person is at home? Likewise, how about another user with calling statistics (A: 80, B: 50, C: 10)?

4.4 When a business makes a loan application to a bank or financial organization, the lender needs to assess the creditability of the borrowers. Let $y = 0$ denote a borrower with a bad record, while $y = 1$ represents a credited borrower. Three features of borrower are represented by X1, X2 and X3 in Table 4.18. Build a prediction model to test a given customer with a credit record (X1, X2, X3) = (−25, 2.5, 0.5). Assess the accuracy of your prediction model.

Table 4.16 The density of nitric oxide measured in various observed areas.

Vehicle Traffic (X1)	Temperature (X2)	Air Humidity (X3)	Wind Velocity (X4)	Density of NO (Y)
1300	20	80	0.45	0.066
948	22.5	69	2.00	0.005
1444	23.0	57	0.50	0.076
1440	21.5	79	2.40	0.011
786	26.5	64	1.5	0.001
1084	28.5	59	3.00	0.003
1652	23.0	84	0.40	0.170
1844	26.0	73	1.00	0.140
1756	29.5	72	0.9	0.156
1116	35.0	92	2.80	0.039
1754	30.0	76	0.80	0.120
1656	20.0	83	1.45	0.059
1200	22.5	69	1.80	0.040
1536	23.0	57	1.50	0.087
1500	21.8	77	0.60	0.120
960	24.8	67	1.50	0.039

Table 4.17 Part of the application information of a smart phone user.

ID	Total Call duration (A)	Volume (B)	Frequency (C)	At home(D)
1	20	45	2	1
2	120	46	4	1
3	90	55	10	0
4	81	56	19	0
5	200	55	8	0

Table 4.18 Sampling data of a bank credit report on borrowers.

X1	X2	X3	Y	X1	X2	X3	Y
−48.2	6.8	1.6	0	43.0	16.4	1.3	1
−49.2	−17.2	0.3	0	47.0	16.0	1.9	1
−19.2	−36.7	0.8	0	−3.3	4.0	2.7	1
−18.1	−6.5	0.9	0	35.0	20.8	1.9	1
−98.0	−20.8	1.7	0	46.7	12.6	0.9	1
−129.0	−14.2	1.3	0	20.8	12.5	2.4	1
−4.0	−15.8	2.1	0	33.0	23.6	1.5	1
−8.7	−36.3	2.8	0	26.1	10.4	2.1	1
−59.2	−12.8	2.1	0	68.6	13.8	1.6	1
−13.1	−17.6	0.9	0	37.3	33.4	3.5	1
−38.0	1.6	1.2	0	59.0	23.1	5.5	1
−57.9	0.7	0.8	0	49.6	23.8	1.9	1
−8.8	−9.1	0.9	0	12.5	7.0	1.8	1
−64.7	−4.0	0.1	0	37.3	34.1	1.5	1
−11.4	4.8	0.9	0	35.3	4.2	0.9	1

4.5 When the body muscles contract, the electromyography (EMG) signals are generated on the skin's surface (Table 4.19). EMG signals can be used to control a computer, as a kind of user interface. The purpose is to devise a device that can detect EMG signals characterized by three feature parameters: frequency, strength and time. You can develop a computer program and use decision tree modeling to extract a set of rules to perform a rule-based classification of the muscle actions or gestures needed to control part of the computer operations, such as power on and off, keyboard or mouse operations, etc.

Table 4.19 Experimental data of EMG and corresponding classification of actions.

Frequency (F)	Strength (S)	Time (T)	Action (A)
1	810	1	A1
1	864	0.5	A2
1	485	1	A3
1	950	0.5	A2
1	1003	0.5	A2
1	524	1	A3
1	736	0.5	A4
1	661	0.5	A4
2	*	*	A5

4.6 A credit card enables the cardholder to borrow money from the card issuing bank, facilitating advance cash withdrawals or payment for goods. The bank expects the customer to pay back by a certain deadline each month. The bank studies statistic as to whether a custom pays back borrowed money on a credit card in time or not. There are three features, i.e. Gender, Age and Income, to lead to such a judgment, as shown in Table 4.20. Use a decision or random forest to predict a custom's credit rating. Given the information of a customer as follows: Gender: female, Age: 26–40, and Income: Middle level, estimate whether she would pay back borrowed money on a credit card on time.

Table 4.20 Credit cardholder data from a card issuing ban.

Cardholder ID	Gender(S)	Age(A)	Income(I)	Pay Back Timely ? (W)
1	Male	>40	High	Yes
2	Female	26~40	High	Yes
3	Male	<15	Low	No
4	Female	15~25	Low	No
5	Male	15~25	Middle	Yes
6	Female	15~25	Middle	Yes
7	Male	26~40	High	Yes
8	Female	26~40	Low	No
9	Male	26~40	Low	Yes
10	Female	<15	Middle	No

4.7 For special weather conditions, people would decide whether go out to play tennis according to Table 4.21. Here, we give a dataset of 14 days. Specify all suitable paths on the decision tree that leads to a play decision.

Table 4.21 Weather conditions in two weeks of observation.

Day	Outlook	Humidity	Windy	Play
1	Sunny	High	Weak	No
2	Sunny	High	Strong	No
3	Overcast	High	Weak	Yes
4	Rain	High	Weak	Yes
5	Rain	Normal	Weak	Yes
6	Rain	Normal	Strong	No
7	Overcast	Normal	Strong	Yes
8	Sunny	High	Weak	No
9	Sunny	Normal	Weak	Yes
10	Rain	Normal	Weak	Yes
11	Sunny	Normal	Strong	Yes
12	Overcast	High	Strong	Yes
13	Overcast	Normal	Weak	Yes
14	Rain	High	Strong	No

4.8 We all know the advantages of having regular exercise. But the weather conditions may prevent us from going out to exercise. Table 4.22 records Cindy's exercise logs for two weeks. Use the Bayesian network to estimate the probability that Cindy should go to play tennis, assuming her partner is available and it is a sunny day.

Table 4.22 Cindy's outdoor exercise records in two weeks.

Day	Weather	Play	Day	Weather	Play
1	Sunny	No	8	Rainy	No
2	Overcast	Yes	9	Sunny	Yes
3	Rainy	Yes	10	Rainy	Yes
4	Sunny	Yes	11	Sunny	No
5	Sunny	Yes	12	Overcast	Yes
6	Overcast	Yes	13	Overcast	Yes
7	Rainy	No	14	Rainy	No

References

1 E. Alpaydin, *Introduction to Machine Learning*. The MIT Press, 2010.
2 C.M. Bishop, *Pattern Recognition and Machine Learning*. Springer, 2006.
3 D.E. Goldberg and J.H. Holland, Genetic algorithms and machine learning. *Machine Learning*, 3(2), 95–99, 1988.

4 R. Kohavi and F. Provost, *Glossary of terms. Machine Learning*, 30: 271–274, 1998.

5 P.T. Langley, The changing science of machine learning. *Machine Learning*, 82(3), 275–279, 2011.

6 D.J. MacKay, *Information Theory, Inference, and Learning Algorithms*. Cambridge University Press, 2003.

7 H. Mannila, Data mining: machine learning, statistics, and databases. *IEEE International Conference on Scientific and Statistical Database Management*, 1966.

8 M. Mohri, A. Rostamizadeh and A. Talwalkar, *Foundations of Machine Learning*. MIT Press, 2012.

9 T. Mitchell, *Machine Learning*. McGraw Hill, 1997.

10 V. Vapnik, *Statistical Learning Theory*. Wiley-Interscience, 1998.

11 I. Witten and E. Frank, *Data Mining: Practical Machine Learning Tools and Techniques*. Morgan Kaufmann, 664 pp., 2011.

12 J. Zhang, et al., Evolutionary computation meets machine learning: A survey. *IEEE Computational Intelligence Magazine*, 6(4), 68–75, 2011

13 V. Vapnik, *The Nature of Statistical Learning Theory*. Springer Science & Business Media, 2013.

14 T. Kohonen, The self-organizing map. *Proceedings of the IEEE*, 78(9), 1464–1480, 1990.

15 W.S. Torgerson, *Theory and Methods of Scaling*, 1958.

16 L. Breiman, Bagging predictors. *Machine Learning*, 24(2), 123–140, 1996.

17 Y, Freund and R.E. Schapire, A decision-theoretic generalization of on-line learning and an application to boosting. *Journal of Computer and System Sciences*, 55(1), 119–139, 1997.

18 J.R. Quinlan, *C4. 5: programs for machine learning*. Elsevier, 2014.

19 L. Breiman, Random forests. *Machine Learning*, 45(1), 5–32, 2001.

5

Unsupervised Machine Learning Algorithms

CHAPTER OUTLINE

5.1 Introduction and Association Analysis, 205
    5.1.1 Introduction to Unsupervised Machine Learning, 205
    5.1.2 Association Analysis and A priori Principle, 206
    5.1.3 Association Rule Generation, 210
5.2 Clustering Methods without Labels, 213
    5.2.1 Cluster Analysis for Prediction and Forecasting, 213
    5.2.2 K-means Clustering for Classification, 214
    5.2.3 Agglomerative Hierarchical Clustering, 217
    5.2.4 Density-based Clustering, 221
5.3 Dimensionality Reduction and Other Algorithms, 225
    5.3.1 Dimensionality Reduction Methods, 225
    5.3.2 Principal Component Analysis (PCA), 226
    5.3.3 Semi-Supervised Machine Learning Methods, 231
5.4 How to Choose Machine Learning Algorithms?, 233
    5.4.1 Performance Metrics and Model Fitting, 233
    5.4.2 Methods to Reduce Model Over-Fitting, 237
    5.4.3 Methods to Avoid Model Under-Fitting, 240
    5.4.4 Effects of Using Different Loss Functions, 242
5.5 Conclusions, 243

5.1 Introduction and Association Analysis

In this chapter, we introduce several major classes of unsupervised machine learning algorithms. First, we study data association analysis methods for unsupervised machine learning. Other unsupervised and semi-supervised machine learning methods are presented in subsequent sections. Machine learning performance metrics and a selection method for various ML algorithms are given in Section 5.4.

5.1.1 Introduction to Unsupervised Machine Learning

In unsupervised learning, the learner must work out a function to describe a hidden structure from unlabeled data. Since the examples given are unlabeled, there is no error or reward signal to evaluate a potential solution. This distinguishes unsupervised learning from supervised learning and reinforcement learning. The unsupervised

Big-Data Analytics for Cloud, IoT and Cognitive Computing, First Edition. Kai Hwang and Min Chen.
© 2017 John Wiley & Sons Ltd. Published 2017 by John Wiley & Sons Ltd.
Companion Website: http://www.wiley.com/go/hwangIOT

approach is related to two fundamental capabilities: i) the density estimation in input data statistics; and ii) the ability to summarize and explain key data features.

Unsupervised machine learning demands more skill on data mining, data structuring, data preprocessing, feature extraction and pattern recognition. Without the help of labeled samples, the user must sort out the unstructured data to obtain the associations among data items, cluster data with similarity, reduce the dimension of the feature space, or change the representation format to enable visualization, etc. Many machine learning methods applied in unsupervised learning are based on data-mining methods to preprocess the unlabeled data. Major approaches to unsupervised learning include the following classes:

- **Association Analysis:** A priori principle and association rules are studied in Section 5.1.2 to 5.1.4;
- **Data Clustering:** Linear clustering, logistic clustering, k-means, KNN (K nearest neighbor), hierarchical and density-based clustering methods are studied in Section 5.2;
- **Dimensionality Reduction:** Dimension reduction, principal component analysis (PCA) and singular value decomposition (SVD) are studied in Section 5.2.

There are also artificial neural network (ANN) models, self-organizing maps (SOM) and adaptive resonance theory (ART) for unsupervised machine learning. We will learn ANN and its extensions for deep learning in Chapter 8. The SOM is a topographic organization in which nearby locations on the map represent inputs with similar properties. ART allows the user to control the degree of similarity between members of the same clusters. The SOM and ART will not be covered in this book. Some semi-supervised methods will be covered in Section 5.3.3, including reinforcement and representation learning.

5.1.2 Association Analysis and A priori Principle

Association analysis, also known as association mining, refers to finding frequent patterns, associations, correlation or causal structures that exist in sets of projects and collection of objects in the transaction data, relational data or other information carriers. In layman's terms, association analysis is a way to find out the interesting association hidden in large datasets. The discovered links are expressed in association rules: $X \rightarrow Y$, where X and Y are data objects or patterns. The rule indicates a strong connection between the X and Y. The most common application of association analysis is to link shopping basket data with customers or transaction ID. Table 5.1 shows such an association.

Table 5.1 Association linking shopping basket data with buyers.

Buyer ID	Itemset
1	{milk, beer, diapers}
2	{cola, beer, bread, diapers}
3	{bread, milk, diapers, cola}
4	{baby food, beer, diapers, milk}
5	{apple, water, egg, diapers}

Through observation, we can see that some shoppers who order diapers also buy milk. That shows there is a strong connection between diapers and milk sales. You use the rule: $\{diapers \rightarrow milk\}$. For the shopping basket data in Table 5.1, we conclude that each line corresponds to a transaction, corresponds to an order $I = \{i_1, i_2, \cdots, i_d\}$ is a collection of all items in the shopping basket data, and $T = \{t_1, t_2, \cdots, t_N\}$ is a collection of all transactions. We will use these notations to introduce the concept of association rules.

The set of items included in each transaction t_i is a subset of I. In an association analysis, a set of items is defined as a collection of 0 or more items. If an itemset contains k items, it is called a k-item set. For example, {cola, beer, bread, diapers} is 4-item set. An important attribute of itemset is its support count defined as the number of transactions that contain a specific set of items. Mathematically, the support count for the itemset X is expressed as

$$\sigma(X) = \left|\{t_i | X \subseteq t_i, t_i \in T\}\right| \tag{5.1}$$

In Equation (5.1), the notation $|\cdot|$ represents the cardinality of a set. For example, in terms of the itemset {milk, beer, diapers}, the support count of {milk, beer, diapers} is 2. Because only two transactions contain the three items, they are associated with BuyerID 1 and BuyerID 4, as shown in Table 5.1. To visualize the association rules, the following notation and assumption is used:

$$X \rightarrow Y, \ X \cap Y = \emptyset \tag{5.2}$$

We define the degree of support $s(\cdot)$ and confidence level $c(\cdot)$ to represent the strength of association rules, where the degree of support $s(\cdot)$ is represented by the frequency of the fact that the rule is reflected in the dataset, and confidence level $c(\cdot)$ means the frequency of the fact that Y appears in the transactions containing X. Mathematical expressions are

$$s(X \rightarrow Y) = \frac{\sigma(X \cup Y)}{N}$$
$$c(X \rightarrow Y) = \frac{\sigma(X \cup Y)}{\sigma(X)} \tag{5.3}$$

where N is the total number of transactions. Obviously, the greater the degree of support and confidence level, the greater the intensity of the association rules.

The object of the association analysis is to find the association rule whose support degree and confidence level are relatively large in a given transaction set. This process is defined as association rule discovery. Its mathematical formula is defined as

$$\left\{X \rightarrow Y \ \middle| \ \left\{ \begin{array}{l} s(X \rightarrow Y) \geq minsup \\ c(X \rightarrow Y) \geq minconf \end{array} \right\} \right. \tag{5.4}$$

among which, $X \rightarrow Y$ is a rule, *minsup* is the threshold value of support degree, and *minconf* is the threshold value of confidence level. Namely, the object is to find all the association rules where the support degree is greater than or equal to *minsup* and the confidence level is greater than or equal to *minconf*.

How to discover the association rules is the key problem. It is usually a simple method to enumerate all possible rules, but it is impractical for a set with large number of transactions. For datasets that contain d items the total number of association rules that may exist equals $R = 3^d - 2^{d+1} + 1$. For example, the dataset that contains 7 items has 1932 association rules. Therefore, in order to better find out the association rules, we introduce the concept of frequent itemsets and strong rules.

For itemset X and its subset X_i, the number of rules is $\sigma(X) \le \sigma(X_i)$, because a transaction that contains a certain set of items must also contains the subset of this set. The frequent itemset is defined as a set of items that satisfy the minimum support count threshold, namely all its subsets are frequent sets of items. The strong rules are defined as the association rules whose confidence level is high in frequent items. Thus, two major subtasks discovered in the association rule are: i) to find out all frequent itemsets, which are known as the generation of frequent sets; and ii) to find out all the strong rules, which are known as the generation of strong rules.

The first thing to do is to discover the association rules. The frequent itemsets demand an algorithm to specify its generation procedure. By definition of frequent itemsets, we see that if an itemset is frequent, then all subsets of it must also be frequent. This is known as the a priori principle. To the contrary, if an itemset is infrequent, so all of its supersets are infrequent. Using this principle, the strategy is based on support count to prune the exponential set. This technique utilizes the anti-monotone trait of the support degree, meaning that the support degree of an itemset can never exceed that of its subset.

Algorithm 5.1   Generation of the A priori Frequent Itemset

Input: T: Dataset that contains transactions
        minsup: Threshold of support degree
Output: All frequent item sets
Procedure:
1) Suppose $k = 1$
2) While
3) Find all the k-itemsets, constitute of the candidate collection of k-itemsets, C_k, create a collection of frequent k- itemsets, F_k
4)   for Each candidate itemset $c \in C_k$
5)   Make its support degree $\sigma(c) = 0$
6)   for each transaction $t \in T$
7)   if Transaction t includes all the items in c
8) $\sigma(c) = \sigma(c) + 1$
9)   end if
10)   end for
11)   if $\sigma(c) \ge minsup$
12)   Add c into Collection F_k
13)   end if
14)   end for
15) $k = k + 1$
16)   until $F_k \ne \emptyset$
17)   Output $F = \cup F_k$

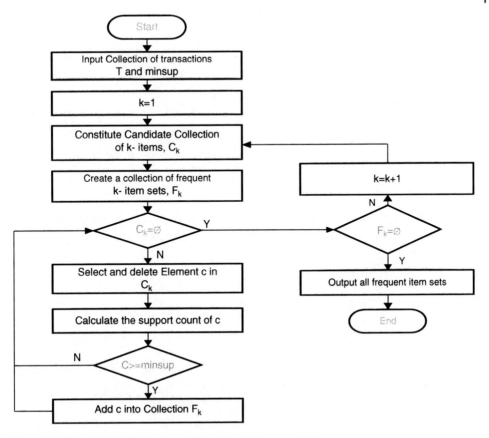

Figure 5.1 Algorithm 5.1 illustrated by a flow chart with more details.

According to the a priori principle, the algorithm of the generation of frequent itemset is given below. This algorithm generates the frequent itemsets and mines the association rules. It uses pruning technique based on support degree to solve the exponential explosion problem. The specific steps of the generation of a priori frequent itemsets are formally specified in Algorithm 5.1.

Algorithm 5.1 is further illustrated by the flow chart in Figure 5.1. The key point is how to generate many candidate itemsets C_k. There are three methods to prune unnecessary itemsets. Table 5.2 presents the complexity (order of magnitude) of the three pruning methods. Only brief descriptions are given in the right-hand column. These methods are applied in Example 5.1 numerically.

Example 5.1   Using A priori Principle to Predict Price Rising in a Department Store

Table 5.3 gives the price data of commercial goods in a department store during the first eight months of a given year. We use number 1 to refer to a price increase and 0 for no increase. These data are used to analyze the price relations as to whether there is a link between a pair of goods. Using the methods in Table 5.2 and the steps specified in Algorithm 5.1, the frequent itemsets are generated at the end.

Table 5.2 Complexity of three itemset pruning methods.

Method	Complexity	Description
Exhaustive method	$O\left(\sum_{k=1}^{d} kC_d^k\right) = O(d \cdot 2^{d-1})$	Upper bound to enumerate all possible itemsets, where d is the total number of data items under consideration.
$F_{k-1} \times F_1$ Method	$O\left(\sum_k k\|F_{k-1}\|\|F_1\|\right)$	Use of frequent 1-itemset to extend the frequent k-1 itemsets, in order to generate the frequent k-itemsets, where $\| \cdot \|$ is the set cardinality.
$F_{k-1} \times F_{k-1}$ Method	$O\left(\sum_k k\|F_{k-1}\|\|F_{k-1}\|\right)$	Upper bound for combining frequent k-1 itemsets to generate the frequent k-itemsets.

Here, we set minsup and minconf to 0.4 and 0.6, respectively. $F_{k-1} \times F_1$ method is used to generate k-candidate itemsets to determine frequent itemsets. The process includes the following steps:

1) First, the support degree of candidate 1-itemsets can be calculated:

$$\sigma(A) = 6, \ \sigma(B) = 4, \ \sigma(C) = 5, \ \sigma(D) = 2, \ \sigma(E) = 3.$$

2) According to the confidence threshold 0.6, B, D and E can be pruned, and thus obtaining frequent 1-itemsets $\{A\}$, $\{C\}$.
3) Using the method $F_{k-1} \times F_1$ can generate the following candidate 2-itemsets: $\{A, C\}$.
4) Calculate the support degree of candidate 2-itemsets: $\sigma(\{A, C\}) = 5$.
5) Finally, we obtain all the k-frequent itemsets as follows: $\{A\}$, $\{C\}$, $\{A, C\}$. ■

5.1.3 Association Rule Generation

After the frequent itemsets are generated, each of the frequent itemsets and their combination can satisfy the threshold of the support degree. We describe the rule pruning technique based on a concept, called degree of confidence. If the enumeration method is used, each k-frequent itemset can generate as many as $2^k - 2$ association rules. For

Table 5.3 Reported price variation of commercial goods in a department store.

Month Good	Item A	Item B	Item C	Item D	Item E
1	1	0	1	0	1
2	0	1	0	1	0
3	1	0	1	0	0
4	0	1	0	0	1
5	1	0	0	0	0
6	1	1	1	0	1
7	1	1	1	0	0
8	1	0	1	1	0

example, if the itemset is $\{1, 2, 3\}$, a frequent 3-itemset, it can generate six rules as the follows:

$$\{1, 2\} \rightarrow \{3\}, \ \{1, 3\} \rightarrow \{2\}, \ \{2, 3\} \rightarrow \{1\},$$
$$\{1\} \rightarrow \{2, 3\}, \ \{2\} \rightarrow \{1, 3\}, \ \{3\} \rightarrow \{1, 2\} \tag{5.5}$$

The number of rules generated by this approach is too large, and it does not necessarily meet the requirements of the confidence threshold. So we need the confidence measure to reduce the number of rules to achieve pruning. Consider the following scenario, if the two rules $X' \rightarrow Y - X'$, $X \rightarrow Y - X$ meet the requirement of $X' \subset X$, and their confidence levels are respectively:

$$c(X' \rightarrow Y - X') = \frac{\sigma(Y)}{\sigma(X')}$$
$$c(X \rightarrow Y - X) = \frac{\sigma(Y)}{\sigma(X)} \tag{5.6}$$

From the above, for a set of items that have the inclusive relationship $\sigma(X') \geq \sigma(X)$ exists. So the confidence level of the previous rule in the above equation must not exceed the latter confidence level. As a result, we have the association rule: if the rule $X \rightarrow Y - X$ does not satisfy the confidence threshold, the rules such as $X' \rightarrow Y - X'$ $(X' \subset X)$ will not satisfy the confidence threshold.

Based on the above theorem, the algorithm of the generation of A priori rules is put forward. The algorithm uses a layer-by-layer method to generate association rules, in which each layer corresponds to the number of items in the rules. Initially, all rules with high confidence are extracted from the rule which will only contain one item after the extraction. Then these rules are used to generate new candidate rules. Specific steps are specified in Figure 5.2 for the generation of A priori rules.

The algorithm of the generation of A priori rules does not need to scan the dataset again to calculate the confidence level of the candidate rules, because we can use the support count of the generation of frequent items to determine the degree of confidence level for each rule. The algorithm flow is shown in Figure 5.2.

Example 5.2 Physical Check-up to Link Symptoms to Diseases

Table 5.4 is a data collection of people whose physical examinations are not qualified with fatty liver, obesity, high blood pressure, diabetes and kidney stones from a general hospital of level II in Wuhan, among which, 1 refers to suffering from the disease and 0 means no. These data are used to analyze whether there is a link between these diseases.

There is often a relationship between different diseases. One disease can be derived from another. Relationships found between diseases can help doctors to improve diagnostic efficiency and reduce the rates of misdiagnosis. Through observing the data in Table 5.4 and utilizing correlation analysis, these data are used to analyze whether there is a link between these diseases.

To find out whether there is an association between the sample transactions, we first need to determine all the frequent itemsets in the transaction dataset. Then we use the frequent item to generate association rules. Here, we assume that the support and confidence thresholds are 0.4 and 0.6, respectively. A, B, C, D, E respectively refers to fatty

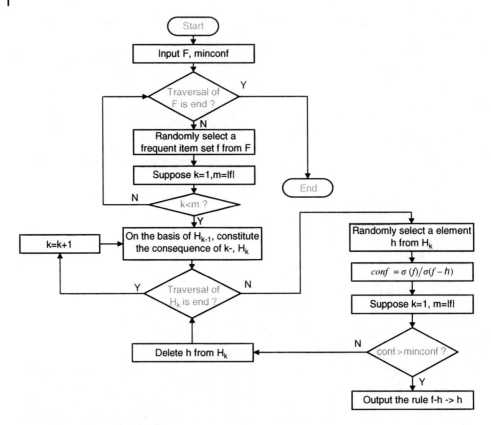

Figure 5.2 The flow chart for the generation of A priori rules.

liver, obesity, high blood pressure, diabetes and kidney stones. The process and rules of The process of the generation of frequent itemsets and rules is mainly as follows:

1) Use the method $F_{k-1} \times F_1$ to generate k-candidate itemsets to determine frequent itemsets.

Table 5.4 Physical examination record of some unqualified group.

No	Fatty liver	Obesity	High blood pressure	Diabetes	Kidney stones
1	1	1	1	0	0
2	1	0	0	0	1
3	0	1	0	1	0
4	1	1	0	0	0
5	0	1	1	0	0
6	1	1	1	0	0
7	1	1	0	0	1
8	1	1	0	1	0
9	1	0	1	0	0
10	0	0	0	0	1

a) Calculate the outcome of candidate 1-itemsets as follows:

$$\sigma(a) = 7, \ \sigma(b) = 7, \ \sigma(c) = 4, \ \sigma(d) = 2, \ \sigma(e) = 3.$$

b) According to the by support threshold 0.4, d and e can be pruned. Obtain the frequent 1-itemsets: $\{a\}, \{b\}, \{c\}$.

c) Using the method $F_{k-1} \times F_1$, generate the following candidate 2-itemsets: $\{a, b\}, \{a, c\}, \{b, c\}$

d) Calculate the support degree of 2-itemsets: $\sigma(\{a, b\}) = 5, \sigma(\{a, c\}) = 3$, $\sigma(\{b, c\}) = 3$

e) Note that $\{a, c\}, \{b, c\}$ can be cut off. The frequent 2-itemsets can be derived $\{a, b\}$.

f) Reusing the method $F_{k-1} \times F_1$, the following candidate 3-itemsets are generated as $\{a, b, c\}$.

g) Its support count is $\sigma(\{a, b, c\}) = 2$, so prune the item. Thus we get the k-frequent itemsets as follows: $\{a\}, \{b\}, \{c\}, \{a, b\}$.

2) Use A priori rules algorithm to generate association rules. We need to make sure that the number of items in frequent itemset is more than 2. Then calculate frequent items such that only $\{a, b\}$ meets the requirements. For frequent itemset $\{a, b\}$:

o) The consequence of 1-item that generates rules: $H_1 = \{a, b\}$.

p) Rules that can be generated are: $a \rightarrow b, \ b \rightarrow a$.

q) Calculate the confidence level of these rules: $c(a \rightarrow b) = \frac{5}{7}, \ c(b \rightarrow a) = \frac{5}{7}$.

r) Therefore, the rules $a \rightarrow b, \ b \rightarrow a$ can meet the requirement of the confidence threshold and can be used as the association rules. ∎

In fact, *a* and *b* respectively refer to fatty liver and obesity. The above association rules indicate that people who suffer from fatty liver are overweight people. Likewise, overweight people generally have a certain degree of fatty liver. The association rules can remind you to pay attention to your diet, undergo regular physical examinations and prevent fatty liver when you are overweight.

5.2 Clustering Methods without Labels

We can utilize classification algorithm to analyze labeled data, but how to discover the hidden information about the unlabeled data and how to discover the relationship among data? The common analytical method is the clustering method, which is one of the classical unsupervised learning methods. Clustering methods divide data into meaningful or useful groups (called clusters). In terms of data analysis, cluster is the potential class, while clustering analysis is the technique to find this class automatically. This section introduces three cluster methods: K-means clustering, agglomerative hierarchical clustering and density-based clustering.

5.2.1 Cluster Analysis for Prediction and Forecasting

Cluster analysis assigns a set of observations to group a sample data space into clusters. Data elements in the same class are similar according to some predefined similarity metrics. The clusters are separated by dissimilar features or properties. Other clustering methods are based on estimated density and graph connectivity. Cluster analysis is aimed to separate data for classification purpose. It is a process to divide data objects into clusters. Let X be the set of n data objects and X_i the cluster label. The clusters are the disjoint subsets defined bellow:

$$X = \bigcup_{i=1}^{n} X_i, \; X_i \cap X_j = \emptyset \; (i \neq j) \tag{5.7}$$

Example 5.3   Cluster Analysis of Hospital Examination Records
Figure 5.3 shows an example of the cluster analysis of a hospital's physical examination records. The physical examination groups are divided into a conformity group and a non-conformity group based on clustering of characteristics. Non-conformity may be divided into a subgroup with hyperlipemia and a subgroup of heart disease. In the same way, the hyperlipemia group can be divided into high-risk and low-risk subgroups.

The difference between clustering and classification is that clustering-based division is uncertain. From the perspective of machine learning, clustering is an unsupervised learning process with a constant search for clusters. The classification is a supervised learning process to divide existing objects into different groups with various labels. Clustering often requires the algorithm to determine the labels by themselves. So how to do clustering if given certain objects or datasets? This requires the design of specific algorithms for clustering. K-means clustering is a basic clustering method.   ∎

5.2.2   K-means Clustering for Classification

Assume that the dataset D contains n objects in Euclidean space. We need to divide objects in the D into k clusters $C_1, C_2, \cdots, C_k$, making $1 \leq i, j \leq k, \; C_i \subset D, \; C_i \cap C_j \neq \emptyset$.

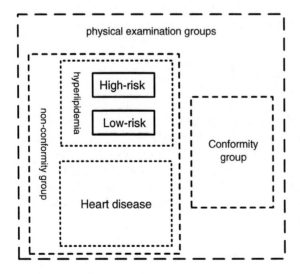

Figure 5.3 Clustering of items in a hospital's physical examination reports.

It is necessary to evaluate the quality of the division by defining an objective function, which has the object of high similarity in a cluster and low inter-cluster similarity. In order to embody a cluster more visually, the centroid heart of a cluster is defined to represent the cluster, which is defined as

$$\bar{x}_{C_i} = \frac{\sum\limits_{i=1}^{n_i} \vec{x}_i}{n_i}, \quad i = 1, 2, \cdots, k \tag{5.8}$$

where n_i denotes the number of elements in a cluster, and $\vec{x}_i$ denotes the vector coordinate of cluster elements. Then $\bar{x}_{C_i}$ denotes the centroid's coordinates of C_i. Use $d(x, y)$ to denote the Euclidean distance between the two vectors. The objective function is defined as

$$E = \sum_{i=1}^{k} \sum_{x \in C_i} [d(x, \bar{x}_{C_i})]^2 \tag{5.9}$$

Assess the quality of division with the above objective function E. In fact, the objective function E is the error sum of squares of all objects in datasets D to the centroid of a cluster. Thus, the objective of K-means is described as follows. For a given dataset and given k, find a group of clusters $C_1, C_2, \cdots, C_k$ in order to minimize the objective function E, namely:

$$\min E = \min \sum_{i=1}^{k} \sum_{x \in C_i} [d(x, \bar{x}_{C_i})]^2 \tag{5.10}$$

The K-mean Clustering method is specified in Algorithm 5.3.

Algorithm 5.3 K-means Clustering

Input: k: The number of result clusters
       D: The data set containing n objects
Output: Set of k clusters
Procedure:
1) Randomly select k objects from D as the initial k clusters
2) According to the mean of objects in each cluster, divide the remaining objects into the nearest cluster
3) Re-calculate the mean of objects in each cluster
4) Until no longer changes.

Example 5.4 Using K-mean Clustering to Classify Patients into Three Clusters

Hyperlipemia is a common disease, which is due to high levels of blood lipids. Thus, in the physical examination, the contents of triglyceride and total cholesterol in the blood

Table 5.5 Hospital's physical check-up data for Example 5.4.

Serial No	Triglyceride (mmol/L)	Total cholesterol (mmol/L)	Serial No	Triglyceride (mmol/L)	Total cholesterol (mmol/L)
1	1.33	4.19	10	2.63	5.62
2	1.94	5.47	11	1.95	5.02
3	1.31	4.32	12	1.13	4.34
4	2.48	5.64	13	2.64	5.64
5	1.84	5.17	14	1.86	5.33
6	2.75	6.35	15	1.25	3.18
7	1.45	4.68	16	1.30	4.36
8	1.33	3.96	17	1.94	5.39
9	2.43	5.62	18	1.90	5.19

are always used to determine whether the subjects are suffering from hyperlipemia. Therefore, according to the two indexes discussed above, people can be divided into two categories, i.e. normal people and patients with the disease. Table 5.5 is the dataset of triglyceride and total cholesterol contents of physical examinations in a typical hospital. In order to divide these people into different groups, it is necessary to conduct cluster analysis.

According to the table above, all the datasets can be obtained as

$$D = \{(1.33, 4.19), (1.94, 5.47), \cdots, (2.43, 5.62), (1.90, 5.19)\}$$

First, to determine the number of clusters, assuming we need to divide into three groups identified by $k = 3$. Second, it is necessary to select three objects randomly as the initial cluster and obtain three objects by means of the random number to constitute the initial cluster, respectively:

$$C_1 = \{(1.94, 5.47)\}, C_2 = \{(1.30, 4.36)\}, C_3 = \{(1.86, 5.33)\}$$

Select the objects in D as per the nearest Euclidean distance and put them into the three clusters above. The object $e = (1.33, 4.19)$, for example, the Euclidean distance of the object to the three clusters are

$$d_{(e, C_1)} = \sum_{i=1}^{n} (x_{ei} - y_{C_1 i})^2 = (1.33 - 1.94)^2 + (4.19 - 5.47)^2 = 2.0105$$

$$d_{(e, C_2)} = \sum_{i=1}^{n} (x_{ei} - y_{C_2 i})^2 = (1.33 - 1.30)^2 + (4.19 - 4.36)^2 = 0.0298$$

$$d_{(e, C_3)} = \sum_{i=1}^{n} (x_{ei} - y_{C_3 i})^2 = (1.33 - 1.86)^2 + (4.19 - 5.33)^2 = 1.5805$$

If the object is nearest to the cluster C_2, it should be divided into the cluster C_2. In this way, we may obtain the following results:

$$C_1 = \{(2.48, 5.64), (2.64, 5.64), (2.63, 5.62),$$
$$(2.75, 6.35), (2.43, 5.62), (1.94, 5.47), (1.94, 5.39)\}$$

$$C_2 = \{(1.33, 4.19), (1.31, 4.32), (1.13, 4.34),$$
$$(1.30, 4.36), (1.25, 4.18), (1.45, 4.68), (1.33, 3.96)\}$$

$$C_3 = \{(1.95, 5.02), (1.84, 5.17), (1.86, 5.33), (1.90, 5.19)\}$$

Then recalculate the mean of cluster objects and obtain the following results:

$$\bar{v}_{C_1} = \left(\frac{2.48 + 2.64 + \cdots + 1.94}{7}, \frac{5.64 + 5.64 + \cdots + 5.39}{7} \right) = (2.4014, 5.6757)$$

$$\bar{v}_{C_2} = \left(\frac{1.33 + 1.31 + \cdots + 1.33}{7}, \frac{4.19 + 4.32 + \cdots + 3.96}{7} \right) = (1.3000, 4.1471)$$

$$\bar{v}_{C_3} = \left(\frac{1.95 + 1.84 + \cdots + 1.90}{4}, \frac{5.02 + 5.17 + \cdots + 5.19}{4} \right) = (1.8875, 5.1775)$$

Due to the difference in means and initial cluster, reallocate each object of the dataset *D* in the similar way of putting the first division objects into each cluster. We can obtain the following results:

$$C_1 = \{(2.48, 5.64), (2.64, 5.64), (2.63, 5.62), (2.75, 6.35), (2.43, 5.62)\}$$

$$C_2 = \{(1.33, 4.19), (1.31, 4.32), (1.13, 4.34), (1.30, 4.36), (1.25, 4.18),$$
$$(1.45, 4.68), (1.33, 3.96)\}$$

$$C_3 = \{(1.95, 5.02), (1.84, 5.17), (1.86, 5.33), (1.90, 5.19),$$
$$(1.94, 5.47), (1.94, 5.39)\}$$

The mean values and relocated means can be very close to terminate the process. This ends up with the final classification, the classification results of which are shown in Figure 5.4. Thus, these physically examined people in this hospital can be grouped into three categories, namely, normal people, people with slight symptoms or having potential to become sick, and people with hyperlipemia. The hospital may give different recommendations to different groups for specialized treatments. ∎

5.2.3 Agglomerative Hierarchical Clustering

Hierarchical clustering and K-means clustering are two traditional clustering ways but with different starting points. K-means clustering is based on the given number of clusters and gather the raw data objects to each cluster for the final clustering results. Hierarchical clustering does not require a given number of categories. It starts with each object and gradually gathers each object based on the adjacent matrix of such an object

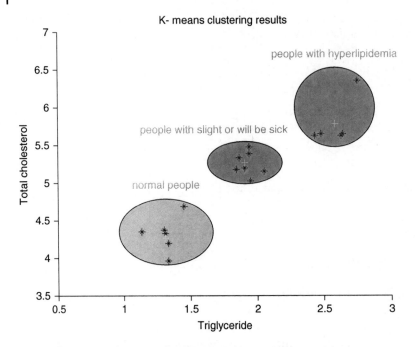

Figure 5.4 K-means clustering of patients into three treating groups.

until all objects are owned by a class (or from the overall, gradually separates each object until each object is in the same category). Therefore, hierarchical clustering includes two categories:

1) **Agglomerative hierarchical clustering:** Start with individual objects against a cluster, merge the two nearest objects or clusters, until all objects are in one cluster (namely, all collections data).

2) **Divisive hierarchical clustering:** Begin from the cluster containing all the points (i.e. the collection of all data), dividing a cluster from each division, and get the two clusters which are farthest from each other, until it cannot be divided (namely, only a single point cluster left).

Agglomerative hierarchical clustering requires a constant merger of the two most adjacent clusters. It needs to determine the proximity of each cluster, so a specific criteria must be given for this measurement. This is the key to agglomerative hierarchical clustering, for different measurement criteria may come up with different clustering results. There are five common definitions of proximity ways, namely single-chain, whole-chain, the group average, the Ward method and the centroid method. Table 5.6 describes the definition and simple explanation of the five proximities.

Note, where C_i, C_j are different clusters, x_i, x_j are the objects of cluster, n_i, n_j are the number of objects in the cluster, e_{pre} is the error before merger, and e_{after} is error after merger. Objects can be regarded as a single-point cluster, as proximity between this object and the cluster can be seen as proximity between cluster and cluster. The first three methods are visualized in Figure 5.5.

Table 5.6 Five common chains to determine the proximity among clusters.

Definition	Formula	Description
Single-chain	$\min d(x_i, x_j), x_i \in C_i x_j \in C_j$	The proximity of clusters is defined by *MIN* as the distance between two closest points in clusters
The whole chain	$\max d(x_i, x_j), x_i \in C_i x_j \in C_j$	*MAX* is the distance between two solstices of two clusters (usually use the Euclidean distance)
Group average	$\dfrac{\sum\limits_{i=1}^{n_i}\sum\limits_{j=1}^{n_j} d(x_i, x_j)}{n_i n_j}, x_i \in C_i x_j \in C_j$	The average distance between two cluster midpoints (usually use Euclidean distance)
Ward method	$\min \Delta e = \min(e_{after} - e_{pre})$	Merging two clusters to make the minimum increment of the square error of clustering
Centroid method	$\min d(v_{C_i}, v_{C_j})$	This min function defines the distance between two centroids of the clusters (using Euclidean distance)

Algorithm 5.4   Generation of Cluster Tree Map

Input: D: The data set contains n objects
Output: Clustering result tree map
Procedure:
1) Taking each object as a cluster, calculating the proximity between clusters, obtaining the proximity matrix; while
2) According to the proximity of clusters, merge the nearest two clusters
3) Recalculate proximity matrix of clusters
4) Until only one cluster is left.

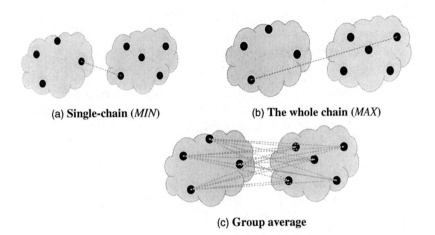

(a) **Single-chain** (*MIN*)　　　　　(b) **The whole chain** (*MAX*)

(c) **Group average**

Figure 5.5 Proximity representation of clusters.

Table 5.7 Part of a hospital physical check-up data.

Serial No.	Height (cm)	Weight (kg)	Heartbeat (times/min)
1	154	45.5	59
2	165	65.4	108
3	166.5	76.2	58
4	166.5	74.7	54
5	161	55.6	45
6	165.5	62.3	58

Example 5.5 Clustering Analysis of Hospital Check-up Data

Table 5.7 gives a dataset of weight, height and heartbeat of some unqualified people in the physical examination. We need to conduct clustering analysis for them.

As shown in Table 5.7, all the datasets can be obtained as

$$D = \{(154, 45.5, 59), (165, 65.4, 108), \cdots, (165.5, 62.3, 58)\}$$

Since the data units of the physical examination items are not unified, standardization shall be done to eliminate the influence on the results of the unit. The standardized results are

$$data\_st = \begin{pmatrix} 0.92 & 0.60 & 0.55 \\ 0.99 & 0.86 & 1 \\ 1 & 1 & 0.54 \\ 1 & 0.98 & 0.50 \\ 0.97 & 0.73 & 0.42 \\ 0.99 & 0.82 & 0.54 \end{pmatrix}$$

Using the Euclidean distance as the proximity of cluster, the proximity matrix can be calculated as follows

$$dist = \begin{pmatrix} 0 & 0.53 & 0.41 & 0.39 & 0.19 & 0.23 \\ 0.53 & 0 & 0.48 & 0.51 & 0.60 & 0.46 \\ 0.41 & 0.48 & 0 & 0.04 & 0.30 & 0.18 \\ 0.39 & 0.51 & 0.04 & 0 & 0.27 & 0.17 \\ 0.19 & 0.60 & 0.30 & 0.27 & 0 & 0.15 \\ 0.23 & 0.46 & 0.18 & 0.17 & 0.15 & 0 \end{pmatrix}$$

It can be seen that the proximity of cluster 3 and cluster 4 is the minimum 0.04. Then merge these two clusters, recalculate the proximity of each cluster and adopt the method of single chain (*MIN* method) as the definition of proximity. This produces

$$cluster: \quad 1 \quad\quad 2 \quad\quad 3,4 \quad\quad 5 \quad\quad 6$$

$$dist = \begin{pmatrix} 0 & 0.53 & 0.39 & 0.19 & 0.23 \\ 0.53 & 0 & 0.48 & 0.60 & 0.46 \\ 0.39 & 0.48 & 0 & 0.27 & 0.17 \\ 0.19 & 0.60 & 0.27 & 0 & 0.15 \\ 0.23 & 0.46 & 0.17 & 0.15 & 0 \end{pmatrix}$$

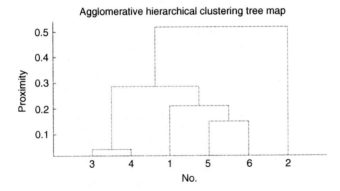

Figure 5.6 Tree map for an agglomerative hierarchical clustering.

It can be seen that the proximity of cluster 5 and cluster 6 is the minimum 0.15. Then merge these two clusters, recalculate the proximity of each cluster and repeat until there is only one cluster. The merging order is respectively $3, 4 \rightarrow 5, 6 \rightarrow 1, \{5, 6\} \rightarrow \{3, 4\}, \{1, \{5, 6\}\} \rightarrow \{\{3, 4\}, \{1, \{5, 6\}\}\}, 2$. An agglomerative hierarchical clustering result tree map is shown in Figure 5.6.

From the results, the No. 2 physically examined person has differences from the others. From the table data, we find that the heartbeat of No. 2 is fast, while the others are too slow. From Figure 5.6, we see that No. 3 and No. 4 physically examined persons are very similar (weights are almost the same and the heights are both relatively similar), clustered into one group. ∎

5.2.4 Density-based Clustering

K-means clustering and agglomerative hierarchical clustering normally can only discover globular clusters, but not clusters of arbitrary shapes, such as ring-like clusters, etc. In real life, however, there are various kinds of shapes that are not spherical, but S-shaped or ring-like, etc. As a result, it is hard for k-means or hierarchical clustering to satisfy the practical requirements, especially when it involves the classification of the latter outliers of noise, which are usually in the interior of the ring or stay outside the groups.

In order to look for such kind of outliers, it is necessary to create clusters of arbitrary shape. One point of view is to divide the spatial data into different kinds of zones in accordance with data density. Each zone corresponds to a certain cluster, insulating the outlier. Such kinds of density-based clustering is one way to solve the problem of outliers. This section mainly discusses one kind of density-based spatial clustering of applications with noise (DBSCAN). The points in the data space can be classified into the following three types according to the intensive degree: Density-based clustering is listed in Table 5.8 and specified by Algorithm 5.5:

1) **Core point:** is the point within the dense areas. Its neighborhood is determined by the distance function (Euclidean distance is commonly used), the distance parameter

Table 5.8 Three types of data density points.

Type	Formula	Description
Core point	$\begin{cases} card(\{x : d(x,a) \leq Eps\}) \geq MinPts \\ x \in D \end{cases}$	$card()$ is the number of obtained set elements, $d(x,a)$ is the distance function, a is the core point, Eps is a distance parameter and $MinPts$ is the threshold value applied.
Frontier point	$\begin{cases} card(\{x : d(x,b) \leq Eps\}) < MinPts \\ x \in D,\ b \in A \end{cases}$	b is the frontier point, Eps is the distance, $MinPts$ is the threshold value of the number of internal point and A refers to the neighborhood collection of the core point.
Noise point	$\begin{cases} card(\{x : d(x,c) \leq Eps\}) < MinPts \\ x \in D,\ c \notin A \end{cases}$	$d()$ is the number of obtaining set elements, $d(x,c)$ refers to the distance function, c is the noise point, Eps is the distance, $MinPts$ is the threshold and A is the collection of core points

specified by the user and the threshold value of the number of internal points. If this point is the core one, then the number of the points in defined fields would surpass the given threshold value.

2) **Frontier point**: is the point on the edge of the dense areas. The number of the points within the neighborhood of this point is less than the threshold value of the number of internal points specified by the user, but this point is located in the neighborhood interior of one certain core point.

3) **Noise point**: is the point in the sparse areas. The number of the points within the neighborhood of this point is less than the threshold value of the number of internal points specified by the user. But this point is not located in the neighborhood interior of any core point.

Algorithm 5.5   Using Density-based Clustering of Data Objects

---

Input: D: the data set, which contains n subjects

   Eps: distance parameter. $MinPts$: neighborhood density threshold value

Output: *type*: density-based clustering analysis result, that is the relevant type of data object

Procedure:

1)   Randomly select a object p that has not been labeled, mark this object
2)   Calculate the neighborhood density Pts of this object
3)   if $Pts \geq MinPts$
4)   Set up a new cluster C, and add p to C
5)   Find out all the neighborhood objects of this object, forming collection N
6)   for each object P' within N
7)   If p' has not been labeled, mark this object
8)   If the neighborhood density of p' is larger than $MinPts$
9)   Find out all the neighborhood objects of this object and add to N
10)   else mark p' as the frontier point
11)   If p' does not belong to any member of cluster, add p' to C
12)   end

13)   Mark the object within cluster *C* as the core point, output *C*
14) otherwise mark *p* as the noise point
15) end
16) Define *type*, and taking use of it to all the objects, represent the noise point, frontier point and core point with −1, 0, 1
17) Until all the objects have been marked.

Three point types are shown in Figure 5.7. The circles are core points, the rectangles are frontier points, and the triangles are noise points. The number of the points within some certain points is defined as the neighborhood density. If both objects *p* and *q* are core points, and one is within the neighborhood, the two objects are density-related:

$$\begin{cases} d(p,q) \leq Eps \\ p, q \in A \end{cases} \qquad (5.11)$$

The expression $d(p,q)$ refers to a distance function, and *A* refers to the neighborhood collection of the core point. The so-called density-reachable refers to the two objects connected by a series of direct density-reachable objects. The two objects can be seen as the core point or the frontier point. The purpose of DBSCAN is to find out the core point, frontier point and noise point. The steps of an algorithm are shown in Algorithm 5.5.

Example 5.6   Using Data Density to Perform Clustering in Blood Cell Analysis
Table 5.9 provides the data collection of the white and red cells content of some physically examined people in a hospital in Wuhan, China. It needs to be pointed out that the abnormal person among the examined group may be the person whose examination data is wrong.

Based on the table above, the whole datasets can be obtained as

$$D = \{(9.4, 5.33), (6.0, 4.26), \cdots, (5.0, 4.44), (5.6, 6.78)\}$$

The neighborhood density threshold value and the distance parameter (Euclidean distance) pointed out here are

$$\begin{cases} MinPts = 4 \\ Eps = 0.9016 \end{cases}$$

Figure 5.7 The core point, frontier point and noise point in two clusters.

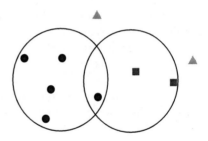

Table 5.9 White and red cells data for Example 5.6

White cells	Red cells	White cells	Red cells	White cells	Red cells
9.4	5.33	6.6	4.41	4	4.43
6	4.26	5.4	4.62	8.6	5.15
6	4.62	6	4.92	8.7	5.43
6	4.12	8.6	5.44	5.5	5
5.5	5.45	6.5	5.34	5	5.95
6	5.90	4.2	4.54	4.7	5.04
5.5	5.73	3.5	4.80	5.6	5.42
4.8	4.51	4.9	4.46	2.1	3.79
5.9	4.24	3	4.79	7.8	5.73
5	4.46	5.8	5.20	4.5	4.35
4.8	3.97	3	4.17	12.6	5.27
3.6	4.46	8.1	4.82	4.4	5.32
7.5	5.51	5.1	4.16	5.6	4.39
8.3	4.92	6.9	5.18	4.6	3.74
8.6	5.97	6.3	3.99	5	4.44
5.3	5.33	6.8	3.91	5.6	6.78
4.2	4.87	5.9	4.29		

Randomly select an object $p(4.8, 4.51)$, calculate the distance between each object to this object iteratively. For example, the distance between object p and the first object (9.4, 5.33) in Table 5.9 is

$$d(p, q) = \sqrt{(9.4 - 4.8)^2 + (5.33 - 4.51)^2} = 4.67$$

Obviously, the result is larger than $Eps = 0.9016$. Thus this object is not within the neighborhood of p. As another example, the distance between object (5, 4.46) and object p is

$$d(p, q) = \sqrt{(5 - 4.8)^2 + (4.46 - 4.51)^2} = 0.21$$

Obviously, the result is less than $Eps = 0.9016$. Thus this object is within the neighborhood of p. After calculation, such kind of objects in this example have a total of 15, so the neighborhood density of this object is $Pts_v = 15 > MinPts = 4$.

Thus, object p(4.8, 4.51) is the core object. Repeat the procedure for the other objects within the neighborhood of object p. For example, (5, 4.46), the neighborhood density of this object is 14, and it is in the neighborhood of object p. Thus this object and object p are density-reachable, and shall be marked as the core point. If one certain object and core point are density-reachable and the neighborhood density is no less than $MinPts = 4$, then mark the object as the core point.

If one certain object and core point are density-reachable but the neighborhood density is less than $MinPts = 4$, mark this object as the frontier point. If one certain object

Figure 5.8 The result figure of density-based clustering analysis.

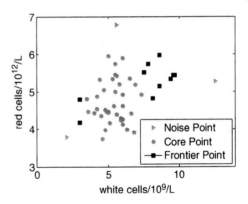

and core point are not density-reachable, then mark this object as the noise point. In this way, the obtained set of noise points is $\{(2.1, 3.79), (5.6, 6.78), (9.7, 5.43)\}$. The density-based clustering result is shown in Figure 5.8. ∎

As depicted in Figure 5.8, the shapes after the clustering are irregular, and it is not difficult to pick out the core point, frontier point and noise point. We can easily find out that the points at the bottom left, but the top and the right-hand position appear to be wrong in terms of the white and red cells content. The corresponding examined people need to be rechecked so as to further confirm the result.

5.3 Dimensionality Reduction and Other Algorithms

Under high-dimensional reduction, the distance (such as Euclidean distance) between points is quite similar or any two vectors are orthogonal and thus causing difficulties in classification, regression and especially clustering. The phenomenon is called "curse of dimensionality". Many dimensionality reduction algorithms are proposed to solve the problem.

Dimensionality reduction refers to the transfer of the points in high-dimensional space to low-dimensional space through the mapping function to relieve the "curse of dimensionality". Dimensionality reduction may not only reduce the correlation of data, but also accelerate the operation speed of algorithm (decrease of data volume). This chapter will explain the core idea of the dimensionality reduction algorithm.

5.3.1 Dimensionality Reduction Methods

Dimensionality reduction in the machine learning field refers to mapping the data points in high-dimensional space to low-dimensional space with certain mapping methods. The essence of dimensionality reduction is learning a mapping function: $f: x \rightarrow y$, where x is the expression of original data points in vector expression form. y is the expression

Table 5.10 Dimensionality reduction methods for machine learning.

Methods	Basic Ideas
Principal Component Analysis (PCA)	Use several aggregate indicators (principal component) to replace all indicators in original data
Singular Value Decomposition (SVD)	Take singular value in matrix to resolve. Select the larger singular value and abandon the smaller singular value to reduce matrix dimension
Factor Analysis (FA)	Find out the intrinsic link of each property through analyzing data structure to find out the generality of property (factor)
Partial Least Squares Method	Integrating the advantages of PCA, canonical correlation analysis method and multivariate linear regression analysis method. Dimensionality reduction and prediction may be achieved
Sammon Mapping	Whilst keeping the point-point distance structure, map the data in high-dimensional space to low-dimensional space
Discriminate Analysis (DA)	Project the data (points) in high-dimensional space with class labels to low-dimensional space, making it classified in low-dimensional space.
Locally Linear Embedding (LLE)	As a kind of nonlinear dimensionality reduction algorithm, it may make the dimensionality reduction data retain the original manifold structure.
Laplacian Eigenmaps	We need the related points (connected points in the map) to be close to each other in the space after dimensionality reduction

of a low-dimensional vector after data point mapping. Generally, the dimension of y is lower than x. f may be explicit, implicit, linear or nonlinear (Table 5.10).

At present, most dimensionality reduction algorithms process vector expression data, while some dimensionality reduction algorithms process high-order tensor expression data. The reason to use dimensionality reduction data is that there is redundant information and noise information in the original high-dimensional space and it may cause errors and reduce accuracy in practical application (i.e. image identification). Through dimensionality reduction, we wish to reduce errors caused by redundant information and improve recognition accuracy (or other applications). Or, we wish to seek out the essential structure characteristics of data through the dimensionality reduction algorithm. Linear dimensionality reduction includes PCA and linear discriminant analysis methods, and nonlinear dimensionality reduction is represented by LLE and isometric feature mapping methods.

5.3.2 Principal Component Analysis (PCA)

In the actual situation, the object has many property compositions. For example, the medical examination report of the human body consists of many physical examination items. Each property is a reflection of the object. There is more or less correlation between these objects. The correlation causes information overlapping. The high overlapping and correlation of property information (variable or characteristics) may pose many obstacles to the application and data analysis of statistical methods. Property dimensionality reduction is required to solve the information overlapping, which may greatly reduce the number of variables participating in data modeling, and will not cause information loss. PCA is a kind of analysis method widely used to effectively reduce variable dimension.

PCA is designed to transfer multiple indicators (variable in the regression) to several aggregate indicators (principal component) with dimensionality reduction ideas. Each principal component may reflect most information of original variables, and the information included is not repeated. In general cases, each principal component is the linear combination of the original variable, and each principal component is unrelated. The method may summarize the complex factors to several principal components while introducing many variables to simplify the problem and obtain the scientific and effective data information.

It is important to note that there is information loss in PCA, regardless of the decrease in property dimensions. This loss of information may be amplified in machine learning algorithm iteration, causing inaccurate conclusions. Therefore, careful consideration should be taken when using PCA. Principal components are several new variables comprehensively formed by original variables. It is called the first principal component, the second principal component, etc. according to the information volume in the principal component. There are several relations between principal components and original variables:

1) Principal component retains most information of original variables.
2) Number of principal component is much less than that of original variables.
3) Each principal component is unrelated.
4) Each principal component is the linear combination of original variables.

The purpose of PCA is to recombine the related variables to a group of new unrelated comprehensive variables to replace the original variables. Generally, the mathematically processing method is the linear combination of the original variables as the new comprehensive variables. How to choose from so many combinations? If the first linear combination (the first comprehensive variable) is denoted as F_1, we need it to reflect more information of the original variables. In PCA, "information" is measured by variance, namely if $Var(F_1)$ is larger, it indicates F_1 contains more information. Therefore, the variance selected in all linear combinations is largest, so F_1 is called the first principal component. If the first principal component is insufficient to represent the information of p variables, we consider selecting the second linear combination. To effectively reflect the original information, the information in F_1 will not appear in F_2. The expr F_2 ession is $Cov(F_1, F_2) = 0$, and is called the second principal component. We may construct the 3rd, 4th and p_{th} principal component by doing like this.

Supposing there are n evaluation objects (sample, such as the person conducting physical examinations) and m evaluation indicators (such as height, weight, etc.), it may compose a matrix sized $n \times m$. It is denoted as $x = (x_{ij})_{n \times m}$, where $x_i, i = 1, 2, \cdots, m$ is column vector. The matrix is called an evaluation matrix.

After obtaining the evaluation matrix, the general steps of PCA are shown as follows:

1) Calculate the mean value $\bar{x} = \frac{1}{n}\sum_{i=1}^{n} x_{ij}$ and variance $S_j = \sqrt{\sum_{i=1}^{n} (x_{ij} - \bar{x}_j)/(n-1)}$ of the original sample data. The mean value and standard deviation are calculated in each column.

2) Calculate standard data $X_{ij} = {(x_{ij} - \bar{x}_j)}/{S_j}$ and evaluation matrix changes to the matrix after standardization:

$$X = \begin{bmatrix} X_{11} & X_{12} & \cdots & X_{1m} \\ X_{21} & X_{22} & \cdots & X_{2m} \\ \vdots & \vdots & \ddots & \vdots \\ X_{n1} & X_{n2} & \cdots & X_{nm} \end{bmatrix} = (X_1, X_2, \cdots, X_m) \tag{5.12}$$

3) Apply the matrix after standardization to calculate the correlation matrix $C = (c_{ij})_{m \times m}$ of each evaluation indicator (or covariance matrix), thus C is the symmetric and positive matrix. Therefore $c_{ij} = X_i^T X_j / (n - 1)$.

4) Calculate the characteristic value λ and characteristic vector ξ of the correlation matrix (or covariance matrix). Arrange the characteristic values in decreasing order: $\lambda_1 > \lambda_2 > \cdots > \lambda_m$, and then arrange characteristic vectors corresponding to the characteristic value. Supposing the j characteristic vector is $\xi_j = (\xi_{1j}, \xi_{2j}, \cdots, \xi_{mj})^T$, then the j principal component is

$$F_j = \xi_j^T X = \xi_{1j} X_1 + \xi_{2j} X_2 + \cdots + \xi_{mj} X_m \tag{5.13}$$

When $j = 1$, F_1 is the first principal component.

5) According to the characteristic value of the correlation matrix, calculate contribution rate η and the accumulative contribution rate Q of the principal component is

$$\eta_i = \frac{\lambda_i}{\lambda_1 + \lambda_1 + \cdots + \lambda_m}, \quad Q_i = \eta_1 + \eta_2 + \cdots + \eta_i, \quad i = 1, 2, \dots, m \tag{5.14}$$

6) Finally, according to the contribution rate designated by the user, determine the number of principal components and obtain the principal component of the evaluation matrix (Figure 5.9). Generally, the contribution rates are 0.85, 0.9 and 0.95. Three different contribution rate levels are determined according to the specific scenario. The general steps of PCA are shown below:

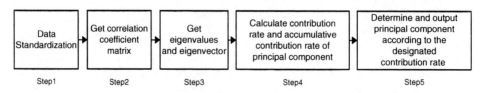

Figure 5.9 Principal Component Analysis (PCA) steps.

Table 5.11 Patient data for PCA classification in Example 5.7.

Id	Triglyceride	Total cholesterol	Hdl-c	Ldl-c	Age	Weight	Total protein	Blood sugar
1	1.05	3.28	1.35	1.8	60	56.8	66.8	5.6
2	1.43	5.5	1.66	3.69	68	57.4	79.4	5.3
3	1.16	3.97	1.27	2.55	68	70.7	74.7	5.4
4	6.8	5.95	0.97	2.87	50	80.1	74	5.6
5	3.06	5.25	0.9	3.81	48	82.7	72.4	5.8
6	1.18	5.88	1.77	3.87	53	63.5	78	5.2
7	2.53	6.45	1.43	4.18	57	61.3	75	7.3
8	1.6	5.3	1.27	3.74	47	64.9	73.6	5.4
9	3.02	4.95	0.95	3.53	39	88.2	79	4.6
10	2.57	6.61	1.56	4.27	60	63	80	5.6

Example 5.7   Principal Component Analysis of Patient Data

Table 5.11 is the set of triglyceride, total cholesterol, high-density lipoprotein choles-terol (hdl-c), low density lipoprotein cholesterol (ldl-c), age, weight, total protein and blood sugar levels in physical examination data in a grade-A hospital of the second class in Wuhan City, China. Use PCA to determine the principal component of persons to achieve dimensionality reduction of data.

Because the data in each column reflects different aspects of the persons conducting the physical examinations and the indicator unit is different, we standardize the original data. For example, the indicator of No. 1 person is given as $x'_{11} = \frac{x_{11}}{\max(x_1)} = \frac{1.05}{6.8} = 0.15$, represented by the following evaluation matrix and correlation matrix:

$$x = \begin{bmatrix} 0.15 & 0.50 & \cdots & 0.77 \\ 0.21 & 0.83 & \cdots & 0.73 \\ \vdots & \vdots & \ddots & \vdots \\ 0.38 & 1 & \cdots & 0.77 \end{bmatrix} \qquad corr(x) = \begin{bmatrix} 1 & 0.40 & \cdots & 0.09 \\ 0.40 & 1 & \cdots & 0.35 \\ \vdots & \vdots & \ddots & \vdots \\ 0.09 & 0.35 & \cdots & 1 \end{bmatrix}$$

Calculate characteristic value and characteristic vector according to the correlation matrix:

$$\lambda = [2.96, 2.65, 1.33, 0.62, 0.33, 0.0024, 0.07, 0.036]$$

where the characteristic vector corresponding to the first characteristic value is

$$\xi_1 = [00.42, 0.02, 0.53, 0.06, 0.46, -0.54, 0.07, 0.16]^T$$

Calculate the contribution rate of each principal component and plot, as in Figure 5.10. The appointed contribution rate is 85%. We may calculate the principal component as:

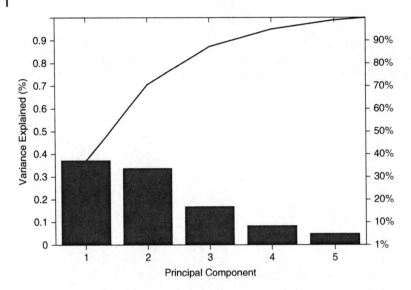

Figure 5.10 Contribution rate of principal component.

The explanation of the above three principal components to each physical examination indicator $(X_1, X_2, \cdots, X_8)$ is shown in Figure 5.11. Therefore, use PCA to determine three principal components:

$$F_1 = \sum_i \xi_{1i} x_{1i} \ , F_2 = \sum_i \xi_{2i} x_{2i} \ , F_3 = \sum_i \xi_{3i} x_{3i} \quad i = 1, 2, \cdots, m \tag{5.15}$$

Here, m = 8, which is the physical examination indicator. We may use three principal components to reflect eight indicators in the physical examination data. The information retention rate is 86.86%, which greatly reduces the dimensions of the data and facilitates the data analysis in later stages. ∎

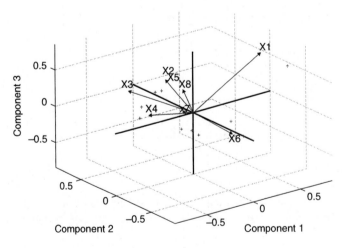

Figure 5.11 Explanation of principal component to physical examination indicator.

5.3.3 Semi-Supervised Machine Learning Methods

In this subsection, we introduce three alternative ML algorithms that differ from the supervised machine learning. Most unsupervised learning algorithms aim at discovering better representations of the input provided. Only the basic concepts of these learning models are given below. These three methods are not qualified as totally unsupervised ML algorithms presented in the previous sections.

5.3.3.1 Reinforcement Machine Learning

This is considered an unsupervised ML algorithm. The correct input/output pairs are never presented, nor sub-optimal actions explicitly corrected. This method expects users to take proactive action to reinforce the quality of the input data to help the prediction accuracy. This is considered a long-term performance reward. A reinforced learning algorithm demands a policy that links the states of the prediction model to the levels of reinforcement actions to be taken. The idea of reinforcement learning is inspired by behavioral psychology. For example, reinforcement actions can be related to game theory, control theory, operations research, information theory, crowd intelligence, statistics and genetic algorithms.

The ultimate goal is to reach some form of equilibrium under bounded rationality. Some researchers also relate reinforcement learning by a Markov decision process (MDP) using dynamic programming techniques. Reinforcement actions are not initiated by supervised learning. The emphasis is to achieve on-line performance. We need to find the proper tradeoff between exploration of unknown data exploitation from knowledge sorted from available data. To reinforce the learning process, the user must first define the optimality. Instead of using brute force, users can use a value-function approach based on Monte Carlo or temporal difference methods. Also, we can consider the direct policy search approach.

We can also consider an inverse reinforcement learning (IRL) method. Here, no reward function is given. Instead, the user figures out a policy under some observed behavior. The purpose is to mimic the observed behavior toward optimality. If the IRL process deviates from the observed behavioral course, the trainer needs a contingency plan to return the track to stability. This is essentially a trial and error approach, by which the user repeats the observed behavior multiple times with small changes each time.

5.3.3.2 Representation Machine Learning

This ML approach attempts to preserve the crucial information in input data, while transformation is done with the data to yield a better unsupervised model. This could be done at the pre-processing stage before performing classification or predictions. This may demand reconstruction of the inputs with some unknown data distribution. Classical examples of representation learning include the PCA and cluster analysis presented in Sections 6.1 and 6.2. This method is also known as feature learning. The learner attempts to learn a feature through transformation of raw data input into a representation that can better improve the prediction model.

This method allows a computer to learn a specific task using the features and to learn the features themselves to improve the learning process. Feature learning is motivated by the fact that the classification demands simpler input data to reduce computational complexity. The real-world data such as images, video and sensor measurements are often very complex. The learner must discover useful features or representations from raw data. Traditional hand-crafted features often require expensive human labor and often rely on expert knowledge.

Toward the design of efficient feature learning techniques to automate the learning process, we have two approaches based on the division between supervised and unsupervised learning:

1) Supervised feature learning is conducted with labeled input data. Examples include artificial neural networks, multilayer perceptron and supervised dictionary learning.

2) Unsupervised feature learning generates features with unlabeled input data. Examples include dictionary learning, independent component analysis, autoencoders, matrix factorization and various forms of clustering introduced previously: https://en.wikipedia.org/wiki/Feature_learning - cite_note-coates2011-3

5.3.3.3 Semi-supervised Machine Learning

This approach offers a mixture between supervised and unsupervised learning. In this case, the trainer is given an incomplete training dataset with some of the target outputs (labels) missing. Transduction is a special case of this principle where the entire set of problems is known at the learning time, except that parts of the targets are missing. In a way, both reinforcement and representation algorithms are subclasses of semi-supervised ML methods.

Many machine-learning researchers found that the joint use of unlabeled data with a small amount of labeled data can improve the learning accuracy. The discovery of some useful labeled data often demands domain expertise or a set of physical experiments to be conducted. The cost associated with the labeling process prevents the use of a fully labeled training set. In other words, the use of partially labeled data is more plausible.

As a matter of fact, semi-supervised learning is closer to human learning due our capability to handle fuzziness. Three basic assumptions on semi-supervised learning are given below. In order to make any use of unlabeled data, we must assume some data distribution. Different semi-supervised learning algorithms may assume at least one of the following assumptions (sources: Wikipedia https://en.wikipedia.org/wiki/Semi-supervised_learning 2016):

- **Smoothness assumption:** Sample data points which are close to each other are more likely to share a label. This is also generally assumed in supervised learning. This assumption may lead to a preference for geometrically simple decision boundaries. In the case of semi-supervised learning, the smoothness assumption yields a preference for decision boundaries in low-density regions.
- **Cluster assumption:** The data tend to form discrete clusters, and points in the same cluster are more likely to share a label. Sharing a label may be spread across multiple clusters, an assumption related to feature learning with clustering algorithms.
- **Manifold assumption:** The data lie approximately on a manifold of much lower dimension than the input space. In this case, we learn the manifold using both the labeled and unlabeled data to avoid the problem of dimensionality. Thus, semi-supervised learning can proceed using distances and densities defined on the manifold.

The manifold assumption is practical when high-dimensional datasets are encountered. For instance, the human voice is controlled by a few vocal cords, and images of

Figure 5.12 An example to illustrate semi-supervised machine learning.

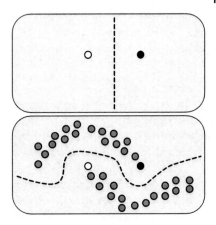

various facial expressions are controlled by a few muscles. We would like in these cases to use distances and smoothness in the natural data space, rather than in the space of all possible acoustic waves or images respectively. The following example shows the advantage of semi-supervised machine learning.

Example 5.8   Semi-Supervised Machine Learning
This example is from Wikipedia (https://en.wikipedia.org/wiki/Semi-supervised_learning). The purpose is to show the influence of unlabeled data on semi-supervised learning. The top panel in Figure 5.12 shows a decision boundary we might adopt after seeing only one positive (white circle) and one negative (black circle) example.

The bottom panel shows a decision boundary we might adopt if, in addition to the two labeled examples, we were given a collection of unlabeled data (gray circles). This could be viewed as performing clustering and then labeling the clusters with the labeled data, pushing the decision boundary away from high-density regions, or learning a 1-D manifold where the data resides.   ∎

5.4   How to Choose Machine Learning Algorithms?

Methods to select the right model for machine learning are studied below. Some strategies and plausible solutions are introduced. We consider data comprehension through visualization, ML algorithm selection, and over-fitting or under-fitting solutions. Finally, we present a procedure for ML algorithm selection. We also discuss the advantages and disadvantages of using different loss functions.

5.4.1   Performance Metrics and Model Fitting

Each ML algorithm has its own application potential. Given a dataset, the performance of a given algorithm may be excellent, but that of another algorithm may be the opposite. Furthermore, changing to a different dataset may also drastically change the conclusion. Thus, it is rather difficult to judge which algorithm is more excellent than others in the general cases. It is critical to introduce some common metrics to evaluate ML algorithms. Some metrics may be adopted to reveal the relative merits. Others may be used to find similar algorithms that could be easier to implement.

5.4.1.1 Performance Metrics of ML Algorithms

We consider three fundamental metrics to satisfy various performance requirements as stated:

1) **Accuracy:** This is the most important criterion to evaluate ML performance, based on testing the dataset. There are two cases: over-fitting or under-fitting algorithms. Obviously, the higher performance exhibited by the training set, the better the fit of the algorithm.
2) **Training time:** This refers to the convergence speed of an algorithm, or the time needed to establish the optimality of a working model. Obviously, the shorter the training time, the better the model built to perform with a lower implement cost.
3) **Linearity:** This is a model property reflecting the complexity of the ML algorithm applied. Linear performance implies some form of scalable performance. In practice, linear algorithms with lower complexity are more often desired, because they may lead to shorter training times or even higher accuracy at a reduced cost.

5.4.1.2 Data Preprocessing

Before analyzing data, the data growth pattern and correlation among data must be revealed. This demands data visualization, especially when large or multi-dimensional datasets are encountered. Because only 2-D or 3-D graphs can be displayed, preprocessing is required to reduce the dimensions of data space to a fewer dimensions.

Data quality affects the effectiveness of the ML training process and thus the performance. To achieve the above performance goals, we consider several methods to enhance the data quality during data discovery, collection, preparation and preprocessing stages. The purpose is to make the data more complete, relevant and regulated to be used as training data or yield higher cross validation results:

- **Filling of missing data:** Due to incomplete statistics or unrecognizable handwritten records, we cannot guarantee full datum in each line and each column of a raw dataset. In this case, to reconstruct missing data is desirable. Generally, Mean/mode completion or hot deck imputation are adopted for filling in missing data to make them more complete to meet our needs.
- **Preprocessing of incorrect data:** Often we encounter some data that are obviously incorrect due to typos or recording error. Sometimes, the data could be deviated from regularity for being too large or too small in values. These demand data fitting or some interpolation or extrapolation methods to streamline that data.
- **Regularization of data:** Many data features and their physical units are very different. If two data units differ by several orders of magnitude, the normalization or standardization process is needed. To this end, Equation (5.19) is used, where x is the unregulated or un-normalized data and x' is the regulated or normalized data. The regularization process is governed by one of these computations:

$$\begin{cases} x' = \dfrac{x}{\max(x)} \\ x' = \dfrac{x - \min(x)}{\max(x) - \min(x)} \end{cases} \qquad (5.16)$$

- **Visualization Support:** For multidimensional data, visualization is carried out by feature extraction and dimension reduction. The users may want to visualize the

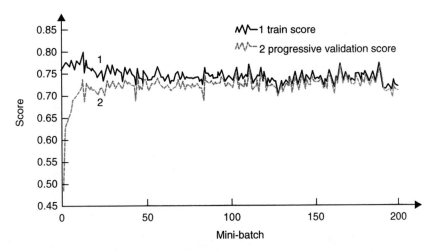

Figure 5.13 The training score and cross-validation score match nicely in a well-fitting machine learning model created.

principal features first. A dimension reduction method is adopted to eliminate some insignificant features. For example, numerical numbers can be converted from recorded data to digital or graphical forms.

5.4.1.3 Machine Learning Performance Scores

In order to quantify the performance of an ML algorithm, we can define some performance scores. These scores are normalized as a percentage with 100% for the perfect score and small fractions for lower scores. This score is often a weighted function of all three performance metrics introduced in Section 5.4.1. Difference user groups may apply different weighting functions to emphasize their preferred choices. Often the accuracy weights the highest and the training time may be the secondary. The linearity could be the least important or simply ignored if the learner is limited by implementation costs.

The performance of an ML algorithm is often plotted as a learning performance curve, as shown in Figure 5.13. In this learning curve, the score is shown on the y-axis against the training samples or the testing data size on the x-axis. There are two competing scores illustrated in such a performance curve. The training score is driven by the training dataset applied. The cross validation score is based on the progressive testing of all incoming data. In general, the training score is higher than the validation score because the model is built from the training dataset. Figure 5.13 shows an ideal case, where the two scores converge quickly after sufficient testing by a mini batch of data.

5.4.1.4 Model Fitting Cases in Machine Learning Process

We consider below two model under-fitting cases in the process of choosing an acceptable machine learning algorithm to apply under various performance conditions of the training and testing datasets:

- **Over-Fitting Modeling**: This is the case where the training score is very high, but the cross-validation score is very low for testing the datasets applied. As shown in

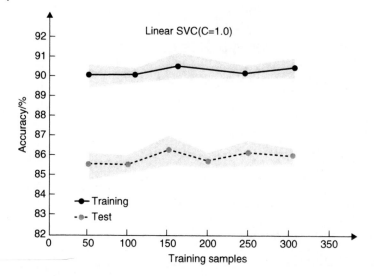

Figure 5.14 The over-fitting case when creating a learning model using the linear-SVC algorithm with a small dataset of up to 160 samples.

Figure 5.14, the two scores are separated far apart from each other. This status implies that the model fits the training set very closely. However, the model has ignored the noise margins in the validation dataset. In other words, the training set is heavily biased on a particular training dataset. This sample dataset stays far away from common data distribution or characteristics in general applications. In this case, the over-fitting model simply cannot model the testing data accurately.

- **Under-Fitting Modeling**: This is the case where the model produced by a given training set ends up with a very low score performance, which is far below the user's expectation. The under-fitting phenomenon implies that a poor training set was chosen and the trained model so obtained cannot perform well on real testing datasets. Therefore, the model is totally unacceptable to users.

Both over-fitting and under-fitting are not acceptable. This implies that we have to choose the proper training dataset that can represent the general datasets. In subsequent subsections, we will suggest a number of methods to cope with these two shortcomings in machine learning modeling. In summary, an ideal model must work well in both the training dataset and other datasets in general applications.

With the increase of sample data size, the training score decreases slightly while small increase of cross-validation score is observed. This is texted on the Linear-SVC algorithm with a regulation factor C = 1. In general, the training score is often higher than the cross-validation score. But the gap between them should be minimized by all means. This implies that the model is more often falling into an over-fitting case. When we follow the behavior of the training set, we have to be concerned about lowering the cross-validation score. We will attack the over-fitting problem in Section 5.4.2 and the under-fitting problem in Section 5.4.3.

In general, the training score is often higher than the cross-validation score. This implies that the model is more often falling into an over-fitting case. Thus, the model is making every effort to follow the behavior of the training set. The lower cross-validation score is under the influence of having much higher noise in the testing dataset, so we must overcome the difficulties coming from both over-fitting and under-fitting problems. Some approaches are given in the next two sections.

5.4.2 Methods to Reduce Model Over-Fitting

The main reason for over-fitting is that the model deliberately memorizes the distribution properties of the training samples. In other words, the model being created is overly biased by the sample data behavior. The over-fitting model scores very highly on a particular training set, but scores badly on other datasets. In other words, the big score gaps must be closed up across the various datasets applied. Listed below are several methods to reduce this adverse effect.

5.4.3.1 Increasing the Training Data Size

Increasing the quantity of samples may make the training set more representative to cover more variety and scarcity of data. Increasing in samples applied reflects the noise effects better, with the mean value of the noise being reduced to zero. That is, the influence of noise on the testing data could be greatly reduced. The common method to increase sample size is to collect more data under the same scenario. Sometimes, manual labeling is added to generate some artificial training samples. For instance, we can apply image recognition, mirror transform and rotation to enlarge the sample quantity. Even though these operations may be labor-intensive, the method enhances the dependency of samples. This will improve the model by avoiding training biases.

Example 5.9 Enlarging the Sample Dataset for the Linear SVC Algorithm
As shown in Figure 5.15, the sample dataset is now enlarged from 150 to 400. This enlarged dataset has resulted in good convergence of the score curves as the dataset increases beyond 200. The two scores become very close to each other as the sample data size increases beyond 300. ∎

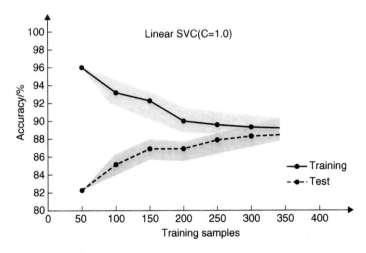

Figure 5.15 Reducing the model over-fitting effects by enlarging the training set to 800 samples.

Under circumstances with small sample data size that cannot be increased further, we can reduce the noise effect by transforming the existing sample set, such as by using wavelet analysis. The purpose is to reduce the mean noise to zero. In the meantime, the noise variance is also reduced, thus reducing the influence of noise on all data to be tested. As training samples increase, the difference between the training-score and cross-validation score could be reduced, as demonstrated by the following example.

5.4.2.2 Feature Screening and Dimension Reduction Methods

Sometimes we may have a large training dataset that is characterized by many sample features. By revealing the correlation between features, we can cut off some features to reduce the over-fitting effect. Those features with limited representative power are removed. This is called feature screening or dimension reduction. In fact, we can traverse all combination styles of features and select the more important features. In the case of samples with high dimensionality, association analysis or correlation analysis may be adopted to eliminate some weak features by reducing the dimensions.

Occasionally it can be difficult to determine the relations between orthogonal features. In this case, the PCA algorithm applies dimension reduction. In the case where the dimensionality of feature space is not high, we conduct feature screening to decrease the complexity of the model. There exist three approaches methods for doing so: i) decreasing the degree of polynomial in the ML model; ii) reducing the layers of artificial neural networks and quantity of nodes in each layer; and iii) increasing the bandwidth of the RBF-kernel in the SVM algorithm.

Example 5.10   Using Fewer Features (Dimensions) to Reduce the Over-Fitting Effects

We can apply an association analysis to assess various feature impacts in the PCA algorithm. In Figure 5.16, we demonstrate the effects of using fewer features in the Linear-SVC algorithm. In this case, feature 7 and feature 8 are selected manually after

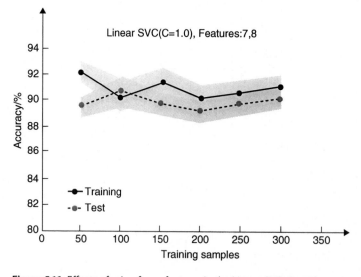

Figure 5.16 Effects of using fewer features in the Linear-SVC algorithm.

observation of their heavier roles in the learning process. Sometimes it is difficult to determine the relations between orthogonal features. In this case, the PCA algorithm should be applied for dimension reduction. ∎

5.4.2.3 Effects of Data Regularization

By adjusting data regularization parameters, we can reduce the over-fitting effects to some extent. Grid-search may be conducted on the cross-validation set to find the optimum regularization parameter. To this end, we have just seen the course of selecting features with SelectKBest in the sklearn.feature_selection. As mentioned above, this course may be very slow in cases of features with high dimensionality. We have to discriminate against some features through some data regularization methods, as in the two cases:

1) **L1-regularization:** This regularization method makes the characteristic weights sparsely distributed. In other words, characteristics, which are not important to the final results, can be assigned with zero weight.
2) **L2-regularization:** This method scatters the feature weights on various feature dimensions as far as possible. Scattering prevents weight from concentrating on certain dimensions.

Example 5.11 Applying the L1 Data Regularization to Reduce the Over-Fitting Effects

We apply the L1-regularization in Figure 5.17 to make the feature weights sparsely distributed in the Linear-SVC algorithm in classification applications. This method automatically discriminates against the features with very low or zero weights. Considering all the weights of 5-D, 9-D, 11-D, 12-D, 17-D and 18-D features, we keep the 11-D feature for having the highest weight. The weight factor is marked as C = 1.0 in Figure 5.17. With a small size of 300 samples, the training and testing scores converge to each other nicely. ∎

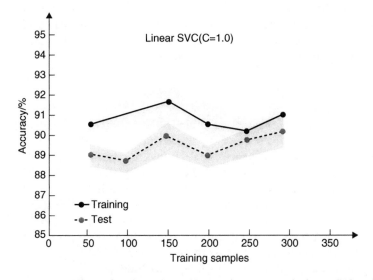

Figure 5.17 Effects of applying the L1 data regularization on the linear-SVC performance.

5.4.3   Methods to Avoid Model Under-Fitting

Under-fitting takes place in two situations: i) the dataset is poorly prepared, and simply cannot perform well in training and validation processes; and ii) the machine learning algorithm is wrongly chosen, considering the nature of the problem environment. In other words, different datasets may apply to the chosen algorithm differently. For this reason, the under-fitting problem is difficult to solve completely. The more feasible approach is to find ways to avoid the under-fitting problem. In this section, we show two methods to reduce the under-fitting effects on performance scores. In Section 5.4.4, we will suggest an intuitive method to select the best-fit machine learning algorithm out of five categories at the highest functional level.

5.4.3.1   Mixed Parameter Changes

Consider the under-fitting problem when using an SVM (Support Vector Machine) model for solving a classification problem. One way is to utilize an artificial neural network (ANN) to train the system to yield a better model fit. In another example of model under-fitting, we can modify the kernel function to cover the case of non-linear classification. For example, we can replace an SGD (Stochastic Gradient Descent) classifier with a multi-layer ANN. Here the **kernel-approximation** is adopted to complete the task. Example 5.12 shows the modification of two parameters in the Linear SVC algorithm, shown in previous examples, to yield a better fit to the SVC learning model development.

Example 5.12   Changing the Linear-SVC Model with Reduced $C = 0.1$ and L1 Penalty

The change in score on data is small after iteration of 50 mini-batches of sampling data. The scores are low to reflect under-fitting. The performance deteriorates rapidly in the case of using an under-fitting model. For the LinearSVC model we have tested in previous examples, we could reduce the regularization factor C to 0.1 from 1 and apply the L1 regularization penalty at the same time. Figure 5.18 plots the improved high scores (around 0.91) in both scores across a wide range of sample dataset sizes from 50 to 300. Thus, through this mixed change of model parameters, we end up with a fairly close match between the training score and cross-validation scores.   ■

5.4.3.2   Changing the Loss Functions

Machine learning problems also can be viewed as a minimization of some loss function of the training examples. Loss functions express the discrepancy between the trained model prediction and the actual problem instances. For example, the classification problem requires the user to assign a label to such instances, and by using the trained model to predict the labels of training samples, loss function then reflects the differences of these two kinds of label set. Thus, the loss function reveals the effects of losing the expected performance of an ML algorithm. An optimized algorithm should minimize the loss in a training set, while machine learning is concerned with minimizing the loss in unseen samples. The selection of loss function is critical to obtain a better or optimal prediction model. We consider below five design choices of loss functions. Their effects are plotted in Figure 5.19.

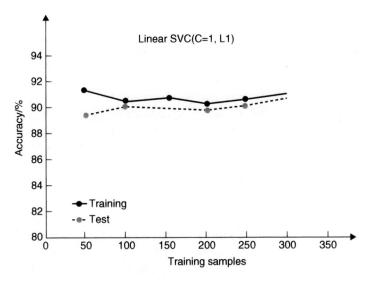

Figure 5.18 Under-Fitting results in the Linear-SVC algorithm.

1) **Zero-one loss function**: This policy offers a very sharp division between success and failure. The 0–1 loss function counts the number of miss-predictions in the classification problems. However, it is a non-convex function, not practical in real-life applications.

2) **Hinge loss function:** This is often used in SVM (Support Vector Machines) applications for its relative strength to reflect the unusual sensitivity to noise effects. This function is not supported by the probabilistic distributions.

3) **Log loss function:** This loss function can reflect the probabilistic distribution. In multi-class classification, we need to know the confidence of the classification. The

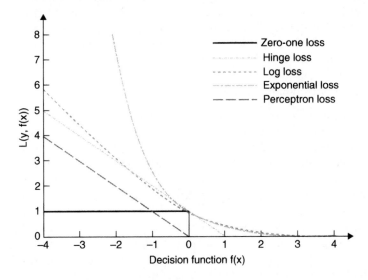

Figure 5.19 Effects of using different loss functions in machine learning model selection.

log-loss function is rather suitable. However, the shortcoming lies in lower sensitivity to noise and lack of judgment strength.

4) **Exponential loss function:** This has been applied in AdaBoost. It is very sensitive to separation from the crowd and noises. Its prediction style is simple and effective in dealing with boosting algorithms.

5) **Perceptron loss function:** This can be regarded as a variation from the hinge loss. Hinge loss poses a heavy penalty in misjudgment of the boundary points, while perceptron loss is satisfied with accurate classification from sample data. This score ignores the distance from the judgment boundary. The advantage is that it is simpler than using the hinge loss function. The shortcoming lies in the fact that it offers a weaker model to apply to general problems, due to lack of a max-margin boundary.

5.4.3.3 Other Model Modifications or The Ensemble Approach

The PCA (Principal Component Analysis) algorithm studied in Section 5.3.2 offers a dimension reduction approach to reduce model complexity. We can also consider using several principal components to interconnect the data elements. Besides, the independence of each principal component is strong, therefore it greatly reduces the internal connection among the data.

The emergence of the ensemble algorithm provides another solution to the under-fitting problem, where each individual model does not perform well in a given dataset. We can consider using several algorithms concurrently in the same dataset, then choose the one that best fits the performance scores. As an example, applying the Adaboost and Decision Tree models jointly to improve the accuracy of the prediction results.

5.4.4 Effects of Using Different Loss Functions

Given the datasets from a known application domain, the following procedure in Algorithm 5.6 shows how to select the proper machine learning algorithm, based on the dataset characteristics and performance requirement. Five categories of machine learning algorithms are considered. In general, the following options can be used to solve the under-fitting problems. These methods appear, in particular, to improve the classification problem, since the model performance is so sensitive to the datasets applied. We consider three options in selecting the datasets. The dataset selection is driven by the performance demand. Three selection options are given below:

1) **Common Datasets:** Dividing the original dataset into two parts: with equal characteristics and distributions in the training set and testing set. This subdivision should result in a model performance to avoid either over-fitting or under-fitting problems.

2) **Cross Validation:** Dividing the original dataset into k parts and selecting a part in turn as a test set, with the remaining as the training set. This demands k validation test runs. This model performance shows the average accuracy of the model over many subdivided test sets.

3) **Bootstrap Cycle:** Randomly sampling with replacement of some data elements repeatedly in different training samples. Let the sampled data be the training set, with the remaining as the test sets. Repeat these sampling cycles k times. We may end up with a weighted mean performance of all test sets applied.

Algorithm 5.6   Selecting Machine Learning Algorithm from five Categories

---

Input: The input dataset
Output: Algorithm category
Procedure:
1) Preprocessing to improve data quality (regulation could be delayed to model process)
2) Visualization requirements (selecting algorithm based on visualization results)
3) Define Objective Function (focusing on feature properties or expected results)
4) If feature property is chosen, choose a feature correlation algorithm (Category 1)
5) Or choose expected results
6) Subdivide the entire data set (training dataset versus testing dataset)
7) Are labels present in dataset?
8) If yes, then exit labels
9) Choose a classification algorithm (Category 2)
10) Or only partial labels present
11) Choose a semi-unsupervised learning algorithm (Category 3)
12) Or no label exists
13) Choose a clustering algorithm (Category 4)
14) Execute the model obtained
15) Measure the results (making predictions)
16) Obtain testing scores
17) If the score is satisfactory
18) Output the results
19) Or the accuracy score is too low
20) Choose an ensemble algorithm (Category 5), go to Step 4
21) Repeat preset number of iterations
22) The output is doubtful, so choose a different dataset or reduce the standard.

5.5   Conclusions

Machine learning is high in demand with the rise of data science and the big data industry. More and more scholars begin to focus on this area and an increasing number of algorithms have been proposed. This chapter focuses on unsupervised learning and semi-supervised learning in machine learning. The last section of this chapter introduces how to choose a suitable algorithm among many machine learning algorithms. More details of various ML algorithms can be found in the references below.

Homework Problems

5.1 Table 5.12 provides the abscissa and ordinate of data points in a machine learning experiment. Apply the K-means clustering algorithm to subdivide these points into three clusters using the Euclidean distance function. You must identify the

Table 5.12 Abscissa and ordinate of some data points.

Point ID	Abscissa	Ordinate	Point ID	Abscissa	Ordinate
1	0	0	6	4	11
2	2	3	7	6	9
3	4	2	8	8	10
4	0	6	9	12	6
5	3	10	10	7	9

centers (centroids) and show the detailed clustering process step by step. Draw a 2-D Euclidean space diagram to show the final partition results on the 10 data points and the cluster boundaries.

5.2 You have learned four different clustering methods in Section 5.2. Distinguish their fundamental differences in methodology, strength and weakness. Analyze the computational complexity and implementation requirements on a chosen cloud if an extremely large dataset is processed. Discuss the scenario where each method fits best. Based on the similarity or distance function applied, you should identify one real-life application for each clustering method. Justify your observations and claims with analytical reasoning and numerical performance assessment, with data available from the public domain or literature.

5.3 There is always a definite link between commercial commodities and their labeled prices in department stores. The pricing policy is what you are asked to work out with the small dataset given in Table 5.13. There are five products that have been observed for 8 months for their price variations. The binary value "1" represents the price increase during the past 8 months. The "0" marks no increase in price of a given product item. Work out a set of association rules to specify the price policy. Apply the rules to determine the price of a new product column. Justify the association rule you have derived and applied.

5.4 The development level of a city is assessed by many indicators, such as population, total volume of passenger transport and freight transport. Table 5.14 shows six

Table 5.13 Goods price rising conditions.

Goods, Month	Item A	Item B	Item C	Item D	Item E
1	1	0	1	0	1
2	0	1	0	1	0
3	1	0	1	0	0
4	0	1	0	0	1
5	1	0	0	0	0
6	1	1	1	0	1
7	1	1	1	0	0
8	1	0	1	1	0

Table 5.14 Social and economic indicators of eight Chinese cities.

City	ILP	TGOV	TIOV	TVPT	TVFT	FB
Beijing	1249.90	1.84	2.00	2.03	4.56	2.79
Tianjin	910.17	1.59	2.26	0.33	2.63	1.13
Shijiazhuang	875.40	2.92	0.69	0.29	0.19	0.71
Taiyuan	299.92	0.24	0.27	0.19	1.19	0.39
Hohhot	207.78	0.37	0.08	0.24	0.26	0.14
Shenyang	677.08	1.30	0.58	0.78	1.54	0.90
Dalian	545.31	1.88	0.84	1.08	1.92	0.76
Changchun	691.23	1.85	0.60	0.48	0.95	0.48

social and economic indicators for eight cities in China The column headings: IL, TGOV, TIOV, TVPT, TVFT and FB denote the total income level (in 10,000 yuan), total agricultural output (10 billion yuan), total industrial output (100 billion yuan), total transport values (100 million yuan), total freight transport value (100 million yuan) and financial budget (100 billion yuan), respectively. Use the principal component analysis (PCA) method to rank the development level of these cities. Give complete reasoning on the dimensionality reduction performed in ranking the cities.

5.5 In order to determine whether students suffer from hyperlipemia disease when the semester begins, a physical examination is required to detect triglyceride, The metrics tested include cholesterol, high-density lipoprotein and low-density lipoprotein, etc. Due to human error, there is data missing from the list of physical examinations. Based on the data given in Table 5.15, select an appropriate machine learning algorithm to build a classification model to predict whether a student is suffering from hyperlipemia or not.

Table 5.15 Physical examination data and the status of hyperlipemia.

Id	Triglyceride	Total Cholesterol	High-Density Lipoprotein	Low-Density Lipoprotein	Hyperlipemia or not
1	1.05	3.28	1.35	1.8	No
2	1.43	5.5	1.66	3.69	No
3	1.16	3.97	1.27	2.55	Yes
4	6.8	5.95	0.97	2.87	Yes
5	3.06	5.25	0.9	3.81	Yes
6	1.18	5.88	1.77	3.87	No
7	2.53	6.45	1.43	4.18	Yes
8	1.6	5.3	1.27	3.74	No
9	3.02	4.95	0.95	3.53	Yes
10	2.57	6.61	1.56	4.27	Yes

Table 5.16 Growing status of plants in different environments.

Plant Number	Humidity (%RH)	Temperature (OC)	Light (light intensity)	CO2 (ppm)	Growing Status
1	64.14	23.04	1.87	817	0
2	65.97	23.11	36.99	702	0
3	65.3	21.01	6.36	803	1
4	71.75	20.58	125.82	822	1
5	63.6	21.53	94.23	772	0
6	64.51	21.47	58.47	888	1
7	65.01	22.03	3.19	719	0
8	66.98	23.66	14.23	754	0
9	67.73	21.61	16.49	760	1
10	67.04	20	6.68	890	1
11	67.79	19.86	121.1	842	1
12	65.6	20.82	15.92	694	0
13	64.92	23.06	86.38	849	1
14	65.8	23.67	86.56	752	0
15	64.91	22.48	73.74	806	1

5.6 A number of factors have been suggested to assess the growth condition of green-house plants, such as humidity, temperature, light, content of CO_2, etc. Given the data in Table 5.16 for a garden with 15 plants, evaluate the growing conditions of these 15 plants. We use "1" to denote the condition of growing well and "0" otherwise. By analyzing these data, apply the SVM model to estimate the growth condition of plants in an environment characterized by the vector {68.08, 20.27, 59.25, 775}.

5.7 Moderate drinking is good to increase blood circulation, but excessive drinking can harm health. Alcohol has been proven to have a paralysis effect on the human brain. Table 5.17 shows the relevant properties of 10 beer brands. You are asked to

Table 5.17 Descriptive properties of 10 beer brands.

Brand Beers	Heat (Joule)	Sodium (mmol/L)	Alcohol (degrees)	Price($)
Budweise	144	19	4.7	0.43
Ionenbra	157	15	4.9	0.48
Kronenso	170	7	5.2	0.73
Oldmin	145	23	4.6	0.26
Sudeiser	113	6	3.7	0.44
Coors	140	16	4.6	0.44
Coorslic	102	15	4.1	0.46
Kkirin	149	6	5	0.79
Olympia	72	6	2.9	0.46
Schite	97	7	4.2	0.47

use this dataset to analyze their paralysis effects. Define an objective function using any of the unsupervised machine learning models you have learned in this chapter. The purpose is to classify the damaging degree of these brands of beers. You may need some medical knowledge to define this paralysis model correctly. Check with healthcare experts or consult some authority, or dig out help from Wikipedia or Google search.

5.8 In Section 5.5, you have studied some selection criterion of machine learning (ML) algorithms to match with the application demands. The purpose is to make predictions, forecasting or classification of large datasets more accurately or efficiently. Briefly answer the following five questions on ML algorithm selection. Justify your answers with reasoning or by example cases:

a) Compile a table to suggest the key performance metrics that should be applied for each ML algorithm you have learned so far in Chapters 4 and 5. Justify your table entries with reasoning by applying an example that you know of.

b) Define the performance score of a machine learning method, such as those presented in Figure 5.13.

c) Distinguish between over-fitting and under-fitting cases in choosing an ML prediction model.

d) Define the different loss functions used in plotting those curves in Figure 5.19.

e) Explain the concepts of common datasets, cross-validation and bootstrap cycles in ML algorithm selection.

References

1 H. Trevor, R. Tibshirani and J. Friedman, *The Elements of Statistical Learning: Data mining, inference and prediction.* New York: Springer. pp. 485–586, 2009.

2 A. Ranjan, *A New Approach for Blind Source Separation of Convolutive Sources,* ISBN 978-3-639-07797-1 (this book focuses on unsupervised learning with Blind Source Separation), 2008.

3 C. Ding and X. He, K-means clustering via Principal Component Analysis. *Proceedings of the International Conference on Machine Learning* (ICML 2004), 225–232, July 2004.

4 P. Drineas, P.A. Frieze, R. Kannan, S. Vempala and V. Vinay, Clustering large graphs via the singular value decomposition. *Machine Learning,* 56, 9–33. Retrieved 2012-08-02, 2004.

5 Y. Bengio, et al., Representation learning: A review and new perspectives. *Pattern Analysis and Machine Intelligence,* 35(8), 1798–1828, 2013.

6 H.P. Kriegel, P. Kröger and A. Zimek, Clustering high-dimensional data. *ACM Transactions on Knowledge Discovery from Data,* 3(1), 2009.

7 C. Böhm, K Kailing, H.-P. Kriegel and P. Kröger, Density connected clustering with local subspace preferences. *4th IEEE International Conference on Data Mining* (ICDM'04), p. 27. 2004.

8 S.J. Bradtke, S.J. Andrew and G. Barto, Learning to predict by the method of temporal differences. *Machine Learning,* Springer, 22, 33–57, 1996.

9 L.P. Kaelbling, M.L. Littman and A.W. Moore, Reinforcement learning: a survey. *Journal of Artificial Intelligence Research,* 4, 237–285, 1996.

10 R. Sutton and A. Barto, *Reinforcement Learning: An Introduction.* MIT Press, 1998.

11 I. Szita, and S. Csaba, *Model-based Reinforcement Learning with Nearly Tight Exploration Complexity Bounds* (PDF). ICML, Omnipress, pp. 1031–1038, 2010.

12 O. Chapelle, B. Schölkopf, and A. Zien, *Semi-supervised Learning.* Cambridge, MA, MIT Press. 2006.

13 J. Ratsaby and S. Venkatesh, Learning from a mixture of labeled and unlabeled examples with parametric side information. *Proceedings of the Eighth Annual Conference on Computational Learning Theory,* 412–417, 1995.

14 X. Zhu and A. Goldberg, *Introduction to Semi-Supervised Learning.* Morgan & Claypool, 2009.

15 R. Agrawal and J.C. Shafer, Parallel mining of association rules. *IEEE Transactions on Knowledge & Data Engineering,* 6, 962–969. 1996.

16 R. Agrawal, T. Imieliński and A. Swami, Mining association rules between sets of items in large databases. *ACM SIGMOD Record,* 22(2), 207–216, 1993.

17 M.B. Eisen, P.T. Spellman, P.O. Brown, et al., Cluster analysis and display of genome-wide expression patterns. *Proceedings of the National Academy of Sciences,* 95(25), 14863–14868, 1998.

18 J. MacQueen, Some methods for classification and analysis of multivariate observations. *Proceedings of the 5th Berkeley Symposium in Mathematical Statistics and Probability,* 1(14): 281–297, 1967.

19 N. Jardine and R. Sibson, *Mathematical taxonomy.* London, John Wiley, 1971.

20 M. Ester, H.P. Kriegel, J. Sander, et al., A density-based algorithm for discovering clusters in large spatial databases with noise. 96(34), 226–231, 1996

21 S. Wold, K. Esbensen and P. Geladi, Principal component analysis. *Chemometrics and Intelligent Laboratory Systems,* 2(1–3), 37–52, 1987.

22 L. Breiman, J. Friedman, C.J. Stone, et al., *Classification and Regression Trees.* CRC press, 1984.

23 R. Kohavi, A study of cross-validation and bootstrap for accuracy estimation and model selection. 4(2), 1137–1145, 1995.

6

Deep Learning with Artificial Neural Networks

CHAPTER OUTLINE

6.1 Introduction, 249
    6.1.1 Deep Learning Mimics Human Senses, 249
    6.1.2 Biological Neurons versus Artificial Neurons, 251
    6.1.3 Deep Learning versus Shallow Learning, 254
6.2 Artificial Neural Networks (ANN), 256
    6.2.1 Single Layer Artificial Neural Networks, 256
    6.2.2 Multilayer Artificial Neural Network, 257
    6.2.3 Forward Propagation and Back Propagation in ANN, 258
6.3 Stacked AutoEncoder and Deep Belief Network, 264
    6.3.1 AutoEncoder, 264
    6.3.2 Stacked AutoEncoder, 267
    6.3.3 Restricted Boltzmann Machine, 269
    6.3.4 Deep Belief Networks, 275
6.4 Convolutional Neural Networks (CNN) and Extensions, 277
    6.4.1 Convolution in CNN, 277
    6.4.2 Pooling in CNN, 280
    6.4.3 Deep Convolutional Neural Networks, 282
    6.4.4 Other Deep Learning Networks, 283
6.5 Conclusions, 287

6.1 Introduction

Deep learning simulates the operations in layers of artificial neural networks. This is heavily used to extract and learn features from data. A multilayer neural network includes one input layer, one output layer and multiple hidden layers. The connection strength between neurons is adjusted in the learning process. Common deep learning architectures are introduced in subsequent sections, including the basic ANN, convolutional neural networks, deep belief network and recurrent neural network, etc.

6.1.1 Deep Learning Mimics Human Senses

In March 2016, AlphaGo generated high publicity and debate on human-machine competition in intelligence. After five rounds of competition, finally the computer beat Sedol Lee, a world-class Go player. Go is a complicated game, as it is well known that only

Big-Data Analytics for Cloud, IoT and Cognitive Computing, First Edition. Kai Hwang and Min Chen.
© 2017 John Wiley & Sons Ltd. Published 2017 by John Wiley & Sons Ltd.
Companion Website: http://www.wiley.com/go/hwangIOT

human intelligence can cope with the complexity involved. No professional athlete has been beaten by Go software before. Twenty years ago, computer Deep Blue used the method of searching algorithm to beat international chess master Garry Kasparov in an international chess match.

Playing Go is more difficult than playing other chess games. The computer-implemented AlphaGo combines deep learning and tree search algorithms to make smart decisions in placing the pawns. For the first time, Google AlphaGo has reached an almost human level in playing Go, intelligently without emotional disturbance. This represents a major step in advancing artificial intelligence to achieve human levels of performance.

Another reported advance was made at the Google Brain Project. In June 2012, tens of millions of random images from YouTube were recognized by a computer platform built over 16,000 CPU cores at Google. They use a training model over a deep neural network built with 1 billion artificial neurons. This model system identified basic features of images, learned how to compose these features, and automatically identified the image of a cat. During the training, the system did not obtain the information of "This is a cat", but comprehended the concept of "cat" itself. The project leader Andrew Ng said: "We directly put massive data into the artificial system and the system learns from data, automatically."

From the victory of AlphaGo to the success of Google Brain Project, it seems that deep learning has the capability of self-learning. The meaningful question to ask is: How can deep learning compete with humans through self-learning? If we want to judge whether a quadrangle is square or not, the rationale analytical approach is to seek features of a square, such as the same length for the four sides and four 90-degree corner angles. This requires comprehension of the concept of a right angle and the length of the side view, as demonstrated in Figure 6.1.

If we show a square image to a boy and tell him that this is a square, he would identify a square accurately after several tries. The method of rationally identifying a square is similar to the method where feature identification is designed artificially. But the way a child identifies a square follows a perceptual method. In a rational way, it is easy to describe and realize this problem with a computer. However, it is easy for a human to understand many problems in reality, but it is hard for a computer to comprehend and solve these problems in a rational way.

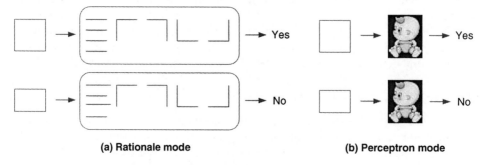

(a) Rationale mode   (b) Perceptron mode

Figure 6.1 Rationale versus perceptron modes to recognize a square object.

For instance, if we want to identify people through photos by a rational method through a computer, it requires to determine which features in a human face can be used for identification, such as nose, eyes, eyebrows and mouth, etc. Of course, it is difficult to choose appropriate features which can accurately distinguish people. Enormous influence would be brought by factors such as the change of light in photos, difference in shooting angle, and whether glasses are worn or not.

Let us consider a child's recognition of a person as an example. The child does not need to seek the features of the person to be recognized. But he can accurately identify the person after seeing that person or his/her photos several times. The change of light in photos, difference in shooting angle, and whether glasses are worn would not influence the identification. We may interpret that a child recognizes a person by impression. There exists some kind of mapping between the input photos and the output name in a human memory.

With the development of computer applications, people increasingly realize that rational or analytical methods would be inefficient or impossible when solving many problems in the real world. The mechanism that people do things intuitively seems quite efficient in front of modern science and technology. This intuitive method or the method of following one's heart could be simply interpreted as establishing certain mapping between input and output. But it is still unknown for us how the human brain realizes encoding, processing and storage of information with 100 billion neurons.

The main contribution of David Hubel and Torsten Wiesel (winners of the 1981 Nobel Prize in medicine) is that they found out that the information processing of the visual system (i.e. visual cortex) is hierarchical, as shown in Figure 6.2. At John Hopkins University, in 1958, they were studying the correspondence between pupil area and neurons in the cerebral cortex. By many experiments, it has been proven that there is some kind of correspondence between stimulation received by the pupils and different visual neurons located in the posterior cerebral cortex. They found a kind of neuron which they named as "orientation selective cell". When the pupil captures the edge of an object, and if this edge points to a certain direction, the corresponding neurons will be active.

The information processing of the human visual system was interpreted as extracting edge features from area V1, and extracting shape features or some constituent parts of an objective from area V2. Then higher levels of understanding are reached. From low- to high-level features, the abstraction degree increases. A combination of low-level features serves as input to higher level. Thus, higher level features reveal more semantics. As abstraction increases, there is less context confusion, which is good for classification or identification purposes.

6.1.2 Biological Neurons versus Artificial Neurons

The human brain has a very complicated structure. But its constitutional unit is the neuron, which produces output (excitement) per input. The hierarchical information processing of the human brain is realized through numerous neurons that are interconnected. In the biological neuron modeled in Figure 6.3(a), the left end of the dendrite is connected to the cytomembrane as the input, while the right end of the axon is the output. What the neuron mainly outputs is an electrical impulse. There are a lot of branches of dendrites and axons, with the end of an axon often connected to a dendrite of other neurons.

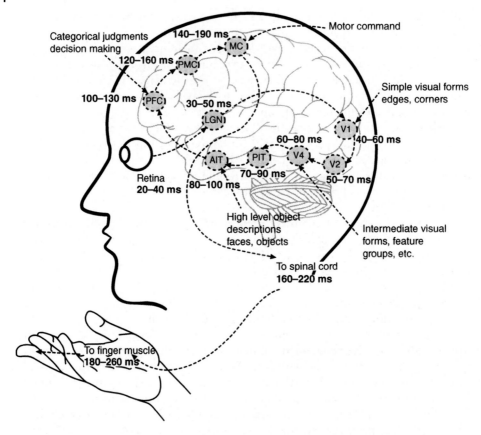

Figure 6.2 Hierarchy signal flows of human visual cortex in the brain, retina and fingers.

The neuron obtains input from upper layer neurons, produces output and transmits it to the neuron in the next layer. If the human brain can be simulated, neurons should be simulated firstly. Figure 6.3(b) shows the structure of an artificial neuron. The inputs to an artificial neuron are all from external stimulating signals, denoted by x_i for $i = 1$, 2, ...n. The artificial neuron calculates a weighted sum of the input signals, where the weights are denoted as w_i for $i = 1, 2, ..., n$. A nonlinear function is applied to produce the output signal y. The following nonlinear sigmoid function was suggested to model the operation of an artificial neuron, as shown in Figure 6.3(b):

$$y = Sig \bmod(x) = \frac{1}{1 + e^{-x}} \tag{6.1}$$

where x represents the sum of weighted inputs.

In 2006, an article by Hinton in *Science* inspired a new era of deep learning. Artificial neural networks with multiple self-learning hidden layers were suggested in that article. Each hidden layer includes several neurons. The output of the previous layer is made as the input of the next layer. The structure of such a deep neural network first adopts an artificial neuron to simulate a biological neuron in the human brain. Then, the layer-wise

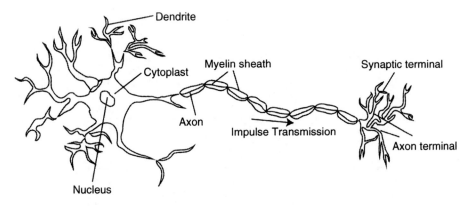

(a) Biological neuron in human brain

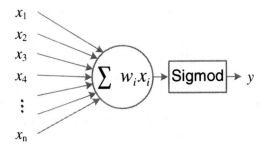

(b) Structure of an artificial neuron

Figure 6.3 Schematic diagrams of biological neuron versus artificial neuron.

learning structure of the deep network simulates a hierarchical structure of information processing by the human brain.

The main conclusions in that article are:

1) The learning capability to obtain features by a deep artificial neural network with multiple hidden layers is strong. What is more, the features obtained by progressive learning in multiple layers can represent data accurately;
2) A layer-wise pre-training method solves difficulty in training ANN. Meanwhile, unsupervised learning is adopted during layer-wise pre-training.

As shown in Figure 6.4, the regions V_1 and H_1 compose the first layer with V_1 as input and H_1 as output, where the data in V_1 comes from original data. V_2 and H_2 compose the second layer. The input of V_2 comes from the output of H_1, while H_2 is the output in second layer.

In summary, the success of deep learning depends on the following factors: improvement in algorithm, realizing layer-wise feature extraction, simulating capability of the human brain in learning, and simulating a hierarchical structure of the human brain during information processing. Besides, there are two external reasons to make deep learning popular. One is the adoption of GPU and the improvement of the computers' computation capability to support the large-scale training of a deep neural network. The

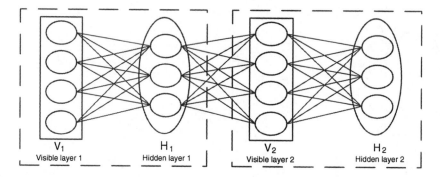

Figure 6.4 Concept of deep learning with an ANN having two hidden layers.

other is the convenience of acquiring a large amount of training data in the era of big data with IoT sensing.

Though human beings can obtain the abstract value of big data by the power of deep learning, there is still a significant gap between current AI and the simulation of the human brain with high fidelity. For example, only a few times are needed to teach a child to recognize a person, and the child can adapt to any light effects and appearance changes. However, if we want a computer to recognize a person, a huge number of stored images are needed for learning, and it is hard for the computer to adapt to the changes in light effects, clothing, glasses or other factors.

6.1.3   Deep Learning versus Shallow Learning

A deep neural network (DNN) is an artificial neural network (ANN) with multiple hidden layers of units between the input and output layers. DNNs can model more complex non-linear relationships than shallow neural networks. In order to recognize simple patterns, basic classification tools based on shallow learning, for example decision trees, SVM, etc., are good enough. With the increase in the number of input features, ANN starts to exhibit its superior performance.

Furthermore, when patterns become more complex, shallow neural networks become unusable, since the number of nodes required in each layer grows exponentially with the increasing number of possible patterns. Then training becomes expensive and accuracy starts to suffer. Thus, when a pattern becomes very complex, deep learning is really required. Giving facial recognition as an example, shallow learning or shallow neural nets are infeasible, so the only practical choice is deep learning through deep nets. The important reason for deep learning to outperform all of their competitors is that computation capacity is upgraded extensively to make the training process much faster than ever before.

At each layer of a deep learning algorithm, the signal is transformed by a processing unit, like an artificial neuron, whose parameters are "learned" through training. There is no universally agreed upper threshold of depth dividing shallow learning by shallow neural nets from deep learning, but most researchers in the field agree that deep learning has multiple nonlinear layers (CAP > 2) and Schmidhuber considers CAP > 10 to be very deep learning. [https://en.wikipedia.org/wiki/Deep_learning]

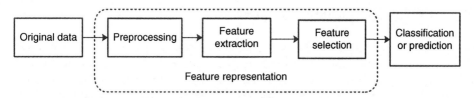

Figure 6.5 Process for classification or prediction by feature representation.

Representation learning offers a way to represent data more accurately through feature representation, as illustrated in Figure 6.5. It adopts the complicated features of the data to represent original input data. It is applied in many fields of machine learning, such as image recognition, voice recognition, natural language understanding, weather forecasting and content recommendations, etc. The processes for solving problems of classification or prediction are shown in Figure 6.5.

After obtaining original data, we conduct preprocessing first, followed by feature extraction and feature selection. With these features, classification or prediction can be achieved. The combination of data preprocessing, feature extraction and feature selection is called feature representation. Finding a good feature representation plays an important role in obtaining high accuracy of final classification or prediction. The handcrafted selection of features requires professional knowledge, and the efficacy of selected features is questionable. With autonomic feature learning, deep learning solves this problem efficiently.

The concept of deep learning derives from the development of ANN. The structure of deep learning often includes multiple hidden layers, and learning representation of original data is conducted layer by layer. Through a combination of low-level features, deep learning forms more abstract representation of attributes or high-level features. The main difference between deep learning and other machine learning methods is the capability of "feature learning". It can be interpreted as the situation where "deep model" is a method and "feature learning" is the objective.

Deep learning adjusts learning models that has multiple hidden layers through training and learning with plenty of data, then obtains layer-based representation from the original data. Thus it learns effective feature representation of data, and finally improves the accuracy in classification or prediction. Deep learning differs from shallow learning in four aspects:

a) It emphasizes the depth of the ANN structure. Compared to conventional shallow learning, more hidden layers are utilized in deep learning.
b) The importance of feature learning is highlighted. By the use of layer-wise feature transformation, data features from original space are represented by the features in a new feature space. With this method, classification or prediction becomes easier and more accurate.
c) Deep learning derives from ANN. However, their training models are different. The layer-wise training is adopted in deep learning, which solves the problem of the vanishing gradient.
d) Plenty of data are utilized to learn the features in deep learning, which is not a must in shallow learning.

6.2 Artificial Neural Networks (ANN)

Artificial neural network (ANN) is a kind of abstract mathematical model that aims to reflect structure and function of the human brain. It is widely used in many fields such as pattern recognition, picture processing, intelligent control, combinatorial optimization, financial prediction and management, communication, robotics and expert systems. There are many similarities between ANN and biological neural networks in the human brain. ANN consists of a group of connected input/output units. Each connection is expressed as a weighted edge. In the learning stage, we adjust these weights based on the gap between predicted output and labeled test data.

6.2.1 Single Layer Artificial Neural Networks

The perceptron is the simplest ANN, which includes an input layer and an output layer without a hidden layer. The input layer node is used for receiving data, while the output layer node yields output data. The structure chart of the perceptron is shown in Figure 6.6. Since we simulate the perceptron as the human nervous system, the input node corresponds to the input neuron and the output node corresponds to the decision-making neuron, while the weight parameter corresponds to strength of connection between neurons. By constantly stimulating neurons, the human brain can obtain unknown knowledge. An activation function, $f(x)$, is used to mimic the stimulation of a neuron in the human brain. This is how the artificial neural network gets its name.

From the perspective of mathematics, each input item corresponds to an attribute of object, while weight stands for the degree by which the attribute reflects the object. Multiplied together with the degree of deviation, the input x is obtained. Then, the output is calculated

$$x = w_1 x_1 + w_2 x_2 + \cdots + w_n x_n + b \rightarrow y = f(x) \tag{6.2}$$

Usually, we may not necessarily obtain ideal results. In the strict sense, $\hat{y}$ should be adopted to stand for the output result of perceptron. The equation of the model is $\hat{y} = f(w \cdot x)$, where, w and x are n-dimensional vectors. Typically, sigmoid function (sig mod $(x) = \frac{1}{1+e^{-x}}$) or hyperbolic tangent function ($\tanh(x) = \frac{e^x - e^{-x}}{e^x + e^{-x}}$), are used for $f(x)$, as shown in Figure 6.7.

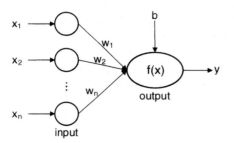

Figure 6.6 Conceptual diagram of a perceptron machine.

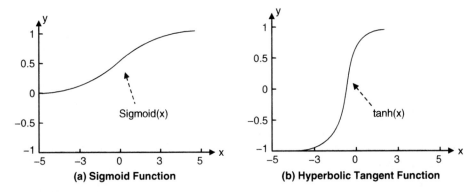

(a) Sigmoid Function   **(b) Hyperbolic Tangent Function**

Figure 6.7 Common activation functions for the perceptron.

If we expect good results, appropriate weights are needed. However, we cannot know which value should be set to each weight in advance. Therefore, the value of weight must be adjusted dynamically during training. The weight renewal equation is shown as

$$w_j^{(k+1)} = w_j^{(k)} + \lambda\left(y_i - \hat{y}_i^{(k)}\right)x_{ij} \quad j = 1, 2, \cdots n \tag{6.3}$$

where, $w_j^{(k)}$ is the weight value of input node j after iterations of k times, λ is known as learning rate, and x_{ij} is the input value of node j in the ith training data sample.

The learning rate is within the interval of $[0, 1]$. If λ is close to 0, the new weight value is mainly influenced by old weight value. The learning rate is slow, but the optimal weight value may be found easily. If λ is close to 1, the new weight value is mainly influenced by the current adjustment amount. The learning rate is fast, but it may skip the optimal weight value. Therefore, under some circumstances, the value of λ would be larger in several previous iterations, but it would be reduced gradually in following iterations.

6.2.2   Multilayer Artificial Neural Network

Perceptron is a neural network with two layers, i.e. input layer and output player. By comparison, a multilayer artificial neural network is composed of one input layer, one or more hidden layer(s) and one output layer, as shown in Figure 6.8. The main unit of ANN is the neuron. There are three basic elements of a neuron:

Figure 6.8 Structure of a two-layer artificial neural network.

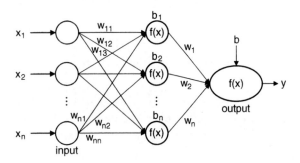

1) a group of connections, corresponding to synapses of a biological neuron. The connection strength is expressed by the weight value of each connection. The weight value represents activation if it is positive, while it represents suppression when the value is negative. The mathematical equation is

$$\begin{cases} w = (w_1, w_2, \cdots, w_n) \\ w_i = (w_{i1}, w_{i2}, \cdots, w_{in}) \quad i = 1, 2, \cdots n \end{cases}$$

(6.4)

2) one summation unit. It is used to work out the weighted sums (linear combination) for each input signal, and generally together with an offset or threshold. Its mathematical equation is

$$\begin{cases} \mu_k = \sum_{j=1}^{n} w_{kj} x_j \\ v_k = \mu_k + b_k \end{cases}$$

(6.5)

3) one nonlinear activation function. It plays a role of nonlinear mapping and restricts the output amplitude of neuron within a certain range [often (0, 1) or (−1, 1)]. Its mathematical equation is

$$y_k = f(v_k)$$

(6.6)

where $f(\cdot)$ is an activation function.

There is no uniform regulation for the number of hidden layers in an artificial neural network; the number of neurons in input, output and each hidden layer, and how to select the activation function of neurons in each layer. Also there is no standard for some specific cases, which need to be chosen independently or chosen as per personal experience. Therefore, there is a certain heuristic nature on the choice of network, and this is why the artificial neural network is deemed as a heuristic algorithm. Four steps to generate an ANN model are given below in Figure 6.9:

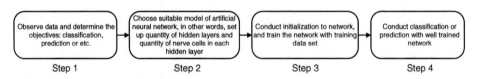

Observe data and determine the objectives: classification, prediction or etc.	Choose suitable model of artificial neural network, in other words, set up quantity of hidden layers and quantity of nerve cells in each hidden layer	Conduct initialization to network, and train the network with training data set	Conduct classification or prediction with well trained network
Step 1	Step 2	Step 3	Step 4

Figure 6.9 General steps for modeling an artificial neural network

6.2.3 Forward Propagation and Back Propagation in ANN

Like the perceptron model, for a multilayer network, how to obtain a set of appropriate weights to let the network have a specific function and a practical application value is important. The artificial neural network solves this problem with a back propagation algorithm. Before introducing back propagation algorithms, we need to know how the network propagates forward.

6.2.3.1. Forward Propagation

The forward propagation starts from the input layer towards a hidden layer. As for hidden unit i, its input is h_i^k, which stands for the input of hidden unit i in layer k, while b_i^k stands for the offset of hidden unit i in layer k. The corresponding output state is

$$h_i^k = \sum_{j=1}^n w_{ij}x_j + b_i^k \rightarrow H_i^k = f(h_i^k) = f\left(\sum_{j=1}^n w_{ij}x_j + b_i\right) \tag{6.7}$$

For convenience, we often let $x_0 = b$, $w_{i0} = 1$. Then the equation of forward propagation from hidden units of layer k to layer $k + 1$ is

$$\begin{cases} h_i^{k+1} = \displaystyle\sum_{j=1}^{m_k} w_{ij}^k h_j^k \\ H_i^{k+1} = f(h_i^{k+1}) = f\left(\displaystyle\sum_{j=1}^n w_{ij}^k h_j^k\right) \end{cases} \quad i = 1, 2, \cdots, m_{k+1} \tag{6.8}$$

where m_k stands for the quantity of neurons in hidden units of layer k, and w_{ij}^k stands for weight vector matrix from layer k to layer $k+1$. The final output is obtained as

$$O_i = f\left(\sum_{j=1}^{m_{M-1}} w_{ij}^{M-1} H_j^{M-1}\right) \quad i = 1, 2, \cdots, m_o \tag{6.9}$$

where m_o stands for the number of output units (there can be multiple outputs in artificial neural network, but generally one output would be set up by default), M stands for total number of layers of artificial neural network, and O_i stands for the outcome value of output unit i.

Example 6.1   Forward Propagation-based Output Prediction in ANN
In an ANN, each set of inputs are modified by unique weights and biases. As shown in Figure 6.10(a), when calculating the activation of the third neuron in the first hidden layer, the first input was modified by weight of 2, the second by 6, the third by 4, and then a bias of 5 is added on the top. Each activation is unique, because each edge has unique weight and each node has unique bias.   ∎

This simple activation will flood across the entire network. The first set of inputs is passed to the first hidden layer, as shown in Figure 6.10(b). The activation of the first hidden layer passes to the next hidden layer, as shown in Figure 6.10(c). Until it reaches the output layer, the score of each output node brings impact on the outcome of classification, as shown in Figure 6.10(d). Such a procedure of classification in ANN is called forward propagation, which will be repeated for another set of inputs.

6.2.3.2. Backward Propagation

Equations 6.8 and 6.9 describe how the input data of neural networks are propagated forward. Next, we will introduce the back propagation algorithm and how to update the weight w_{ij} through a learning or training process. We hope that the output of the artificial neural network is identical with standard values of the training sample. This kind of output is named an ideal output. Actually, it is impossible to accurately achieve

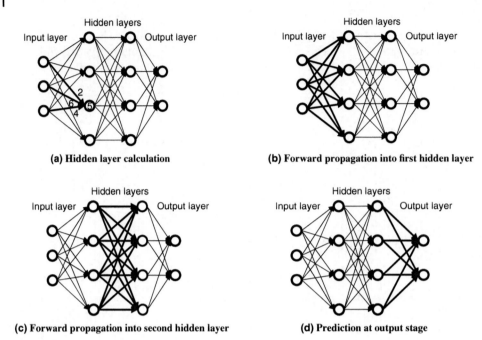

(a) Hidden layer calculation

(b) Forward propagation into first hidden layer

(c) Forward propagation into second hidden layer

(d) Prediction at output stage

Figure 6.10 Forward Propagation based output prediction in a simple ANN with two hidden layers and four neurons at each layer.

this objective. We could only hope the actual output is as close as possible to the ideal output.

The symbols i and s represent the outcome value of output unit i if the training sample is denoted as s. O_i^s stands for the outcome value of output unit i if the training sample is s. Thus, the problem of finding a group of appropriate weights naturally comes down to the problem that $E(W)$ reaches a minimum by figuring out appropriate values of W, as shown below:

$$E(W) = \frac{1}{2}\sum_{i,s}\left(T_i^s - O_i^s\right)^2 = \frac{1}{2}\sum_{i,s}\left(T_i^s - f\left(\sum_{j=1}^{m_{M-1}} w_{ij}^{M-1} H_j^{M-1}\right)\right)^2$$

$$\to \min E(W) \quad i = 1, 2, \cdots, m_o \tag{6.10}$$

As for each variable w_{ij}^k, this is a continuously differentiable nonlinear function. In order to work out the minimum, we generally adopt the steepest descent method. As per this method, we constantly update weight in the direction of the negative gradient until the conditions set up by the customer are satisfied. The so-called direction of gradient is to work out the partial derivative of function:

Assume the weight is $w_{ij}^{(k)}$ after renewal at the kth time. If $\nabla E(W) \neq 0$, then the renewed weight at the $(k+1)$th time is expressed by

$$\nabla E(W) = \frac{\partial E}{\partial w_{ij}^k} \to w_{ij}^{(k+1)} = w_{ij}^{(k)} - \eta \nabla E\left(w_{ij}^{(k)}\right) \tag{6.11}$$

where, η is the learning rate of that network. It plays the same role as learning rate λ in perceptron. When $\nabla E(W) = 0$ or $\nabla E(W) < \varepsilon$ (ε is permissible error), it stops renewing. w_{ij}^k, at this time, will be the final weight of the artificial neural network. The process by which the network constantly adjusts the weight is called the learning process of the artificial neural network. The algorithm utilized in this learning process is called the backward propagation algorithm of network.

Example 6.2 Backward Propagation based Weights/Biases Corrections in ANN

The accuracy of prediction depends on weights and biases. The goal is to make the predicted output as close to the actual output as possible. Just as in the other machine learning methods, the key to improve the accuracy is training. Let y denote the output of forward propagation, and y* denote the correct output. The cost denoted by (y − y*), is the difference between y and y*. After enormous times of training process, the cost should be decreased more and more.

During training, ANN adjusts weights and biases step by step until the predicted output matches the actual output. To achieve this, three steps are taken:

1) When updating the weights between the first neuron in the output layer and the neurons in the second hidden layer and the bias of the first output neuron, the error between forward propagation of the output and its actual result needs to be calculated first. The error is 3 through computing.
2) Then, the gradient of each weight and bias is calculated. For example, the weights and bias are 5, 3, 7, 2, 6, respectively, as shown in Figure 6.11(a). Then, the corresponding gradients are −3, 5, 2, −4, −7.
3) Finally, the updated weights and biases can be calculated, such as $5 − 0.1 \times (−3) = 5.3$, where 0.1 is the learning rate set by the user. In Figure 6.11(b), the bias of the node is revised as follows: $6 − 0.1 \times (−7) = 6.7$.

This simple error will flood across the entire network. As shown in Figure 6.11(c), the output error will backward propagate to the second hidden layer. The associated weights and biases will be updated accordingly. There is the same operation in Figure 6.11(d).

Such operation will be repeated until the error is propagated to the input layer. At this time, the weights and biases of the whole network are updated, as shown in Figure 6.11(e). Such a procedure of updating weights in ANN is called backward propagation, which will be repeated for another set of errors. ∎

The backward propagation process of neural networks reveals that the influence of error propagation is getting smaller and smaller, which will limit the number of hidden layers in a network. If the number of hidden layers is too large, the error will not be passed to several previous layers in the backward propagation process, which results in the incapable updating of corresponding weights and biases.

Example 6.3 Hyperlipemia Diagnosis Using an Artificial Neural Network

For instance, Table 6.1 is a dataset of triglyceride, high-density lipoprotein, low-density lipoprotein and whether hyperlipemia or not ("1" for yes and "0" for no) in health

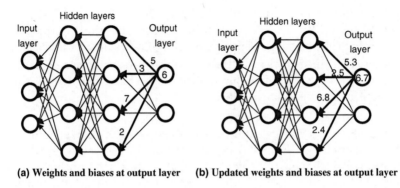

(a) Weights and biases at output layer   **(b)** Updated weights and biases at output layer

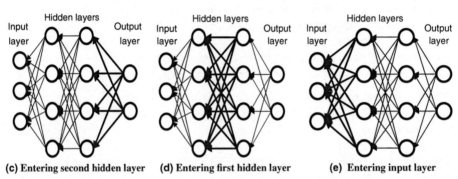

(c) Entering second hidden layer   **(d)** Entering first hidden layer   **(e)** Entering input layer

Figure 6.11 Backward propagation based output prediction in a simple ANN with two hidden layers and four neurons per layer.

Table 6.1 Patient examination data for those suspected to have hyperlipemia.

Patient ID	Triglyceride (mmol/L)	Total Cholesterol (mmol/L)	High-Density Lipoprotein (mmol/L)	Low-Density Lipoprotein (mmol/L)	Hyperlipemia or not
1	3.62	7	2.75	3.13	1
2	1.65	6.06	1.1	5.15	1
3	1.81	6.62	1.62	4.8	1
4	2.26	5.58	1.67	3.49	1
5	2.65	5.89	1.29	3.83	1
6	1.88	5.4	1.27	3.83	1
7	5.57	6.12	0.98	3.4	1
8	6.13	1	4.14	1.65	0
9	5.97	1.06	4.67	2.82	0
10	6.27	1.17	4.43	1.22	0
11	4.87	1.47	3.04	2.22	0
12	6.2	1.53	4.16	2.84	0
13	5.54	1.36	3.63	1.01	0
14	3.24	1.35	1.82	0.97	0

Table 6.2 Table of parameters for artificial neural network.

Neurons at input layer	Hidden layers	Neurons in hidden layers	Neurons in output layer
4	1	5	1

Permissible error	Times for training	Learning rate	Activation function
10–3	10,000	0.9	Tansig and purelin

examination data of people in a hospital. Let us attempt to conduct preliminary judgment on whether a person who received the health examination has hyperlipemia if his or her health examination data are in the sequence {3.16, 5.20, 0.97, 3.49}.

From the data in the table, it is known that this problem is a dichotomy problem ("1" for hyperlipemia or "0" for healthy) with four attributes. Therefore, we can conduct prediction and classification using the artificial neural network.

As there are not enough sample data for training in this case, it is not necessary to set up too many hidden layers and neurons. Here one hidden layer is set up, and the quantity of neurons in each layer is five. The Tansig function is chosen as an activation function between input layer and hidden layer, while the purelin function is chosen as the function between the hidden layer and output layer (choosing other functions has little effect on the results of this case). Its network parameters are listed in Table 6.2.

Then we train the network with the data in Table 6.1 above. MATLAB is used for programming. The training process of the network is shown in Figure 6.12(a). The error between actual output of the network in the training process and ideal output is reduced gradually. A satisfactory state is reached after the second times of backward propagation. The final training results are shown in Figure 6.12(b). The neural network classifier divides the training data into two categories.

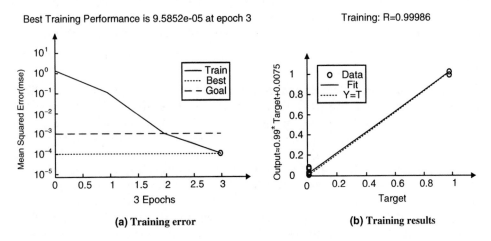

(a) Training error

(b) Training results

Figure 6.12 Training error and results on the ANN in Example 6.3.

The training data are divided into both ends and form two classes. The class 0 stands for healthy while the class 1 stands for hyperlipemia. The results of classification are $\{1, 1, 1, 1, 1, 1, 1, 0, 0, 0, 0, 0, 0, 0\}$. The accuracy for classification reaches 100%, so this network can be used for prediction. Finally, let us predict whether a person whose data are $\{3.16, 5.20, 0.97, 3.49\}$ respectively has hyperlipemia or not, with the artificial neural network mentioned above. The result is $class = 1$. Therefore, we can predict the person has hyperlipemia. ∎

6.3   Stacked AutoEncoder and Deep Belief Network

When training ANN, cost value, i.e. the gap between ANN predicted output and actual output, is used to adjust weights and biases over and over again throughout the training process. The progress of training follows the tendency of gradient, which is analogous to a slope. The training process is like rolling a rock down a slope. A rock moves quickly along the surface if the gradient is high. When the gradient is small, the training process of ANN is slow. However, the gradient could potentially vanish during backward propogation.

Typically, the gradient is much smaller in earlier layers. As a result, the early layers are hard to train. However, the early layers correspond to basic pattern and building block, especially in facial recognition. The error will propagate in the following layers in ANN. In the years before 2006, there was no way to train DNN, due to the fundamental problem of the vanishing gradient during training process. This problem can be solved by replacing the conventional layer by AutoEncoder, which automatically finds the pattern by reconstructing input. The vanishing gradient problem will be eliminated in stacked AutoEncoder. We will introduce AutoEncoder and stacked AutoEncoder in Sections 6.3.1 and 6.3.2, respectively.

In Sections 6.3.3 and 6.3.4, we introduce Restricted Boltzmann Machine (RBM) and Deep Belief Networks (DBN) structure, training methods and applications. RBM contains two layers: a visible layer and a hidden layer. The two layers are undirected connected. There is no connection between neurons in the same layer. RBM trains the network parameters using the unsupervised method. DBN contains multiple RBMs, where the hidden layer of the previous RBM works as the visible layer of the next RBM.

6.3.1   AutoEncoder

The AutoEncoder can be treated as a special ANN. There are sample data but no corresponding label data in this stage of network training. Instead, AutoEncoder extracts output data to reconstruct input data and compare it with original input data. After many iterations, the value of the objective function reaches its optimality, which means that the reconstructed input data is able to approximate the original input data to a maximum extent. AutoEncoder is a self-supervised learning tool and belongs to supervised training. Figure 6.13 shows an example of learning with four elements composing a circle I.

Let O denote the right answer, i.e. the circle is composed of four identical sectors. The result of the first learning O_1' consists of four rectangles. The calculated error between

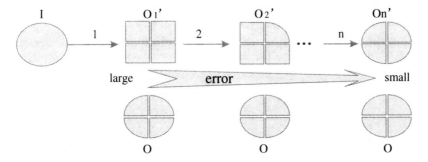

Figure 6.13 Composition of supervised learning cycle.

O_1' and O is relatively large. This error is referred to improve the model in the second learning. As shown in Figure 6.13, the result O_2' is composed of three rectangles and one sector. The error between O_2' and O is reduced and is used once again to modify the model. Such a learning process will repeat for n times. Finally, result On' reveals that the circle consists of four sectors.

When the error between On' and O reaches a minimum, the learning process is terminated. During the whole learning process, we use current output and the correct answer to calculate the error. Step by step, we adjust the knowledge and learn gradually to get the anticipated answer: the circle is composed of four identical sectors. This is so-called supervised learning, i.e. when the problem (input data) and correct answer (label) are known, the current answer is adjusted continuously to reach or equal the final correct answer.

With the supervised learning method, all input data (samples) of neutral network training correspond to their expected values (labels). The difference between the current output value and expected value is used to adjust parameters at all input and output layers. The error will reach the minimum after many iterations. Figure 6.14(a) shows the workflow structure of a supervised neutral network, including the input layer, one

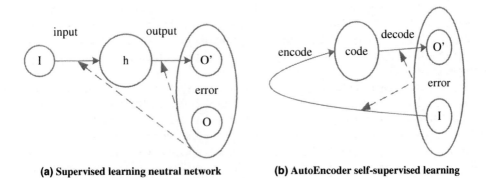

(a) Supervised learning neutral network   **(b) AutoEncoder self-supervised learning**

Figure 6.14 Supervised learning in an ANN versus self-supervised learning in AutoEncoder.

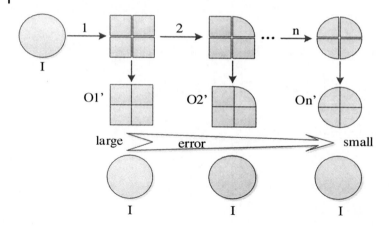

Figure 6.15 Composition of self-supervised learning cycle.

hidden layer and the output layer. The output value O' is derived from input data I through the hidden layer h. O means the label of I. The error between O' and O is calculated. Then, backward propagation is used to adjust the network parameters. With the increasing number of iterations, the error is reduced until a minimized value is obtained.

Figure 6.15 shows the self-supervised version of the example in Figure 6.13. The input data of circle I are known, but no reference answer is given. How can we know the correctness of an output result? The only way is to compose the output result and verify whether it is equivalent to I (i.e. a circle) or not. We derive four rectangles from the first learning and combine them to get the result O_1'. The calculation error between O_1' and I is relatively large. Thus we modify the knowledge of combination based on the error.

We derive three rectangles and one sector from the second learning and combine them to get the result O_2'. The calculation error between O_2' and I is reduced and the knowledge is modified once again based on the error. After repeating such learning processes for n times, On' reveals the knowledge of combining the four same sectors. Finally, the calculation error between On' and I is reduced to zero, and the desired knowledge is obtained without knowing the correct answer in advance. AutoEncoder is a self-supervised learning tool. Since the correct answer is not given, its input data also works as the labeled data. Figure 6.14(b) shows the workflow of self-supervised learning in the AutoEncoder.

The input data I represents the m-dimension vector $I \in R^m$. Self-supervised learning of AutoEncoder consists of two parts: encoder and decoder. By the encoding process, *code*, which is a n-dimension vector $code \in R^n$, is calculated. By the decoding process, O' is reconstructed, where $O' \in R^m$ represents an m-dimension vector. Then, the error between O' and I is obtained. By the use of a stochastic gradient descent, the parameters of encoder and decoder are adjusted for error reduction. When the error between I and O' is minimized, code can be considered as the incarnation of I. In other words, code is a kind of feature representation extracted from I.

Algorithm 6.1   Construction of an AutoEncoder

Input: T: Sample set
Output: Feature representation of input data
Procedure:
1) Initialize parameter set $\theta=\{w_1, w_2, b_1, b_2,\}$
2) Encode: Calculate the representation of the hidden layer
3) Decode: Use the representation of the hidden layer to reconstruct input
4) Calculate $L_{recon}(I, O')$ and objective function value $J(\theta)$
5) Judge whether or not $J(\theta)$ meets end condition?
6) If yes, return 7), else return 6).
7) Modify the parameter set with backward propagation and return 2);
8) End

The brief algorithm of AutoEncoder is presented in Algorithm 6.1, which includes three main steps:

1) **Step 1 – Encode:** Convert input data I into *code* of the hidden layer by $code = f(I) = s_1(w_1 \cdot I + b_1)$, where $w_1 \in R^{m \times n}$ and $b_1 \in R^n$. S_1 is an activate function. The sigmoid or hyperbolic tangent function can be used.
2) **Step 2 – Decode:** Based on the above code, reconstruct input value I by equation $g(code) = s_2(w_2 \cdot code + b_2)$, where $w_2 \in R^{n \times m}$ and $b_2 \in R^m$. The activate function S_2 is the same as S_1.
3) **Step 3 – Calculate square error:** $L_{recon}(I, O') = \|I - O'\|^2$, which is the error cost function. Error minimization is achieved by optimizing the objective function: $J(\theta) = \sum_{I \in D} L(I, g(f(I))\theta = \{w_1, w_2, b_1, b_2\}$

Through AutoEncoder, feature representation is obtained to represent original input by code. For the purpose of classification, we still need a classifier. The classifier is connected with the hidden layer of AutoEncoder. Both SVM or softmax can be used as the classifier. The supervised training method such as stochastic gradient descent can be used to train the classifier. The code obtained from AutoEncoder works as input to the classifier, while its output (Y' in Figure 6.16) is compared to labeled data (Y) for supervised fine tuning.

6.3.2   Stacked AutoEncoder

Stacked AutoEncoder (SAE) is a neutral network with several hidden layers between the input layer and the output layer, while each hidden layer corresponds to an AutoEncoder. Figure 6.17 shows the structure of a stacked AutoEncoder, which includes multi-layer AutoEncoder and classifier.

6.3.2.1.   Multi-layer AutoEncoder
The original input data are used in the first AutoEncoder layer. After going through several rounds of encoding and decoding, the reconstruction error is gradually minimized

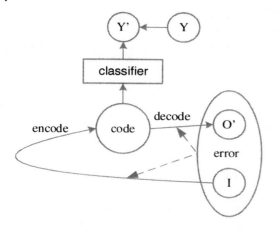

Figure 6.16 Classification process by AutoEncoder.

and encoder and decoder parameters are iteratively updated in the first layer. Finally, we obtain the code of the first layer, which represents the feature of the original input data. After constructing the network structure of the first AutoEncoder layer, the second AutoEncoder layer is trained in the same way. But the difference is that the output code of the first layer is treated as the input data of the second layer.

The algorithm of training a multi-layer encoder is an iterative version of Algorithm 6.1. Let n denote the number of layers in SAE. Let T_n denote the number of sample dataset. For each sample data x_m, $m = 1,2,3,..., T_n$, Algorithm 6.1 will be conducted for n times iteratively. The output code of the former layer is always treated as the input of the latter layer. Such a multi-layer training will contribute to obtaining representation of a multi-layer feature of original input data. Finally, the network of multi-layer AutoEncoder is constructed.

6.3.2.2. Supervised Fine Tuning

Figure 6.18 shows a map of training SAE. The classifier of SAE is connected with the final layer of AutoEncoder. There are two methods for supervised fine tuning. One is to adjust classifier parameters only. The other is to adjust the parameters of the classifier and all AutoEncoder layers. The marks of No. 1 to No. 5 in Figure 6.18 represent the sequence of operations in the training. There are two No. 5 operations, which represent two kinds of fine-tuning operations. We summarize the five steps for using the algorithm of parameter fine tuning in SAE:

Step 1: Substantial unlabeled data are used to train the multi-layer AutoEncoder. And multi-layer data feature extraction is constructed.

Step 2: Obtain code at the highest layer AutoEncoder.

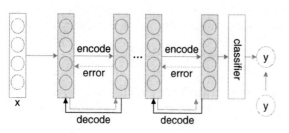

Figure 6.17 Structure of a stacked AutoEncoder.

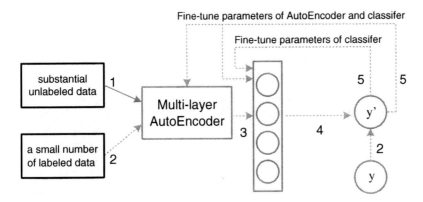

Figure 6.18 Sketch map of training stacked AutoEncoder.

Step 3: Calculate classification result Y′ (i.e. output of the classifier). Calculate error between Y and Y′ based on cost function. Note that a small number of labeled data will be utilized.

Step 4: Judge whether or not end condition is met based on cost function? If yes, the structure of SAE is well trained, and the supervised fine tuning of parameters is terminated. Otherwise, continue with Step 5.

Step 5: Adjust the parameters of classifier (adjustment for the parameters of multi-layer AutoEncoder is optional) via stochastic gradient descent. Then return to Step 3.

6.3.3 Restricted Boltzmann Machine

The restricted Boltzmann machine (RBM) is a neural network model that can realize unsupervised learning. It includes two layers, visible layer V and hidden layer H, which are connected by an undirected graph. There is no connection among neurons in the same layer. In this section, we only introduce the V and H as the binary units. The input of RBM is an m-dimensional vector data V, where $V = (v_1, v_2,...,v_m)$ and $v_i \in \{0, 1\}$. v_i stands for the binary state of neuron *i* in the visible layer. The output of RBM is an n-dimensional vector H, where $H = (h_1, h_2,..., h_n)$ and $h_j \in \{0, 1\}$. h_j stands for the binary state of neuron *j* in the hidden layer (Figure 6.19).

Now, we give a simple example to understand the learning process of RBM, as shown Figure 6.20. The goal is to obtain the answer of the following question: Which shapes compose the input graph? There are only two kinds of components in the graph, i.e. square and triangle. Let us use code 1 and code 0 to represent square shape and triangle shape, respectively. Let us assume the coding sequences are upper-left corner, upper-right corner, lower-left corner and lower-right corner. Then, the input graph corresponds to a four digit code, i.e. 1011. In Figure 6.20, we obtain layer H by the mapping from layer V to layer H. Then we use symmetric mapping to reconstruct layer V based on layer H. As shown in Figure 6.20, we perform the following operations:

1) A code of 1011 is obtained as V. Through mapping, the expression of 01 in layer H is calculated, which means the input graph consists of triangles. Then, symmetrical mapping is adopted to obtain 0011 as the value of V1.

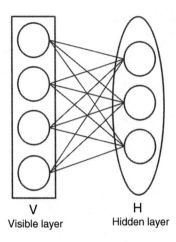

Figure 6.19 The structure of a single stage of restricted Boltzmann machine (RBM).

2) Calculate the error between the distribution of V and V1, and revise the mapping parameters according to the error.

3) Repeat step 1) and step 2) with new mapping. Conduct training and establish RBM after completion of training. It includes layer V, layer H and the mapping between the two layers.

As seen from Figure 6.20, what we ultimately want is to find a good *Mapping*. Now we describes contrastive divergence (CD) algorithm, which can quickly obtain Mapping.

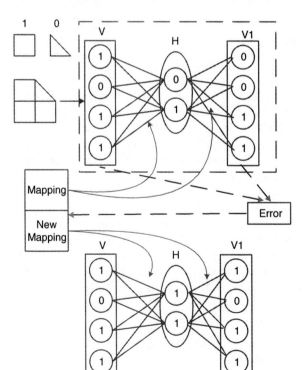

Figure 6.20 Schematic diagram for learning image composition by RBM.

We define $\theta = (w, bv, bh)$ as Mapping parameters to be learned from the RBM network. w denotes a set of weights between visible layer V and hidden layer H, $w \in R^{m \times n}$. w_{ij} is the weight between visible neuron i and hidden neuron j. bv is vector composed of deviation of each neuron in the visible layer, and bv_i stands for the deviation value of visible neuron i, $bv \in R^m$. bh is vector composed of deviation of each neuron in the hidden layer, $bh \in R^n$. bh_j stands for deviation value of hidden neuron j. The task of learning RBM is to establish the RBM network structure or obtain the optimal parameter θ^* by CD learning.

RBM learning algorithm utilizes the Boltzmann distribution and solves the parameter θ through maximum likelihood estimation. In other words, $P(v \mid \theta)$ is subject to the Boltzmann distribution:

$$P(v \mid \theta) = \frac{\sum\limits_{h} e^{-E(v, h \mid \theta)}}{Z(\theta)} \tag{6.12}$$

where $E(v, h \mid \theta) = -\sum\limits_{i=1}^{m} bv_i v_i - \sum\limits_{j=1}^{n} bh_j h_j - \sum\limits_{i=1}^{m} \sum\limits_{j=1}^{n} v_i w_{ij} h_j$, $Z(\theta) = \sum\limits_{v,h} e^{-E(v, h \mid \theta)}$

The maximum likelihood function is described in Equation 6.13, which can be solved by the gradient descent method:

$$L(\theta) = \sum\limits_{t=1}^{T} \log P(v^{(t)} \mid \theta) \tag{6.13}$$

Adopt Equation (6.14) to calculate the activation probability of hidden neuron j in the hidden layer, i.e. calculate the probability when the state of hidden neuron j is equal to 1. Thus we can obtain the state h of the hidden layer:

$$P(h_{1j} = 1 \mid v_1, \theta) = \sigma \left(bh_j + \sum\limits_{i=1}^{m} v_{1i} w_{ij} \right) \tag{6.14}$$

where function σ is the sigmoid function. We summarize five steps to calculate the $P(h_1 = 1 \mid v_1, \theta)$:

Step 1: Input state of visible layer v_1, network parameter θ, number of neurons in visible layer m, number of neurons in hidden layer n.

Step 2: $j = 1$.

Step 3: Calculate activation probability for neuron in the hidden layer as Equation (6.14).

Step 4: As per uniform distribution, produce a random floating point number that is between 0 and 1. If it is less than $P(h_{1j} = 1 \mid v_1, \theta)$ the value of h_{1j} is 1; otherwise the value is 0.

Step 5: $j{+}{+}$.

Step 6: If $j < m$, then return to Step 3.

Algorithm 6.2   Rapid learning algorithm based on Contrastive Divergence

---

Input: X: a training sample – original inputted datum x
  m: number of neurons in hidden layer
  λ: learning rate
  P: iterative numbers of training
Output:
  Establish RBM; network parameter $\theta = \{w, bh, bv\}$
Procedure:
1) Initialization: initial state V_1 for neuron in visible layer; $V_1 = x$; for initialization, $\theta = \{w, bh, bv\}$
2) for t = 1,2,3,…P
3) Calculate activation probability for all neurons in the hidden layer, $P(h_1 = 1|v_1, \theta)$
4) Calculate activation probability for all neurons in the hidden layer, V_2
5) Calculate activation probability for all neurons in the hidden layer, $P(h_2 = 1|v_2, \theta)$
6) Renew weight: $w = w + \lambda(P(h_1 = 1|v_1,\theta)v_1^T - P(h_2 = 1|v_2,\theta)v_2^T)$
7) Renew deviation in visible layer: $bv = bv + \lambda(v_1 - v_2)$
8) Renew deviation in hidden layer: $bh = bh + \lambda(P(h_1 = 1|v_1,\theta) - P(h_2 = 1|v_2,\theta))$
9) end

After obtaining all states in the hidden layer, the activation probability of neuron i in the visible layer can be calculated by symmetrically utilizing Equation (6.15). Then, the activation state for neuron i can be obtained by utilizing the result of activation probability $v_i \in \{0, 1\}$.

$$P(v_{2i} = 1 \mid h_1, \theta) = \sigma\left(bv_i + \sum_{j=1}^{n} w_{ij} h_{1j} \right) \tag{6.15}$$

The algorithm to calculate the activation probability of the neuron in the visible layer is similar with the hidden layer, as follows:

Step 1: Input state of hidden layer h_1, network parameter θ, number of neurons in visible layer m, number of neurons in hidden layer n.
Step 2: $I = 1$.
Step 3: Calculate activation probability for neurons in visible layer, as Equation (6.15)
Step 4: As per uniform distribution, produce a random floating point number that is between 0 and 1. If it is less than $P\left(v_{2i} = 1 \mid h_1, \theta\right)$, the value of v_{2j} is 1; otherwise value is 0.
Step 5: $i{++}$
Step 6: If $I < n$, then return to Step 3.

Example 6.4   Recommend Movies with Restricted Boltzman Machine
We can use the RBM model to recommend movies to users. Utilizing the known users' rating data to construct the RBM model, this model will be adopted to predict users' rating for all movies. First, we sort out all of the rating data in descending order. Then,

Table 6.3 Movie rating by viewers.

id	Movie 1	Movie 2	Movie 3	Movie 4
User1	3	4	4	1
User15	3	5	0	0

we can obtain a movie which gets the highest rating and that users have never watched it before. Thus we can recommend it to users.

Assuming there are four movies, the movies' ratings are integers and vary from 1 to 5, and 0 denotes no rating. Table 6.3 shows the rating of user 1 and user 15.

The steps of recommending movies with restricted Boltzman machine are as below:

Step 1: Dataset and RBM structure

The ratings of all movies by one user can be represented by a 5×4 matrix v, where $v(i, j) = 1$ means the user rate i for movie j. Thus, the rating matrices of user 1 and user 15 are as

$$v_1 = \begin{pmatrix} 0 & 0 & 0 & 1 \\ 0 & 0 & 0 & 0 \\ 1 & 0 & 0 & 0 \\ 0 & 1 & 1 & 0 \\ 0 & 0 & 0 & 0 \end{pmatrix} \quad v_{15} = \begin{pmatrix} 0 & 0 & 0 & 0 \\ 0 & 0 & 0 & 0 \\ 1 & 0 & 0 & 0 \\ 0 & 0 & 0 & 0 \\ 0 & 1 & 0 & 0 \end{pmatrix}$$

Let the quantity of neurons in visible layers and hidden layers be 20 and 5, respectively in the RBM model. We can transform the rating matrix into a vector with 20 elements. Thus v_1 and v_{15} can be transformed into $\{0,0,1,0,0,0,0,0,1,0, 0,0,0,1,0, 1,0, 0,0,0\}$ and $\{0,0,1,0,0,0,0,0,0,1, 0,0,0,0,0, 0,0, 0,0,0\}$, respectively.

Step 2: Training

After inputting users rating data, we can utilize Algorithm 6.2 to train RBM. The corresponding deviations of visible layers can be obtained as

$$a = \begin{pmatrix} -0.6 & -0.6 & -0.3 & 0 \\ -0.3 & -0.3 & 0.6 & 0.3 \\ 0.6 & 0.3 & 0 & -0.6 \\ -0.3 & 0.3 & 0.6 & 0.0 \\ -0.3 & 0.3 & -0.9 & 0 \end{pmatrix}$$

The deviations of hidden layers are $b = (-1.2 \ -0.6 \ -0.6 - 0.3 \ -0.3)$.

The weight matrix is a 20×5 matrix, where it can be represented by five matrices according neurons of hidden layers. Each matrix denotes the connection weights among 20 neurons of visible layer and 1 neuron of hidden layer.

Step 3: The movie recommendation

1) Input the rating data of user 15, and utilize Equation (6.16) to calculate the activate probability of all hidden units, i.e. *ph*= (0.0214, 0.0151, 0.0453, 0.1404, 0.6583). The weights and deviations of hidden layers can be obtained through training:

$$p(h_j = 1|V) = \frac{1}{1 + \exp\left(-b_j - \sum_{i=1}^{M} \sum_{k=1}^{K} v_i^k W_{ij}^k\right)} \tag{6.16}$$

$$w(:,:,1) = \begin{pmatrix} -0.8388 & -0.1559 & -1.1827 & -0.2224 \\ -0.7873 & 0.0986 & -0.0791 & -0.8191 \\ -0.6809 & -1.0458 & -0.2480 & -0.3867 \\ -1.2027 & 0.0872 & -0.1243 & -0.5868 \\ -1.1445 & -0.6589 & -0.8836 & -0.1172 \end{pmatrix}$$

$$w(:,:,2) = \begin{pmatrix} -0.1580 & -0.6287 & 0.3352 & -0.2182 \\ 0.1031 & 0.0961 & 0.3511 & -0.2471 \\ 0.1854 & 0.6668 & 0.4663 & -0.1070 \\ -0.1052 & -0.2801 & -0.2151 & -0.7534 \\ -0.2325 & -0.0457 & -0.0993 & 0.4049 \end{pmatrix}$$

$$w(:,:,3) = \begin{pmatrix} 0.0467 & -0.2369 & -0.0054 & 0.5772 \\ -0.0050 & -1.1134 & 0.1793 & 0.0143 \\ 0.5374 & -0.2505 & -0.1696 & 0.2379 \\ 0.5298 & -0.1375 & 0.4546 & -0.8972 \\ 0.8843 & -0.2688 & -0.6814 & -0.3714 \end{pmatrix}$$

$$w(:,:,4) = \begin{pmatrix} -0.8423 & 0.0999 & -0.7604 & 0.0074 \\ -0.3207 & -0.6556 & 0.4505 & 0.2922 \\ 1.1088 & -0.1351 & -0.1854 & -0.2619 \\ 0.4764 & 0.2176 & 0.2992 & 0.0226 \\ 0.4378 & 0.1666 & -0.6949 & -0.2281 \end{pmatrix}$$

$$w(:,:,5) = \begin{pmatrix} -0.7458 & -0.5607 & -0.0101 & 0.1658 \\ -0.4698 & 0.0969 & 0.4129 & 0.7707 \\ 0.7059 & 0.7355 & 0.0868 & -0.3635 \\ 0.5583 & 0.2992 & 0.4809 & -0.1271 \\ 0.7589 & 1.2223 & -0.2460 & 0.3042 \end{pmatrix}$$

The uniform distribution generates a random floating point number between 0 and 1. If it is less than ph_j, then $h_j = 1$, otherwise $h_j = 0$. Then we can get $h = (0, 0, 0, 0, 1)$.

2) According to the activate probability *ph* of hidden layers calculated in the previous step, use Equation (6.17) to calculate the activate probability *pv* of visible layers. The weight matrix and deviation of the visible layer can be obtained by training. We can calculate the corresponding activate probability of every rating k for each movie i, where $k = 1,...,5$. $pv(i.j)$ means the probability of movie j rating i:

$$p(v_i^k = 1|h) = \frac{1}{1 + \exp\left(-a_i^k - \sum_{j=1}^{F} W_{ij}^k h_j\right)} \qquad (6.17)$$

$$pv = \begin{pmatrix} 0.2066 & 0.2385 & 0.4231 & 0.5414 \\ 0.3165 & 0.4494 & 0.7336 & 0.7447 \\ 0.7868 & 0.7380 & 0.5217 & 0.2762 \\ 0.5642 & 0.6455 & 0.7467 & 0.4683 \\ 0.6128 & 0.8209 & 0.2412 & 0.5755 \end{pmatrix}$$

3) We choose the highest probability of each column as the rating by user 15 to movie i. For example, for movie 1, the probability of the rating 1,2,3,4,5 is respectively 0.2066, 0.3165, 0.7868, 0.5642 and 0.6128. The highest probability is 0.7868, corresponding rating is 3, so user 15 rates movie 1 as 3. After deducing the rest from this, the user's rating for the four movie is (3,5,4,2).
4) Because user 15 have not rated movie 3 and movie 4, it is likely that user 15 has not seen these two movies. According to ratings, we recommend movie 3 first, and movie 4 second. ∎

6.3.4 Deep Belief Networks

Deep belief network (DBN) is a hybrid deep learning model, which was proposed by Hinton et al. in 2006. Figure 6.21(a) shows that a DBN includes one visible layer V and n hidden layers. DBN is composed of n stacked RBM, which means the hidden layer of the previous RBM is the visible layer of the next RBM. The original input is visible layer V. This layer V, together with hidden layer H_1, consists of one RBM. H_1 is the visible layer V_2 of the second RBM. This hidden layer H_1, together with hidden layer H_2, consists of another RBM and so on. All adjacent two layers form an RBM.

In Figure 6.21(a), the visible layer and the hidden layer of the top layer are part of the undirected connection, which is known as associative memory. The RBM visible layer in the top layer consists of hidden layer H_{n-1} in the previous RBM and category labels. The training of DBN is divided into two parts: unsupervised training and supervised fine tuning. Unsupervised training uses a large number of data without labels to train RBM one by one. Supervised fine tuning uses a small amount of data with labels to finely adjust the parameters of each layer in the whole network.

Unsupervised training adopts original input V as the visible layer of the first RBM, using the method introduced in Section 6.3.1 to train RBM_1 and fix the connection parameters until the end of the training. Then we get the hidden layer H_1 and let this H_1

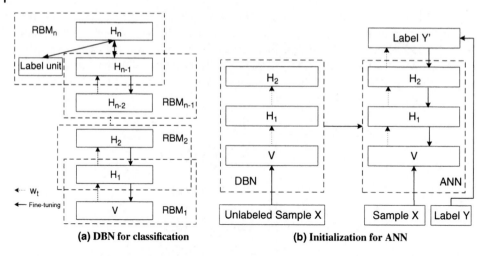

(a) DBN for classification **(b) Initialization for ANN**

Figure 6.21 The structure of a deep belief network (DBN).

be the visible layer V_2 of the second RBM. A similar method is applied to train RBM_2 and obtain the hidden layer H_2. Repeat this process until all the RBM training is done. The unsupervised training of multi-layer RBM is given in Algorithm 6.3.

Fine-tuning uses sample data as the input data of the visible layer of DBN and the label of the sample as a part of the visible layer of the top RBM layer. The category labels data y of the sample are expressed with neurons. In other words, if there are m kinds of category labels data of the sample, there will be m neurons to express them. Setting the neuron that corresponds to the category is equal to 1. The BP algorithm can be used to adjust network parameters when utilizing DBN for fine tuning.

DBN cannot only be used to classify directly, but also can use the trained network parameters to conduct ANN initialization. This application mainly includes two parts: unsupervised training DBN and supervised fine tune neural networks. As shown in Figure 6.21(b), we can input sample data x without labels and training DBN by the unsupervised training algorithm above to get the connection parameters between each layer. It is the same with DBN to define the number of neutral network layers and neutrons of each layer. We can use the parameters of DBN obtained from training of the initial neutral network. Then we input sample data x with labels into the neutral network. Finally, we use the correct classification y and y', which we obtained above to calculate the error and the training method of neutral networks to adjust the parameters of each layer.

Algorithm 6.3 Unsupervised training of multi-layer RBM

Input: V: Training data
   r_n: The number of RBM layers
Output: The activation status of each neuron in visible layer V
procedure:

(Continued)

1) $V_1 = V$
2) for t = 1 to rn
3) Initial parameter $\theta_t = \{w_t, bh_t, bv_t\}$ of the t_{th} RBM network
4) Use contrast divergence algorithm to train t_{th} RBM and get h_t
5) t++;
6) $V_t = H_{t-1}$
7) end

6.4 Convolutional Neural Networks (CNN) and Extensions

The convolutional neural network (CNN) is a kind of feed-forward neural network, which uses convolution and reduces the quantity of weights in the network and reduces complexity of calculations compared with traditional feed-forward neural networks. This kind of network structure is similar to biological neural networks. The CNN belongs to the supervised learning method, and is widely applied to voice recognition and image field. The convolutions and pooling were introduced earlier. The training process of CNN is also presented.

The CNN is composed of many layers. Generally, it includes such basic components as input, convolution, pooling, fully connected and output layers. We need to decide how many convolution layers and pooling layers should be utilized and what kind of classifier should be selected according to each specific application problem, just like piling up building blocks. Figure 6.22 shows the structure of a convolutional neural network utilized by LeNet-5. It includes 7 layers, i.e. 3 convolution, 2 pooling, 1 fully connected and 1 output layer. The concept is illustrated in Figure 6.22, based on the work of LeCun (1998) [12].

6.4.1 Convolution in CNN

In the following, we explain the concept of convolution on a CNN with an application of image understanding. When considering the need to process an image of 500 × 500 pixels, the quantity of neurons in the input layer should be set to 500 × 500. We assume a set 10^8 neurons in the hidden layer. Each connection between one neuron in the input layer and one neuron in the hidden layer should be set as a

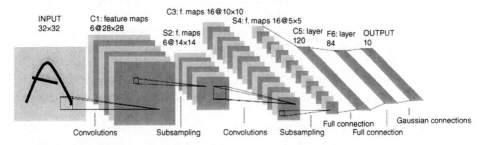

Figure 6.22 Convolutional Neural Network utilized in LeNet-5.

weight parameter. Here let us compare the number of weight parameters needed in the two cases when using fully connected neural networks and using locally connected neural networks.

When establishing a fully connected neural network to deal with the image, the quantity of weight parameters between the input layer and the hidden layer will be $500 \times 500 \times 10^8 = 25 \times 10^{12}$. Understanding a large image with the method of full connection faces the problem that the parameters are too many and the computational burden too large. People can only see part of the image information at any one time. Using the method of people understanding the image as a reference, we can design a filter to extract the local features of an image and apply it to understand the whole image.

In other words, we use a filter to realize the local connection between the input layer and the hidden layer. Assume a 10×10 filter is designed to imitate human eyes to visualize the local image region. Then a hidden layer neuron is connected to a 10×10 area of the input layer through the filter. The hidden layer has 10^8 hidden neurons, so the quantity of filters between the hidden layer and the input layer is 10^8. Each connection corresponds to a 10×10 area of the input layer through a filter. Thus the quantity of connection weight parameters between input layer and hidden layer becomes $10 \times 10 \times 10^8 = 10^{10}$.

While reducing the quantity of weights from 25×10^{12} to 10^{10} by changing full connection to local connection, the problem that the weight parameters are too many and the computational burden is too large is still unsolved, because there are intrinsic features in natural images. In other words, the statistic features for one part of an image are the same as for those for other parts. This means the features learned from one part of an image can also be utilized for other parts. Therefore, for all the locations of the same image, we can use the same learning features. A filter is a matrix of weights and represents local features of an image.

Then the same filter can be utilized for all the locations of an image naturally. 10^8 filters of 10×10 correspond to different 10^6 areas of 10×10 of an image. If the filters are completely identical, which means local features are utilized for the whole image, there is 1 filter with 100 weight parameters between the input layer and the hidden layer. By sharing weight, the quantity of weight parameter is reduced from 25×10^{12} to 100, which reduces the quantity of weight parameters and computational burden greatly. These images were provided by Yann LeCun and Marc'Aurelio Ranzato in 2013 [12].

The concept of local connection and weight sharing that we use achieves convolution operation. The filter of 10×10 is exactly a convolution kernel. A convolution kernel represents just one kind of local feature of an image. When we need to represent more local features, we can use multiple convolution kernels. If the first convolution layer of Figure 6.22 has six filters, then we can gain six feature maps of hidden layers by convolution operations.

Example 6.5 How Convolution Works for Building Convolutional Neural Network

We can understand how to realize the convolution through the convolution operation for an image of 8×8, as shown in Figure 6.23. The dimension of convolution kernel is

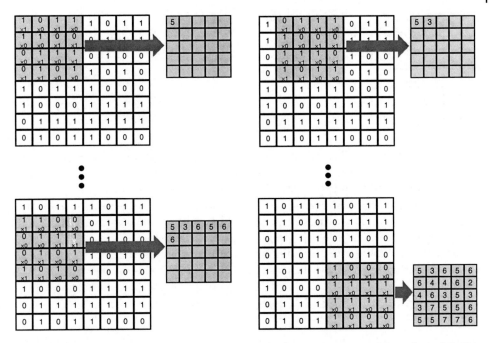

Figure 6.23 Schematic diagram for a convolutional ANN (CNN) (source: http://ufldl.stanford.edu/wiki/index.php/UFLDL_Tutorial).

4×4; and the feature matrix is

$$w = \begin{pmatrix} 1 & 0 & 1 & 0 \\ 0 & 0 & 1 & 1 \\ 0 & 1 & 0 & 1 \\ 1 & 1 & 0 & 0 \end{pmatrix}$$

First, we extract an image x_1 of 4×4 from the image of 8×8 for convolution operation with feature matrix. Here, we obtain the value y_1 for the first neuron in the hidden layer by utilizing equation $y_i = w \cdot x_i$. The step size of convolution is set to 1. We continue to extract image x_2 of 4×4, and obtain the value y_2 for the second neuron through convolution operation. We repeat the aforementioned steps until the traverse of the whole image is complete. After the calculation for all values of neuron in the hidden layer is complete, a feature map corresponding to a convolution kernel is obtained.

Usually, we calculate values of the output feature map in the hidden layer by utilizing the activation function. The frequently used activation functions are: sigmoid function $[\sigma(x) = \frac{1}{1+e^{-x}}]$, hyperbolic tangent function $[\tanh(x) = \frac{e^x - e^{-x}}{e^x + e^{-x}}]$ and RELU function $[\text{RELU}(x) = \max(0, x)]$.

Assuming the number of input feature maps of convolution layer l is n, we adopt the equation $y_j = f(\sum_{i=1}^{n} (w_{ij} * x_i + b_i))$ to calculate the output feature map in convolution layer l, where b stands for deviation, w for weight matrix and f for activation function.

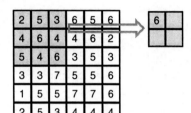

Figure 6.24 The concept of pooling from the 6 x 6 grid to a 2 x 2 grid (source: http://ufldl.stanford.edu/wiki/index.php/UFLDL_Tutorial).

If convolution layer l has m filters, the number of weight matrix w is $n \times m$ corresponds to the m filters, and convolution layer l will have m output maps.

The quantity of neurons in the hidden layer is $n_y = (|\frac{n_{l-1}-n_k}{s}| + 1) \times (|\frac{m_{l-1}-m_k}{s}| + 1) \times m$, where the dimension of input data is $n_{l-1} \times m_{l-1}$, the size of filter is $n_k \times m_k$, the step size of convolution is s (the distance that the convolution moves at each time) and the quantity of filters is m. As shown in Figure 6.23, the items of schematic diagram of convolution are 8×8 size of input data, 4×4 convolution window, 1 step size of convolution, 1 feature map and the quantity of neurons in the hidden layer is

$$n_l = \left(\left|\frac{8-4}{1}\right| + 1\right) \times \left(\left|\frac{8-4}{1}\right| + 1\right) \times 1 = 5 \times 5$$

■

6.4.2 Pooling in CNN

A feature map or feature of an image is obtained by convolution. But when using such features to train the classifier directly, we face the challenge of a huge computational burden. For instance, as for an image of 96×96 pixels, assuming 400 convolution filters are utilized, the convolution dimension is 8×8, and each feature graph includes $(96 - 8 + 1) \times (96 - 8 + 1) = 89^2 = 7921$-dimensional convolution features. As there are 400 filters, each input image sample would obtain $89^2 \times 400 = 3,168,400$ hidden neurons. This may involve a heavy computation overhead.

Common images have an attribute of static nature. The features that are useful in one image area are very likely to be applicable in another area. Therefore, in order to describe large images, we can conduct aggregation statistics for features at different locations. For instance, people can calculate the mean value (or maximum value) in an area of image. The statistical features obtained by such aggregation cannot only reduce dimensionality but also improve the results (by preventing over-fitting). The operation of such aggregation is called pooling. As per different computational methods, it is divided into mean pooling and maximum pooling. Figure 6.24 shows the pooling operation of 3×3 for an image of 6×6; the image is divided into four areas that do not overlap with each other. Figure 6.24 shows the result after maximum pooling in one area. The feature graph after pooling is 2×2.

Example 6.6 Convolution and pooling for CNN

In recent years, CNN has been widely used in digital image processing with the rapid development of CNN. For example, using this DeepID convolutional neural network, the correct recognition rate of the human face can reach a maximum of 99.15%. This

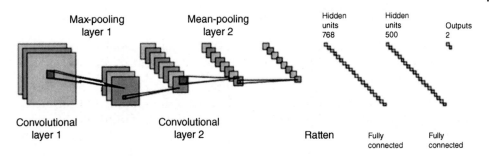

Figure 6.25 Schematic diagrams of convolutional neural network.

technique can play an important role in the search for missing persons and the prevention of terrorist crime. Figure 6.25 shows CNN in use.

If the given input image is as shown in Figure 6.26(a), the image size is 6 × 8. We adopt the size of convolution kernels as 3 × 3 and the size of one feature graph in convolutional layer 1 as $((6 - 3) + 1) \times ((8 - 3) + 1) = 4 \times 6$. Assuming we use three filters, the corresponding weight matrices are:

$$w_1 = \begin{bmatrix} 1 & 0 & 1 \\ 0 & 0 & 0 \\ 1 & 0 & 1 \end{bmatrix}, \quad w_2 = \begin{bmatrix} 0 & 0 & 1 \\ 0 & 1 & 0 \\ 0 & 0 & 0 \end{bmatrix}, \quad w_3 = \begin{bmatrix} 0 & 0 & 1 \\ 0 & 1 & 0 \\ 1 & 0 & 0 \end{bmatrix}$$

Assume deviation $b = -10$, the activation function $RELU(x) = \max(0, x)$. In order to obtain the feature graphs of convolutional layer 1, we need the following operations:

Step 1: Use w_1 to perform convolution of input data. The result is shown in Figure 6.26(b).

Step 2: Figure 6.26(c) shows the result with added deviation.

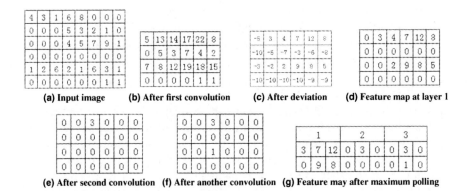

Figure 6.26 Successive convolutional and pooling steps in a CNN.

Step 3: After activation, we obtain the feature map 1 of convolutional layer 1, as showed in Figure 6.27(d).

Step 4: Repeating the above steps over weight matrix w_2 and w_3, we obtain the feature maps 2 and 3 of convolutional layer 1, as showed in Figures 6.27(e) and (f).

In order to obtain the feature graphs of max-pooling layer 1, we choose the maximum value of every non-overlapping 2×2 area in each output feature map and conduct a 2×2 max-pooling operation. Figure 6.27(g) shows the resulting feature map after the max-pooling at layer 1. ∎

6.4.3   Deep Convolutional Neural Networks

In fact, the learning of the convolutional neural network is to obtain the mapping relationship between input and output through a large quantity of learning of data with tags. But this mapping relation between input and output is hard to express with mathematical precision. When the training of such mapping relations is completed, the corresponding output data can be obtained through mapping by inputting data into the network.

The training of the convolutional neural network is similar to the BP network. It is divided into two stages, one is forward propagation to calculate output and the other is backward propagation for parameter adjusting with error. The algorithm for forward propagation is shown in Algorithm 6.4. During the course of forward propagation, we input sample data x into a convolutional neural network, conduct operation on input data layer by layer, make the output data of the previous layer as the input data of next layer, and finally obtain the output result of y′.

During backward propagation, we calculate the error between right tag y of input data x and the output result y', transmit the error and adjust parameters layer by layer from the output layer until it reaches the input layer. Detailed steps are as follows:

Step 1: y stands for tag of sample data, y' stands for output through calculation, calculate error: $O = y - y'$, Calculate cost function: $E = \frac{1}{2} \sum_{N} \sum_{K} (y - y')^2$, N stands for number of samples, K stands for classes.

Step 2: Calculate derivative of error E to weight w: $\frac{\partial E}{\partial w}$ layer by layer from output to input layer, renew the weight by using $w = w + \Delta w = w + \lambda \frac{\partial E}{\partial w}$.

Step 3: By utilizing Algorithm 6.4 from line 2 to line 15, calculate y'.

Step 4: Judge whether the terminal condition of backward propagation is achieved; if not, conduct Step 1, or end the training.

6.4.3.1.   Setup for Each Layers of the LeNet-5 Image Experiment

The input data are image data of 32×32. Layer C1 is a convolution layer and 6 filters of 5×5 are adopted for the convolution operation. The step size of convolution is 1, and 6 feature graphs of 28×28 are obtained. Each neuron in the feature graph is connected to an area of 5×5 input. There are 156 parameters in layer C1 for training: there are 25, i.e. 5×5 weight parameters and one deviation parameter for each filter, and there are six filters. So there are 156, i.e. $(25 + 1) \times 6$ parameters in total. The algorithm is given below:

Algorithm 6.4   Forward propagation in CNN

Input: x: sample data
Output: y′: output through calculation
Procedure:
1)   Conduct initialization to all parameters in n layers
2) $p_1 = x$
3)   for I = 1,2,...n
4)   if i is convolution layer
5)   Conduct convolution operation for p_i, and output q_i
6)   i++;
7) $p_i = q_{i-1}$
8)   end if
9)   if i is pooling layer
10)   Conduct pooling operation for p_i, and output q_i
11)   i++;
12) $p_i = q_{i-1}$
13)   end if
14) end
15) Output y′ through calculation

Layer S2 is a pooling layer. We conduct a maxpooling operation of 2×2 for 6 feature graphs for the output of layer C1. Then 6 feature graphs of 14×14 are obtained. As for layer C3, we conduct a convolution operation to output layer S2 with 16 convolution kernels of 5×5. Thus, 16 feature graphs with 10×10 neurons are obtained. Each feature graph in layer C3 is connected to all the 6 feature graphs, which are the output of layer S2.

Layer S4 is a pooling layer. We conduct a maxpooling operation of 2×2 for 16 feature graphs that are the output of layer C3. Then 16 feature graphs of 5×5 are obtained. Layer C5 is also a convolution layer and includes 120 filters of 5×5, and 120 feature graphs can be obtained. Each neural in the feature graph is connected to the areas of 5×5 in all 16 units in layer S4. There are 84 neurons (in the design of output layer, the quantity of neurons is set to 84) in layer F6, with full connection to layer C5. Just as in a classical neural network, the dot product between input vector and weight vector is calculated in layer F6, and an offset is also added. Then it transmits the result to the sigmoid function to produce the state of Unit i.

6.4.4   Other Deep Learning Networks

Deep learning architecture includes input layer, output layer and several hidden layers. Deep learning architecture means a deep neutral network, which has forward propagation and reverse learning. There are many types of deep learning architecture. Most of these architectures are used to change the common architecture. Here we divide deep learning architecture into three types according to the connectionist models of neutrons: fully connected, locally connected, and many other deep learning networks, as shown in Figure 6.27.

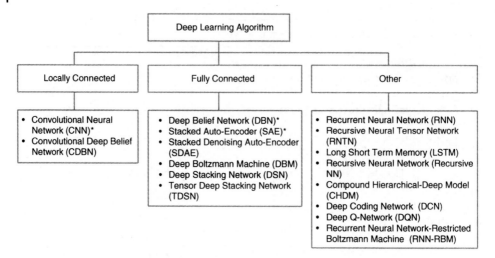

Figure 6.27 The architectural classification of various deep learning models. (Those marked with * are covered in this book.)

6.4.4.1. Connectivity of Deep Learning Networks

- **Fully connected networks:** In the traditional neutral network, the connections between layers from input layer, hidden layer to output layer are fully connected. One neutron in the previous layer connects with every neuron in the next layer. Fully connected deep learning architectures include Deep Belief Network (DBN), Deep Boltzmann Machine (DBM), Stacked Auto-Encoder (SAE), Stacked Denoising Auto-Encoder (SDAE), Deep Stacking Network (DSN) and Tensor Deep Stacking Network (TDSN).

- **Locally connected Networks:** Locally connected deep learning architecture means the connection mode between input layer and output layer is locally connected. This kind of deep learning architecture takes Convolutional Neural Network (CNN) as the representative class. It uses the concept of partial connection and weight sharing of convolutional operation to describe the overall local features. Thus, it reduces the amount of weight greatly. Convolutional Deep Belief Networks (CDBN) are also locally connected.

- **Other:** This class includes Recurrent Neural Network (RNN), Recursive Neural Tensor Network (RNTN) and Long Short Term Memory (LSTM), etc. Other related networks include the Recurrent Neural Network-Restricted Boltzmann Machine (RNN-RBM), Deep Q-Network (DQN), Compound Hierarchical-Deep Models (CHDM) and Deep Coding Network (DPCN), etc. Conventional ANNs, locally connected or fully connected, may have limited applicability, because they perform badly or become powerless when dealing with data streams. We introduce the recurrent neural networks (RNN) as follows:

6.4.4.2. Recurrent Neural Networks (RNNs)

An RNN corresponds to an ANN with three layers at each time point, so the training of this is similar to a traditional ANN. However, an RNN considers current output of a data stream also related to the previous output. That means information processing at

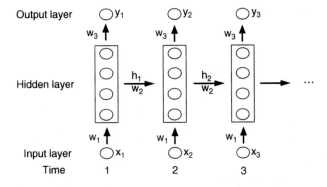

Figure 6.28 The structure of recurrent neural networks (RNN).

the current time needs to consider the output from the last time. Training a single layer RNN for 100 time steps is equivalent to training a feed forward network with hundreds of layers, as shown in Figure 6.28. When an RNN processes a sequence of data, the previous output will feedback as part of the input data. The RNN must remember the previous output for calculating the current output iteratively. There exist connections between the nodes of hidden layers in the network structure. The input of hidden layer needs to use the output of the input layer and the output of itself iteratively.

Most deep learning networks are feedforward networks, such as SAE, and DBN, which means the signal process flow in one layer is unidirectional from input to output. Unlike feedforward neural networks, RNN receives a sequence of inputs and also produces sequence values as output. RNN is a neural network including temporal behavior. This implies that the output of a sequence is fed as an input to the next input. RNNs appeal is to model language or speech recognition processes. The nodes between hidden layers are no longer unconnected but connected, and the inputs of the hidden layer include not only the current input but also the output of the hidden layer from last time.

At each time point t, the RNN corresponds to an ANN with three layers. The input and output of RNN at time t are represented as x_t and y_t', respectively, and the hidden layer is represented as h_t. We use the same network parameters (w_1, w_2, w_3) at all times, in which the connection weight between input and hidden layer is w_1, the weight between hidden layer of time $t-1$ and hidden layer of time t is w_2, and the weight between hidden layer and output layer is w_3, as illustrated in Figure 6.29. The forward computation is done as follows: the input at time t is x_t, the value h_t of the hidden layer is computed by the current input value x_t and the value h_{t-1} of the hidden layer at time $t-1$, then the output value y_t' is obtained while regarding h_t as the input of the output layer. Figure 6.29 attempts to reveal the differences between an RNN and an ANN.

6.4.4.3. Recursive Neural Tensor Networks (RNTN)

Recursive neural tensor network (RNTN) has a recursive deep neural network structure. This class was suggested for processing input data with variable lengths or making multistage predictions. The RNTN and RNN both have recursive behaviors [22]. They differ as follows: The RNN is the recursion of time sequencing and the RNTN is the recursion of data structure, called tensors (to be studied in Chapter 9).

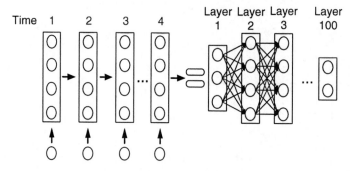

Figure 6.29 Contrast between RNN and ANN architectures.

6.4.4.4. Input and Output Relationships in Different Neural Networks

RNN receives a sequence of inputs and also produces a sequence of outputs. According to different applications, there are different forms of input or output pairs, which are shown in Figure 6.30 in four cases. In Figure 6.30(a), the I/O structure is especially appealing to image capturing applications. Figure 6.30(b) shows the I/O structure as having multiple inputs with a single output, which matches with document classification.

In Figure 6.30(c), both input and output are shown as sequential. This is practiced in RNN for video streaming applications, frame by frame. This architecture is also suitable for statistical prediction of the future situation. In Figure 6.30(d), we input the known data at time 1 and time 2, and the prediction starts at time 3. After inputting the data

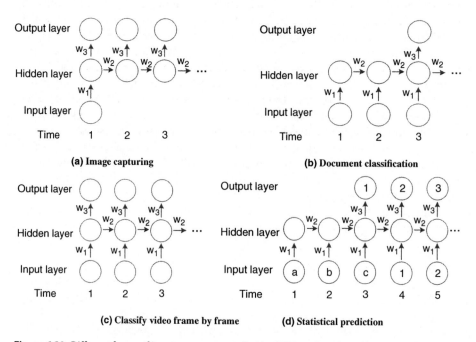

Figure 6.30 Different forms of input or output applied in different deep learning applications.

at time 3, we get the output result 1. This implies that we have predicted the data at the next time as 1. In the same way, we get the output result 2 after inputting the data 1 at time 4 and predicting the data at time 5 as 2.

6.4.4.5. Other Deep Learning Neural Networks

- **Convolutional Deep Belief Networks:**(CDBN) is a network structure which combines CNN with DBN. It can be utilized to solve the problems of extending DBN to process images with full size and high dimension.
- **Deep Q-Networks (DQN):**DQN is deep neural network structure, put forward by Google Deep-Mind. It combines reinforcement learning method Q-learning and artificial neural network.
- **Deep Boltzmann Machines (DBM):** (DBM) includes one visible cell layer and a series of hidden cell layers. There is no connection among the same layer. DBM is a deep structure of stacking several RBM, and there are undirected connections between any two layers.
- **Stacked Denoising Auto-Encoder (SDAE):**The structure of Stacked Denoising Auto-Encoders (SDAE) is similar to stacked auto-encoder. The only difference is changing AE to Denoising Auto-Encoder (DAE). DAE utilizes unsupervised training methods, which include three steps, i.e. corrupting, encoder and decoder.
- **Deep Stacking Network (DSN):**DSN uses simple neural network modules to stack deep networks, and the number of modules is uncertain. The output of each module is a category. The input of the module in the first layer is the initial data. From the second layer on, the input of modules is the series connection of initial data x and output y of the previous layers.
- **Tensor Deep Stacking Network (TDSN):**This TDSN is the extension of Deep Stacking Networks (DSN). It includes many stacked blocks. Each stacked block includes three layers, i.e. input layer x, two parallel hidden layers h_1 and h_2, and output layer y.
- **Long Short Term Memory (LSTM):** (LSTM) is the improvement of RNN, which adds memory modules in hidden layers of basic RNN. LSTM can solve weak influence problems of hidden layers in previous time points to the hidden layers in following time points when using basic RNN for training.
- **Deep Coding Networks (DPCN):** (DPCN) is a hierarchical generative model, which is a deep learning network that can use context data to realize self-update.
- **Compound Hierarchical-Deep Model (CHDM):**This model is composed of deep networks with non-parametric Bayesian models. Features can be learned using deep architectures such as DBN, DBM, stacked auto encoder, etc.
- **Recurrent Neural Network-Restricted Boltzmann Machine (RNN-RBM):** (RNN-RBM) is a kind of recurrent temporal RBM.

6.5 Conclusions

In this chapter, we introduce deep learning in detail, including its concept, representative deep learning algorithms and the training process. In Section 6.1, through the comparison of deep learning and shallow learning, the concept of deep learning is easily understood. In Section 6.2, we introduce the basis of deep learning, i.e. artificial neural network. Then, popular deep learning algorithms, such as SAE, DBN and CNN, are detailed in Sections 6.3 and 6.4. Additional deep learning methods will be treated in Chapter 9, where deep learning applications are presented with a software platform TensorFlow in DeepMind applications.

Homework Problems

6.1 Table 6.4 shows the Iris flower data set with only two species: setosa (denoted by "1"), and versicolor (denoted by "0"). We can differentiate between these data items by their petal length, petal width, sepal length and sepal width. Design an ANN model to classify the Iris flowers using a clustering approach:

1) Compute the number of neurons in the input layer of the neural network, and illustrate which flower's features are represented by these neurons, respectively.
2) Explain the number of neurons in the output layer, and how these neurons represent the categories of flowers.
3) Simply illustrate the process of training and classification and interpret the final clustering results.

Table 6.4 Sample data of Iris flowers characterized in four attributes.

ID No.	Petal Length	Petal Width	Sepal length	Sepal Width	Species
1	5.1	3.5	1.4	0.2	1
2	7.0	3.2	4.7	1.4	0
3	5.2	3.4	1.6	0.3	1

6.2 There are six optional courses for students in a school whose numbers are (1, 2, 3, 4, 5, 6). The grades for each course are represented as (A, B, C). Build a DBN model to predict the grades of some students, and the grades of courses as input of the network, then predict the grade of the sixth course. Given that the input data of each neuron in input layer of DBN is 0 or 1, then:

1) Design an input method for students' grades of courses, and explain how this method realizes the input of students' grades. And if so, how much neurons are in the visual layer?
2) If the grades of Jerry are (A, B, A, C, B), please write out the corresponding input data.

6.3 Many gas sensors face a cross-sensitivity problem, i.e. using a gas sensor is often unable to accurately detect the presence of poisonous gas. We can solve the problem by using an array of sensors to detect the cross-sensitivity characteristics over an artificial neural network. Table 6.5 shows three kinds of gas sensor measurements. The gas condition 1 refers to the existence of gas and 0 means no gas. Design an ANN model with the given data to distinguish the gas type characterized by X_1:0.4, X_2:0.5, X_3:0.4.

6.4 The semiconductor gas sensor is a sensor whose resistance will change in the presence of gas. We can determine the gas concentration according to the change in

Table 6.5 Data of gas sensors and corresponding gas conditions.

Sensitivity(X_1)	Sensitivity(X_2)	Sensitivity(X_3)	Gas A (Y_1)	Gas B (Y_2)
0.63	0.56	0.68	1	0
0.55	0.44	0.65	0	1
0.46	0.78	0.64	0	1
0.37	0.55	0.44	1	1
0.58	0.43	0.33	1	0
0.65	0.79	0.35	0	0
0.89	0.35	0.40	0	1
0.58	0.99	0.36	0	1
0.54	0.89	0.32	1	1
0.40	0.55	0.31	1	0
0.69	0.38	0.39	1	0

resistance ratio (sensitivity). However, the resistance of the semiconductor sensor will also vary with temperature and humidity. The dataset of 16 groups corresponding to the sensor sensitivity is given in Table 6.6. Use this dataset to design an artificial neural network model to speculate the gas concentration with X_1:28, X_2:50 and X_3:0.4.

Table 6.6 Temperature and humidity and gas concentration to measure sensor sensitivity.

Temperature(X_1)	Air humidity(X_2)	Sensitivity (X_3)	Concentration of gas (Y)
20	45	0.50	20
22.5	60	0.46	23
23.0	57	0.43	33
21.5	57	0.44	34
26.5	64	0.33	45
28.5	59	0.35	44
23.0	37	0.40	41
26.0	66	0.36	47
29.5	72	0.32	45
35.0	83	0.31	48
30.0	76	0.29	56
20.0	45	0.45	39
22.5	77	0.39	40
23.0	57	0.35	52
21.8	46	0.39	48
24.8	67	0.32	51

6.5 Use a convolutional neural network (Figure 6.31) to perform image classification. The image has an input layer with 32 × 32 resolution, and the network includes a convolution layer (C1) and a maxpooling layer (P1). Follow the steps below to carry out the classification task.

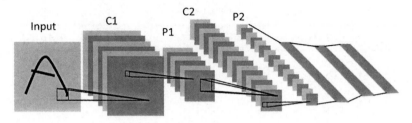

Figure 6.31 Structure diagram of convolution neural network for image classification.

1) Assuming the convolution kernel size of C1 in CNN is 5 × 5, stride is 3 and the number of feature maps is 6, calculate the size of each feature map in C1.
2) The size of the pooling area in P1 is 2 × 2; calculate the size of each feature map in the pooling layer.
3) Assuming the convolution kernel size of C1 in CNN is 3 x 3, stride is 1 and number of feature maps is 6, calculate the size of each feature map in C1.
4) The size of the pooling area in P1 is 3 × 3; calculate the size of each feature map in the pooling layer.

6.6 In handwritten numeral recognition, the usage of the Stacked AutoEncoder produces a result with high accuracy. In order to simplify its training process, we give a simple structure figure of Stacked AutoEncoder, as shown in Figure 6.32. The given structure includes one input layer (L1), two hidden layers (L2 and L3) and one classifier (L4). The input dataset includes a large number of unlabeled data and a small number of labeled data. By using supervised parameter fine tuning, calculate the number of parameters corresponding to the network and write the training steps of this Stacked AutoEncoder network.

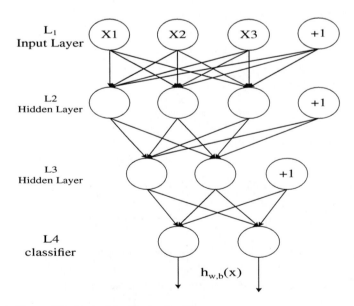

Figure 6.32 Stacked AutoEndcoder diagram.

6.7 Consider a handwritten numeral recognition network with three layers: a convolution layer, a max-pooling layer and an output layer. Write a program to calculate the feature graph after the convolution layer and max-pooling layer. The characteristic matrix of the convolution layer must be designed. The size of pool area is 2×2, and the input matrix of 8×8, as shown in Table 6.7.

Table 6.7 Input image data matrix of 8×8.

5	3	17	8	34	137	45	0
0	20	0	0	204	13	0	6
4	0	0	253	0	0	0	2
0	0	198	0	5	0	3	0
6	186	0	146	0	7	0	2
0	139	0	0	176	0	0	0
0	157	0	0	154	0	2	0
4	0	173	182	0	0	0	0

6.8 There are 6 neurons in the visual layer and 4 neurons in the hidden layer in an RBM. Given the input vector of neurons in the visual layer as $(0, 1, 1, 0, 1, 0)$, the connection weights are

$$w = \begin{pmatrix} -0.2 & -0.1 & -0.4 & 0 \\ -0.1 & -0.3 & 0.2 & 0.3 \\ 0.6 & 0.3 & 0 & -0.6 \\ -0.3 & 0.5 & 0.4 & 0.0 \\ -0.1 & 0.3 & -0.9 & 0 \\ -0.1 & 0 & -0.4 & 0 \end{pmatrix}$$

The bias of the visual layer is $bv = (0.1, 0.3, 0.2, 0, 0.1, 0)$ and the bias of the hidden layer is $bh = (0.1, 0.2, 0.1, 0)$. The random number is 0.6. Calculate the value of neurons according to the random number and the probability that neuron value is 1. Use Equation (6.14) to calculate the value of neurons in the hidden layer based on the input value in the visual layer. According to the calculated value of neurons in the hidden layer, use Equation (6.15) to calculate the neurons at the output layer.

References

1 Y. Bengio, A. Courville and P. Vincent, Representation learning: A review and new perspectives. *Pattern Analysis and Machine Intelligence, IEEE Transactions*, 35(8), 1798–1828, 2013.

2 N. Boulanger-Lewandowski, Y. Bengio and P. Vincent, Modeling temporal dependencies in high-dimensional sequences: Application to polyphonic music generation and transcription. preprint arXiv:1206.6392, 2012.

3 R. Chalasani and J. Principe, Deep predictive coding networks. 1–13. 1301–3541, 2013.

4 L. Deng and D. Yu, Deep Convex Net: A scalable architecture for speech pattern classification (PDF). *Proceedings of Interspeech*, 2285–2288, 2011.

5 A. Fischer and C. Igel, Training restricted Boltzmann machines: an introduction. *Pattern Recognition*, 47(1), 25–39, 2014.

6 F. Gers, N. Schraudolph and J. Schmidhuber, Learning precise timing with LSTM recurrent networks. *Journal of Machine Learning Research*, 3, 115–143, 2002.

7 A. Graves, A. Mohamed and G. Hinton, Speech recognition with deep recurrent neural networks. *IEEE International Conference on Acoustics, Speech and Signal Processing* (ICASSP), 6645–6649, 2013.

8 G. Hinton and R. Salakhutdinov, Efficient learning of deep Boltzmann machines. 3, 448–455, 2009.

9 G.A. Hinton, A practical guide to training restricted Boltzmann machines. *Momentum*, 9(1), 926, 2010.

10 H. Lee, R. Grosse, R. Ranganath and A.Y. Ng, Convolutional deep belief networks for scalable unsupervised learning of hierarchical representations. *ICML*, 609–616, 2009.

11 B. Hutchinson, D. Li and Y. Dong, Tensor deep stacking networks. *IEEE Transactions on Pattern Analysis and Machine Intelligence*, 1–15, 1944–1957, 2012.

12 Y. LeCun, L. Botto, Y. Bengio, et al., Gradient-based learning applied to document recognition. *Proceedings of the IEEE*, 86(11), 2278–2324, 1998.

13 V. Mnih, et al., Human-level control through deep reinforcement learning. *Nature*, 518, 529–533, 2015.

14 V. Pascal, L. Hugo and L. Isabelle, et al., *Stacked Denoising AutoEncoders: Learning Useful Representations in a Deep Network with a Local Denoising Criterion*, 2010.

15 S. Rifai, Y. Bengio and A. Courville, et al., *Disentangling Factors of Variation for Facial Expression Recognition*. Computer Vision–ECCV. Springer Berlin Heidelberg, 808–822, 2012.

16 R. Salakhutdinov, A. Mnih and G. Hinton, Restricted Boltzmann machines for collaborative filtering. *ACM Proceedings of the 24th International Conference on Machine Learning*, 791–798, 2007.

17 R. Salakhutdinov, J.B. Tenenbaum and A. Torralba, Learning with hierarchical-deep models. *IEEE Transactions on Pattern Analysis and Machine Intelligence*, 35(8), 1958–1971, 2013.

18 J. Schmidhuber, Learning complex, extended sequences using the principle of history compression. *Neural Computation*, 4(2), 234–242, 1992.

19 J. Schmidhuber, Deep learning in neural networks: An overview. *Neural Networks*, 61, 85–117, 2015.

20 Y. Sun, X. Wang and X. Tang, Deep learning face representation from predicting 10,000 classes. *Proceedings of the IEEE Conference on Computer Vision and Pattern Recognition*, 1891–1898, 2014.

21 R. Socher, J. Pennington and E.H. Huang, et al., Semi-supervised recursive AutoEncoders for predicting sentiment distributions. *Proceedings of the Conference on Empirical Methods in Natural Language Processing. Association for Computational Linguistics*, 151–161, 2011.

22 R. Socher, et al., Recursive deep models for semantic compositionality over a sentiment treebank. *Proceedings of the IEEE Conference on Empirical Methods in Natural Language Processing*, 2013.

Part 3

Big Data Analytics for Health-Care and Cognitive Learning

7

Machine Learning for Big Data in Healthcare Applications

CHAPTER OUTLINE

7.1 Healthcare Problems and Machine Learning Tools, 295
    7.1.1 Healthcare and Chronic Disease Detection Problem, 295
    7.1.2 Software Libraries for Machine Learning Applications, 298
7.2 IoT-based Healthcare Systems and Applications, 299
    7.2.1 IoT Sensing for Body Signals, 300
    7.2.2 Healthcare Monitoring System, 301
    7.2.3 Physical Exercise Promotion and Smart Clothing, 304
    7.2.4 Healthcare Robotics and Mobile Health Cloud, 305
7.3 Big Data Analytics for Healthcare Applications, 310
    7.3.1 Healthcare Big Data Preprocessing, 310
    7.3.2 Predictive Analytics for Disease Detection, 312
    7.3.3 Performance Analysis of Five Disease Detection Methods, 316
    7.3.4 Mobile Big Data for Disease Control, 320
7.4 Emotion-Control Healthcare Applications, 322
    7.4.1 Mental Healthcare System, 323
    7.4.2 Emotion-Control Computing and Services, 323
    7.4.3 Emotion Interaction through IoT and Clouds, 327
    7.4.4 Emotion-Control via Robotics Technologies, 329
    7.4.5 A 5G Cloud-Centric Healthcare System, 332
7.5 Conclusions, 335

7.1 Healthcare Problems and Machine Learning Tools

This chapter is devoted to the applications of predictive analytics in healthcare and disease detection. First, we review some IoT-supported healthcare systems. We focus on healthcare monitoring and physical exercise promotion systems. These medical domain requirements are assessed first. Then, we present the analytic solution systems using machine learning techniques supported by clouds, mobile devices and IoT resources.

7.1.1 Healthcare and Chronic Disease Detection Problem

In 2015, the World Health Organization (WHO) released a worldwide report on ageing and health. This report raises the serious concerns on global population ageing. The population over 60 years of age was projected to increase from 12% in 2015 to 22% by

Big-Data Analytics for Cloud, IoT and Cognitive Computing, First Edition. Kai Hwang and Min Chen.
© 2017 John Wiley & Sons Ltd. Published 2017 by John Wiley & Sons Ltd.
Companion Website: http://www.wiley.com/go/hwangIOT

2050. With a twice growing speed, the number of elderly people aged 60 and over will reach 2 billion during next 35 years. The situation in Asian countries is even worse, for example, Japan will have 30% elderly in her population in the next 10 years.

By 2050, the ageing population in many countries will rise to a similar level, which causes a series of problems all around the world. The medical systems in many countries are taking on heavy burdens, while the quantity of medical facilities and personnel is seriously inadequate. One possible solution is incorporation of both wearable computing and IoT technology into health monitoring services. Compared to typical healthcare problems such as population ageing, the care for chronic disease becomes more and more important nowadays.

With the changing economy and environment of human society, the acceleration of chronic disease has become the top threat to human health. And the morbidity keeps rising. However, it is not easily accessible for people to use public health services because of the shortage in medical resources and facilities. Those medical resources and systems are focused in urban cities based on population and capital. Up to now, the medical and health systems in some countries (especially the developing countries) are mostly intended to cope with acute diseases and infectious diseases, where prevention and treatment for chronic diseases are not emphasized yet.

Surprisingly, the improvement of living standards pushes the rise in chronic disease. In the US, 50% of people suffer from one or multiple kinds of chronic diseases at different levels. Eighty percent of medical funds are used to treat chronic disease. In 2015, the US spent around $2.7 trillion on chronic disease treatment. This accounts for 18% of the US GDP. The expensive medical expenditure places an enormous financial burden on society and government.

The main causes of chronic diseases include three factors. They are unchangeable factors, changeable factors and those factors hard to change. Age and heredity belong to the unchangeable factors and account for 20% in the causes of chronic diseases, as shown in Figure 7.1. Living circumstances are critical for one's physical condition, which is hard to change arbitrarily.

In 2015, the WHO produced a report on chronic diseases. It lists the four major chronic disease types, i.e. cardiovascular diseases, cancers, chronic respiratory diseases and diabetes mellitus. The report indicates that in 2012, most of non-communicable disease deaths were caused by these four diseases among under 70-year-old people. Cardiovascular diseases took the largest proportion of chronic deaths under the age of 70 (37%), followed by cancers (27%) and chronic respiratory diseases (8%). Diabetes took up 4% of deaths and other factors accounted for approximately 24% of deaths.

In addition to environmental factors, worldwide social and economic trends, such as population ageing, urbanization and globalization, also impact on the cause of chronic diseases. Population ageing is the direct reason for rising numbers of chronic diseased patients and urbanization makes environmental pollution worse. For example, the heavy PM2.5 and haze have stimulated the increase in lung disease. Another aspect is globalization. People are getting used to communicating with friends by mobile devices. The new technologies on social, mobile and networking are making an urban life more convenient. However, these advances also create a variety of unhealthy lifestyles. For example, sitting in front of computer for too long and lack of physical exercise causing obesity problems, etc.

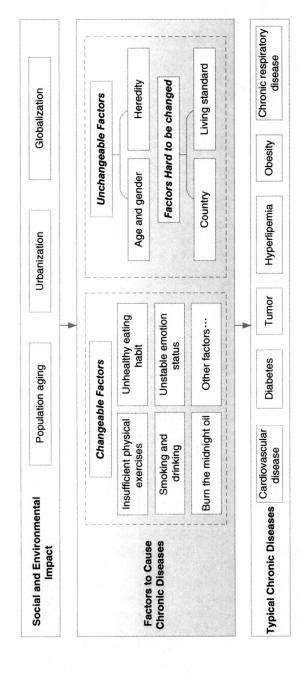

Figure 7.1 Factors that affect the detection accuracy in detecting chronic diseases.

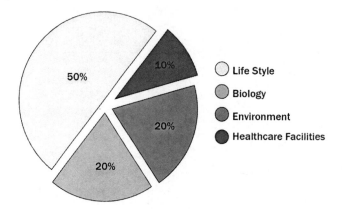

Figure 7.2 Determinants of health (statistics from centers for disease control in 2003).

According to a recent WHO report, the determinants of health comes down to five different factors. In fact, health facilities, such as surgeons and medical centers, can solve only 10% of medical problems. Fifty percent is dependent on lifestyle such as living habits, eating styles and exercises. Twenty percent lies in the environment and the remaining 20% is due to biological factors such as heredity. This shows that most of the causes are lifestyle-related. That is why we should concentrate more on health surveillance rather than after treatment, as shown in Figure 7.2. Due to its intrinsic long-term features, chronic disease is not acute enough to be treated in hospital. That is why national governments are spending lots of money on this problem. Sustainable health monitoring is critical to solve this challenging issue.

7.1.2 Software Libraries for Machine Learning Applications

In executing ML tasks, we need to create application programs, or use existing codes, toolkits, benchmarks from open sources or purchase from service providers. To match with task requirements, the best approach is to write your own application codes. This approach involves the algorithm selection, toolkits and dataset collection, program coding and test runs repeated until perfection. With limited experts or programmers, it is more convenient to apply existing codes or benchmarks.

In Table 7.1, we identify a few software toolkits that can help users to select a suitable program for data analytics. Surprisingly, many of these ML packages are from open source. Readers may check the developer websites for more details of the functionality and capability of those programs or runtime support systems provided.

Only brief introductory information is given here. We can dig much deeper with Google TensorFlow framework. The Spark and TensorFlow libraries have enriched our capability to develop new ML or DL applications. For a lot of cognitive activities, a human (even a new-born baby) can perform easily but not always certainly, but now we can train a computer to handle those screening and filtering tasks routinely to save us time and augment our decision processes with better evidence or supporting bases.

Table 7.1 Commonly available machine learning toolkits.

Toolkit or Framework, Language, Website of Developer	Short Description of Functionality and Capability
Scikit-learn, Python, http://scikit-learn.org/stable/	Built with NumPy and Matplotlib, provides simple and efficient mathematical tools for data mining and big data analysis
Shogun, C++, http://www.shogun-toolbox.org/	SWIG interfaces enable communication between C++ and target languages Python, Octave, R, Java, C#, etc., focusing on SVM kernel functions
Accord, Aforge.net,.NET, http://accord.codeplex.com/ http://www.aforgenet.com/ framework	Applied for audio/image processing in face detection and image stitch-on SIFT, supporting real-time mobile computing with ANNs or decision trees
Mohout, Hadoop, https://mahout.apache.org/	Using MapReduce to run on a single or multiple nodes of a Hadoop cluster, greatly improving the data volume
MLlib, Spark http://spark.apache.org/mllib/	MLlib is designed to enable many ML algorithms to run fast on large clusters. It supports personalized ML code design
Cloudera, Hadoop, http://www.cloudera.com/	Provided by Cloudera Hadoop distribution, enabling machine learning models to run on real-time data flow, such as spam email filtering
GoLearn, Go, https://github.com/sjwhitworth/golearn	Developed by Go with Google to support customized code design with simple tools to extend data structure and source code
Weka, Java, http://weka.wikispaces.com/	Weka is designed for data mining, preprocessing, classification, regression and clustering applications with visualization support
CUDA-Convnet, C++, https://code.google.com/p/cuda-convnet	CUDA is a speed-up toolkit of GPU, while CUDA-Convnet is a machine learning library for ANNs based on using fast GPU clusters
ConvNetJS, JavaScript, http://www-cs-faculty.stanford.edu/ people/karpathy/convnetjs/	An online training service for deep learning, which helps users understand the algorithms intuitively by showing some simple demos
FBLearner Flow, Python, https://code.facebook.com/posts/1072626246134461/	This platform reuses many algorithms in different products, by stretching into thousands of customized experiments of simulation. It also offers automatic generation of user interface experiences from Python codes

7.2 IoT-based Healthcare Systems and Applications

Health Internet of Things (Health-IoT) is devoted to solving medical health problems, and also has an important realistic meaning for promoting the development of the medical health industry and improving people's quality of life. Compared with the traditional things-oriented IoT, the Health-IoT is "human-centric", and all network accesses, data analyses and services are conducted surrounding humans. For example, the sensor at the data collection layer is not a common sensor, but a body sensor for collecting physiological health parameters.

The previous Health-IoT emphasized the design of a human body sensor and the collection of human body physiological data, but did not fully consider the users' mobility. Therefore, it is inconvenient to use in daily life and may even adversely affect daily life. The development of the mobile internet brings the integration of physical world, cyber world and social network, thus generating Cyber-Physical Society Systems (CPSS). Integrating the Health-IoT into CPSS, allows users to obtain the services and convenience brought by mobile health and mobile medical treatment, while user's mobility is not limited and the social network space is an inevitable trend for the development of Health-IoT.

Traditional IoT has been widely applied in the traffic, logistics and retail industries. With its maturity, the IoT attracts people's attention in the field of healthcare. However, lots of applications, which promote health service to families or individuals by utilizing IoT technology, later were proven to be unsuccessful. Due to its importance to improve medical treatment quality and service efficiency, the Health-IoT is a milestone in health information development. It will play an important role in improving people's health levels and enhancing their quality of life.

7.2.1 IoT Sensing for Body Signals

The physiological information collection is the basis of the Health-IoT, while the sensor is the most important link of physiological information collection, and it is the bridge between the physiological world and the electronic system. The sensing device is responsible for collecting the physiological data from the human body, and these data will help users check their own physical situation and help doctors in their diagnose.

According to users' demand for mobile medical treatment and health system, the physiological information collecting devices in the applications of the Health-IoT are divided into two large categories, one category collects the physiological information through sensing components integrated on universal mobile devices (GMD: General Mobile Device) (i.e. mobile phone); and the other refers to dedicated medical health collecting device (MHS: Medical Health Sensor), which collects health information by designing and integrating one or multiple dedicated health sensors. The following refers to respective features of these two kinds of collecting devices.

The universal mobile collecting devices possess the advantage of low cost as well as convenience in carrying and using. However, they also have disadvantages. For example, the precision of data collection is low and the collected physiological information types are limited. A complete Medical Healthcare System (MHS) is often equipped with the following devices or sensors, as shown in Figure 7.3.

Based on MHS, there are following concerns for IoT sensing of body signals:

- **Embedded Sensors:**The MHS device adopts dedicated sensors, and possesses the advantage of high collecting precision, but also features the disadvantages of high cost and insufficient portability and usability. This kind of device possesses the following features.
- **Wearability:**Most MHSs must be placed on the human body so as to collect precise data, for its data collection targets the vital signs of humans. Therefore, almost all existing medical health collecting devices take wearability as the basic requirement. In this case, the users' comfort must be considered and the accuracy of the data collected

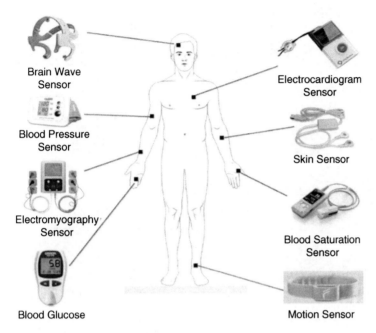

Figure 7.3 The layout of common human body sensors.

must be guaranteed during the collection procedure. The layout of common human body sensors are shown in Figure 7.3.

- **Long working time:**The method of the dedicated medical health collecting device varies with universal mobile collecting devices. The purpose of the former one is to collect data from the human body over a relatively long time period, which requires the high power supply capability of MHS.
- **Stability:**MHS still can collect data normally when users are taking strenuous exercise or in extreme environment.
- **Low participation degree of users:**Different from the method of GMD, the functions of MHS are relatively independent, and most MHS devices do not need the intervention of users during the data collecting procedure, and users only need to start up the power source, and the MHS will then start collecting.
- **Possessing data interim storage mechanism:**The weight and dimensions of MHS may be limited strictly to meet the requirements of a wearable feature. Therefore, most MHS devices will not integrate the data transmission module, but will select the data storage module with relatively small dimensions, and adopt the data interim storage mechanism to store the collected data in advance, and then transmit the data through other network access devices.

7.2.2 Healthcare Monitoring System

In recent years, remote health monitoring for the home environment has developed rapidly, and has integrated the health sensor, wireless communication and cloud computing. This has become a typical use of Health-IoT and cloud systems. The data collected by the sensor can be transmitted to a mobile phone, while the mobile phone

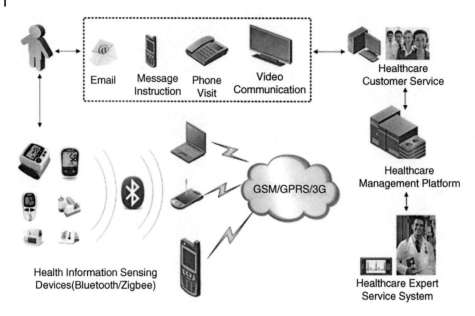

Figure 7.4 Common health monitoring system based on community services.

and the sensor can be connected through Bluetooth, and the data then transmitted to the health management service platform in the clouds.

This kind of application is especially applicable to the elderly, patients with chronic diseases and from sub-health groups. It can monitor the physiological parameters of people, including blood oxygen/pulse, blood pressure, blood glucose, ECG, body temperature and respiration. Figure 7.4 refers to the overall architecture of a common health monitoring system based on the community service. Services are usually provided by the health monitoring system, as shown in Table 7.2. As the simplified version, a dedicated health sensing device can be connected with an intelligent mobile phone through Bluetooth. The detected physiological data are transmitted to the mobile phone for visualization.

Different health monitoring systems have their specific features, and suit various groups of a population, such as the elderly, empty nesters, and patients with chronic diseases, etc. In the following, we classify the health monitoring systems into the following categories:

- **Health Cyber-Physical System:** Health-oriented mobile Cyber-Physical System (CPS) plays a vital role in existing medical monitoring applications, such as diagnosis, disease treatment and emergency rescue, etc. Some electronic medical intelligent network systems suitable for a large number of patients have been designed. The End-to-End delay of medical information delivery is the main concern, especially in the event of an accident, or in the period when there is an epidemic outbreak.
- **Mobile Health Monitoring:** Several years ago, a mobile health monitoring system based on portable medical equipment and smart phones was proposed. Smart phones are used to collect physiological signals from the human body from a variety of health monitoring devices by virtue of dedicated smart phone application software. Then

Table 7.2 Common health monitoring services.

No.	Service Contents	Service method
1	Providing 24 h remote ECG/blood pressure/blood glucose/blood oxygen/pulse/respiration/sleeping	Real-time monitoring service
2	Providing real-time warning of monitoring abnormality	Short message
3	Providing the service of notifying relatives of monitoring information	Short message
4	Providing the service of booking expert consultancy	Video or short message
5	Providing the emergency calling and aid service	Automatic telephone calling
6	Providing the family positioning service	Positioning
7	Regular health assessment report service	Short message or email
8	Regular health promotion care service	Short message or email
9	Regular follow-up service	Telephone
10	Life-long health record management service	Website inquiry
11	User data self-help inquiry service	Website inquiry
12	Providing 24 h consulting hotline service	Telephone

those physiological signals are transmitted to medical centers. If necessary, it can also notify caregivers and medical emergency institutions using the short message service of mobile phone.

- **Wearable Computing for Health Monitoring:** Over a long period, wearable devices and wearable computing are the key research topics to enable health monitoring. As new kind of body sensor nodes, the smart phone and smart watch are adopted to measure SpO_2 and heart rate; however, such measurement data has low accuracy, few signal types and limited medical uses (Table 7.3).

Table 7.3 Several common health monitoring devices.

Name of Device	Monitoring content	Additional functions
Blood pressure monitor	Blood pressure	Recording the historical blood pressure data
e-health Cloud Blood pressure monitor	Blood pressure	Integrating the cloud platform, historical data curves and transmitting distress information
Sunstudy GPS LBS	Tracking the elderly	Mobile phone communication, SOS distress help-seeking alarm and successively dialing three numbers; uploading the tracking position regularly and low-power alarm
Smart blood pressure device	Blood pressure and heart rate	The blood pressure and heart rate monitoring may avoid atrial fibrillation by contacting doctors to obtain the right treatment and know the situations of other patients
jWatch wristwatch	Blood pressure and heart rate	Data analysis and manual calling center
Remote infant monitoring	Monitoring infants	Monitoring infants from a distance and add other guardians

- **Health Internet of Things:** Health IoT is another way to provide a health monitoring service. The mobile sensing, localization and network analysis based on IoT technologies can be used for healthcare.
- **Ambient Assisted Living:** Ambient Assisted Living (AAL) aims at improving the life quality of patients, and it can notify relevant relatives, caregivers and healthcare experts. AAL-related technologies include sensing technology, physiological signal monitoring, home environment monitoring, video-based sensing, smart home technology, pattern analysis and machine learning.
- **Body Area Network based Health Monitoring:** Existing work on the body area network (BAN) focuses on sensor nodes energy saving, intra-BAN network design, implantable micro-sensors, physiological signal acquisition, etc. A portable smart wearable health monitoring system based on BAN has been developed. However, stability, sustainability and reliability of the system need to be improved.

7.2.3   Physical Exercise Promotion and Smart Clothing

With the rise in wearable devices and people's increasing attention to health, the exercise promotion industry based on wearable devices develops vigorously. The wearable devices can record the amount of exercise, food consumption and sleeping status of users each day, thus effectively supervising and urging them to increase the amount of exercise to keep the body healthy. A communication architecture of exercise promotion device has been proposed, as shown in Figure 7.5.

Professional exercise promotion devices can measure various physical indexes such as heartbeat and respiration more exactly, monitor their data including speed, running distance and endurance on the sports ground and provide support for improving exercise achievements. Thus, coaches can know the status of their team members more visually, and select the most suitable athletes to participate in a sporting event.

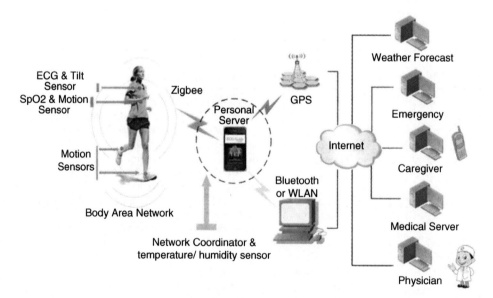

Figure 7.5 Communication architecture of exercise promotion devices.

| Sports bracelet | Heart Rate | Fitness tracker |

| Sport adornment | Smart heart rate watch | Step speed sensor |

Figure 7.6 Exercise promotion products available in 2016

The exercise promotion products at present are almost wearable, such as the smart wristband, heart rate strip and smart wristwatch, as shown in Figure 7.6. These devices can realize exercise step counting, exercise tracking, heart rate monitoring, as well as real-time exercise and sleep monitoring, sleep tracking and quality, diet tracking, calorie consumption and calorie burning, emotional tracking, distance course and counting, motion reminder, customized alarm, smart alarm clock, and smart no-sound alarm clock.

Example 7.1   Smart Clothing Application Software and Testbed Setting
Nowadays, smart clothing becomes an innovative wearable device for physical exercise promotion. The definition of smart clothing is given in the example: smart clothing is a kind of new system that integrates various micro-sensors for physical signals collection. Compared with traditional wearable devices, the smart clothing has the following features: convenient, comfortable, washable, highly reliable and durable.

In smart clothing, body sensors are integrated into the textile, which takes various factors into consideration, such as sensor type, strategic location for sensor placement and layout of flexible electricity cable. The fabric of the smart clothing adopts an elastic textile fabric, which is suitable for wearing next to skin. The smart clothing APP software installed in a mobile phone is shown in Figure 7.7(a), and the testbed of smart clothing systems is shown in Figure 7.7(b).   ∎

7.2.4   Healthcare Robotics and Mobile Health Cloud

Cloud computing is a new type of computing and service mode based on the Internet. Through this method, pooling hardware and software resources and information can be supplied to the service requester on the basis of requirement. The traditional robots are always restricted in the hardware and software functions where there are serious

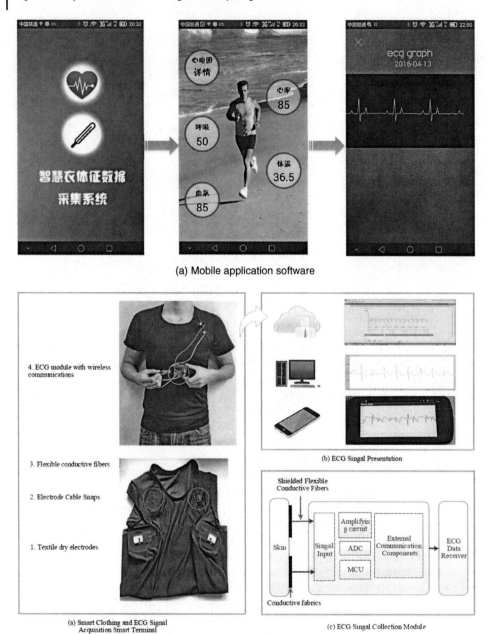

Figure 7.7 Smart clothing application software and testbed settings.

problems. But the cloud computing, as a good support for the robot technology, can easily combine cloud computing with robot technology to build a cloud robot.

As a frontend equipment, the robot takes charge of signal collection, specific action performances and some simple tasks in terms of analysis and process, while the more complicated tasks are offloaded to the cloud. By the use of its strong storage and computation capacity, the cloud builds effective models by applying ML algorithms and transmits the results of analysis back to the robots. The robot will also handle some computations locally based on its available resources.

Example 7.2   Mobile Devices, Robots and Cloud Environment for Healthcare
Figure 7.8 shows the collection of mobile devices, robots and clouds for healthcare applications. Integration of the robot and cloud computing technology in a healthcare system can greatly improve the service quality and level. Users apply wearable devices to collect physiological data, and then the collected data is forwarded to the remote cloud platform by the robot. The robot can store sensory data, interact with humans and integrate a variety of wireless communication modules including ZigBee, WiFi and LTE. The cloud is used to store large-scale health data, health analysis and prediction, and provide personalized service.

Robotics technology has a great influence on society, the economy and people's lives. The development of wireless network and cloud computing technologies pave the way for the robot moving from the industrial control field to the service field. Currently, the robot on the market mainly focuses on early child education, entertainment and domestic service (i.e. the cleaning robot). Most of them are controlled by software with customized functions. Networked robots enable remote operations and management. Lack of efficient communication links and learning ability is the major drawback in today's robotic-cloud interactions systems. ∎

The cloud robot architecture is divided into two tiers: machine to machine (M2M) level and the machine to cloud (M2C) level. In the M2M level, a group of robots are connected to each other via a wireless network to form an *ad hoc* robot collaborative cloud infrastructure. In the M2C layer, it provides a shared computing and storage resource pool, allowing the robot to offload computing tasks to the cloud. Google's research group has developed a smart phone-driven, learning through the cloud, robot system. Figure 7.8 shows the architecture of robotics and cloud-assisted healthcare systems.

Figure 7.9 shows an example of a mobile health cloud system. From end to clouds, the mobile health cloud system involves smart clothing, mobile phone, communication gateway, health cloud system and datacenter, etc. The related software includes smart clothing related software, smart phone application software, cloud-assisted big data analysis tools, etc. Software of each part needs to be developed separately, and eventually to be integrated into service packages for pervasive access.

The whole software system involves the embedded system development, mobile APPs and cloud deployment coupled with big data technology. Smart clothing software development needs to capture physiological signals. The communications, data storage, alarm system and other functions are constrained by low power consumption and embedded computing capacity. The smart clothing APP installed in a mobile phone is shown in Figure 7.7(a).

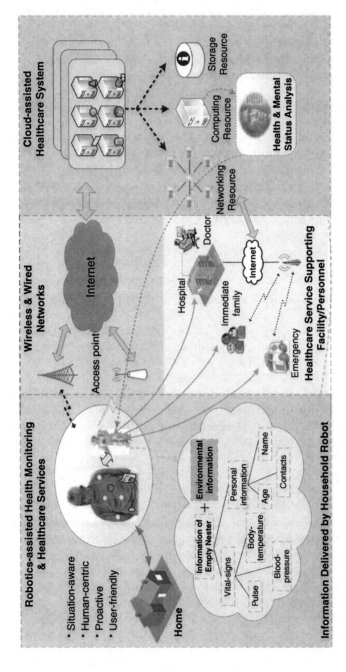

Figure 7.8 Robotics and cloud-assisted healthcare system.

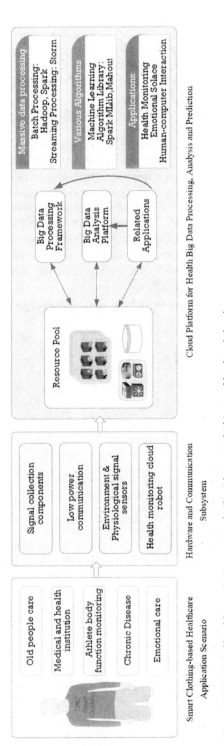

Figure 7.9 A typical health monitoring system built with smart clothing and backend cloud.

Smart clothing software must support two main functions: i) interconnect with body sensors for body signal acquisition with adjustable parameters and upload the data collected by smart clothing to the cloud; ii) provide personalized health services for users and show the users' all kinds of physiological indicators, bring convenience for users to query the historical data, receive alarm message and health guidance sent by the cloud, and remind the users of their health precautions.

Mobile cloud software produces the intelligence based on a centralized system. First, we need to construct a resource management tool to coordinate computing, storage and network resources. With the assistance of the cloud resource manager, a dynamic allocation mechanism can be applied to access cloud resources for smart clothing-based healthcare applications. In order to provide more accurate health advice and diagnosis, data statistics and machine learning library, API for big data analytics on cloud need to be enabled to predict the hidden development trend of a user's status. The cloud can also provide services between the user and the third-party medical and health institutions. The cloud software is the foundation of the smart clothing system, while mobile phone application provides the bridge to these services.

7.3 Big Data Analytics for Healthcare Applications

With big data growth in the biomedical and healthcare communities, analysis of medical data benefits early disease detection, patient care and community services. However, the analysis accuracy is reduced when the quality of medical data is incomplete or missing in various attribute dimensions. Moreover, different regions exhibit unique characteristics regarding regional diseases, which complicates the assessment of disease outbreaks. In this section, we streamline machine learning models and algorithms, especially for the detection of chronic disease outbreak in identified communities. We experiment with the modified detection models over real-life hospital data collected at from central China from 2012 to 2014.

To overcome the difficulty of incomplete data, we develop a new matrix decomposition method to reconstruct the missing data. We identified the regional chronic diseases such as hyperlipemia and diabetes, and consulted with hospital experts to extract representative characteristics of the disease. A new risk assessment model is developed using five machine learning models: naive Bayesian (NB), k-nearest neighbor (KNN), support vector machine (SVM), artificial neural network (ANN) and decision tree (DT). Comparing the relative performance of these prediction models, we find that the DT and SVM methods display higher performance than other models for detecting chronic diseases. The detection accuracy rate can be trained to as high as 90%.

7.3.1 Healthcare Big Data Preprocessing

The application of health big data is closely related with the sustainability of health monitoring. From the data collection point of view, without long-term physiological data collection supported by sustainable health monitoring, the data volume cannot reach the level of big data. From the cloud point of view, health big data analytics on clouds provide intelligence for more efficient health monitoring and make it more sustainable.

Generally, big data is of great significance in optimizing the costs of public and private health systems. Health big data is promoting healthy lifestyles and activities, avoiding the occurrence of chronic diseases (i.e. hypertension), slowing chronic diseases and transferring dependent patients into the monitoring center. In today's era of big data, it becomes possible to collect massive medical and health data on the basis of wearable devices along with the application of large amounts of body area network business platforms. The research on human activity recognition by using big data technology research has become an important research direction of healthcare big data.

In this section, we will discuss the healthcare preprocessing based on real data from a hospital in Wuhan, China. The data provided by the hospital include EHR, medical image data and gene data. The data covers a total of over 30,000 patients. Four important tables were extracted from the medical dataset:

- **Disease table:** the number of diseases and the corresponding disease name;
- **Results table:** the patient's examination results and the doctor's advice;
- **Patient table:** the patient's basic information, such as gender, age, living habits and inspection items;
- **Patient-disease table:** patient records.

For example, Table 7.4 gives an example of a physical examination data, including the patient's statistics, life habits, examination items and results, the patient's disease, healthcare costs incurred by the patient and the doctor's advice. In 2012, hyperlipemia did not appear in a large number of patients. However, there was a high-risk population of hyperlipemia (i.e. high triglycerides); thus, we developed a risk model for hyperlipemia to identify the disease early. We are concerned about the number of examination failures and the proportion of men and women and their average annual expenditure on healthcare. The number of people who fail the physical examination increases every year. There were more male patients than female patients in this region. That is, the disease is sensitive to gender differences. The increasing rate of chronic disease is reflected by patients' medical expenses.

Before data imputation, we first used data integration for data pre-processing. The accuracy of risk prediction depends on the diversity feature of the hospital data. We can integrate the medical data to guarantee data atomicity: i.e. we integrated the height and weight to obtain the body mass index (BMI). Latent variables are those variables that cannot be directly observed in a specific model. The latent factor models are presented to explain the observable variables in terms of the latent variables. The matrix factorization approach is one of the most successful realizations of latent factor models.

Table 7.4 Medical-related terms often found in hospital data base.

Item	Description
Demographics	Patient's gender, age, etc.
Living habits	Whether the patient smokes, whether he has a genetic history, etc.
Examination results	Includes 132 items, such as blood, etc.
Diseases	Diseases the patients is suffering from, such as hypertension, diabetes, etc.
Healthcare cost	The patient's expenses in detail.
Doctor advice	The doctor's advice regarding the patient's disease, the state of the risk.

7.3.2 Predictive Analytics for Disease Detection

We have learned machine learning algorithms in Chapters 5 and 6 for supervised and unsupervised approaches, respectively. In this section, we present three concrete health-care application examples in using predictive analytics based on five distinct machine learning algorithms, namely logistic regression, Baysian classifier, decision tree, KNN and SVM methods. In the next section, we will compare more choices of performance metrics to make the suitable choice of machine learning models for chronic disease detection.

Example 7.3 Predictive Disease Diagnosis using Logistic Regression

Table 7.5 lists a dataset of triglyceride, total cholesterol content, high-density lipoprotein, low-density lipoprotein and hyperlipemia or not ("1" for yes and "0" for no). These are collected from health examination data in a hospital in Wuhan, China. Let us attempt to conduct preliminary judgment on whether the person has hyperlipemia, if his or her health examination data are {3.16, 5.20, 0.97, 3.49} in a sequence.

To detect hyperlipemia, we choose a logistic regression approach with "1" for hyperlipemia or "0" for healthy, considering four attributes (features). First, we extract the four attributes and combine them into one attribute, as $z = \beta_0 + \beta_1 x_1 + \beta_2 x_2 + \beta_3 x_3 + \beta_4 x_4$, where x_1, x_2, x_3, x_4 stand for triglyceride, total cholesterol content, high-density lipoprotein and low-density lipoprotein respectively, and z stands for the feature after combination. Second, estimate weight β by using the maximum likelihood method, adopt software MATLAB here, and conduct iteration solution to likelihood equation set with Newton-Raphson Method.

In accordance with results above, β_2 is relatively large; thus it can be seen that whether one person has hyperlipemia or not is largely influenced by total cholesterol

Table 7.5 Health examination data for patients with hyperlipemia.

Patient ID	Triglyceride	Total Cholesterol	High-Density Lipoprotein	Low-Density Lipoprotein	Whether hyperlipemia or not
1	3.62	7	2.75	3.13	1
2	1.65	6.06	1.1	5.15	1
3	1.81	6.62	1.62	4.8	1
4	2.26	5.58	1.67	3.49	1
5	2.65	5.89	1.29	3.83	1
6	1.88	5.4	1.27	3.83	1
7	5.57	6.12	0.98	3.4	1
8	6.13	1	4.14	1.65	0
9	5.97	1.06	4.67	2.82	0
10	6.27	1.17	4.43	1.22	0
11	4.87	1.47	3.04	2.22	0
12	6.2	1.53	4.16	2.84	0
13	5.54	1.36	3.63	1.01	0
14	3.24	1.35	1.82	0.97	0

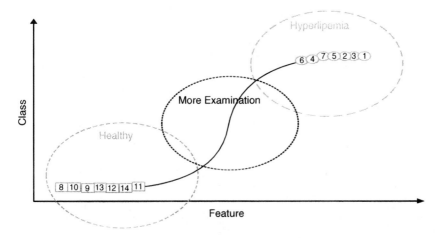

Figure 7.10 Classification results using logistic regression in Example 7.3.

content measured in the health examination. Then work out the class for each sample in the training dataset by use of the sigmoid function. The results are *class* = [1, 1, 1, 1, 1, 1, 1, 0, 0, 0, 0, 0, 0, 0]. The result is shown as Figure 7.10.

$$\beta_0 = -132.3, \beta_1 = -3.1, \beta_2 = 39.6, \beta_3 = -2.9, \beta_4 = 3.2$$

The number in the figure stands for ID of the person tested, and the circles in the dotted line stand for class. It can be seen from the figure that the accuracy of classification with logistic regression in this instance is 100%, thus this model could be adopted for prediction. Lastly, let us predict whether a person whose data are {3.16, 5.20, 0.97, 3.49} respectively has hyperlipemia. Adopt the model above and conduct solving-equation-by-substitution, then *class* = 1 .Therefore, that person is predicted to have hyperlipemia. ∎

Example 7.4   Use of Baysian Classifier in Diabetic Analysis and Prediction
This example analyzes diabetic patients and predicts whether they have acquired the disease. The prediction is based on training from sample data on labeled patients on their obesity and blood sugar content. The sample data are given in Table 7.6. Here, *Yes* stands for obesity or diabetic patients and *No* for normal weight or healthy persons.

For simplicity, we denote attribute *A* for obesity and attribute *B* for blood sugar content. Based on the statistics from Table 7.7, we obtain the following probability distributions on patient obesity and blood sugar content. To predict the class label of a person who received the health examination, if $X = (A = Yes, B = 7.9)$, the calculation of $P(Yes|X)$ and $P(No|X)$ is required. Using the statistics data, we have:

$$\begin{cases} P(A = Yes\,|Yes\,) = \dfrac{3}{4} & P(A = No\,|Yes\,) = \dfrac{1}{4} \\[2mm] P(A = Yes\,|No\,) = \dfrac{2}{5} & P(A = No\,|No\,) = \dfrac{3}{5} \end{cases} \begin{cases} P(Yes\,) = \dfrac{4}{9} \\[2mm] P(No\,) = \dfrac{5}{9} \end{cases}$$

Table 7.6 Health examination data of diabetics patients.

id	Obesity(A)	Blood Sugar Content(B) (mmol/L)	Diabetics Patient or Not
1	No	14.3	Yes
2	No	4.7	No
3	Yes	17.5	Yes
4	Yes	7.9	Yes
5	Yes	5.0	No
6	No	4.6	No
7	No	5.1	No
8	Yes	7.6	Yes
9	Yes	5.3	No

As for index of blood sugar content, if class is *Yes*, then:

$$\begin{cases} \bar{x}_{yes} = \dfrac{14.3 + 17.5 + 7.9 + 7.6}{4} = 11.83 \\ s^2_{yes} = \dfrac{(14.3 - 11.83)^2 + (17.5 - 11.83)^2 + \cdots + (7.6 - 11.83)^2}{4} = 18.15 \end{cases}$$

If the class is *No*, then

$$\begin{cases} \bar{x}_{yes} = \dfrac{4.7 + 5.0 + 4.6 + 5.1 + 5.3}{5} = 4.94 \\ s^2_{yes} = \dfrac{(4.7 - 4.94)^2 + (5.0 - 4.94)^2 + \cdots + (5.3 - 4.94)^2}{5} = 0.07 \end{cases}$$

With Gaussian distribution in blood sugar content, we have

$$\begin{cases} P(B = 7.9 \mid Yes) = \dfrac{1}{\sqrt{2\pi} \times \sqrt{18.15}} e^{-\frac{(7.9-11.83)^2}{2\times18.15}} = 0.062 \\ P(B = 7.9 \mid No) = \dfrac{1}{\sqrt{2\pi} \times \sqrt{0.07}} e^{-\frac{(7.9-4.94)^2}{2\times0.07}} = 9.98 \times 10^{-28} \end{cases}$$

At the moment, conduct classification for X with naive Bayesian classification method:

$$P(X \mid Yes) = P(A = Yes \mid Yes)P(B = 7.9 \mid Yes) = \frac{3}{4} \times 0.062 = 0.0465$$

Table 7.7 Probabilistic results on patient obesity and blood sugar content.

Diabetics	Obesity Yes	Obesity No	Blood Sugar Content (mmol/L) Mean Value	Blood Sugar Content (mmol/L) Variance
Yes	3/4	1/4	11.83	18.15
No	2/5	3/5	4.94	0.07

Table 7.8 Labeled samples from examination reports of 20 hyperlipemia patients.

Patient ID	Triglyceride (mmol/L)	Total Cholesterol (mmol/L)	High-Density Lipoprotein (mmol/L)	Low-Density Lipoprotein (mmol/L)	Hyperlipemia or not
1	3.07	5.45	0.9	4.02	1
2	0.57	3.59	1.43	2.14	0
3	2.24	6	1.27	4.43	1
4	1.95	6.18	1.57	4.16	1
5	0.87	4.96	1.36	3.61	0
6	8.11	5.08	0.73	2.05	1
7	1.33	5.73	1.88	3.71	1
8	7.77	3.84	0.53	1.63	1
9	8.84	6.09	0.95	2.28	0
10	4.17	5.87	1.33	3.61	1
11	1.52	6.11	1.29	4.58	1
12	1.11	4.62	1.63	2.85	0
13	1.67	5.11	1.64	3.06	0
14	0.87	3.45	1.25	1.92	0
15	0.61	4.05	1.87	2.05	0
16	9.96	4.57	0.53	1.73	1
17	1.38	5.61	1.77	3.62	0
18	1.65	5.1	1.77	3.16	0
19	1.22	5.71	1.53	3.93	1
20	1.65	5.24	1.47	3.41	1

In a similar way, the probability of $P(X|No)$ is obtained as follows with errors estimated:

$$P(X|No) = P(A = Yes|No)P(B = 7.9|No) = \frac{2}{5} \times 9.98 \times 10^{-28} = 3.99 \times 10^{-28}$$

$$\begin{cases} P(Yes\,|X) = \dfrac{P(X|Yes)P(Yes)}{P(X)} = \varepsilon \times \dfrac{4}{9} \times 0.062 = \varepsilon \times 0.0276 \\ p(No\,|X) = \dfrac{P(X|No)P(No)}{P(X)} = \varepsilon \times \dfrac{5}{9} \times 3.99 \times 10^{-28} = \varepsilon \times 2.218 \times 10^{-28} \end{cases} \qquad \varepsilon = \frac{1}{P(X)}$$

We get $P(Yes\,|X)P(X) = 0.0276 > 2.218 \times 10^{-28} = P(X)P(No\,|X)$. Therefore, the class of the person is *Yes* if $X = (A = Yes, B = 7.9)$. Thus, the person has acquired diabetes. ∎

Example 7.5 Selection for Hyperlipemia Detection Methods over Medical Data
In order to determine whether students suffer from hyperlipemia, a physical examination is conducted to measure the triglyceride, total cholesterol, high-density lipoprotein and low-density lipoprotein, and other projects. Table 7.8 lists the raw data of 20 students who were tested. Here, those students detected to have acquired hyperlipemia are marked by a "1" and those who have not by a "0" in the right-hand column.

Table 7.9 Measured performance of three competing classifer choices.

ML Algorithm	Memory Demand (in KB)	Training Time (in second)	Accuracy
Decision Tree	1,768	1.226	90%
KNN	556	0.741	100%
SVM	256	0.196	100%

Based on the small samples obtained, select the appropriate machine classifier to build a machine learning system to detect potential problems in students. Three candidate classifier methods are under consideration. Since the sample data is rather small, the final choice may not be able to cover a truly big data case. We use the example mainly for illustrating the selection choice.

By observing the sample datasets, we know all data have class labels, so this can be solved by a supervised classification method. Table 7.9 summarizes the memory demand, training time and accuracy measured by the use of the three candidate machine learning methods. In terms of accuracy demand, obviously the KNN and SVM methods are perfect to serve our purpose. If memory demand and training time are important, the SVM method is an even better choice. ∎

7.3.3 Performance Analysis of Five Disease Detection Methods

Big data can be applied to predict whether a person is among the high-risk population for a certain chronic disease, based on their personal information such as age, gender, the prevalence of symptoms, medical history and living habits (e.g. smoking or not, etc.). For example, we can specify a risk prediction model using the supervised machine learning method studied in Chapters 5. Figure 7.11 lists five distinct machine learning methods, namely naive Bayesian (NB), k-nearest neighbor (KNN), SVM, neural network (NN) and decision trees (DT) that we use for disease detection.

The model's basic framework is shown in Figure 7.11. We randomly divide the data into training data and test data, and the ratio of the training set and the testing set is 3:1. The methods mentioned above are used to train the model.

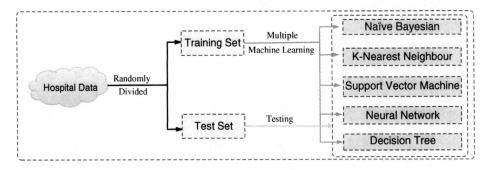

Figure 7.11 Five machine learning models for disease prediction based on medical big data.

7.3.3.1   Prediction using Nearest Neighbor Algorithm

NB classification is a simple probabilistic classifier presented in Section 6.3.3. Based on a patient's input feature vector $x = (x_1, x_2, \ldots, x_n)$, we can calculate $p(x|c_i)$ and the prior probability distribution $p(c_i)$. Bayesian theorem, $p(c_i|x) = \dfrac{p(c_i)p(x|c_i)}{p(x)}$, is applied to obtain the posteriori probability distribution, $p(c_i|x)$. Through solving the problem of $\mathrm{argmax}_{c_i} p(c_i|x)$, the NB classifier can predict the disease of a patient.

7.3.3.2   Risk Prediction using the Nearest Neighbor Algorithm

KNN was discussed in Section 4.3.2. In this example, we use Euclidean distance. Based on the medical big data, $x = (x_1, x_2, \ldots, x_n)$ and $y = (y_1, y_2, \ldots, y_n)$ are the characteristic vectors of two given patients, with each of the vector containing n characteristics. The Euclidean distance between two patients is calculated as follows: $d(x, y) = \sqrt{\sum_{i=1}^{n} (y_i - x_i)^2}$. The parameter K is sensitive to the model performance. We choose from 5 to 25 in typical healthcare applications. For the dataset we used, when $K = 10$, the model exhibits the highest performance. Thus, we set K to 10.

7.3.3.3   Prediction using Support Vector Machine

SVM was studied in Section 4.3.4. It is used to find a max hyperplane to divide an n-dimensional space into subspaces. In typical medical applications, the patient's characteristics vector $x = (x_1, x_2, \ldots, x_n)$ is linearly inseparable. To map the data to a transformed feature space, using kernel-based learning, it is easier to classify the linear decision surfaces and, therefore, to reformulate the problem so that the data are mapped explicitly to this space. The kernel function can have many forms. Here, we use the radial basis function (RBF) kernel. The SVM classifier can be implemented using the LibSVM library.

7.3.3.4   Prediction using Neural Network

NN classifiers were invented by mimicking biological neural networks. In this example, we need to set parameters first: i) the number of layers. The NN model contains four layers generally, including an input layer, two hidden layers and an output layer and; ii) the number of neurons in each layer. Here, the dimension of the input layer is equal to the number of patient's characteristics. The input is denoted by $x = (x_1, x_2, \ldots, x_n)$. In this example, we set 10 neurons in the first hidden layer, while setting 5 as the number of neurons in the second hidden layer. The output only has two results, i.e. high-risk or low-risk. Thus, the output layer only contains two neurons.

After constructing the structure of NN, we need to train the model. For each connection weight w and bias b in each layer, we use the back propagation algorithm. For the activation function, we apply the sigmoid function.

7.3.3.5   Prediction using Decision Trees

Decision Trees (DT) based classification was presented in Section 4.3.1. Its basic idea is that an object is classified by minimizing the data impurity, which is determined by the use of information gain. The information gain is based on the concept of entropy, whose definition is as follows: $H(S) = -\sum_i p_i \log p_i$, in which $p_i = |C_{i,s}|/|S|$

is the non-zero probability of C_i. The expected information required for the classification of S according to attribute A is denoted by $H_A(S)$. Then, we can obtain $H_A(S) = \sum_{v \in V} |S_v|/|S|H(S_v)$, where v represents the v subsets divided from S according to attribute A. We can then obtain the information gain as follows: $\text{Gain}(S, A) = H(S) - H_A(S)$.

To improve the model, the 10-fold cross-validation method is used on the training set, where data from the testing participant are not used in the training phase. Let TP, FP, TN and FN be the true positive (the number of legitimate instances correctly predicted), false positive (the number of legitimate instances incorrectly predicted), true negative (the number of negative instances correctly predicted) and false negative (the number of negative instances incorrectly predicted), respectively. We define four measurements: accuracy, precision, recall and F1-Measure as follows:

$$\text{Accuracy} = \frac{TP + TN}{TP + FP + TN + FN} \tag{7.1}$$

$$\text{Precision} = \frac{TP}{TP + FP} \tag{7.2}$$

$$\text{Recall} = \frac{TP}{TP + FN} \tag{7.3}$$

$$\text{F1} - \text{Measure} = \frac{2 \times Precision \times Recall}{Precision + Recall} \tag{7.4}$$

The F1-Measure is the weighted harmonic mean of the precision and recall represents the overall performance. In addition to the evaluation criteria above, we most often use the receiver operating characteristic (ROC) curve and the area under the curve (AUC) to evaluate the pros and cons of the classifier. The ROC curve shows the trade-off between the true positive rate (TPR) and the false positive rate (FPR), in which $TPR = TP/(TP + FN)$ and $TFR = FP/(FP + TN)$. When the area is closer to 1, the better the model.

Example 7.6 Prediction of High-Risk Disease with Five Machine Learning Algorithms

The inputs to the model are the attribute values of the patient, denoted by $x = (x_1, x_2, \ldots, x_n)$. The output value is $C = \{c_0, c_1\}$, where c_0 indicates whether the patient is amongst the hyperlipemia high-risk population class, and c_1 indicates whether the patient is amongst the hyperlipemia low-risk population class. We concern about the accuracy, precision, recall and F1-Measure of the hospital's dataset. The DT has the highest accuracy in the training set and the test set. The relative performance and training time of five machine learning models are given in Figure 7.12.

Figure 7.12(a) plots the accuracy, precision, recall rate and F1 performance of all five prediction methods. Based on the datasets we have processed, they all perform the same range between 82% and 95%. Considering accuracy alone, SVM and DT methods are higher around 92%, while the other three methods stay around 90%. By precision measure, we find that NN and DT are better than KNN, which is lowest around 80%. In terms of recall rate, the KNN method is the highest, while the other four algorithms stay at the

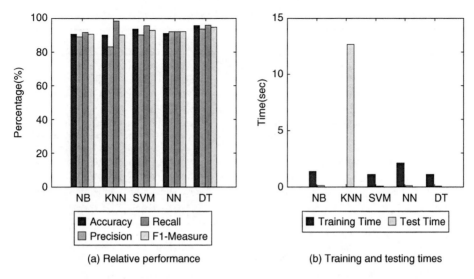

(a) Relative performance   (b) Training and testing times

Figure 7.12 Relative performance of 5 machine learning methods for disease prediction.

same level above 90%. Finally, the DT has the highest F1 measure of 95%, while others stay around 90%.

In summary, in terms of training time, as plotted in Figure 7.12(b), we find KNN takes a much longer time to be trained, while the rest have much lower training times. Based on these results, we rank the DT method as the highest in performance and the KNN method as the lowest in overall scores. However, we have to indicate that this ranking result is by no means the same in general situations. The relative performance is very sensitive to the dataset size and characteristics. By ROC results, we find that SVM exhibits better performance for high-dimensional cases, whereas the DT works better for low-dimensional cases (Figure 7.13). Finally, we summarize the pros and cons of using these five machine learning models in Table 7.10. ∎

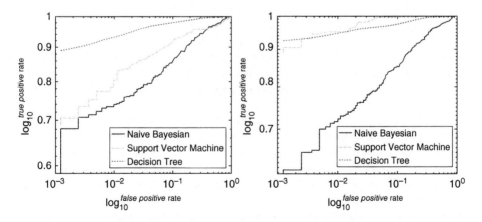

Figure 7.13 ROC curve of the disease prediction results using hospital data.

Table 7.10 Strength and weakness of disease detection methods reported in Example 7.6.

Algorithm	Strength	Weakness
Naïve Bayesian	Easy to implement; strong robustness to variation in independent attributes under noise impacts, the training time is short and detection time fast	Attribute assumptions occurs independently. Generally, the accuracy of the classification is not as high as other methods
K-Nearest Neighbor	Easy to understand; there is no assumption about the distribution of the dataset; the data can be multi-dimensional	Classification speed is slow; all training sets must be stored in the memory to gain in processing speed and is sensitive to noise disturbance
Support Vector Machine	Can handle high-dimensional data; generally, the accuracy is high; the abnormal value has good processing abilities	With high dimension, needs a good kernel function; training time is longer with high demands for storage and CPU power
Neural Network	Handles multiple feature data; classification speed is fast; it can address redundant characteristics	Training time is relatively long; sensitive to the concentration noise
Decision Tree	Less dependence on data distribution. Classification of data is fast and easy to interpret detection results	Is prone to the problem of data fragments; the good DT tools are difficult to find

7.3.4 Mobile Big Data for Disease Control

The traditional approach to analyze disease mobility patterns is often based on household surveys and information provided from census data. These traditionally collected datasets suffer from recall bias and limitations in the size of the population sample involved in the analysis, mainly due to excessive costs in the acquisition of the data and its timing. Human mobility models cloud-assisted derived from mobile network data have the potential to overcome the shortcomings of traditional methods.

What is interesting and powerful is the fact that mobile phones are connected, leaving a digital trace behind, which can be used to analyze and model human behavior at individual and aggregate levels. The analysis of these digital traces has already been successfully applied in a variety of fields, including urban planning, modeling human mobility, and understanding social network structures or measuring economic development. And it will be applied in cloud-assisted disease control. With the popularity of mobile-cellular and cloud platforms, there is tremendous potential for using different types of mobile network data for public health and disease control. More and more studies have focused on the opportunity to model population mobility and to characterize disease spreading.

The past few years have seen a dramatic growth in mobile traffic. The global cellular network traffic from mobile devices is expected to surpass 24 exabytes (an exabyte is approximately equal to 1018 bytes) per month by 2019, which is nine times larger than the traffic served by the existing cellular network in 2014. Such a huge volume of mobile traffic forms large-scale mobile big data. This provides the most convenient data resource to analyze the population mobility for cloud-assisted disease control.

Individual and aggregated human mobility is certainly a key variable to measure, model and predict public health. Human mobility models can be built from passively collected mobile network data, with great promise to help decision making in disease control, particularly when fighting against an infectious disease, facing the risk of a pandemic or when dealing with the consequences of a natural disaster. In order to expedite the adoption of mobile data for disease control, people need to collect the mobile phone data of the patients, such as event-driven mobile phone CDR (Call Detail Records), mobile phone location data, signal triangulation of mobile locations like GPS, and so on. Each one of the types of mobile data has its own technical strengths and limitations, so we need to combine them to model the mobility of the patient crowd.

In scenarios of disease control, it is necessary and important to combine the mobile phone data with variables from external data sources, such as public health information or medical records, weather data, air quality data and social information of patients. The mass volume of the mobile phone data and the linkage of different datasets pose both technical and privacy challenges that need to be addressed. In cloud-assisted disease control systems, people use the cloud as a platform for data collecting, data storage, data transmission and the computing resource for big data analysis technique.

For example, the typical mobility variables in CDRs include the number of base stations used, radius of gyration (i.e. the root mean squared distance between base stations), the total distance traveled and the diameter of the area of influence. This refers to the graphical area where user activities are taking place. This could be measured as the maximum distance between base stations. In the transmission of malaria, we may need to analyze the CDRs of almost 15 million Kenyan mobile subscribers by using an epidemic spread model. The approach was grounded in the fact that human mobility contributes more to the spread of malaria than that by mosquito dispersal.

In addition to understanding population mobility in cases of epidemics or natural disasters, mining mobile network data can provide valuable information for ongoing routine public health surveillance. After Haiti's earthquake in January 2010, followed by a cholera outbreak in October 2010, researchers at the Karolinska Institute in Sweden analyzed daily movement data from 2 million mobile phones. They were able to identify critical areas of the cholera outbreak and quantify the population that was affected by the disaster and their movements in the following period. This study illustrated the tremendous value for disease control and emergency services officials of mobile network data when made available directly after a disaster takes place.

From the perspective of public health and disease control, mining mobile network data with cloud-assistance can potentially enable us to identify patient populations and disease situations in which an intervention (i.e. a message, a phone call or a visit) can trigger positive behavioral change or encourage adherence to the therapy, which would contribute to improving disease control efficiency and lower healthcare costs. However, there are many challenges in using cloud platforms for disease control with mobile data. Data privacy and database security are also setting some limits. For example, due to regulatory and legal limitations and lack of technical expertise, many rescue initiatives were called off to stop the outbreak of Ebola in Africa.

The overall methods of data analytics for disease control are shown in Figure 7.14. This study used general data mining, including data pre-processing, data-mining models and data post-processing. Medical big data must be discussed with the doctor to obtain an understanding of the problem and the data. The hospital's data were stored in the cloud. To protect the user's privacy and security, we created a security access mechanism. We first pre-processed the data, including the processing and dimension

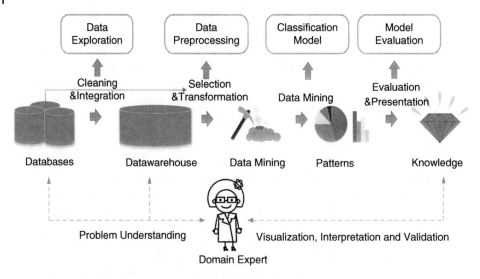

Figure 7.14 Methods for the high-risk patient prediction process encompassing exploration, preprocessing and evaluation stages.

reduction of missing values, repeat values and exception values. According to the doctor's opinion to extract feature values, we used machine learning algorithms to evaluate the patient's risk model; finally, the best model was selected via evaluation using the mathematical method.

Aggregation was performed on the training data by implementing the demographics, risk factors, vulnerability on which the pre-processing was performed and transformation of the input data. Data cleaning included cleaning and pre-processing the data by deciding which strategies to use in handling missing fields and to alter the data according to the requirements. We first identified uncertain, inaccurate, incomplete or unreasonable medical data and then modified or deleted them to improve the data quality.

In the clean-up process, we examined the format, integrity, reasonableness and limitations of the data. Data cleaning is of vital importance for maintaining the consistency and accuracy of the data analysis. The accuracy of risk prediction depends on the diversity feature of the hospital data. We can integrate the medical data to guarantee data atomicity, i.e. we integrated the height and weight to obtain BMI. According to the discussion with a domain expert and Pearson's correlation analyses, we extracted the user's statistical characteristics and some of the characteristics associated with hyperlipemia and living habits (i.e. smoking).

7.4 Emotion-Control Healthcare Applications

The emerging research on human–machine emotional interactions is based on wearable computing to the context of IoT sensing and big data analytics on clouds. To enable automated emotion caring with the help of machines, the system must be designed to collect data on human's emotions, expressions or gestures. Emotion-control poses higher requirements on the amount and quality of body signals than traditional healthcare. Some emotion-control healthcare requires the affective interactions with the users. In this section, we address the relevant issues and review some solution schemes proposed in recent years.

7.4.1 Mental Healthcare System

Emotion care helps those who suffer from mental problems or are trapped in deep depression or frustration in their daily lives. This includes aged or people living alone, families under the poverty line, retarded or under-privileged citizens, long-distance truck drivers, and psychologically diseased patients, etc. To solve the problem, many civilized societies have social workers or policy forces to help out. Here, we study how machine intelligence can be employed to assist or provide augmented help beyond human caring agents. One can apply some physiological or cytological indexes to detect human emotions.

When finding a person in a very low mood, the system should raise some alert to the victim or to those who care for them. For example, voice reminders or playing music, etc. can be applied to stop an emergency situation or suicidal attempt. An emotion detection robot can be designed to guide the patient's emotion state. Emotion interaction commands can be aided by cloud or IoT resources. Emotion detection using a Wearable 2.0 standard can be designed to use comprehensive physiological index values, which are monitored by IoT devices (including smart phones) or smart machines like intelligent robotic systems. Emotion detection is based on human expressions or gestures. Designing a dedicated mobile application may be helpful to detect an angry state to avoid inappropriate responses. Other approaches include integrating social workers' data, location information, mobile phone call records, etc, in automated emotion detection systems.

To provide proper and effective emotion care, we need to develop an emotion model based on physiological data training in the cloud. The system should establish unique responses for different user emotion patterns. For example, to use ECG (Electrocardiography), the signal is transmitted to the cloud via wisdom clothing with ECG acquisition and transmission function. When the cloud receives the ECG data, it will conduct analysis and processing in real time. Next, according to the user's unique identification, the user's emotional state is predicted by the trained model, while the other data collected from mobile terminal can assist emotion prediction.

When detecting that the user has negative emotions, an immediate call is made to the relevant equipment and resources to emotionally interact with users. For example, with a sadness emotion, in order to play music which can ease the grief for the user, the system can even send a command to a robot in the home and let the robot emotionally interact with user through a series of methods of actions, voice, etc. And finally, the system realizes the effect of emotional care. As shown in Figure 7.15, the population that needs emotional care includes empty-nest people, depressive patients, autism children, long-distance drivers, pilots and spacemen, prisoners or slaves, etc.

7.4.2 Emotion-Control Computing and Services

Although the development of sensors and wearable devices has spawned a plethora of mobile, pervasive and intelligent applications as well as new service models, users'

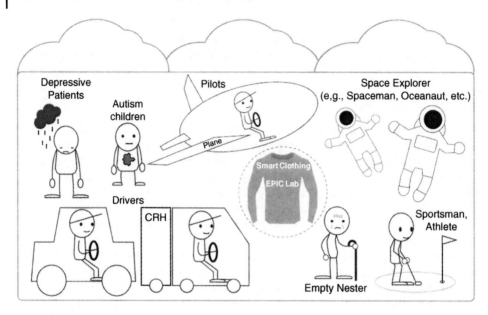

Figure 7.15 Mental healthcare for special groups of populations.

psychological status is meeting the challenge to deal with the increasing demands of emotional care. Most existing emotion-aware applications sense emotion by the relationship between the user's emotion and behavioral patterns of the mobile phone usage. However, the inference accuracy of emotion recognition is either limited by the small-scale data collected by smart phones, or dependent on labor-intensive manual labeling processes, which limits the provision of sufficient emotion-oriented care. Thus, the major purpose of such applications is for smart phone-based entertainment.

7.4.2.1 Data Collection and Feature Extraction

Wearable devices and mobile phones are used to collect data every 30 minutes. The data collected are then categorized into physical data, cyber data and social network data. Physical data consists of physiological data, activity level, location information, environmental, phone screen on/off and body videos. Cyber data includes phone call logs, SMS logs, emails logs and application usage logs. Social network data includes SNSs. On the other hand, the user's emotional status is obtained mainly through the following two methods: i) self-label by the user; and ii) label through transfer learning. Table 7.11 shows the data collection in detail. Data preprocessing mainly contains the following four aspects: data cleaning, eliminate redundancy, data integration and time series normalization.

We divide the data into three classes: statistical data, time-series data and content data. We obtain the features of the physical data, cyber data and social network data. For physical data, for example calls, SMS, email, heart rate, breathing rate, skin temperature and sleep time, we count the number of each attribute. For time-series data, for example the activity level, with ranges between low, medium and high, representing a person being static, walking and running. With location information, we cluster our time-series of location data through the DBSCAN, which can obtain the locations that the user

Table 7.11 Various data types in providing emotion control services.

Data Style	Data Type	Usage Cue
Physical Data	Physiological data	Heart rate, Breathing rate, Skin temperature, Duration time of sleep
	Activity level	Static, Walking, Running
	Location	Latitude and longitude coordinates, User retention time
	Environmental	Temperature, Humidity
	Phone screen on/off	The time screen on/off
	Body video	Facial expression, Head movement, Eye blink, and Behavioral video
Cyber Data	Calls	No. of incoming/outgoing calls, Average call duration, No. of missed calls
	SMS	No. of messages, The length of the messages, Content of each SMS
	Emails	No. of sent/receive emails
	Application	Numbers Office Apps, Maps, Games, Chat, Camera and Video/Music Apps
Social Network Data	SNS	The user ID and screen name, No. of friends, Content post, repost and comment, Image post, repost and comment, Content or Image create time

visits. For content data, we utilize SentiWordNet to filter emotional-aware words with scores belonging to $[-1, -0.4] \cup [0.4, 1]$.

7.4.4.2 Transfer Learning based Labeling for Emotion Detection

Typically, each person has his/her own behavioral pattern in terms of behaviors state and living habits, i.e. different people may have different physiological signals and living habits under the same emotions. As shown in Figure 7.16, various people express their emotion of happiness by difference behaviors, which can be sensed by multimodal

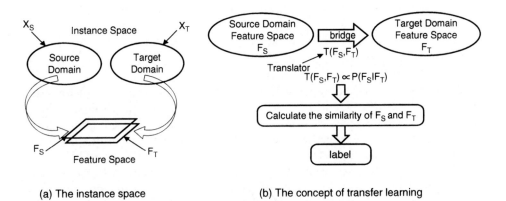

(a) The instance space   (b) The concept of transfer learning

Figure 7.16 Instance space and feature space for transfer machine learning.

person-centric data. One key penetrating point is to match a single type of emotion with various user's behaviors through transfer learning. The concept of transfer learning is illustrated below. Various data types are given in Table 7.11 in providing emotion control services.

Let X_S be the source instance space, i.e. the data collected which have mood label, and let X_T be the target instance space, i.e. the data collected which does not have mood label. F_S and F_T are the feature spaces corresponding to X_S and X_T, respectively. As shown in the Figure 7.16(a), C denotes the label space of a number of emotional modes: {happiness, sadness, fear, anger, disgust, surprise}. The transfer learning model applies a Markov chain $(c \rightarrow f_s \rightarrow f_t \rightarrow x_t)$, where $x_t \in X_T, f_t \in F_T, f_s \in F_S$ and $c \in C$.

Our goal is to estimate the conditional probability $p(c|x_t)$. First, we need to find a translator $T(f_t, f_s) \propto p(f_t|f_s)$ to link the two feature spaces. The similarity of features is used to judge the similarity of feature domains. As shown in the Figure 7.16(b), we link the feature f_s and f_t through the following equation:

$$D_{JS}(P_T||P_S) = \frac{1}{2}(D_{KL}(P_T||M) + D_{KL}(P_S||M)) \tag{7.5}$$

where $M = 1/2(P_S + P_T)$ and the KL-divergence D_{KL} is defined as

$$D_{KL}(P_T||P_S) = \sum_{x \in X} P_T(x) \log \frac{P_T(x)}{P_S(x)} \tag{7.6}$$

For time-series data, we first normalize them into $[0, 1]$. Time series collected from source domain and target domain are denoted by M_S and M_T, respectively. Dynamic time warping (DTW) is used to measure the similarity of M_S and M_T as

$$D(i,j) = d(m_i, n_j) + \min\{D(i-1,j), D(i,j-1), D(i-1,j-1)\} \tag{7.7}$$

where $d(m_i, n_j) = \sqrt{(m_i - n_j)^2}, m_i \in M_S, n_j \in M_T$. With the decreasing of $D(i,j)$, M_S and M_T become more similar. So we take the low-n similar sequences out. Now we link the f_t and f_s, so we can calculate the top-N most probability sequences label.

For the text, we extract the word which scores between $[-1, -0.4] \cup [0.4, 1]$. According to SentiWordNet, the vectors of scores from source and target domains are denoted by V_S and V_T. Now we use cosine similarity to measure the similarity between V_S and V_T as

$$\cos(\theta) = \frac{V_S \cdot V_T}{||V_S|| \cdot ||V_T||} \tag{7.8}$$

Now we link the f_s and f_t, so we can calculate the top-N most probability vector label. As shown in the Figure 7.17, the P_S is the probability distribution of f_s from the source domain, for example plot the frequency of body temperature value. For physiological data, call, SMS, email and application, we adopt the same method to estimated distribution. P_T is the probability distribution of f_t from the target domain, since the Jensen–Shannon divergence is widely used for measuring the similarity between two probability distributions. $D_{JS}(P_T||P_S)$ equals to zero if and only if the two distributions P_T and P_S are identical. So we take the low-n similar distributions out. Now we link the f_t and f_s, so we can calculate the top-N most probability distributions label.

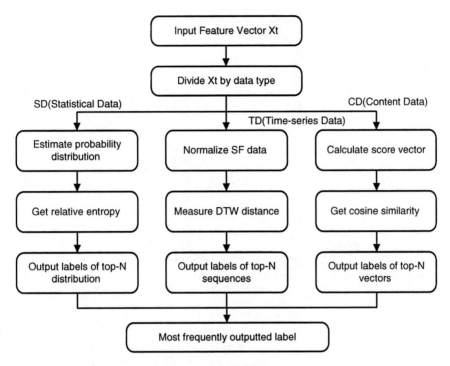

Figure 7.17 The concept of transfer learning for emotion labeling.

7.4.3 Emotion Interaction through IoT and Clouds

Traditional affective prediction has resulted from analyzing one type of emotional data. This may lead to inaccuracy in validating the detection results. To overcome this difficulty, we present an emotion detection architecture, named the AIWAC in Figure 7.18. AIWAC stands for Affective Interaction through Wearable Computing and Cloud. The system collects emotional data from multiple sources: namely the cyber, physical and social spaces. In the physical space, the user's physiological data is collected, including various body signals, such as EEG, ECG, electromyography (EMG), blood pressure, blood oxygen and respiration.

In cyber space, we use a computer to collect, store and transfer the user's facial and/or behavioral video contents. In the social space, the user's profile, behavioral data and interactive social contents are extracted. With the availability of social networking services, IoT frameworks (shown in Chapter 2) and 4G/5G mobile networks, the affective data collected is truly a big data source over a long observation period. The AIWAC provides users with physiological and psychological healthcare support. As shown in Figure 7.18, AIWAC is developed into three layers: i) user terminal layer with wearable devices for physiology data collection and emotional feedback; ii) communication layer; and iii) cloud layer for affective interaction. These layers are specified below.

7.4.3.1 User Terminal Layer

This layer consists of wearable and smart devices, wherein wearable devices are mainly used for collecting various physiological data, such as EEG, ECG, electromyography

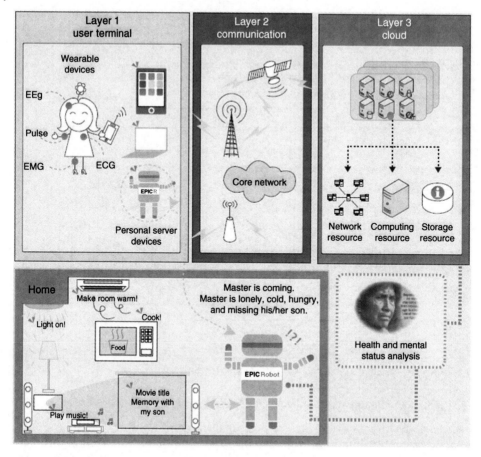

Figure 7.18 Layered architecture of the AIWAC emotion monitory system (reprinted with permission from Zhang et al., 2015 [17]).

(EMG), blood pressure, blood oxygen, respiration, etc., while smart devices provide support for emotional interaction. In many cases, the terminal is a wearable as well as a smart device. We use a robotic terminal to provide a high-fidelity affective interaction and presentation, and especially the robot is designed with an anthropomorphic appearance and human behavioral patterns (voice, smile, nod and other actions).

7.4.3.2 Communication Layer

This layer consists of a store-and-forward module and a communication access module, and smart phone, computer, tablet, and any other smart devices with 2G, 3G, 4G or WIFI access function, are integrated with these two modules. These devices need software support to receive various real-time physiological and psychological data transmitted from the user terminal layer, and preprocess, format and classify these data (including coding, decoding, filtering and other operations).Through the communication access module, the preprocessed data are sent to cloud via mobile or other networks.

This layer is the core of AIWAC, which provides physiological and psychological data analysis via data centers on the cloud platform. The data center is mainly responsible for data storage, feature extraction and classification, and individual emotion modeling. With the massive computing power of cloud-based services, AIWAC is able to efficiently respond to an affective request from the user terminal. In addition, AIWAC can provide public health monitoring based on big physiological and psychological data.

7.4.3.3 The Cloud Layer

Affective cloud performance depends on the quality of data collected. The larger the dataset collected, the higher the accuracy of the emotional analysis will be. However, it is difficult to meet the requirement for collecting emotional data with limited resources of wearable devices. Hence, we result to the help of a backend cloud to perform most of the signal analytics operations.

Example 7.7   The AIWAC emotion monitory system Developed at Huazhong University of Science and Technology

This AIWAC system is a research prototype built at the Huazhong University of Science and Technology, China in 2015. The idea is illustrated in Figure 7.18, where the cloud resources are abundant to perform the operations required in the system. This media cloud platform is used to store, manage and analyze emotional data from a multi-dimensional space. The goal is to achieve fast emotion interactive services for mobile users. Mobile cloud computing technology is employed to overcome the shortcomings of poor time and space constraints in handheld mobile devices or wearable sensors. Results of cloud sentimental analysis are fed back to the clients.

When emotional interaction is temporarily interrupted and the user environment changes, cloud needs to quickly perceive and optimize the allocation of resources in a new environment to continue the interaction. Since the user's emotions are affected by many factors, as various as possible data should be collected by wearable devices in order to make a timely and accurate judgment of the user's emotions. Furthermore, it is a great challenge to evaluate which kind of data is useful for sentiment analysis. First, modeling should be made based on the factors affecting the user's emotions. Then based on the established emotional perception model, we need assistance to decide which wearable devices to use to collect essential data.

For humanized and intelligent feedback, emotional interaction should be affinity. With accurate analysis and prediction of user's emotions, a variety of humanized ways for emotional interaction will directly affect the user's experience. We intend to build an intelligent upright walking robot by integrating interdisciplinary study results in many fields. A high biofidelity robot integrated with multiple sensors can work together with other smart devices to sense environmental information. The robot will become one of the most intimate, emotionally dependable front-end carriers for emotional interaction with people. Meanwhile, relying on wireless communication and cloud computing technology, the robot can provide mobile intelligence.   ■

7.4.4   Emotion-Control via Robotics Technologies

In recent years, robot research has become one of the most popular research fields in industry and academia. Especially the humanoid intelligent robot has drawn a great amount of interest. While promoting industrial robots, countries worldwide are paying more and more attention to the intelligent service robot. The application domain of robots is developing gradually from industry to family and personal service. With the development of research on robot products with autonomous ability and intelligence, humans will be freed from simple, monotonous and dangerous tasks.

The humanoid robot has made great progress, but is also facing many technical challenges to make it fully integrated into human life, among which to equip the human robot with emotional interaction ability is one of the most challenging problems. In the past, most robots were designed to perform repetitive work in accordance with programs written in advance. They usually did not have autonomous capability. They were not intelligent or their intelligence level was very low. They were not aware of human feelings. In Figure 7.19, humanoid robotics are shown with affective interactions between AIWAC and the clients.

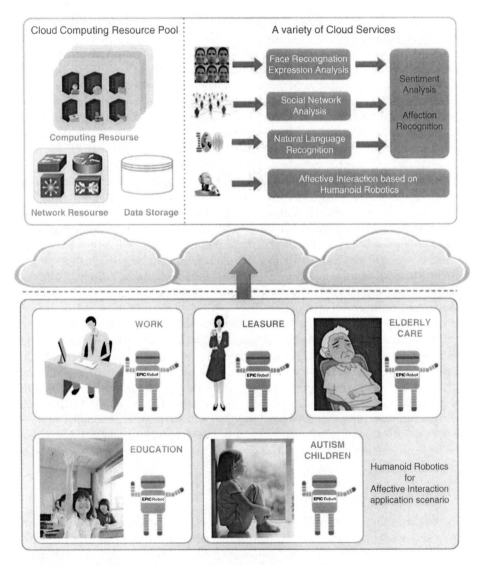

Figure 7.19 Humanoid robotics for affective interactions between AIWAC and clients.

With cloud computing technology, there is no need for users to understand every detail of the cloud computing infrastructure, the corresponding professional knowledge or the direct control. The traditional robots are always restricted in the hardware and software functions where there are serious problems. But the cloud computing, as a good support to the robot technology, can easily combine the cloud computing with the robot technology to build a cloud robot. As a front-end equipment, the robot takes charge in signal collection, specific action performance and some simple tasks of analysis and processing, while the more complicated tasks which need a large-scale computing cluster will depend on the cloud. The cloud itself has strong storage and calculating ability, training, learning and building effective models by advanced machine learning algorithm and transmitting the results of calculation or analysis back to the robots. In that way, the robot will be provided with the second-wise brain with the help of cloud's strong analysis and processing abilities.

We train the robot with the ability of emotion interaction by combining cloud computing technology with the humanoid robot. Intelligent perception and cognition are integrated into the robot to enhance its intelligence levels. Multiple wireless communication technologies are adopted to ensure the stability and reliability of the communication of the robot and the cloud platform. As the robot is the front end to communicate with people, in order to ensure the high quality of human–computer interaction, the robot must also have an approachable humanoid appearance, with basic human actions and expressions.

In order to make the humanoid robot capable of emotional interaction, we need to analyze a large amount of data related with emotions (i.e. human's expressions, languages, actions, words and pictures used in social network, etc.), but the robot is unable to complete the task of resource analysis due to its limited processing and storage capacity. Cloud computing has changed the traditional software delivery model, providing computing, storage and network resources to the user in the way of service.

The system architecture is divided into three layers, i.e. user, robot and cloud service (Figure 7.19). User means the user of the robot, and also the object of the emotional interaction. In order to improve the accuracy of emotion recognition, the user will be required to wear wearable devices (i.e. smart watch or smart bracelet) to collect the user's physiological indicators (e.g. body temperature, heart rate and gait, etc.). The data acquired by these wearable devices is sent to the back-end cloud platform through the robot. As a large number of computing and storage tasks are completed by the cloud platform, the reliability of the network connection between the robot and the cloud platform is particularly important.

To ensure the smooth communication of the robot and the cloud platform, the robot needs to be inserted with a variety of wireless communication modules (4G-LTE, 3G, WiFi), and can automatically switch network connection in different communication modules. In order to realize the emotional interaction, the robot needs to be configured with audio and video sensors, LED lights and other components. The robot body must be flexible enough to complete a variety of actions. To perceive the environment information of the user's position, the robot also needs to be integrated with a variety of environmental sensors.

The cloud platform adopts big data storage and computing engines based on Hadoop and Spark, with the help of sentiment analysis algorithm based on deep learning and integrates the data collected by the robot and the user's social network data to complete the analysis and the predication of the user's emotion condition. The cloud issues the emotion analysis results and the emotional interaction instructions to the robot, and makes the robot complete the specific interactive tasks. During the emotional interaction, the robot will report the effect of real-time emotional interaction to the platform. The cloud platform adjusts the emotional interaction timely according to the robot's feedback. As shown in Figure 7.20, the robot components include the head, upper limb, leg, sensing device, communication, etc.

The cloud system is the brain of the humanoid robot intelligence and the storage center of data. The cloud receives a steady stream of data from robots and social networks. Data from the robot include the robot's perception of the surrounding environment, human physiological signals and other related data (i.e. human expressions, sounds, movements, etc.). Social network data sources include user's Micro blog, shared photos, videos, etc. Because there are a wide variety of data, the data needs to be distributed to the corresponding storage engine according to the types of the data and the requirements of sentimental analysis.

The robot captures video by camera in real time, and positions out human facial expressions by captured videos, and then sends the expression images to remote cloud platform for expression identification. The cloud platform can train the human facial expression module with large amounts of human facial data, and recognize the facial expressions transmitted by the robot based on the training module so as to identify the emotional states of the human (i.e. happy or depressed). At the same time, the robot also accepts the user's voice and physiological signals (e.g. heart rate, blood pressure), and the surrounding environment signals, and then sends the data to the cloud. The cloud collects user data in social networks. Finally, the cloud predicts the user's emotional state by data fusion analysis. The cloud platform sends affective interaction instructions to the front-end robot based on the results of emotional prediction. The purpose is to instruct the robot to take proper action, as illustrated in Figure 7.20.

7.4.5 A 5G Cloud-Centric Healthcare System

Typically, cognitive applications have high requirements in terms of latency and reliability. The 5G mobile network is aimed at breaking the limitations of time and space for cognitive systems. The enhanced mobile bandwidth guarantees faster access to multimedia content, services and data for human-centric applications. In Figure 7.21, the concept of the smart cognitive system is illustrated with the following features:

- Through 5G future telecommunication technologies, sensors, cognitive devices and robots interact smoothly with ultra-reliable low latency communications.
- The design of networking is enhanced so that it can move data quickly. For the retrieval or access of stored big data, 5G networks connect terminal devices and datacenters at a very fast rate, facilitating quick learning response.
- Learning from data is the heart of cognitive computing, and a cloud datacenter is the main hardware facility for advanced learning.
- Cognitive computing requires a wealth of data available, as clouds are implemented and configured to store and process those data.

To build a smart cognitive system in the 5G era, the system needs to include three functional components:

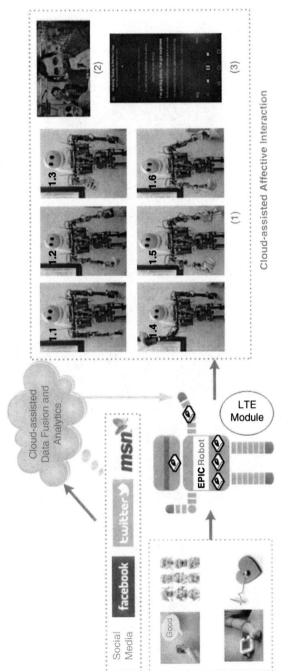

Figure 7.20 Robot affection interaction based on cloud computing.

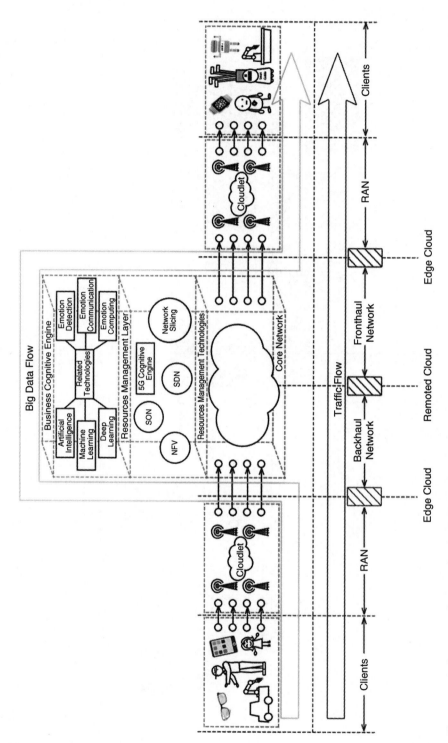

Figure 7.21 Architecture of a smart cloud/IoT/5G based cognitive system.

1) **Behavioral interaction terminal:** cognitive behaviors in a cognitive system should be displayed in terminals; in order to achieve this, robots of varied types and increasingly powerful functions are favorable alternatives;

2) **Environmental perception component:** realization of cognition should be based on big data, and the cognitive component should realize the comprehensive perception of hearing, vision, touch and human emotion;

3) **Cognitive reasoning component:** the intelligent cognitive reasoning model can effectively simulate human cognitive process, and related technologies including AI, machine learning, deep learning, cloud computing and other effective tools utilized to establish cognitive reasoning model.

The system is divided into three layers: The first layer is built with smart terminals, cloud-based RAN and cloud-based Core Network. The heterogeneous access networks interconnect smart terminals, such as smart phones, smart watches, robots, smart cars and other devices. The edge cloud and remote cloud are the infrastructures to support the realization of cognitive functions in terms of storage and computing resources. The second layer is for resource management to support a resource cognitive engine to achieve resource optimization and high energy efficiency. The third layer provides data cognitive capability. In data cognitive engine, AI and big data learning techniques are employed for cognitive big data analytics, such as in the domain of healthcare. The big data flow represents the process of massive data collection, storage and analysis with the support of cloud or IoT. The traffic flow consists of packets and control messages during users' end-to-end communications.

Two archetypal applications of the smart cognition system are shown in Figure 7.22. In telemedicine, remote surgery may be designed to save life in the domain of healthcare. Using the 5G network, the critical operation action and haptic perception of the surgeon will be mapped to the robot arm in the remote operating table with very short delay and high reliability. In addition, all vital data of the patient can be processed with analytics tools at remote cloud real-timely to guide the rescue team to carry out some preliminary life-saving operations before transporting the patient to the hospital. The second archetypal application is to detect human emotions with the help of smart robots, which interact with clouds to execute some responsive actions to calm patients. A lot of research experiments have been suggested in the past. The cloud/IoT based system may help to solve emotion control problems in the future.

7.5 Conclusions

In this chapter, we have focused on big data application in the bio-medical and healthcare areas. However, the datasets we have tested in the illustrated example cases are not sufficiently large in scale to draw a general conclusion on TB or PB datasets. This chapter needs the background from previous chapters. Big data and clouds both demand a major overhaul of our educational programs in science and technology. There is no unique or general solution to big-data problems, due to heavy dependence on specific application domains.

We must leverage the use of clouds and big-data analytics in storing, processing and mining big data, which changes rapidly in time and space. The clouds, mobile, IoT

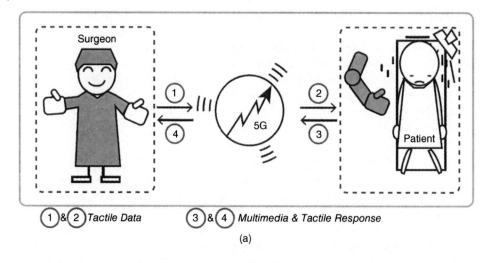

1 & 2 *Tactile Data*　　　3 & 4 *Multimedia & Tactile Response*

(a)

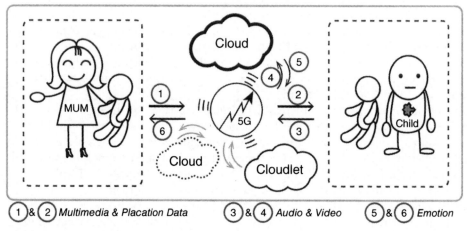

1 & 2 *Multimedia & Placation Data*　　　3 & 4 *Audio & Video*　　　5 & 6 *Emotion*

Figure 7.22 Two applications of a smart cognitive system.

and social networks are changing our world, reshaping human relations, promoting the global economy and triggering societal and political reforms on a world-scale. Those machine learning methods may perform differently, if non-medical or non-healthcare datasets are processed or tested. However, learning the machine learning methodologies is more important in general big data science and cloud computing applications.

Homework Problems

7.1 Build a demo system of healthcare monitoring based on big data technology. Detailed requirements and suggestions are:

  a) You can use TI CC2530 Development Toolkit-CC2530DK or CrossBow TelosB. At least one physiological signal can be collected, such as body temperature, heartbeat rate or oxygen saturation of blood.

b) Physiological signal should be transmitted to a Hadoop or Spark big data process platform in a specified period. Achieve a simple analysis and visual presentation for collected physiological data.

7.2 In today's society, social networks has become an important tools for people to communicate. Besides, more and more people express their ideas and emotions on social networks. Thus, emotion analysis based on social network data has a strong practical significance. Now provide a group of text datasets extracted from Twitter[1], where text language type is Arabic and the text sample numbers of positive emotions and negative emotions are both 1000, which were manually tagged by three linguistic experts. The RNN algorithm in deep learning has a great effect in the processing of text classification. Now, please complete an application of the classification for this dataset based on the RNN algorithm and compare the classification results with the algorithm used in the literature[2]. If the accuracy is lower than the algorithm in the literature, please try to debug the application in order to improve the accuracy of classification.

7.3 Nowadays, cancer has become a major killer, in which breast cancer has affected a high proportion of women patients. Thus, there is a great practical significance for effective diagnosis of breast cancer. There exists a group of standard datasets for breast cancer detection.

Design and implement an application of breast cancer diagnosis based on the machine learning algorithm by using a tool of machine learning such as Spark MLlib and selecting an appropriate machine learning algorithm. Based on the existed dataset and the application achieved by yourself, please think about how to improve the accuracy of breast cancer diagnosis as much as possible. The basic information of the dataset is shown in Table 7.12.

Table 7.12 Attributes and data characteristics for cancer detection.

Property	Value
Number of Instances	699
Number of Attributes	10
Property of Attributes	01. Sample code number: id number
	02. Clump Thickness: 1–10
	Uniformity of Cell Size: 1–10
	Uniformity of Cell Shape: 1–10
	Marginal Adhesion: 1–10
	Single Epithelial Cell Size: 1–10
	Bare Nuclei: 1–10
	Bland Chromatin: 1–10
	Normal Nucleoli: 1–10
	Mitoses: 1–10
Class	2 for benign, 4 for malignant

Download URL of DataSet: http://archive.ics.uci.edu/ml/datasets/Breast+Cancer+Wisconsin+%28Original%29

Download URL of DataSet: ttp://archive.ics.uci.edu/ml/datasets/Twitter+Data+set+for+Arabic+Sentiment+Analysis

Download URL of Literature: http://ieeexplore.ieee.org/xpl/articleDetails.jsp?arnumber=6716448&newsearch=true&queryText=Arabic%20Sentiment%20Analysis:%20Corpus-based%20and%20Lexicon-based

7.4 Data analysis has applications in many fields. We can make use of a large amount of weather data to calculate the probability of a sunny day or a rainy day. Can you build an application that can analyze the climate data and predict the weather? You may need knowledge of the Naive Bayesian and you can use the datasets by the following link: http://cdiac.ornl.gov/ftp/ndp026b/

7.5 Facebook is one of the most popular social-media platforms nowadays. A billion of people share their experiences of their daily lives on Facebook. Some topics are very interesting and attract many people to discuss them together. Could you build an application to find out the items associated with hot topics based on the technology of data analysis? You may also need to use the web crawler technology to collect data. Here is some useful information:

- You should have a Facebook account and register the generated key hash on Facebook for your application.
- The official documentation can be found by this link: http://developers.facebook.com/docs/reference/api/
- You can use this URL to collect some personalized information: https://graph.facebook.com/fql?q=SELECT status_id, time, source, message FROM status where uid=me()&access_token=

7.6 Usually, a health monitoring system adopts wearable or smart devices to collect various physiological data. If emotional care is required, the system needs stronger machine intelligence to enable emotion interaction. Among various physiological detection methods, EEG can accurately record brain activity. Through the analysis of EEG pattern data, we can effectively diagnose epilepsy, mental illness, etc. There exists a large study to examine EEG correlations of genetic predisposition to alcoholism. It contains measurements from 64 electrodes placed on the scalp sampled at 256 Hz. Combining with machine learning related knowledge and using the toolkit Weka, ConvNetJS, etc., try to design an application of whether a patient have a genetic predisposition to alcoholism or not, based on this EEG dataset. Download URL of EEG dataset: http://archive.ics.uci.edu/ml/datasets/EEG+Database

7.7 In recent years, research on robotics has become increasingly popular. In the emotion-control field, humanoid robotics has exhibited their advantages in affective interactions. In [1], there is a wall-following robot navigation dataset. The data were collected as the SCITOS G5 robot navigated through the room following the wall in a clockwise direction, for four rounds, using 24 ultrasound sensors arranged in a circle around its "waist".

Download them and try to use nonlinear neural classifiers, such as the MLP network, to conduct analysis and processing of this dataset combined with the knowledge you have learned. Then compare the results with the classification using a recurrent neural network (e.g. Elman network). In order to let the wall-following robot finish those tasks successfully, you shall improve the accuracy of the neural classifiers as much as possible based on the merits of the two approaches. Download URL of wall-following robot navigation dataset: http://archive.ics.uci.edu/ml/datasets/Wall-Following+Robot+Navigation+Data

7.8 Parkinson's disease (PD) is a chronic disease caused by movement disorder of the central nervous system and the dysfunction of basal ganglia. Typically, gait is an important indicator to identify and evaluate PD. In order to evaluate gait changes of the elderly with Parkinson's disease continuously without human intervention, pressure of foot step can be measured when PD patients walk, and the mode of center of pressure (CoP) can be obtained. Figure out the differences of CoP between normal people and PD patients. Which statement is correct?
   a) The pressure sensors are deployed under the PD patient's foot.
   b) The pressure sensors are installed on the ground.
   c) In order to obtain CoP, the pressure of front, middle or back parts of foot should be collected.
   d) Measure the pressure data when the PD patient is standing or walking.

References

1 P. Groves, B. Kayyali, D. Knott and S. Van Kuiken, The "big data" revolution in healthcare. *McKinsey Quarterly*, 2013.
2 P.B. Jensen, I.J. Jensen and S. Brunak, Mining electronic health records: towards better research applications and clinical care. *Nat. Rev. Gene*, 13, 395–405. 2012.
3 D.W. Bates, S. Saria, L. Ohno-Machado, A. Shah and G. Escobar, Big data in health care: using analytics to identify and manage high-risk and high-cost patients. *Health. Affairs*, 33, 1123–1131, 2014.
4 D. Oliver, F. Daly, F.C. Martin and M.E. McMurdo Risk factors and risk assessment tools for falls in hospital in-patients: a systematic review. *Age Ageing*, 33, 122–130, 2004.
5 S. Marcoon, A.M. Chang, B. Lee, R. Salhi and J.E. Hollander, Heart score to further risk stratify patients with low TIMI scores. *Critical Pathways in Cardiology*, 12, 1–5, 2013.
6 S. Bandyopadhyay, et al., Data mining for censored time-to-event data: A Bayesian network model for predicting cardiovascular risk from electronic health record data. *Data. Min. Knowl. Disc.*, 1–37, 2014.
7 B. Qian, X. Wang, N. Cao, H. Li and Y.-G. Jiang, A relative similarity based method for interactive patient risk prediction. *Data. Min. Knowl. Disc.*, 1–24, 2014.
8 A. Singh, et al., Incorporating temporal EHR data in predictive models for risk stratification of renal function deterioration. *J. Biomed. Inform.*, 53, 220–228, 2015.
9 X. Chen, KATZLDA: Katz measure for the lncRAN-disease association prediction. *Sci. Rep-UK*, 5, 2015.
10 J.C. Ho, C.H. Lee and J. Ghosh, Septic shock prediction for patients with missing data. ACM *Transactions on Management Information Systems* (TMIS), 5(1), 2014.

11 R.S. Basu, et al., Dynamic hierarchical classification for patient risk-of-readmission. *Proceedings of the 21th ACM SIGKDD International Conference on Knowledge Discovery and Data Mining*, 1691–1700, 2015.

12 Z. Huang, W. Dong and H. Duan. A probabilistic topic model for clinical risk stratification from electronic health records. *J. Biomed. Informa.*, 58, 28–36, 2015.

13 E. Frias-Martinez, G. Williamson and V. Frias-Martinez. An agent-based model of epidemic spread using human mobility and social network information. *Proceedings of the IEEE Third International Conference on Privacy, Security, Risk and Trust*. Boston: IEEE. 57–64, 2011.

14 C.O. Buckee, A. Wesolowski, N.N. Eagle, E. Hansen and R.W. Snow, Mobile phones and malaria: modeling human and parasite travel. *Travel Med. Infect. Dis.*, 11(1):15–22, 2013.

15 L. Bengtsson, X. Lu, A. Thorson, R. Garfield and J. von Schreeb, Improved response to disasters and outbreaks by tracking population movements with mobile phone network data: a post-earthquake geospatial study in Haiti. *PLoS Med.*, 8(8), 2011.

16 J. Xie, S. Kelley and B.K. Szymanski, 2013. Overlapping community detection in networks: The state-of-the-art and comparative study. *ACM Comput. Surv.*, 459(4), Article 43, August 2013.

17 M. Chen, Y. Zhang, Y. Li, et al., AIWAC: affective interaction through wearable computing and cloud technology. *Wireless Communications, IEEE*, 22(1), 20–27, 2015.

18 R. Costa, D. Carneiro, P. Novais, et al., Ambient assisted living. *Proceedings of the 3rd Symposium of Ubiquitous Computing and Ambient Intelligence 2008*. Springer, Berlin Heidelberg, 86–94, 2009.

19 A. Costanzo, A, Faro, D. Giordano, et al., Mobile cyber physical systems for health care: Functions, ambient ontology and e-diagnostics. *Proceedings of the 13th IEEE Annual Consumer Communications and Networking Conference* (CCNC), *IEEE*, 972–975, 2016.

20 L.G. Jaimes, J. Calderon, H. Lopez, et al., Trends in mobile cyber-physical systems for health just-in time interventions. *SoutheastCon, IEEE*, 1–6, 2015.

21 I. Tabas and C.K. Glass, Anti-inflammatory therapy in chronic disease: challenges and opportunities. *Science*, 339(6116), 166–172, 2013.

22 S. Murali, F.J. Rincon Vallejos and D.A. Atienza Alonso, Wearable device for physical and emotional health monitoring. *Computing in Cardiology*. 42(EPFL-CONF-213467): 121–124, 2015.

23 J. Wan, C. Zou, S. Ullah, et al., Cloud-enabled wireless body area networks for pervasive healthcare. *Network, IEEE*, 27(5), 56–61, 2013.

24 M.M. Rodgers, P.V. Pai and R.S. Conroy. Recent advances in wearable sensors for health monitoring. *Sensors Journal, IEEE*, 15(6), 3119–3126. 2015.

25 C.W. Mundt, K.N. Montgomery, U.E. Udoh, et al., A multiparameter wearable physiologic monitoring system for space and terrestrial applications. *Proceedings of the IEEE Transactions on Information Technology in Biomedicine*, 9(3), 382–391, 2005.

26 H.C. Chao, S. Zeadally and B, Hu, Wearable computing for healthcare. *Journal of Medical Systems*, 40(4), 1–3, 2016.

27 M. Chen, Y. Ma, S. Ullah, et al., ROCHAS: robotics and cloud-assisted healthcare system for empty nester. *Proceedings of the 8th International Conference on Body Area Networks*. ICST (Institute for Computer Sciences, Social-Informatics and Telecommunications Engineering), 217–220, 2013.

28 C. Lavel and Z. Callejas, Sentiment analysis: from opinion mining to human-agent interaction, 2016.

29 S. Jerritta, M. Murugappan, K. Wan, et al., Emotion detection from QRS complex of ECG signals using Hurst Exponent for different age groups. *Humane Association Conference on Affective Computing and Intelligent Interaction* (ACII), *IEEE*, 849–854, 2013.

30 G. Castellano, L Kessous and G. Caridakis, *Emotion Recognition through Multiple Modalities: Face, Body Gesture, Speech. Affect and Emotion in Human–Computer Interaction.* Springer, Berlin Heidelberg, 92–103, 2008.

31 M. Soleymani, S. Asghari Esfeden, Y. Fu, et al., Analysis of EEG signals and facial expressions for continuous emotion detection, 2015.

32 E. Cambria, Affective computing and sentiment analysis. *IEEE Intelligent Systems*, 31(2), 102–107, 2016.

33 S. Zhao, Affective computing of image emotion perceptions. *Proceedings of the Ninth ACM International Conference on Web Search and Data Mining. ACM*, 703–703, 2016.

34 *The Oxford Handbook of Affective Computing.* Oxford University Press, US, 2014.

35 J. Broekens, T. Bosse and S.C. Marsella, Challenges in computational modeling of affective processes. *IEEE Transactions on Affective Computing*, 4(3), 242–245, 2013.

36 M. Chen, Y. Zhang, Y. Li, et al., EMC: emotion-aware mobile cloud computing in 5G Network. *IEEE*, 29(2), 32–38, 2015.

37 M. Chen, Y. Ma, Y. Hao, Y. Li, D. Wu, Y. Zhang and E. Song, CP-Robot: Cloud-assisted pillow robot for emotion sensing and interaction. *ICST IndustrialIoT*, 2016.

38 M. Simsek, A. Aijaz, M. Dohler, J. Sachs, and G. Fettweis, 5G-enabled tactile internet. *IEEE Journal on Selected Areas in Communications*, 34(3), 460–473, 2016.

8

Deep Reinforcement Learning and Social Media Analytics

CHAPTER OUTLINE

8.1 Deep Learning Systems and Social Media Industry, 343
    8.1.1 Deep Learning Systems and Software Support, 343
    8.1.2 Reinforcement Learning Principles, 346
    8.1.3 Social-Media Industry and Global Impact, 347
8.2 Text and Image Recognition using ANN and CNN, 348
    8.2.1 Numeral Recognition using TensorFlow for ANN, 349
    8.2.2 Numeral Recognition using Convolutional Neural Networks, 352
    8.2.3 Convolutional Neural Networks for Face Recognition, 356
    8.2.4 Medical Text Analytics by Convolutional Neural Networks, 357
8.3 DeepMind with Deep Reinforcement Learning, 362
    8.3.1 Google DeepMind AI Programs, 362
    8.3.2 Deep Reinforcement Learning Algorithm, 364
    8.3.3 Google AlphaGo Game Competition, 367
    8.3.4 Flappybird Game using Reinforcement Learning, 371
8.4 Data Analytics for Social-Media Applications, 375
    8.4.1 Big Data Requirements in Social-Media Applications, 375
    8.4.2 Social Networks and Graph Analytics, 377
    8.4.3 Predictive Analytics Software Tools, 383
    8.4.4 Community Detection in Social Networks, 386
8.5 Conclusions, 390

8.1 Deep Learning Systems and Social Media Industry

In this chapter, we introduce the software libraries or platforms that have been developed by industry and academia for machine learning (ML) and deep learning (DL) applications. As studied in earlier chapters, deep learning is part of a broader family of machine learning methods. The difference lies in the learning representations of data. For example, the inspection of an X-ray image is represented in many ways such as vectors, matrices or tensors. Some of the representations are inspired by advances in neuroscience.

8.1.1 Deep Learning Systems and Software Support

So far, we have learned machine learning and deep learning algorithms. With huge amounts of data, the clouds have sufficient resources to train the model to perfection.

Big-Data Analytics for Cloud, IoT and Cognitive Computing, First Edition. Kai Hwang and Min Chen.
© 2017 John Wiley & Sons Ltd. Published 2017 by John Wiley & Sons Ltd.
Companion Website: http://www.wiley.com/go/hwangIOT

Table 8.1 Comparison of five open source software libraries for deep learning applications.

Software, Creator, Language(s)/ Interface, License, and Website	Platform(s), Software Tools	DL Models Supported	A Brief Description
Caffe, Berkeley Vision and Learning Center, C++, Python, MATLAB, BSD2, http://caffe.berkeleyvision.org/	AWS, OSX, Windows, OpenCL, CUDA	RNN, CNN	A DL framework adopts a pure C++/ CUDA architecture for easy switch between CPU and GPU
CNTK, Microsoft, C++, Python, .NET, Free, http://github.com/Microsoft/CNTK	Windows, Linux, OpenMP, CUDA	RNN, CNN	A free DL software for cross platform applications
TensorFlow, Google Brain Team, C/C++, Python, Apache 2.0, https://www.tensorflow.org/	OpenCL on roadmap, CUDA	RNN, CNN, RBM, DBN	Based on DistBelief, allowing tensor to flow through ANN graph from one end to another
Theano, U. of Montreal, SD, Python http://deeplearning.net/ software/theano	Cross platform, Open MP, CUDA	RNN, CNN, RBM, DBN	A framework using Torch for a modular ANN library supporting joint GPU and CPU operations
Torch, Ronan Collobert, C, Lua, BSD, http://torch.ch/	Linux, Android, OSX, iOS, OpenCL	RNN, CNN, RBM, DBN	Built with iTorch and fbcunn, to improve ANN performance in computer vision and natural language processing

Deep learning is certainly an extended field of machine learning. It aims at obtaining abstract high-level features through the combination of low-level features. We build artificial neural networks to simulate the learning and analysis functions of the human brain, to understand various types of big data such as image, audio and text.

Five deep learning software libraries are compared in Table 8.1, in terms of modeling capability, interfaces, performance, cross platform and reported performance. Modeling capability is the key metric to assess their usefulness in deep learning applications. We evaluate each toolkit's ability to train common and state-of-the-art neural networks. The neural network toolkits include those ANNs developed in recent years, such as ConvNets CNN: AlexNet, OxfordNet, GoogLeNet; RNN: plain RNN, LSTM/GRU, bidirectional RNN, etc.

Caffe is the most popular toolkit within the computer vision community. In general, its support for recurrent networks and language modeling is limited due to its legacy architecture. Caffe has a pycaffe interface but that is a mere secondary alternative to the command line interface. The model has to be defined in Google protobuf. CNTK, a unified deep-learning toolkit by Microsoft Research, is better known in the speech community than in the general DL community. Like TensorFlow and Theano, CNTK is specified as a symbolic graph of vector operations, such as matrix add/multiply or convolution. A layer in the neural network is just a composition of those operations. The fine granularity of the building blocks (operations) allows users to invent new complex layer types.

TensorFlow supports state-of-the-art models: RNN, CNN, RBM and DBN; so do Theano and Torch. TensorFlow uses symbolic graph of vector operations approach, and its every computational flow is constructed as a static graph. That makes some computations difficult, such as beam search. TensorFlow supports two interfaces: Python and C++.

Theano has implementation for most state-of-the-art neural networks. This software pioneered the trend of using a symbolic graph for programming a network. Its symbolic API makes implementing RNNs easy and efficient. The lack of low-level interface makes Theano less attractive for industrial users. Torch supports the convolutional neural networks nicely. The native interface for temporal convolution in Torch makes it more intuitive to use. Torch runs on LuaJIT, which is very fast. However, Lua is not a mainstream language, which limits its application prospective. All deep learning software packages run on computer system or cloud clusters built with both CPU, GPU or TPU accelerators.

A lot of deep learning service products have been developed by social and web service industries, including Facebook, Google, Microsoft, Twitter, Baidu and WeChat, etc. Here we review several example ML or DL systems from industry. For example, many of the Google's new products are related to upgrade the Google search engine. By learning the underlying technology and development tools, we can develop our own applications to meet specific demands. By no means, do we act in favor of any particular product. Readers are encouraged to learn from the high-quality service products from all of the IT and network companies.

Certainly, deep learning with ANNs has been proven to have some impressive successes in recent years. As we have reviewed in Table 8.1, a lot of interesting ML and DL products and systems are developed by industry and academia. For example, Google search engine's success in recent years is achieved by adding many new intelligent features. When it got started with the PageRank system by its cofounders, the search was rather rudimentary. Over the years, intelligent service products like Gmail, Google Map, YouTube and some personalized search functions, are added into Google services. In this context, many productivity tools are also developed by major IT companies; notable ones are Apple's Apps Store, AWS machine learning library, Spark MLlib package, Google's TensorFlow platform, etc.

Microsoft Office 365 offers the cloud-based Outlook Web Access (OWA) to manage the emails of tens of thousands of organizations. Similarly, iCloud offers free email services to lock up their iPhone or iPad users. Other interesting products include Apple's Siri and fingerprint ID, Google's WatsApp and Scholars, SalesForce CRM services, Tencent's WeChat and Microsoft OneDrive, etc. These human-centric applications all have built some machine intelligence features. These features must satisfy massive numbers of individual clients, as well as many enterprises in business, education and government sectors.

On March 15, 2016, Google introduced the Google Analytics 360 Suite. This is a suite of integrated data and marketing analytics products, designed specifically to meet the needs of enterprise-class marketers. This may compete with existing marketing cloud offerings by Adobe, Oracle, Salesforce and IBM. Today's machine translation systems attempt to cover almost 100 different languages, including handwriting recognition. Speech can be used as input, and translated text can be pronounced through speech synthesis. The software uses corpus linguistics techniques, where the program "learns" from professionally translated documents.

Besides speech/language processing, machine perception, automated image understanding, vision analysis and AR/VR products are very hot products in the IT and entertainment industries. To give our readers a feeling of the cutting edge technology of bringing AI into today's clouds, we now examine the Google Brain Project for developing machine learning systems and cognitive service products.

8.1.2 Reinforcement Learning Principles

We have introduced the basic definition of reinforcement learning (RL) in Chapter 5. The operational principles of RL will be further illustrated in this section. The use of RL algorithms will be given in Section 8.3, along with the case study of Google DeepMind programs to achieve maximal reward in the deep learning process. The RL is indeed a subclass of unsupervised ML, because the correct input/output pairs are never presented. David Silver of Google DeepMind has given a tutorial on reinforcement learning, which was applied in the AlphaGo program.

Reinforcement learning is considered as a general-purpose framework of artificial intelligence. Mathematically, a Markov decision process (MDP) is applied in the learning environment. The RL emphasizes online performance by finding a balance between exploration of unknown territory and exploitation of current knowledge in the decision process. Formally, an RL model is built with the following five constituting parts:

1) A learning environment characterized by a set of states;
2) A set of actions that can be taken by RL agents. Each action influences the agent's future states. The agent has the capacity to assess the long-term consequences of its actions;
3) Rules of transitions between the RL states;
4) Rules that determine the immediate reward of a state transition;
5) Rules that specify what the agent can observe.

The above rules are often stochastic or probabilistic. The observation involves the scalar reward associated with the last transition. An RL agent interacts with its environment in discrete time steps. There exist tradeoffs between long-term and short-term rewards. RL algorithms have been applied successfully in robot control, elevator scheduling, cognitive radio, logistical problem solving and game playing like chess, checkers, Go and Atari games, etc. In a nutshell, the idea is to select actions to maximize the future rewards. This is very similar to the situation where students try various study methods to earn the best score so as to achieve a satisfying career as the future reward.

RL algorithms encourage the use of samples to optimize performance and the use of function approximation to deal with large environments. These two features make RL especially effective in handling three machine learning environments: i) a known model environment short of an analytic solution; ii) a simulation-based optimization environment; and iii) an environment enabling information collecting by interacting with it. Fundamental assumptions on the reinforcement learning environments include the following:

- All events are episodic as a sequence of episodes. An episode ends when some terminal state is reached.
- No matter what course of actions the agent may take, termination is inevitable.
- The expectation of the total reward is well-defined for any policy and any initial distribution over the states.

An intelligent person must be able to work out an RL algorithm to find a policy with maximum expected gain. The algorithm needs to search for optimal policy to achieve maximal rewards. Often, we apply deterministic stationary policies, which select the actions deterministically, based only on the current or last state visited. There are a number of approaches in designing reinforcement learning algorithms.

A brute-force method is to choose the policy with the largest expected return. The major difficulty with this approach is that the policy choices could be very large or even infinite. Value function approaches attempt to find a policy that maximizes the return by maintaining a set of estimates of expected returns for some policy. These methods rely on the theory of MDPs, where optimality is defined as stronger than the one above. A policy is called optimal if it achieves the best expected return from any initial state. It is well-known from the theory of MDPs that an optimal policy always results in choosing optimal actions with the highest value of each state.

Other RL schemes include the time-difference method, which allows the policy to change before the award values are settled. A direct policy search method finds a good policy by searching directly from a policy space. Both gradient-based and gradient-free methods belong to this class. Gradient-based methods start with a mapping from a finite-dimensional (parameter) space to the space of policies. Policy search methods are often too slow to converge to the optimal choice. Reinforcement learning is often tied to models for human skill learning or acquisition. In Section 8.3, we apply the reinforcement learning idea to implement the AlphaGo program.

8.1.3 Social-Media Industry and Global Impact

In Chapter 7, we have studied big data analytics for building automated healthcare systems with smart clothing, robotics and clouds. This has provided personalized medicine and prescriptive analytics, clinical risk intervention and predictive analytics to reduce waste, automate external and internal reporting of patient data, use standardized medical terms, and provide patient registries and real-time caring solutions. In the education area, we also see progress in training students in big data applications.

The social-media industry is moving away from flat media such as newspapers, magazines and television shows. Instead, e-books, mobile payment, Uber cars, on-line shopping and social networking are gradually becoming the main stream. The trick is to catch or target users at optimal times in ideal locations. The ultimate aim is to convey a message or content that is in line with the consumer's mindset. For example, e-newspapers and e-books are replacing hardcopy books and newspapers.

Targeting of consumers is closely tied to the data-capture method, much more than it has been in the past. This is best seen by finding the correlation of IoT and big data.

Various IoT sensing technologies have transformed the way media industry, business companies and even governments operate. This has affected economic growth and competitiveness. The social media industry provides computer-mediated tools that allow people or companies to create, share or exchange information. (https://en .wikipedia.org/wiki/Social_media#cite_note-Buettner2016b-1). Social media services are presented in the following four areas in our daily activities:

- Social media services are part of Web 2.0 web service applications.
- User-generated content is the lifeblood of the social media organism.
- Users create service-specific profiles for social media organizations and websites.
- Social media facilitate the development of online social networks in societal and business activities.

Social media enables fundamental changes to communication between businesses, organizations, communities and individuals. These changes demand the social media industry to operate from many sources to many receivers. This differs from traditional media that operates from one source to many receivers. Social media technologies take on many different forms including blogs, business networks, enterprise social networks, forums, microblogs, photo sharing, products/services review, social bookmarking, social gaming, social networks, video sharing and virtual worlds, etc.

Example 8.1 Social-Media Applications Programming Interfaces (APIs)
Application programming interfaces (APIs) are the first software tools to access a computer, website or cloud platform. These APIs enable users or programmers to start using the system being programmed. Social media APIs are used in social networking, instant messages, dating services, Citylife, personal, location service, hobbies, travel, crowd sourcing, blogging, Chat, messaging and Avators, etc. Table 8.2 lists ten representative APIs for social-media big data applications. We characterize each API by its functionality, protocol, data format and security applied.

All computer, cloud and social media providers have their own API tools. Readers should visit their websites to learn the specific API tools to be used in their big data mining, preprocessing, machine learning and analytics applications. Among them, REST is known for the most popular protocol, JASON JSON is the most used format, and API key for most security control. Those listed above are only some representative ones, and there are many more for various IT companies and social websites. ∎

8.2 Text and Image Recognition using ANN and CNN

This section introduces how to utilize artificial neural networks (ANN) and convolution neural networks (CNN) to achieve handwritten numeral recognition. We give the pseudo-code to help readers understand the structure of the deep learning algorithm applied. The details of ANN and CNN were treated in Chapter 6. We apply the CNN in human face recognition and medical text analytics. Handwritten numeral recognition is a classification problem. As shown in Figure 8.1, the input is the handwritten numeral image and the output are the numbers transformed from the image. In order for readers to learn and practice easily, we use a classic handwritten numeral set, MNIST,

Table 8.2 Social media application programming interfaces (APIs).

API Name	Functionality	Protocol applied	Data Format	Security
Facebook Graph API	Facebook social graph processing, community detection and finding friends, etc.	REST	JSON	OAuth
Google+ API	To provide access of Google+, a social media website with link, status and photo options	REST	JSON	API key, OAuth
Social Mention API	Programmatic access to interact with Social Mention website, a RESTful API	HTTP	PHP	API key
Delicious API	Allow users to access, edit and search for bookmarks	REST	JSON, RSS	OAuth, HTTP/Basic
MySpace API	To access various MySpace functions and integrate application into MySpace	Javascript	Unknown	OAuth
Meetup API	To use the Topics, Groups and Events created by Meetup into their own applications	REST	JSON, XML KML, RSS	PAith, API key
FindMeOn API v.1,0	Programmatic access to the social media search and management functions of FindMeOn	HTTP	JSON	API key
Fliptop API	Person API to get social data based on email address, or utilize Twitter/Facebook handles to elicit data return	REST	JSON, XML	API key
Cisco JTAPI	Cisco Java Telephony API allows Java applications to interact with telephony resources	SOAP, HTTP	XML	SSL Support
YouTube Data API v3.0	Perform actions available on the YouTube website	REST, HTTP	JSON	API key

as application datasets. MNIST includes 60,000 images of handwritten numerals, and each image is 28 × 28 pixels.

8.2.1 Numeral Recognition using TensorFlow for ANN

The following example shows how to use TensorFlow in programming an artificial neural network (ANN), called the MINST classifier. With this example, readers can gain

Figure 8.1 A deep learning system for recognizing handwritten numerals.

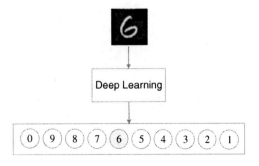

concrete insights on TensorFlow operations. This classifier system can be applied to hand-written numeral recognition. ANN was introduced in section 7.2.

Example 8.2   Programming an ANN by TensorFlow

We consider the construction of a 4-layer ANN, called the MNIST classifier. There are four steps to construct their ANN. We specify the procedure of each step, separately, using pseudo codes with comments, which are rather close to Python codes.

Step 1: Collect the data: We use the MNIST data which is taken from Yann LeCun's website: http://yann.lecun.com/index.html. TensorFlow has included some Python code (named input_data.py). The data will be installed when running the downloaded files. We import it by a Python code import input_data. The Python codes and its explanation are specified below:

```
# import tensorflow, numpy and input_data to this program
import tensorflow as tf
import numpy as np
import input_data
# load the data
mnist = input_data.read_data_sets("MNIST_data/", one_hot=True)
trX, trY, teX, teY = mnist.train.images, mnist.train.labels,
 mnist.test.images,
mnist.test.labels
```

Step 2: Construct the ANN model: We select a 4-layer neural network to construct the classifier, which contains one input layer, two hidden layers and one output layer. The Python code for this step is given below. The following code defines the model explicitly. There are two hidden layers and three dropouts. The dropout means that some node weight does not work in the network, the work of those nodes being temporarily considered as part of the network structure, but its weight was preserved (only temporarily not update). The tf.matmul is a multiply function and the tf.nn.relu is a kind of activation function:

```
// The following is for weight initialization in the ANN
   construction
def init_weights(shape):
return tf.Variable(tf.random_normal(shape, stddev=0.01))
def model(X, w_h, w_h2, w_o, p_drop_input, p_drop_hidden):
X = tf.nn.dropout(X, p_drop_input) #dropout
h = tf.nn.relu(tf.matmul(X, w_h))
h = tf.nn.dropout(h, p_drop_hidden) # dropout
h2 = tf.nn.relu(tf.matmul(h, w_h2))
h2 = tf.nn.dropout(h2, p_drop_hidden) # dropout
return tf.matmul(h2, w_o)
```

The following code defines the placeholder. X is not a specific value, but a placeholder, a value that we will input when we ask TensorFlow to run a computation. We want to input any number of MNIST images, each flattened into a 784-dimensional vector. We represent this as a 2-D tensor of floating-point numbers, with a shape [None, 784]. Here None means that a dimension can be of any length. Similarly, Y is a 10-dimensional vector which stands for 10 numbers, through weight initialization. The entity w_h is a 784 × 625 matrix, w_h2 a 625 × 625 matrix, and w_o a 625 × 10 matrix:

```
X = tf.placeholder("float", [None, 784])
Y = tf.placeholder("float", [None, 10])
w_h = init_weights([784, 625])
w_h2 = init_weights([625, 625])
w_o = init_weights([625, 10]) // Define p_keep as the
                                probability of dropout
p_keep_input = tf.placeholder("float")
p_keep_hidden = tf.placeholder("float") // The model is
                                        set as follows
py_x = model(X, w_h, w_h2, w_o, p_keep_input, p_keep_hidden)
```

Step 3: **Train the model:** By comparing the output of training data and its labels, the algorithm will adjust the parameters of the network. The Python code is given below: this part defines the cross-entropy as the loss function. Then we ask TensorFlow to minimize cross-entropy using the RMSPropOptimizer algorithm. argmax is an extremely useful function, which gives us the index of the highest entry in a tensor along some axes. For example, tf.argmax(y,1) is the label our model has for each input, while tf.argmax(y_,1) is the correct label. We can use tf.equal to check if the prediction is correct:

```
cost = tf.reduce_mean(tf.nn.softmax_cross_entropy_with_logits
  (py_x, Y))
train_op = tf.train.RMSPropOptimizer(0.001, 0.9).minimize(cost)
predict_op = tf.argmax(py_x, 1) //Create a session object to
                                launch the graph
sess = tf.Session()
init = tf.initialize_all_variables()
sess.run(init)
for i in range(100):
 or start, end in zip(range(0, len(trX), 128), range(128,
len(trX), 128)):
sess.run(train_op, feed_dict = {X: trX[start:end],
    Y: trY[start:end], p_keep_input: 0.8, p_keep_hidden: 0.5})
  print i, np.mean(np.argmax(teY, axis=1) ==
  sess.run(predict_op, feed_dict= {X: teX, Y: teY,
  p_keep_input: 1.0, p_keep_hidden: 1.0}
  endfor
  endfor
```

Step 4: **Test the network:** The algorithm will compare the output of the test data and its corresponding label and calculate the accuracy. The training data is used to train the parameters of the model, but the test data is not used to train the parameters. So we can use test data to obtain the accuracy of the train model. As shown in Figure 8.2, the accuracy becomes higher after each training. After training the system for 100 times, the accuracy of 0.9851 was achieved. ∎

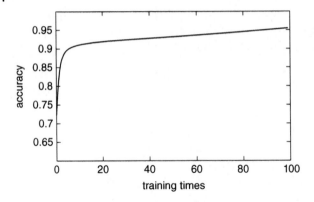

Figure 8.2 Results of TensorFlow based on programming an artificial neural network.

8.2.2 Numeral Recognition using Convolutional Neural Networks

The intermediate layer extracts features and classifies with CNN, as shown in Figure 8.3, namely utilizing CNN to realize handwritten numeral recognition. An all-purpose MNIST dataset of handwritten numerals is adopted in the input layer. With multiple convolution layers, pooling layers and a fully connected layer, the recognition result can be obtained in the output layer.

8.2.2.1. Structure of Convolutional Neural Network (CNN)

The structure of a 5-deep learning layer in a convolutional neural network (CNN) is shown in Figure 8.3. There are two convolution layers in this structure. Each convolution

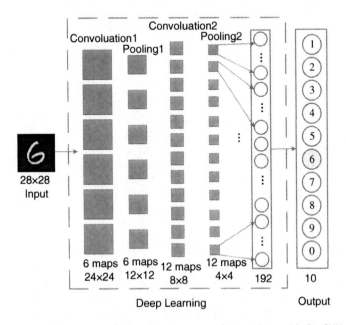

Figure 8.3 Structure for handwritten numeral recognition with the CNN network.

layer is closely followed by a pooling layer. The last layer is a fully connected layer and the output classification is conducted finally. This CNN graph is modified from the work of Rasmus Palm: http://github.com/rasmusbergpalm/DeepLearnToolbox

Example 8.3 Use of Convolutional Neural Network for Numeral Recognition

For the same purpose as in the above two examples, we want to recognize the handwritten numerals using the MNIST dataset and CNN construction:

1) **Input:** Input x is the handwritten numeral of 28×28 pixels.
2) **Convolution 1:** The size of the convolution kernel of the first convolution layer is 5×5 with 6 feature maps, i.e. 1×6 weight matrix w_{ij} is adopted, where $w_{ij} \in R^{5 \times 5}$. It conducts computation for the feature graph with $y_j = f(\sum_i (w_{ij} * x_i + b_i))$, where f is the sigmoid function, namely $f(x) = \frac{1}{1+e^{-x}}$. $J = \{1,2,\ldots,6\}$ stands for serial number (SN) of output feature map and i stands for SN of input feature map. The size of the output feature map obtained is 24×24. The output feature graph in this layer will go to the next layer, Pooling 1 as input.
3) **Pooling 1:** The first Pooling (subsample) layer adopts maximum pooling operation and selects the maximum value in each non-overlapping area of 2×2 as output. The 6 output feature maps of pooling layer 1 will go to the next layer Convolution 2 as input.
4) **Convolution 2:** The size of the convolution kernel in this layer is 5×5 and 12 convolution kernels are adopted, i.e. 6×12 weight matrices w_{ij} are adopted, where $w_{ij} \in R^{5 \times 5}$. We conduct computation for the feature map with $y_j = f(\sum_i (w_{ij} * x_i + b_i))$, where f is the sigmoid function, $j = \{1,2,\ldots,12\}$ is the SN of output feature map, and $i = \{1,2,\ldots,6\}$ is the SN of input feature map. Twelve output feature graphs of 8×8 are obtained in this layer as output will function as input feature map of Pooling 2.
5) **Pooling 2:** Utilize maximum pooling operation to select the maximum value in each non-overlapping area of 2×2 as output. There are 12 feature maps of 4×4 in total.
6) **Full connect:** Each output feature map of pooling layers will be unfolded into a vector of 1×16, and 12 feature graphs are connected into a vector of 1×192.
7) **Output:** It adopts softmax classifier for classification and outputs the classification result. The result of Figure 8.3 is $\{6\}$.

The implementation of the handwritten numeral recognition system with the CNN network includes four detailed steps, as described below:

Step 1: Load dataset

First, we need to load the dataset and preprocess the train set train_x and label set train_y, respectively. Similarly, we also need to preprocess test dataset test_x and label set test_y. The pseudo-code of these tests is given below:

```
load mnist_uint8;
train_x = double(reshape(train_x',28,28,50000))/255;
test_x = double(reshape(test_x',28,28,10000))/255;
train_y = double(train_y');
```

Step 2: Initialization in CNN

In this step, we need to initialize the structure of the convolution layer and the pooling layer; for the convolution layer, the number of convolution kernel (output maps) and the size of convolution kernel (layerCkernel). For pooling layer, the size of pooling area (layerScale) should be specified. The pseudo-code is given below:

```
layerNumber=5
layer(1, 'i') // Input layer
layer(2, 'c', 6, 5) // Convolution layer, 6 5x5 kernel,
                        layerCkernel=5, layerName='c', outputmaps=6
layer (3, 'p', 2) // Pooling layer, 2x2 Pooling,
                        layerScale=2, layerName='p'
layer (4, 'c', 12, 5) // Convolution layer, 12 5x5 kernel,
                        layerCkernel=5, layerName='c', outputpmaps=12
layer (5, 'p',2) //Pooling layer, 2 x 2 Pooling,
                        layerScale=2, layerName='p'
```

For each pooling layer, the size of the feature map (map size) should be initialized. For each convolution layer, we need to configure several parameters, such as connection weight (w), bias (b), and the size of feature map (map size). After the initialization is finished at Layer l, its output feature maps will be utilized as the input feature maps of Layer ± 1. The pseudo-code is shown below:

```
for l = 1 to layerNumber
        if layer(l).layerName= 'p' // Pooling layer
                layer(l).mapsize = layer(l).mapsize /
                layer(l).layerScale
        endif
        if layer(l).layerName='c' // Convolution layer
                layer(l).mapsize = layer(l).mapsize -
                layer(l).layerCkernel+ 1;
                for j = 1 to layer(l).outputmaps % output map
                        for i = 1 to layer(l).mapsize %
                        input map
                                layer(l).w(j) =rand(i,i)
                                layer(l).b(j) = 0;
                        endfor
                endfor
        endif
        layer(l+1).inputmaps= layer(l).outputmaps;
        layer(l+1).mapsize= layer(l).mapsize;
endfor
```

Step 3: Training CNN

During the training stage, we first input the handwritten numeral images. Output classes of input images will be obtained after the forward propagating algorithm goes through all of the layers at the CNN. Then, a backward propagating algorithm is used to calculate the error between output class and label class, by a layer-wise method starting from output layer to input layer. Finally, we adjust the parameters of each layer, in order to decrease the error. After training is completed, the network parameters are fixed to obtain a well-trained CNN. This step includes function cnnff(), function cnnbp() and updatepara(), and the pseudo-code is shown as below:

1) **CNN forward propagating:** Function cnnff() is used to return the numeral recognition results. The input image data first enters Layer 1, and passes Layer 2 to reach the last Layer (denoted by layer number). Finally, the classification result, y', will be obtained at the output layer. If the current layer is the convolution layer, all of input feature maps will be utilized for the convolution operation to obtain the output feature map. If the current layer is the pooling layer, a max-Pooling operation will be performed for all of the input feature maps:

```
layer (1) =x; // x is sample data set
inputmaps = 1;
for l = 2 to layerNumber
          if layerName= 'c'
                  for i=1 to outputmaps
                              initialize every outputmaps
                              Calculate convolution of inputmap
                              get outputmaps
                  endfor
          endif
          if layersname= 's'
                  for j = 1 to inputmaps
                              Figure out maximum values in layer
                              Scale area
                  endfor
          endif
                  layer(l+1). inputmaps= layer(l+1).outputmaps
endfor
Calculate output for full connection layer
Multiple classifier outputs of classification y'
```

2) **CNN backward propagating:** Based on the output of forward propagating (y') and label data (y), error and cost function will be calculated. From the last layer (layerNumber+1) down to the first layer, the error is backward propagated. The pseudo-code of the function cnnbp() is given below:

```
error = y'- y; // Recognition error
L = 1/2*sum(error^ 2) / size(error); // Loss function
// back propagating error
for i= layerNumber+1 to 1 step -1 // layerNumber+1 is the
                                       number of layers
 Calculate error of layer of No i
endfor
```

3) **Update weights:** This operation is applied from the input layer to the fully connected layer. If the current layer is not the Pooling layer, weights and bias

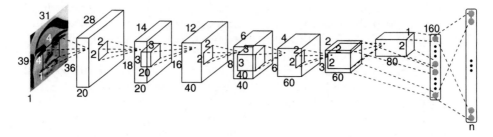

Figure 8.4 Structure of the Deep ID human face recognition system with a CNN with 10 layers including the I/O layers.

between Layer l and Layer l−1 will be updated. The pseudo-code of the function updatepara() for CNN parameters updating is given below:

```
for i= 2 to layerNumber+1 // layerNumber+1 is total
   number of layers
            // update weights of each layer except the
               Pooling layer.
            if layerName != 'p'
                    Update the connection weights between
                       the i-th layer and (i-1)-th layer
                    Update bias of i-th layer
         endif
   endfor
```

4) **Test CNN**

The final testing requires the input test_x and utilize cnnff() to output the recognition results. The testing tag set test_y is used for testing the accuracy of the recognition process. ∎

8.2.3 Convolutional Neural Networks for Face Recognition

Human face recognition is a very important research direction in computer vision field. At present, in this field, deep learning has reached or exceeded the human level. For example, the recognition rate for an LFW dataset is 99.47%, which is higher than the value 99.25% on this dataset by human eyes. In an LFW dataset, there are 13,233 images of 5749 persons, and the images are obtained from Yahoo News. There is only one image for 4069 persons, and there are multiple images for 1680 persons.

Figure 8.4 shows the structure of CNN adopted in Deep ID algorithm, proposed by The Chinese University of Hong Kong in 2014, whose purpose is human face recognition. The Deep ID algorithm includes four convolution layers, three pooling layers and one full connection layer. The recognition rate for the human face in the LFW dataset with such a CNN achieves 97.45%.

Now, we specify the Deep ID algorithm as follows:

- **Input:** the input layer are the human face images of 39 × 31 pixels, each in an LFW dataset.

- **Convolution 1:** In convolution layer 1, the algorithm sets the size of convolution kernel as 4×4, and uses 20 convolution kernels. Thus, in this layer, 20 weight matrixes of 4×4 need be set. Furthermore, the convolution step is set to 1. After convolution, we can obtain 20 feature graphs, and the size of each feature graph is $((39 - 4) + 1) \times ((28 - 4) + 1) = 36 \times 28$. For each feature map x, function $RELU(x) = max(0,x)$ is used as the activation function.
- **Pooling 1:** In pooling layer 1, the algorithm conducts maximum pooling for each non-overlapping area of 2×2 pooling for 20 feature graphs output by previous layer convolution 1. After pooling, we can also obtain 20 feature graphs, and now the size of each feature graph is $(36/2) \times (28/2) = 18 \times 14$.
- **Convolution 2:** In convolution layer 2, the algorithm uses the output of previous layer pooling 1 as input. The size of convolution kernel is 3×3, and 40 convolution kernels (40 weight matrixes of 3×3) are adopted. Similar with convolution 1, the convolution step is also set to 1. Thus, 40 feature graphs will be obtained after convolution, and the size of each feature graph is $((18 - 3) + 1) \times ((14 - 3) + 1) = 16 \times 12$. We also use RELU function as activation function.
- **Pooling 2:** In pooling layer 2, the algorithm conducts the operation for 40 feature graphs output by the previous layer convolution 2, and conducts maximum pooling for each non-overlapping area of 2×2. Then 40 feature graphs will be obtained, and the size of each feature graph is $(16/2) \times (12/2) = 8 \times 6$.
- **Convolution 3:** In convolution layer 3, the algorithm uses the output of the previous layer pooling 2 as the input. The size of the convolution kernel is 3×3, and 60 convolution kernels (60 weight matrixes of 3×3 will be set up) are adopted. Similar to convolution layers 1 and 2, the convolution step is set to 1. Sixty feature graphs will be obtained after convolution, and the size of each feature graph is $((8 - 3) + 1) \times ((6 - 3) + 1) = 6 \times 4$. The activation function is the RELU function.
- **Pooling 3:** In pooling layer 3, the algorithm conducts operations for 60 feature graphs output by previous layer convolution 3, and conduct maximum pooling for each non-overlapping area of 2×2. Then 60 feature graphs will be obtained, and the size of each feature graph is $(6/2) \times (4/2) = 3 \times 2$.
- **Convolution 4:** In the convolution layer 4, the algorithm uses the output of previous layer pooling 3 as input. The size of convolution kernel is 2×2, and 80 convolution kernels (80 weight matrixes of 2×2) are adopted. The convolution step is set to 1. Eighty feature graphs will be obtained after convolution, and the size of each feature graph is $((3 - 2) + 1) \times ((2 - 2) + 1) = 2 \times 1$. The activation function is the RELU function.
- **Deep ID:** In this algorithm, the Deep ID is the full connection layer and contains 160 hidden neurons which conduct full connection to convolution 4 and pooling 3.
- **Softmax (output layer):** utilizes the softmax classifier and outputs the recognition results.

8.2.4   Medical Text Analytics by Convolutional Neural Networks

In order to conduct text comprehension with the deep learning method, we first need to conduct digitized expression for the text, then use deep learning algorithm for feature extraction and text understanding. The application of this approach is illustrated below for medical text analysis.

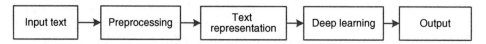

Figure 8.5 The process of text classification with deep learning.

8.2.4.1. Word Embedding via Deep Learning

Figure 8.5 shows the steps of text comprehension with deep learning. Similar methods can be adopted in medical text comprehension as well. In this section, we will introduce the detailed course where we extract the representation features of medical text and then adopt them to comprehend medical text with the deep learning method. We use risk assessment for diseases with the medical text as an example.

Before the use of deep learning for natural language understanding, each word should be transformed from text to digitalized representation first. Generally, we adopt the method of word embedding for representation. Conducting word representation with word embedding is to establish a vocabulary where one word corresponds to one vector. There are two representation methods of word embedding: one-hot representation and distributed representation. One-hot representation is simpler and more direct. The quantity of total words in the vocabulary is also the dimension of vectors.

But there is only one value equal to 1 in the vector composition of each word, while other values are equal to 0. In this method, the unique value is adopted to identify each word, so this is a sparse method. When word embedding is established, the semantic relation between two different words is not taken into consideration. There is no relation between the vectors, even for words with similar semanteme, called a "word gap". As the dimension of word embedding is equal to the quantity of total words, the computational burden for application in some tasks is too high and may cause a dimension disaster.

Figure 8.6 shows a text representation with one-hot representation method. With the Distributed Representation method, each word is represented by a real number vector, such as [0.792, −0.177, −0.107, 0.109, −0.542, ...]. Thus, the dimension of vectors is much less than the quantity of total words. If Word Embedding is established with the Distributed Representation method, large amounts of real text corpus will be needed for training and learning. Tool Word2vec is often used to train word embedding. The dimension of the vector will be determined in the process of learning word embedding.

For instance, the dimension could be set to 50. With this method, the word embedding introduces semanteme of words, i.e. the closeness among words makes their word vectors closer in the vector space. Figure 8.7 shows a text representation with a

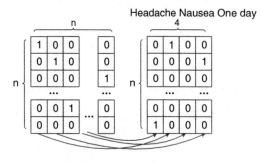

Figure 8.6 One-hot representation for word embedding.

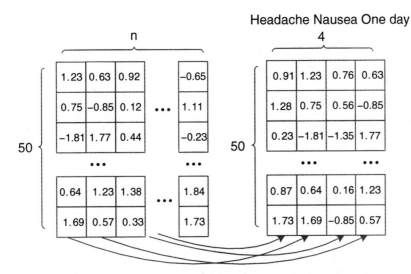

Figure 8.7 Distributed Representation for word embedding.

distributed representation method. Compared with one-hot representation, the dimension of word embedding is largely reduced and the distance of vectors between relevant semanteme or similar semanteme is close.

Word Embedding is a matrix $D = R^{d \times |C|}$, where d is the dimension for word embedding and $|C|$ is the number of words in the vocabulary. The locations of words in the vocabulary are stored in C. There is only one location that is equal to 1 for a vector corresponding to each word. Vector representation for a word i in the vocabulary is stored in the ith column, i.e. of vector matrix of Word Embedding. When transforming text into digitized words, it extracts vector representation t for each word c from vector matrix of Word Embedding.

Each input text sample $x(x_1, x_2, \ldots, x_N)$ includes N words. We search the vector representation xw_n corresponding to each word x_n in a text from word embedding by $t = D \cdot C$. The word embedding representation $xw(xw_1, xw_2, \ldots, xw_N)$ will be obtained for the input sample.

8.2.4.2. Medical Text Analytics using the CNN

Figure 8.8 shows a model of medical text comprehension based on a convolutional neural network. The model mainly includes three parts:

1) **Setup Word Embedding:** it extracts historical data of the patient in clinical notes, conducts data cleaning and data preprocessing, and trains word embedding with processed data as corpus. N-skip gram algorithm or other algorithms in word2vec may be adopted to train word embedding. Dimension is set for word embedding.
2) **Train CNN to learn features of medical text:** it chooses data of a disease from data in clinical notes; after data cleaning and data preprocessing, it selects "Patient Complaint", "Diagnosis Record through Interrogation", etc. And the data becomes sample data. Then conducts digitized representation for the sample data with word

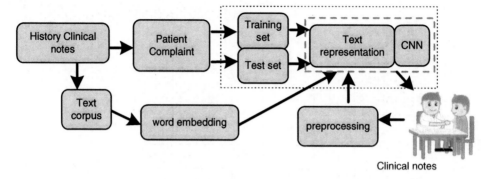

Figure 8.8 Model for risk disease assessment through medical text learning using CNN network.

embedding, and inputs the results into CNN for supervised learning of features in risk assessment of diseases.

3) **Test and application:** the processes of test and application are the same. It inputs "Patient Complaint" and disease-relevant text data, conducts preprocessing and text representation for the data, inputs results into CNN and outputs the result of risk assessment of diseases.

8.2.4.3. Convolutional Neural Network Construction

For word embedding representation $xw(xw_1, xw_2, ..., xw_N)$ of input text, it calculates the convolution vector s_n^{sc} for each word in xw in sequence. The calculation of the convolution vector for word n is given in Figure 8.9. The size of convolution window is d^s. With current word n at the center, intercepting d^s words from the input text and connecting the vectors of these words, we obtain $S_n \in R^{dd^s}$ with $S_n = (xw_{n-(d^s-1)/2}, ..., xw_n, ... xw_{n+(d^s-1)/2})^T$. The system calculates the convolution vector s_n^{sc} for the word n using the following equation, where $w^1 \in R^{l^{sc} \times dd^s}$ is the weight matrix and b^1 is its deviation:

$$s_n^{sc} = w^1 s_n + b^1 \tag{8.1}$$

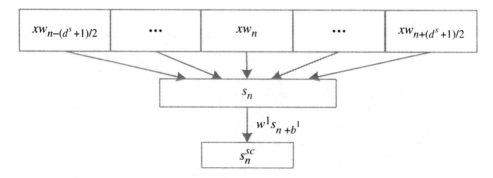

Figure 8.9 Convolution for word xw_n (word No. n).

The variable s_n^{sc} stands for h_n^1, the expression of word xw_n in the hidden layer. After obtaining h_n^1, we calculate the output h_n^2 of the hidden layer with the tanh-function $(\tanh = \frac{e^x - e^{-x}}{e^x + e^{-x}})$ and make it the input of the next hidden layer:

$$h_n^2 = \tanh(w^1 s_n + b^1) \tag{8.2}$$

1) **Pooling layer:** The output of the convolution layer is used as the input of pooling layer. The maximum values among N elements in h_n^2 is calculated by

$$h^3 = max_{1 \leq n \leq N} h_n^2 \tag{8.3}$$

The pooling operation is divided into maximum pooling operation and average pooling operation. Here we conduct maximum pooling operation because the function of each word in the text is not completely equal, i.e. the elements that play a vital role in the text would be selected by maximum pooling operation. The samples have different lengths, so do the input $x(x_1, x_2, ..., x_N)$. However, the text will be transformed into a vector with fixed length after it goes through the convolution layer and the pooling layer:

2) **Output layer:** There is a full connection layer of neural networks after the pooling layer. Softmax classifier is adopted to output classification results:

$$h^4 = w^4 h^3 + b^4 \rightarrow y_i = \frac{e^{h_i^4}}{\sum_{m=1}^{n} e^{h_m^4}} \tag{8.4}$$

where n shows there are n classes. We define all parameters that require training as parameter set $\theta = \{w^1, w^4, b^1, b^4\}$

The objective of training is to learn the maximum log-likelihood value of θ. We utilize random numbers as initialization parameter of θ and stochastic gradient descent for training of parameter θ. As for parameter revision, we utilize the following expression, D is the training sample set, $class_y$ is accurate classification of the sample and α is the learning rate:

$$\max_\theta \sum_{y \in D} \log p\left(class_y | D, \theta\right) \rightarrow \theta = \theta + \alpha \frac{\partial \log p\left(class_y | D, \theta\right)}{\partial \theta} \tag{8.5}$$

8.2.4.4. Medical Text Comprehension with CNN Network

The pseudo-code for the disease risk assessment model in medical text comprehension with the CNN network is specified in Algorithm 8.1. Medical text data include training set X and test set X', with corresponding results data of diagnosis from doctors divided into training label set Y and test label set Y'.

First, we read one medical text data x from X, then represent it as a vector, finally obtaining the predicted result y* after the convolution layer, pooling layer and fully connection layer. The update of parameter θ in this CNN is completed through the backward propagation algorithm. The CNN after training can be used for risk assessment of a disease according to medical text. In the same way, we use the test set X' and corresponding label set Y' to test the model. We get the predicted result y* and contrast it with the true label in Y' to estimate the performance of the CNN.

Algorithm 8.1   Creation of CNN for Text Recognition

Input: X: Training sample, original input data in clinical notes

Y: Tag for training sample, corresponding disease diagnosis result of patient in clinical notes

Output: Create CNN, network parameter $\theta = \{w^1, w^4, b^1, b^4\}$, test result

Algorithm:

1) **Initialization:** $c = 5$ //the size of convolution kernel;

$T = 50$ // the size of sample batch

2) **for** $I = 1,2, ..., I$ // (I is the number of iterations)

3) **for** $j = 1,2, ..., m$ // (m is the number of sample batches)

4) Read in a sample batch x and corresponding tag y

5) Vector representation for data x (as for each word, search its vector representation in word embedding).

6) **for** n = 1,2, ..., T

7) Work out number of words (n) in sample

8) Calculate convolution

9) Max-Pooling for n words

10) Connect full connection layer with softmax classifier for classification, get result y_n^*.

11) **End**

12) Use the backward propagation algorithm to update θ with Formula 10.5

13) **End**

8.3   DeepMind with Deep Reinforcement Learning

In this section, we study the DeepMind technology that is currently in use by Google artificial intelligence programs. The Deep Reinforcement Learning scheme is presented along with its applications in AlphaGo and other game programs at Google cloud.

8.3.1   Google DeepMind AI Programs

In 2010, a British artificial intelligence company started the DeepMind Technologies, which has received "Company of The Year" Award by the Cambridge Computer laboratory in the UK. Subsequently, in 2014, DeepMind was merged with Google at a price of £500 million. This project applies convolutional deep networks that learn to play video games in a fashion that mimics the short-term memory of the human brain. Go is a very complex game for both human players and computers, due to the huge search space involved.

In 1997, IBM's computer Deep Blue beat world chess champion Garry Kasparov in an open match. Ever since then, the strongest AI program to play Go only reached about amateur 5-dan level, which still could not beat a professional Go player without handicaps. For example, the software program Zen, running on a four PC cluster, beat Masaki Takemiya (9p) two times at 5- and 4-stone handicap. The program Crazy Stone beat Yoshio Ishida (9p) at 4-stone handicap.

The Go game is played with black and white stones on a 19×19 mesh board. The game has a search tree complexity equal to b^d, where b is the game's breadth (number of the illegal moves at each state) and d is the depth (number of moves before the game is over). This means that brute force search is impossible for computers to evaluate who is winning. In the past, no computers have ever beaten human Go players until March 2016. In fact, Go is much more complex than any other games such as the chess. This is attributed to the much larger number of possibilities on the Go game board. The complexity involves deep steps that even professional players cannot keep track of beyond certain steps with possible rewards accurately evaluated.

The AlphaGo research project was formed around 2014 to test how well a neural network using deep learning can win over Go professional players. It represents a significant improvement over previous Go programs. AlphaGo running on multiple computers won 500 games played against other Go programs. The distributed system used in the October 2015 match was using 1202 CPUs and 176 GPUs. In January 2016, the team published a paper in the journal *Nature* that described the algorithms used in AlphaGo. In March 2016, this computer program beat Lee Sedol, a 9-dan Go player in the world with 4 to 1 in a 5-game match.

AlphaGo was not specifically trained to face Lee and it won the game entirely out of machine intelligence without handicap. Although it lost to Lee in the fourth game, and Lee resigned the final game, giving a final score of 4 games to 1 in favor of AlphaGo. In recognition of beating Lee, AlphaGo was awarded an honorary 9-dan by the Korea Baduk Association. The Google DeepMind program is aimed to solve very difficult intelligence problems that leverage machine learning and neuroscience systems.

The AlphaGo and Lee match proves that computers can be trained to formalize human intelligence processes. In addition to the Go match, seven Atari video games: *Pong, Breakout, Space Invaders, Seaquest, Beamrider, Enduro* and *Q*bert* were also tested using similar computer programs. All of these games involve strategic thinking out of imperfect or uncertain information content. DeepMind claims that their AI program is not pre-programmed. Each move is limited to 2 seconds. The program learns from experience using only raw pixels as data input. Technically, the program uses deep learning on a convolutional neural network.

The DeepMind team has proposed a novel scheme Q-learning, based on reinforcement learning. Figure 8.10 shows the schematic system diagram of a Google's Reinforcement Learn Architecture, known as *Gorila*. This system was implemented on large clusters of servers at Google. With 64 search threads, a distributed cluster of 1930 CPUs and 280 GPUs was used in the AlphaGo and Lee competition. Parallel acting generates new interactions with distributed replay memory to save iterations. Parallel learning computes gradients from replayed iterations. The distributed CNN updates the network with gradients.

Google DeepMind has combined deep learning and reinforcement algorithm to achieve human level performance in several innovative AI applications. The new algorithm is called deep reinforcement learning (DRL). The DRL adopts a group of agents to select the best actions. The first DRL approach is known as the Deep Q-network (DQN), proposed by David Silver of DeepMind. He is also one of the AlphaGo authors. The DQN combines CNN and Q-network algorithms. The Q-network is used to assess the reward after an agent executes a specific action. The functions of other boxes in

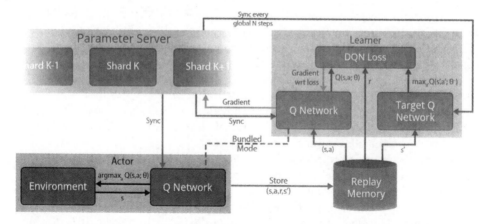

Figure 8.10 The Gorila architecture for implementing the Google reinforcement learning system (reprinted with permission from David Silver, Google DeepMind, http://www0.cs.ucl.ac.uk/staff/d.silver/web/ Resources_files/).

Figure 8.10 will become more transparent in Section 8.5.2, where the DRL algorithm is presented.

The intelligence program learns to play the game directly after a sufficient number of learning plays. For most games, DeepMind plays well below the current world record. For example, the application of the DeepMind program for 3-D video games, such as Doom, was still under development in 2016. According to DeepMind cofounder, Mustafa Suleyman, DeepMind technologies also extend their applications to a Deep-Mind Health program. This program is mainly designed to provide clinical services to the healthcare community. This will open up intelligent healthcare services, which benefit all the patients. In what follows, we introduce the DeepMind approach by combining deep learning with reinforcement learning ideas. Then we examine the algorithms used in AlphaGo and in the Floppybird game, including their implementation and learning process applied.

8.3.2 Deep Reinforcement Learning Algorithm

As introduced in Section 8.1.2, the DRL process is mainly displayed by interactions between the learning agents and its working environment. The reinforcement learning offers an algorithm to solve sequential decision-making problems. Cumulative reward is maximized by software agents after taking a series of actions in a working environment. Without knowing any rules in advance, an agent observes the current environmental state and tries some actions to improve the deep learning process. A reward is the feedback to the agent by adjusting its action strategy. After numerous adjustments, the reinforcement algorithm obtains the knowledge of optimal actions to achieve the best results for a specific situation in the decision environment.

Figure 8.11 shows the interaction of an agent and its environment during the learning process. At each time t, the agent receives a state s_t. and executes an action a_t . Then, it receives an observation o_t. and a reward r_t associated with the action. The environment

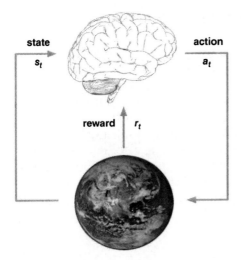

state

s_t

action

a_t

reward r_t

- ► At each step t the agent:
  - ► Receives state s_t
  - ► Receives scalar reward r_t
  - ► Executes action a_t
- ► The environment:
  - ► Receives action a_t
  - ► Emits state s_t
  - ► Emits scalar reward r_t

Figure 8.11 Interaction of an agent and environment in deep learning (reprinted with permission from David Silver's presentation at the International Conference on Machine Learning, ICML 2016) [20].

is typically formulated as a Markov decision process (MDP) to allow the agent to interact with it. After receiving an action, the environment emits a state and a scalar reward. The goal of reinforcement learning is to accumulate the rewards, as many as possible at successive steps. A sequence of observation, action and reward, $\{o_1, r_1, a_1, \cdots, a_{t-1}, o_t, r_t\}$, forms an experience, while the state is a function of the experience, i.e.:

$$s_t = f(o_1, r_1, a_1, \cdots, a_{t-1}, o_t, r_t) \tag{8.6}$$

AlphaGo's algorithm uses a Monte Carlo tree search (MCTS) to find its moves based on knowledge previously "learned" by machine learning. A deep learning ANN is used by extensive training, both from human and computer play. The MCTS is guided by a "value network" and a "policy network", both implemented using deep neural network technology. A limited amount of game-specific feature detection is applied to the input at the pre-processing stage, before it is sent to the neural networks.

The system's neural networks were initially bootstrapped from human gameplay expertise. AlphaGo was initially trained to mimic human play by attempting to match the moves of expert players from recorded historical games, using a database of around 30 million moves. Once it had reached a certain degree of proficiency, it was trained further to become set to play large numbers of games against other instances of itself. This was done with reinforcement learning to improve its play. The purpose is to avoid wasting the opponent's time. The program is programmed to resign if its assessment of win probability falls beneath a given threshold. For the AlphaGo-Lee 2016 match, the resignation threshold was set at 20%.

In the 33rd International Conference on Machine Learning (ICML 2016), Silver et al. presented the application details of DeepMind by using the DRL approach. Specifically, a value function, policy and model are represented by a deep neural network. In a DRL approach, AI is achieved by reinforcement learning and deep learning jointly. The human-level task can be solved by a single agent with reinforcement learning to achieve the objective set by the deep learning mechanism. After the action is selected by the agent, policy and value function play important roles in its performance:

1) **Policy:** is a behavior function selecting actions given states. There are two typical policies. One is the deterministic policy which definitely executes some action a under a specific state s, i.e. a $= \pi(s)$. The other is stochastic policy, which means there is a probability to perform some action a under state s, i.e. $\pi(a|s) = P[a|s]$.

2) **Value function:** predicts the future reward, and evaluates the efficacy of an action or state. For example, $Q^{\pi}(s, a)$ is the expected total reward from state s and action a under policy π. It calculates the expected value of the accumulated reward obtained in future states, i.e. $t + 1, t + 2, t + 3...$, etc. However, the future reward is discounted as time passes. The discount-factor $\gamma \in [0, 1]$ is applied to decrease the award in a future state. There is no perfect model to predict what will exactly happen in the future:

$$Q^{\pi}(a|s) = E[r_{t+1} + \gamma r_{t+2} + \gamma^2 t_{t+3} + \cdots |s, a] \tag{8.7}$$

The goal is to obtain the maximum value of $Q^{\pi}(s, a)$. The optimal policy is obtained by maximizing the value function as

$$Q^*(s, a) = E[r_{t+1} + \gamma \max_{a_{t+1}} Q^*(s_{t+1}, a_{t+1})|s, a] \tag{8.8}$$

Equation 8.8 was attributed to Bellman, who uses dynamic programming to achieve the optimal value through multiple iterations. Give an action a under state s, a reward r_{t+1} is obtained at state s_{t+1}. In order to achieve the maximum Q value, the state s_{t+1} needs to be optimal. Similarly, the Q value of state s_{t+2} should be optimized to guarantee the optimal Q-value of state s_{t+2}, etc. The iterative process goes on until the final state. When the number of states and actions is small, a state action table can be built to record the optimal Q-value. For infinite states, approximation function is needed to represent the relationship among state, action and value. The Neural network is the best choice for this purpose.

The DQN provides three stable solutions to overcome the above problem: i) uses experience replay to break correlations in data and bring us back to an independent and identically distributed (iid) setting. We store all past policies in replay memory and learn from them; ii) freeze the target Q-network to avoid oscillations and break correlations between Q-network and the target; and iii) clip rewards or normalize network adaptively to a sensible range. This demands the use of a robust gradient method.

Compared to conventional RL, DQN adopts neural network to calculate the Q value. For each state as an input, the individual Q value will be calculated for each action. After a single forward propagation of the neural network, Q values for all actions are updated. Given a transit $< s, a, r, s' >$, the Q value table updating algorithm is given below:

1) Perform forward propagation starting from current state s and obtain predicted Q value for all actions;
2) Perform forward propagation starting from the next state s', calculate the maximum Q value, i.e. max $Q(s', a')$;
3) Set the target Q value $r + \gamma$ max $Q(s', a')$ based on the calculated result at Step 2 and the predicted value $Q(s, a)$ calculated by step 1.

4) Update weight s of the neural network by the backward propagation algorithm. The loss function is shown as

$$L = \frac{1}{2} \underbrace{[r + \max Q(s', a')}_{target} - \underbrace{Q(s, a)}_{prediction}]^2 \tag{8.9}$$

5) The model refers to a descriptive expression to specify the agent behavior in the learning environment. The designer can interact with the model and learn from the experiment. Each action of the agent is based on a certain environment. For such environment, the next state of the agent has many possible situations, and it is hard to determine exactly which is the next state, that is to say, the transition probability of the agent going into a specific next state, and the possible reward cannot be confirmed. As long as the environment changes, the agent has to traverse all the possible next state every time, leading to a decline in the efficiency of learning. As a result, the agent must be able to take appropriate action strategies based on the current environment and past experience, in view of the situation that the environment is unknown or under constant change.

If the agent learns the optimal policy only by value iteration without learning from the model, the experience of each learning knowledge will not be fully used, which leads to the relatively slow convergence rate and a sub-optimal solution rather than the optimal solution. Although the application of RL is successful, its feature state needs to be manually set. Thus, it is difficult to handle complex scenes, and sometimes meets the problem, the dimension disaster. In DQN, DL is introduced to learn features automatically. Thus, combining RL and DL enables the automatic learning of the features in dynamic scenes, while the learning decision, i.e. action, is optimally selected by RL

8.3.3 Google AlphaGo Game Competition

The AlphaGo program is built with four functional parts: Policy Network, Fast Rollout, Value Network and Monte Carlo Tree Search (MCTS). Fast rollout network is trained by linear model utilizing local features, which has high speed but low accuracy, while Policy Network has low speed but high accuracy, which is implemented using a deep convolution neural network based on global features. Value Network estimates who would win given the current state, black chessman or white.MCTS combined is guided by the three parts above.

8.3.3.1. CNN Construction in AlphaGo and its Training Process

The Go game is played on a 19×19 grid board, as shown in Figure 8.12. Black and white stones are placed on the board, one at a time by two players alternately. Once the stones of the same color are fully surrounded by the opponent's stones, they will be removed from the board. The winner ends up by controlling the larger areas. It is essentially a seize-and-control game. The game involves a large search space in every move of the stone. A convolution neural network (CNN) can be built (Figure 8.12), based on the successive insertions of the stones in the strategic grid locations from the left-hand side to the right-hand side.

Figure 8.13 illustrates the neural network training process using human expert positions. The learn pipeline flows from the left to the right. Expert successive positions

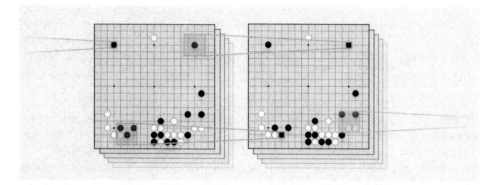

Figure 8.12 Convolutional neural network construction over the Go playing board.

serve as the inputs. The policy network starts with a supervised learning algorithm to maximize the likelihood by stochastic gradient decent. After self play, the policy network is reinforced using the RL algorithm. The system then moves to generate self-play data to feed the value network to assess its rewarding values. This process is repeated with many iterations until the winning condition is met. The supervised learning and reinforcement learning are explained in Example 8.4.

Example 8.4   Supervised and Reinforcement Learning of Policy Networks before Feeding the Self-Play Data into the Value Network using Regression
This example shows the specific training details of supervised learning followed by reinforcement learning on the policy networks. Then the trainer applies regression to assess the rewards in the value network. The policy network uses a 12-layer convolutional neural network with games of self-play as its training data. The training algorithm for the RL process attempts to maximize the wins z by gradient reinforcement learning, i.e.:

$$\Delta\sigma \propto \frac{\partial \log p_\sigma(a|s)}{\partial \sigma} z \tag{8.10}$$

where s is the state, a the action and σ the reward. The policy networks should be trained for one week on 50 GPUs on servers in Google cloud. Then, an excellent result is that the policy network is equivalent to the 3 amateur dan with an accuracy of 80% versus 57% on held out test data from the supervised learning.

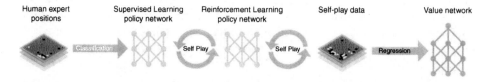

Figure 8.13 Self-play training pipeline between policy network and value networks (reprinted with permission from David Silver, Google DeepMind, http://icml.cc/2016/tutorials/AlphaGo-tutorial-slides.pdf) [20].

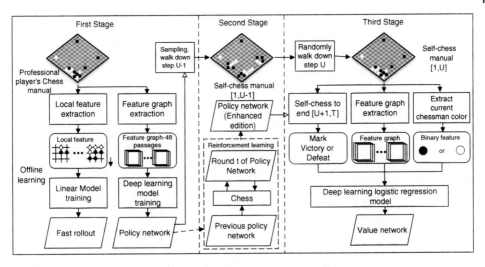

Figure 8.14 The off-line learning process of the AlphaGo program (courtesy of artwork by Lu Wang and Yiming Miao, Huazhong University of Science and Technology, China).

The value network applies 12 layers of CNN to perform the reinforcement learning. This CNN is similar to that used in the policy network. The training data of 30 million positions are used from human expert games (KGM 5+ dan). Its training, the algorithm minimizes the mean square error θ by a stochastic gradient descent method characterized by

$$\Delta\theta \propto \frac{\partial v_\theta(s)}{\partial \theta}(z - v_\theta(s)) \tag{8.11}$$

The training of the value network is done similar to that of the policy network. The entire pipeline of policy and value networks can achieve a first strong position evaluation that has never been achieved previously by other Go programs. ∎

8.3.3.2. System Architecture for Deep Reinforcement Learning in AlphaGo Program

In Figure 8.14, we provide a schematic block diagram to illustrate the data flow in the AlphaGo program in three learning stages: The three stages are functionally described below:

Stage 1: This stage performs off-line deep learning, as shown in the left-hand side Figure 8.14. A supervised deep learning method is implemented against a professional player's chess manual. The purpose is to perform two tasks in parallel: i) local feature extraction with a linear model training to generate fast rollout for use in the Monte Carlo Tree search (Figure 8.15); and ii) run feature graph in 48 passes with a deal learning model to update the policy network for use in the next two stages of Figure 8.14 and in the on-line execution process in Figure 8.15.

Stage 2: This stage updates the previous policy network through reinforcement learning to an enhanced edition of the policy network, ready for use in Stage 3. A

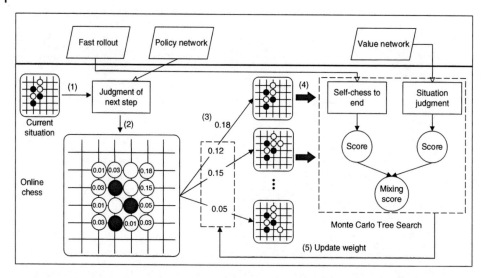

Figure 8.15 The on-line playing process of the AlphaGo game (courtesy of Artwork by Xiaobo Shi and Ping Zhou, Huazhong University of Science and Technology, China).

self-chess manual is used to sample the random walk from step u-1 to step u to be carried out at Stage 3.

Stage 3: This stage applies the self chess manual at step u in three parallel tasks to mark victory or defeat and extract useful features and current chessman color. The outputs of the three tasks are merged to feed into the deep learning logistic regression model in order to work with value network. The updated rollout, policy network and value network will be used in the on-line execution process in the five steps specified in Figure 8.15.

8.3.3.3. Execution Steps in Online AlphaGo Match with a Human Player

In Figure 8.15, we show five execution steps in the on-line AlphaGo program. Essentially, these steps use the updated policy network to make a decision in the next stone placement using the Monte Carlo tree search. The five steps are briefly specified below:

Step 1: Extract feature based on current state of placed stones.

Step 2: Estimate the probability that each empty location will be located with policy network.

Step 3: Compute the weight for the next move on each empty location based on the initial value probability.

Step 4: Check the value network and fast rollout network to update scores. Here fast rollout demands high speed rather than high accuracy. Repeat this score process iteratively after each move in the match. The rate of winning is estimated at each insertion location. The value network gets the estimated result on each state.

Step 5: Choose the decision with a maximum weight to make the next move. The update of these weights can be done in parallel. If the times of visiting a location exceed a certain value, the next step is searched on the next layer in Monte Carlo Tree.

The MCTS performs the following tasks using the value network and policy network, collaboratively:

1) Choose several possible strategies that the opponent would choose for their next move based on the current situation.
2) Judging the strategies of the opponent, choose a move that benefits most to traverse the right subtree. The search tree of AlphaGo will not expand all the nodes, except along the optimal path of the subtree traversed.
3) How to decide the best action in the next move requires an estimation of the probability of winning with the value network. A Monte Carlo tree search needs to predict deeper results along the tree layers. The mutually supportive results of these two networks are key for AlphaGo to win the game.
4) After deciding the best action to take, we estimate the possible next moves of the opponent and corresponding strategies through policy network based on the location of best action.

In summary, AlphaGo's algorithm combines deep learning and reinforcement learning, trained with human players and machine Go manuals. The reinforcement learning method is based on the Monte Carlo search tree of the value network and the policy network, which are both implemented with deep neural networks.

Example 8.5   Reported Performance Results on Monte-Carlo Tree Search
The MCTS process essentially exhausts all possible moves and rewards. Building a large lookahead search tree to cover millions of possibilities, the 19 × 19 AlphaGo program uses MCTS to end up with high accuracy. The value network is trained to predict expert human moves, using the large database of professional Go games. Detailed performance data can be found in David Silver, Google DeepMind, http://www0.cs.ucl.ac.uk/staff/d.silver/web/Resources_files/deep_rl.pdf

The predictive accuracy of the 12-layer CNN reaches 55%, which is a significant improvement over the 31% and 39% predictive accuracy reported for earlier Go programs. The neural network is considerably stronger than the traditional search-based program GnuGo, and its performance is on a par with MoGo for 100,000 rollouts per move. The Pachi runs a reduced search of 10,000 rollouts per move. It wins about 11% of games against Pachi, with 100,000 rollouts per move.   ∎

8.3.4   Flappybird Game using Reinforcement Learning

One of DQN's representative applications is playing Atari 2006, a collection of popular entertainment computer games. It includes 49 independent games, such as Breakout and other classic games. The input of the algorithm consists of the image of game screen and the game score. Without knowing the rules of the games, the DQN learns how to play the games by itself and find the best strategy to play. Figure 8.16 shows the Artari game setting involving the joystick and the slide control to play the game. The interplay among the learning state, action and reward is shown by the arrows.

Example 8.6   Deep Q Network works the Neural Network in Artari Games
Flappybird is a simple game based on using the DQN, as illustrated by the flowchart in Figure 8.17. The player must control a bird so as not to fly too high or too low to hit

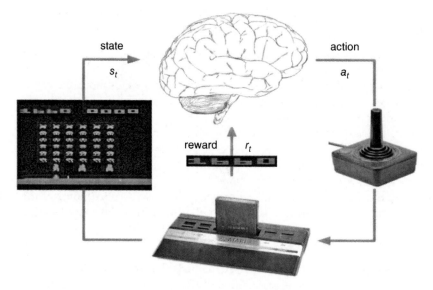

Figure 8.16 Reinforcement learning applied in Artari game play.

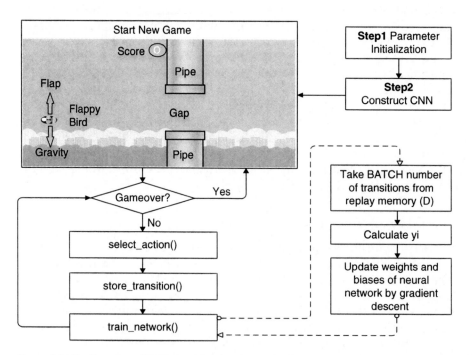

Figure 8.17 The flowchart of DQN algorithm for playing the Flappybird game.

the water pipes. This CNN includes three convolution layers and one full connection layers. In the game, there are two actions that the player can take: to press the "up" key, which makes the bird jump upward or not pressing any key, which makes it descend at a constant rate. The pseudo code for creating the CNN is given below:

```
def createNetwork():
  # Weight of neural network
  # Input layer
  # Hidden layer
    # Output layer
      Qvalue= tf.matmul(h_fc1, W_fc2) + b_fc2 // Predict the value of Q
      return s, Qvalue, h_fc1
      a = tf.placeholder("float", [None, ACTIONS]) // Allocating space
                                                      to action
      y = tf.placeholder("float", [None]) // y is the Q value of
                                             optimal goal
Qvalue_action = tf.reduce_sum(tf.mul(Qvalue, a), reduction_indices=1)
      //Neural network prediction value
cost = tf.reduce_mean(tf.square(y - Qvalue_action)) // Loss function
train_step = tf.train.AdamOptimizer(1e-6).minimize(cost)
      //Neural network optimization by minimizing the loss function
```

The construction of the CNN follows the cascade of input four images, three convolution layers and one full connection layer, and the output action as illustrated in Figure 8.18. Setting the ACTIONS=2 means that Flappybird only has two actions, either "up" or "down". In order to solve such an asynchronous problem, the algorithm sets FRAME_PER_ACTION as the number of samples before an action. The parameter GAMMA is the discount factor γ of future reward. The REPLAY_MEMORY represents the capacity of replay memory. Collected samples are time-series data and there exits overlapping between samples. The efficiency is low if the updating process of Q value is performed each time a sample is obtained.

The samples are stored in replay memory with the form of the sequence $(\phi_t, a_t, r_t, \phi_{t+1})$ and then extracts BATCH (the number of minibatch taken out from the

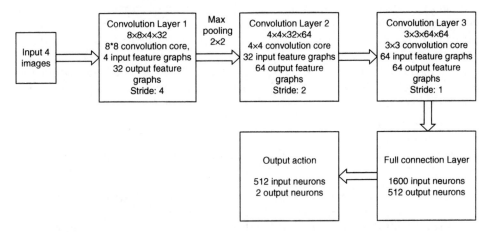

Figure 8.18 The construction of the convolutional neural network used in the FlappyBird Game.

replay memory each time) sequences randomly to conduct training. In most cases, the game scenes can be captured in a very short time, while feature coding by DL and policy building by RL are computing-intensive with a longer delay. Thus, when every new frame appears during game playing, it needs to check whether the agent finishes the calculation.

Every four frames of game screen together as a training sample. After obtaining a new image, the next state will move forward one frame to ensure that the image is still four frames. Then, the training sample will get the operation set. As for each sample, we should initialize states s_1 first. Now begin the game. After received samples, we can choose action a_t in two ways:

1) Randomly select action a_t based on epsilon, which will not decrease over time.
2) Input current state into the network to compute the Q value for each action chosen for the next move.

This implies that choosing the action a_t will result in an optimal Q value being calculated. The pseudo-code for selecting the actions is given below:

```
def select_action():
Qvalue_t = Qvalue.eval(feed_dict={s : [s_t]})[0] // get Qvalue_t through
                                                     neural network
 a_t = np.zeros([ACTIONS]) // allocate space for action
 action_index = 0 // index for action
if t % FRAME_PER_ACTION == 0: // each action skips on frame of samples
 if random.random() <= epsilon: //randomly choose one action
  action_index = random.randrange(ACTIONS)
  a_t [random.randrange(ACTIONS)] = 1
 else: // take action based on the best policy
  action_index = np.argmax(Qvalue_t) // predict all the Q values for
    each action, and choose the action with maximum Q value
  a_t [action_index] = 1
else: a_t [0] = 1 //do nothing
```

The training of the deep CNN is performed by the following pseudo-code. Reward r_t and image input x_{t+1} of the next network will be obtained when action a_t is executed in the emulator, then put the sequence $(\phi_t, a_t, r_t, \phi_{t+1})$ into the playback pool. If the capacity of the playback pool is full, discard the sequences that were input the earliest. The inputs are only images and scores of the game, the action outputs after training with convolution neural network. Due to no labels, reinforcement learning is applied and the decision is made, each time choosing the action with the maximum value as the output. The following pseudo code is self-explanatory with comments:

```
def train_network():
if t > OBSERVE:
 minibatch = random.sample(D, BATCH)   //choose BATCH sequences from D
 s_j_batch = [d[0] for d in minibatch] //current state of corresponding
                                          sequence
 a_batch = [d[1] for d in minibatch] //action of corresponding sequence
 r_batch = [d[2] for d in minibatch] //reward of corresponding sequence
 s_j1_batch = [d[3] for d in minibatch] //next state of corresponding
                                          sequence
```

```
y_batch = [] //allocate space for y
Qvalue_j1_batch = Qvalue.eval(feed_dict = {s : s_j1_batch})
// compute the max Q value for the next state
 for i in range(0, len(minibatch)):
 terminal = minibatch[i][4] //next state of sequence
 if terminal:
 y_batch.append(r_batch[i])
 else:
 y_batch.append(r_batch[i] + GAMMA X np.max(Qvalue_j1_batch[i]))
 train_step.run(feed_dict = {
 y : y_batch,
 a : a_batch,
 s : s_j_batch})
```

∎

8.4 Data Analytics for Social-Media Applications

Social media is a major source of big data aggregation in our daily activities. In this section, we assess data analytics technologies applied in the social-media industry and its impact on all works of life. Then we study social networks and graph analysis of social communities. Finally, we present smart cloud resources needed to support big-data analytics applications. Online social networks are formed with individuals or organizations over the Internet. These individual or organizational entities are related, connected or associated with special interests or specific dependencies.

The building of social networks is based on personal friendship, kinship, professional orientations, common interests, financial exchange, community or racial groups, religious or political beliefs, knowledge or prestige, celebrity fans, etc. In a social network, nodes represent the individuals, and the ties between the nodes represent the relationships such as friendship, kinship and colleagueship. Online social networking services are built to reflect the social relations among people. These services are introduced as communication tools among people. Traditional online communities are more group oriented, while modern social websites are mostly built individually.

8.4.1 Big Data Requirements in Social-Media Applications

We review below typical requirements in big data applications in the social media domain, marketing profits from microblogs and video streaming. Consumer services prefer using forums and mobile systems. Sales enjoy products/service reviews mostly. Human resources prefer to leverage business networks. Most organizations apply enterprise social networks. Mobile social-media users make use of the location- and/or time-sensitive features of the big dataset collected. They aim to manage customer relations, sales promotions and incentive programs as assessed in the four areas described below:

1) **Marketing research:** In mobile social media applications, the users often collect data from offline consumer movements first, before they move to online companies. Online data collections could escalate rapidly to a large amount. They have to be handled timely in a streaming mode continuously. The requirement is to keep all concerned parties or firms well informed with the exact times of transactions and the comments made during the transactions or social network visits.

2) **Communication in social-media exchanges:** Mobile social media communication takes two forms: business-to-consumer (B2C), in which a company may establish a connection to a consumer based on its location and provide reviews about user-generated content. For example, McDonald's offered $5 and $10 gift cards to 100 users randomly selected among those checking in at one of its restaurants. This promotion increased sales by 33% and resulted in many blog posts and news feeds through Twitter messages.

3) **Sales promotions and discounts:** Although customers have had to use printed coupons in the past, mobile social media allows companies to tailor promotions to specific users at specific times. For example, when launching its California-Cancun service, Virgin America offered passengers two flights to Mexico for the price of one. Relationship development and loyalty programs could be established to enhance long-term relationships with customers. For example, companies may construct loyalty programs to allow customers who check in regularly at a location to earn discounts or perks.

4) **e-Commerce:** Mobile social media applications such as Amazon.com and Pinterest have started to influence an upward trend in the popularity and accessibility of e-commerce, or online purchases. Such e-commerce events could be conducted as B2B (business-to-business), B2C (business-to-customer), C2B (customer-to-business or C2C (customer-to-customer in a peer-to-peer (P2P) fashion). Recently, O2O transactions are also taking place as online to offline or offline to online sales or business exchanges.

Table 8.3 provides a list of the leading 14 social networks based on the number of active user accounts, as of April 2016. Obviously, Facebook and WhatsApp are both very successful in attracting users. In China, the QQ and WeChat users are booming rapidly, which involves almost two-thirds of the population of China. Gladwell has indicated that social media are built around weak ties. For example, social media's role in democratizing media participation may fall short of ideals, allowing anyone with an Internet connection to become a content creator. This may be able to empower the "active" users to inspire the "passive" ones. But international survey data suggest online media audience members are largely passive consumers, while content creation is dominated by a few. The following example assesses the plus and minus of the social networks industry in recent years.

Table 8.3 Top 14 Social Networks based on Global User Population in 2016.

Social Network	Active Users	Social Network	Active Users
Facebook	1.59 Billion	Twitter	320 Million
WhatsApp	1.00 Billion	Baidue Tieba	300 Million
QQ	853 Million	Skype	300 Million
WeChat	697 Million	Viber	249 Million
Qzone	640 Million	Sina Weibo	222 Million
Tumblr	555 Million	Line	215 Million
Instagram	400 Million	Snapchat	200 Million

Example 8.7   Positive and Negative Impacts of Some Social Networks

Social media fosters the communication industry. Social networks have impacted our daily lives and pushed for some societal changes. Obviously, the influence impacts of social networks increase with their user populations. Facebook and Twitter provide open forums for their users to make connections, share information and open up discussions on public or private issues. They have even affected the US presidential election and triggered some political reforms or revolutions in certain parts of the world.

People worldwide are taking advantage of social media for its convenience at almost no cost to the general public. We review a few cases of social network events to assess their positive and negative impacts. Circles of friends, business groups, political and special-interest groups can openly discuss their concerns on these platforms. For example, a positive outlook in using the social networks may address the health, safety and social issues, such as alcohol control, drug prevention, avoiding sex abuse or domestic violence, and stopping organized crime. All of these should be encouraged, revealing the bright and positive side of our society.

On the negative side, there are some very bad effects such as spreading unhealthy rumors, smashing people's reputations at random, causing riots in neighborhoods, and racial tensions in a country. As an extreme example, if a person displays a suicidal scene on line, it may trigger youngsters or desperate persons to follow. Pornography, if not regulated, may spread wider to poison young generations. Illegal medicine sales or drug abuse may hurt many innocent people.

In summary, we see some positive effects of free speech and the promotion of harmony in social values. However, if we do not learn from the negative consequences by letting the guns become totally out of control and allowing unleashed freedom to hurt innocent people en masse, all of us will suffer eventually. The conclusion is that negative usage of social networks must be regulated by law and order enforcement. Social networks should not be allowed to head in immoral or unhealthy directions.   ∎

8.4.2   Social Networks and Graph Analytics

The social network is useful in social sciences to study relationships between individuals, groups, organizations or even entire societies. The term is used to describe a social structure determined by such interactions. The ties between constituting members represent the convergence of various social contacts. An axiom to understanding social interaction is that it is based on the properties of relations between and within the social group. Due to the existence of many different relations, network analytics are useful to a broad range of social network construction. In social science, this study is related to anthropology, biology, communication studies, economics, geography, information science, organizational studies, social psychology, sociology and sociolinguistics.

In general, social networks are self-organizing, emergent and complex, such that a globally coherent pattern appears from the local interaction of the elements that make up the system. These patterns become more apparent as network size increases. However, a global network analysis of all interpersonal relationships in the world is not feasible. Practical limitations are due to ethics, participant recruitment and economics considerations.

8.4.2.1. Levels of Social-Media Networking

The nuances of a local system may be lost in large network analysis, hence the quality of information may be more important than its scale for understanding network properties. Thus, social networks are analyzed at the scale relevant to the researcher's theoretical question. Although levels of analysis are not necessarily mutually exclusive, there are three general levels into which networks may fall: micro-level, meso-level and macro-level. The following example shows their differences in the formation of those social networks.

Example 8.8   Construction of Social Networks in Three Levels

At the micro-level, social network research typically begins with an individual, snow-balling as social relationships are traced, or may begin with a small group of individuals in a particular social context. This shown in Figure 8.19(a), where small groups are formed, on average, with a hundred or less peer nodes. Member nodes in the same group may have more ties of edge connections. Different groups (or called community) are loosely connected with far fewer edge connections.   ∎

Rather than tracing interpersonal interactions, macro-level social networks generally expand from the outcomes of greater interactions, such as economic or other resources. Large-scale networks is a term somewhat synonymous with "macro-level" social networks, as demonstrated in Figure 8.19(b). These are often used in social, computer or behavioral sciences in connection with economics classes, professional societies or political affiliations.

The meso-level theories begin with a population size that falls between the micro- and macro-levels. However, meso-level may also refer to networks that are specifically designed to reveal connections between micro- and macro-levels. Meso-level networks are low density and may exhibit causal processes distinct from interpersonal micro-level networks. In Figure 8.19(b), the macro-level network graph may far exceed the cutoff boundary being shown at all sides of the network. The circled network groups are at the micro-level, while the thick linkages among micro-groups correspond to the

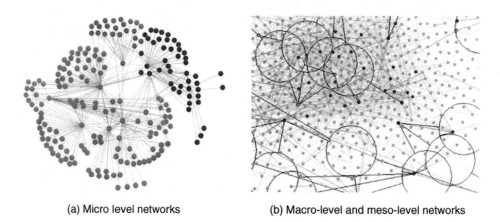

(a) Micro level networks   (b) Macro-level and meso-level networks

Figure 8.19 Micro-level, meso-level and macro-level construction of social networks.

meso-level connections. Several micro-networks tied to a few central nodes form the so-called meso-networks.

8.4.2.2. Social Graph Characteristic

Social network analysis has emerged as a key technique in modern sociology. Characterizing the existing relationship among a person's social group is the main task in social network analysis. Also, users are facing a so-called "small-world" society, where all people are related in a short chain of social acquaintances, one way or another. All social networks are not so chaotic or random as once assumed, but rather they have underlying structures. Social relationships are often mapped into directed or undirected graphs, sometimes called acquaintance graphs or simply social connection graphs.

The nodes in a social graph correspond to the users or actors and the graph edges or links refer to the ties or relationships among the nodes. The graphs can be complex and hierarchically structured to reflect relationships at all levels. There can be many kinds of ties between the nodes. Social networks operate from family level up to national and global levels. There are pros and cons of social networks. Most free societies welcome social networks. For political or religious reasons, some countries block the use of social networks to prevent possible abuses:

- **Social Network Graph Properties:** The social networks play a critical role in problem solving, running an organization, and calculating the degree to which individuals succeed in achieving their goals. A social network is simply a map of all of relevant ties between all actor nodes. The network can also be used to measure social capital – the value that an individual gets from the social network. These concepts are often displayed in a social network graph. An example social-network graph is shown in Figure 8.20. The black dots are the nodes (users) and the edges link the nodes under specified tie relationships. Listed below are some interesting properties of a social graph.

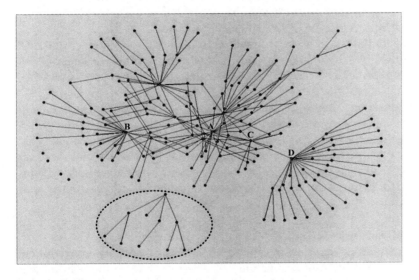

Figure 8.20 The graph representation of a social network.

- **Node Degree, Reach, Path Length and Betweenness:** The node degree is the number of immediate node neighbors of a node. The reach is defined as the degree by which any member of a network can reach other members of the network. Path length measures the distance between pairs of nodes in the network. Average path length is the average of these distances between all pairs of nodes. Betweenness reveals the extent to which a node lies between other nodes in the network. This measures the number of people who a person is connected indirectly to through their direct links.
- **Closeness and Cohesion:** The degree an individual is near to all other individuals in a network (directly or indirectly). It reflects the ability to access information through the network members. Thus, closeness is the inverse of the sum of the shortest distances between each individual and every other person in the network. Cohesion is the degree to which actors are connected directly to each other by cohesive bonds. Groups are identified as "cliques" if every individual is directly tied to every other individual.
- **Centrality and Centralization:** Centrality indicates the social power of a node based on how well they "connect" the network. Nodes A, B and D in Figure 8.20 are all centrality nodes with different node degrees.
- **Social Circles or clusters:** This refers to some structured groups. If there is less stringency of direct contact or as structurally cohesive blocks, then a social circle can be created either loosely or tightly, depending on the stringency rules applied. Those nodes inside the circle of Figure 8.20 form a cluster. The clustering coefficient is the likelihood that two associates of a node are associates themselves.
- **Centralized versus Decentralized Networks:** Centrality gives a rough indication of the social power of a node based on how well they "connect" the network. Betweenness, closeness and degree are all measures of centrality. A centralized network has its links dispersed around one or a few nodes, while a decentralized network is one in which there is little variation between the number of links that each node possesses.
- **Bridge and Local Bridge:** An edge is a bridge if deleting it would cause its endpoints to lie in different clusters or components of a graph. For example, the edge between nodes C and D in Figure 8.20 is a bridge. The endpoints of a local bridge share no common neighbors. A local bridge is contained in a cycle.
- **Prestige and Radiality:** In a social graph, prestige describes a node's centrality. "Degree Prestige", "Proximity Prestige" and "Status Prestige" are all measures of Prestige. Radiality is the degree to which a network reaches out and provides novel information and influence.
- **Structural Cohesion, Equivalence and Holes:** Structural cohesion is the minimum number of members who, if removed from a group, would disconnect the group. Structural equivalence refers to the extent to which the nodes have a common set of linkages to other nodes. These nodes do not have any ties to each other. A structural hole can be filled by connecting one or more links to reach other nodes. This is related to the social capital: by linking two disconnected people, we can control their communication.

8.4.2.3. Social Graph Analysis Example

Online social networking services are put together through identity, conversation, sharing, telepresence, relationship, affiliation, etc. These are offered through Internet access and web services. Early online social network services include job hunting,

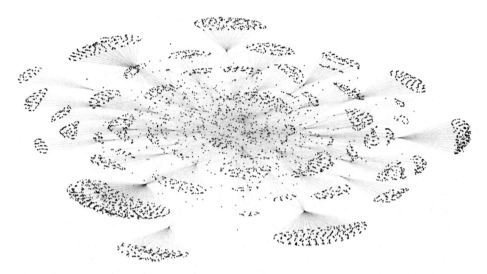

Figure 8.21 Graph representation of a social network.

dating or bulletin board services, etc. The traditional online communities are organized in different groups based on different interests and regions, while modern social networking websites are always individual-oriented or follow peer-to-peer interactions. Listed below are some ideas in providing online social networking services:

1) Personal page or profiles for each user linked by social connections;
2) The social graph traverse along specific social links or networks;
3) Communication tools between the participants or registered users;
4) Share special information like music, photos, videos, etc. with friends or professional groups;
5) Operating a community in special niche topic areas such as healthcare, sports, hobbies, etc.;
6) Customized software tools or databases may be needed to set up the social network services;
7) Strong customer loyalty and viral membership growth are typical in social network communities;
8) Social networks have revenues by selling premium memberships and access to premium content.

Example 8.9 Graph Representations of An e-Mail Exchange Network

In Figure 8.21, we show a 430-node network of email exchanges within a small research laboratory. Only internal email exchanges are shown; emails to and from external sources are not shown here. The edges correspond to those who have sent emails to each other. The number of edges could easily reach 200,000 if fully connected. Here we see only a partially connected graph with roughly 5000 edges.

At the University of Southern California, an email exchange network like this may have to cover 40,000 nodes. This may end up as a connection graph with 1.5 million email exchange edges. If the external emails are included, the email network would be significantly enlarged to cover 10 millions of nodes on a global scale. ∎

Twitter does not copy all offline relationships onto the websites. Hence, the attraction to use Twitter is far less than Facebook at present. On the other hand, Facebook is not as open as Twitter. These features make people trust Facebook more than Twitter, because the concerns of privacy would lead people choose a more closed system.

Last but not least, Facebook is more complex in functionalities than Twitter. Although Twitter has plenty of third-party applications, it is still not convenient for beginning users. Facebook has embedded many common features in the websites. If someone does not like to explore third-party applications for some common functions, they would go to Facebook instead of Twitter, based on the current trend.

8.4.2.4. Filtering Techniques and Recommender Systems

We need to build recommender systems for movies, tourism and restaurants to make our daily-life activities better organized, convenient and enjoyable; social or collaborative filtering of unwanted data by polling the opinions of the mass to make decision based on ratings. Content-based filtering is needed to recommend items based on features of products and ratings by users. Demographic filtering helps making decisions based on demographic information of the users. Finally, knowledge-based filtering makes wise decisions based on expertise knowledge and peer reputations, etc. Hybrid filtering combines the advantages of the above filtering techniques to make even smarter decisions.

8.4.2.5. Pushing Data Analytics for Cloud/Network Security Enforcement

This is a hot research area to apply big data for cyber security enforcement. Big data analytics is much needed in network security, enterprise events analytics, netflow monitoring to identify botnets, detection of persistent threats, data sharing, provenance, and governance techniques for trust management with reputation systems.

8.4.2.6. Cloud Support of IoT and Social Network Applications

In cyber-physical systems (CPS), analytical algorithms can perform more accurately in system configuration, physical knowledge and working principles. To integrate, manage and analyze machinery, we desire to handle data more efficiently during different stages of the machine life cycle. The coupling model between human and machines is greatly facilitated by the use of cloud storage and analytics systems. This involves the sensing, storage, synchronization, synthesis and service operations.

Smart and pervasive cloud applications are in high demand by individuals, homes, communities, companies and governments, etc. These include coordinated calendar, itinerary, job management, events, and consumer record management (CRM) services. Other interest areas include cooperative word processing, on-line presentations, web-based desktops, sharing on-line documents, datasets, photos, videos and databases, content distribution, etc. Deployment of conventional clusters, grid, P2P and social networking applications are very much in demand in the cloud environments. Earthbound applications may demand elasticity and parallelism to avoid large data movement and to reduce storage costs.

8.4.2.7. Online Social Network Architecture

It is desirable to customize the OSN to sustain the competition in this field. The social network provider should choose a brand name with its own API interfaces and profile variables. The chosen forum categories must be relevant to the sufficiently large user community. The OSN platform must include specific functionalities that make it easy for users to join and enjoy the services. Furthermore, the provider must prove the online marketing concept to attract members to join and leave freely. Highly sophisticated software, virtualized datacenters, or processing and storage cloud platforms are needed.

The social network community must operate reliably with high availability and performance. Logically, the OSN provides a P2P platform. However, modern popular social networking services are all built with the client-server architecture for easy management and maintenance. This means that all blog entries, photos, videos and social network relations are stored and managed by private clouds owned by the service providers. With hundreds of millions of users, the large social network site must maintain large datacenters. To serve the clients better, many of the datacenters are virtualized to provide standard and personalized cloud services at all levels.

Example 8.10   Cloud Mashup for MapReduce Detection of Spam in a Message Stream
The idea of using MapReduce to filter out spam in a mashup of two cloud platforms is shown in Figure 8.22. Here, we assume unknown spam is embedded within a legitimate blog stream from Twitter applications. This data stream could be very large, in the TB or PB range, so we have to apply the Amazon EC2 cloud to implement a Naïve Bayesian classifier to detect the presence of spam in the data stream. The Baysian classifier is trained by comparing the detected results with some labeled samples to improve the classification accuracy.

On the input side at the left end, initial checking of URL links can eliminate some known spam. The blog stream flows through the MapReduce engine from left to right. We apply Map function to map out the input file to different machine instances, and the Reduce function for Naive Bayesian classifier construction. The training of the Baysian classifier is done by using the feedback of detected results against some spam with known labels. With an input data stream of 1 TB, the EC2 spam detection can be done in less than 10 seconds, comparing 1000 seconds needed to detect the spam on a desktop computer. The detection accuracy achieved was reported higher than 90%. ∎

8.4.3   Predictive Analytics Software Tools

Some commercial predictive analytics tools are introduced below. These tools are indispensable in social media and business applications of big data resources. They can be applied in many important real applications that use data mining, machine learning and statistics techniques to extract information from business or government datasets. The purpose is to reveal hidden patterns and trends and predict future outcomes. Both open source and commercial analytics tools are available from large or small software companies or research organizations, such as IBM, SAP, Oracle, MATLAB, SAS, Predixion, etc.

8.4.3.1.   Predictive Analytics Applications
Important applications of predictive analytics software are listed below. Most of them are related financial matters, marketing analysis, healthcare and social management, etc.

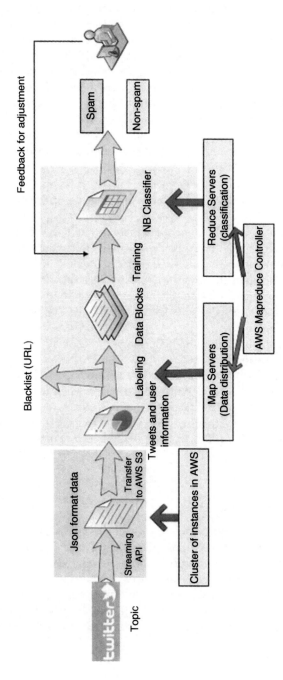

Figure 8.22 Detection of spam from 1 TB of Twitter blogs on EC2 cluster using Baysian classifier (reprinted with permission from Y. Shi, S. Abilliash and K. Hwang, IEEE Mobile Cloud, 2015) [23].

Both regression and machine learning techniques are often applied in implementing these applications:

- Analytical customer relationship management (CRM);
- Clinical decision support and disease prediction;
- Fraud detection, loan approval and collection analytics;
- Child protection, healthcare and elderly caring;
- Customer retention and direct marketing;
- Portfolio, product or economical prediction;
- Underwriting and risk management.

8.4.3.2. Commercial Software for Predictive Analytics

In Table 8.4, we summarize the functionality and application domains of five representative predictive analytics software packages. These are selected from a long list of 31 predictive analytics packages reported at https://www.predictiveanalyticstoday.com/what-is-predictive-analytics/

IBM offers a predictive analytics portfolio that meets the specific needs of different users. This package includes: the IBM SPSS analytic server, collection, statistics and modeler; analytical decision management, social-media analytics; and IBM analytic answers. The IBM SPSS Modeler offers an extensive predictive analytics platform that is designed to bring predictive intelligence to decisions made by individuals, groups, systems and business enterprises. The solution provides a range of advanced algorithms and techniques that include text analytics, entity analytics, decision management and optimization. IBM SPSS statistics is an integrated family of products that addresses the entire analytical process, from planning to data collection to analysis, reporting and deployment.

SAP Predictive Analytics helps to understand the customers, provide targeted products and services, and reduce risk. This software works with the existing data

Table 8.4 Top five commercial predictive analytics software systems.

Software Name	Functionality and Application Domains
IBM Predictive Analytics	Predictive analytics portfolio from IBM includes SPSS Modeler, Analytical Decision Management, Social Media Analytics, SPSS Data Collection, Statistics, Analytic Server and Analytic Answers
SAS Predictive Analytics	SAS supports predictive, descriptive modeling, data mining, text analytics, forecasting, optimization, simulation and experimental design
SAP Predictive Analytics	SAP predictive analytics software works with existing data environment as well as with the SAP Business Objects BI Platform to mine and analyze the business data, anticipate business changes, drive smarter and more strategic decision making
GraphLab Create	A machine learning platform from Dato that enables data scientists and app developers to easily create intelligent apps at scale
Predixion	The very cloud-based predictive modeling platform back in 2010. It supports end-to-end predictive analytics capabilities from data shaping to deployment. Models evolved from machine learning libraries by Microsoft SQL Analysis Services, R and Apache Mahout

environment as well as with the SAP BusinessObjects BI Platform to mine and analyze the business data, anticipate business changes, and drive smarter and more strategic decision making. They perform intuitive, iterative or real-time predictive modeling, advanced data visualization and integration. GraphLab Create is a machine learning platform from Dato that enables data scientists and app developers to easily create intelligent apps at scale. Their package offers to clean the data, develop features, train a model and create a predictive service.

Oracle Data Mining (ODM) contains several data mining and data analysis algorithms for classification, prediction, regression, association, feature selection, anomaly detection, feature extraction and specialized analytics. It also provides means for the creation, management and operational deployment of data mining models inside the database environment. The Oracle Spreadsheet Add-In provides predictive analytics operations within a Microsoft Excel spreadsheet.

Predixion released the first Cloud-based predictive modeling platform back in 2010. Predixion Insight is available in public, private or hybrid Cloud environments, as well as on premises and supports complete end-to-end predictive analytics capabilities from data shaping to deployment. Models in Predixion are created by leveraging various integrated Machine Learning libraries such as Microsoft SQL Server Analysis Services, R or Apache Mahout. The SAS software for predictive analytics applications are described in Example 8.11.

Example 8.11   SAS Analytics for Predictive and Descriptive Modeling

SAS Predictive Analytics provides a commercial software package for integrated predictive, descriptive modeling, data mining, text analytics, forecasting, optimization, simulation and experimental design. The application domains of SAS Analytics include predictive analytics, data mining, visual analytics, forecasting, econometrics and time series analysis. The package can also be applied in model management and monitoring, operations research, quality improvement, statistics, text analytics and analytics for Microsoft Office.

The predictive analytics and data-mining components build descriptive and predictive models and deploy results throughout an enterprise. The functionalities include exploratory data analysis, model development and deployment, high performance data mining, credit analysis, analytics acceleration, scoring acceleration, and model management and monitoring. The SAS Enterprise Miner streamlines the data-mining process to create accurate models. The SAS output dashboard display tables, histograms, ROC chart, and a range diagrams in reporting prediction results.   ∎

8.4.4   Community Detection in Social Networks

In social science, a community (or a cluster) is formed by a group of people under some bounding relations. Detecting communities is of great importance in sociology, biology and computer science. The community structure is often represented by social graphs. Each social graph for a well-formed community is organized as a set of nodes (vertices), with many edges joining internal nodes of the community and a few edges linking to external nodes in the original global graph. The communities could be either disjoint or overlapping. Disjoint communities do not share nodes, while overlapping communities do share some nodes.

For simplicity, to present the community detection problem and its solutions, we consider here only disjoint communities, by which there are more edges inside the community than edges linking to external nodes in the social graph under study. In an autonomy sense, communities are subgraphs with higher cohesion with internal nodes and very light connection with the rest of the graph system. We focus on the subgraph representing a community with some common properties. The formation of a community subgraph follows some similarity function among its nodes. As illustrated in Figure 8.23, six graph operations can change the graph topology. Like a human community, the social graph can also vary during its life cycle.

Communities are defined as self-maintained subgraphs in a global graph. For social network analysis, we follow four subgraph properties: complete mutuality, reachability, node degree and internal versus external cohesion in defining a community graph. The global criteria to identify communities with different community formation rules. The global graph may have some global properties that are shared by neighboring communities. However, each community subgraph may have its unique rules to form the community structure. A random subgraph is expected to have no such a structure.

Community detection refers to the process of detecting the existence of a community structure in a large social graph. A null model is used to verify whether the graph being studied displays a particular community structure or not. The most popular null model corresponds to random subgraphs of the global graph. Random subgraphs have edges that are rewired randomly. However, the expected node degree matches that of the global graph. This null model is the basic concept behind the concept of modularity of the original graph. A social graph with good modularity implies that it can be easily portioned into as many as can be partitioned into a function, which evaluates the goodness of partitions of a graph into clusters.

Modularity enables the detection of a community structure. Graph clustering is often performed based on modularity properties. Various clustering techniques: basic

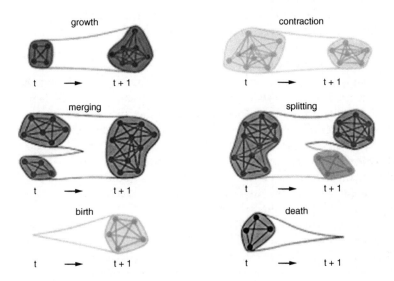

Figure 8.23 Forming a community graph by join, leave, growth, merging, splitting and contraction.

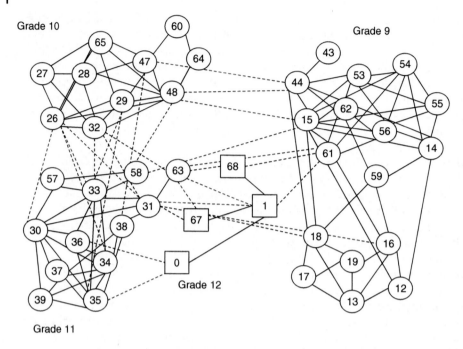

Figure 8.24 High school class formation based on the grade membership of students [22].

clustering, k-mean and hierarchical clustering (Chapter 5) can be applied here for detecting communities. A social subgraph is a community if the number of edges inside the subgraph exceeds that of a random subgraph in a null model. This expected number is an average over all possible realizations of the null model. Node similarity is natural to group nodes to form a community. For example, we can compute the similarity between each node pair of vertices by some predefined criterion. Another important measure of node similarity is based on properties of random walks on graphs.

Example 8.12 High School Community Detection Based on Grade Classes

This example shows a simple social graph for grouping high-school children based on their grade classes. Each grade class is called a community here. The problem of community detection is to distinguish the grade classes based on the courses students are taking in the same year. Certainly, this is an overlapped community detection problem, because some students could be labeled as in 2 grade classes. The graph shown in Figure 8.24 partitions 69 students into 6 grade classes labeled Grade 7 to Grade 12. The edges demonstrated their classroom relations by taking the same common courses. Obviously, students in the same grade are often taking a similar set of courses. Therefore, there exist more internal edge connections among them.

Due to age differences or scheduling conflicts, some courses are shared by students across adjacent grade levels or even two or more levels apart due to their study progress delays. These are shown by the cross-grade or distance edge connections. Of course, there are fewer cross-grade edges than those internal edges in the same grade community. It turns out that Grades 7 and 12 students are easier to separate from the rest. Grades 9 and 10 students have more cross edges than those of other grades. This social graph clearly demonstrates the differences between internal and external edges affiliated with different grade communities. The boundary between communities can be detected based on the distributed connections among the students. The data plotted in Figure 8.24, is from the original work by Xie et al., 2013 [22]. ∎

To detect community affiliation in a social graph, we realize that non-overlapped communities are easier to detect than the overlapped cases, and list three methods to detect communities in a social graph. The methods are distinguished by the membership affiliation rules applied, which results in three methods based on spin-spin interactions, random walks and synchronization:

1) **Spin-spin model:** A spinning system is used to spin among q possible states. The interaction is ferromagnetic, i.e. it favors spin alignment, so at zero temperature all spins are in the same state. If anti-ferromagnetic interactions are also present, the ground state of the system may not be the one where all spins are aligned, but a state where different spin values coexist, in homogeneous clusters. With community structures, and the interactions are between neighboring spins, it is likely that the structural clusters could be recovered from like-value spin clusters of the system, as there are many more interactions inside communities than outside.

2) **Random walks:** Random walks are useful to find communities. If a graph has a strong community structure, a random walker spends a long time inside a community due to the high density of internal edges and consequent number of paths that could be followed. Here we describe the most popular clustering algorithms based on random walks. All of them can be trivially extended to the case of weighted graphs.

3) **Synchronization:** In a synchronized state, the units of the system are in the same or similar state(s) at every time. Synchronization has also been applied to find communities in graphs. If oscillators are placed at the vertices, with initial random phases, and have nearest-neighbor interactions, oscillators in the same community synchronize first, whereas a full synchronization requires a longer time. So, if we follow the time evolution of the process, states with synchronized clusters of vertices can be stable and long-lived, so are easily recognized.

The ultimate goal of clustering algorithms is trying to infer properties of and relationships between vertices, which are not available from direct observation/measurement. Still, there are also applications aimed at understanding real systems. Some results have been already mentioned in the previous sections. This section is supposed to give a flavor of what can be done by using clustering algorithms. Therefore, the list of works presented here is by no means exhaustive. Most studies focus on biological and social networks. We mention a few applications to other types of networks as well.

Other social-media networks also exist in today's IT world and are briefly introduced below. These networks also generate big datasets that can feed into clouds in making analytics decisions:

- **Collaboration Networks:** In such a social network, individuals are linked together for common interest or business collaborations. Collaboration is done through an implicit objective concept of acquaintance. For instance, we may consider another individual as a friend, while the latter may disagree. A formal collaboration team is put together through special agreement or attachment. The best example is the virtual organization involving IBM, Apple and Motorola in developing the PowerPC computer series in the past.

The analysis of the structure of scientific collaboration networks has exerted a large influence on the development of modern network science. Scientific collaboration is associated with co-authorship. Two scientists are linked if they have co-authored at least one paper together. Information about co-authorship can be extracted from the large databases of published work in various fields. Some of the collaboration networks are attached with private clouds for intellectual copyright protection purpose.

- **Citation networks:** have been used to understand the citation patterns of authors and to disclose relationships between disciplines. Rosvall and Bergstrom have used a citation network of over 6000 scientific journals to derive a map of science. They used a clustering technique based on compressing the information on random walks taking place on the citation graph. A random walk follows the flow of citations from one field to another, and the fields emerge naturally from the clustering analysis.
- **Legislative networks:** enable us to deduce association between politicians through their parliamentary activity, which may be related or not to party affiliation. Numerous studies on this subject were done by using Library data from the US Congress. They examined the community structure of networks of committees in the US House of Representatives. Committees sharing common members are connected by weighted edges. Hierarchical clustering reveals close connections between some of the committees.

Palla et al. [19] have pioneered the study of overlapping social communities. The detection of such dynamically changing social communities is much more involved than that of static or disjoint communities. There is no consensus about a quantitative definition of the concept of overlapping community, because it depends on the method adopted. Intuitively, we would expect that community clusters share nodes at their borders. This idea has inspired many interesting detection algorithms. Dynamic social graphs that vary with time are also more difficult to evaluate. This could be studied using time-stamped datasets. Tracking the evolution of community structure with time is crucial to uncover how communities are generated and how they interact with each other dynamically.

8.5 Conclusions

Many interesting cognitive functions can be built with deep learning tools over various types of artificial neural networks. In particular, we show the use of TensorFlow for implementing cognitive intelligence system on today's clouds. We also study the reinforcement learning method. In particular, we study the combined use of deep learning and reinforcement learning, which has been applied successfully in the DeepMind

AlphaGo game match. The predictive analytics are shown to be powerful in supporting big data application in social networks, like community detection and screening friend circles.

Homework Problems

8.1 Through data mining and analyzing electronic health record (EHR), various advantages can be achieved for future medical research and clinic medicine. Please enumerate a few such advantages, such as the corresponding challenges?

8.2 Design a healthcare system which consists of body sensors and wearable devices to collect human physiological signals. This system should possess the following functions: real-time monitoring, disease prediction and early detection of chronic diseases.

8.3 Design a monitoring and management system which can optimize the distribution of medical resources and facilitate the data sharing for such resources. List a few features of this system in terms of intelligence and networking, etc.

8.4 In recent years, video analytics has become a hot topic, especially for security checks through video tracking, which is useful to protect personal and property safety. Traditional security technology emphasizes real-time response and the effectiveness of verification. So video presentation with high-resolution, no loss and low delay has been the main development direction of the security industry over the past few years. Nowadays, we see cameras for city surveillance everywhere.

With increasing use of high-definition cameras, how to effectively transmit the large amount of video data has become a key issue. In addition, tracking criminals to obtain their location information is time-consuming and labor-intensive. Please describe how to use artificial intelligence and machine learning technology to analyze massive video samples, automatically track the target and work out the moving path according to the feature of the target.

8.5 Design a system that can monitor the mental and physical conditions of the worker who operates dangerous machines (i.e. special vehicles, airplanes and nuclear power plants). Such a system design should utilize IoT, image sensing and physiological signals technology.

8.6 The incidence of leukemia among young people has increased, which requires stem cell transplantation as the compulsory treatment. After the transplant, patients have to stay at home for 12 to 24 months. The traditional approach requires the patient to send their healthcare report to the medical team who takes charge of nursing and medical treatment.

In order to skip arduous and unpleasant feelings of the patients during rehabilitation, a video system can be designed to assist the communications between patients and medical team via smart phone, tablet or personal computer. Meanwhile, the personal data of the patients can be easily accessed through a web-based system. Especially, if a gaming element is added to such a remote data retrieving system, the patients' mood can be improved during the daily report. With more practical and frequent healthcare data, the medical team can monitor the patient's health status more accurately and timely and provide more effective treatment:

1) About the video system, which statements are correct?
   a. We need a highly flexible framework of data, in order to meet the requirements of custom health parameters.
   b. External data sources transfer through the e-health data service bus to the database.
   c. Data can only be hard to define, not soft definition.
   d. Game is given priority with smart phones and tablets, but can also be conducted on a web browser.

2) Video game system workflow includes three steps: data definition; create a configuration file; and plan a game task. When distributing small games to patients, the task can specify a group of patients with physical therapy practice according to patients' health status evaluated by the medical team. Write your thoughts on the above three steps.

8.7 The shortage of medical resources makes it inconvenient to see a doctor or access medical facilities. With the development of IoT technology, please think about some methods to alleviate this? Would you like to list some challenging applications in this field? About the solutions of building intelligent agricultural system, discuss how to implement each solution with up-to-date wireless, sensor and GPS technologies:

a) Wireless sensor network technology is applied in intelligent agricultural systems to achieve the data collection and control.

b) A smart agricultural greenhouse equipped with wireless sensors to monitor the environmental like air/soil temperature, humidity, moisture, light and CO_2 concentration.

8.8 Study Sections 8.2.2 and 8.2.3 to understand how to use DBN and CNN for handwritten numeral recognition. Based on Mnist dataset and the information covered in Section 7.3.2, use stack auto-encoder (SAE) to implement handwritten numeral recognition. You need to specify steps and pseudo-codes of SAE for handwritten numeral recognition, and provide detailed programming codes.

8.9 Handwriting numeral recognition and human face recognition belong to image classification problems. Both of them can be solved by CNN. First, study Section 7.4 and 8.2.3 to understand how to use CNN. Then, study Section 8.2.1 and 8.2.2 to understand how to use CNN for image understanding and medical text analytics. Finally, write down both similarities and differences between CNN-based image classification and medical text analytics. You need to illustrate the details from the aspect of convolution operation and pooling operation, respectively.

8.10 AlexNet, a network architecture proposed by Alex, won the championship in the ImageNet Large Visual Recognition Challenge in 2012. AlexNet is the improvement of CNN network model applied to image recognition, and this network structure has some new and novel functions. Use TensorFlow platform and realize the AlexNet with TensorFlow. Check the website: https://www.tensorflow.org/ for recent progress of TensorFlow. This homework requires you to provide program codes and show the steps of building an AlexNet for handwritten digital recognition with TensorFlow.

References

1 G.A. Miller, The cognitive revolution: a historical perspective. *Trends in Cognitive Sciences*, 7: 141–144, 2003.

2 D. Gardner and G.M. Shepherd, A gateway to the future of Neuroinformatics. *Neuroinformatics*, 2(3): 271–274.

3 A. Zaslavsky, C. Perera and D. Georgakopoulos, Sensing as a service and big data. *Proceedings of the International Conference on Advanced. Cloud Computing* (ACC), Bangalore, India, July 2012, pp. 21–29, 2004.

4 G. Lo, A. Suresh, S. Gonzalez-Valenzuela, L. Stocco and V.C.M. Leung, A wireless sensor system for motion analysis of Parkinson's disease patients. *Proceedings of the. IEEE PerCom*, Seattle, WA, March 2011.

5 M. Chen, S. Gonzalez, A. Vasilakos, H. Cao and V. Leung, Body area networks: a survey. *ACM/Springer Mobile Networks and Applications (MONET)*, 16(2), 171–193, April 2010.

6 M. Chen, NDNC-BAN: Supporting Rich Media Healthcare Services via Named Data Networking in Cloud-assisted Wireless Body Area Networks. Information Sciences, 284(10), 142–156, Nov. 2014.

7 H. Li and J. Tan, Heartbeat driven medium access control for body sensor networks. *Proceedings of the ACM SIGMOBILE*, San Juan, Puerto Rico, 2007.

8 L. Deng, and D. Yu, Deep learning: methods and applications. *Foundations and Trends in Signal Processing*, 7: 3–4, 2014.

9 Y. Bengio, Learning deep architectures for AI. *Foundations and Trends in Machine Learning*, 2(1): 1–127, 2009.

10 J. Schmidhuber, Deep learning in neural networks: an overview. *Neural Networks*, 61: 85–117, 2015.

11 K. Hwang, G. Fo and J. Dongarra, *Distributed and Cloud Computing*. Mogan Kaufmann, 2012.

12 Y. Bengio, Y. LeCun and G.E Hinton, Deep learning. *Nature*, 521: 436–444, 2015.

13 I. Arel, D.C. Rose, and T.P. Karnowski, Deep machine learning – a new frontier in artificial intelligence research – a survey paper by *IEEE Computational Intelligence Magazine*, 2013.

14 Google Cloud BigQuary: https://cloud.google.com/bigquery/

15 Google Cloud Datalab: https://cloud.google.com/datalab/

16 A. Krizhevsky, I. Sutskever and G.E. Hinton, Imagenet classification with deep convolutional neural networks. *Advances in Neural Information Processing Systems*, 1097–1105, 2012.

17 R. Collobert, Deep learning for efficient discriminative parsing. *Proceedings of the Fourteenth International Conference on Artificial Intelligence and Statistics (AISTATS)*, 224–232, 2011.

18 T. Mikolov, K. Chen, G. Corrado and J. Dean, Efficient estimation of word representations in vector space. *Proceedings of Workshop at International Conference on Learning Representations*, 2013.

19 G. Palla, I. Derenyi, I. Farkas and T. Vicsek. Uncovering the overlapping community structure of complex networks in nature and society. *Nature*, 435(7043), 814, 2005.

20 D. Silver, A. Huang, C. Maddison, A. Guez, L. Sifre, et al., Mastering the game of Go with deep neural networks and tree search. *Nature*, 529(7587), 484–489, 2016.

21 N. Jouppi, *Google Supercharges Machine Learning Tasks with TPU Custom Chip*. Google Cloud Platform Blog, Google. May 18, 2016.

22 J. Xie, et al., Overlapping community detection in networks. *ACM Computing Survey*, August 2013.

23 Y. Shi, S. Abhilash and K. Hwang, Cloudlet mesh for securing mobile clouds from intrusions and network attacks. *IEEE Mobile Computing*, San Francisco, April 2, 2015.

Index

A

AAL. *See* Ambient assisted living
Accuracy, performance metrics of ML
    algorithms, 234
Active GPS (aGPS), 134
Adaboost, 162
Adaptive resonance theory (ART), 206
ADC. *See* Analog-to-digital converter
Ad hoc networking, 22, 88, 109, 112, 127,
    132
Advanced antenna systems, 20
Affective interaction through wearable
    computing and cloud (AIWAC),
    327
  cloud layer, 329
  communication layer, 328–329
  emotion monitory system, 329
  user terminal layer, 327–328
Agglomerative hierarchical clustering,
    217–221
  tree map for, 221
aGPS. *See* Active GPS
AI. *See* Artificial intelligence
AIWAC. *See* Affective interaction through
    wearable computing and cloud
Algorithms selection, machine learning,
    233–243
  data preprocessing, 234–235
  ensemble approach, 242
  model fitting cases, 235–242
  over-fitting model, methods to reduce,
    237–239

performance metrics, 233, 234
performance scores, 235
under-fitting model, methods to avoid,
    240–242
AlphaGo, Google, 249–250, 363, 365
  CNN construction in training process,
    367–369
  match with human player, 370–371
  system architecture for deep
    reinforcement learning in, 369–370
Amazon Machine Images (AMI), 78–79
Amazon S3, storage service, 81–82
Amazon Web Service (AWS), 49
  architecture over distributed datacenters,
    78–79
  cloud, 65–68
    services in, 79–82
  Elastic Compute Cloud (EC2) for IaaS,
    78–79
  infrastructure, 67
  S3 architecture with block-oriented data
    operations, 81–82
Ambient assisted living (AAL), 304
AMI. *See* Amazon Machine Images
Analog signal-based sensors, 124
Analog-to-digital converter (ADC), 126
ANN. *See* Artificial neural networks
Antenna, RFID, 119–120
AODE. *See* Averaged one dependence
    estimators
Application programming interfaces (APIs),
    for social-media industry, 348, 349

Big-Data Analytics for Cloud, IoT and Cognitive Computing, First Edition. Kai Hwang and Min Chen.
© 2017 John Wiley & Sons Ltd. Published 2017 by John Wiley & Sons Ltd.
Companion Website: http://www.wiley.com/go/hwangIOT

Applications, big data, 34
  categories, 35
  commercial, 34–35
  in enterprises, 36–37
  healthcare and medical, 37–38
  network, 35–36
A priori knowledge, 164
A priori principle, 206–210
  algorithm, for frequent itemsets,
    208–209
  example, 209–210
  flow chart, 209, 212
AR. *See* Augmented reality
ART. *See* Adaptive resonance theory
Artificial intelligence (AI), 40, 157
Artificial neural networks (ANN), 159, 160,
    206, 256, 344
  AutoEncoder, 264–267
  back propagation in, 259–264
  deep learning with, 253–255, 345
  forward propagation in, 259
  hyperlipemia diagnosis using, 261–264
  modeling, steps for, 258
  multilayer, 257–258
  numeral recognition using TensorFlow
    for, 349–352
  versus RNN, 285, 286
  single layer, 256–257
  text and image recognition using,
    348–362
Artificial neurons *versus* biological neurons,
    251–254
Association analysis, 206–210
Association rule
  generation, 210–213
  learning, 159, 160
Augmented reality (AR), 148
AutoEncoder, 264–267
  classification process by, 268
  construction of, 267
  multi-layer, 267–268
Automobile speeding check, RFID to,
    121
Averaged one dependence estimators
    (AODE), 162
AWS. *See* Amazon Web Service

B

Back propagation, in artificial neural
    networks, 259–264
BANs. *See* Body area networks
Bayesian belief networks, 191–194
  in diabetes prediction, 194
  for predictive analytics, 192
Bayesian classifiers, 188–191
  in diabetic analysis and prediction,
    313–315
Bayesian methods, 159, 160
  Bayesian classifiers, 188–191
  belief networks, 191–194
  for classification, 187–194
Bayesian theorem, 188
Beamrider, Atari video game, 363
Big data
  acquisition, 24–32
  analysis, 25
  applications, machine intelligence to,
    32–42 (*See also* Applications, big
    data)
  bluetooth devices and networks and,
    22–23
  characteristics, 4
  cloud platform architecture, 56
  computing, enabling technologies for,
    3–16
  database models of, 26–27
  data science and, 4–7
  economic gains of, 24–25
  and emerging technologies, 7–13
  five V's of, 4
  generation, 25–26
  growth of, 24–25
  industry, 12–13
  mobile cellular core networks and,
    19–20
  mobile core networks and, 21–22
  mobile devices and, 20–21
  mobile Internet edge networks and,
    22–23
  preprocessing, 27–30
  processing engine, workflow in, 57
  quality control of, 26
  representation, 26–27

requirements in social-media industry, 375–377

research, development and applications, challenges in, 6–7

SMACT technologies and, 13–16

social-media industry and, 347–348

social networks and, 17–19

storage, 25, 29

value chain, 24–25

web service sites and, 17–19

WiFi networks and, 23

Big data acquisition, 24, 27–28

data cleaning, 29

data integration, 30

log files, 28

methods, 27

network data, 28

sensors, 28

Big data analytics, 16

cloud resources for, 55–57

evolution, 30–32

goal of, 24

for healthcare applications, 310–322

machine learning models for disease prediction, 316–320

Big data storage, 25, 29

clouds models for, 52–55

requirements, 55

BigTable, 84

Bioelectrical sensors, 125–126

Biological neurons *versus* artificial neurons, 251–254

Block reduction rate (BRR), 97

Block Storage (Cinder), 73

Bluetooth networks, 22–23

Body area networks (BANs), 22, 118, 131–134

communications system, 133

data rate, 133

deployment and density, 132–133

health monitoring and, 304

latency of, 133

mobility of, 133–134

versus WSNs, 132–134

Body sensors, 124, 125

Body signals, IoT sensing of, 300–301

Brain-inspired computer, 38–39

Brain-inspired computing chips and systems, 140–142

China's Cambricon Project, 141–142

Google's Brain Team Projects, 142–145

IBM SyNAPSE Program, 140–141

Breakout, Atari video game, 363

BRR. *See* Block reduction rate

Business cloud services, 52

C

Caffe, 344

Cambricon, 141

CDBN. *See* Convolutional deep belief networks

Cellular networks, 19–20

CHDM. *See* Compound hierarchical-deep model

China's Cambricon Project, 141–142

Chronic disease detection, machine learning tools and, 295–298

Chubby, 84

Citation networks, 390

Classification trees, 172

Cloning of virtual machines, 69

Cloud-based radio access network (C-RAN), 22, 115–116

Cloud-centric IoT system applications, 114–116

Cloud computing, 8–9, 20, 45–46

advantages of, 50

characteristics, 48–49

defined, 54

features, 49

generic architecture of, 47–48

mobile, infrastructure of, 23–24

models and services, 45–57

versus on-premise computing, 12

over Internet, 10–11

service-level agreements for, 77

taxonomy, 46–49

technological convergence in, 10–11

virtual machines in, 48–49

CloudFront, 78

Cloudlets
  gateways, mobile clouds and, 88–91
  mesh architecture, 92
  VM synthesis in, 91
Clouds
  architecture, 47–48
    application layer, 51
    infrastructure layer, 50–51
    platform layer, 51
  AWS, 65–68, 79–82
  big data analytics and, 55–57
  community, 49
  data analytics evolution over, 30–32
  development trends, 47
  emotion interaction through, 327–329
  hybrid, 49
  infrastructure management, 68–69
  Internet, 54–55
  mashup services, 91–97
  mobile, 88–97
  models for big data storage and
    processing, 52–55
  OpenStack systems, 65–68
  platforms
    for analytics applications, 31–32
    architecture, 56, 65–68
    for big data processing, 31–32
    design goals, 52
    families of, 49
  private, 49
  public, 49
  service platforms, layered development
    of, 50–52
  service providers, 52
  taxonomy, 46–49
  technologies in hardware, software and
    networking, 46
  VMWare systems, 66–68
CloudWatch, 78
Cluster analysis
  of hospital examination records, 214
  for prediction and forecasting,
    213–214
Clustering analysis, 159, 160
CNN. *See* Convolutional neural network
CNTK, 344–345
COBWEB, 162

Code division multiple access (GSM)
  communications, 21
Cognitive computing, 38–39
  applications of, 40–42
  augmented application, 146–149
  brain-inspired computing chips and
    systems, 140–142
  cognitive science in, 139–140
  and current computers, 39–40
  fields, 40
  IoT contexts for, 145–146
  neuroinformatics and, 39, 40, 139–140
  system features of, 39
  technologies, 139–149
  virtual reality application, 146–149
Cognitive science, 139–140
Collaboration networks, 389–390
Collective intelligence, 38
Co-location cloud services, Savvis, 53–55
Commercial applications, big data,
  34–35
Communication
  chips, 129
  in social-media exchanges, big data and,
    376
Community clouds, 49
Community detection, in social networks,
  386–390
Compound hierarchical-deep model
  (CHDM), 287
Computer virtualization, 58
Container orchestration tools, 74
Container scheduling, 74
Convolutional deep belief networks
  (CDBN), 287
Convolutional neural network (CNN),
  277
  construction, 360–361
  convolution in, 277–280
  deep, 282–283
  for face recognition, 356–357
  forward propagation in, 283
  in LeNet-5, 277
  medical text analytics by, 357–362
  numeral recognition using, 352–356
  for playing Flappybird game, 371–375
  pooling in, 280–282

structure for handwritten numeral recognition with, 352–353
text and image recognition using, 348–362
CPS. *See* Cyber physical system
CPSS. *See* Cyber-physical society systems
C-RAN. *See* Cloud-based radio access network
Crowdsourcing, 38
Cyber-physical society systems (CPSS), 300
Cyber physical system (CPS), 118, 302, 382

D

DA. *See* Discriminate analysis
DAE. *See* Denoising auto-encoders
Dashboard (Horizon), 73
Data
  acquisition, 5, 25
  analysis, 5, 25, 31
  generation, 5, 25–26
  Internet, 25
  storage, 5, 25, 29
  unstructured, 5
  value of, 4
  varieties of, 4
  velocity of, 4
  veracity of, 4
  volumes of, 4
Data aggregation, 16
Data analytics, 6
  for social-media applications, 375–390
Database models, of big data, 26–27
Datacenters, 12–13, 47
Data cleaning, 29
Data collection, 28
Data integration, 16, 27, 30
Data mining, 15–16, 27
  versus machine learning, 32–34
Data regularization, 239
Data science
  applications, 5
  defined, 5
  evolution of, 4–5
  functional components of, 6–7
Data scientists, 5
Data transformation, 27
DBM. *See* Deep Boltzmann machines

DBN. *See* Deep belief network
DBSCAN. *See* Density-based spatial clustering of applications with noise
DCNN. *See* Deep convolutional neural networks (DCNN)
Decision trees methods, 159, 160
  for bank loan approval, 173
  for machine learning, 171–175
  prediction using ID3 algorithm, 174–175
  rule extraction from, 179
Deep belief network (DBN), 275–277
  structure of, 276
Deep Boltzmann machines (DBM), 287
Deep coding networks (DPCN), 287
Deep convolutional neural networks (DCNN), 144–145, 282–283
Deep learning (DL), 249
  with ANN, 253–255
  biological neurons *versus* artificial neurons, 251–254
  deep belief network, 275–277
  human senses and, 249–251
  methods, 159, 161
  networks, 283–287
  open source software libraries for, 344
  versus shallow learning, 254–255
  and software support, 343–346
  word embedding via, 358–359
Deep learning networks, 283–287
  connectivity of, 284
  input and output relationships in, 286–287
  recurrent neural networks, 284–285
  recursive neural tensor network, 285–286
DeepMind AI programs, Google, 362–364
Deep neural network (DNN), 254
Deep Q-networks (DQN), 287, 363, 366–367
  algorithm for playing Flappybird game, 372
  for playing Flappybird game, 371–375
Deep recurrent neural networks (DRNN), 144
Deep reinforcement learning (DRL), 363
  algorithm, 364–367
Deep stacking network (DSN), 287
Denoising auto-encoders (DAE), 287

Density-based clustering, 221–225
  in blood cell analysis, 223–225
  core point, 221–222
  of data objects, 222–223
  frontier point, 222
  noise point, 222
Density-based spatial clustering of
      applications with noise (DBSCAN),
      221–222
DevPay, Amazon, 78
Digital signal-based sensors, 124
Dimensionality reduction methods for ML,
      159, 161, 225–226
Discriminate analysis (DA), 226
Disease detection
  performance analysis of, 316–320
  predictive analytics for, 312–316
Divisive hierarchical clustering, 218
DL. *See* Deep learning
DNN. *See* Deep neural network
Docker containers, 62–64
  hypervisor-created VMs *versus,*
      64–65
Docker engine, 62–63
  versus hypervisors, 64
Docker virtualization, 63
DPCN. *See* Deep coding networks
DQN. *See* Deep Q-network; Deep
      Q-networks
DRL. *See* Deep reinforcement learning
DRNN. *See* Deep recurrent neural
      networks
Dropbox, 82
DSN. *See* Deep stacking network

E

EC2. *See* Elastic Compute Cloud
e-Commerce, big data and, 376
ECS. *See* Elastic container service
e-Labeling, RFID for, 120
Elastic Compute Cloud (EC2), 78–79
Elastic container service (ECS), 65
Electrocardiographic sensors, 125
Electrochemical sensors, 125
Emotion-control computing and services,
      323–327
  data collection, 324–325

emotion detection, transfer learning
      based labeling for, 325–327
  feature extraction, 324–325
Emotion-control healthcare applications,
      322–335
  computing and services, 323–327
  emotion interaction through IoT and
      clouds, 327–329
  5G cloud-centric healthcare system,
      332–335
  mental healthcare system, 323
  via robotics technologies, 329–332
Emotion labeling, transfer learning for,
      325–327
Enduro, Atari video game, 363
Ensemble methods, 159, 161
  random forests and, 195–200
Enterprises applications, big data in, 36–37
Environmental surveillance sensors, 124
Escherichia Coli, 37
Eucalyptus
  for cloud resource management, 76
  for virtual networking of private cloud,
      71
Exercise promotion devices, 304–305
Expanded log format (W3C), 28
Exponential loss functions, 242

F

FA. *See* Factor analysis
Facebook, 17
  application distribution, 18
  infrastructure, 18
  platform architecture, 17–19
  service functionality of, 19
Face recognition, CNN for, 356–357
Factor analysis (FA), 226
Fifth generation (5G) wireless access
      technologies, 19–20, 21–22
File systems storage, big data, 29
Find My Friends, iCloud, 53
First generation (1G) wireless access
      technologies, 19, 20–21
Five V's of big data, 4
Flappybird game using reinforcement
      learning, 371–375
Forest-RI, 195, 197

Forward propagation, in artificial neural networks, 259, 260
Fourth generation (4G) wireless access technologies, 19–20, 21

G

GAE. *See* Google App Engine
Garnter Research, 7
5G cloud-centric healthcare system, 332–335
General mobile device (GMD), 300
GFS. *See* Google's file systems
Gilder's law, 8
Global positioning system (GPS), 13, 15
  in China, 138
  developed in USA, 113–114, 138
  in EU, 138
  features, 138
  operating principles of, 136–137
  passive *versus* active, 136
  in Russia, 138
  satellite technology for, 112–113
  sensors in, 134–139
  triangulation location calculation method, 137–138
  worldwide deployment status, 138–139
Global system for mobile (GSM) communications, 21
GMD. *See* General mobile device
Google Analytics 360 Suite, 345–346
Google App Engine (GAE), 49, 83–86
  functionality of, 86
  platform for PaaS operations, 85
Google's Brain Projects, 142–145, 250
Google's file systems (GFS), 29, 84
Go player, 249–250, 363
Gorila, Google's reinforcement learn architecture, 363, 364
3GPP, 20
GPS. *See* Global positioning system
Graph analytics, social networks and, 377–383

H

Hardware virtualization, 58–59, 68
  full virtualization, 59

para-virtualization, 59
partial virtualization, 59
Healthcare
  applications
    big data analytics for, 310–322
    emotion-control, 322–335
  big data analytics for, 310–322
  big data preprocessing, 310–311
  and medical applications, of big data, 37–38
  mobile big data for disease control, 320–321
  monitoring system, 300–304
  performance analysis of disease detection, 316–320
  predictive analytics for disease detection, 312–316
  problems and machine learning tools, 295–299
    chronic disease detection, 295–298
    software libraries, 298–299
  robotics, 305–310
Health Internet of Things (Health-IoT), 299–310
  for body signals, 300–301
  healthcare monitoring system, 300–304
  healthcare robotics, 305–310
  mobile health cloud, 305–310
  physical exercise promotion, 304–305
  smart clothing and, 304–305
Hierarchical clustering, 217–221
High-performance computing (HPC), 9–10
High-throughput computing (HTC), 9–10
Hinge loss function, 241
HPC. *See* High-performance computing
HTC. *See* High-throughput computing
Human body sensors, 300–301
Human brain
  artificial neuron in, 251–254
  biological neuron in, 251–254
Hybrid clouds, 49
  VMWare packages for building, 75–77
Hype cycle, for emerging technologies, 7–9
Hyper V hypervisor, 60, 61
Hypervisors, 58–59
  versus Docker engine, 64
  for virtual machines, 60–62

I

IaaS. *See* Infrastructure as a Service
IBM Blue Cloud, 49
IBM SyNAPSE Program, 140–141
iCloud, Apple, 53
Identity Service (Keystone), 73–74
IIS log format (Microsoft), 28
Inertial motion sensors, 124–125
Infrastructure as a Service (IaaS), 12, 51,
    67, 68
  case studies of, 77–88
  clouds, 78
  Elastic Compute Cloud (EC2) for, 78–79
  open-source software packages for, 71–73
Instance-based learning algorithms, 159,
    160
Instruction set architecture (ISA), 59, 60
Internet, 10
  cloud computing and, 10–11, 47–48,
    54–55
  data, 25
  mobile, 16
  radio-access networks with, 22
  wireless, 16
Internet of Things (IoT), 13, 15–16
  application domains, 107–108
  architectural and wireless support,
    110–111
  challenges of, 107
  for cognitive computing, 145–146
  with cyber systems, 117
  emotion interaction through, 327–329
  enabling technologies of, 106–108
  with environments, interaction
    frameworks, 116–118
  evolution of, 106–108
  global positioning, satellite technology
    for, 112–114
  healthcare systems and applications,
    299–310
  LBS for, 134
  with local positioning technology,
    111–112
  local *versus* global positioning
    technologies, 111–114
  radio frequency identification technology
    and, 108–109
  research, 107
  in retailing and logistics services, 122
  sensors and sensor networks technology
    and, 109
  smart power grid and, 114
  social-media industry and, 347–348
  standalone *versus* cloud-centric
    applications, 114–116
  in supply chain management, 122–123
  synergistic technologies of, 106–108
  wireless sensor network technology and,
    109–110
Intranets, radio-access networks with, 22
Inverse reinforcement learning (IRL)
    method, 231
IoT. *See* Internet of Things
iPlant, 36
IRL. *See* Inverse reinforcement learning
ISA. *See* Instruction set architecture
Iterative dichotomiser 3 algorithm tagging,
    173–175

K

KDD. *See* Knowledge discovery and data
    mining
K-means clustering
  algorithm, 215
  for classification, 214–217
Knowledge discovery and data mining
    (KDD), 5
Knowledge engineering, 40
Knowledge representation, 27
KVM hypervisor, 60, 61

L

Languages, 40
Laplacian eigenmaps, 226
LBS. *See* Location-based service
Learning and memory mechanisms, 40
Learning vector quantization (LVQ),
    162
Legislative networks, 390
Linearity, performance metrics of ML
    algorithms, 234
Linear regression analysis methods, ML
  healthcare data analysis with, 168–169
  multivariate, 167–168

for prediction and forecast, 166–169
  unitary, 166–167
Linguistics, 40
Linkedin, 14, 17
LLE. *See* Locally linear embedding
Locally linear embedding (LLE), 226
Local positioning systems, 111–112
Location-based service (LBS), 134
Log files, 28
Logistic regression analysis methods, ML
  for classification, 169–171
  steps for, 171
Log loss function, 241–242
Long short term memory (LSTM), 287
Loss functions, ML
  changing in, 240–242
  effects of, 242–243
  exponential, 242
  hinge, 241
  log, 241–242
  perceptron, 242
  zero-one, 241
L1-regularization, 239
L2-regularization, 239
LSTM. *See* Long short term memory
LVQ. *See* Learning vector quantization

M

Machine intelligence, 32
  and big data applications, 32–42
Machine learning (ML), 16, 82
  algorithms, 157–164
    based on learning styles, 158–159
    based on similarity testing,
      159–162
    categories of, 159–162
    selection, 233–243
    supervised, 162–163, 163–164,
      171–187
    unsupervised, 163–164, 205–243
  applications
    software libraries for, 298–299
  AWS cloud service and, 82
  versus data mining, 32–34
  decision trees for, 171–175
  dimensionality reduction methods for,
    225–226

healthcare problems and tools of,
  295–299
regression analysis methods for
  concepts of, 164–166
  linear, 166–169
  logistic, 169–171
reinforcement learning, 34, 231
  representation, 231–232
  rule-based classification, 175–180
  selection of algorithms, 233–243
    data preprocessing, 234–235
    ensemble approach, 242
    model fitting cases, 235–242
    over-fitting model, methods to reduce,
      237–239
    performance metrics, 233, 234
    performance scores, 235
    under-fitting model, methods to avoid,
      240–242
  semi-supervised, 159
  supervised, 34, 158, 171–187
  techniques, 34
  toolkits, 299
  transfer learning, 34
  unsupervised, 34, 158, 205–243
Machine to machine (M2M)
  communication, 118
Mapping, 270–271
MapReduce, 84
Marketing research, big data and, 375
Markov decision processes (MDPs), 34, 346,
  365
Mashup services
  clouds, 91–97
  composition of, 96–97
  in healthcare applications, 93–94
  quality of, 94–95
  quality of experience, 95
  skyline discovery of, 95–96
Maximal margin hyperplane, 185–186
MCC. *See* Mobile cloud computing
MCTS. *See* Monte Carlo tree search
MDPs. *See* Markov decision processes
Medical health sensors (MHS), 300–301
Medical text analytics by CNN, 357–362
  algorithm, 362
  CNN construction, 360–361

Medical text analytics by CNN (*Continued*)
text comprehension, 361–362
word embedding via deep learning, 358–359
Memory-based learning. *See* Instance-based learning algorithms
Merchandize tagging, RFID for, 120
MHS. *See* Medical health sensors
Microprocessors, 129
Microsoft Azure, 49
Microsoft Office 365, 345
MIMO. *See* Multi-input multi-output
MINST classifier, 349–352
ML. *See* Machine learning
M2M. *See* Machine to machine
Mobile big data for disease control, 320–321
Mobile cellular core networks, 19–20
five generations of, 19–20
Mobile cloud computing (MCC), 23–24
architecture of, 23
IoT and, 107
Mobile clouds, 88–97
and cloudlet gateways, 88–91
Mobile core networks, 21–22
for cellular telecommunication, 21
radio-access networks with, 22
Mobile devices, 20–21
Mobile health cloud, 305–310
Mobile health monitoring, 302–303
Mobile Internet, 16
Mobile Internet edge networks, 22–23
Monte Carlo tree search (MCTS), 365
example, 371
Moore's law, 8
Multi-input multi-output (MIMO), 20
Multilayer artificial neural networks, 257–258
Multi-layer AutoEncoder, 267–268
Multivariate linear regression analysis methods, ML, 167–168

N

Naive Bayesian (NB), 162, 188
classification process, 189
networks, 191–194
NAS. *See* Network-attached storage

National Institute of Standard and Technology (NIST), 48
Naur, Peter, 4
NB. *See* Naive Bayesian
Nearest neighbor classifier, 181–183
flow chart for, 182
hyperlipemia prediction using, 183
Network applications, big data, 35–36
Network-attached storage (NAS), 56
Network data acquisition, 28
Network Functions Virtualization (NFV), 20
Networking (Neutron), 73
Neural computer. *See* Brain-inspired computer
Neuroinformatics, 40, 139–140
Neurons, biological *versus* artificial, 251–254
NFV. *See* Network Functions Virtualization
NIST. *See* National Institute of Standard and Technology
Node, sensors, 126–127, 128–129
operating system in, 130
Nova, OpenStack systems, 73
Numeral recognition
using convolutional neural network, 352–356
using TensorFlow for artificial neural networks, 349–352

O

On-premises computing *versus* cloud computing, 12
OpenSSL, 19
Open source software libraries for DL, 344
OpenStack orchestration (Magnum), 75
OpenStack systems
clouds, 65–68
compute (Nova), 73
for constructing private clouds, 70–74
functional modules, 73–74
storage (Swift), 73
Optical sensors, 125
Orchestration, 74
Ordered rules, 176
Outlook Web Access (OWA), 345

Over-fitting model, methods to reduce, 237–239
  data regularization, effects of, 239
  dimension reduction methods, 238–239
  feature screening, 238–239
  increasing training data size, 237–238

P

PaaS. *See* Platform as a Service
PAN. *See* Personal area network
Partial least squares method, 226
PCA. *See* Principal component analysis
Peer-to-Peer (P2P) networks, 10
Perceptron loss functions, 242
Perceptron machine
  activation functions for, 257
  conceptual diagram of, 256
Performance analysis of disease detection, 316–320
  decision trees, prediction using, 317–318
  nearest neighbor algorithm
    prediction using, 317
    risk prediction using, 317
  neural network, prediction using, 317
  support vector machine, prediction using, 317
Personal area network (PAN), 22
Physical machines, 60
Piconet, 22
Platform as a Service (PaaS) clouds model, 12, 51, 67, 68
  case studies of, 77–88
  Google App Engine, 83–86
Point reduction rate (PPR), 97
Pong, Atari video game, 363
PPR. *See* Point reduction rate
Predictive analytics applications, 383–385, 385–386
  commercial software for, 385–386
  for disease detection, 312–316
Preprocessing, big data, 27–30
  operations, 27
Principal component analysis (PCA) for ML, 226–230
  evaluation matrix and, 227–228
  of patient data, 229–230

purpose of, 227
  steps, 228
Private clouds, 49
Processing engines, 27
Proximity, of clusters, 218–219
Public clouds, 49
Public log file format (NCSA), 28

Q

Q*bert, Atari video game, 363
Q-network, 363–364
QoMS. *See* Quality of mashup service
QQ network, 17
Quality control, of big data, 26
Quality of experience (QoE), mashup services, 95
Quality of mashup service (QoMS), 94–95

R

Radio-frequency identification (RFID), 13, 15, 29, 108–109, 119
  antenna, 119–120
  architecture, 120–121
  to automobile speeding check, 121
  backend system, 109, 121
  for merchandize tagging/e-labeling, 120
  readers, 109, 119–120, 121
  tags, 109, 119, 121
Radios access networks (RAN), 21, 22
  with Internet, 22
  with Intranets, 22
  with mobile core networks, 22
RAN. *See* Radios access networks
Random forests, ensemble methods and, 195–200
  for decision making in classification, 197
  diabetics prediction using, 197–200
Random walks, 389
RBM. *See* Restricted Boltzmann machine
RC2. *See* Research compute cloud
RDMA. *See* Remote direct memory access
Readers, RFID, 109, 119–120, 121
Real-time vehicle tracking, 134–135
Recurrent neural network-restricted Boltzmann machine (RNN-RBM), 287

Recurrent neural networks (RNNs), 284–285
  versus artificial neural networks, 285, 286
  input and output relationships in, 286–287
Recursive neural tensor network (RNTN), 285–286
Regression algorithms, 159, 160
Regression analysis methods for ML
  concepts of, 164–166
  linear, 166–169
  logistic, 169–171
Regularization algorithms, ML, 160
Reinforcement machine learning, 34, 231
  algorithms, 346–347
  in Artari game play, 371–375
  environments, 346–347
  Flappybird game using, 371–375
  principles, 346–347
Remote direct memory access (RDMA), 70
Remote radio heads (RRH), 22, 116
Representation machine learning, 231–232, 255
Representation models, big data, 26–27
Research compute cloud (RC2), 49
Resources virtualization, 58
Restricted Boltzmann machine (RBM)
  learning image composition, 269–271
  rapid learning algorithm, 272
  recommend movies with, 272–275
  single stage, structure of, 269–270
Retailing and logistics services, IoT in, 122
RFID. *See* Radio-frequency identification
RNN-RBM. *See* Recurrent neural network-restricted Boltzmann machine
RNNs. *See* Recurrent neural networks
RNTN. *See* Recursive neural tensor network
Robotics technologies
  emotion-control via, 329–332
  for healthcare, 305–310
Rote classifier, 181
RRH. *See* Remote radio heads
Rule-based classification techniques, 175–180
  applicability of, 176
  decision tree, rule extraction from, 179

  diabetes prediction using, 179–180
  direct rule, rule extraction with, 177–179
  exhaustive rule, 176
  general and specific properties, rule generation strategies between, 178
  mutual exclusion rule, 176
  ordered rules, 176
  unordered rules, 176

S

SaaS. *See* Software as a Service
SAE. *See* Stacked AutoEncoder
Salesforce clouds, 49, 86–88
Sales promotions and discounts, big data and, 376
Sammon mapping, 226
SAN. *See* Storage area network
Savvis, 53–54
  co-location cloud services, 53–55
  content delivery network (CDN) services, 54
Scientific applications, big data, 36
SDAE. *See* Stacked denoising auto-encoders
SDN. *See* Software-defined networking
Seaquest, Atari video game, 363
Search engines, 27
Second generation (2G) wireless access technologies, 19, 21
Self-organizing maps (SOM), 162, 206
Self-supervised learning cycle, 266
Semi-supervised machine learning, 159, 232–233
  reinforcement machine learning, 231
  representation machine learning, 231–232
Sensor networks, 109, 127
  for environmental protection, 129
Sensors, 28, 109, 124
  analog signal-based, 124
  architecture design, 126–127
  BANs, 131–134
  bioelectrical, 125–126
  for body sensing, 124
  communication chips and, 129
  digital signal-based, 124
  electrochemical, 125
  as energy-supplying devices, 128–129

environmental surveillance, 124
expansibility of, 127–128
flexibility of, 127–128
in GPS, 134–139
hardware, 124–130
inertial motion, 124–125
microprocessors and, 129
node, 126–127
operating systems in, 130
optical, 125
power management in, 126, 127
price and size of, 127
robustness, 128
smart phones and, 130–131
temperature, 125
WSNs, 131–134
Service-level agreements (SLA), for cloud
computing, 77
Service oriented architecture (SOA), 11, 65,
67
Single layer artificial neural networks,
256–257
Singular value decomposition (SVD), 162,
226
SLA. *See* Service-level agreements
SMACT technologies, 13
big data analytics and, 15–16
characterization of, 14
fusion for future demand, 16
interactions among technologies,
15–16
Internet of Things (IoT), 13
IoT domains and, 15–16
mobile systems and, 15–16
social networks and, 15–16
subsystems, interactions among, 15
Smart clothing, 304–305, 310
"Smart earth," IBM, 16
Smart phones
for healthcare applications, 131
sensors and, 130–131
Smart power grid, 114
SOA. *See* Service oriented architecture
Social engine, Facebook, 18
Social-media industry
APIs, 348, 349
big data and, 347–348, 375–377

data analytics for, 375–390
IoT and, 347–348
Social networks, 376
big data and, 17–19
cloud support of IoT and, 382
community detection in, 386–390
filtering techniques, 382
graph
analysis example, 380–382
analytics, 377–383
characteristic, 379–380
levels of, 378–379
online architecture, 382–383
positive and negative impacts of, 377
pushing data analytics for cloud/network
security enforcement, 382
recommender systems, 382
SMACT technologies and, 15–16
Software as a Service (SaaS) clouds model,
12, 46, 51
case studies of, 77–88
platforms and their service, 86–88
Salesforce clouds, 86–88
Software-defined networking (SDN), 20
Software libraries, for ML applications,
298–299
Solid state drive (SSD), 56
SOM. *See* Self-organizing maps
Space Invaders, Atari video game, 363
Spatial Crowdsourcing, 38
Spin-spin model, 389
SSD. *See* Solid state drive
Stacked AutoEncoder (SAE), 267–269
multi-layer AutoEncoder, 267–268
sketch map of training, 269
structure of, 268
supervised fine tuning, 268–269
Stacked denoising auto-encoders (SDAE),
287
Standalone IoT applications, 114–116
Storage, big data, 25, 29, 55
Storage area network (SAN), 56
Supervised machine learning, 34, 158, 265
algorithms, 162–163, 171–187
in ANN *versus* AutoEncoder, 265–266
cycle, 265
decision trees for, 171–175

Supervised machine learning (*Continued*)
   nearest neighbor classifier, 181–183
   rule-based classification, 175–180
   support vector machines, 183–187
Supply chain management, IoT in, 122–123
Support vector machines (SVM), 159, 161
   classification using, 183–184
   formal model, 186
   linear decision boundary, 184–185
   maximal margin hyperplane, 185–186
   non-linear hyperplanes, 186–187
SVD. *See* Singular value decomposition
SVM. *See* Support vector machines
Swift storage rings and route, 73
Synchronization, 389

T

Tags, RFID, 109, 119, 121
TDSN. *See* Tensor deep stacking network
Technologies
   clouds, in hardware, software and
      networking, 46
   cognitive computing, 139–149
   convergence of, 10–11
   evolutional trend, 9–10
   GPS, 112–114
   high-risk, 8
   HPC *versus* HTC, 9–10
   hype cycle for emerging, 7–9
   for Internet of Things, 105–111
   local *versus* global positioning in IoT,
      111–114
   mature, 9
   radio-frequency identification, 13, 15, 29,
      108–109, 119–123
   sensors and sensor networks, 109
   SMACT, 13–16
   utility computing, 11
   virtual reality (VR), 146–149
   wireless, 19–20
   wireless sensor network, 109–110
Temperature sensors, 125
Tencent QQ, 17
Tensor deep stacking network (TDSN), 287
TensorFlow, 344–345
Tensors, 56
Theano, 344, 345

Third generation (3G) wireless access
   technologies, 19, 21
Training time, performance metrics of ML
   algorithms, 234
Transfer learning, 34
   for emotion labeling, 325–327
TruthNorth processor, 140–141
Twitter, 17

U

Under-fitting model, methods to avoid,
   240–242
   loss functions, changing in, 240–242
   mixed parameter changes, 240
Uniform resource locators (URLs), 28
Unitary linear regression analysis methods,
   ML, 166–167
Unordered rules, 176
Unstructured data, 5
Unsupervised machine learning, 34, 158
   adaptive resonance theory for, 206
   algorithms, 163–164, 205–243
   approaches to, 206
   artificial neural network for, 206
   association analysis and, 206–210
   association rule generation and,
      210–213
   cluster analysis for prediction and
      forecasting, 213–214
   density-based clustering and, 221–225
   dimensionality reduction methods for,
      225–226
   hierarchical clustering and, 217–221
   introduction to, 205–206
   K-means clustering for classification,
      214–217
   principal component analysis for,
      226–230
   a priori principle and, 206–210
   reinforcement machine learning, 231
   representation machine learning,
      231–232
   self-organizing maps for, 206
   semi-supervised machine learning,
      232–233
URLs. *See* Uniform resource locators
Utility computing, 11

V

Value of big data, 4
Varieties of big data, 4
VBS. *See* Virtual base station
Velocity of big data, 4
Veracity of big data, 4
Video games, 148
Virtual base station (VBS) pools, 116
VirtualBox hypervisor, 60, 61
Virtualization, 57–58
  abstraction levels of, 59–60
  computer, 58
  Docker, 63
  hardware, 58–59
Virtual machine monitors (VMMs), 58–59
  for virtual machines, 60
Virtual machines (VMs), 48–49
  architecture, 60–62
  cloning for disaster recovery, 69
  versus computers, 60–62
  creation of, 57–62
  deployment of, 64–65
  Docker engine *versus* hypervisors for, 64
  hosted, 61
  hypervisor-created VMs *versus* Docker
    containers, 64–65
  hypervisors and, 60–62
  live migration of, 69–70
  management, 68–69
  resources virtualization, 58
  synthesis in cloudlets, 91
Virtual memory, 58
Virtual private network (VPN), 60
Virtual reality (VR), 146–149
  and education, 149
  in training, 149
VMMs. *See* Virtual machine monitors
VMs. *See* Virtual machines
VMWare Player hypervisor, 60, 61–62
VMWare systems
  clouds, 66–68
  packages for building hybrid clouds,
    75–77
  vSphere 6, 75–77

Volumes of big data, 4
VPN. *See* Virtual private network
VR. *See* Virtual reality
vSphere 6, 75–77

W

Wearable computing, for health
    monitoring, 303
Web crawler, 28
Web 2.0 services, 11, 46
Web service sites
  big data and, 17–19
WHAN. *See* Wireless home-area network
WiFi networks, 22, 23
WiMax networks, 22
Wireless home-area network (WHAN), 22,
    109
Wireless Internet, 16, 22
Wireless local-area network (WLAN),
    22
Wireless sensor networks (WSNs),
    109–110, 117–118, 131–134
  versus BAN, 132–134
  data rate, 133
  deployment and density, 132–133
  features of, 132
  generations of, 132
  latency of, 133
  mobility of, 133–134
Wireless technologies, 19–20
WLAN. *See* Wireless local-area network
Word embedding
  distributed representation for, 359
  one-hot representation for, 358
  via deep learning (DL), 358–359
WSNs. *See* Wireless sensor networks

X

XEN hypervisor, 60, 61–62, 70

Z

Zero-one loss function, 241
ZigBee networks, 22, 110